# ADVENTURES
## IN THE

# B

# MOVIE
# TRADE

## BRIAN TRENCHARD-SMITH

ADVENTURES IN THE B MOVIE TRADE

Copyright © 2020 by Brian Trenchard-Smith

Cover and interior formatting

by Kevin G. Summers

This book is dedicated to the love of my life for the past 45 years, *Margaret*, whose inspiration, patience, counsel and editorial skill helped me to the finish line.

ADVENTURES IN THE B MOVIE TRADE is a work of nonfiction, written as an historical record, in the hope that all who seek a career in Cinema and Television find it educational. And amusing.

## ABOUT THE AUTHOR

Most books start with a quick summary of the author's career. Let's cut to the chase. Everything you need to know about the author is in the book.

# CONTENTS

SPECIAL THANKS ............................................................................................ 5

ACKNOWLEDGEMENTS ................................................................................ 6

PROLOGUE ...................................................................................................... 7

PART I | BEGINNINGS ................................................................................... 11

    CHAPTER 1 | *Nosce Teipsum* ................................................................... *13*

    CHAPTER 2 | Formative Impressions ....................................................... 20

    CHAPTER 3 | "Come to Sunny Wellington" ............................................. 25

    CHAPTER 4 | Studio Tours ........................................................................ 32

    CHAPTER 5 | Breaking In........................................................................... 39

    CHAPTER 6 | *Un Chien Andalou* ............................................................. *44*

PART II | AUSTRALIA .................................................................................... 49

    CHAPTER 7 | The Land of My Father ...................................................... 51

    CHAPTER 8 | Frontier Television .............................................................. 57

    CHAPTER 9 | Further Explorations ........................................................... 66

    CHAPTER 10 | National Screen Service ................................................... 71

    CHAPTER 11 | TCN Nine .......................................................................... 78

    CHAPTER 12 | Promos and Productions ................................................... 86

    CHAPTER 13 | Clip Shows to Docudramas .............................................. 91

PART III | TRENCHARD PRODUCTIONS PTY LTD .................................. 97

    CHAPTER 14 | Going It Alone................................................................... 99

    CHAPTER 15 | Building the Company ...................................................... 116

    CHAPTER 16 | Bruce Lee .......................................................................... 130

    CHAPTER 17 | Grant Page ......................................................................... 137

    CHAPTER 18 | *The Man from Hong Kong* .............................................. *148*

    CHAPTER 19 | Cannes '75 ........................................................................ 170

    CHAPTER 20 | *MFHK:* Censors and Critics............................................. 173

    CHAPTER 21 | Margaret ............................................................................ 182

    CHAPTER 22 | *Death Cheaters* ............................................................... *186*

PART IV | AN AMERICAN INTERLUDE ..................................................... 197

    CHAPTER 23 | *Stunt Rock* ....................................................................... *199*

    CHAPTER 24 | At the Corner of Mickey Avenue and Dopey Drive............ 207

CHAPTER 25 | *Dangerous Summer*....................................................................*209*

CHAPTER 26 | *Día de los Assassinos*.................................................*214*

CHAPTER 27 | *Blood Tide*...................................................................*223*

PART V | RETURN TO OZ.......................................................................225

CHAPTER 28 | Ozploitation...................................................................227

CHAPTER 29 | *BMX Bandits*................................................................*233*

CHAPTER 30 | *Frog Dreaming*............................................................*240*

CHAPTER 31 | *Jenny Kissed Me*.........................................................*247*

CHAPTER 32 | *Dead End Drive-In*.......................................................*251*

CHAPTER 33 | Doldrums......................................................................265

CHAPTER 34 | The *Panther* Pictures.....................................................266

CHAPTER 35 | *The Siege of Firebase Gloria*........................................*278*

CHAPTER 36 | Taking Stock..................................................................298

PART VI | BACK IN THE USA...............................................................301

CHAPTER 37 | Starting Over.................................................................303

CHAPTER 38 | Animalflix.....................................................................312

CHAPTER 39 | Fight for Survival..........................................................334

CHAPTER 40 | Sci-Fi...........................................................................338

CHAPTER 41 | Horror Comedy.............................................................363

CHAPTER 42 | War Films.....................................................................391

CHAPTER 43 | Supernatural Thrillers....................................................421

CHAPTER 44 | Whodunits and Action Thrillers......................................437

CHAPTER 45 | TV Melodramas............................................................470

CHAPTER 46 | Sex Comedies...............................................................496

CHAPTER 47 | Epics............................................................................509

CHAPTER 48 | Film Doctoring.............................................................562

CHAPTER 49 | *Alice Through the Multiverse*.......................................*574*

EPILOGUE........................................................................................577

# SPECIAL THANKS:

Mark Hartley, Julian Beaumont, Richard Harrington Hawes,
James Mongtomery, Ed Fawkes, Joe Dante,
Elizabeth Stanley, Mick Garris, Richard Christian Matheson,
Thomas Révay, Steven Lowy, Nick Dawson, Jeff Harrison, David Baxter,
Steve & Bennique Blasini, Jerry Offsay, Jon Brown, Steve Jarchow,
Paul Colichman, Jeff Schenck, Kirk Shaw, Jeffery M. Hayes. Martin Fink.

# ACKNOWLEDGEMENTS

Essays I wrote about Bruce Lee, Day of the Assassins, The Siege of Firebase Gloria, Turkey Shoot, DC 9/11: Time of Crisis, Aztec Rex, Leprechaun in Space have been published on line across Talkhouse Film, Cine-Bazar, and Trailers from Hell. I have revised and expanded on them here. Trailers From Hell is a goldmine of Cinema factoids with almost two thousand mini-lectures from a range of distinguished film makers curated by Joe Dante (*Gremlins 1 & 2, The Howling,* among many favorites). If the name of a movie, or a star or director mentioned here piques your interest, you'll probably find the subject covered at trailersfromhell.com.

Many photographs are from my personal collection. Screengrabs from my own movies are reproduced here under the doctrine of Fair Use: Section 107 of the Copyright Act relating to criticism, comment, scholarship and research. Other photographers for whose contribution I am grateful are: Liane Hentscher (*Long Lost Son*) Robbie Buchanan (*Dead End Drive In*), Connie Minney (*The Stuntmen*), Jon Dowding (*Frog Dreaming*) Kevin Broadribb (*The Man From Hong Kong & Danger Freaks*) Jim Heath (*Night of the Demons 2, Leprechaun 3 & 4*), Mark (Tubby) Taylor (*Absolute Deception, Drive Hard*) David Moir (*Chemistry*) Grace Atkins *(Tides of War, Aztec Rex),* Adrian Carr, Sarah Badat Richardson.

Thanks to Anthony Ginnane for stills from our mutual endeavors.

Thanks to the National Film and Sound Archive of Australia for their valuable contribution to cultural preservation. They weren't involved with this book, but staff I have worked with, past and present, deserve a nod.

Additional perspective: I finished writing this book just before the 2020 pandemic stopped the recorded entertainment industry in its tracks, changing film making, distribution and exhibition for the foreseeable future. Studios and broadcasters have now developed new methodology to facilitate covid-free production till a reliable vaccine is available. Indie movies may still enjoy the romance of all-location photography and close actor interaction, but big movies will minimize employee contact by requiring each department to leave the set once its function is completed. Actors on the LED-screen stage will be inserted into photo-real crowds and environments via ever improving digital technology. Some crew functions will be automated or carried out by robotic equipment. Might take the fun out of things, I fear, having been lucky to have enjoyed 50 years of close proximity with cast and crew. There's certainly a brave new movie world ahead. It gives this book a fin de siècle quality.

# PROLOGUE

Life is a movie, or so it seems to me. And every movie needs a teaser:

INTERIOR. LONDON UNDERGROUND PLATFORM—DAY

London 1983. Commuters stand in silent groups awaiting the next rattling arrival on the Piccadilly Line.

"Work, consume, be silent, die…" is etched on the faces of many. The Thatcher Years.

Only two men are having a conversation; one, a young movie geek, the other, a national newspaper film critic.

MOVIE GEEK

Glad the mail strike is over.

The Critic grunted assent. They stare at a nearby movie poster for TURKEY SHOOT, which mimics a *Hunter with His Kill* trophy photograph — a tall, muscular, bald-headed man carrying an M16 stands with his foot on the corpse of a beautiful young woman while other hunters stand behind.

MOVIE GEEK
That's the bloke from Mad Max…Roger Ward! He played Fifi. Gotta to see that.

The gleaming dome combines with the curvature of the paramilitary hunter's mustache to conjure a diabolically evil face, a leer coloring the edges of cruel resolve.

Emblazoned beside the (18) 'X' Certificate: the admonitory tag line: "NO FILM FOR CHICKENS."

CRITIC
"They haven't press-screened it, so it's obviously trash. If I bother to catch it, I might give it a paragraph. Looks vile and sadistic to me."

Vile, sadistic and trashy, with the added bonus of Roger Ward, sounds pretty good to the movie geek.

CUT TO:

INTERIOR. FILM CRITIC'S OFFICE — DAY

With the end of the mail strike, there is a mountain of correspondence on the Critic's desk. The camera ZOOMS into a slender package, about six inches long, triggering:

EXPOSITION FLASHBACK: a fast-cut montage of images—at a crowded post office, a dozen identical packages, neatly wrapped and addressed to critics at all the leading publications, are weighed and sorted by a depressed employee.

RESUME CRITIC'S OFFICE:

The Critic spies the package. Ah, Swag. Promising. There's often a gift to cajole attendance at a screening. He rips open the package, and immediately his nostrils are assaulted by a foul, pungent aroma. There, in a loose paper wrapper, is A ROTTING CHICKEN'S FOOT! The luckless appendage had set out on its adventure through the strike afflicted British postal system some eleven days before and was now at the height of putrefaction.

The Critic grabs the accompanying card, an invitation to the press screening of TURKEY SHOOT, mailed on the day before the mail strike, arriving now on the day of the screening. If he leaves immediately, he will get there just in time. This insult to his dignity and stature must be addressed.

CUT TO: 1940s STYLE MONTAGE

The Critic watches the movie, scribbling furiously on a pad.

Other nasally affronted critics pound their office typewriters about each sensational act.

Superimposed titles of some of their phrases glide past camera.

"cut in half by a bulldozer!"
"riddled with arrows!"
"half man/half beast!"
"mass nude scene!"

Closeups of London Underground commuters reading newspapers intently.
Closeups of reviews excoriating the film.

The words "senselessly violent" lift off the page, moving towards camera. As they do so, the word "senselessly" fades out, leaving only the word "violent" to dominate the frame. Each male reader takes this in, along with detailed examples of at least six depraved-fun sequences he and his mates would love to see, starting with "mass nude scene!"

CUT TO:

EXTERIOR. WARNER WEST END 2 THEATER—NIGHT

The Critic is crossing Leicester Square to get the train home. A light dusting of snow is falling. He sees there is a line round the block of the adjacent Theatre. It is the line for the movie TURKEY SHOOT.

—*//—*

The first week's box office figures for Turkey Shoot set the house record for a February opening at the Warner West End 2. Despite a blizzard! With a helpful assist from British postal workers. Yes, truly, Enterprise—Turkey Shoot's U.K. distributor—did mail invitations containing chicken feet to select media to suggest the film's undercurrent of humor, resulting in humorless media coverage way beyond expectation. Perhaps box office was also influenced by the fact that early in the Iron Lady's reign we gave the name Thatcher to the sadistic commandant of the B.F. Skinner Re-Education and Behavior Modification Camp, as a deliberate political jab. So effective a jab, in fact, that a subsequent UK DVD release retitled the film *Blood Camp Thatcher*.

*Turkey Shoot* broke box-office records in some Australian drive-ins, scored a U.S. theatrical release, albeit with MPAA cuts, and ultimately video audiences across the globe discovered it as a guilty pleasure. Inclusion in Mark Hartley's *Not Quite Hollywood: The Wild, Untold Story of Ozploitation!* documentary expanded its fanbase further.

At the reception that followed the premiere of HBO's *Norma Jean and Marilyn* in 1996, to which its writer and my close friend Jill Isaacs had invited me, Mira Sorvino introduced me to her then-boyfriend Quentin Tarantino. I gave my name and he said: "You made Turkey Shoot!" He went on to list all the things he liked about the film, including: "I loved that scene where the Guard from Hell beats that girl to death on the parade ground while she tries to recite the dissident's mea culpa." Which Quentin then recited verbatim!

"I am a deviate, the lowest form of life on earth. The Re-education and Behavior Modification Center is my salvation. I will obey the state, my parents and you, Sir…"

Wow! I was astonished.

"Freedom is obedience, Obedience is work. Work is Life… What were you thinking, man?" asked Quentin, "That was great!"

At the Sydney premiere of *Kill Bill: Volume 1*, Quentin dedicated the screening to Turkey Shoot, causing a ripple of shock through the assembled glitterati.

Quentin quickly responded: "If you don't like Brian Trenchard-Smith, then you're not going to like this movie. And you can fuck off right now."

As he put it later: "I like to stick a lighted weed in the ass of the snob."

Quentin Tarantino is *forgotten cinema*'s walking, talking Smithsonian Museum. It was good of him to give me his nod. Fellow director Australian director Adrian Carr snapped us chatting at a BAFTA awards ceremony.

My career has never achieved great heights. I take that philosophically. I am so lucky to have been able to play in the business/art hybrid that I love for over fifty years. Like Bill and Ted, I've had many excellent adventures. So I'm sharing my adventures, successes, and many mistakes to amuse movie nerds worldwide, and perhaps be food for thought and lessons to learn for aspiring filmmakers. No doubt vanity and self-congratulation play a part, too. I was so fortunate to have been part of the Australian Cinema and TV Renaissance of the 1970s, but in this book, those years are recalled from my perspective only. There are many other Aussie movie battlers whose stories and achievements should be told, but I will leave that to others. In telling my story, I'm going to ignore the advice I have given to many writers I have worked with: cut to the chase. I will occasionally pause along the way to muse on old technology, social changes, favorite movies, trailers, camera style, editing, music, visual effects, etc., a wide range of Cinema trivia that I find interesting in the hope that you will too. My Id will occasionally surface. Perhaps it will offer some insight on the demons that drive directors, and this director particularly.

Snack on what interests you.

# PART I
## BEGINNINGS

# CHAPTER 1
## Nosce Teipsum

The name Trenchard first appeared in England after the Norman Conquest of 1066 CE. It is derived from the Old French word *trenchire*, originally referring to a man who cuts meat, but it came to mean a *man of war* or *swordsman* (a particular sort of butcher). A love of fencing would seem to be my heritage. The first record of a Trenchard was found in the county of Dorset around 1100, where Paganus Trenchard and his heirs were granted the lands of Hordhill in the Isle of Wight. The grandsons of Paganus, Robert, Alexander and Hugh Trenchard, witnessed the deed, which suggests that Paganus was old enough to have fought in the Battle of Hastings that installed William the Conqueror as king. Likely these lands were a reward for faithful service.

The Trenchard descendants, traced through Church records of births and deaths from 1143 onwards, were frequently servants of the state: burghers, sheriffs, judges, knights, politicians. Sir John Trenchard earned his knighthood by fighting on the winning side of the Wars of the Roses. A subsequent Sir John Trenchard became Secretary of State to joint monarchs William and Mary in 1692. Hugh Trenchard born in 1873, regarded as the father of the Royal Air Force, was awarded a peerage and became the 1st Viscount Trenchard in 1936. The Trenchard motto from the 17th century on has been: *Nosce Teipsum*. Know thyself. Still working on that.

Here's the relevant aspect of the family tree. On August 4, 1803, in the Dorset town of Winsham Crewkerne, Miss Elizabeth Trenchard married Mr. Robert Smith. When their son William was born, he was christened William John Trenchard-Smith. In order to preserve the Trenchard lineage on the distaff side, they fused the family names. William's son Edward Trenchard-Smith sought his fortune in Australia. He married in Maryborough, Queensland on August 27, 1863, and fathered nine children. One son, Oliver, born in Balmain, Sydney, was my grandfather. He was often away on business, and a heavy-handed disciplinarian towards his four sons when at home. According to my uncle Lloyd, the youngest, he beat my father Eric with a leather belt when Eric was a rebellious 12-year-old. The family moved to Auckland for a few years, then returned to Chatswood in Sydney, where his father wanted Eric to study accountancy and join the family business. Eric nurtured dreams of becoming a pilot, and yearned for a way to escape. Then a perfect opportunity presented itself. The Australian Air Force was small with few openings, but Britain's Royal Air Force was offering short service commissions lasting three years to Australian and New Zealand volunteers in order to build a reserve of trained pilots in case of future war. My father jumped at the chance. At age twenty, Eric Trenchard-Smith sailed to England, just as I, at the same age, would sail to Australia to pursue my own dream.

When he signed up for flying school, my father decided to uncouple his hyphenated surname and become Eric T. Smith. There was a reason for this. Sir Hugh Montague Trenchard had been the pioneering leader of the Royal Flying Corps during the Great War, which later through his efforts became the Royal Air Force. Trenchard achieved the highest rank—Chief of the Air Staff. For my father to use his full surname might be seen as an attempt to capitalize on the Trenchard renown. My father was a modest man. He wanted no special privileges. Nor did he need any. His rating as a pilot was "Exceptional". Nine months after leaving flying school, he was sent back to be an instructor. He soon earned the nickname "Expert Eric". My father did meet Viscount Trenchard when he came to a graduation parade of newly-minted Pilot Officers at the RAF Cranwell Flying School. Somehow Viscount Trenchard knew of my father's then middle name.

"I understand you're from the Australian branch of the family," Viscount Trenchard said, and he invited my father to a weekend house party at his residence. One of those *Downton Abbey* sorts of things. My father was a good tennis player, a useful social asset in those days.

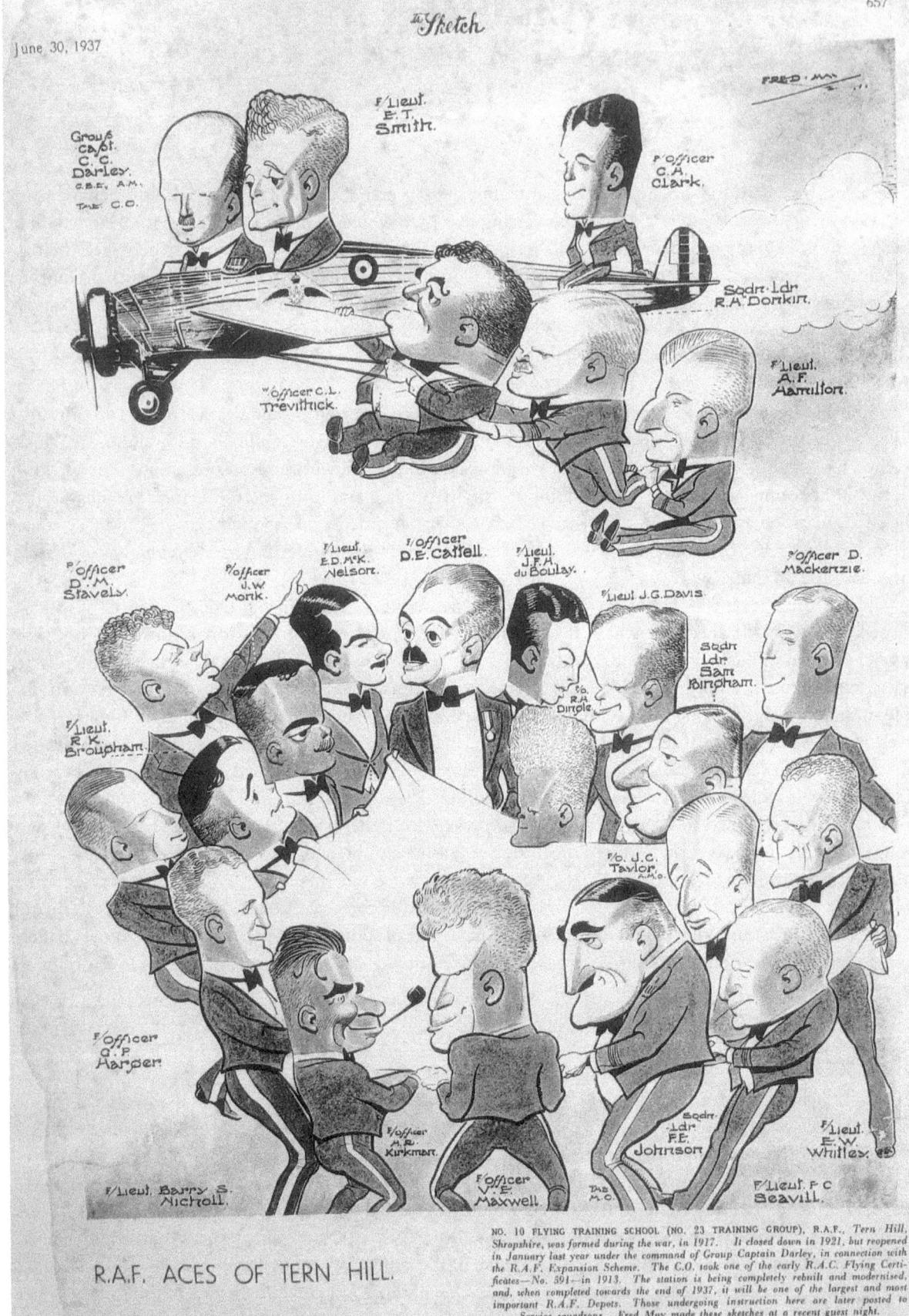

R.A.F. ACES OF TERN HILL.

NO. 10 FLYING TRAINING SCHOOL (NO. 23 TRAINING GROUP), R.A.F., Tern Hill, Shropshire, was formed during the war, in 1917. It closed down in 1921, but reopened in January last year under the command of Group Captain Darley, in connection with the R.A.F. Expansion Scheme. The C.O. took one of the early R.A.C. Flying Certificates—No. 591—in 1913. The station is being completely rebuilt and modernised, and, when completed towards the end of 1937, it will be one of the largest and most important R.A.F. Depots. Those undergoing instruction here are later posted to Service squadrons. Fred May made these sketches at a recent guest night.

At the end of his short service commission, my father was offered a full commission (rare), which he accepted, going on to serve for twenty-five years. He trained instructors in the training of pilots, and flew night fighters in the Battle of Britain. On February 17 1941 Squadron Leader E.T.Smith flying Hurricane Z 3246 was one of three pilots shot down during operation Circus 13, escorting bombers on a raid over France. Smoke filled the cockpit. He turned the plane upside down, opened the cockpit canopy, and dropped out, parachuting into a field surrounded by German soldiers. He told me that an officer addressed him with the words that became a cliché in postwar movies: "For you the war is over…"

My father was dispatched to prison camp. Luckily, perhaps, because a month later the fighter squadron he was set to command was wiped out while attacking E-Boats in the English Channel. It was considered the duty of British POWs to attempt escape. At Stalag Luft Three, he dug tunnels for what would become known as The Great Escape. There were twenty men ahead of him in the tunnel when the sound of gunfire indicated the operation had been discovered. Lucky again. Only three men who had escaped reached freedom. Fifty of those who were recaptured were shot by the SS. Had my father gotten out, he might have been among them. He was moved to Poland, where he made another attempt, The Warburg Wire Job. One moonless night, prisoners disabled the camp generator with a razor blade across its terminals. In total darkness, my father and several dozen other POWs placed a ladder made from bed boards against the inner perimeter fence, and then set a plank across to the outer fence. My father fell between the fences; when the sentries opened fire, he could sense bullets kicking up the sand around him. This attempt earned him thirty days in the cooler on bread and water.

After the war, Dad commanded a number of RAF bases. The last two years of his career were spent commuting to London each day to a desk job at the Air Ministry. Or so he told us, because he had signed the Official Secrets Act. In fact, he was working for MI6, helping to plan spy flights over Eastern Europe.

My mother was born Vera Eileen Baxter and lived in Putney, London. Her father was an Irish merchant sea captain who was often away. When my mother was eight years old, her father returned home and told his daughter that she would never see her mother again. He had discovered that his wife had been unfaithful and was instituting divorce proceedings. Young Vera was immediately taken to Northern Ireland to be looked after by her aunts, who resented the imposition. The psychological damage inflicted by this traumatic event would last throughout her life.

Her aunts put Vera into a series of Dickensian boarding schools, the first of which expelled her when they learned she was "a child of divorce." Subsequent schools were imbued with the same prejudice. For four years Vera was often cold, hungry, and made to feel inferior. Finally, her mother regained custody, having married the man who had been the cause of the divorce. Vera moved back to England to live with her mother and her new stepfather, Mr. Fred Medwin, who occasionally drank to excess and flew into rages.

Mr. John Baxter, her actual father, disowned Vera when she succumbed to pressure to assume her stepfather's surname. She never heard from her father again. Another blow upon the wound.

Once back in England, Vera went to better schools, including a Belgian convent school which specialized in teaching the girls to be good cooks, a skill my mother often displayed. Education over, it was my mother's dream to become an actress, perhaps to receive from an audience the approval she had been denied throughout her formative years.

Due to a financial downturn, the family could not afford to send her to RADA. She interviewed with agents, some of whom made it clear what the price of representation would be. She declined. But there were four movie studios—Pinewood, Beaconsfield, Denham, and Elstree—not far from Cookham where she lived. She signed up to do crowd work, which she enjoyed. Occasionally she was the lighting stand-in for Diana Churchill.

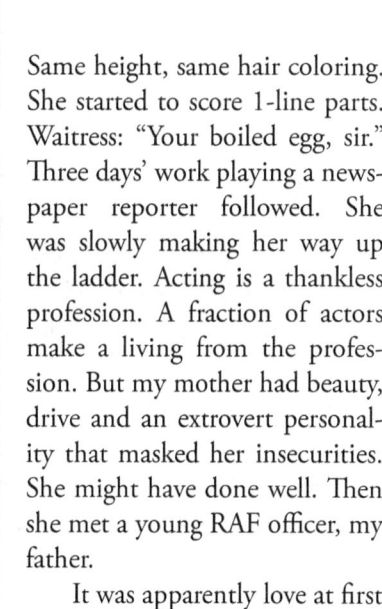

Same height, same hair coloring. She started to score 1-line parts. Waitress: "Your boiled egg, sir." Three days' work playing a newspaper reporter followed. She was slowly making her way up the ladder. Acting is a thankless profession. A fraction of actors make a living from the profession. But my mother had beauty, drive and an extrovert personality that masked her insecurities. She might have done well. Then she met a young RAF officer, my father.

It was apparently love at first sight. They were married within six months.

The nomadic life of the RAF in those days meant that her career was put aside. A few months

later the war came. Then in February 1941, the feared orange telegram arrived from the War Office: "Missing in action over occupied France." It took a month for her to learn his fate. The Nazi radio propagandist known as Lord Haw Haw would sometimes include in his broadcast the names of half-a-dozen recently captured British servicemen. My mother got a call telling her that her husband's name was on the list. Four years of separation and anxiety followed, particularly after the execution of 50 Stalag Luft Three escapees was announced. The Russian army liberated the camp in Poland to which my father had been transferred in March 1945.

If my father was a quiet man before the war, he was a quieter man on his return. Like many POWs he experienced survivor guilt. In the first year after Victory in Europe Day, there was an unspoken stig-

ma applied by many who had suffered bereavement to those who "... sat out the war in a cheap German hotel." My father's old squadron had been chosen to participate in victory parade flyovers in America. He was denied the opportunity to lead it and was replaced by a recent fighter ace. A squadron led by a former prisoner of war did not fit the desired PR image. When my mother took my father shopping for the first time since his capture over four years before, if she waved at a friend across the street, he would hide in the nearest shop rather than be introduced. It was always hard to get him to talk about the war. This is common among veterans who have experienced combat and deprivation.

I was born a year after my father's return.

# CHAPTER 2
## Formative Impressions

My mother's diary reveals that after my birth, on June 1, 1946, the doctor showed her my umbilical cord. It seems I had been an active baby in the womb, creating a loop in the cord and swimming through it, causing the cord to form into a knot. The attending doctor said that this was most unusual and could have been fatal.

I can hear a 1983 critic now: "...a few more days and the world would have been spared *Turkey Shoot...*"

My father had been promoted to Wing Commander during the war, and in 1949 was given command of Royal Air Force Station Castel Benito in Libya. Said Benito Mussolini had suffered the fate all fascist dictators deserve five years before, and the town was renamed Idris during my father's tenure. On the 9th of April 1951 he attended a Royal Air Force Ball in Malta given in honor of the visiting Princess Elizabeth, who would become Queen the following February upon the death of her father, King George VI. All twelve attending officers were given one dance each with the Princess. In my father's case, it was a foxtrot. He told me that the Princess was amply endowed and that he was glad to have the length of arm sufficient to avoid accidental contact with the royal bosoms. He also recounted that the future Queen was charming and seemed genuinely interested in him, his Australian background, what RAF life was like. Princess Elizabeth herself had served in the Women's Auxiliary Territorial service as a mechanic and truck driver during the war, and her new husband Prince Philip was a Navy man.

After the dance, Princess Elizabeth sat down with my father, and ordered a glass of Orangeade. When the waiter put the glass down, he spilled a little. My father had been taught always to carry a spare clean handkerchief to a social gathering. He was able immediately to pull it out and mop up the little puddle, softening the embarrassment of the waiter and getting a smile from the Princess. (You may be certain that if you have any social encounter with me, I will come equipped for

LUQ___ C. 9 APL 51. ROYAL AIR FORCE BALL, PHOENICIA HOTEL, MALTA.

spillage.) The future Queen continued to ask questions till it was time to dance and converse with the next officer. I have sympathy for the Royal Family. Being on duty, under the microscope, all day, every day, for life, is a taxing job. The Netflix series *The Crown* is illuminating. The royal diadem is really an iron vise.

In Libya, from age two to age five, I lived the consummate British child's colonial experience. I have flashes of memories from those years: a snake crawling up the vines and through my nursery window, a servant chopping it into pieces with a spade before my eyes; another member of the Libyan staff who kept a scorpion in a matchbox and as a party trick would entice it to crawl up his bare arm and back into confinement in front of anxious but delighted guests; being headbutted by a neighbor's pet ram and knocked to the ground. I remember my parents eating couscous with an Arab sheikh on a carpet spread under the trees of an orange grove, a member of his entourage placing me on his lap onto a saddle atop a stallion for a gentle circuit of the grove. On this occasion, the sheikh presented my father with an Italian-made roulette set, which I still possess. Before we departed from Libya, I had begun to speak English with an Italian intonation, like my nanny, Sandra. These memories are not unlike those J.R.R. Tolkien reported of his earliest years in Bloemfontein, South Africa over half a century earlier, nor, I suspect, of countless thousands of British children abroad. The contrast between the colonial and subsequent British experience was inherently dramatic, I think, setting off a rich imaginative life,

It was during my father's posting to Libya that I saw my first moving image. A 16mm print of a movie was being projected on a sheet hung from a clothesline outside the Officers Mess. I was sitting on my mother's lap among a gathering of British servicemen and their families enjoying Cinema under the stars. *Going to the pictures* was a weekly habit for many in the UK, so these screenings helped morale for those on tours of duty far from home. I vaguely recall a column of horsemen and dust. Perhaps this film was a Western. I remember nothing more, but this magical window into another world resonated strongly within me. I'm sure I paid the projector some attention. It was a 'gadget', a giant flashlight that created pictures that moved, and boys of my era loved 'gadgets'. Four years later I would get to touch one of these marvels, when I was at prep school back in England.

42.—MARSHCOURT : ENTRANCE FRONT FROM NORTH-WEST

In 1954, a month before my eighth birthday, as expected of British boys in my social stratum, it was time to attend boarding school, where I would spend eight months each year until I was eighteen. Separation from my parents was a shock to me and very hard on my mother, since initially, boys were only allowed a parental visit every three weeks. Yet my parents wanted the best for me in life, and boarding school was the established path. The first was Marsh Court in Stockbridge, Hampshire, a good school which encouraged interest in the arts. Marsh Court had once been a lavish stately home, commissioned in 1901 by Herbert "Johnnie" Johnson, a trader on the London Stock Exchange where he had accumulated a fortune of half a million pounds (about £62 million today). Renowned architect Sir Edwin Landseer Lutyens, noted for imaginative fusions of architectural styles, designed and built the house from locally-quarried rectangular chalk blocks, its masonry interspersed with black flint and red tiles. In 1930, the Stock Market crash wiped out Mr. Johnson's fortune and he was forced to sell. Subsequent buyers allowed the high-maintenance property to deteriorate, and after being requisitioned as a WWII hospital, the estate was sold for demolition and subdivision. Enter Maurice and Mary Wright, idealistic schoolteachers, who saved this unique Lutyens creation by offering to turn the estate into a school. Seven years later, I became a pupil.

You can imagine my awe at first sight of the imposing Tudor exterior, the gardens, terraces, ponds and pergolas, and the trademark Lutyens twisted brick chimneys. A long hallway of hexagonal tiles was lined with the mounted heads of animals Mr. Johnson had shot on hunting trips to Africa, as were most rooms in the building. Each dormitory was named after a particular trophy: Eland, Gazelle, Hartebeest, Buffalo, Swordfish, and Rhino. Reprehensible as I find big game hunting, five formative years around effigies of these noble beasts may have stimulated my enduring interest in all creatures great and small.

A dry moat, crossed by a stone bridge, surrounded the front courtyard where we all performed calisthenics each morning. In the oak-paneled ballroom we were taught boxing, and encouraged to roller skate after lessons and all day on weekends. Physical fitness, self-reliance, and sports—rugby, soccer, cricket, swimming—were a strong focus of the curriculum, along with Latin, Greek, and Bible study. Headmaster Maurice Wright believed in "muscular Christianity," hymns at morning and evening prayers, Bible class on Sunday, with an emphasis on the Old Testament. I became proficient at reciting catalogues of smiting and begetting. Heroes. Villains. Great stories. Works for me. But Organized Religion did not take root, though the question "What is the meaning of life?" has never left my mind.

Mr. Wright pushed all of us hard, particularly me, whom he saw as an attention-seeking only child who needed to be cut down to size for his own good. Wing Commander E.T. Smith had resumed the family name of Trenchard-Smith when he retired from the RAF in 1955. Mr. Wright urged me unsuccessfully to drop the Trenchard, the sin being self-vaunting by association: "A blacksmith was a noble profession, nothing wrong with being a Smith." He growled a lot. He was a big bear of a man who played rugby hard till he was fifty-one. In a practice session, he would on occasion wait until the *wing three quarter* (i.e. quarterback) had the ball, then chase him down the *wing*, whipping his calves with a hazel switch, shouting "Run, boy, run!" But he did introduce me to the novels of Raphael Sabatini, The Sea Hawk, and Captain Blood.

We were both in awe and afraid of Mr. Wright, known to us as "whacker" for his use of the cane, which was more humiliating than painful. I was caned twice, first at nine. It was a shock because I had not received corporal punishment at home. Thereafter I just accepted the risk when I chose to misbehave. In his memoir *Marsh Court—The Missing Years*, published in 2015, onetime pupil Francis James tells of an occasion where Mr. Wright hung a recalcitrant boy out of a window, holding him over a thirty-foot drop to the garden below by the scruff of his neck and belt buckle. Through instruction or discipline Mr. Wright was determined to make every boy achieve his full potential.

I wrote a play in my final year (age twelve) that was going to be performed, but was then canceled. Welcome to Showbiz, kid. The school screened 16mm films and cartoons once every three weeks in the library. There were a few Disney cartoons in color, but lots of black and white prints of Popeye. Feature titles I remember were *The Mark of Zorro* (Tyrone Power version), the Ealing comedy *The Lavender Hill Mob*, and the documentary *Conquest of Everest*, recently climbed by Edmund Hillary and Tenzing Norgay. The son of one of the climbers was a pupil at the school.

The master in charge of this activity was Mr. David Watkinson. You don't forget the names of those teachers who expand your universe. He had noticed that I would watch as he threaded the film through the picture gate onto the take-up spool of a projector he had assembled from spare parts. Forgive me if I indulge in a chunk of antique technology nostalgia. In those days, cinema projectors used carbon rods rather than incandescent light bulbs to throw the image onto a screen some distance away. These retractable carbon rods were rigged nose to nose inside a protective housing, then electrically ignited. By slowly winding a knob, the rods were drawn a couple of inches apart, while the electric current maintained an arc between them. The resulting carbon vapor in the arc was extremely luminous, then rendered more intense by a concave mirror which directed the light at the picture gate, as the film ran through it. The projector lens expanded the image onto the screen beyond. As the rods slowly burned away, the distance between them had to be regularly adjusted in order to maintain the arc, which Mr. Watkinson monitored through a panel of protective welding glass. He gave me this job a number of times in my final prep school year so that he could attend to other duties, returning in twenty-five minutes to change the half-hour-long reel.

There was no projection box. I stood beside Mr. Watkinson's Frankenstein creation, complete with homemade venting system and watched the beam of light reach across a full-sized billiards table over the heads of seventy kids to illuminate a screen in front of them and make them laugh. I rotated the knob to keep the carbons arcing, feeling I was not only an audience member but part of the process of putting on a show. It felt good to watch my schoolmates laugh. Perhaps that experience was the seed…

Mr. Watkinson moonlighted on weekends as a projectionist at a cinema in nearby Winchester and on one Saturday afternoon he took me with him. Lewis Milestone's Korean War movie *Pork Chop Hill* starring Gregory Peck was playing. I spent a couple of hours in the projection box watching the process at a professional level. I learned how uninterrupted screenings of the whole movie—unlike the school's reel-by-reel presentation—were achieved by two alternating projectors mounted side by side. Today, entertainment is delivered by an impersonal keystroke. I admire the picture showmen of old. There was a romance to the work.

At the end of each reel, the film had two small cue marks, stamped in the top corner of the frame, eight seconds and one second respectively before the last frame. Upon seeing the first cue mark, Mr. Watkinson would roll the other projector which was set eight seconds ahead of the first frame of incoming picture, but with its beam of light sealed within the projection box by a closed sliding panel. Upon seeing the second cue, the changeover cue, he quickly slid the panel, opening up the incoming reel, while shutting off light from the outgoing reel.

In *Dead End Drive-In*, I gave a nod to this technique. When Crabs (Ned Manning) stalks the police who stole his tires, I set up a tracking shot moving with him at the crouch across the front of the projection box under the beams of light, just as the projector changeover took place above him. The visit to

the beating heart of a cinema increased my fascination with the medium but it took another year before I had that "Eureka!" moment.

# CHAPTER 3
## "Come to Sunny Wellington"

After returning from North Africa our family had settled in the small English village of Odiham in Hampshire, where my father commanded the RAF base for several years. In 1953, a joint operation by the CIA and MI6 overthrew the elected government of Iran under its Prime Minister, Mohammad Mosaddegh, and installed Reza Pahlavi as Shah. My father's duties did not include this covert operation which was both immoral and a serious foreign policy mistake.

One day said Shah arrived at RAF Odiham, wearing the uniform of Marshal of the Imperial Iranian Air Force. It was my father's task to show him a range of aircraft to consider purchasing. The Shah was a qualified pilot, and enjoyed talking about the technical details of planes, so my father, offered him an aircraft of his choice to try out.

"No, I have generals for that," replied the Shah. But he bought a lot of planes, spending more money on his air force than on his army or navy.

My father loved flying. His logbook recorded flights in over eighty different types of aircraft: Sopwith Camel, Bristol Bulldog, Walrus, P-38, Catalina, Vampire, to name but a few. But the jet age meant instrument flying, and that was not as much fun as seeing the ground a thousand feet below, navigating by following railway lines. He decided he would settle in Odiham, Hampshire, and see out the remainder of the minimum twenty-five years' service required for retirement at the Air Ministry in London. He could have elected to stay on another ten years and get full retirement, but he wanted a shot at a new career before it was too late. At age forty-five he started a small finance company which was successful enough to afford me an excellent education.

Odiham, my hometown for fifteen years. About three thousand people, seven pubs, one picture palace—the Regal. At age thirteen I was for the first time allowed to go to the movies on a winter's night by myself. Yes. My mother, bless her, was overprotective, hence my later flirtation with stunts. To get to the Regal on the outskirts of town, I had to walk through the cemetery of the Norman era church. Eerie shadows. Wisps of fog. Knowing I was going to see a film crafted by a director dubbed the Master of Suspense made the graveyard all the spookier.

*Vertigo* was on its rerelease, making its way through the secondary circuit of British cinemas that played two double bills, three days each, per week, then a pair of older reissues on Sunday evening. Hitchcock's richly atmospheric story of obsession had not been a commercial hit in America or the UK, so on reissue it was paired with a Rory Calhoun B western, *Four Guns to the Border*.

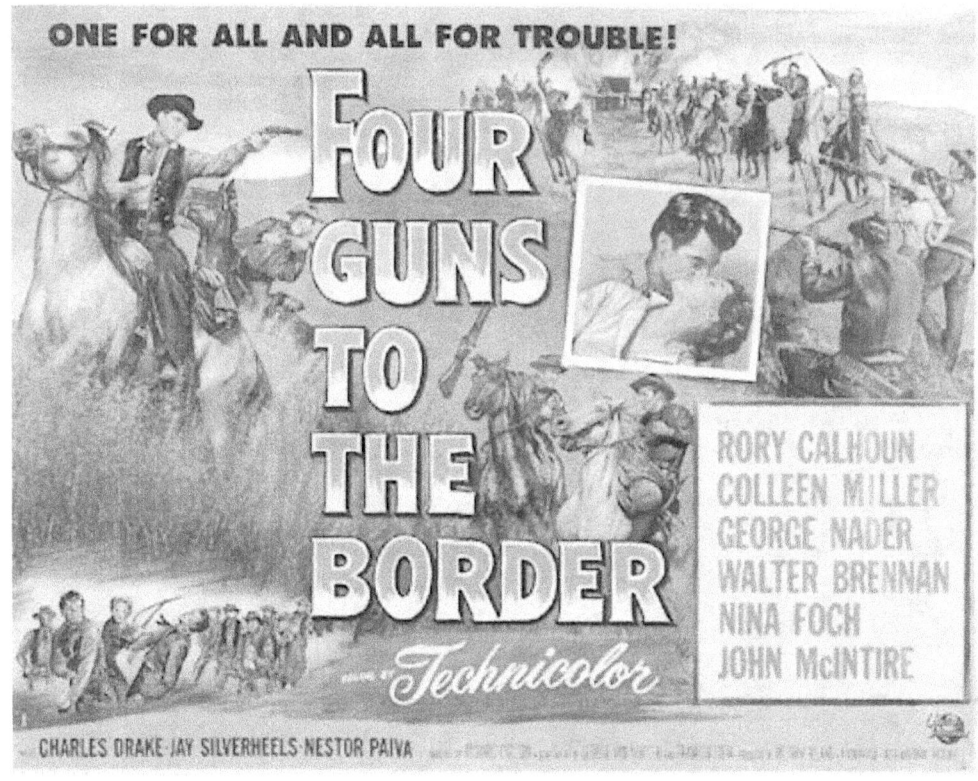

In 1980 I would take a course in acting from one of the *Four Guns* cast, Nina Foch (*The Ten Commandments*). Barry Manilow was in the class too, displaying a flair for comedy. But that's another story.

Even a dull western in color was better than those on UK's monochrome TV. ("Color," the experts said in the 1920s, "It's just a fad.") At the time my cinema education was limited to reading occasional copies of the US movie magazine *Photoplay*, but I was beginning to notice technical things like back projection. Interior car scenes particularly. Something about the traffic in the rear window didn't look real. Why was this? In *Four Guns to the Border*, the change in lighting when studio sets of the desert were intercut with actual desert photography jarred to my developing eye. Why didn't they shoot the whole movie out of doors? The reason I had been asking myself such questions did not coalesce till that night.

When *Vertigo* began with the stunning Saul Bass title sequence propelled by Bernard Herrmann's score, something took hold of me. I had seen films before, but this time I was transported into a new universe, rich in color, dark in motivation. My first encounter with an antihero. And who better to confuse your loyalties than the inherently sympathetic James Stewart? Of course, at age thirteen, some of the moral dilemmas and sexual undertones escaped me, but the film took me on an emotional thrill ride. I loved the way it made me feel, and I knew then and there that I wanted to make other people feel that way, too. Vertigo was my *eureka* moment. I knew that when I left school in five years, I would have to do what grown ups do – work for a living. Going to the Cinema gave me great pleasure. People get paid to make movies. OK, that's what I will do. Thus my ambition was born. Luck and persistence gave me opportunity. My pleasure became my vocation.

Why do I love movies as passionately as I do? Probably the same reason as any film maker. Remember *The Purple Rose of Cairo* when Jeff Daniels steps out of the screen into the audience. Part of me wants to step out of the audience into the screen not only to engage with the story but also to study its making. I can do both simultaneously. One does not distract or detract from the other. It's a complete meal.

In that year, I transferred from Marsh Court to Wellington College, considered to be one of the top English public schools, after Eton, Harrow and Marlborough. At six feet tall I was expected to be talented on the rugby field. Wrong. As an only child I had been cosseted somewhat, shielded from the bumps and scrapes of childhood play. I was timid. Tall for my age yet physically underconfident. My attitude to a combat sport was that it helped to have a weapon. I was quite a dangerous player at field hockey till I lost my two front teeth—after years of braces—while tackling a fellow high stick combatant from behind. Such accidents were a rare occurrence. We were generally well-supervised.

The sport I was most drawn to was fencing. The addictive rush of flèche, parry, counter parry, coulé, coupé, dégagé! continues to this day. I'll be fencing for as long as my knees hold out. Fencing resonated with a favorite genre, largely discovered on black and white television—the swashbuckler. Anything with a sword fight. Pirates, gladiators, I was not discriminating. Errol Flynn was my hero. (Twenty years later I would take a foil lesson from Errol Flynn's tutor and frequent double, Ralph Faulkner, at his salon in Hollywood. When I first met Ralph Faulkner, he was eighty-two years old, leaning on a crutch six weeks after hernia surgery, and was partially blind, yet his blade always found mine.) Wellington engaged an excellent fencing instructor, Sgt. Roberts, who trained the fencing team at the Royal Military Academy Sandhurst two miles away. My skills advanced under his tuition. Height and length of arm helped. I eventually captained the school team when we beat Eton in foil. Here I am spoiling *take one* of the team photo.

Every year quite a few Wellington pupils went straight from school to officer training at Sandhurst. Wellington had been founded in the memory of the Duke of Wellington (battle of Waterloo 1815) to provide education for the sons of officers killed in Britain's wars, and later opened to qualifying students. I was originally slated to go to Cranwell, a school favored by the RAF. My father's service secured me a place there. But because my common entrance exam had scored so high, my parents were offered a place for me at Wellington, a more prestigious school. From 1959 to 1964 I was in The Murray, named for Sir George Murray (like all dormitories and houses at the school it honored one of the Iron Duke's generals). There was a strong sense of military tradition at Wellington which I embraced, being the son of an RAF officer growing up in the home counties of England. So you'd think I would have been an outstanding member off the Cadet Force. Wrong again. I have an inherently antiauthoritarian streak. I was caned twice for general insolence.

Corporal punishment as practiced at Wellington in those days is an interesting experience to deconstruct. The Head Prefect of the House or Dormitory would give reasons to the House Master why a boy needed to be caned, either for a specific "beatable offense," like being caught smoking or being "generally Bolshie," as in my case. The condemned would be informed of the sentence in the late afternoon. You could appeal to the House Master or your parents, but that was deemed "weak and cowardly." Bend over. Take it like a man. When all students were in their cubicles at *lights out*, your name would be called. You were to carry your chair, over which you would bend to receive punishment, down to the communal bathroom where sentence would be carried out, and once it was, carry it back, while your dormitory mates listened for sniffles to see if the beating had produced tears. Corporal punishment, like capital punishment, is given sanction through ritual.

The Prefect assigned to give me six of the best was two years my senior. There had been friction between us for some time. He saw me as an irreverent show-off and bad influence. Could I crimp his satisfaction in his moment of domination? I arranged for friends to ask me as we passed his cubicle if I was worried about the caning later that night. I boasted loudly that it would not hurt because I would wear padding under my pajama bottoms. He fell for it and obtained permission, if justified, to extend the beating. After six hard blows landed, he told me he knew I had "cheated", and instructed me to pull down the pajama bottoms, remove the padding so he could start again. I duly dropped trou. No padding. I stared him down. Thus, in a small way, I had the last word. The second time I was beaten, it was by a prefect I liked and admired, Hamish McGregor. I don't remember what my infraction was, probably my flair for insolence, but Hamish was assigned to carry it out. He took no pleasure in it. In the strange dynamic between torturer and victim, I just wanted to impress him with how well I would take it.

Senior boys caning junior boys was abolished a couple of years later, but corporal punishment had been a tradition at UK Public Schools for hundreds of years. Inevitably the opportunity to inflict authorized pain on another person without consequences attracted those of a sadistic bent. A realistic depiction of such an official beating can be found in Lindsay Anderson's award-winning film *If*, which made Malcolm McDowell a star. He gives a great performance in the caning scene, which is all the more effective for so much of it being played in one static shot. By coincidence, six years later I made a trailer for *If*. Lindsay Anderson hated it and made his own. More about that later.

I was an only child, used to being the center of attention at home, but away from my parents nearly eight months of the year, in a controlled social environment where I had to find my place among an evolving peer group. I was not one of the cool kids.

Strike One: Over six feet tall, yet unskilled in rugby. My sport was fencing, which, curiously for a combat sport, was regarded by the rugger buggers as "only for fairies."

Strike Two: Strange sense of humor.

Strike Three: Always talking about films. "When you leave school, T-Smith," as I was called, "are you planning to live at the Cinema?" a master enquired with more than a hint of scorn. "If I can," I replied with a smile…

In fact, I was living at the Cinema as often as I dared. Although going to "halls of public entertainment" was strictly forbidden, my friend Richard Harrington-Hawes and I would borrow bicycles and sneak off to the Palace Aldershot to see double bills on the occasional Sunday afternoon. *Psycho & The War of the Worlds*. That's a four course dinner. Then ride seven miles back in the rain without lights. Eventually the school would reward my interest in Cinema and encourage me in that direction.

At thirteen, I discovered irony. And paradox. I also discovered that my parents were not happily married, but had stayed together for my sake. It had a profound effect on me. I did not feel worthy of their sacrifice. But I resolved to make them proud of me in some way, so that they would feel that their sacrifice was worthwhile. This issue fueled my career drive.

My five years at Wellington College proved to be good for the career I had in mind. A film production is an army on the move, requiring strategic planning, organizational support, and strong leadership. Serving in the Combined Cadet Corps, participating in sports, captaining the fencing team, gave me a good grounding. I joined the Drama Group run by an English teacher, J.M.O. Curtis, who had staged Shakespeare plays in the Japanese POW camp Changi to help fellow inmates hang on to their sanity. Mr. Curtis was a decent man whose unexpected flashes of temper would now be diagnosed as PTSD. When I was fifteen, he directed Christopher Marlowe's *Edward the Second* as the end of term play, and cast me in two small parts, the Elder Spencer (silver hair and beard) and Lightborne (clean shaven), the proud regicide. While some historians question the accuracy of Marlowe's account, Lightborne's words clearly outline the method of murder: *See that in the next roome I have a fier,/And get me a spit, and let it be red hote*, because the text as written was sacred. However, school authorities obliged me to smother the luckless King with a mattress, lest murder by molten metal sodomy, as per Marlowe, be too confronting to an audience of six hundred boarding school boys and the attending parents of the cast.

*Edward the Second* opened up opportunity. Citing my fencing experience, I volunteered to stage the battle scene in the middle of the play, but my choreography of sword, shield and halberd combat was considered potentially dangerous and was abandoned after the dress rehearsal. But my Lightborne, the King's assassin, got good reviews. I was apparently "chilling", so I won further roles.

My next attempt at fight choreography was in *King Lear*. I was playing Oswald, who fights Edgar and loses. Before he dies, Oswald has five vital lines that enable Edgar to find the lost King on the barren moor. I set the fight up as Oswald's sword versus Edgar's quarterstaff. After countering a series of thrusts, Edgar disarms Oswald, knocks him to the ground, then picks up the sword and stabs him in the belly. Unfortunately, during one performance, I fell with some momentum, sliding backwards along the stage. This caused the costume to be pulled tightly around my throat. Before I could adjust it, Edgar knelt down and stabbed me. I lay in direct profile to the audience so from their perspective a thrust to my midsection would look like it entered my stomach, as I simultaneously cried out in pain. Unfortunately, Edgar stabbed low, beside my thigh, so it looked to the audience like a thrust to the groin. At the same time the costume constricting my throat turned my baritone cry into a falsetto "EEEK!" The full house erupted in gales of laughter. I wanted to die. I wanted Oswald to die, but he couldn't until he said those vital lines that lead Edgar to Lear. Guffaws turned to titters as I gasped out my final speech.

My gaffe was forgiven and I went on to perform in Aristophanes' *Lysistrata*, playing the lecherous magistrate Creon. In one scene I had to chase a "woman" (played by another boy as per ancient Greek tradition) around the stage. His flimsy costume snagged a nail in the scenery, ripping it off, leaving him standing in his underwear, clearly male. Howls of laughter from the audience. (As you can see, my school acting career was accident-prone.) In Jean Anouilh's *Becket*, I played Gilbert Foliot, Bishop of London. At one point he is called upon to read from a scroll to which I secured a cheat sheet. Why learn the lines when you can just read them? Hubris and Murphy's Law go hand in hand. The cheat sheet fell out of the scroll and I had to pick it up in front of the audience. Oh, the embarrassment. But a good lesson. I sang in the chorus of Gilbert and Sullivan's *Ruddigore*, and finally achieved a leading role in Waterhouse & Hall's WWII play *The Long and the Short and the Tall*. Appropriately, I played Private Bamforth, a cynical, antiauthoritarian barrack room lawyer, who eventually becomes the conscience of the patrol. It's a showy part, crackling with anger and wit. Peter O'Toole got great reviews when he created the role at the Royal Court Theater in 1959. The role suited me and I got a nice notice from the school magazine.

At this point, I belonged to the 300-member Film Society and the school had admitted me to the Film Circle, a group of twelve students for whom art films were screened, lectures by documentary makers presented, and visits to studios organized. "Come to Sunny Wellington" is the mildly ironic title of a film I would make about the school in my final year.

# CHAPTER 4
## Studio Tours

In May of 1962 the Film Circle spent a day at Pinewood Studios, where the first James Bond movie, *Dr. No*, was shooting pickups. We watched several takes of a sleeping Sean Connery waking up, gun in hand, on a 10-foot square patch of sand and tropical shrubbery, positioned in the middle of an empty soundstage. I think it was Bond's reaction to the iconic image of stunning bikini-clad Ursula Andress coming out of the water, that had been shot in Jamaica. We went on to tour the sets that had not yet been struck. I can tell you that production designer Ken Adam's spectacular nuclear reactor set was a lot smaller than it looked on the screen. That opened my eyes to the power of lenses when I saw the finished movie a year later.

I learned later that getting the right director for *Dr. No* had not been easy. The three hottest British directors of the day, Bryan Forbes, Ken Hughes and Guy Hamilton, all turned the picture down. In the end the producers selected Terence Young, who had displayed a flair for action scenes in *The Red Beret* (US title: *Paratrooper*), which he had directed for producer Cubby Broccoli eight years before. He was also an experienced writer with his own vision for the Bond movies. The cold war Bond of Ian Fleming's books was a serious man. The mantle of Richard Hannay or Bulldog Drummond, popular spy heroes of a prior generation, weighed heavily upon him. But Terence Young argued that the screen Bond needed more humor and charm for audiences to engage with him. Sean Connery acknowledged that he had emulated Terence Young as Bond, because Young was in many ways the character Ian Fleming had written: Saville Row suits, fast cars, champagne tastes; an adventurer. He'd been a tank commander in World War II. Excellent training for the film industry. It's a tribute to Terence Young's skill as director that he made *Dr. No* look as big and as rich as it does. He is said to have worked in a calm, authoritative manner. His daughter reports that there were rarely any notes in his script, or shot lists. He had the whole film in his head, every day.

Terence Young directed *Dr. No* to test the boundaries of the UK 'A' Certificate. An 'A' would allow all age groups to attend, provided the under-16s were accompanied by an adult. Several cuts were made to the violence, and the British Board of Film Censors took particular exception to the controversial scene of Bond repeatedly shooting an unarmed man. Professor Dent had just emptied his pistol into what he believed to be Bond's sleeping body only to find Bond sitting across the room, his Walther PPK leveled. He shoots Dent twice, the second time as the man lies face down on the floor. In fact, Young filmed Connery pumping four more bullets into the prone man's back to pay off Bond's line: "You've had your six." There had followed a face-to-face meeting with the Chief Censor John Trevelyan, where Young, as a WWII veteran, argued: "wartime justification." No agent on active duty would leave to chance the possibility that Professor Dent might survive the single shot and warn Dr. No. John Trevelyan allowed two bullets.

The visit to Pinewood studios in May 1962 was inspiring. I became all the more determined to make movies my career. By a stroke of luck, my first job in the business came in July that year during the summer holidays. Wellington College had been rented for a week as the exterior location for *Tamahine*, a comedy set in a British public school. Extras were needed. Hey, I'm your man.

Nancy Kwan, who came to fame in *The World of Suzy Wong* two years earlier, was cast as the titular Tamahine, a young Polynesian girl uprooted from her free-spirited island life and required to live with her guardian, headmaster of a stuffy British boarding school. The resulting culture clash provided some amusement, but on balance the comedy was light to the point of weightlessness, despite the efforts of a top British supporting cast. Dennis Price, Coral Browne, Dick Bentley, Derek Nimmo, Justine Lord, Michael Gough, Allan Cuthbertson, Howard Marion-Crawford, were all familiar faces in British movies and television in the 1950s and 60s. I was in Heaven. I was on a movie set. I could watch how movies were made. Super!

One of the first things I noticed about the process was the "hurry up and wait" factor, relays of crew performing specific functions while others watched before taking their turn. Director of Photography Geoffrey Unsworth and his team positioned the camera, then set big arc lamps to augment the sunlight, and smooth away harsh contrast. The film was being shot in the 2.35:1 anamorphic ratio to exploit the spectacular Wellington architecture. A decision had been made to shoot exteriors in full sun whenever possible, and the sun had just emerged from half an hour behind a bank of clouds. Actors were hurriedly summoned, taking their designated positions. Makeup and hair personnel—*Fluff and Buff*, as a producer I later worked for called them—quickly checked each actor, particularly the ladies, for imperfections acquired during the delay. Director Philip Leacock was about to roll camera when his chief electrician, the "gaffer", who was always squinting at the sky through a tinted monocle, shook his head. The sun would go behind a cloud, altering the camera's exposure in mid-shot, before the dialogue in the scene was concluded. Geoffrey Unsworth con-

curred. Everyone held their positions for about a minute, the actors still as statues, *Fluff and Buff* circling and pecking like hungry birds. This is fascinating, I thought. So many parts to the machine, all must be in coordination, yet chance plays a part in the end result.

*Tamahine* was nominated by the British Academy of Film and Television Arts for Best British Cinematography (Colour). It did not win, but it was sumptuous to look at when I saw it, together with my fellow extras, on opening night at the Empire, Leicester Square. I had had the privilege of watching, albeit from a distance, one of the great cinematographers of the twentieth century. Geoffrey Unsworth worked on nearly ninety films, including Kubrick's *2001: A Space Odyssey* and Donner's *Superman*. He scored multiple BAFTA awards and two Oscars for Bob Fosse's *Cabaret* and Ro-

man Polanski's *Tess*, during which he died of a heart attack at age sixty-four. Shooting all year 'round can take its toll.

With my customary modesty, I told the Assistant Director managing the crowd scenes that I planned to make films when I left school, and would be grateful if the producer would give me some advice. To the surprise of my friends, a meeting was arranged. *Tamahine* was John Bryan's tenth film as a producer while simultaneously maintaining a parallel career as a top production designer. Such duality was rare in those days, though he admitted he made more money designing sets than producing movies. He was a charming man with a dry sense of humor. "When they put their arm around you," he said, putting his arm across my shoulders, "Just remember, they're feeling for where to stick the knife." He spent most of our conversation telling me why I should avoid the film business. But he did invite me and the Wellington College Film Circle to visit him at Shepperton Studios the following year, where he would be production designer on a big historical drama as yet uncast.

So in June the following year, there I was, with six Film Circle members, on the set of *Becket*. I have a particular memory of that day. Elizabeth Taylor arrived on the set during the lunch break with a small entourage. We spotty-faced teenagers gazed at the icon with awe. She smiled acknowledgment, but her face really lit up at the sight of her husband, Richard Burton, returning to the set with his co-star Peter O'Toole. Burton clearly saw her but walked right past her without acknowledgment. The Cut Direct. I saw the smile change to a jab of hurt. Hmm, stars had human foibles too.

Later in the shoot Peter O'Toole, a seasoned practical joker, replaced a nude actress in his bed with a complicit Elizabeth Taylor, and covered her with a blanket before Burton returned to the set for the scene. The cameras rolled. The director Peter Glenville called action. Henry the Second and Thomas à Becket began a spirited conversation. Then on cue O'Toole pulled back the blanket revealing not the peasant wench but Mrs. Burton. Mr. Burton was not amused. *Becket*'s editor, Anne Coates, later said she wished she had kept a copy of that take.

I enjoy historical drama where the moral conflicts have contemporary relevance, even if the author is a little free with the facts on record. Jean Anouilh's hit stage play *Becket*, on which the film is based, is a French take on a piece of British 12th century history. It goes like this: King Henry II of England has trouble with the English clergy who take their orders from Rome. When the Archbishop of Canterbury dies, Henry has a bright idea. He appoints his old drinking-and-wenching buddy, Thomas à Becket, a lowly deacon of the Church, to be the new Archbishop. Problem solved. But Becket finds he cannot dissemble to God. He takes his role as the leader of the Church seriously and provides more successful opposition to Henry than the previous Archbishop had done. "Will no one rid me of this meddlesome priest?" Henry challenges. Four of his knights see an opportunity to impress their monarch. They ride to Canterbury Cathedral and hack Becket to death on the altar steps. King Henry eventually performs public penance and Becket is canonized. It's a tragic story of intimate friends who become ideological enemies in a clash between Church and State.

In his play, Anouilh tampered with history in a number of ways to serve his agenda. Among Anouilh's deliberate inaccuracies, Thomas à Becket was not a Saxon as written. He was an Anglo-Norman like Henry. Nor were the English clergy all Saxon while the nobility were all Norman, behaving like rival soccer teams. Anouilh also examined the collaboration between a conquered people and their conquerors, an issue which had particular resonance for his fellow Frenchmen, still processing the Nazi occupation of the early 1940s, although you get little of that in the film version. What you do get is dialogue full of meaty speeches and aphorisms which give Burton and O'Toole, two of the greatest actors of their generation, opportunities to perform at the height of their powers.

We were given a tour of the enormous sets. Shepperton Studios Stage H barely contained an actual size replica of the inside of Canterbury Cathedral, the largest set that had yet been built in Europe. This was the work of our host, the film's production designer John Bryan, whom I had met the previous year at the location shoot of *Tamahine* at Wellington. He took pleasure in showing us an old school Hollywood device for making a large set even bigger at minimal expense: the *perspective miniature*. He had commissioned a miniature of the half of the cathedral dome that was visible from inside the front entrance. This miniature was semicircular, three feet in diameter, and painted in fine detail. The dome was then suspended from wires above the camera and lowered into a wide angle shot of the cathedral, so that it sat in perfect alignment with the top edge of the set. A split diopter lens on the camera then balanced the focus between the foreground miniature and the deep background beyond. Bryan explained that same effect could also be achieved by a matte painting of the dome on a sheet of glass positioned in front of the camera in the same alignment with the walls beyond. I could sense John Bryan's joy in the classic tricks of the trade. But the stress of his twin careers as producer and designer took its toll. He died of a heart attack three years later, aged fifty-seven.

The visit to Shepperton Studios spurred me to shoot a film of my own. Two of my friends had 8mm cameras. I paid for a 4-minute roll of Kodachrome, and Francis De Wilde filmed me and a fencing buddy dueling with foils without protective masks and gloves. Unwise, but no injuries. Gerald Towell's camera had a zoom lens, so he and I got together to shoot two Kodachrome rolls with the imaginative title: *The Chase*.

Wellington College was about two miles away from the Broadmoor Hospital for the criminally insane. Famed gangster Ronnie Kray was kept there till he died. The 'Yorkshire Ripper' is a current inmate. Alongside Broadmoor's 50-foot wall, we staged the escape of "a lunatic." Fellow drama class buddy Mike Jones jumped into frame, waving a WWI bayonet before charging into the surrounding woods looking for someone to kill. The hapless victim, of course, was myself, an innocent fellow out for a stroll, who turns tail and runs at the sight of this raging maniac and ends up being stabbed and rolling down the steep slope of a quarry. The final shot displayed my corpse with a Hammer Films-level bloodstain on my stomach, courtesy of tomato ketchup borrowed from the school kitchen. We filmed the chase through different forest vistas over a couple of Sunday afternoons, shooting in sequence in order to edit in the camera. We had no editing equipment, but could play the processed reel as shot on Gerald's 8mm projector. There were some interesting shots; a running figure brushing a foreground frond into the lens. I found I liked low wide angles. (Who doesn't?) So perhaps my filmic instincts tended, from the get-go, towards heightened reality rather than realism.

Two Canadian documentary producers gave a lecture to the Film Circle and showed Satyajit Ray's documentary on the Indian poet Rabindranath Tagore. We in turn subjected them to my homicidal nightmare, *The Chase*. The Canadians were remarkably kind under the circumstances. They told me I had a good eye for locations. That was encouragement enough. And yes, I have a good eye…

This led to the school asking me to make a record of the school's principal activities over a 12-month period. They loaned me a camera and gave me new rolls of 8mm whenever I asked. Record architecture, seasonal looks, sports, traditions—was the brief. It was to be shown to parents of prospective students. I expanded on that somewhat, adding a staged caning scene, shots of the Cadet Corps Drill Cadre goose stepping and performing actual Turkish arms drill, much more flamboyant than its British counterpart. And of course, a battle scene. Why not? I had access to troops, weapons and pyrotechnics. "Thunder flashes," as they were called, were used in training as grenade simulators. Not much thunder, not much flash, but the smoke helped create a battle atmosphere. It was a short scene of a wave of troops assaulting a small trench line. I realized that the best shots were handheld behind the defenders viewing the charging attackers beyond. A year later, I saw the textbook battle movie *Zulu* and its influence is evident in my own war films *Sahara* and *The Siege of Firebase Gloria*.

Though I did not fully appreciate it till after I left, Wellington had a transformational effect on me. I was a brash yet insecure, nonconformist kid, poor at math and science, but articulate in speech and essay writing. I was in trouble several times for disciplinary infractions. But my Latin and Greek teacher Sandy Entwhistle saw that punishment was not the cure for what ailed me. He mentored me, introducing me to Italian opera and great literature. He found out what I was passionate about, then persuaded the school to give me opportunities to practice it, first on stage and then with a camera. Having tea and biscuits with Sandy Entwhistle, and the benefit of his advice, elevated my self-esteem. At the end of WWII, before becoming a teacher, Sandy had joined the War Graves Commission and spent two years locating and reburying British dead, during which time he became a heavy smoker. I went to visit him in 1969 and found that he had died of lung cancer at the age of forty-five. A sad loss to the school and to generations of pupils he would have positively influenced, as he did me.

In my final year I became more popular. Captaining both a fencing and an athletics team was good for my social development. With a group of friends, I cowrote, directed and acted in a comedy sketch revue entitled "Carmen Heroidum."

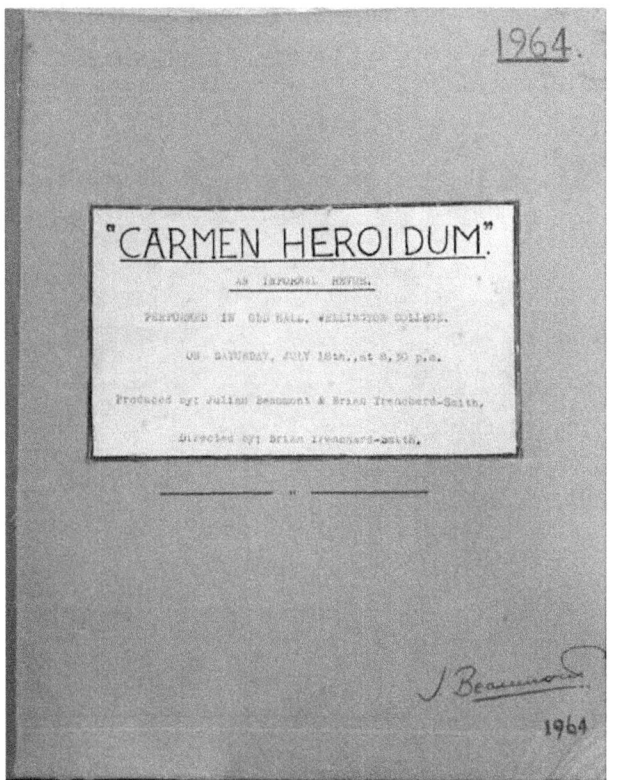
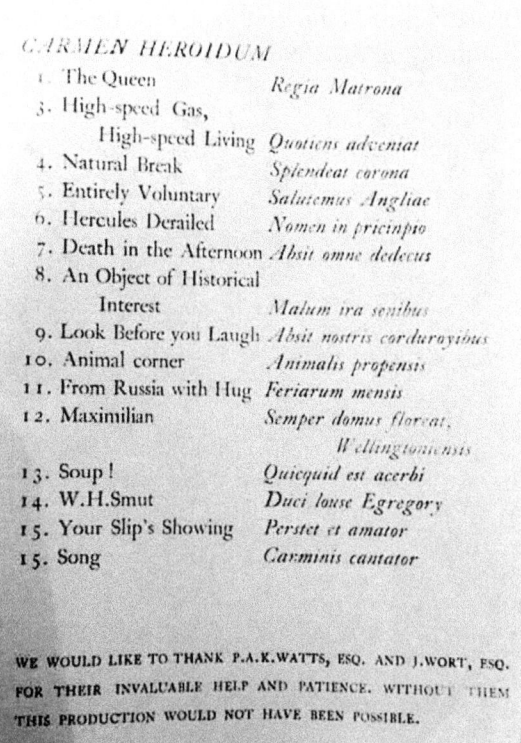

The title mocked the school song. We lifted a few ideas from the subversive underground paper *Private Eye*, and made irreverent fun, full of wordplay and non sequiturs, of movies, TV commercials, the cadet corps, and the gas board. Certainly, trailers and sword-and-sandal movies were on my mind when I wrote the Hollywood Epic sketch "Hercules Derailed," during which I declaimed wildly hyperbolic promo lines. This purple prose was in fact lifted from an actual press kit for *The Last Days of Pompeii* (1960). Those who are familiar with my contributions to *Trailers From Hell* can imagine how much fun I had with this material. Better still, imagine the great trailer narrator Don Lafontaine thunder-throating his way through lines like these:

*See the yawning jaws of the flesh-ripping alligator death pit!*
*The martyred Christians thrown to the gaping fangs of hungry lions!*
*The mob-swallowing earthquake that plunges the city into bottomless chasms!*
*The dungeons of a thousand terrors for the shrieking damned!*

Our cultural satire was not on the level of "Beyond the Fringe," the Oxford and Cambridge University show that made stars on the West End stage of all four of its writer performers. "Carmen Heroidum" at its best was middle class schoolboy humor, irreverent and absurdist, appealing to a sensibility that within a few years would find expression in *Monty Python's Flying Circus*. At 8:30 on the last night of our last term we performed it in front of two hundred pupils and staff. One sketch was banned by the master in charge at dress rehearsal, but we performed it with gusto anyway. We could not be punished because we were leaving school for good the next morning. Among my fellow miscreants and performers was coproducer/performer Julian Beaumont, one of my best friends at Wellington, who remains so to this day. Julian later moved to Australia to pursue a successful career in banking. He was awarded the Order of Australia Medal (OAM) for service to the arts and the health and care of the aged. A remarkable man. Our performer/pianist Pete 'Fingers' Wingfield contributed many musical jokes to the production. He became a successful keyboard player, singer/songwriter, record producer and music journalist, playing with such greats as B.B. King, Olivia Newton John and Paul McCartney. His hit single "Eighteen with a Bullet" later featured on the soundtrack to the 1998 film *Lock, Stock and Two Smoking Barrels*.

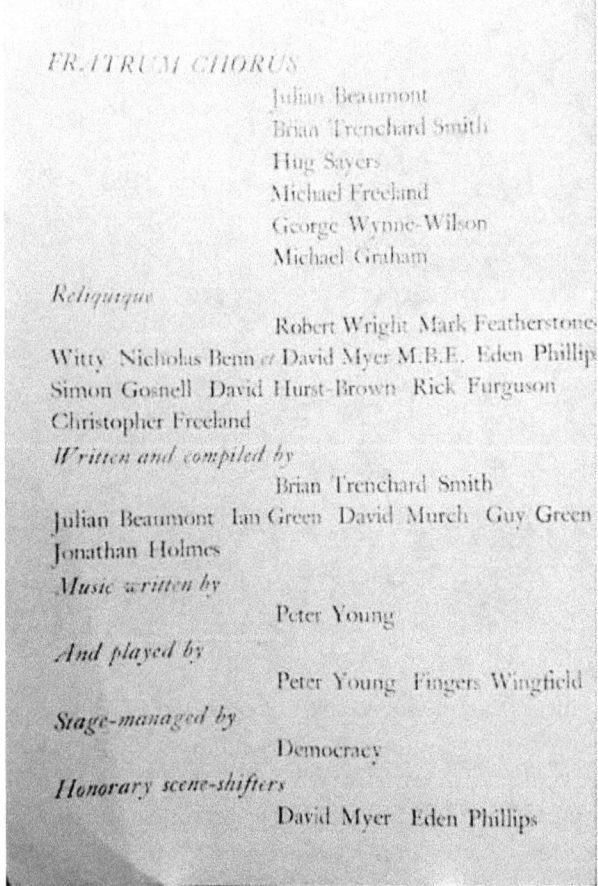

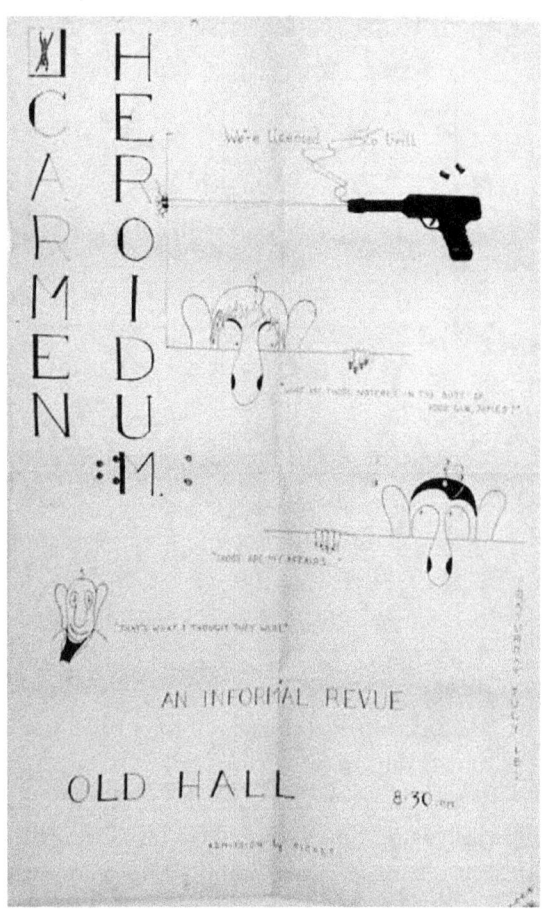

There was genuine applause when "Carmen Heroidum" ended. Everyone had had a good laugh. Positive buzz from an audience is addictive. I found I loved putting on a show. Wellington had prepared me for my chosen career.

# CHAPTER 5
## Breaking In

I left school in July 1964, returned home, and started editing the year's footage of Wellington College activities. My girlfriend at the time, Lisa, who later became a successful interior designer, watched me splicing different strips of 8mm film together for the school project. I shot titles on white cards, edited ten rolls of film down to five, and prepared a music score to accompany the film on a Grundig tape recorder. I loved epic scores, so transferred sections from Miklos Rozsa's *El Cid*, and Dimitri Tiomkin's *The Alamo* and Alex North's *Spartacus* from LP vinyl to ¼-inch tape. That certainly added a surreal quality to the images. The resultant extravaganza was the aforementioned "Come to Sunny Wellington." The school did show it to parents of prospective pupils for a while, but the only copy has since been lost.

Lisa mentioned my epic to her father, an executive at the Central Electricity Generating Board. The CEGB had a few reels of 16mm film shot by a staff member to demonstrate how electricity pylons could be delivered onto farmland by helicopter rather than trucks, thereby reducing compensation for damage to farmers' fields. They needed someone to "organize" the footage. They provided me with 16mm splicer and hand wind viewer, and I put the shots together as best I could. The CEGB was happy and paid me five pounds. It gave me confidence immediately to look for a job in the film business.

I had offers from Bristol and Manchester Universities based on my 4 A Level grades to continue my Classics and History studies. Why didn't I consider the London School of Film Technique? But I was tired of Academia. With the impatience of youth, I saw it as delay. I wanted to get started straightaway. Was it a mistake to bypass formal education in my chosen profession? Maybe. But today I wouldn't encourage high school leavers to incur massive student debt to obtain an entry level diploma for such an uncertain profession.

My parents had no connections in the movie business but had been supportive of my desire to make movies my career ever since I had announced it five years earlier. Particularly my mother, who regularly took me to plays at London West End theaters during school holidays. My father took me to many a Western and Hollywood epic till I got my driving license. My plan to get into the game was to walk up and down Wardour Street, where the offices of many film distributors and production companies congregated. I would walk in and ask to see the personnel officer, stating I wanted a job and could shoot and edit film. I did not get past the doorman at Hammer House. (Ah, what might have been…) But I did get a hearing from E.J. Fancey, owner of E.J. Fancey Productions and Border Films. They acquired "continental films" as they were known, skin flicks and genre thrillers dubbed into English. He booked them into independent theaters outside the Rank and Associated British Cinema circuits, which offered second run movies and first run exploitation fare at cheaper admission prices.

Border Films needed an editing room assistant to carry out the many cuts required by the British Board of Film Censors in prints supplied from Europe, where movies were getting racier. So when Mr. Fancey heard that a public school graduate was at the front desk claiming to know how to edit film, albeit 16mm, he had me shown straight into his office. I have always been "good in the room" (that's agent speak for interview technique), so I caught the train home with a job at seven pounds sterling a week, less tax. What I did not know during the interview, although it might not have made any difference, was Mr. Fancy's somewhat colorful background. Around 1940/41 E.J. Fancey was arrested for stabbing his company accountant in the groin. The man had accused Mr. Fancey of running the finances of his company "close to the wind." The dispute had become violent. The accountant had a leg amputated as a result of the injury, yet was uncooperative when the case came to trial, resulting in the prosecution treating the victim as a hostile witness. It seemed he had been 'softened up' before the hearing. E.J. Fancey's prison sentence was short.

I soon found out that the company also sailed a little "close to the wind" with the censor. They had me faithfully execute the censor's cuts for films released in the London area, the orbit of the BBFC's staff, then put some or all of the cuts back into the prints destined for the provinces. Exhibitors did not care; the stronger a film's content the better. Word of mouth ("Ooh! You can see her tits..!") would increase box office within days. Violence was similarly reinserted. To get *Scheherazade*, a French epic shot in 70mm, passed by the BBFC with a 'U' (Universal Exhibition) certificate, (the predecessor to 'G' rating), I had to reduce twelve lashes in a whipping scene to

three on camera. A few prints played London and Home Counties as per the BBFC's specs, but in the prints destined for the Midlands and north, hero Gérard Barray received the full punishment. I doubt if that did much for box office, but the company mindset was crass and cynical. Thinking nobody in the provinces would have heard of the Arabian Nights story of Scheherazade, they retitled the movie *Scorching Sands*. I had a pretty good idea who would get the blame if the BBFC discovered these shenanigans and saw little likelihood of promotion into more creative areas, so after a few months I left.

Again I prowled Soho and Wardour Street, looking for film production company offices. I had tried the recognized approach of applying in writing to major film and TV companies. That had produced only two interviews, from BBC and Grenada TV. It had taken months to find out that I had not made the cut. I took to pounding the pavement again in the hope that my enthusiasm would coincide with a company's need. I spied a sign on a doorway in Meard Street: Reflex Films, whose main business was shooting news magazine material in the UK for foreign television stations, particularly France. So I walked in and offered my services, adding that I could speak rudimentary French.

Like Border Films, Reflex was a company operating on the fringe of the business, below the radar of the Association of Cinematograph, Television and Allied Technicians, which governed employment in the British film industry. The ACTT at that time required all film workers to be members of the union and ran a closed shop that in reality restricted new membership to applicants with union connections. Reflex gave me casual work a few times, at half the union rate. I regarded it as an apprenticeship, grateful to be paid to learn how to load 16mm Eclair cameras (their magazines jammed easily) and handle the clapperboard. I was so excited my first time with the camera crew that I declaimed all the information on the board, including the date, the director and cameraman's names, scene and take number before executing the synchronizing clap. Stares of disbelief all around.

A friend of my mother got me a week's work at the London Press Exchange, the advertising agency at which he was an executive. In a small basement studio, LPE made draft commercials cheaply to test on an audience of potential consumers. The version deemed to be the most persuasive was put into full scale production. One of the commercials I worked on was for Handy Andy, a cleaning fluid. To emphasize its fast-acting power in the "*Wipes the shelf clean in one easy stroke!*" shots, the dirt on the shelf was a layer of vacuum cleaner dust, easy to sweep away. It was my job to reapply the dust after each take. And to be certain that not a speck was left behind by the miracle product, a strip of felt was attached to the underneath of the sponge to catch any stragglers. In the linoleum floor mopping shots, the dried stains had to look real, so the actual cleansing product used was Flash, the very product this Handy Andy campaign was being mounted to outsell, because Flash was actually better at first wipe. Those five days provided an interesting window on the world of advertising.

While still trying to break into the film business, I worked for my father's small company as a book-keeper. Acting was a good distraction. I dabbled in it, but never saw it as a likely career path.

Students—from different parts of the South of England—are briefed at a rehearsal of "Luther," by John Osborne, which they are to present in the Elmhurst Studio Theatre tonight and tomorrow afternoon and evening

A friend, (Tony Covell, kneeling) staged a two-performance production of John Osborne's *Luther* at a local dance school with a 50-seat theater. He offered me a small but juicy part—Dominican Inquisitor Bishop Johan Tetzel, the most successful vendor of Indulgences at the time of the Reformation. He would be a wealthy televangelist today. Here's Osborne's evocative stage direction for the character:

*He is splendidly equipped to be an ecclesiastical huckster, with alive, silver hair, the powerfully calculating voice, range and technique of a trained orator, the terrible, riveting charm of a dedicated professional able to winkle coppers out of the pockets of the poor and desperate.*

Tetzel's only scene is a speech from the pulpit, offering indulgences not just for past sins but for sins yet to be committed. At eighteen years old, I hardly looked the part, but in each performance, I knew that I nailed it, receiving that addictive buzz stage actors get when they know that the audience is eating out of their hand.

Watching my friend put the production of *Luther* together spurred me to try my hand, too. I booked the same dance studio in Camberley for three nights in mid-December 1964. Any profits from the performances would be donated to a local assisted care facility, the Kingsclear Old Folks Home.

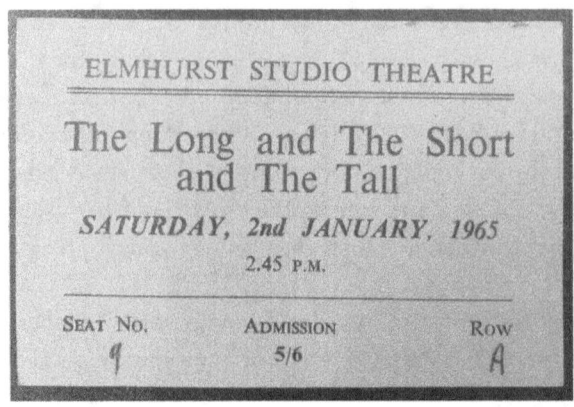

ELMHURST STUDIO THEATRE

The Long and The Short
and The Tall

SATURDAY, 2nd JANUARY, 1965

2.45 P.M.

| SEAT No. | ADMISSION | ROW |
|---|---|---|
| 9 | 5/6 | A |

The play I chose was the one with which I was most familiar, *The Long and the Short and the Tall*. Again I played Private Bamforth. With school mentor Sandy Entwhistle's help, I succeeded in persuading school authorities to loan me not only the jungle green uniforms and webbing, but seven .303 Lee Enfield rifles from the Cadet Corps armory. Their firing pins were long gone. Even so, those were more trusting times.

I persuaded a lumber yard to give me discarded plywood with which to build the broken down Malayan hut in which the play is set. I was able to recruit all but one of the original Wellington College cast now out in the adult world like myself. Rupert Frazer again played Whittaker, the nervous radio operator. Rupert was determined to be a professional actor. To showcase him (and naturally myself) I sent invitations to all the leading London theater critics. What was I thinking? Does *Waiting for Guffman* spring to mind? Where does chutzpah end and hubris begin? Only one critic wrote back, offering his regrets and wishing us luck. Surprisingly, this was Bernard Levin, by reputation the most acid-tongued critic of West End Theater.

He made also regular appearances on David Frost's satirical show *That Was the Week That Was*, broadcast live on Saturday nights. I remember seeing the episode in which the husband of an actress, whose one-woman show Levin had recently panned, leapt out of the studio audience and started swinging punches at him. Levin had been hosting a discussion panel on nuclear disarmament. As stagehands dragged the man away, Levin quipped: "Now let's get back to nonviolence." Impressive. The clip is on Utube: https://

youtu.be/3EelRI_oRPY Incidentally, the future author, broadcaster and publisher Arianna Huffington was Levin's lover throughout the 1970s. After his death, she wrote: "He wasn't just the big love of my life, he was a mentor as a writer and a role model as a thinker." Levin was a man at the top of his game, but still polite enough to reply to an invitation from a nobody.

We did get one review, from the local *Camberley Times*, calling the play "Teenage Triumph." The entire cast and crew were under age nineteen. I received compliments for:

*...[my] skillful enactment of the role of Bamforth, the reluctant rebellious private, who talks, and talks. Delivered in the Harold Steptoe brand of cockney, well suited to the character, he obtained the maximum from every line.*

Bad weather affected one night's receipts, so we made a net loss of about twenty pounds, but my parents, bless them, sent ten pounds to the Kingsclear Old Folks Home, anyway. Itwas an early lesson in the uncertain economics of Showbiz. Rupert Frazer went on to a solid career, working for all the major British theater companies, and racking up eighty-six credits in film and television, including playing young Christian Bale's father in Spielberg's *Empire of the Sun*.

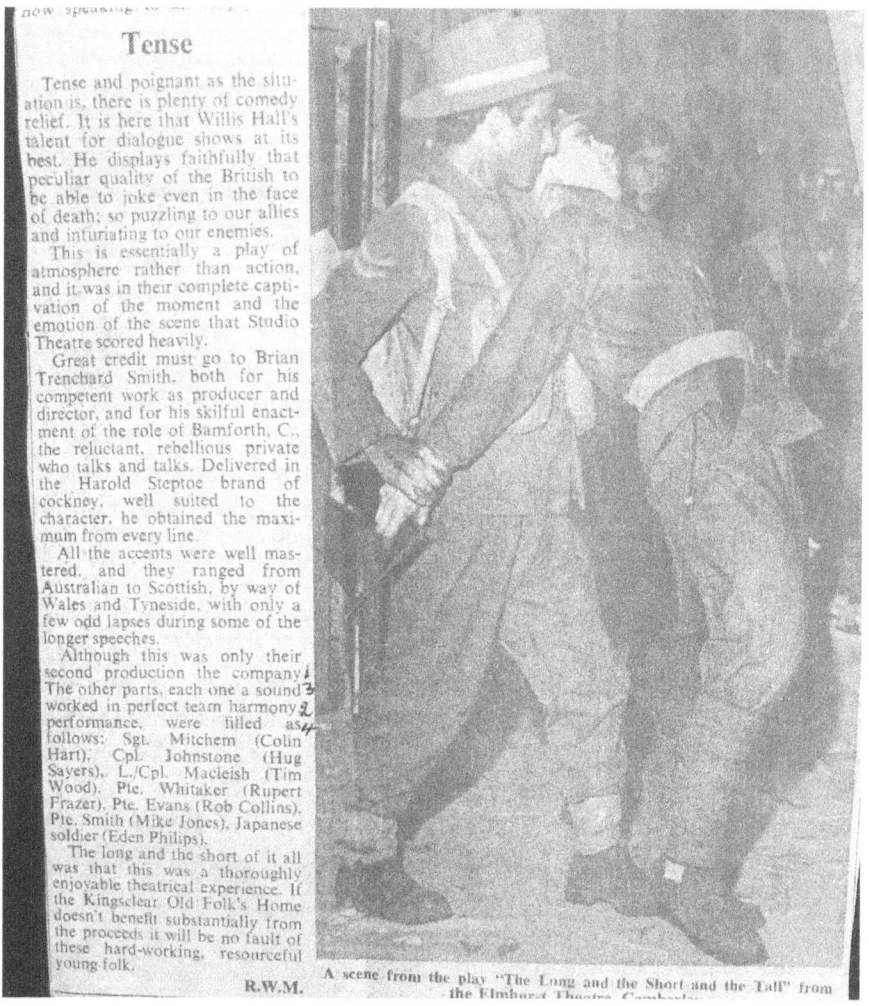

### Tense

Tense and poignant as the situation is, there is plenty of comedy relief. It is here that Willis Hall's talent for dialogue shows at its best. He displays faithfully that peculiar quality of the British to be able to joke even in the face of death; so puzzling to our allies and infuriating to our enemies.

This is essentially a play of atmosphere rather than action, and it was in their complete captivation of the moment and the emotion of the scene that Studio Theatre scored heavily.

Great credit must go to Brian Trenchard Smith, both for his competent work as producer and director, and for his skilful enactment of the role of Bamforth, C., the reluctant, rebellious private who talks and talks. Delivered in the Harold Steptoe brand of cockney, well suited to the character, he obtained the maximum from every line.

All the accents were well mastered, and they ranged from Australian to Scottish, by way of Wales and Tyneside, with only a few odd lapses during some of the longer speeches.

Although this was only their second production the company worked in perfect team harmony. The other parts, each one a sound performance, were filled as follows: Sgt. Mitchem (Colin Hart), Cpl. Johnstone (Hug Sayers), L./Cpl. Macleish (Tim Wood), Pte. Whitaker (Rupert Frazer), Pte. Evans (Rob Collins), Pte. Smith (Mike Jones), Japanese soldier (Eden Philips).

The long and the short of it all was that this was a thoroughly enjoyable theatrical experience. If the Kingsclear Old Folk's Home doesn't benefit substantially from the proceeds it will be no fault of these hard-working, resourceful young folk.

**R.W.M.**

A scene from the play "The Long and the Short and the Tall" from the Elmhurst Theatre, Cambridge.

Fate was not kind to Hugh Sayers, who returned to the role of Corporal Johnstone, and grew even better in the part. After the play, Hugh entered the Royal Military Academy Sandhurst as planned. He rose to Captain in the Welsh Guards by age twenty-six, when he was assigned to the Governor of Bermuda Sir Richard Sharples, as his aide-de-camp. At midnight on March 10, 1973, following a dinner party, Captain Sayers and the Governor were taking the Governor's Great Dane for a walk round Government House when they were ambushed by members of the Black Berets, a radical Marxist group seeking Bermuda's independence from Britain. They opened fire with automatic weapons. Hugh was reportedly killed instantly, falling with his hand in his pocket reaching for his gun. It was the night of the annual police ball and the governor's residence had only one guard on duty. The two men convicted of these and other murders were the last men hanged under British rule worldwide. Hugh, or Hug, as he was known in our group, was smart, funny and a good friend. He had a fine future ahead of him, cut short by a meaningless act of violence, which retarded rather than advanced its purported cause. My anger and dismay at this loss did not change my view that capital punishment is morally wrong.

# CHAPTER 6
## *Un Chien Andalou*

While continuing to apply for an entry level position in the business, I tried my hand at screenwriting. I had no idea what the proper formatting was, and wrote it as a series of shots. Dialogue was sparse, characters one-dimensional. Hammer was the company I really wanted to work for. They had just released *The Secret of Blood Island*, a follow up to their reviled but hugely successful *The Camp on Blood Island*, so I tried writing a treatment, proposing a third film, *Escape from Blood Island*. I mailed it in. No response. *The Secret of Blood Island* fizzled at the box office. The public taste for another Japanese war atrocity movie had waned. I would have done better to have tried adding to Hammer's *Dracula* or *Frankenstein* franchises.

A year after leaving school, I had made no real progress getting my foot in the door. Perhaps I shouldn't have left that first job with E.J. Fancey's Border Films, I wondered. I was both frustrated and hungry for a bit of adventure. Family friends had a cottage in the South of France they would be leaving for a month. I was welcome to stay. So I took the ferry from Southampton and went hitchhiking to the cottage in Èze-sur-Mer. I had left my comfort zone. Everything was new and exciting. I had £15 in my pocket to last the month. I can still remember the movies I saw along the way.

In Paris, after checking into a cheap pension (eight francs a night) on the Left Bank, I walked a block to a small cinema that happened to be showing *Le Masque du Demon* (US: *Black Sunday*), the Mario Bava classic banned in England, but still playing revival screenings in France five years after its original release. As I took one of the few remaining front row seats, a buzz rippled through the audience. I overheard whispers that Salvador Dali had just entered the theater and was taking a seat at the back of the hall. I turned 'round and just caught a glimpse of that signature mustache as the lights went down…

Bava shot the film in Rome with the Italian cast performing in English alongside the soon to be iconic Barbara Steele. She was never shown a script, just handed pages to be shot at the beginning of each day, but the film made her a star. Perhaps because my limited French meant that I only got the broad beats of the story, the French dubbed version seemed to give all dialogue scenes more gravitas and authenticity. With no apparently dumb line to take me out of the movie, I was quickly sucked into Bava's atmospheric world of cobweb-strewn crypts, where scorpions scuttle from the eye sockets of a skull.

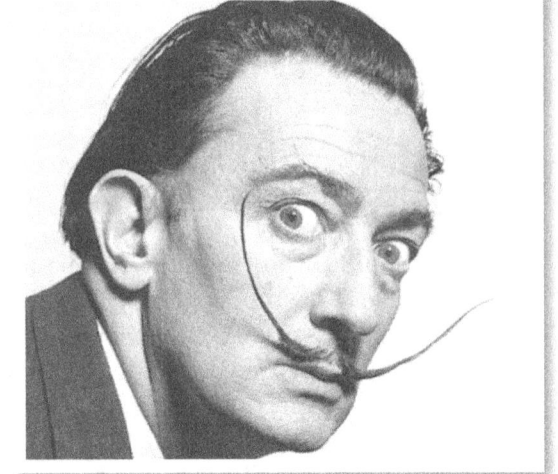

Twenty years' experience as a top Italian cinematographer informed all Bava's subsequent twenty-five movies as director. His use of color in his *gialli* is phenomenal, but this, his masterpiece, is in black and white. The sets were actually designed and painted in monochrome—no color at all—adding to the dark mood for the cast. It was only the third horror film produced in Italy in the sound era (Mussolini banned the genre during his dictatorship). The opening scene in which Barbara Steele is branded and a spiked mask hammered into her face, gushing blood, explains the sensitive British censor's ban in 1960, listing the film in official records as "Unnecessarily gruesome." Now the uncut DVD is categorized '15+'. When the movie ended and the lights came up, Salvador Dali's seat was empty.

Pity. There was a story I would have loved to have told him…

At age seventeen, I had become president of Wellington College's Film Circle, and decided to open selected screenings to a wider audience of fellow students in the Science Lecture Theater. The raked bench and desk seats were filled with 120 or so pupils, their visiting parents, and school staff, awaiting the start of a 16mm screening of a classic from the silent era. I had booked the German expressionist film *The Cabinet of Doctor Caligari* (1920). I had seen brief clips of *Caligari* on the BBC. Looked cool. Wanted to see it.

I had also needed a short to screen first, as was the custom, something running under twenty minutes. Cruising down the running-time column, I found *Un Chien Andalou* (1929), clocking in at eighteen minutes. I figured it was some Robert Flaherty-esque nature study of the wild dogs of Andalusia. Neither *Caligari* nor *Andalou* were categorized "adults only" in the Gaumont/British 16mm catalogue, so screening them did not require permission from school authorities. These were just titles in a column of more titles and rental prices. Somehow the two words Bunuel-Dali in the director's column of *Un Chien Andalou* rang no warning bells for me. Perhaps because I was rushed, perhaps because the filmmakers triggering my research interest at that time were mainly Hollywood directors, viz. Hitchcock, Mann, Aldrich, Fuller, Corman—perhaps because my Greek exam was pending, I gave the film's profile no further thought, made the booking and hurried off to class.

CUT TO: Three weeks later.

Signaling the projectionist to start, I walked to my seat in the front row, aware that many of my peers were wondering how an old silent film, other than one by Charlie Chaplin, could possibly be fun. Why was I inflicting this on them? At the same time, parents and teachers were telling them how culturally enriching the experience would be.

The lights went down and the first images appeared…

"Once upon a time" reads the caption in French,

Oh, it's a fairy tale…

A man (Bunuel), smoking furiously, hones the blade of a cutthroat razor on a leather strap, carefully testing its sharpness on his thumbnail.

Interesting…

He walks onto the balcony and stands beside a woman seated in a deck chair, gazing at a full moon. Then he bends down and pries open the woman's eyelid…

OK. You definitely have my attention.

A thin cloud slides across the moon.

The razor slices open the eyeball. Liquid spews.

AAAAGH!

A collective gasp as a hundred people respond to Bunuel and Dali's symbolic statement that we have to "look at life with new eyes." Still alarmingly real today, it was in fact a dead calf's eyeball that was slit.

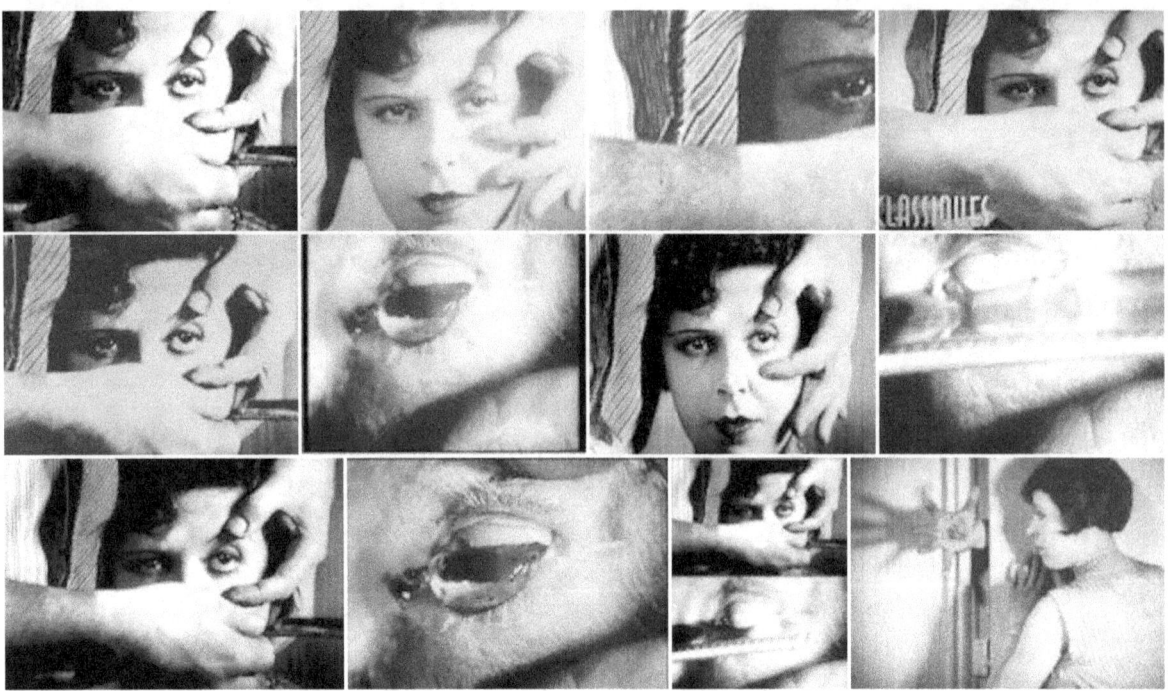

A typically British hierarchical quandary was now at hand. Ambushed in front of children by provocative imagery, every adult wanted to stop the film, but whose responsibility was it? Dali and Bunuel would have been vastly amused by their critique of bourgeois inertia generating polite paralysis within this little British audience. As indecision and nervous body language prevailed, the film continued with more incendiary shots. A hermaphrodite pokes at a severed hand in the street. Ants pour out of a hole in its palm. A man is physically restrained from raping a woman by the weight of two priests, and by two grand pianos on which lie two dead donkeys, all of which are attached to ropes he drags behind him. To my peers this was a rare dish of forbidden fruit. T-S has really done it this time…

Luis Bunuel and Salvador Dali's assault on the Catholic Church was finally too much, even for the faculty of a decidedly Protestant school. As hands began fondling a woman's naked buttocks, the projector ground to a halt. The lights came up. I was sitting in the front row and felt the pressure of hundreds of eyeballs on the back of my head. Much coughing and muttering. He's in trouble. He did it. Deliberately. A prank. No, I didn't, I wanted to say. It was an accident. I had merely broken the Eleventh Commandment: Thou shalt not assume. After a very long two minutes the projector spluttered into life again and *Caligari* rolled. I think German Expressionism proved to be less entertaining to my peers than Spanish Surrealism. Up to this point, I was not one of the cool kids. Until this moment…I had just thrown a cultural water balloon, drenching faculty with embarrassment. I did not program screenings without vetting thereafter. But for a while, I was cool. I think Dali would have appreciated the tale.

But I digress.

I hitchhiked on from Paris. I forget which town I reached (maybe Lyon?) where I saw another masterpiece in black and white—*317th Platoon*, about a group of soldiers trapped behind enemy lines during France's Indo-China war. It has stuck with me ever since because I had never seen a war film like it. *317th* was directed by Pierre Schoendoerffer, an Army cameraman who had been a POW of that conflict, captured at the battle of Dîen Biên Phû. After his liberation in 1954, he wrote books and directed films. This movie version of his own novel, also named *317ᵗʰ Platoon*, has an intense immediacy, shot with documentary realism by the great Raoul Coutard as if every angle is the point of view of a fellow soldier. You are there, trudging with the soldiers through the hot, humid jungle in monsoonal rain. Many are afflicted by dysentery and diarrhea. Monkeys are constantly screeching, making it hard for the soldiers to hear approaching Viet Minh, who seem to be active all over the forest. Firefights are brief and inconclusive. The badly injured suf-

fer and die in agony. The green lieutenant is idealistic and caring. Men are killed as a result. His experienced adjutant is a cynical realist, whose worst predictions always come to pass. We see the two men gradually develop respect for one another, before the final death-defying charge to the nearest French outpost. *317ᵗʰ Platoon* is about the craft of soldiering in defeat rather than victory. It's one of the great war films, one I might never have seen had I not been hitchhiking through France that year.

Next I met up with schoolfriend and revue coproducer Julian Beaumont in Grenoble, where he was enrolled in the University, preparing for his successful banking career. We picked a movie at random—*Le gentleman de Cocody*—because the poster suggested lively escapism.

We were not disappointed. It introduced me to the work of prolific writer/director Christian-Jaque, and the Rémy Julienne stunt driving team. Released a year later in the UK and America as *Ivory Coast Adventure*, and shot in spectacular locations, as the title suggests, it was a light-hearted Bond-inspired spy drama with a wry Gallic flavor. The local audience laughed at quite a few things I did not understand, but Julian and I came out feeling we'd had our money's worth of fun. With 2,027,645 admissions, it was one of the top-grossing movies in France in 1965. I'm sure *Cocody* was referenced in Michel Hazanavicius' pair of *OSS:117* pictures. I would watch out for Christian-Jaque movies thereafter.

My French was improving as I reached Marseilles, where I saw two Jean-Paul Belmondo films, both directed by someone unknown to me—Henri Verneuil. As I found out from *Week-end à Zuydcoote* and *Cent mille dollars au soleil*, Henri Verneuil's genre pictures were the equal of any Hollywood action directors' whose films had passed through my local cinema in England in the early 1960s. *Cent mille dollars au soleil*, co-written by Verneuil, is a buddy comedy/double cross/truck chase/heist movie, or with the advantage of hindsight, *The Good, The Bad, And The Ugly on Wheels*, because the characters display the same hardboiled *Dollars* cynicism that was influencing Euro scripts at the time.

I was new to Belmondo. So here he was, in his rakish street rogue persona, and his star quality was evident from the first scene. Same goes for *That Man from Rio*, for which he performed all his own stunts. He was always interesting, even if a film was below par.

Belmondo obviously respected Henri Verneuil's expertise, starring for him in four more films. I sense that Henri Verneuil is somewhat undervalued by Cinema historians today, but for me he brought a solid professionalism and a particular sensibility to any subject he took on.

I briefly worked as a gardener in Èze-sur-Mer, where I tended all plants, even the weeds, earning enough money for a train fare back to the ferry at Le Havre, then home. But I was thoroughly infected with wanderlust, which would surface acutely as my attempts to break into the film business kept hitting brick walls. One way into the film industry was to get a job at a laboratory. Working for two years in the lab, getting used to the aroma of formic acid, would qualify me for admittance to the union, the Association of Cinematograph, Television and Allied Technicians, a requirement across all crafts. Even then I would have to work in the lab for two more years before I could change my union grade and become a junior assistant in the cutting room. Then, assuming I showed sufficient skill, I might rise to top editor, say by age thirty-five. Then and only then would I be likely to be given a chance to direct a feature film. Patience was not my leading virtue in those days.

I decided to try my luck in the land of my father—Australia.

# PART II
## AUSTRALIA

# CHAPTER 7
## The Land of My Father

Although Hollywood and British companies occasionally shot movies there (*On the Beach*, *The Sundowners* were two of them), Australia had no self-sustaining feature film industry at the time. But there were three commercial television networks and a government broadcaster, the Australian Broadcasting Commission. Union membership was not a requirement for employment. I had two uncles in Sydney, cousins in Perth and Melbourne and Brisbane. In fact, all the Trenchard-Smiths except us lived in Australia, and had done since the 1860s. As the son of an Australian there were no immigration issues. I had a strong gut instinct that relocation to Australia was the right move, and it was. Australia altered my life and worldview, vastly for the better.

I knew a reference of some kind would be helpful in the job hunt. So I went to the office of Reflex Films, sat down at a typewriter, and wrote a glowing recommendation on company letterhead. Then I told Basil Cox, one of the partners, of my plans, and asked if he would be kind enough to sign it. Luckily he was amused by my effrontery, appended his signature, and wished me luck.

I bought a Russian 8mm camera with an excellent lens to record the journey, and tried to placate my parents, who were worried about whether I would be conscripted to serve in Vietnam. Australia had committed to send 8,000 troops to aid America's war. For my part, I was determined to go to Australia. Let the chips fall where they may. I had enough money saved from my bookkeeping salary to buy a ticket aboard the P&O liner Canberra. Then my voyage was delayed by the British seamen's strike, causing all passengers booked on British ships to be transferred to foreign-owned vessels. As a result, I would arrive in Australia two weeks after my 20th birthday. Those over twenty on arrival in Australia were not eligible for the conscription ballot.

I was transferred to the Achille Lauro. The ship was built to carry 1,250 passengers. By the time we picked up all the European migrants to Australia stranded by the seaman's strike, in Genoa, Naples, Messina, Malta, Piraeus, Beirut, and Port Said, we were carrying 1,700. It made for a lively voyage and an accelerated cultural education. I was able to spend a day in each of those ports, trying to capture them on 8mm. As I took a bus from Piraeus to Athens, I passed by the pier where the iconic scene of Melina Mercouri stripping and swimming was filmed for *Never on a Sunday*. After eight years of studying classical Greek, it was wonderful to walk 'round the Acropolis.

At Suez, I joined a tour that sped at breakneck speed to Cairo, where I saw belly dancing, toured the British Museum, and was shrugged off the back of a camel at the Pyramids. Then it was back on the bus to catch up with the ship as it continued through the Suez Canal. Through the window I filmed miles of military camps in the desert. Egypt was, I think in retrospect, already gearing up for the Six Day War. We boarded a launch at Suez, just as the Achille Lauro sailed past. It did not stop, just slowed enough to deploy a floating pontoon beside a doorway just above the waterline. The launch captain gunned the engine and caught up. Somehow none of us fell into the water getting back on board.

Reaching the Yemeni port of Aden we were advised not to go ashore because a lady on the ship's previous voyage had been killed on the quayside by a grenade. A group of us went ashore anyway. I filmed jeeps full of British soldiers cruising through the streets. There was a palpably tense atmosphere. Britain was experiencing the downside of colonial rule. Fifty plus years later a proxy war still rages in Yemen, with no end in sight.

There was tension on the Achille Lauro, too, during the 9-day leg from Aden to Perth. Just ocean, horizon to horizon, day and night, every day. Overcrowding. Competing Greek and Italian "cabins of ill repute" in the stern. Alcohol. A couple of fights in the bar. People were getting stir crazy. The ship organized trap shooting on the deck, culminating in a contest, which I won. Finally, landfall at Freemantle, Western Australia.

An albatross followed the ship as we sailed on to Melbourne. The runner-up in the trap shooting contest, a migrant from Lebanon, would jokingly aim an imaginary gun at the bird cruising alongside. Bang! Bang! he would exclaim. Trying to explain the implications of *The Rime of The Ancient Mariner* when neither of us spoke the other's language was challenging. The bird followed the ship till it reached Melbourne four days later, then flew safely away. In 1985 the Achille Lauro would be hijacked by terrorists and a decade after that catch fire and sink in the Indian Ocean. The albatross is not to blame.

The ship docked in Melbourne where I met my cousin Teddy Trenchard-Smith for the first time. He was advertising manager at the Melbourne Sun Pictorial, and had set up an interview for me at Crawford Productions, a pioneering company first in radio, now television. They made *Homicide*, Australia's first cop show and a ratings smash. The interview went well and before I re-boarded the ship, I heard from Cousin Teddy that Crawfords were interested in taking me on as a general trainee and that I should get in touch upon landing in Sydney. Sailing into that magnificent harbor on a bright sunny day, past the Opera House under construction, to berth at Circular Quay, with the Bridge bestriding the waterway beyond like a colossus, I knew this was the city for me.

Uncle Ollie, my father's favorite of his three brothers, and his wife Renata picked me up and installed me in their spare room. Ollie was kind enough to drive me across town to my first interview at Channel Seven, and on the way back I saw another TV station along the Epping Highway. Channel Ten had been on air for just under two years. I asked Ollie if he wouldn't mind pulling into their car park, for a minute. I would rush in and leave a resume with the personnel office. Ollie was always happy to help. Perhaps I was mistaken for someone who actually had an appointment, but for some reason I was sent up to the personnel manager's office, a place that had been the site of one of those *stranger than fiction* tales from the annals of Australian Television.

The personnel manager, Mr. Reginald Pendergast, was a pleasant but somewhat nervous man, understandably so, as I learned later. His office was where payroll was distributed. Four months previous, two armed men had burst in, tied him up along with his assistant Jill Hodges, stolen pay packets totaling AUD$8,276, and then vanished. Police suspected an inside job. When one of the robbers, Kevin Harry Wittaker, 24, was arrested, he claimed that a former TV newsreader and quiz show host Chuck Faulkner had advised him on where and when the payroll was vulnerable. After the robbery, he had driven to Faulkner's flat in Double Bay to divide the loot. Police noted that both men were gamblers, frequenting inner city gin rummy clubs, and that Faulkner had paid Wittaker for providing "business contacts." Chuck Faulkner, 44, had been Channel Nine's first news presenter between 1956 and 1964, which made him one of the most recognized faces on Australian television, until he dared to ask Nine's owner and notorious Scrooge Sir Frank Packer for a raise, causing his contract not to be renewed. By 1966, after two divorces and a run of bad luck at the card tables, Chuck was in financial difficulties. Circumstantial evidence and a witness prepared to testify was enough for the police, who charged Chuck with having "incited, moved, procured and counseled" Kevin Wittaker to commit the robbery. But Judge Levine told the jury it would be dangerous to convict Faulkner on the uncorroborated evidence of an alleged accomplice who might be trying to gain a shorter sentence. Chuck was found not guilty, but the legal expenses bankrupted him. However, in an ironic turn of fate, Crawford Productions hired him to play Detective Sergeant Vickers in their new cop show, *Division 4*. He went on to be a series regular for 301 episodes till the show ended in 1975. He moved to America and became a talk show host on radio station WNIS in Norfolk, Virginia until the mid-1980s. Ah, the twists and turns of life.

I was unaware of the robbery and the real trauma Mr. Pendergast and Miss Hodges had suffered in this very room, as they accepted my impromptu arrival and perused my resume. The only opening available at Channel Ten was for the afternoon newsreader position. Would I like to audition? Sure. I came back the next day and sat in front of the camera in the news studio. No teleprompter. Just the script. I read well but was scuppered by my plummy British public-school tones. My voice might have been acceptable on the

BBC's colonial cousin the ABC, but not at the newest commercial network aimed at the broadest audience. Australia has a bit of a love/hate relationship with the mother country.

But the News Director Norm Bennell spotted film editing experience on the glowing reference I had written on Reflex Films letterhead. One of his news film cutters had just given notice. I can do that, I said, confident I would soon learn. Thus I started in Channel Ten's news division two weeks later. In the game at last! If I had not been passing Channel Ten at that time on that day…If I had accepted the Crawfords offer as soon as I landed in Melbourne, my life and body of work might have been completely different. I have benefited from so many examples of serendipity, as you will see.

Senior News Editor Penny Curtis didn't mind being given a trainee. I had used a 16mm hand-wound viewer and cement splicer when I had edited the Central Electricity Generating Board footage. Penny showed me how to use the sound reader for selecting interview sections. She shepherded me through the technique of editing news till I was up to speed. And speed was required, particularly as the clock ticked towards the 6:30 p.m. airtime. The journalist assigned to a particular story would sit with the next available editor who would fast-wind the footage through the viewer. The journalist would say, for example, "Give me the best fifteen seconds of the motorcade arriving, then cut to the interview soundbite starting here and ending there." When the story was assembled the journalist would review, reading the copy over it, and make adjustments to words or image as necessary. Then the stories, generally between twenty-five and forty seconds each, were assembled onto one reel in the designated order with a second of black between each. The reel was loaded onto a telecine machine which would roll each clip, on cue, from the news studio.

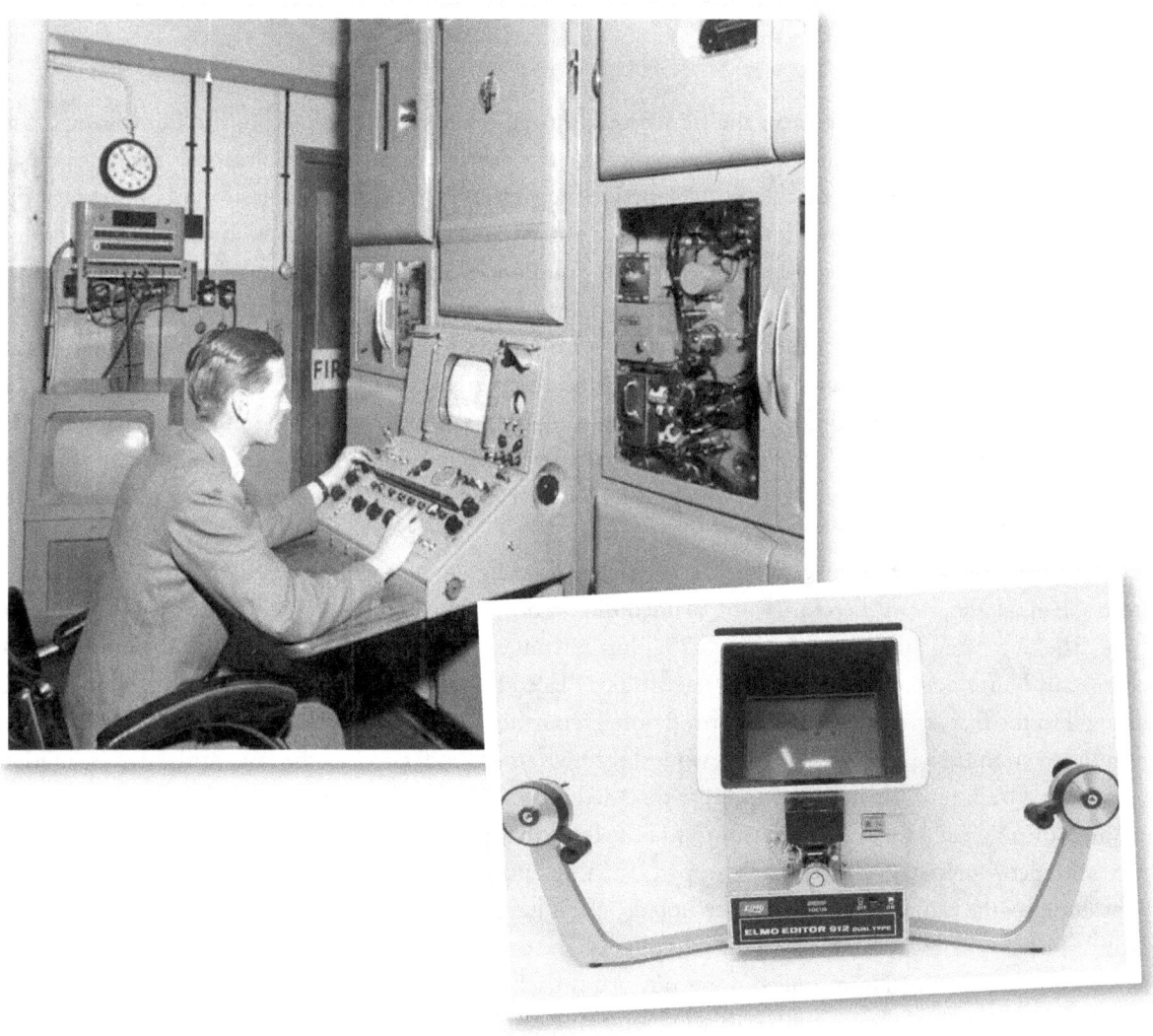

Wearing white gloves to protect the film from dirt and scratches, I would wind the film through the viewer, cut out the relevant shots a frame ahead of the chosen 'in point,' and a frame after the 'out point,' hang them by a sprocket hole on the pin rack beside the viewer. I would swap shots around on the rack till they were in the chosen editorial order. Between eighteen and twenty stories were broadcast each night. Sometimes I was cutting two stories at the same time and once I muddled the footage.

On October 22, 1966 Soviet spy George Blake escaped from Wormwood Scrubs Prison in the UK. There was a rumor on the police radio, which the newsroom monitored, that Blake was on a particular flight to Sydney under a false passport. Our cameraman at the airport got great shots of police unloading tracker dogs from a paddy wagon. Unfortunately, I was cutting a dog show story at the same time, hanging the shots on the same pin rack. When the *escaped spy false alarm* clip went to air, a low angle shot of an Alsatian being led out of the paddy wagon was followed by a poodle striding, head held high, past an appreciative crowd. Ouch!

It was not my worst mistake. When an RAAF Sabre jet fighter crashed near Newcastle, an hour's drive from Channel Ten, news director Norm Bennell did an onsite report himself, arriving back in the nick of time. The film came off the processor at 6:25. "Just one take, put it on a separate reel, get it round to telecine," said Norm before rushing back to the studio. I laced the film through the viewer and sound reader, listened to the first sentence: "This is Norm Bennell reporting to you from the crash site of…" I spliced the numbered countdown leader ahead of it, wound through to the end, checked the last words, then wound it back onto a fresh reel. The telecine operator threaded it up with less than a minute to spare. In the control room, Norm signaled the studio director to roll the lead story and watched his report go to air. After Norm's first sentence—precisely where I had stopped listening and then fast-wound the reel to where the interview ended—the cameraman's voice interrupted: "We'll have to do it again, mate…" "Ah, hell!" exclaimed Norm. Just as well it was not his usual turn of phrase. The cameraman kept rolling expecting Norm to begin again immediately, but Norm pulled notes out of his back pocket and studied them. For eleven seconds. Probably the longest eleven seconds of his TV reporting career. Then he put away the notes and started the report again. He had not told me of his false start, but I had broken the Eleventh Commandment, and by doing so had embarrassed Norm on national television. Luckily, he forgave me.

There were political conflicts within the station's news division. The Head of News, Lionel Hudson, wanted strict neutrality on the Vietnam War issue. Norm Bennell, as his news director, was bitterly opposed to Australia's contribution of 8,000 troops. There were real constraints on how he could slant a story. Only the copy was vetted, not the visuals. But news chief Hudson would watch the broadcast. So he had to be subtle.

I learned how a story could be flavored by which images were selected. When I was assigned the footage of Prime Minister Harold Holt on a State visit to Thailand, Norm said: "Make it look like an armed camp." I chose shots where a military vehicle or body of troops dominated the frame. Rather than a wide angle, I chose a long lens shot of Holt inspecting the guard of honor viewed through a row of soldiers' bayonets gleaming in foreground.

On October 20th, when U.S. President Lyndon Johnson paid a goodwill visit to Australia, Prime Minister Harold Holt, accompanied by New South Wales Premier Robin Askin, showed him round the sights of Sydney. Thousands demonstrated at Hyde Park Corner as his motorcade came into the city from the airport. Some lay on the road to block the cars. This is when Premier Robin Askin uttered his infamous words:

"Ride over the bastards."

The driver ignored the command. Police removed the demonstrators with some vigor.

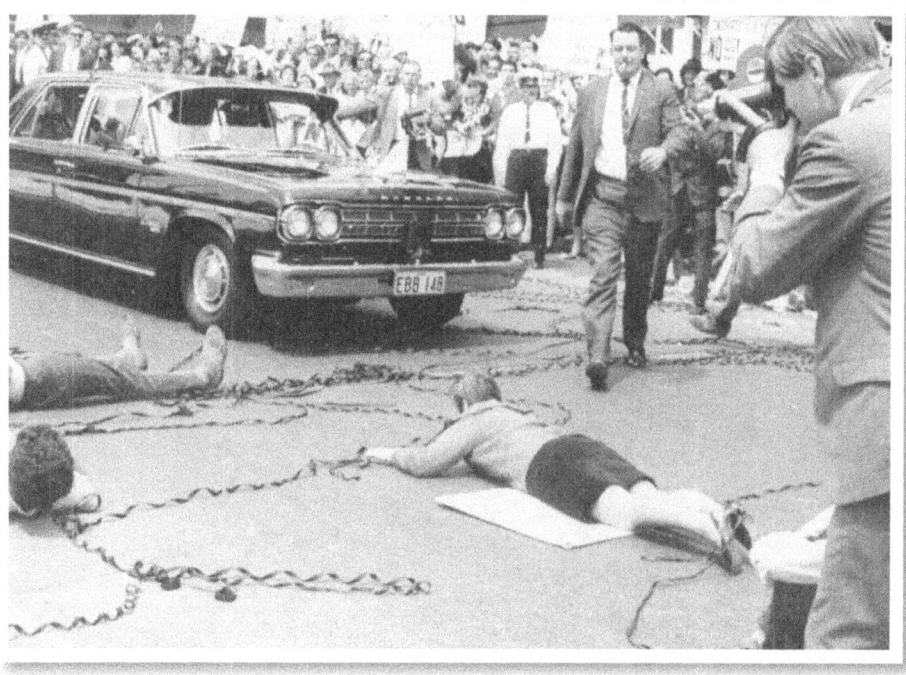

"Make it look as violent as you can" was Norm's instruction. Other news crews shooting from the pavement kept their cameras on tripod. Channel Ten's cameraman Greg Hunter, who would shoot great footage for my *Danger Freaks* show years later, got into the melee, whip panning his handheld Arriflex across the fray, lying down, capturing a dramatic low angle of struggling demonstrators carried past camera. Visnews picked up Ten's coverage, and it showed across the world.

Four months in the news department of an Australian TV station had turned my worldview upside down. The human cost of colonialism was missing from my education. Britain had no troops in Vietnam, so coverage of the war in 1966 was not a dominant issue for UK media. I was ineligible for the ballot, unlike others of my age. The station's music librarian lost her conscripted fiancé in the battle of Long Tan. Vietnam was an ill-advised war, as the French experience showed, but Australia's politicians did not dare break ranks with the United States. Labour Party activists scorned the government's motivation as "Fellas for dollars."

The News Department sent me out as a cameraman/field reporter when they were shorthanded. Once I was sent to Canberra, the nation's capital, to cover Princess Alexandra of Kent, cousin to Queen Elizabeth, planting a tree at Government House. The shrub was already loosely positioned in the ground. All the Princess had to do was heap a last shovelful of dirt onto it for the photo op. I joined the gathered camera crews and photographers, equipped with a clockwork wind Bell & Howell. While we waited for Princess Alexandra to arrive, I took some scene-setting shots, and forgot Rule One of cameras powered by clockwork: rewind after every shot. So, just as the Princess scooped earth onto her shovel, the camera cut out. I rewound frantically, but by the time I was ready to roll again, the Princess had deposited the requisite shovelful of earth at the foot of the shrub and was smiling at the gathered media. Applause all round. Oh God, I've missed the money shot! So without hesitation I asked: "Excuse me, Ma'am, my camera jammed, would you mind doing that again?" Sharp intake of breath issued from British embassy officials who were aghast at this lapse of protocol. But the Princess graciously obliged. Later at the press reception, I was able to thank her. She and her husband Angus Ogilvy were both relaxed and friendly, asked me questions about Australia from a young ex-pat's perspective, before a royal equerry steered them away to more important guests.

As mentioned, I've always had sympathy for the Royal Family. They symbolize British heritage and make an important contribution to tourism. To anti-Royalists they represent an outdated class structure and a drain on the public purse. Lifelong representation of an historic institution is a difficult job, made all the harder by a coprophagic tabloid media.

# CHAPTER 8
## Frontier Television

Channel Ten, just two years old when I joined, felt like frontier television. Everyone was on a learning curve, particularly me. If you volunteered for a new responsibility, there was generally a positive response. When I went to the cinema in England, the Coming Attractions, or Trailers—trailblazers being a possible derivation—had always intrigued me. Why did they choose that bit? I would often wonder. The next week I would see the film in question, noting which elements had been emphasized, perhaps out of proportion, and which aspects had been disguised. There was an art to it and it fascinated me. Channel Ten's promo director Ian Bannerman, hired from the UK, was overworked. I offered to help increase the output, and he was kind enough to give me a shot. When my news shift ended, I would do two hours of overtime a few nights a week. My interest in the manipulation of image for a promotional rather than narrative purpose would ultimately bear fruit. In a parallel career to filmmaking, I would write and produce over 100 trailers and product reels in the UK, Australia, and the United States. But that's another story…

In the "Have a go, mate" culture of Channel Ten, Ian Bannerman had volunteered to host a spoof horror movie show: "The Awful Movie with Deadly Earnest," which would be broadcast live every Friday night at 11 p.m.

Ian, playing Deadly Earnest, would rise from his coffin like a pale male Vampira (or like the 1980s Elvira, Mistress of the Dark, whom Vampira unsuccessfully sued for plagiarism). Then Ian would introduce, in strong satirical vein, a horror movie of the 50s, many of which had had the "good bits" cut out by the Australian censor. In commercial breaks, live to air, he and other volunteers, myself included, spoofed commercials while maintaining a gothic context. I once played a Joe the Gadget Man character selling discounted intravenous feeding tubes to vampires. The senior station management were perhaps in bed at this hour and never saw some of the things we got up to.

In the Channel Ten building, there was much human comedy to observe, as is common in any place of business. Sometimes truth is stranger than fiction. Imagine you are reading a screenplay submitted by an unknown writer, and you come across a scene such as the one I offer here. Come on, you might exclaim, that's absurd, that would never happen.

INT. CHANNEL TEN GENERAL MANAGER'S OFFICE  DAY.
The head of the network affiliate sips tea while reviewing correspondence. His office is distinguished by its neatness. Everything is shipshape, befitting a retired naval officer. His name is REGINALD FOX. The intercom buzzes.

FOX
Yes…

SECRETARY
Bruce Gyngell of Channel Nine is calling.

FOX
Put him on.

What did his opposite number at a rival network, a charming fellow at industry functions—and worse, a CEO with higher ratings—have to say?

FOX
Hello Bruce, what can I do for you?

GYNGELL (V.O.)
Have you seen your Guy Adams column today?

He reaches for the early editions of the two afternoon papers that had been delivered with the tea.

FOX
Oh, no. Have we made a boo-boo?
Is it glaring?

GYNGELL (V.O.)
Well, I guess you could say that.

Fox turns to the page where their weekly column Guy Adams Presents touts the hot shows of the week, all of course to be found on Channel Ten, the bright new TV station in town. There is no such person as Guy Adams. The photo of Mr. Adams that sat in the top corner is in fact that of a suave male model, and the column has been written by several different Channel Ten publicity staffers over the past year. The words "paid announcement" in very small print can be found by a diligent reader.

But what immediately stands out in the half page ad is its signature design: a column of seven paragraphs, the first letter of each being bold, black, and in much larger typeface.

At first glance nothing seems amiss. Then, as Mr. Fox's eyes scroll quickly down the paragraphs, those embossed first letters stop being a vertical acrostic, and unite into discernible words, which read:

F U C K F O X.

CUT TO FLASHBACK SEQUENCE:

Mr. Fox is at his desk studying the proofs for the Guy Adams Presents ad that will appear a few days. Awaiting his approval is a slender woman of thirty-three with striking red hair, his publicity officer JENNY PHILLIPS, whose dress reflects a free spirit.

Mr. Fox crosses out the first word of the top paragraph and replaces it with another. "Fine Trumpeter" becomes "Hot Trumpeter." He looks up at her.

FOX
It's better. Really.

JENNY
If you say so.

CUT BACK TO:
A stunned Mr. Fox. The top paragraph reads "Fine Trumpeter" again.

INTERIOR    TV STATION CORRIDOR

Jenny Phillips rounds a corner and comes face to face with twenty-year old YOUNG FILM EDITOR, whom she had invited into her bed a few times, though not for a while.

> JENNY
> There you are. Wanted to say goodbye.
> Got to be gone in ten minutes.

The word had spread like wildfire.

> YOUNG FILM EDITOR
> You are demented, wonderfully demented!
> Why did you do that?

> JENNY
> I got tired of him changing my copy every week.
> I was going to leave anyway. Sick of the place.
> Time for a change. See ya.

She hugs him, and is gone.

INTERIOR    SENIOR EXECUTIVE'S OFFICE

The senior executive, WINSTON FRECKER, stares at the page, the offending ad flashing like a hazard light. Not a good day to ask if his contract will be renewed when it expires in six weeks. He picks up the phone.

> FRECKER
> Get me the Art Department.

INT. CHANNEL 10 NEWSROOM

A journalist, BARRY, makes an announcement to his colleagues as he displays an empty money bag and a rectangular sheet of white cardboard.

> BARRY
> This just came from upstairs. The whole staff is expected to sign, and make a donation to go towards the cost of the gift. Doesn't have to be more than a dollar.

The staff look at the placard. There is fancy embossed writing along the top with room below for the one hundred plus signatures of the staff.

CLOSE UP OF EMBOSSED WRITING:

It reads "The opinions expressed in the press are not necessarily those of the staff of this station."

INTERIOR   TV STATION EDITING ROOM

The assembled editors stare at the sparsely-filled money bag, and the placard which now has several columns of differing lengths, as new departments add their signatures.

YOUNG FILM EDITOR
So, let me get this straight. Fox's going to be given a cigarette lighter with his initials engraved on it, so that every time he lights up, he can be reminded of the time of he was embarrassed in the press and amongst his peers. "We want to rub balm on your wound, but they were out of balm at the store, so we got salt instead." Right? And what about "not necessarily"? Does it mean it is possible that some of the staff of this station do actually think: "You ought to get fucked"? Like: "We want to make you feel better, but in the interests of statistical accuracy, full disclosure obliges us to acknowledge this possibility. So please accept our humble symbol of your humiliation."

OLDER FILM EDITOR
That about covers it.

The Young Film Editor thinks for a moment,

YOUNG FILM EDITOR
Well, I know someone who would definitely sign if she were here…

He takes a pen and writes "Jenny Phillips" at the top of the far left column of names.

OLDER FILM EDITOR
You're mad!

YOUNG FILM EDITOR
True. It's the Irish in me. But don't worry. You can start your own column over there. I'll just mess with this one…Naturally, as a gesture of solidarity, I'll be signing my own name.

He writes at the bottom of the same column "Jack D. Ripper. "

YOUNG FILM EDITOR
And I think Her Majesty the Queen would want to weigh in on this issue too…

With a different colored pen, he adds "Elizabeth Regina" at the bottom of another column.

INTERIOR   SENIOR EXECUTIVE'S OFFICE

The Senior Executive and Art department Staff stare at the now fully signed placard. As well as "Jack D. Ripper" and "Elizabeth Regina", a couple of other names of questionable veracity in different handwriting have become evident. The presentation is scheduled to begin in five minutes.

FRECKER
Oh dear. That won't do.

INTERIOR. TV STATION CANTEEN

All the station staff that can leave their posts are gathered in the canteen. Mr. Fox has graciously accepted the cigarette lighter from Mr. Frecker, thanked his staff, and is using the momentum of their applause to propel himself from the room.

Fox passes the placard displayed on an easel and sees strips of black masking tape cover signatures in five different places.

That's absurd. True. That could not have happened. It did.

The edition of the afternoon paper sold out before the next delivery from which Jenny's version of The Ad had been pulled. Reporters sent copies to friends overseas. In 1969 Jenny Philips met and later married a struggling artist named Robert Dickerson, who became one of Australia's most eminent painters before his death in 2015. His work is exhibited all over the world, with some paintings selling for north of 100K. Jennifer Dickerson herself became a published poet and author.

We reconnected a few years ago when I needed a painting by a well-known artist for the Lifetime movie *Absolute Deception* which I shot on the Gold Coast of Australia. The scene called for the villain (a Bernie Madoff/Rupert Murdoch hybrid) to boast of his wealth to the heroine, by gesturing the expensive painting he just bought on a whim. To give credibility to his words, the painting shown needed to be by an artist familiar at least to art connoisseurs. The day of the shoot was approaching fast, but I preferred not to quickly photoshop a lookalike Picasso, for instance. The artist should be Australian. We put a call out to art galleries within driving distance, but what renowned artist would allow us to use his work in this way, and at what cost? Then I learned there was a Dickerson painting hanging in a gallery not too far away. It did not take me long to track down Jenny and get her permission. Thus the characters are looking at a well-known Dickerson painting "The Businessman," which underscores the anti-One-percent subtext of this Lifetime potboiler.

Towards the end of 1967, I was getting restless again. So I tried pitching a movie magazine show to another Sydney TV station, TCN Channel Nine. I met with Pat Condon, an executive with overlapping responsibilities in production and promotion, and evident entrepreneurial drive. He would later become one of Australia's leading impresarios, producing concerts and opera and bringing in such artists as Frank Sinatra, Bob Dylan, Tina Turner, Bruce Springsteen, Bob Hope, Sammy Davis Jr, Liza Minnelli, Peter Allen, Elvis Costello, Lou Reed and Simon & Garfunkel, to name a few. Check out his website for just a glimpse of his amazing career.

Pat Condon didn't spark to my idea (well, not until four years later) but he picked up on my promo experience at Channel Ten. The battle for rating supremacy between the three competing commercial networks, which would determine their respective advertising revenues, would start again in early February. He needed someone to create *launch promos* for the new American and British series that comprised the bulk of the prime time drama Channel Nine offered its viewers at that time. Pat wanted a new approach to promos that were flashier than those of Channel Seven, the closest rival. He would try me out for a month at $70 per week and see how I did. Luckily, I did OK. I would work with many of these executives over several happy years. I'll be forever grateful to Pat for the opportunities that sprang from his decision.

EMPLOYEES WHO HAD SERVED THE FIRST TEN YEARS OF
TCN CHANNEL 9 SYDNEY
1956 – 1966

Back row: Jock Harkess  Mike Ramsden  Ian Faircloth  Ron Haynes  Alex Baz (Camera)  Noel Swanson  Peter Skelton
2nd row:  Peter Kinna  Barry Ford  Pat Condon  (Camera)  Brian C.Morelli  Bruce Gyngell  Roy Phillis  Jeff Hancock
Front row:  Peter Cox  Ted Greensil  Vince Florentine  Cyril Bond  Ken Sidery  Jack Maude

The premiering series were dream shows to work on: the debut seasons of the original *Star Trek*, and *Ironside*, the new vehicle for Raymond Burr, star of the long running *Perry Mason* series. There was producer Irwin Allen's personal favorite from his oeuvre, even though it only lasted one season—*Time Tunnel*. I loved the show so much that I made special 30-second promos for fifteen of the thirty episodes. From the UK there were two offbeat British shows: *The Champions*, an espionage/sci-fi/paranormal cocktail, and *Randall & Hopkirk (Deceased)*, a comedy drama about two private eyes, one of whom is a ghost. Neither Brit series went beyond the first season, but each developed a cult following years later on DVD. They rated higher in Australia than in any other country.

In addition to adapting promotional material supplied with each show for the launch, I would add another strand of promos to the campaign that were, in effect, short music videos. It was fairly simple. I would take the standard opening title montage, then replace any bland images with more sexy, violent, high-production-value shots culled from multiple episodes, then incorporate new titles and an Australian voiceover tag line.

During the course of my work I had been introduced to the CEO of Channel Nine, Bruce Gyngell. He was at that time married to the niece of the aforementioned owner of the National Nine Network, Sir Frank Packer, with whom I would have a brief encounter a few years later. Channel Nine won the opening round of the ratings by a handy margin. Whether Nine's high ratings for the week these shows premiered were due to my promos or just the strength of the programs is anybody's guess. But the win made Mr. Gyngell look good to his formidable uncle-in-law. Sir Frank had a habit of firing people who did not deliver results. It was said he even fired an office boy who presumed to talk to him in the elevator. After the ratings success, Bruce Gyngell offered me a fulltime job. I expressed gratitude, but told him, after five months at TCN Nine, that I wanted to expand my experience, particularly of color television, which was a few years away in Australia. To that end I intended to travel to Japan and America, and then visit my parents in England before deciding on my next move.

Then Gyngell spontaneously offered to make me a 16mm kinescope of my best promos to take with me. Kinescope was a process that transferred videotape to film. At that time in Australia all promos were completed on 2-inch videotape in the PAL system. Japan and America broadcast in NTSC. The two systems are incompatible. (The joke is that NTSC means Never The Same Color, whereas PAL is Perfect At Last.) But TV stations everywhere had 16mm film projectors. A short reel of my work would be an invaluable calling card. Just another example of how the kindness of others can assist in the development of a career.

# CHAPTER 9
## Further Explorations

By living frugally, I had saved enough money to book passage on a ship to Japan, for a 3-week stay, then another ship from Japan to Hawaii, a flight to San Francisco, then an open ticket on Pan Am from New York to London. A 3-month travel pass on the Greyhound Bus Line would provide transportation within America. My stay in America would last as long as I could stretch my remaining funds.

The ship docked at Yokkaichi. With friends I had made on the 2-week voyage, I took the bullet train to Tokyo and shared rooms at the Miyako Hotel, a Japanese style ryokan in the suburb of Takadanobaba. One stop away on the Yamate line was Shinjuku, where Tokyo people went for entertainment, rather than the Ginza district which was mainly for tourists. First order of business: see a Japanese movie. It was a routine *chambarra* or samurai picture, more talk than swordplay, but the first Japanese movie I had seen that was shot in color. My study of action staging was expanded by nightly visits to yakuza and samurai movies. Lots of flashing blades and bright red blood. More blood than was ever allowed in western movies. Hmm… food for thought.

We would frequent big tents behind Shinjuku railway station where we ate whale meat and yakitori served robata style with copious amounts of beer and hot sake. It was frequented by students who wanted to learn English from foreigners. I picked up a useful word, "benjo", which I was told was Japanese for toilet. For many subsequent years at sushi bars in Australia and the US, I would drop the word "benjo" either to the greeter or the sushi chef when requesting directions to the bathroom. Their reactions contained a flicker of surprise. It turns out I had been asking Japanese people, not: "Where is the toilet?" but rather: "Where is the shit trench?" Benjo was a macho slang term used by the Yakuza crime clans, derived from the trench dug for fieldworkers to squat over in medieval Japan. Tough guy talk. Perhaps the suspicion of some yakuza affiliation got me a better cut of sushi…

Before leaving Australia, I had a business card printed in English and Japanese identifying me as TCN Channel Nine Promotion Director. I also brought my old Channel Ten photo ID Press Pass, issued to news cameramen and reporters by the New South Wales Police Department the logo of which dominated the front cover. "Television policeman..?" asked one puzzled executive at a Tokyo TV station. But the combination of press pass, business card, and a reel of promos for foreign programs was sufficient to get me in the door to quite a few places just by cold calling. Japanese courtesy and the language barrier notwithstanding, they seemed genuinely to like the vigor of my promos, and I responded in kind when they showed me theirs. At the national public broadcaster NHK I was able to observe color television production of news and variety shows. I was particularly intrigued by the chroma key process, by which a presenter stood at a podium in front of a blue screen, yet the viewer saw him standing in front of a long flight of steps framed by tall classical pillars. This huge set was in fact a 2-foot tall miniature of painted balsa wood, sitting on a platform in front of another camera. Electronic back projection. Cool.

The NHK studio control rooms had panels of fancy wipes more sophisticated than those I had seen in Australia. One intriguing innovation was the audio modulated wipe. A standard barn door or curtain wipe, peeling apart to reveal the incoming image, could be made to pulsate to the rhythm of music or sound effects on the audio track. I would use—and perhaps overuse—this added visual pizzazz in TV commercials for Kay Tel Records' 20 Red Hot Hits two years later.

Moviegoing in Tokyo opened my eyes to cultural differences in Cinema's forbidden fruit, previously unavailable to me due to the vigilance of British and Australian censors. While walking with shipboard friends one morning through Marunouchi, the business district, we noticed a movie theater playing a triple bill of softcore porn, judging by the stills of naked ladies in various dramatic situations, their nipples masked from the passing public with black bars. Nudity in movies was permitted in Japan provided no genitalia were shown. My first experience of sustained screen nudity had been Naked as Nature Intended, a joys of nudism faux documentary released by former employer E.J. Fancey. Happy nudists sitting, legs crossed, in deck chairs, watching friends leaping about on the badminton court, with foreground objects masking their genitalia. These Japanese movies went considerably further than that. All were shot in black and white scope, but one was presented in 3-D…the one playing at that moment. My friends and I pondered. None of us had never seen either soft core porn or 3-D. I'm sure it was the 3-D that carried the day…

We were issued disposable red and green tinted anaglyph glasses, the way audiences experienced 3-D in the early fifties, then were ushered into a small theater. Maybe ten of the fifty seats were occupied. While seeing nudity in 3-D had some initial novelty value, we found the content pretty dispiriting, as much of the simulated sex involved violence. For instance—a man carried a naked semi-conscious girl to a large fish tank in his apartment where he raised piranha. He dipped her buttocks an inch below the surface for the piranha to nibble. The girl chirruped a mixture of pleasure and pain. Ugh. The strong undercurrent of sexual violence began to make us feel soiled by watching. We noticed that the theater was frequented by businessman in suits and ties.. No women. They would only stay for about twenty minutes, then get up and leave. We joined the next group to depart. Apparently these movies provided some kind of therapy for the high-pressured salary man in the banking district.

I saw two American movies during my Japanese visit. In *Wait Until Dark*, the Audrey Hepburn suspense thriller tautly directed by Terence Young, I gasped in shock along with everyone else in the theater when Alan Arkin leaped across the room to grab blind Audrey Hepburn's ankle. A good story well told crosses all cultures.

*Planet of the Apes*, one of Charlton Heston's best, was playing to packed Tokyo houses, subtitled in Japanese. What a fantastic movie it was, directed with epic sweep by Franklin Schaffner, with ground-

breaking prosthetic make up, propelled by an Oscar-winning avant-garde score by Jerry Goldsmith. *Empire Magazine* named it one of the 500 Best Movies of All Time. Seeing the first and best *Apes* in a packed theater in Shinjuku, I was the only *gaijin* in the audience. Everyone around me was as gripped by this science fiction allegory as I was. The actors playing the simian soldiers all wore green jumpsuits (seven years later I would be set on fire while wearing one of those very jumpsuits). At the end of the movie, when the Statue of Liberty was revealed poking out of the sand, evidently a casualty of nuclear war, there was an intake of breath, then a silence that continued as the audience left the hall. The movie's conclusion must have had an unique resonance for that Shinjuku audience twenty-two years after Hiroshima and Nagasaki.

After three weeks in Japan I boarded another ship, and five days later landed in Honolulu. Just in time for my 22nd birthday, which I was lucky to survive. I had rented a Mini Moke to tour Oahu, and when I drove out of the lot onto a 6-lane highway, my internal autopilot was still set to righthand drive Australian and British rules of the road. Consequently, I turned left, rather than right—straight into a fast-approaching wall of cars. I swung the Moke onto the grass verge in the nick of time amid angry hooting of horns. Otherwise, I remember nothing eventful about that trip to Hawaii other than seeing Goldie Hawn in a bikini dancing the twist on *Rowan and Martin's Laugh-In*. In living color what's more! What an infectious personality. Then I caught the 10 p.m. session of *The Graduate* which was on rerelease in Hawaii. Unreleased at that time in Australia, I knew little about it, but the audience, young like myself, was seeing it for the second or third time. Unlike the more reserved British and Australian cinema audiences I was used to, they didn't just laugh at a good dialogue line, they applauded. *The Graduate*'s satire of American social values was a seminal film for this generation of young Americans. But that Great Society was about to suffer a grievous blow, the effects of which linger today. As I boarded the 11 p.m. plane from Honolulu to San Francisco, people were in tears. The news had just announced that Presidential Candidate Robert Kennedy had been mortally wounded by gunshot to the head. It was June 5, 1968.

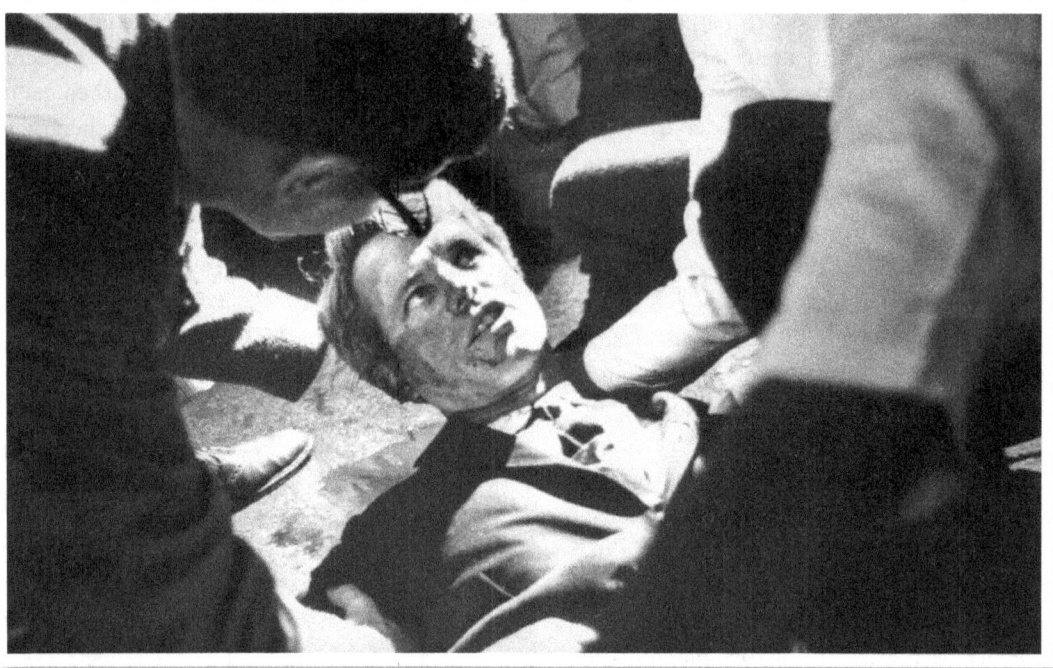

Landing in San Francisco in the morning, I checked into a flophouse on Mission Street, then went walking. The third political assassination in five years had put all passersby in a somber mood. People I spoke with at a diner were shocked, depressed, anxious. What a difference to American domestic policies and international relations Robert Kennedy would have made if he had lived to be elected President. Among other things, he would not have prolonged the Vietnam quagmire as Nixon did.

I needed some movie therapy, and right around the corner the perfect pick-me-up was playing—*The Good, The Bad and The Ugly*. I had seen censored versions of *A Fistful of Dollars* and *For a Few Dollars More* in Australia and had enjoyed their cynical take on the Old West. Aided by a more substantial budget this time, and the comedic skills of Eli Wallach, Sergio Leone's third western gave his operatic style full rein. It influenced me as it has countless filmmakers. When I am thinking about a project at the concept stage, the springboard of my creative instinct is music; the way the scores of Miklos Rosza. Dimitri Tiompkin, Elmer Bernstein and Ennio Morricone make me feel; I want to create images and big moments that would soar accompanied by such music. As I left the theater with Ennio Morricone's glorious, giddy chorus from the graveyard finale still whirling around in my head, I had no idea that later that year I would be making Paramount's European trailer for Leone's next movie, *Once Upon a Time in the West*.

My plan for exploring America was to circle and crisscross the continent by Greyhound Bus using my prepaid unlimited travel pass. First stop: Los Angeles for a few weeks, to broaden my education and build connections. I got a good deal on a weekly rental of a furnished room on Figueroa Street downtown and spent a lot of time at the Los Angeles Public Library on nearby 5th Street, where I devoured books on Cinema. A list of films "condemned" by the Catholic Legion of Decency further fueled a lifelong interest in censorship, a project that I am currently researching.

I set about cold calling TV and Studio promo departments with my "I'll show you mine, you show me yours" offer, which was moderately successful. Perhaps my Anglo-Australian tones had novelty value, and executives fifty years ago could conduct their work day under less pressure. So I got into KCAL TV and 20th Century Fox, which added me to a test audience for *Prudence and the Pill* starring David Niven and Deborah Kerr, a muddled comedy. My view—*Meh*. But I kept it to myself.

Channel Nine's Bruce Gyngell had given me an introduction to Raymond Burr, legendary star of *Perry Mason*, for whose *Ironside* series I had made Australian promos. I spent time on the set, and met Mr. Burr, who shook my hand warmly and instantly invited me to dinner at his house. Sensing that he might have had more than dinner in mind, I thanked him but never called. The public didn't know that Raymond Burr was gay; at that time, it would have meant career death. I later learned that Bruce Gyngell, who had met Burr a number of times, had mischievously effected the introduction to find out if I was gay, a suspicion based apparently on the florid paisley shirts I often wore at work.

Then it was time to go exploring. I took the Greyhound along the West Coast into Canada, up to Montreal, across to New York, down the Eastern Seaboard, into Florida, across the South, then the Southwest, and back to LA, and eventually across the Midwest to New York again. Wherever I went, I found Americans to be welcoming and hospitable to a foreigner like myself. It was a friendlier country then, perhaps. Even the cops were friendly, once they had checked me out…

On a hot July day in Montgomery, Alabama, I was walking down the street in shorts and a colorful Hawaiian shirt, when a police car pulled up beside me. The cops basically accused me of soliciting as a male prostitute. My "Stubbies" style classic Australian work shorts were a few inches shorter than the Alabama custom. My velveteen shirt confirmed their suspicions. Homophobia ran deep in the Deep South, it seemed. But once the cops heard my accent, they could not have been nicer, wanting to hear about life in Australia and England, their allies in WWII.

How long I could afford to stay in America would depend on how long my travelers' checks held out. I had to live on $50 a week. Transport was paid for. Food was relatively cheap. A bowl of chili and beans at the Greyhound Bus Station diner was 50¢. In the South I could get a couple of pieces of Kentucky Fried Chicken for 30¢. The flavor was new to me, and I enjoyed it. So imagine my surprise when I actually met Colonel Sanders in New York a few days before flying to England.

I was walking down a not particularly crowded Lexington Avenue. There, coming towards me, I saw a man I recognized immediately by his signature white suit, goatee beard and shoestring tie, familiar to all patrons of KFC. Is it really him? He got closer. Yes, the Colonel himself.

So being in a cheerful frame of mind, I called out to him:

"Colonel Sanders, I eat your chicken."

Today, accosting a celebrity on the street can result in their security putting you in a headlock. Those were more trusting times.

"Please excuse me, sir," I added, "but it's really good."

And it is, especially when you are hungry. He looked at me, smiled, and stopped to talk. The archetypical Southern gentleman, he asked me where I was from. I told him I had come from Australia and was on my way to England, and like every American I met in 1968 he responded warmly to my mixed origins. The Colonel (a purely honorary title he had given himself) said Kentucky Fried Chicken franchises had been sold to both Australia and the UK, so I would be able to continue my appetite for his "secret recipe" wherever I went. We chatted for a few minutes, then went our separate ways. Serendipity once again.

My principle expense each week was the cost of bed and bath. I sometimes saved a day's accommodation by sleeping on the bus. Taking a 4-hour bus from LA to Bakersfield, catching the next bus back. Who needs eight hours' sleep at age twenty-two? After the YMCA, which was often full up, accommodation was cheapest at the flophouse level. I thought I had a bargain in the 2-storey Ritz Hotel in Pershing Square in LA, which offered a room at the extraordinarily low rate of $12 per week with communal bathroom. It was very run down, smelly, but bearable. Its saving grace was a color TV in the lobby. When I decided to visit the Grand Canyon for four days, I considered leaving my suitcase with the smiling manager, but then thought the better of it. I left it in a locker at the Greyhound Bus Station. Just as well. I came back four days later and the Ritz Hotel was a pile of rubble. It had been demolished as planned, two days after I left.

Sometimes the price of sleep was a dollar-fifty ticket to an all-night movie theater. The downtown grindhouses offered a multipicture bill, three or more movies rotating from noon till 5 a.m. the next morning, when straggling patrons were kicked out. The Orpheum and the Cameo were my favorites. I saw a lot of AIP movies in these venues. I remember Roger Corman's psychedelic *The Trip* and the Vincent Price horror classic *Witchfinder General*. With triple bills like *For a Few Dollars More*, *The Devil's Brigade*, and *Will Penney*, I ended up getting less sleep in a grindhouse than on a Greyhound bus.

On my first visit to New York, I got a meeting at the leading trailer company Kaleidoscope. They showed me a work-in-progress trailer for *The Charge of the Light Brigade* on the Moviola, the film editor's classic workhorse, with an adaptive lens un-squeezing the anamorphic ratio of the film clattering through the picture gate in tandem with the sprocketed magnetic soundtrack. I watched the editor run a section backwards and forwards a few times, then mark frames for trimming with a chinagraph pencil, before lacing image and sound through a synchronizer and making the cuts. While I embrace the economics and speed of digital postproduction, I miss the tactile nature of old school film editing, the hands-on nurturing of the core material. The producers screened my grainy 16mm reel, and were pleasantly complimentary. They recommended that I show my wares to a veteran trailer house in Los Angeles—National Screen Service.

# CHAPTER 10
## National Screen Service

When I eventually arrived back in LA, I used Kaleidoscope's recommendation to get a meeting. My reel seemed to impress them. It had energy, they said, and how did I get away with that much "strong material" in a TV promo? Nobody complained, I responded. They told me that they had a branch of the company in England that made about 70% of the English language trailers for films in Europe, and adapted American trailers for the British market. They were thinking about adding a new writer/producer to the staff. Would I like to be interviewed when I got back to the UK?

On the Greyhound, I zigzagged back across the Midwest to New York, and used my pre-paid flight to the UK. I could have taken more time to explore America, but I had an instinct about that possible job. A few weeks later, smartly suited—no florid shirt—I presented myself at the National Screen Service's production offices at Perivale, West London, to be interviewed by Esther Harris, known as the *doyenne* of British trailer production. She was diminutive of stature, with a warm cheery face. She wore a wig, perhaps because she did not want hairdressing to take time away from work. Trailers were her passion and her pleasure.

A 16mm projector had been set up on her desk. After opening pleasantries, the reel was laced up and rolled. She said she liked the energy of the editing and took me on as the junior of three writer/producers on staff, and taught me how to make trailers for Cinema. Esther never married. I think our relationship was that of a hyperactive nephew indulged but tempered by a wise maiden aunt. You can see her in the front row of a staff photograph taken for a sales brochure. I stand on the right further back, wearing a beard, in an attempt to appear to clients older than twenty-two.

I am surprised to find that Esther Harris's story, an important one, has not been more widely recorded by Cinema historians. This is probably the only picture of her that exists. Was there any other female executive who achieved such prominence in the British film industry prior to the 70s? In those days, the glass ceiling was more of an iron portcullis, but she pushed through it by dogged hard work and making herself indispensable.

Esther Harris was born in the East End of London in 1910. At age sixteen, she went to work as an "office girl" at the British arm of the American trailer production company National Screen Service. Her salary was thirty shillings a week. In one of her few interviews (with British trade paper *Kinematography 1969*), conducted while I worked for her, she explained how she got her foot in the creative door. She had become the secretary to the lead trailer maker Leslie Everleigh:

*Leslie used to take me with him to do the shorthand bits, make notes at the studios…He used to ask my opinion. And I was terribly naïve, because I used to tell him what I really thought…He got fed up of this and said well if you know so much about it, why*

*don't you do it…So the next time I went to the studios with him, instead of taking notes I was making a list of what I wanted. We both wrote scripts and they took mine and not his. That's how I got into it.*

She went on to describe her craft in these terms:

*The purpose of a trailer is to make a bad picture look good and a good one better. Trailer makers are simply publicists on film. It is sometimes necessary to exaggerate. It must be borne in mind that too much subtlety does not pay in mass selling to an audience of so many different degrees of understanding. It is necessary to be just a little larger than life and a little noisier too, as in most cases is the material being publicized. It is not easy to convey the greatness of the stars, the story and the scenes, without using superlatives, but we no longer use the 'super colossal' adjectives.*

When Esther started in the business, usherettes walked the theater aisles selling cigarettes and confectionary while the trailers played.

*We recognize the fact that trailers are wedged in between the popcorn rattling, seat tipping and ice-cream sales.*

Esther's trailer in 1951 for John Huston's *The African Queen* established her expertise on both sides of the Atlantic. She quickly became the star trailer maker at NSS. Esther regarded the trailer as the spearhead of the advertising campaign. The stakeholders—producer, distributor, exhibitor—had a captive audience. Before TV, this was the only way to give customers a glimpse of the product they were being invited to buy next week.

*We do not necessarily choose only those scenes which are the most exciting, whether from a romantic, dramatic or humorous point of view. All kinds of small and inconsequential shots are also taken from every reel and these are eventually melded together to become part of the trailer story. For instance, in the case of a mystery story, any isolated shot which suggested mystery would be utilized, although in the feature there may be nothing mysterious about the shot at all. As an example, we would note shots of footsteps, or of a door being opened by an unseen hand; a telephone ringing; a light being switched on; a shadow against a wall. Shots such as these, out of context, can be exceedingly useful to back a piece of narration or a title and to give the trailer a build-up of atmosphere. A chase, or any kind of fast action, is a wonderful aid to the general pace of the trailer. In fact, the more action the better, since a trailer must keep moving or have something equally arresting to grip the attention.*

While producers only had to deal with the British Board of Film Censors whenever they completed a film, Esther had to deal with them every day. Adult elements allowed in the movie were often not allowed in the trailer.

*We had tremendous censorship problems of course, because every trailer had to be Universal, had to have a U certificate, no matter how A certificate or X certificate the film was… in the early days, you mustn't show a man and woman kissing! It was ridiculous… For a man to slap a woman's face is taboo, although on the other hand, a woman may slap a man's face.*

A good relationship with the BBFC was essential, as NSS' trailer makers frequently found themselves caught in the middle of testy bargaining between the Chief Censor and Hammer Films over the content of their latest horror film. Hammer always wanted the trailer to be as strong as possible. So in the course of introducing me round the distributor and production company clients, Esther set up a lunch at Soho's SPQR restaurant with Chief Censor John Trevelyan.

John Trevelyan
Secretary BBFC 1951—1971

I remember Esther saying to me by way of background: "He's been married four times, and his wives seem to get younger every time." I found him to be urbane, charming, erudite, a commanding figure. He had taken on the difficult task of liberalizing British censorship without incurring the wrath of either boundary-pushing directors or the Conservative establishment. Herding cats, really. His judgmental manner certainly earned him some detractors.

According to film director Roy Ward Baker, a Hammer regular:

*Trevelyan had that schoolmasterly habit of pigeon-holing people. If you were in the box marked 'art cinema' you could tackle anything, however controversial: sex, violence, politics, religion—anything. If you were in 'commercial cinema' you faced obstruction and nit-picking all the way. He chose these categories and allocated everyone according to his estimation of them. He was a sinister mean hypocrite, treating his favorites with nauseating unctuousness.*

Ouch. Personally, I found Trevelyan fascinating and was ready to pick up any pearls of wisdom he cast in my direction. I did attend a couple of screenings in his presence. When the director's cut of *The Last Grenade*, a story of rival mercenaries, starring Stanley Baker and Alex Cord, was projected for him, a splice broke in the first reel just after the opening ambush sequence. The lights went up, while the splice was repaired. Trevelyan spoke, praising in some detail the staging of the action scene he had just witnessed to the director Gordon Flemyng and producer Joseph Shaftel sitting nearby. Trevelyan was certainly literate in film editing.

I had to drop a shot from *The Vampire Lovers* trailer of a girl in a diaphanous nightie walking down stairs. Trevelyan claimed that pubic hair was visible through the nightie. Hammer said the girl was wearing black panties. Trevelyan ruled that the effect was just the same. So the shot disappeared from both the movie and my trailer. Rats! I recall his request of my *Frankenstein Must Be Destroyed* trailer. "Remove nasty sound effects as Frankenstein winds screw into man's head." What an interesting job—writing memos like that all day. His book on the subject of censorship is fascinating.

My first trailer for National Screen Service was for *Day of the Landgrabber*, subsequently retitled *Land Raiders* in the UK because Columbia felt the word 'landgrabber' was too sophisticated for the intended audience.   The producer was Charles Schneer, who produced the Ray Harryhausen stop motion animation classics. He had all his trailers done by National Screen Service. Schneer also created low budget 'B' movies for the co-feature market, pillaging Columbia's library for sequences he could not afford to stage. *East of Sudan* benefited from spectacular scenes lifted from the1939 Alexander Korda version of *The Four Feathers*. *The Black Shield of Falworth* provided battle scenes for his *Siege of the Saxons*. *Land Raiders* raided a number of Columbia westerns of the 1950s, particularly *The Guns of Fort Petticoat*.

In *Land Raiders*, medium close shots of Telly Savalas (*Kojak*) George Maharis (*Route 66*) and other actors were staged against backgrounds in Spain that approximated the topography in the selected stock footage. These new shots were cut into large scale scenes from the Columbia library of Indians attacking a wagon train, Indians attacking a stagecoach, Indian stampeding cattle through a town, and so on—a lot of 'Indian aggression,' in fact, because history is written by the victors. But by the time of *Land Raiders*, those 1950s patriotic 'cavalry vs. Apache' westerns had become retrograde, at least in plot. *Land Raiders* reworked these high production value sequences to portray white villains pretending to be Indians attacking white settlers in order to provoke reprisals and profit thereby. The library footage had been shot on older color stock and had suffered some wear and tear, so the integration of stock with the Spanish shoot was bumpy in a few action scenes, but the studio philosophy was that the core drive-in audience would neither notice nor care. *Land Raiders* had none of the photographic style of the recent crop of Euro westerns. To jazz up the trailer, I used split screens a number of times, a device not normally used for westerns. A panel of four images, each triggered by a gunshot, preceded the main title. Beside some dialogue scenes, I wiped on panels of illustrative action. These days I wince at my purple lines of commentary. But Columbia were happy, wanted no changes, I had made the grade.

Esther Harris taught me the questions to ponder when starting a trailer: what is the audience for the picture? What is the sell the distributor wants? Is the distributor right? Find the through line. Look for commentary lines or a succession of titles that can trigger key scenes, impact moments, and production value shots. Trailers are a subjective medium. One man's meat can be another man's poison, and my trailer for *IF* was certainly Lindsay Anderson's poison when we screened it for him at the Trident Theater, Wardour Street. I was in the back row sitting beside Esther, who had vetted my work and approved it to be shown to client.

FREEZE FRAME: FLASH BACK …

…to three weeks earlier, when Esther and I had both been at the office of Paramount (UK) Publicity Chief Gerry Lewis. No, not Jerry Lewis but Gerry Lewis, the longtime Paramount executive in London. He gave us his brief which I paraphrase from memory as follows: "Do what you like, just don't say it's set in a school." He invoked the old Hollywood adage: School pictures, boxing pictures, prison pictures rarely work at the box office. For every success in these genres there are ten failures. Famous school movie *Goodbye Mr. Chips* starring Robert Donat was a big box office success. The remake (as a musical) starring Peter O'Toole (who for all his gifts could barely sing) was an expensive failure. I thought *If* was a great film.

It particularly resonated with me because the writer based the culture of the fictitious school on a combination of Charterhouse and Wellington, my old school. Gerry Lewis wanted a trailer that broadened the appeal of the movie beyond arthouse. Make it feel youthful, intriguing, vibrant. So I tried to obfuscate the school setting by emulating techniques used in the *Midnight Cowboy* trailer I had seen recently. That trailer made use of dialogue lines from disparate parts of the movie in ironic counterpoint. "Who's that Joe Buck" is a line that gets repeated effectively. I embraced the technique, and made maximum use of the brief scenes with the only girl in the film to give *If*'s trailer a Swinging Sixties kinetic vibe.

BACK TO SCENE:

The trailer played, and the lights came up. Mr. Anderson stood up from the front row where he sat with the writer David Sherwin and yelled at us:

"I don't know what the fuck's going on…You've trashed my film!"

I stammered something about how much I admired his film. Let's just say he was not interested in having his work praised by a 22-year-old and his tongue lashing continued. Esther stepped in and said we would go back to the drawing board, but Lindsay Anderson informed Paramount that he would make his own trailer, thank you, one that was most definitely set in a school. His trailer played UK and Australian theaters, with a title crawl tacked on the end listing its film festival awards.

*If* was a critical and box office success in the UK, so Lindsay Anderson's didactic trailer worked. Would my trailer have expanded the audience further? Who knows? Esther gave me sound advice on client relations—say as little as possible; they want to do the talking. Sometimes she was asked by a producer or director what she thought of the film they had just screened. If inwardly she thought it stank, she would dissemble enthusiastically: "It's a hell of a picture."

National Screen management understood the *If* debacle and continued to assign me to a variety of genres. I did TV spots for another Euro Western, *Kill Them All and Come Back Alone*. This one starred Chuck Connors (*The Rifleman*) and was directed by Enzo G. Castellari. I would meet Enzo, a charming fellow, years later when he came to the US for the premiere of Tarantino's *Inglourious Basterds*, which was inspired by Castellari's 1968 Euro hit *Inglorious Bastards*. I would direct Chuck Connors, a lovable rogue, in one of my worst films, but that story is a few chapters away

I moved up the Euro Western ladder when Esther gave me Sergio Leone's *Once Upon a Time in the West* to handle. I arrived at the Trident Theater at 9 a.m. I was the sole invitee. The lights went down, and that extraordinary dialogue-less sequence sustained tension minute after minute as the gunmen waited for Charles Bronson's train to arrive. It was only when the opening credits started that I realized I was watching the Italian language print without subtitles, but it didn't matter. I grasped the key beats of the story. The stunning visuals supported by Morricone's sweeping hypnotic score allowed me to be immersed in Leone's operatic universe and enjoy it on a wholly sensual level

Paramount gave me no particular brief, other than make it look like "a *Dollars* picture." Not hard. Leone's follow up to *The Good the Bad and the Ugly*, by virtue of its title structure, lent itself to pithy commentary bookmarks. Hence: "The Widow," "The Outlaw," "The Landgrabber," etc. (I liked the word "landgrabber", so I laid it over Henry Fonda's closeup.) I recorded commentary with London based Canadian actor Robert Beatty, who played a lot of Americans in British movies. Paramount (US) then rerecorded it for the US version with one of their regular narrators in the same hard-bitten style.

Here are most of the trailers I can remember making for NSS. You'll find a few of them on YouTube. I've covered some of them on the *Trailers From Hell* website.

| | |
|---|---|
| *A Man Called Sledge* | *Land Raiders* |
| *Before Winter Comes* | *The Last Grenade* |
| *The Bellstone Fox* | *Moon Zero Two* |
| *Bronco Bullfrog* | *Once Upon a Time in the West* |
| *Crossplot* | *Perfect Friday* |
| *Destiny of a Spy* | *The Rise and Rise of Michael Rimmer* |
| *The File of the Golden Goose* | *Run a Crooked Mile* |
| *Frankenstein Must Be Destroyed* | *Take a Girl Like You* |
| *Hellboats* | *Valley of Gwangi* |
| *Horror of Frankenstein* | *The Vampire Lovers* |
| *The Italian Job* | *The Virgin Soldiers* |
| *Julius Caesar* | *You Can't Win Them All* |
| *Kill Them All and Come Back Alone* | *Mission Impossible vs the Mo* |

I have always had an affinity for trailers. As Joe Dante, renowned director and founding guru of *Trailers From Hell* put it: "Any film can be good for two minutes." Perhaps my fascination with trailers led me to think of movies as a series of flashy set pieces linked by a story, rather than a story enlivened by flashy set pieces. For good or ill, this approach to filmmaking had a formative effect on my development as a dramatist.

Towards the end of 1969, my parents separated for the second time. My father gave my mother the house and half the family business, which ticked over on remote control for a few more years. He would live in Sydney on his RAF pension. As December and January were quiet months at NSS for trailers, I took my two weeks annual holiday and added a 6-week leave of absence without pay to join him. My father's apartment in Captain Piper's Road, Vaucluse, had a view of the ocean. Revisiting my old haunts: Bondi Beach, Harbord Beach, the No-Name restaurant in Darlinghurst, the giant screen of the Rose Bay Theater, I realized how much I had missed Australia.

# CHAPTER 11
## TCN Nine

Upon arrival in Sydney, I contacted Pat Condon of Channel Nine to see if he could use another hand with the launch promos for new and returning programs, offering to work over Christmas. The rating season would begin in early February after the summer holiday hiatus. The three commercial networks would launch a barrage of promos in January and duke it out for first place in Ratings Week One. For the rival networks, there was a lot of advertising revenue riding on that opening week's figures. Pat assigned me not to promos but to a special project, a 15-minute presentation tape to be screened to an audience of advertising executives at a champagne breakfast in Studio A. It would be IN COLOR!

Australia would wait five more years before transmitting in color, allowing TV manufacturers to sell existing stock and retool. But the networks all knew the learning curve was steep and they had better get ahead of the game. TCN Nine had entered into a partnership to start a full-color postproduction house they called VTC. This was where I was to do the work. Some of what I had gleaned observing color TV production in Japan and the US paid off here. I delivered a slick fast-paced 18-minute promo for all the new shows, incorporating as many optical effects as VTC's switching console could provide.

I recorded a model—more about her later—dancing sinuously to the strains of John Barry's score for the recently released Bond movie *On Her Majesty's Secret Service*. I turned the shots into a high contrast silhouette of her body that I could use as a keying effect, much as the Bond title sequences did, enabling me to put images or titles inside the silhouette. This gave the presentation a cutting edge look, though this gimmick has been done to death since. The Ad People, a species addicted to eye candy, were impressed, and some major accounts committed to Channel Nine during the champagne breakfast that followed. At the end of the breakfast, Pat Condon introduced me to the new comanaging director of the network, Clyde Packer, older son of the owner, Sir Frank Packer. Bruce Gyngell had left in a row over salary with the notoriously parsimonious Sir Frank. Clyde Packer was very complimentary. When he heard I was going back to a job in England, he said: "If you ever want to come and work for me, we'll fly you back."

The dancing silhouette in the promo was British model Bobo Faulkner, newly arrived in Australia, having separated from her husband, actor Trader Faulkner. She was sharp, with striking chestnut red hair and a wicked sense of humor. Her father had been headmaster at Shaftesbury Grammar School. We bonded over a common English background. I became aware she was in a troubled relationship with successful local impresario Harry M. Miller, who imported top Broadway shows like *Jesus Christ Superstar*. Although I was five years younger, Bobo felt that she could talk to me and I was happy to listen. A few days after the promo screened, I boarded a plane back to my job in London. Two years later, Bobo would connect me with the backer for my first independent film.

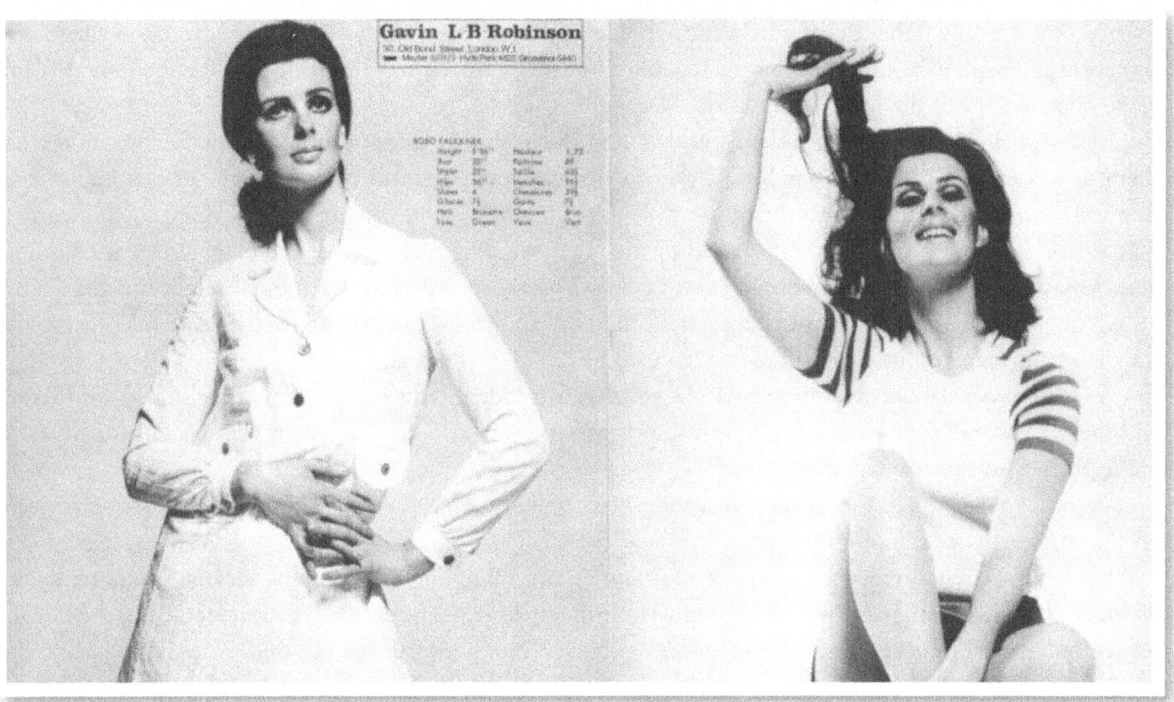

I broke the flight to London in New Delhi for two days where I shot a few reels of 8mm at the Red Fort and the Taj Mahal. I shared a taxi with three other foreigners to the Taj Mahal. On the 3-hour-plus journey, we witnessed a crowd in the middle of a village blocking the road. The cab driver sensed something and started hooting his horn, pushing slowly but firmly through the crowd, till we reached the object of their attention—the body of a small child, covered by a sheet, through which blood was beginning to seep. The driver accelerated away. He said when a hit-and-run accident occurred villagers might attack the next car that came through, particularly if it contained foreigners. On the way back many hours later, we drove through the village again. This time the crowd was smaller, standing quietly on both sides of the road. We asked our driver to explain why the body still lay in the middle of the street, the sheet now soaked in blood and covered in flies. He said that probably the parents were away and were being sent for. The body could not be moved until they could come and see the circumstances for themselves. I had led a sheltered life. India was my first real taste of culture shock, of the poverty and hardship of others.

After two days in Bangkok, I landed in Moscow with prepaid hotel and meals, but only five dollars cash in my pocket. I just had to last two more days, and make it to London, where I could cash a cheque. (How did we ever manage without credit cards?) The hotel was on Red Square. The American who shared my cab from the airport got nervous when I took out my 8mm camera and started shooting through the window.

"Don't do that. You could be arrested."

"What?"

"As a spy! Nothing in the Soviet Union can be filmed without permission."

He was concerned he would be arrested as an accomplice, which would be bad for whatever business he was hoping to accomplish in Moscow. Or perhaps he was a US embassy official, and was in fact himself a spy. He was noncommittal as to the reasons for his visit. Sensing his concern, I finished the shot of undistinguished Moscow buildings and put the camera away. Was it the beginnings a smile I could see on the cabdriver's face in the rearview mirror? Only later that day when I tried to shoot angles of Lenin's tomb did an armed guard wave me away with his Kalashnikov.

So, given my cashflow problem, how to enjoy Moscow on $2.50 a day? I went to the nearby Intourist Office, where I chatted with two employees, fluent in English, aged 'round thirty. Talking about movies, I learned that the only James Bond movie allowed to be seen in Russia was *Goldfinger*, because the villain was perceived as Jewish. The only *Life* magazine allowed to be imported was the issue that featured vivid crime scene photographs of the Manson murders. Decadent America.

I explained my budgetary problem, probably not a wise thing to do, but had an instinct I could trust them. I had enough money to pay for a ticket to the Moscow Circus but not enough for taxi fare to and from the venue and to the airport the next day. Penniless in Moscow was a prospect to be avoided. I learned that Russia had no ballpoint pens. Or, if they did, they were the privilege of the elite. Western ballpoint pens were a valued source of barter currency. Luckily I had three of them. Each one bought me a taxi ride. Thus I got to see bears riding motorbikes and other amazing acts at the Moscow Circus. And I just made the plane on time, despite a slight holdup in customs.

A customs official opened my suitcase to see what forbidden items I might be smuggling out of Russia, and there he found a can containing a 35mm print of my trailer for *Land Raiders* that I had brought with me to Sydney to show to Channel Nine.

"What is this?" asked the Inspector, wondering no doubt what Soviet secrets or embarrassments were on that three minute roll of film?

Explaining what a trailer was—a sales tool—to an official of an anti-capitalist society, when neither of us spoke the other's language, was not going well. I imagined stone faced KGB officers scouring the images for counter revolutionary thought crime. So I extracted the film from the can and started unwinding the countdown leader till I got to the first shots, which were of Apaches on horseback charging to the attack. I got the official to hold the frame up to the light, then I mimed an Apache firing an arrow at the gallop, then a settler getting it in the chest. Other settlers firing back. Bang! Bang! All acted out with some vigor. Several other officials had come over to watch. I unreeled further frames till I reached the main title *Land Raiders*, which I explained incorporated four split screen shots. Well, I was proud of that title design…It was a Python-esque moment. But my ebullient manner and blithe indifference to the possibility I might have committed a serious smuggling infraction seemed to win the day. I was evidently innocent. An Anglo-Australian wearing an Afro shirt in Moscow midwinter, probably mentally ill, but innocent nonetheless.

My return lifted my mother's spirits. Being the only child of separated parents was not easy. I would spend weekends with her, then return to my rented bedsit in Ealing. Great Indian restaurants. Twenty minutes on the tube to Soho and West End Theaters. Back then, a single man could have a good life in the UK on £45 per week.

Reporting to work at NSS, I was given a £5 raise and Hammer's *Horror of Frankenstein* to work on. I liked the work and my work was liked. It was put to me I could rise high in the company when Esther retired. A definite career path was on offer, albeit on the periphery of filmmaking. There was no precedent in 1970 Britain for trailer makers to become directors. How was I to make the jump? Write something people want to make, dummy!

So in the evenings, I wrote a screenplay called *Live a Little, Die a Little* about the adventures of a TV news crew reporting on the Vietnam War. I drew on my observation of the Channel Ten News department, and my brief romance with the aforementioned Jenny Phillips. I submitted it to a well-thought-of literary agent in London, Robin Dalton. To my surprise, she liked it and sent it to Writer/Director Brian Forbes who had just been put in charge of EMI Studios. In a polite refusal letter to Robin Dalton, he did say some good things about it, but a largescale picture set in Australia and Vietnam was not in EMI's plans. Looking at it now (don't!) it's a bit strange and amateurish. But it was practice. As they say, writing is rewriting.

I enjoyed the challenges of trailer making, but with each new film I saw in that incomplete state of gestation that only a select few are privy to—no music or sound effects, no post synch dialogue, no titles, no visual effects—my desire grew to create rather than publicize what was on the screen. After six months I wrote to Clyde Packer at Channel Nine, reminding him of his offer to fly me back. I would make network promos, provided he would give me programs to make as well. He accepted by return, and I handed in my notice. I was leaving a secure job in a calm workplace full of nice people at a company with connections to the highest levels of film distribution. There would be opportunities for lateral movement to studio publicity posts if I wanted to climb that ladder. Esther felt that the future I was choosing was less assured. But she wished me well. We last spoke in 1990 when I was passing through London on my way to a directing gig in Israel, with, at that time, sixteen features to my name. She had been sorry to lose me from NSS, but was pleased that pursuing my dream had worked out. I was subsequently fired from that gig in Israel, but that's another story…

It was a painful personal crossroads for me as well. Should I stay in England to give emotional support to my mother, or do I chase my dream 10,000 miles away? As it turned out I made the better decision for my mother as well as myself. My mother came to Sydney a year later. Reconciliation with my father did not eventuate, but they established a good relationship. She bought a flat in Avalon, where she lived a short walk from the beach for over thirty years, enjoying a happier life than I think she would have remaining, in a small English village with too many memories.

Channel Nine was an exciting place in 1970. The commercial networks had become brasher, more boundary-pushing than the staid government-funded Australian Broadcasting Commission, known among media folk as Aunty. For those of us in commercial television, political sensitivity was years away. My promo for the return season of *The Don Lane Show* featured our announcer Bruce Menzies dressed as an Indian Chief in full feathered headdress sitting by his campfire in front of a wigwam watching a portable TV. He turned to camera, raised one hand, and spoke in a sonorous tone: "How! You don't have to be Jewish to watch *The Don Lane Show*." Offensive on so many levels. But we were oblivious. There were no howls of outrage. Jewish Don Lane thought it was funny. We did not see ourselves as bigoted, sexist, racist, classist, etc., even as we perpetuated stereotypes. Hey, this is just good-natured humor, right? Or so we believed at the time.

I settled back into promos and awaited the first of my promised directing assignments, thinking they would probably be film sequences for a variety show, something simple. Instead Pat Condon assigned me to coproduce a 1-hour TV special, in color, in French, beamed live to France via satellite on Christmas Day from an Avis Rent a Truck, converted to be an Outside Broadcast Unit parked at Manly Beach. From this iconic vantage point, Jacques Chappard, (the French equivalent of famous British documentary host Alan Whicker) would show the French public what a summer Christmas was like in Australia.

The broadcast had to start promptly at 8:45 a.m. Eastern Australian Time on Christmas morning, so that fifteen minutes later at 9 a.m., which was midnight Christmas Eve in Paris, Father Christmas would be sighted at the prow of the Manly Surf Life Saving Club's biggest boat. On cue, a somewhat seasick Santa was rowed through the surf by a team of lifesavers who beached the boat and carried him ashore. Then sixty or more Aboriginal kids from the Far West Children's Home were cued to rush across the beach and meet him at a Christmas tree planted in a good position for all three cameras. As Santa distributed presents, Jacques Chappard welcomed French viewers to *Noel en Australie*, the title of the show.

Prior to the arrival of the French contingent, I had shot film sequences of different aspects of the Aussie Christmas: Australia's new American-style shopping malls, horseracing, surfing, yachting, cricket matches, BBQs, family get-togethers. The footage was transferred to tape at VTC, the network's color facility, and, in an all-night editing session, the French producer Mr. Anjoubault, Mr. Chappard and I put together a number of five-minute sequences which Monsieur Chappard then narrated. We then hastened to Manly Beach at dawn, where our crew were laying cables and setting up cameras. At the Avis Rental Truck that

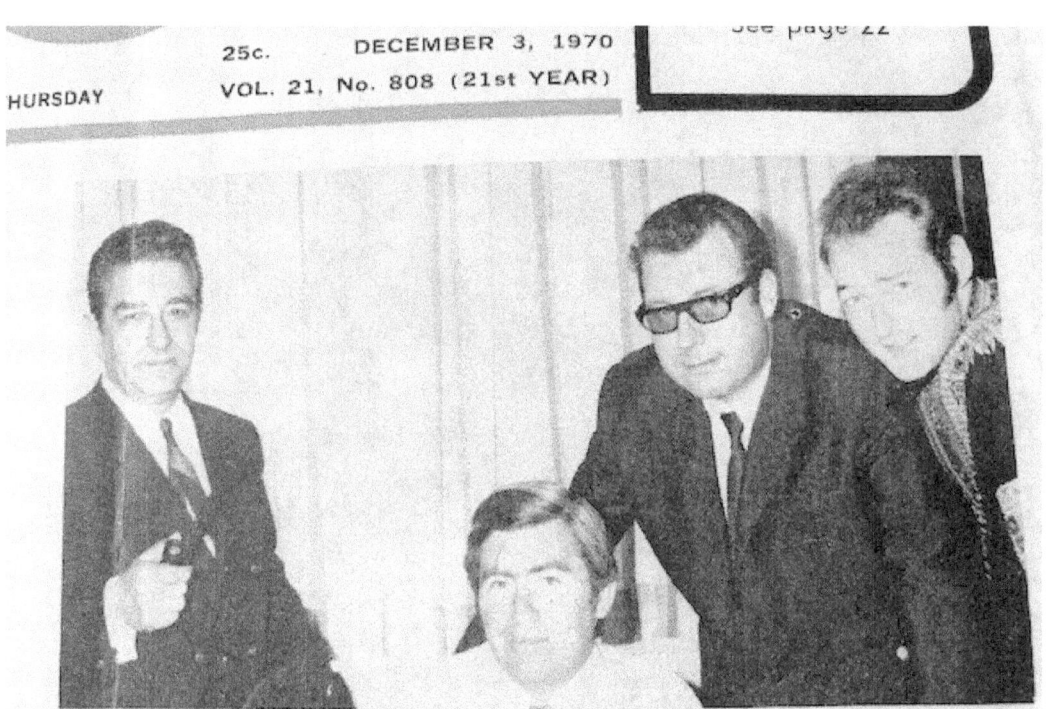

25c.    DECEMBER 3, 1970

THURSDAY    VOL. 21, No. 808 (21st YEAR)

See page 22

Jacques Anjubault of French Television, Pat Condon of TCN, Guy Chausey UTA/Air France and Brian Trenchard-Smith of TCN make final arrangements for the historic telecast at Christmas from Sydney to Paris.

served as a makeshift Outside Broadcast Unit, these prerecorded sequences were rolled into the show at regular intervals on a cue from Mr. Anjoubault sitting beside me and the technical director. It was a think-on-your-feet show, particularly after one of the three cameras went down. Mr. Anjoubault had no English, and I had schoolboy French, but we managed fine. I remember as the Life Saving boat approached through the waves, with the queasy Santa clinging to the prow, he turned to me and said:

"Les raquins! Les raquins!"

Luckily that was a word I *did* know. Shark. He had just heard Jacques Chappard commenting that Australia was surrounded by shark infested seas.

"Camera Three, look for sharks!" is probably a rare instruction from a director in the world of live television, and I am tickled to have had that opportunity. Camera Three dutifully panned back and forth across the waves near the boat. No fins, but the show came together well. Live television is quite the adrenalin rush. TF1 in Paris let Nine executives know they were pleased. I was given a new title: Special Projects Producer.

I was often assigned to beauty pageant shows as associate producer/film sequence director. It's a dirty job but someone's gotta do it... I know, sexist humor. Young girls obliged to parade in swimwear and evening gowns to be judged on their attractiveness by men—such shows were sexist at their core, perpetuating the stereotype of woman as handmaiden or trophy. But young men of my age were oblivious to sexism in 1970. However, there were basic standards of political correctness that I and most Australians observed. So I thought.

*Quest of Quests* was a yearly beauty pageant show broadcast by the Nine Network live across Australia from the ballroom of Sydney's Wentworth Hotel. Two hundred high society guests, fortified by food and liquor, sat at tables to watch twenty-two contestants parade, vying for the crown. In the days leading up to the broadcast, I had shot film sequences on each girl depicting her favorite hobby (for instance, young Belinda Green from Tasmania, later to become Miss World, was a dab hand at finger painting). And there I was, the proverbial eunuch in the harem. Courtesy of the vigilant chaperone and den mother to the girls,

Mrs. Marjorie Colebrook, a tireless organizer and great lady who requested my participation two years running.

My major responsibility during the telecast itself was to ensure that all the contestants and guest judges were at the right place at the right time. The Guest of Honor was former Miss Grenada, Jennifer Hosten, the first black woman to be crowned Miss World. Veteran comedian Bob Hope did the honors. She was a charming statuesque beauty.

Sitting beside Jennifer Hosten at the high table overlooking the ballroom—the rich have their pecking order, too—was the aforementioned owner of the Network, Sir Frank Packer, one of the three robber barons of Australian media, the others being Fairfax and Murdoch. Rupert may be the last man standing now, but Sir Frank was the undisputed titan at the time.

Halfway through the show, I approached the high table to collect Ms. Hosten for her next appearance on the stage. I was wearing a dinner jacket as all crew on the show were required to do. Sir Frank immediately mistook me for a waiter and growled, "Get me a whiskey and soda." So I quickly guided Ms. Hosten to her designated entrance point, then went in search of the requisite whisky and soda. It was not wise to ignore an instruction from Sir Frank.

Given the overworked waitstaff, the quickest solution was to buy the scotch myself from the bar. Back at the high table I placed the tumbler beside Sir Frank and picked up his empty glass. Well, not quite empty. Waste not, want not. Sir Frank's hand clamped firmly around my wrist, and without a word, tipped the dregs into the new glass. You do not fight the hand that feeds you. Actually, it was an indication of how the man had turned a small newspaper into a media empire.

Eventually the winning girls were announced. Winners hug Losers! Tears of Joy! Roll end credits. The live feed to the nation concluded. Just as well. Because at that point the sponsor of the show joined the guest judges on the stage and addressed the audience in the ballroom. Sir John Walton, knighted for his services to commerce, chairman of Waltons Department Stores, offered his thanks to all who had made the show possible. Standing right beside Jennifer Hosten, the very embodiment of Black is Beautiful, he thanked her for coming all the way to Australia. She received enthusiastic applause. Then Sir John turned his attention to the Quest organizer sitting in the audience. He offered particular thanks to "Mrs. Marjorie Colebrook, who has worked like a N***** to get this show together!" Did he see this as an applause line?

There was no discernible intake of breath from the audience, more a moment when two hundred people involuntarily stopped breathing. A sharp silence like a puff of cold air. Sir John went on, oblivious. I was too far back in the hall to gauge Jennifer Hosten's reaction. But she remained on the stage. I am told Sir Frank and Walton offered apologies afterwards. Naturally, it was never reported back then. Today it would be all over social media within seconds.

# CHAPTER 12
## Promos and Productions

Eccentric British comedy star Marty Feldman was touring Australia's capital cities with his one man show. Feldman suffered from thyroid disease and developed Graves' Ophthalmopathy, causing his eyes to protrude and become misaligned. Childhood injuries, a car crash, a boating accident, and reconstructive eye surgery may also have contributed to his appearance. He rose through the ranks of British comedy writers with shows like *Round the Horne*, *The Frost Report*, *At Last the 1948 Show* till he was given his own series, *Marty*, by the BBC. His character fitted the comedic type of Mr. Pest. Rowan Atkinson would explore the same tropes a generation later as Mr. Bean.

When Marty's tour was over, Channel Nine got him to do a half-hour special before he left. A few years earlier at National Screen I had collaborated on the trailer for his first movie *Every Home Should Have One*. Indeed, every home should have a Marty. He proposed a series of filmed sketches that he had performed before, the linking theme being our relationship with the animal kingdom. I was given the chance to direct the sketches. Marty wanted to sing "Let's Talk to the Animals" from *Doctor Doolittle* while roaming through the Taronga Park Zoo. Fantastic! So we shot Marty interacting with as many animals he could get close to, while miming to the playback of the song. I thought he gave Rex Harrison a run for his money.

machine gun battalion, rush in house to save whether they th beforehand and terror, or wheth a nicely organ block that the down, and not the danger unti

The danger nobody saw de film involved Bc Woodham had but he didn't about it.

Smith recall Badcoe, I had charge after ch 100 yards 10 ti pack of equip boiling sun. I anything abo

A far cry from enjoyed filn when zany fu Feldman vis

Marty liked to improvise. One moment did take us by surprise. We were shooting at the gate to the walled rhino enclosure, where a rhino had been induced to come forward to get a snack from his keeper. In the course of singing to the rhino Marty took off his signature cloth cap, reached over the chest-height gate, and hung the cap on the rhino's horn. Then the rhino turned and wandered off, taking Marty's prized possession with him. I clearly remember him climbing up and swinging a leg over the gate. We all yelled at him to stop. I can't recall whether he jumped down to attempt a quick grab and dash, then thought better of it, and climbed back up. I experienced a moment of gut-twisting panic at the potential image of Marty riding the rhino impaled on its horn. I do remember Marty being helped down from the gate by a remonstrating zoo official, who reluctantly went into the enclosure and retrieved Marty's cap.

I wanted to propose TV specials of my own. Only cheap ideas please, they said, so when BOAC offered Channel Nine free tickets on their inaugural 747 Jumbo round-the-world flight, I saw a way to score a twofer. Principally, I would shoot promos with stars of the network's British and American shows, wishing Channel Nine viewers a Merry Christmas. Also to be shot—interviews with any movie stars I could get. That material would be incorporated into 1-hour specials about moviemaking worldwide. Through a contact at the Greater Union Organization, Australia's largest cinema distribution/exhibition company, I was able to line up a few stars willing to publicize their upcoming films. After an horrendous 33-hour flight that touched down in every single city on route it seemed, I was finally in London along with a Channel Nine cameraman and his wife who recorded sound.

First stop Pinewood Studios, where Robert Bolt, writer of *Lawrence of Arabia*, *A Man for All Seasons* and other distinguished works, was making his directorial debut with the story of Lady Caroline Lamb, who was at one point the lover of both the poet Lord Byron and the Duke of Wellington, the victor of Waterloo. Bolt had cast his wife Sarah Miles in the lead. She was a hoot, sprinkling the interview with F-bombs, assuring us that the purple liquid she was sipping from a wine glass was in fact Ribena.

Despite being in the middle of a lavish expensive production (sadly it failed at the box office and Bolt never directed again) both Sarah Miles and Robert Bolt were generous with their time. I found this to be the case throughout the trip. Anthony Quinn, Robert Young, Cesar Romero all had great old Hollywood tales to tell.

Peter Bogdanovich (*The Last Picture Show, What's Up, Doc?*), at the early peak of his directing career, agreed to an interview to promote his upcoming *Paper Moon,* while then girlfriend Cybill Shepherd waited nearby. As we set up the 16mm Auricon camera, he noted its Berthiot zoom lens. "I hate the .zoom" he said,

and explained the difference between a zoom and a dolly shot. A zoom is merely magnification, but in a dolly the relative position of everything within the frame changes. The camera draws the audience towards the point of the shot. Bogdanovich has since written critically acclaimed books on Cinema. I could have listened to him for hours.

In New York, a diverse series of interviews ranging from sweet folk singer Melanie Safka (*Candles in the Rain*) to famously brusque and autocratic director Otto Preminger, twice Oscar nominated for *Laura*, and *The Cardinal*, nicknamed Otto the Ogre in Hollywood. But I found him to be charming with a waspish sense of humor. Perhaps I won his heart by gushing about some of his roving camera 1-shot scenes. He disdained critics volubly, referring to New York critic Judith Crist as "zat Miss Christ!" He concluded

our session with: "I vill come to Australia and zen I vill interview *you.*"

TV stars yanked out of high-pressure schedules at the request of the studio publicity department generally appreciated the break, but their producers did not. Dennis Weaver, star of the *McCloud* series was physically pulled away in mid-interview by a visibly annoyed assistant director. Asking Tony Randall, co-star of *The Odd Couple* series if he wouldn't mind doing a Christmas greeting one more time produced a terse response: "How would you like me to say it?" Ouch. How do I answer that? I could not say, "You sounded bored." Which he did. I forget what I waffled in response. He then repeated the message in exactly the same tone as before. I knew I had a lot to learn about handling actors.

Peter Falk, *Colombo*, was in a Broadway play, Neil Simon's *The Prisoner of Second Avenue*, and didn't want to give up any of his free time. So we lay in wait outside the stage door and ambushed him after the matinee performance. He was not happy, but he did it anyway. That was rude, I know. Ambition sometimes overrides good manners.

I got a range of useful interview material to intercut with behind-the-scenes featurettes supplied by the studios, and spread them over a 2-part showbiz special entitled *The Big Screen Scene*. In Hollywood TV parlance this was a 'clip show.' Such shows need a popular host to link the pieces together. When Darren McGavin (*Kolchak*) came to Sydney for episodes of the American syndicated series *The Evil Touch*, I got him to be the presenter of the first show, shooting his segments in his hotel room. Robert Lansing, whose career totaled ninety-two movies and TV series was also in town for *The Evil Touch*, and presented the second *Big Screen Scene*. After we were done, I asked him for any advice about directing actors he could offer to a young wannabe director. Mr. Lansing said: "Just remember the actor is naked out there. He's baring his soul. You have to create an atmosphere where he can relax and feel comfortable." I've tried to follow his advice.

In part two of *The Big Screen Scene* I staged a stunt sequence, then showed the tricks of the stuntman's trade. This was an idea that I would return to several times over the decade. For this show, I arranged with the Commonwealth Bank in Willoughby Road just down the street from Channel Nine, where many employees including myself had bank accounts, to allow me to film armed bank robbers running out with a bag of cash. A shootout in the street followed, climaxing with a robber on a motorbike crashing through the glass door of an abandoned building. Can you imagine your current bank manager cheerfully consenting to this? But in those days there was a lot of grassroots support for Australian production. Television crews on the street, in your home or workplace, were novel, exciting. Now, well, not so much…

A few days after my first *Big Screen Scene* special went to air, I got a call from an executive with The Greater Union Organization, the largest distribution/exhibition company in Australia. His name was John Fraser and he became the greatest of the many benefactors of my career. John was General Manager of The Greater Union Organization's distribution division British Empire Films, a company name dating from the 20s, wisely abbreviated in 1970 to BEF Film Distributors. BEF supplied Australian screens with films from Paramount, Universal, Disney and the major British studios, foremost of which was The Rank Organization, which owned Pinewood Studios, and more importantly for Australia, at that time a 49% holding in The Greater Union Organization.

I had previously obtained clips to various British movies like *Lady Caroline Lamb* from GUO's publicity department but had not met John Fraser. John said he was calling to congratulate me on the show and invited me to lunch to thank me for the publicity given to upcoming releases. At lunch I discovered John had an encyclopedic memory for films that I could match maybe 70% of the time. We bonded over a mutual fascination with movies and their publicity. We remained friends till he passed away at the age of eighty. John was a kind, witty, buoyant personality to be around. He was gay; I was not. It was never an issue between us. Rather, we had some amusing conversations about our respective romantic lives; in my case, a series of disappointed girlfriends, neglected in favor of my career drive. I learned about gay life in the conservative society that Australia was at that time. Public attitudes had recently evolved from repression to grudging tolerance spiked with homophobic humor.

Only a few years before, people convicted of homosexual acts could be sentenced to up to fourteen years' imprisonment; ironically, their incarceration would take place in the sole company of their own sex. Right, that'll cure 'em… Given the number of gay people I knew in Showbiz, the hypocrisy, injustice, and futility of such a law rankled. It made no sense. Genetic programming determines same sex orientation, not sin or mental illness. It is homophobia that is the disorder, an irrational fear of the Other. The UK Parliament did finally pass decriminalization for consenting adults in 1967. It would take Australia till 1975. I would never have imagined that fifty years later, sin no longer trumped science, and the hitherto unthinkable – gay marriage – would become legal in Australia.

Today my 40-year friendship with John Fraser would be categorized a 'bromance'. Some of my contemporaries snidely suggested more, given John's vital support for my career over the next three years. But we were just fellow movie fanatics, who shared a wish to see a viable Australian film industry develop. At our lunch, I told John Fraser of how much I liked American movie magazines like *Photoplay*, which I would occasionally buy when I lived in England. I told him that I would like to start a similar movie magazine in Australia to be sold in theaters rather than shops. John felt that this might be something that Greater Union could be interested in, so if I could put a few more pieces in place I should bring the project to him. I went back to my office at Channel Nine with my horizons broadened.

# CHAPTER 13
## Clip Shows to Docudramas

The two *Big Screen Scenes* cost virtually nothing but in-house costs. Pat Condon utilized the network's contra-deal relationships with airlines. Hosts Darren McGavin and Robert Lansing were paid not with cash but with round-the-world first-class airfares. The airline was repaid in turn by the network which aired additional commercials to the same value at no charge. Nobody noticed if the commercial break occasionally overran its two minutes. Today's media universe is awash with celebrity interviews and behind-the-scenes coverage. But then Australian television audiences were unaccustomed to seeing so many movie and TV star names in the same program, so ratings and ad revenue were solid.

The network let me spend a little more money on the next one. I proposed *For Valour*, a dramatized documentary about four Australian soldiers, serving in Vietnam, who were awarded the Victoria Cross, Britain's highest award for gallantry, for which soldiers from Commonwealth countries were also eligible. The Australian Army offered technical assistance and access to the Holsworthy Firing Range as a location. The format intercut interviews with brief battle re-enactments, for which I hired Bob Woodham to co-ordinate some stunts.

An ambitious Australian, Woodham had done stunts on *You Only Live Twice* and other films during a spell in England. I had hired him for the bank robbery sequence of *The Big Screen Scene*. Bob had come across an Australian invention, the Waterjel Fire Blanket, soaked in fire retardant jelly, which could be thrown over an electrical fire. Contact with the jelly immediately extinguished the flames. Bob saw Waterjel as a way to do a human torch without the traditional bulky fire suit. This resulted in greater realism for such scenes. He offered to make a fire stunt part of the battle reenactments. It featured in a night ambush and was quite impressive. I went on to film fire stunts many times and ultimately did a few myself. But that's another story...

The nature of courage was my focus rather than political comment on the war. Major Peter Badcoe and Warrant Officer Kevin "Dasher" Wheatley were awarded the Victoria Cross posthumously, so in their cases I interviewed the families. Warrant Officer Simpson had just taken a position as an administrator at the Australian Embassy in Tokyo. I was unable to interview him on camera. But I was able to interview Warrant Officer Keith Payne. His story touched me particularly.

In May 1969 Payne was commanding the 212th Company of the 1st Mobile Strike Force Battalion, leading a company of indigenous Montagnard soldiers when it was ambushed by a strong North Vietnamese force near Ben Het Camp. His company was isolated and, surrounded on three sides, Payne's Montagnard troops began to fall back. Although wounded in both hands and arms, Payne led a fighting retreat to a defensible perimeter, then as night fell, went back up the hill into enemy dominated territory to look for lost or wounded Montagnard soldiers. Over the next three hours he found about forty wounded men. He brought some in himself and organized the rescue of the others. He knew the odds were against his survival if he kept going back up the hill.

At one point, he told me, he sat leaning against a tree and smoked what he thought would be his last cigarette, cupping his hands around it to conceal the flame. In his mind he started speaking to his wife Flo, hoping his psychic message would somehow be received. He was certain that his luck would soon run out. Loyalty to his troops compelled him to persist. He would not stop till he had saved as many as he could. He apologized to her, for putting that loyalty above returning to his family. Luckily, he beat the odds, and saved many lives that would undoubtedly have been lost. It was an extraordinary act of courage and martial skill. Queen Elizabeth II presentsed then-Warrant Officer Payne with the Victoria Cross in Brisbane in April 1970.

The Prime Minister at this time was John Gorton, who was considered something of a war hero himself. A fighter pilot in WWII, he was torpedoed once and crash landed three times, resulting in facial disfigurement. Nonetheless, his personal drive took him all the way to the Prime Minister's office. Would he like to talk about the nature of courage under fire? Nothing ventured, nothing gained, I made my request through official channels, and to my surprise he agreed. I flew to Canberra with a camera crew to interview him. My recollection of his office was that it was quite modest, I thought, for a Prime Minister. He was working at his desk and got up to greet me. When I told him that my father had been a fighter pilot in WWII

and had been shot down just as he had, I sensed I got the interview off on the right foot, but I do not recall after all these years what wisdom on the nature of courage he contributed to the program. I recently discovered the original interview footage and gave it to Australia's National Film and Sound Archive. Australia's most significant engagement in the Vietnam war, the battle of Long Tan (August 8th 1966) has now been made into a moving and spectacular film—*Danger Close*—by Australian director Kriv Stenders.

At that time music royalties were covered by a standard fee per thirty seconds for use of any track from a record sold by Australian music distributors. I found a copy of the soundtrack for *A Last Valley* in the station's music library. Thus I gave a few scenes of *For Valour* the benefit of John Barry's propulsive yet relentlessly tragic score. In hindsight, this was a serious breach of copyright, but at the time nobody questioned it.

But by 1972, Australia's involvement in the Vietnam War was unpopular. Its futility and waste were evident: 60,000 Australians had served, 521 had died, 3,000 had been wounded, and undiagnosed PTSD affected countless veterans. And for what? The protection of the assets of American banks across South East Asia from the threat of communism? For Australia to get trade benefits from America in return? These issues were being strongly debated in the lead up to the Labor Party's massive electoral victory that year. Australia would pull its troops out in January of 1973. *For Valour* found it hard to get a primetime sponsor. The station manager Tom Miller told me he persuaded the Returned Servicemen's League to buy the airtime for AUD$12,000, so it still turned a profit for the network.

In the late 1990s the master tapes of *For Valour* and *The Big Screen Scene* were junked, along with many other black and white programs Channel Nine no longer showed. A 16mm kinescope had been created in 1972 and given to the Returned Servicemen's League, but it too seems lost. However, the story of these four gallant Australians was told once more—with polished production values and greater depth—in a 2009 documentary also entitled *For Valour* directed by Serge Ou.

Among other lost material is a 30-minute documentary called *Rock Set Free*, featuring extracts from the concert by Deep Purple, Manfred Mann, and Free, shot at the Randwick Racecourse on May 9th 1971, in front of 35,000 people. It was an attempt to expand a simple news crew assignment into a TV special. I remember shooting handheld B Roll at the edge of the stage with an ultrawide angle fish eye lens, which I thrust as close to Ritchie Blackmore's guitar as I could get. He gave me a look, but let me continue.

After "The Mighty Quinn" (which went on forever) I interviewed Manfred Mann. Badly.

"Can I help you with your questions?" he asked, a little irritated that his time was being taken by someone who seemed to know nothing about rock and roll.

In hindsight, *Rock Set Free* was priceless footage, albeit in black and white, yet ironically it was never aired because the program department did not believe people would watch it. Now it seems both the news coverage and the program are gone forever. Some color home movie footage of the concert is on Utube: https://youtu.be/VE-zHwAhjASw

My boss Pat Condon and über-boss Clyde Packer continued to be supportive. Clyde decided to hold a screening of *For Valour* for some friends. Among those invited was Bobo Faulkner, the model I had recorded as the dancing silhouette for the ad agency cham-

pagne breakfast two years before. In the meantime Bobo's career had taken off. In addition to modeling and acting in TV drama series, she had cohosted a Melbourne breakfast show, and created *Bobo's Late Show*, introducing midnight movies for the network and its affiliates. By the time of this screening she was no longer involved with impresario Harry M. Miller and brought along her future husband Ralph Rosenblum. Ralph was a Sydney businessman, warmhearted and urbane. He was interested in dabbling in showbiz. *For Valour* impressed him.

"Pity I could not make it in color to reach the world market," or words to that effect, I said to him in subsequent conversation.

"Well, if you ever have any bright ideas..." was his response.

I certainly had, along with a desire to work for myself one day, but did not yet feel ready to leave the security and prospects of a junior executive position at Australia's top rating network. Hey, $120 a week was an OK wage for a single man in 1972. But a couple of months later an event occurred that caused a rethink. Clyde Packer resigned as chairman of Channel Nine after a row with his father. The schism had been a long time coming. Some background into the Packer family's colorful history might be helpful.

Sir Frank Packer had been a successful amateur boxer during his early days of expanding the media interests he inherited from his father. He had a meanspirited, controlling personality. He saw his duty as a parent to be the toughening up of his two sons, Clyde and Kerry, to prepare them for the corporate combat to come as the Packer media empire grew. He was particularly hard on Clyde, the more intellectually inclined of the brothers. Sir Frank is reported to have referred to younger son Kerry, who may have been dyslexic, as "the family idiot." Clyde was to be groomed to take over the family business upon the patriarch's passing. Instead of attending university, as he had wished, Clyde was inducted into the family business. As his father put it: "You go to work for me…You'll learn far more in the school of hard knocks."

Hard knocks were on the curriculum. Clyde and brother Kerry (6 foot 3, 6 foot 2 respectively) were involved in a public brawl when they led an attempt to seize the printing facilities and eject the staff of a newspaper in receivership, the *Anglican Press*, to prevent it being sold to their media rival Rupert Murdoch. Having cleared the building, they boarded up the windows and doors, and attempted to negotiate with the receiver of the bankrupt newspaper. Five tough men were immediately sent by Murdoch to retake the building. The leader of this group was Frank Browne, sports editor of Murdoch's *Sunday Mirror*. Once a professional boxer, Browne had occasionally published a far right political scandal rag called *Things I Hear*. Ten years earlier, Browne and his business partner were jailed for three months for "contempt of Parliament," the only people in Australian history to have been sent to prison by the House of Representatives. While some of his men created a diversion at the front door, Browne broke open a rear toilet window, and gained entry. In the ensuing brawl, Kerry Packer, an amateur boxer as his father had been at his age, took on Frank Browne. It did not go well. For days, Kerry was seen sporting two black eyes under dark glasses, and a badly swollen face. Eventually the battered Packer group fled, all in the one car, because the Murdoch group had sabotaged the tires of the others. Clyde took his share of licks, but his humiliation was more public. The Murdoch group had stationed a photographer to watch the building. "Knight's sons in city brawl" was the frontpage headline in the next day's *Daily Mirror*, above a photo of a menacing-looking Clyde throwing John Willis, the one-legged manager of the *Anglican Press*, into the street.

Despite such devotion to their father's buccaneer ideology, the brothers received scant praise as they worked their way up his corporate ladder. According to author Paul Barry, "Clyde Packer…was also frequently dressed down and abused in public by his father, Sir Frank. Into his late thirties, Clyde was still treated like a stupid, disobedient little boy, until he could take no more and rebelled against such tyranny, splitting clearly and completely with his father." The flashpoint came two years after his father had appointed him to run Channel Nine, an arrangement Clyde later characterized thus: "It was a very equitable arrangement, I had the responsibility and he had the authority."

Sir Frank learned that a Channel Nine current affairs program was about to broadcast an interview with Bob Hawke, then head of the trade union movement, later Prime Minister. Sir Frank, who had used his newspapers shamelessly to campaign against the Labor Party and the unions, banned the interview. Clyde resigned in protest and relinquished all his roles with the family empire. Sir Frank Packer died on May 1, 1974. His estate, valued at around AUD $100 million, passed directly to younger son Kerry. In 1976, Clyde sold his quarter-share of the family business for AUD $4 million to his brother. Kerry went on to become Australia's richest man until his death in 2005. So much for "the family idiot." I met Kerry only once in the mid-1990s while I was bodysurfing at Sydney's Palm Beach. All of 280 pounds, he waded towards me like a galleon under sail. We talked briefly about his brother, then an inviting wave swept us in different directions.

I liked Clyde, not just because he was a supportive boss. He was challenging but fun to work for. I learned a lot. We had the shared experience of ten sometimes lonely years at elite boarding schools. He liked me despite—or perhaps because of—my loud shirts and irreverent sense of humor. We spoke shortly before he left the Channel Nine building for the last time. I could see a weight had been lifted from him. He had thrown off his father's shackles. Now, he said, he could do whatever the hell he wanted, and encouraged me to do the same.

# PART III
## TRENCHARD PRODUCTIONS PTY LTD

# CHAPTER 14
## Going It Alone

It was a big decision to leave the network. For a while an inner voice had been nagging at me…you're twenty-six. Time to strike out on your own. I decided—damn the torpedoes—I am going to start my own little production company. So with a $5,000 investment each from myself and my ever-supportive father, Trenchard Productions Pty. Ltd. was registered on December 1, 1972. I was the sole staff member, operating out of my rented weatherboard house in Fletcher Street, Woollahra. Hard to get a Woollahra address for $100 a month these days…

Bobo Falkner's boyfriend and soon husband, Ralph Rosenblum, financed our first production, *The Stuntmen*, a TV special in color on a budget of $16,000, in return for which he would receive 50% of the profits after recoupment. I made a tentative domestic presale for $16,000 with Channel Nine, ensuring I could repay Ralph. I had left Nine under good terms, and even returned for a few weeks to do promos when my replacement had to take a leave of absence. I could have got maybe $20,000 if I had waited till the film was completed, but presale seemed the prudent decision at the company's outset.

With the help of GUO executive John Fraser, my idea for a quarterly movie magazine came together. It was a 3-way split between publisher Modern Magazines, film exhibitor Greater Union Theaters, and Trenchard Productions, to be sold for fifty cents a copy through GUO and Village theaters. The debut issue entitled *Movie 73* was set for Christmas '72 release. In an intense weekend during my final month at Channel Nine, I wrote short pieces on twenty-seven soon-to-be-released films, generously illustrated by appropriate images from their publicity kits. I worked with Modern Magazines on the layout, then sent the material to Dai Nippon Printing Co in Hong Kong, with an order for a 60-page glossy, 12 pages in color.

My initial editorial described *Movie* in these terms: "…a quarterly film magazine, designed to amuse, inform, and entertain both enthusiasts and casual cinema-goers alike." I urged readers not to throw it away after reading: "Over the months and ultimately

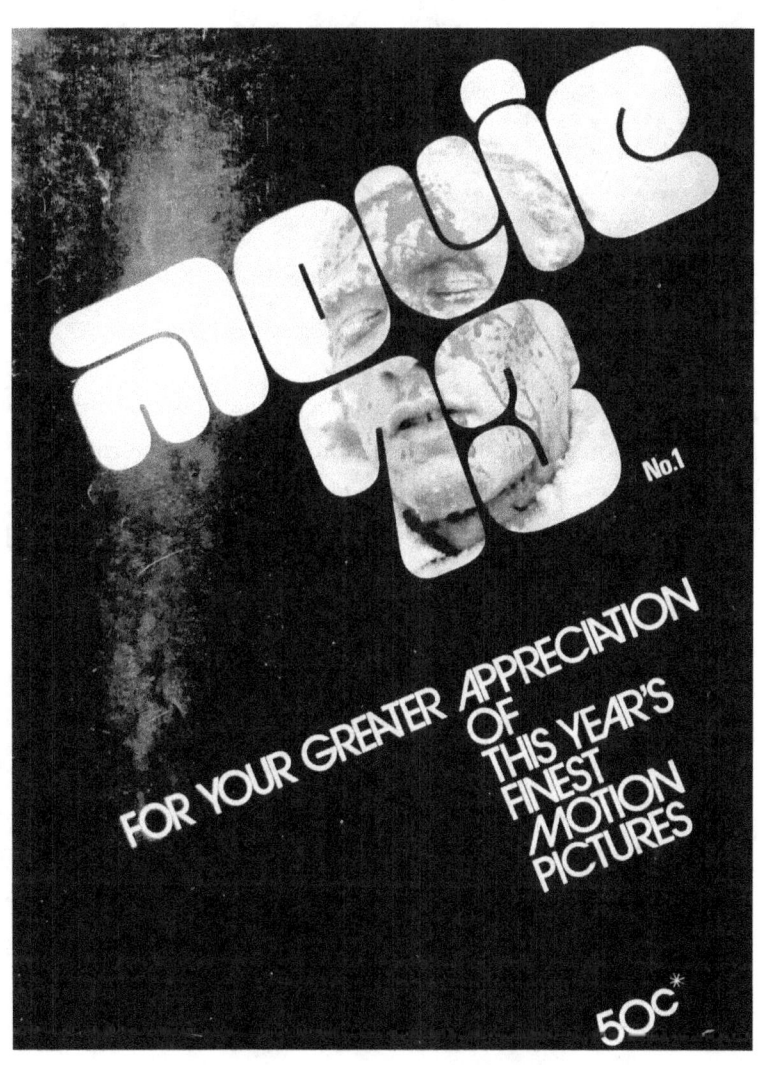

the years, *Movie 73* (*74*, *75*, etc.) will build into a useful reference library that will fill you in on the details of a film, either first release or re-issue, that you are considering seeing." In 2009 I gave one of the last copies of that first issue to the human encyclopedia of movie lore Quentin Tarantino, when *Not Quite Hollywood* filmed a conversation between us.

20,000 copies of *Movie* were printed. 16,000 were sold. The second issue set for end of March '73 was immediately greenlit.

The success of the first issue of *Movie* was a good start for Trenchard Productions. The success of the company's first film would be the key to its future, but the chosen subject matter, movie stunt work, while a fascination of mine, was far from predictable in either execution or market appeal.

*The Stuntman*, a 50-minute color documentary, was devised to play in four parts with an opening teaser and a concluding wrap-up tag to accommodate commercial breaks. Each segment started with a specially created action sequence running between one and two minutes, evoking a particular genre of movie. The rest of the segment featured the methodology and mechanics behind the stunts. Today this is just standard material in any movie's electronic press kit, but for television audiences in the early seventies, it was fresh with a spice of danger.

The opening segment, the most important to hooking the viewer, had to be impressive, so I devised a daylight commando raid that evoked British WWII movies like *The Guns of Navarone*. In my scenario, a group of commandos are interrupted in their sabotage of power lines by enemy troops, who unleash mortar fire and chase the survivors to the edge of a high ocean side cliff. An explosion blows one man to the rocks below, while the others variously abseil down ropes to the getaway craft below.

Because the Army liked *For Valour*, they provided the Holsworthy Firing Range once again free of charge as the location for the ambush, plus troops and four armored personnel carriers to harry my commandos with mortar fire as a training exercise. The Army Engineers blasted a withered gumtree in half behind the fleeing men, their proximity to danger compressed by a long lens.

Next came the clifftop escape sequence. I had chosen a well-known Sydney lookout point, The Gap, the site of a major maritime tragedy.

An anchor from the doomed ship mounted at the top of the cliff beside a commemorative plaque added a sobering vibe. The wreck had happened on the night of 20 August 1857. The Dunbar, carrying 123 passengers and crew, approached Sydney Harbor from the south, in a gale and heavy rain. The ship's captain mistook a smaller break in the coastline known as The Gap for the nearby entrance to Sydney Harbor, and drove the ship onto the rocks. There was only one survivor. Sharks fought over the drowned, while crowds watched helplessly from the cliffs above. Only twenty-two bodies were recovered. Over the years the cliff's macabre past attracted a number of troubled souls who chose plunging off The Gap as the solution to their pain. The tabloid media renamed it "Suicides' Gap." Even though CCTV cameras monitor the site 24/7, it remains among the world's top 10 sites for suicide. But this cliff was an ideal place to shoot the high fall, the solo and tandem abseiling that the commando sequence required. The potential irony in my choice of location was not lost on me that dawn as I waited beside the Dunbar's anchor for crew, stunt team, and Police Rescue Squad to arrive. Because the NSW Police had liked the recruitment commercial I had made for them in my Channel Nine days, I was able to obtain their help in getting crew and equipment safely to the bottom of the cliff.

The man coordinating all the stunts was Bob Woodham, whom I had featured in *For Valour* and *The Big Screen Scene*. He would also carry out the high fall, fall off a horse, be the passenger in a tandem rope slide, crash cars, motorbikes and be set on fire. I gave him $2,000 of the 16K budget, half in advance. Bob saw the film as a showcase for his talents and wanted to excel.

THE STUNTMEN must rank as one of the most hair-raising T.V. Specials ever made. It started as a blow by blow account of how some 25 different types of movie stunts are carried out by professional stuntmen . . . it ended with the stunt co-ordinator claiming 3 world records.
The matter is still sub judice but claims have been made for the highest cliff-fall (100 feet), the longest human torch (40 seconds) and the world's first tandem rope slide. The film was written and directed by Brian Trenchard Smith for his own company Trenchard Productions.

His previous credits include the war film "For Valour", "Marty Feldman in Australia" and "The Big Screen Scene" with Robert Lansing.
THE STUNTMEN creates 4 different types of stunt-packed action sequences, an explosive commando raid, a western ambush, a highly destructive car chase, and a succession of unbelievable motorcycle stunts. Then, making maximum use of the ultra slow motion camera, each stunt is examined from preparation through to execution. The chief stuntmen were Bob Woodham and Herbie Nelson whose films include "You Only Live Twice", "Farenheit 451", "Cleopatra" and "The Guns of Navarone".

Solid action from start to finish, the film has been sold to the National Nine Network in Australia, where it has left all who have seen it gasping.

COLOUR: 48 Mins.

Bob arrived a little frazzled, explained he had just driven 150 miles from an all-night bucks party in Muswellbrook. Bob was a macho guy. He assured me he was fine. I would see how things shaped up. Bob brought a support team with varied experience: Herbie Nelson (*Guns of Navarone*), with whom Bob had teamed up on stunts in the UK, and Warren Campbell, whom he was training to do fire stunts. Playing fellow commandos in the scene were wrestler, writer, novelist and actor Roger Ward (*Mutiny on the Bounty*) and Grant Page, a former commando, trawler fisherman, salesman, jack of all trades. I would have lifelong friendships with Roger and Grant.

At the bottom of the cliff, Bob's team built the customary landing pad for high falls in those days—a 6-foot-high, 25-foot square stack of assembled but empty cardboard boxes. Two layers of mattresses and a tarpaulin were spread on top, then the whole structure was lashed together with ropes. The air trapped in the boxes cushioned the stuntman's fall. Inflatable airbags would soon replace this cumbersome process.

The camera crew under excellent documentary shooter Oscar Scherl (my DP on *For Valour*) captured the preparation of the rig, then set up angles for the fall itself. One camera would run at 400 frames per second, slowing the action down twenty times. It would take ten seconds to get up to speed then run out of film thirty seconds later. The fall had to take place within that window. Two other cameras would capture wide and medium shots. I would also shoot it myself with a clockwork Bell and Howell on the cliff while standing near Bob's takeoff position. He would fall ninety feet.

A crowd now lined the rail, looking down at the rig on the rocks below. Our window of opportunity was narrowing. Spray from the incoming tide hitting the rocks was landing closer and closer to the rig.

If the cardboard boxes got wet, they would lose their effectiveness. Some intermittent gusts of wind had also arisen. Bob dropped a coin from his take off point onto the rig below to focus his aim, and see how wind might affect his trajectory. This was the highest fall Bob had ever done. Even as the tide spray advanced towards the boxes, we would have to wait till the wind dropped. He was always full of confidence and determination but I detected some understandable nervousness.

In the interview just before the jump, I am seen asking: "Are you scared?"
"Yeah, I'm scared," Bob replied.

In the edit, after Bob's admission, I left out his subsequent remarks:

"It's pretty dangerous. It's my form of art, so I'll have to cop it, I guess."

I used that piece elsewhere in the segment, as voice overlay on shots of the preparation of the rig he was to land on. As my response to "Yeah, I'm scared," I just cut to a 2-shot favoring me at the end of the interview.

"OK. Let's do it."

Thus, with editing, I made myself look callous and uncaring. Which was not the case. But perhaps it added to the tension of the scene. Although Bob had signed the standard waiver, absolving the company of responsibility, known in the stunt world as the "blood chit," I was well aware of how serious a decision I was making to move forward.

The moment of truth had arrived. I could call it off or I could stick with the plan. In the few stunts I had filmed to that point, I never felt anyone was in danger of real injury or death. I had told myself: We know the theory, we've gone over the details, it's just a matter of following the plan precisely, right? In fact, stunt work is not an exact science. Accidents still happen all over the movie world. Stuntmen and women still die. Rarely, but it happens. A stuntman's high fall of ninety feet has three possible outcomes—applause, paralysis or a funeral. Whatever happened, I would be responsible. I had created this event. Should I just call a halt, and change the scenario to something without risk, with less dramatic impact? It's a dilemma that all stunt directors face, a dilemma that still gnaws at me every time I shoot action. How can I be absolutely sure that this is absolutely safe?

The gusts of wind died down. Bob got into position. He's the expert, I decided, I have to trust him. Rightly or wrongly, I quarantined my doubts, and called for cameras to roll. I heard Oscar's high speed camera whirr below, then heard him call "Speed!" This was Bob's cue. I rolled my camera.

Bob inched forward to get his toes to the edge of the sloping rim of the sandstone cliff. Then he seemed to slip, then lurch into space, rotating himself into the "tuck" position a stuntman must acquire to land on his back.

Bob hit not the center but the nearside corner of the rig with an echoing thump, penetrating almost to the bottom layer of boxes. The crowd gasped.

Then a hand appeared at the rim of the hole. Warren Campbell gave the thumbs up.

Tumultuous applause from the spectators. Much relief all round, particularly from myself, but also a realization that risk would be a constant factor in the career path I had chosen.

The next stunt was the tandem rope slide. It depended entirely on the expertise of Grant Page, who had flown in from Adelaide for the gig. Drawing on his commando training, he had offered this stunt to the sequence. First he rigged a rope from the highest point of the northern cliff of The Gap across the open water of its concave inlet to the base of the southern cliff, and stretched it as tight as possible.

This represented the commandos' escape route to a waiting zodiac riding the breakers below. Here's how the scene played out: Two commandos arrive at the slide rope. One, played by Bob Woodham, is wounded. We see Grant hoist his buddy onto his shoulder. Then he throws a short piece of rope with a hand toggle on each end across the slide rope. Supporting his burden, he approaches the edge of the cliff. Gripping the toggles tightly, he steps into space and starts to slide down the main rope towards the water 120 feet below. It appears Grant is carrying the weight of two men—364 pounds—by his fingers in each toggle as they accelerate rapidly towards the rocks on the southern side. Judging the best moment, Grant releases his grip on the toggles and they both fall into the sea close to the waiting zodiac, which raced in to scoop them up.

What we reveal later is that there were two hand toggle ropes: a short one, 2 feet across, which we showed up to the moment of takeoff, and another which was used only for the actual slide, identical but twice as long, and looped unseen beneath Bob's body as he lies across Grant's shoulder. This worked as a counterweight to Grant as they slid together. The camera angles were wide enough not show the difference between the two ropes. We believed this trick had never been done before on film. Bob entered it for the Guinness Book of Records, though I am not sure if it was ever accepted.

I was impressed with Grant Page. He had a natural easygoing charisma. If *The Stuntmen* were to become a series, which was my intention if the market responded, he was certainly going to be a regular.

The rest of the shoot went well; slow motion motorbike stunts, plus the full range of horse stunts in an ambush sequence shot on the colonial town movie set at Smoky Dawson's ranch. It was a proud moment when my father played a stagecoach passenger in this first film from our company Trenchard Productions.

Concluding the twelve day shoot was the car chase and fire stunts. The fire gags would provide a big finish to the show. Here's what I had devised: Two payroll bandits played by Bob Woodham and Warren Campbell, are speeding off in their getaway car. A bystander Roger Ward commandeers a car, and gives chase. The crooks hit an old lady, played by Herbie Nelson, pitching him over the hood. They accidentally flick a cigarette into the back of their car, landing beside a leaky gas can, which quickly ignites the whole interior.

In the ensuing panic, they crash the car into a tree, causing them both to fly in slow motion through the windshield on fire. This stunt would be carried out without the customary fire suits. Instead Waterjel, the aforementioned fire-retardant jelly, coating the men's skin would protect them from the flames.

Trailer work had given me many opportunities to study the structure of action sequences. A series of shots, staged separately, would be fluidly edited together to provide the illusion of taking place in real time. If we actually crashed the car into a tree, the windshield might shatter. We had no money for a replacement. We needed to keep it whole till we were ready for the shot where the stuntmen would smash through it. So the solution, time-honored in low budget and TV episodes, was to place the car against the tree, then reverse fast. Both a low angle, with the tree in foreground and the car beyond, plus an angle from the driver's perspective of the imminent collision were shot at twenty frames per second by an under-cranked camera to increase the apparent speed. Then, in postproduction, the shots would be reprinted in reverse, so the car and the driver's perspective now appeared to hurtle towards, not away from the tree. They would be intercut with a reaction shot—the "Oh, shit!" moment—from the driver. Later, as a pickup shot, staged after the

fire stunt had been completed, we set up a close angle of the point of impact between the front bumper and the tree, then rammed the car into the tree for real. Tightly edited, these shots provide a convincing illusion of the crash.

With the car now pressed against the tree, we set up for the main event—the two man fire stunt. We did it twice. First, slow motion cameras covered the blazing men smashing through the windshield on fire. To assist their exit we gently tapped the bottom corner of the glass with a screwdriver, causing the glass to frost. Easier to break through. Shot at 400 frames it looked pretty amazing. For the first time in a fire sequence you can see the actor's face as flying glass and flame swirl around him in ultraslow motion. Then we re-jelled and re-costumed Bob and Warren to do it a second time, now without the windshield. This enabled them, when they were fully alight, to leap out farther across the hood, as if thrown by the impact, and roll off the car.

Waterjel's properties were near-miraculous; I wanted to try it out myself. To provide definitive proof that Waterjel could protect bare skin, I took off my shirt, jelled up my arm from a bucket at my feet. It felt cold and reassuring. Kerosene was squirted on my forearm then ignited with a taper. Flame enveloped my hand and lower forearm.

"I can hold this for... No, I bloody well can't!"

I said, thrusting my arm into the bucket of cold Jel. The flames, it seems, were hotter than I expected. No shit, Sherlock! Such hubris. But I guess you've noticed a pattern in that direction already...

I left this embarrassment in the film, because, it was, after all, a WTF moment, and who can resist those? But it did prove the Jel's efficacy. I was not burned, just had a couple of red marks, where the kerosene squirt bored through the Jel. They went away in days, due to the healing properties of the tea tree oil in the mixture. So I did it again to get the closer angle, still sticking my arm in the bucket pretty damn quick.

I had a healthy respect for fire, but it did not frighten me. Heights frightened me. Still do. But fire gags were a matter of faith in the Jel and the support team. I lacked the reflexes for car chase work. I was a clumsy fighter. Except with an épée. Perhaps this was a stunt I could do, and thereby I would learn how better to stage it. That was my thinking at the time, anyway. Over the next few years I would be set alight from buttocks to shoulders five more times, and be purposely hit by a car twice, breaking the windshield on the second occasion. With hindsight I realize the real driver behind my dabbling in stunts was an issue with physical courage, born of an overprotected childhood, reinforced by failure on the school rugby field. I feared I was not the brave fighter pilot my father was. Perhaps dicing with danger would prove my courage, if only to myself.

I had chosen rising documentary editor Rhonda McGregor to cut *The Stuntmen*. She did a fabulous job, and would edit my next three docos. Tightly edited to forty-eight minutes, scored with library music, a 16mm Ektachrome print was delivered to Channel Nine, which accepted it and I was able to pay Ralph Rosenblum back his $16,000. We would go on to split $15,000 in profits from subsequent international distribution after marketing and sales commission, so for Ralph it was not too bad a return for an 8-month investment. I now had proof of concept: I could make an independently financed film and sell it for a profit.

# CHAPTER 15
## Building the Company

I had developed a relationship with the Australian Film Development Corporation, a government instrumentality created to provide script development and production funding for the emerging film industry. They asked me to do occasional script assessments and promotional work. Head of Production John Daniel, a great supporter, invited me to "help out" on a documentary that needed "creative and administrative guidance." Environmental activist Roland Cantley had received funding for a film entitled *The Last Great Barrier Reef*. Cantley had a big ego and little to no film experience, but his project was worthy. Rising UK media personality David Frost, visiting Australia on other business, had agreed to give two days of his time to some on-location reporting. I was assigned to handle the shoot.

Cantley wanted to show how agricultural pesticides leaching into the ocean off the coast of Queensland were killing the coral and endangering the future of the reef. Sadly prescient, it seems, but at the time angrily disputed by the Queensland State Premier Sir Joh Bjelke-Petersen, a virulent anti-environmental, antiunion, far right conservative, who gerrymandered his way into a 19-year rule of the state. He became known as the Marcos of Queensland. The Labor Party Prime Minister at the time Gough Whitlam described him as "a Bible-bashing bastard—the man is a paranoiac, a bigot and fanatical." Sir Joh's attitude to the free press was simple: "The greatest thing that could happen in Queensland and the nation is when we get rid of all the media. Then we could live in peace and tranquility." (Sound familiar?) Plainclothes State Police shadowed our shoot. Sir Joh claimed that our unit planted fake examples of polluting runoff.

David Frost took it all in stride. I found him to be charming and focused, with a remarkable memory. He only knew me for two days, yet ten years later, encountering me at a media function, he greeted me by name. He had a sense of adventure, and a genuine curiosity about the lives of others. When we were coming in to land at Cairns airport, David asked the pilot of our 6-seater if he could land the plane, while the pilot still retained control. He wanted to understand the job of piloting an aircraft. The pilot, awed by celebrity, complied and talked him through the procedure. Happily, it was an uneventful touchdown. The subsequent editing of all the Barrier Reef material stalled due to Cantley's intransigence. We parted company. To the best of my knowledge, the documentary was never completed. Perhaps the pinnacle of David Frost's remarkable career were the Frost/Nixon interviews, in which he got Nixon to apologize for Watergate.

Luckily, my entry into the freelance market as a TV promo guy coincided with the beginning of the Australian cinema renaissance. And movies needed trailers. Welsh comedian Harry Secombe had come to Australia to shoot a film called *Sun Struck* for a British company. He was one of the comic quartet that had pioneered BBC Radio's *The Goon Show*, alongside Peter Sellers, Spike Milligan, and Michael Bentine. A fish-out-of-water comedy starring Harry Secombe set in a country rarely seen on the big screen at that time was expected to do very well in British cinemas. (It didn't.) Greater Union's John Fraser, who would be distributing the film locally, recommended me for the trailer, citing my work for National Screen Service in the UK. NSS would normally have done this trailer. Esther Harris, my mentor there, was pleased I got the gig. It was the first of dozens of trailers I would make for Australian films over the years. Clients and distributors were happy, but by today's standards my trailers are a bit ponderous, and all are too long.

To develop a trailer company, I needed equipment and human resources. From the outset, my business mantra had been: Hire no permanent staff and buy no plant. Overhead can be the killer of small business. The solution was to subcontract as needed. All cast and crew of *The Stuntman* were subcontractors. I applied the same principle to trailers. Thus began my long association with Alan Lake's company, Film Production Services (FPS). For seventeen years I put all my trailers, all the postproduction of my movies and TV shows through FPS, which became my de facto office. It was a mutually beneficial arrangement. I recommended FPS to other filmmakers. Peter Weir edited *The Year of Living Dangerously* and *Witness* there.

Alan Lake ran a happy company of enthusiastic newcomers and seasoned pros. He personally edited a number of my projects. Peter Fletcher edited many of my trailers. Ron Williams edited *Danger Freaks* and *The Man from Hong Kong*. Amongst the FPS staff was Lee Smith, a fresh-faced lanky 18-year-old with a laconic sense of humor. Years later he would co-edit two of my films, *Turkey Shoot* with Alan Lake (without credit) and *Dead End Drive In* (with credit.) His skills and taste attracted the attention of Peter Weir, editing four of his films. He became Christopher Nolan's editor for his first six pictures. Lee's interweaving of the different time frames in *Dunkirk* till they unite at the climax is truly masterful and deserved the Academy Award. FPS was a great place to encourage young talent. Sue Blainey and Noellene Westcombe were editing assistants on *BMX Bandits* and many of my trailers. They also went on to editing careers in Hollywood.

For a few years I was the primary trailer maker in Australia. Here's a list of the trailers I remember: Sunstruck, Libido, Alvin Purple, Peterson, Picnic at Hanging Rock, Mad Dog Morgan, Storm Boy, The Love Epidemic, The Man From Hong Kong, Death Cheaters, Break of Day, Summerfield, The Irishman, The Killing of Angel Street, Snapshot, Thirst, The FJ Holden, The Journalist, The Last Wave, My Brilliant Career, Stir, Money Movers, Blue Fin, Long Weekend, In Search of Anna, The Fourth Wish, Harlequin, Manganine, The Mango Tree, Turkey Shoot, Midnite Spares, The Dark Room, Goodbye Paradise, Fast Talking, BMX Bandits, Aussie Assault, The Right Hand Man, Dead End Drive In, The Highest Honor, The Coolangatta Gold, Hoodwink, Careful He Might Hear You, Jennie Kissed Me, The Survivor, The Light Horsemen, Belinda, The Place at the Coast, Fair Game, Stunt Rock, The Siege of Firebase Gloria, Eliza Fraser, Weekend of Shadows, Cappuchino, Touch and Go, Breaker Morant, Freedom, Kathy's Child, A City's Child, Journey Among Women, Race for the Yankee Zephyr, Maybe This Time, The Settlement, The Club, Danger Freaks, Short Changed, Chain Reaction, Going Sane, Best of Friends, Crosstalk, Molly, Newsfront, Marco Polo Versus The Red Dragon, Tail of a Tiger, The Panther Pictures, etc.

My second Australian trailer was for *Libido*, a portmanteau feature aimed at arthouse audiences consisting of four shorts, linked by a common theme—the torments that accompany human sexuality: jealousy, promiscuity, loss of innocence, and the moral conflicts of a nun and priest in love. The stories, dealing with gender politics and the cultural upheaval of the early 70s, showcased the work of four directors, two of whom, Tim Burstall and Fred Schepisi, went on to solid careers. One segment was the screenwriting debut of eminent playwright David Williamson with rising star Jack Thompson in the lead. It was a perfect showcase for his screen persona. The Priest/Nun story was written by celebrated author Thomas Keneally, who would go on to write *Schindler's List* (originally *Schindler's Ark*).

The distributor admired *Libido's* quality but was concerned about its commercial appeal. No worries, I said, and suggested a 2-pronged attack, each promotional tool targeting different audiences. First a trailer full of sex and comedy, which the David Williamson *portrait of Australian misogyny* segment, ably directed by David Baker provided. It was lower brow in tone than the other stories; this would be balanced by a behind the scenes TV documentary to

118

emphasize the high-minded intention of the film., reflected in the Burstall and Schepisi segments. (In the UK and Spain Schepisi's low key depiction of a love affair between a priest and a nun was dropped.) Basically, the "TV Special" was a clip show, like *The Big Screen Scene*, intercutting tasteful dramatic moments with cast and creatives' interviews. Quick and cheap to make. These days it would be a 10-minute electronic press kit at most. But in 1973, with public interest in the emerging Australian film industry growing, a network put *The Making of Libido* on at 9 p.m.

Next was the trailer for Tim Burstall's *Alvin Purple*, a comedy about a reluctant male sex symbol, whom women find irresistible. "A man with a big future in front of him," as my narrator intoned. Roadshow's Alan Finney masterminded the successful publicity campaign.

Again I backed it up with a 1-hour Special—*Inside Alvin Purple*—which I presold to Channel Seven. Even though Australian TV had recently liberalized its policy on nudity, I knew I was skirting the boundary with the graphic nature of the clips. The network submitted it to the Broadcasting Control Board a week before the airdate. The Board promptly banned it. Even better, I thought, and leaked the news to a journalist friend.

"Sex movie documentary banned!" screamed the headline in the afternoon tabloid.

What cuts would you like? I asked the Board. The list was not too bad. I quickly re-submitted, and the Board, under pressure from the Fairfax media group that owned Channel Seven, passed the revised version.

"Banned sex movie doco to be shown!" exulted the tabloid.

A few days later, it screened to high ratings. Then the movie opened to queues 'round the block. Not because of my promo efforts, though they helped, but because Australian audiences, after years of censorship, were ready for a madcap local comedy about a reluctant sex symbol pursued by every woman he meets. As word of mouth spread it became a date movie. *Alvin Purple* cost $200,000 and grossed $5 million at the national box office.

Thus I came to the attention of Graham Burke, then CEO of Village Roadshow, *Alvin Purple*'s distributor/exhibitor. In 1954, Graham Burke and his partner Roc Kirby had pioneered drive-in theaters in Australia, then acquired hardtops in all capital cities. Twenty years later Village Roadshow had its own distribution division, which handled releases for major Hollywood companies, the largest of which was Warner Bros, a partnership that would ultimately go global. Graham Burke approached me with what he called "a wicked idea." Would I like to make a feature length theatrically released dramatized documentary about sexually transmitted diseases entitled *The Love Epidemic*? Never met a green light I didn't like…

The availability of reliable birth control and rapidly-changing mores had altered the landscape of sexuality beyond recognition. The newly created 'R 'Rating (over 18) was offering Australians sights and sounds they had never seen before at a public venue. The novelty would wear off in time, but a low budget black and white feature documentary entitled *A Study in Pornography*, that blended analysis with exploitation of its taboo subject, had done well in selected theaters. Graham Burke knew that the first feature to examine another taboo subject, the dark side of sexual liberation, would also draw an audience; a public health shock-doc, with legitimate erotic content, that would play the traditional inner city 'R'-rated grindhouses, followed by a drive-in release. It could be made cheaply and could be licensed for remakes by foreign producers in their own languages. He had a distributor in England interested in shooting a British version of the Australian prototype.

I suggested a comedic approach to relax the audience, sugar the pill, make it entertaining as well as educational, ostensibly an old fashioned VD film but spiced with comedy sketches and some wry commentary. It was my first attempt to concoct a genre hybrid. Graham Burke accepted my pitch. The deal was: write, produce and direct a feature length documentary on a budget of $33,000, including my fee (3K). A percentage of profits would be negotiated. Shoot it in 16mm; Village Roadshow would then pay for the blowup to 35mm. I was off to the races. Whoopee!

I shot the film in bursts over a period of months. The picture starts with a bang, so to speak. Two people meet at a wild party and are mutually attracted. After watching a strip tease, they become aroused and slip into a vacant bedroom to have sex. I intercut their softcore level lovemaking with shots of a telex machine printing out American gonorrhea and syphilis statistics (subtlety is not my strong suit). I wanted the film's message to hit home right from the start. As the couple relax in postcoital bliss, he turns to her and asks: "By the way, what's your name?" In this way the potential consequences of casual sex would be introduced. Well-regarded comedy writer/actor Michael Lawrence penned four comedy sketches, the best of which was a debate between Syphilis and Gonorrhea as to which of them should have jurisdiction over the body they have both just entered. I used the interior of the Bunnerong Power Station to represent the internal organs of the freshly infected. Veteran actors John Ewart and Barry Lovett, dressed in boiler suits and hardhats, respectively played "Syph" and "Gon". It was my first and only experience with drunk actors, arriving midway between pickled and legless. Embarrassed perhaps by the material they were portraying, they'd had an extended liquid lunch and were fluffing lines with impish guilt. I was tempted to express annoyance, but remembered Robert Lansing's advice to me that actors are naked out there, do all you can to reduce their embarrassment and make them feel cherished. So I jollied the fellas along and it helped. They got it together.

A joke in that sketch that always gets a laugh was unplanned. In the middle of a shot, a previously dark illuminated sign behind Syph & Gon suddenly flashed into life, pulsing on and off, with the accompanying sound of a klaxon. It read "Load Coming On." Bunnerong was a standby power station, through which power was occasionally routed, as it was on this occasion. The word "Load" was both a legitimate term in the power industry and slang in Australia for gonorrhea. I cite it as one of those serendipity moments that you just have to go with when they occur.

In research, I came across the Siege of Naples in 1495, which is the first recorded outbreak of syphilis in Europe. The origin of this disease remains unknown. There are two primary hypotheses. The Columbian theory posits that mercenaries returning to Europe from Columbus' voyage to the New World in 1492 brought the disease back with them. They joined the French army at the siege of Naples in 1494. The sharing of prostitutes led to the disease spreading like wildfire. In contradiction, the pre-Columbian theory proposes that syphilis previously existed in Europe but went unrecognized, citing that the symptoms of syphilis in its tertiary form were described by Hippocrates, legendary physician of classical Greece, regarded as the founder of Western medicine. A quasi-medical documentary with a battle scene? Hmm. Tempting.

Could I, given my low budget, stage a medieval siege to provide a backdrop for this information? I knew there was a medieval theme park named Kryall Castle being built outside Ballarat in Victoria. This could provide a production value location. With the aid of Grant Page and Roger Ward, plus twenty burly members of the Viking Society of Australasia, dressed in a variety of anachronistic costumes, we recreated the siege, complete with cannon fire, battering rams, a 4-horse cavalry charge and a lethal broad sword duel.

I must confess it was my desire to shoot a costume battle scene that was the true driver of this sequence. I also saw an opportunity to put some pizzazz into the largely interior/talking head visuals of *The Love Epidemic*. The cost of the Kryall Castle footage would be split with my planned stunt series *Dangerfreaks*, to be headlined by Grant Page. Even though the show wasn't financed yet, I was confident it would be, so I had been stockpiling little low-cost shoots of stunt-oriented material.

Despite the fact that there was no more nudity and sex after the first three minutes, the audience did not seem to care. The taboo subject matter gripped them. *The Love Epidemic* opened on January 5th 1975 with an 'R' (18) rating in two small theaters in Sydney and Melbourne, grossing 15K each in its first week. Similar bookings in other capital cities and drive in achieved a gross box office of AUD$367,000, delivering about 180K in film rental to Roadshow, with home video to come. Not bad for a 50K production cost and 25K in Prints & Ads.

The *Love Epidemic* was part public health, part exploitation documentary. The introduction of the 'R' rating four years earlier enabled the release of numerous softcore movies and sex documentaries from Europe and America. This trend had not yet lost its novelty value in Australia. The exploitation elements would guarantee an audience, some of whom might possibly modify their sexual behavior as a result. I was able to secure the cooperation of the New South Wales Health Department to film sequences at their STD clinic at Albion Street. Promotion of safe sex was a factor in the creation of *The Love Epidemic*, but the principal objective of its backers, as with all movies, was to make money, which was why Graham Burke had commissioned me to make it through his production affiliate Hexagon. In the year following the screening of *The Love Epidemic*, according to a spokesperson from the NSW Department of Health, the number of persons seeking screening for venereal disease at the Albion Street Clinic in Sydney trebled. So the film was not without its social benefit.

While I juggled trailer assignments and these piecemeal shoots, I got my *Movie 73* magazine publisher to fund a world trip to interview stars and directors of upcoming releases. The second issue had printed 25,000 copies, and sold 22,000. The magazine had a future. I would try to sell *The Stuntmen* in the UK and the United States during the trip. To get *The*

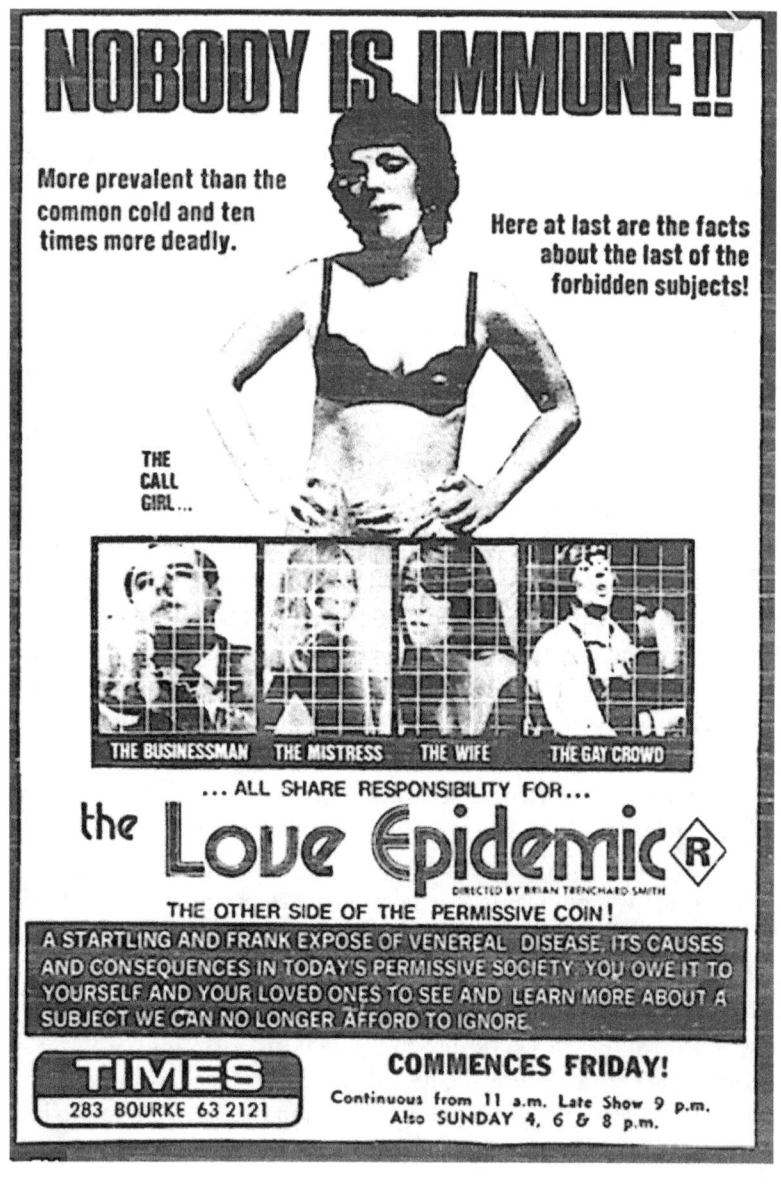

*Stuntmen* some visibility, I had entered the film into the documentary category of the Sydney Film Festival, sponsored by tobacco company Benson and Hedges (nicotine pushers polishing their image by promoting culture). If you want to know why the tobacco company relinquished such an enduring endorsement vehicle, and you are not squeamish, read on.

Two young filmmakers, Hayden Keenan and Esben Storm, entered their film into the short film category. It was just one slow motion shot, taken from underneath a glass table pointing up at a blurry shape. A smaller shape detached itself from the larger shape and floated down, landing on the glass. The focus sharpened to reveal that a substantial turd had dropped from a man's buttocks above, which then descended, smearing it up and down, round and round in patterns on the glass, while the voices of pretentious critics discussed the wondrous artistry of the painting. The title of the film was *A Motion Picture*.

Benson and Hedges learned of the potentially inflammatory content and demanded the film not be screened. But David Stratton, who was running the Festival, declined. He had promised filmmakers that their work would be shown regardless of content. Benson and Hedges threatened to withdraw their sponsorship of future festivals. To his credit David Stratton stuck to his agreement and showed *A Motion Picture* as agreed. Much of the Rose Bay Cinema audience quickly fled to the foyer once the focus sharpened. Benson and Hedges declined to sponsor the festival again. David Stratton nonetheless found other sponsors for the annual Sydney Film Festival which continues to this day. He became a revered movie critic and energetic promoter of Cinema for the next four decades.

*The Stuntmen* won Best Documentary. My father went on stage and received the award for me, because I was overseas on the aforementioned mission: Sell my film. In New York I got Screen Gems (TV Division of Columbia, now Sony) to distribute *The Stuntmen* outside of Australia. An early sale was made to the prestigious BBC documentary series *Man Alive*, for US$13K. Less 40% commission and cost of prints. Aye, there's the rub…

I had told John Fraser at GUO about my forthcoming trip. He then asked me to make a stop in Hong Kong and gave me an introduction to producer Raymond Chow, whose company Golden Harvest had achieved three smash hits in a row across the Asian box office with the new martial arts star Bruce Lee. We viewed the films together. *The Big Boss*, *Fists of Fury*, and *Way of the Dragon* took fight scenes to a whole new level. GUO would be distributing dubbed versions of these films in Australia. Bruce Lee's first English language film, *Enter the Dragon*, was in postproduction at Warner Brothers. It was clear Lee was about to become an international star.

I met Raymond Chow and his American executive Andre Morgan, who was fluent in Mandarin and Cantonese. Bruce Lee was in Hollywood recording post synch dialogue for *Enter the Dragon*. To Chow and Morgan I proposed that a 1-hour TV special on this new movie phenomenon featuring interviews with themselves and Bruce Lee would be a great promotional aid worldwide. GUO would finance it. They agreed and were eager to help. At the same time an idea formed in the back of my mind, what about a Bruce Lee movie set in Australia? He could be a take-no-prisoners Chinese Dirty Harry who comes to Australia and makes mayhem everywhere. I needed some ducks in a row before I pitched and started noodling an outline as I flew on to England.

Among my interview subjects in the UK was Kate O'Mara ( *1963 Dr. Who)* She was a real trouper with a long career, well cast as Joan Collins' sister in the 80's series Dynasty.

Comedian Reg Varney had just completed his third *On The Buses* movie spin-off from the successful TV series which was popular in Australia. Those sideburns. That tie. OMG.

I visited Oscar, Tony, Golden Globe, and Bafta Award winning actress Patricia Neal, whose film *Baxter* was coming up for release. She was married to British author Roald Dahl, and we met at their house in Buckinghamshire. She was a remarkable woman, whose life was full of triumph and heartache. In fact she described it as "a Greek tragedy." When she was twenty-three, she began an affair with married costar, 48-year-old Gary Cooper, who forced her to have an abortion, and on one occasion struck her in the face after Kirk Douglas, in Cooper's opinion, paid too much attention to her. Guilt over her abortion haunted her for the rest of her life. When the affair ended, she had a nervous breakdown. Subsequently she had five chil-

● **BELOW:** Australian film-maker Brian Trenchard Smith, who made *The Man From Hong Kong*, met up with actress Kate O'Mara during a trip to England.

dren with Roald Dahl but suffered through grievous injury to a son and the death of a daughter. While pregnant in 1965, a series of strokes put her in a coma for twenty-one days. Luckily her daughter Lucy was born healthy. Through three years of grueling rehab Neal relearned how to walk and talk. "I think I'm just stubborn, that's all," she said. By 1968 her recovery was sufficiently complete to go back to work, earning a second Academy Award nomination for *The Subject Was Roses*. Patricia Neal was a fine example of Old Hollywood royalty.

Equally gracious and generous with his time was Edward Woodward, star of British TV's spy series *Callan*, which had launched him into movies. I told him I had made the UK trailer for his crime thriller

*The File of the Golden Goose*, in which he costarred with Yul Brynner. Our interview was about his upcoming movie *The Wicker Man*, for which he had high hopes, but which sadly would be reedited and mis-released, before becoming the cult favorite it is today. We had an enjoyable tea and biscuits on his back lawn.

Next was Jon Finch. I had made trailers for his early work in Hammer horrors *The Vampire Lovers* and *Horror of Frankenstein*. That helped get the interview started. It was his starring role in Hitchcock's *Frenzy* that I hoped would produce some amusing Hitchcock anecdotes. But his relationship with the Master of Suspense was not a happy one. Finch had told reporters before the shoot that Hitchcock was perhaps "past his prime" (Finch said he was misquoted). He found the script "a little quaint" and that actors might need to improvise to fill it out. He had even dared to offer Hitchcock a critique of the dialogue. Finch paid dearly for this misstep.

Before a take Hitch would ask pointedly in front of the whole crew if he was "satisfied with his lines." If Finch wanted to change a single word, Hitch would make a big deal of halting filming till writer Anthony Schaffer could be found and consulted. If during a take, Finch strayed in the slightest way from the printed text, the continuity girl would interrupt with a correction. But if supporting actress Vivienne Merchant (then married to playwright Harold Pinter) offered to embroider a scene with some business, or an aside, Hitch would allow it. Finch got no love or support from his director on the set, nor many of the closeups he was expecting. With the net effect that his character appears off balance throughout, as in fact a man unjustly accused of murder might well be. Hitchcock seemed more interested in studying the murderer's reactions. So was Hitch psychologically manipulating his actor towards a more truthful performance, or was it punishment? Whatever the reason, Finch felt badly treated.

British comic Frankie Howerd provided a happier interview. He was coming up in the spook spoof— *The House on Nightmare Park*. His Roman Empire comedy series *Up Pompeii*, and its movie spinoff were popular in Australia. *Nightmare Park* was intended to trigger a franchise with his outrageous character spoofing genre after genre, much as the *Carry On* series did, thirty-one times, from *Carry on Sergeant* (1958) to *Carry on Columbus* (1992). What made Frankie Howerd an unique comedian of his day was his ability to feign innocence about his blatantly risqué double entendre, while mockingly censuring the audience for finding them funny. The interview took place in Clyde Packer's suite at the Savoy Hotel, London.

A few months after Clyde Packer had resigned from Channel Nine, he invited me into his social circle; not the inner circle (Michael Willesee, John Cornel, Paul Hogan); I was more on the periphery, but from time to time I did get invitations to gatherings, like his 37th birthday party at Prunier's Chiswick Garden's restaurant in Woollahra. At one point during the festivities, a 4-foot high birthday cake decorated with candles was wheeled in. A section swung open, and out stepped a scantily clad busty blonde, Abigail, sex siren on the hit soap opera *Number 96*, so called because *Number 69* was considered a little too obvious.

To bring Frankie Howerd, one of Britain's top comedy stars of the day, to Clyde Packer's suite to make us laugh for two hours was a way to repay his hospitality. Former Miss World Ann Sydney was an additional guest. Clyde ordered room service. We ate, drank and were merry. Unlike his father, I always found Clyde to be generous. He spontaneously gave me a chauffeur-driven Rolls Royce to use for a day when his plans changed just before he was to use it. It's paid for, you take it. Why not, I thought, thanked Clyde, and took a trip round my childhood haunts in Hampshire.

Some of my contemporaries in the industry did not care for Clyde. Maybe because of his infamous father, whose ruthlessness and hard right politics Clyde did not share. Clyde was smart, cultured, a *bon vivant*, yet often I detected a sadness about him. He was a little closed off, a trait with which I had sympathy. He was a big man, conscious of his weight which he seemed unable to control. He was never quite comfortable in his own skin. For my part, I tried to be fun in his company. One weekend later that year when we both found ourselves in Los Angeles, we went barhopping with a couple of his girlfriends and associates, ending up somehow at a strip club on Sunset, The Body Shop. My first and last visit to such an establishment. That night happened to be "Amateur Night," on which contestants competed for prizes. Channeling John Cleese, I introduced Clyde to the manager as Lord Packer from Australia, and requested a good table. After a momentary double take, Clyde went with it. The manager was impressed that foreign aristocracy were patronizing his establishment. Clyde and I were made "judges", and at one point found ourselves on stage with the finalists. Sometimes my inner Monty Python just takes over.

# CHAPTER 16
## Bruce Lee

On July 20, 1973 I boarded a Cathay Pacific flight from Sydney to Hong Kong to shoot my documentary about Bruce Lee, a superstar in Asia but virtually unknown to western audiences—as yet. The forthcoming release of his first English language action picture, *Enter the Dragon*, would change all that. I had negotiated with his producer Raymond Chow to interview him for a wide-ranging documentary on Asian martial arts movies to be entitled *World of Kung Fu*. Golden Harvest had agreed to supply footage from Bruce Lee's movies, including *Game of Death*, still in production. In my briefcase was a 6-page outline I had written about a Chinese Dirty Harry sent to Sydney on a routine extradition, who goes after the local crime lord, causing major mayhem, with opportunities for stunt-packed action scenes. And of course a car chase. The grenade in the mouth/confession scene was in this early incarnation but there were as yet no hang glider sequences. There was subtext poking fun at racist attitudes to Asia prevalent in Australia at the time. If the interview with Bruce went well, if I felt we had connected, I would pitch the outline to Raymond Chow.

The plane touched down at Jakarta airport to refuel. I went to stretch my legs in the transit lounge. Staring me in the face was the front page of an English language newspaper with the headline "Bruce Lee Dies!" Utter shock. My heart sank. He was only thirty-two, the very epitome of physical fitness, a man who trained five hours a day, yet he was cut down by cerebral edema variously attributed to heatstroke, an epileptic seizure, or by an allergic reaction to hashish and/or Equagesic, a drug prescribed as a muscle relaxant. My cameraman was booked to fly the next day, my funds were committed. Before recounting what happened next, I want reflect on Bruce Lee through the prism of his films.

Much has been written about Lee Jun-Fan and his legacy. The official website at http://www.brucelee. com/ provides extensive biographical details that will give you a sense of the man, his extraordinary journey, and his cultural impact. Here is a brief snapshot: At age seventeen, Bruce Lee won both the Hong Kong Inter School Boxing Championships with six TKOs, and the Crown Colony Ballroom Dancing Championship with his version of the Cha Cha. It's that mixture of ferocity and grace that would make his movie martial arts style unique. When Hollywood hired him to be Kato, the sidekick in the short-lived *Green Hornet* series at the princely sum of $400 an episode, Bruce Lee stole the show, and became a symbol of national pride to Asian audiences. Then Hong Kong producer Raymond Chow offered him a 2-picture deal at $15,000 apiece.

His first film—*Táng Shān Dà Xiōng/The Big Boss*, also known as *The Chinese Connection*, is roughhewn, has lousy lighting, but delivers the goods in the second half. My favorite *Big Boss* big gasp moment was when Bruce slammed a handsaw into the brain of a luckless opponent with a mighty downswing (cut in most countries!).

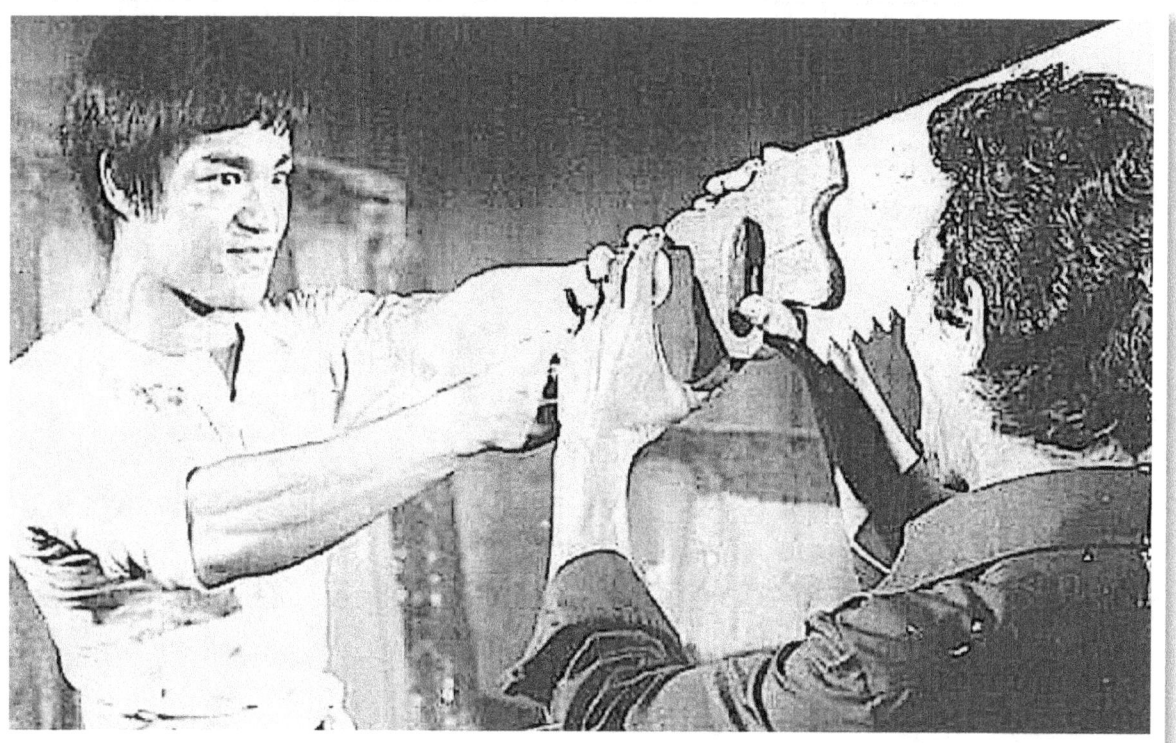

But the persona Bruce projected across Hong Kong media was quite different from the violent defender of the oppressed he portrayed in the movie, which ignored his unique sense of humor. Hong Kong audiences loved his impromptu appearances on Cantonese live TV. He would invade a talk show or a comedy sketch already underway, cracking jokes, while pretending to be lost, drunk, or belligerent. He widened his fanbase, as one media source wryly observed, by becoming "every Chinese mother's favorite naughty son."

His second film—*Jing Wǔ Mén/Fist of Fury*—still concentrated on his martial skill. It was a more polished production and even bigger smash at the Hong Kong box office than *The Big Boss*. In Australia, John Fraser at Greater Union released *Fist of Fury* first, then held *The Big Boss/Chinese Connection* till after *Enter the Dragon* premiered to huge box-office across the world, a successful strategy. At the expiration of their 2-picture deal, Bruce Lee and Raymond Chow formed a partnership company. Their first venture, *Meng Long Guo Jiang* (literally, *The Fierce Dragon Crosses*

*the River*), cost a little over $100,000. Worldwide theatrical gross has now been estimated at $85M. Nice! It's also known as *Return of The Dragon* (you can spend a long time down the wormhole of retitled Kung Fu flics and still be confused). But "Dragon" became the buzzword for multiple Bruce Lee wannabe movies from that moment on.

*Way of the Dragon* (the English language title), written, produced, and directed by Bruce Lee, was the first Hong Kong film to shoot in Europe, and one over which Bruce had total creative control and the freedom to display his comedic side. So for his hero he contrived an archetypal Chinese country bumpkin, a man so unfamiliar with western plumbing that he squats on top of the toilet seat. Not many films show a hero challenged by a bowel emergency three times in the first twenty minutes! In the Cantonese trailer (https://www.youtube.com/watch?v=6Mv3p5w6IlM), you may notice an outrageously gay villain. But

Bruce was not homophobic. He believed in being true to one's core. His philosophy is quoted many times: Be yourself.

The humor overall is pretty broad, aimed at Asian audience sensibilities. Lee planned to remake the film tuned for American audiences in a San Francisco setting. His hero is an eastern version of the archetypal western hero, exemplified in Shane, the iconic Alan Ladd western: A pugilist anxious to hang up his fists is forced to go lethal in defense of the innocent, in this case a family-owned Chinese restaurant in Rome menaced by mafia thugs. A martial arts hero needs plenty of fist fodder on which to demonstrate his expertise. Bruce brought in some top opponents, such as Ing-Sik Whang, a Grandmaster of hapkido, and Chuck Norris, undefeated world middleweight karate champion. Bruce had met Chuck Norris at a tournament a few years earlier, and both of them gave martial arts tuition to Hollywood figures like Stirling Silliphant, James Coburn and Steve McQueen. So Bruce asked Chuck to be his opponent in the set piece duel to the death in the Roman Colosseum. The fight follows the classic pattern of villain beating up hero till hero finds weaknesses in villain's technique then counterattacks, wearing him down till the final killer blow. This sequence launched Chuck Norris' movie career.

But the movie needed a considerable supply of Caucasians for Bruce to beat up. Exteriors were shot in Rome, but interiors, where most of these slugfests took place, were staged at a Kowloon warehouse. The casting director had to scour the bars and hostels of the colony looking for gwai-tau, "ghost heads," the generic Cantonese term for a non-Chinese person, and specifically: unemployed foreigners of thuggish appearance. The pay was US$12 a day. One eager recruit, John Derbyshire, wrote about his two days of work on a fight scene that would run a few minutes in the finished film, but was described in Lee's script by four Chinese characters—*Li da xi ren*—"Lee strikes the Westerners." Mr. Derbyshire provided an insight into Bruce Lee's handling of actors. "Hey, Slim," Bruce would call him in recognition of Derbyshire's tall lean physique, "let's try that again—and this time look mean. You hate me, remember? I'm a runty obnoxious little Chink, just stole your woman, trashed your car and pissed in your beer. Whadd'ya gonna do to me? Huh? Whadd'ya gonna do? Come on..." Pretty effective direction, I say.

In September 1972, Bruce Lee started shooting *The Game of Death*, an ambitious concept infused with his own philosophy. His original script built to a climax where Bruce would have to fight his way up a multistory pagoda, and on each level vanquish a new highly-skilled opponent by defining and exploiting the fatal flaw in his adversary's style. Allegorically, the flaws in fighting style were intended to represent different human failings. Think *Kung Fu* versus *The 7 Deadly Sins*. But the shoot was interrupted by the need to proceed immediately with *Enter the Dragon*, the coproduction Raymond Chow had negotiated with Warners. Before he could resume production on *The Game of Death*, Bruce Lee suddenly died.

It took five years for Raymond Chow's Golden Harvest company to figure out a way to finish the movie with only eleven minutes seven seconds, when edited, of usable Bruce Lee footage. Chow brought in his *Enter the Dragon* director Robert Clouse. They abandoned Lee's original script and devised a whole new plot where Bruce plays—guess what—a martial arts movie star at the peak of his fame, whose family is threatened by a ruthless drug syndicate led by Hugh O'Brien, once TV's Wyatt Earp. Bruce survives an assassination attempt but is wounded—guess where—in the face, so he has plastic surgery to disguise his appearance and fakes his own death. The film, in questionable taste, even incorporates footage from Bruce Lee's actual funeral. The stage is then set for Bruce to appear in numerous disguises, dark glasses, false beards, motorcycle helmets...while being played by body doubles Yuen Biao and Taekwondo master Tai Chung Kim for the high kicks. Some ill-matching close ups of Bruce Lee from his first three movies are cut into these new fights. But it's the fights that Bruce had actually shot that audiences came to see. His combat with Kareem Abdul-Jabbar is worth the price of admission alone. To justify the jumpsuit Bruce wore for the Pagoda fights, the film dresses a bunch of henchmen in striped jumpsuits, and has Bruce's double steal a yellow and black striped one in time for the climax. It's been paid homage in several films and video games since, most notably in Quentin Tarantino's *Kill Bill Volume 1*, when yellow jump-suited Uma Thurman slices and dices the *Crazy 88*.

Chow hoped to broaden the audience beyond Bruce Lee fans, by casting two Oscar winners in supporting roles: Dean Jagger, who had won for *Twelve O'Clock High*, and Gig Young, who won for *They Shoot Horses, Don't They?* On October 19, 1978, just after *The Game of Death* was released, 64-year-old Gig Young, a victim of lifelong alcoholism and crippling insecurity, shot his 31-year-old fifth wife Kim Schmidt in the head during the third week of their marriage, before putting the pistol in his mouth. Consequently, *The Game of Death* has a macabre cult appeal because it contains the final performances of both a suicide murderer and a superstar in the same movie.

But Bruce Lee's final film in no way diminishes his legacy. His box office success helped break down racial barriers, and empowered minorities because at last there was an internationally beloved movie hero who wasn't white! If *Way of The Dragon* established him as an innovative and eccentric auteur, then *Enter the Dragon*'s international success would have given him the power to greenlight his projects and control his vision, much like Quentin Tarantino today.

Bruce Lee was only thirty-two, with a grasp of the dynamics of screen action that was ahead of the curve. He planned to put spiritual content and Asian values into his forthcoming Hollywood movies. What might his oeuvre have contained if he were still directing today in his seventies and beyond, like Scorsese, Spielberg, Eastwood and Ridley Scott? In *Fist of Fury*, there's an underlying message of national pride common to all his films, epitomized when Bruce high kicks a sign that once actually hung at the entrance to a Shanghai public park reading "No Dogs or Chinese Allowed." The message is reinforced by the final image of the film, a freeze frame of Bruce fearlessly leaping at a firing squad. Bruce is saying: "We Chinese are not inferior. We are formidable. Watch out." Half a century later, it seems prescient.

Bruce Lee's death was keenly felt in Hong Kong. I was able to get footage of the estimated 20,000 people that jammed Kowloon streets the day of his memorial. There was a similar response at his subsequent funeral in Seattle. Steve McQueen and James Coburn were among the pallbearers.

Despite his grief and the daily business of running a studio, Raymond Chow found the time to give me an interview, as did Run Run Shaw and Andre Morgan, amongst others. So I ended up making a tribute to Bruce Lee, rather than the revealing documentary I had planned. I sold *World of Kung Fu* to Channel Seven (trying to expand my sales relationship beyond Channel Nine). It rated well a couple of months later.

I also wrote and published two editions of a magazine also entitled *The World of Kung Fu*, packed with pictures of Lee and other Hong Kong action stars. But my idea for a Dirty Harry style HK/Australia co-production would have to wait for better circumstances.

On August 2nd, a few days after my return to Sydney, Bob Woodham, lead performer in *The Stuntmen*, died. He was only thirty-four. Rheumatic fever as a child had left him with an enlarged left ventricle. He decided before he was much older to schedule open heart surgery to repair damaged valves. The operation was successful and he felt well enough to discharge himself from hospital ahead of schedule. Three weeks later while jogging round the block he collapsed and died. Such a pity. He would have had a great future in the developing Australian film industry which at that stage had few experienced stuntmen.

The stars of my first two films *The Stuntmen* and *World of Kung Fu* had both died unexpectedly and young within ten days. "Top Producer's Death Jinx" was the headline in a weekly news magazine.

# TOP PRODUCER'S DEATH JINX!

A TOP Sydney television producer believes he is jinxed following the death of two TV personalities — one an international star — with whom he has been closely associated.

"It really is a most eerie sensation," said producer Brian Trenchard-Smith, "to have the stars of two films die within a fortnight of each other."

The personalities who have died are Bruce Lee, the big-name star of a series of Kung Fu movies to be released in Australia next month, and Bob Woodham, the star of the award-winning feature film The Stuntman.

When he spoke with TV WEEK Brian Trenchard-Smith was still shocked following the news of Bob Woodham's death.

He had flown in from Hong Kong two days previously after the death of Chinese actor Bruce Lee, who was to star in a special being produced on location in Hong Kong.

"It is a great tragedy that these two talented men should die so young," Brian said.

During a recent overseas trip Brian met actor Bruce Lee while he was filming in Hong Kong.

Realising the potential interest in the Kung Fu movies, Brian decided to return to Hong Kong and make a special documentary on the work of Bruce Lee.

"I spent several weeks back in Sydney planning the special," Brian said, "then caught a plane back to Hong Kong two days before we were due to start filming.

"I was sitting in Hong Kong airport a few minutes after my arrival when I saw the newspaper headlines 'Bruce Lee Dies' splashed all over the front page.

"At that stage I had no idea what I would do. An Australian film crew had flown to Hong Kong with me and we had spent a lot of money preparing for the special.

"The alternative was to go ahead with the special — making it a tribute to Bruce."

Brian went ahead with the project, this time filming the actor's funeral as well as gathering material from several of his films.

"The funeral was the most spectacular sight I have ever seen," Brian said.

"More than 20,000 people filed past the body.

"The cause of death was not definitely known, but the local papers believed he had died of a heart attack. He was only 32 years old."

Then, two days after his return to Sydney, Brian was told of the death of stuntman Bob Woodham.

Bob, who was also 32, had died suddenly of a heart attack while recovering from open-heart surgery.

The Stuntmen, the movie in which Bob starred, had recently been awarded the Best Documentary of the Year award at the Sydney Film Festival.

His death sent a shock wave through the Sydney television and film industry. ◆

● BELOW: Brian Trenchard-Smith with English comic Marty Feldman at work on a special in Sydney.

Sadly, Marty Feldman also died too young at 48, after a massive heart attack brought on by shellfish poisoning during the filming of Yellowbeard. A great loss to comedy.

# CHAPTER 17
## Grant Page

There was only one person who could replace Bob Woodham as the focus of a stunt series. That was Grant Page, who had devised the tandem rope slide for *The Stuntmen*. Although his role was small, Grant's charisma was evident in the film whenever he spoke to camera. So I flew to Adelaide and hung out for a couple of days at his house with his wife Joy, and their sons Jeremy Genghis and Leroy Odin.

Grant tried to teach me how to ride a motorbike on deserted Seven Mile Beach. I managed to ride it into the sea! (I'm just not a two-wheel person.) He told me he could ski on the sand barefoot, towed by dune buggy, one he wanted to build out of spare parts with big airplane tires, one that could reach a speed of one hundred kilometers an hour both in forward and reverse gears. It would be a bush basher that could barge obstacles aside, and what it could not move it could go over. He would call it Buttercup. It would subsequently feature in Danger Freaks and Death Cheaters.

Recreational aviation using foot-launched hang gliders was just beginning to develop a following in Australia. As yet "kite flying" had only been seen on TV in news magazine pieces. No one had put it on the big screen in a drama. Naturally, Grant was already learning to fly. As I watched him cruising the wind lifts off Sellecks Beach, a specific scene came to me: Inspector Fang Sing Leng of Hong Kong Special Branch is piloting a hang glider over Sydney Harbor, like an eagle in search of prey, landing on the roof of the villain's penthouse. In previous drafts, as I expanded the premise, the hero had infiltrated by scaling the building freehand. Aerial targeting was more spectacular. I felt a rush of creative joy. I could give the hero a nail biting, hu-

man fly climb to get into another building, the Martial Arts Academy, earlier in the story, and top it with a hang glider attack in the climax. So how does he get a hang glider when he needs one? Easy—make Caroline, the journalist Fang meets in Hong Kong, a kite flyer. The screenplay was falling into place.

My research into hang gliding prompted me to whip up a quick 60 page photo magazine on the subject with friend Michael Falloon.

Grant had quite an appetite for physical challenges. I began to see him as more than a stuntman/spokesperson in documentaries. He could be another Errol Flynn, the Australian who became a Hollywood swashbuckling star of the 1930s and 40s. Grant could be an actor, seen to be doing his own stunts, as Tom Cruise later would in the *Mission Impossible* series. So I decided to go further than make Grant the headliner in my as yet unfunded series of stunt specials. I offered him a 5-year contract of management, during which I would

go fly a kite

By Michael Z. Falloon
and Brian Trenchard Smith

$1·50*

TOP AUSTRALIAN EXPERTS TELL:
• HOW IT'S DONE
• WHERE TO LEARN

create TV and feature film vehicles for him, and negotiate his contracts for other movie stunt work. I would have his name above the title of a movie in five years. In fact, it only took three.

Grant and I became friends. We had a few formative factors in common. Both of us had fathers who fought in WWII. Grant's father went to war a private and came back as a Lt. Colonel. My father fought in the Battle of Britain and spent four years in German POW camps, twice caught trying to escape. Both men excelled in their fields. Grant and I recognized we were both driven by a need to live up to the examples of our fathers. Heroic war stories influenced the culture of 1950s boys' private schools, which Grant and I attended on opposite sides of the globe, providing a subconscious martial driver to our choice of careers. Grant trained to be a commando because he liked to overcome physical challenges. I staged a battle scene with the school cadet corps for my 8mm camera, because epic conflicts featured in my fantasy life.

During a training exercise, Grant once carried a fellow commando with a broken leg all the way up North Head, which for non-Australian readers, stands 300 feet high and looks out over the spectacular entrance to Sydney Harbor. When Grant recounted what happened—the story is reenacted in *Danger Freaks*—I confessed that I could never do that. I have always had a real fear of heights.

Grant offered to help me defeat that phobia. He would talk me down the fisherman's walk on North Head—a descending zigzag of ledges that he had climbed in his commando days. Some of the ledges are wide, some are narrow, but always navigable. Anglers, carrying their rods and buckets, take this path down to the rocks below every day. Grant put it this way: You can step across a 2-foot gap marked in chalk on the floor without fear, but put that gap 300 feet up in the air, fear enters the equation. But it's still the same 2-foot gap regardless, with no impediment to stepping across, other than an emotional response to the height. You have to suppress the emotional context and concentrate on obeying the same laws of physics as you would at ground level. Fear is the enemy of precision. If I followed his instructions exactly, I would be fine. I accepted the offer. It was time to prove to myself that I had courage.

By some twenty feet down North Head, I knew I had made a terrible mistake. Fisherman casting the rods below looked like ants. What kept me going was the consideration that the way back up looked as perilous as the way ahead, not to mention the shame of failure. Grant was meticulous in his instructions about handholds and foot placement: "Put your left hand there, put your right hand there. Then move your left leg onto the next ledge there, etc." Grant showed how a climber should maintain three points of contact with the rock face at all times. Only move a leg or an arm if you have support from three other limbs. I was just settling into a rhythm when we came across a rounded promontory jutting out from the cliff face blocking the ledge. The only way around was to swing the leading leg over the rock without knowing where the ledge started on the other side or its width. Was it a foothold or just a toehold? I froze. The irresponsibility of my choice came home to me, as if for the first time. I thought of my parents and how their lives would be blighted by my death. I would die a fool in most people's eyes.

Strangely, I found myself thinking at this critical moment of an arcane piece of movie equipment, and visualizing a shot I had never seen done before. The AN-N6 Eyemo was a light camera holding only fifty feet of 16mm film, mounted in the wings of British fighters during WWII to provide a visual record of each dogfight for accurate kill count. What if this camera was strapped to my wrist, focused back along my outstretched arm? What a cool shot would result if I reached for a handhold above, swinging the horizontal to the vertical, revealing the drop below. That approach would prove the actor was actually doing the climb, and was not crawling along a fake cliff on the studio floor with a back projection playing behind him, and a wind machine ruffling his hair. It's bizarre that this would enter my mind at such an extreme juncture, but it gave me the impetus to continue. I grasped two firm handholds and swung my leg out into space round the rock. My foot found the ledge on the other side.

When we reached the bottom, the fisherman expressed surprise we had taken the "old route." The chains and spikes and other climbing aids in the cliff face had recently been removed and reinstalled along an easier ladder of ledges 100 yards further round of the cliff. When we reached the top again via the new route, I gazed out across Sydney Harbor as if I had just reached the summit of Everest. Grant was right. If I absolutely had to, I could do it. Somehow. Did it cure my fear of heights? No. But I understood the enemy better now. So I wrote myself a scene for *The Man from Hong Kong*. I would be the luckless thug who fights the hero on top of a descending elevator.

Grant and I have had a long and mutually beneficial association. He is an amazing talent, a fascinating human being, and a loyal friend. Ten years ago, he asked me to write a foreword to his autobiography *Man on Fire*. It will give you a sense of the man and his skills.

I started the foreword as if it were the opening scene in a screenplay for a WWII commando movie…

EXTERIOR—CLIFFTOP—SUNDOWN

Superimpose title: CRETE, GREEK ISLANDS, 1941.

A Messerschmitt strafes an Australian Army truck as it hurtles up a steep wooded incline towards the cliff edge 200 yards away.

The bullets strike the gas tank and the back of the truck explodes in a fiery cloud.

The driver, Grant, a gallant Australian Warrant Officer (AWO), with an army pack slung over his shoulder, dives from the vehicle, before the flames engulf him. In the same shot, the truck smashes into a tree.

The precious pack contains "The McGuffin," the secret key to Allied victory in WWII. The AWO must get it to the commando waiting in a Zodiac, riding the waves at the base of the cliff ahead. He disappears into the woods.

A Wehrmacht motorcyclist with a machine gunner in the sidecar pauses beside a tree, scanning for their target. The AWO drops down out of the tree, chops and kicks them out of their seats, then guns the bike up towards the cliff, smashing through bushes. Platoons of German infantry are rushing up the cliff in pursuit, their Schmeissers blazing.

Bullets chew up the nearby ground as the AWO skids the bike to a halt inches from the cliff edge, where his abseiling rope is tethered ready for the final stage of his escape. He snaps the rope into the karabina on his body belt with a single loop and positions himself for his slide down the cliff.

Suddenly, a German soldier with a flamethrower runs out of the bushes. A cloud of napalm hits the AWO in the back, lighting up his army greatcoat as he leaps into space and freefalls 300 feet down the rope.

The plume of flame coming off his back is huge, but the air rush keeps the flames from spreading over his face as he reaches a velocity of thirty miles an hour, with the rocky shore below fast approaching. Grabbing the rope with padded gloves, he decelerates just in time.

Wham! Still a hard landing. AWO shakes off the pain, sheds the blazing greatcoat then takes the precious pack to the water's edge. Just a few feet away, the getaway Zodiac is riding the current.

As the AWO prepares to jump, a shark's fin slowly cuts through the water between him and the waiting vessel…

OK, so jumping the shark is a little over the top, even for me…

But I offer this amalgam of favorite WWII action clichés as being representative of the range of challenges, creative and industrial, that a director of action movies faces. Precision driving, leaping from a blazing vehicle, martial arts combat, extreme motorcycling, abseiling while a human torch—these are many chapters in the stuntman's handbook. To realize them all on the screen would normally require the director to select a team of stuntmen, each a specialist. And each one would have to be a passable double for the hero.

On the other hand, you could just hire Grant Page. He'd even fight the shark for you.

Grant can do all these stunts, as his book *Man on Fire* will show you. And you'll get a small measure of the man's personal charm. It's a portrait of a quintessential Australian character, a man who refuses to define life in narrow terms. Most people accept that age weighs upon us, gravity holds us down, death awaits us if we dare too much. Not necessarily, says Grant, as he successfully tampers with the laws of physics and probability. Since childhood he has been imbued with that '*have a go*' spirit. It's a quality that has distinguished Australian achievers in all fields of endeavor and is clearly present in Grant, now 80+ years young, at time of writing, and still going strong. Grant deserves a pedestal in Hollywood Stuntmen's Hall of Fame alongside Yakima Canutt, Hal Needham, and Buddy Joe Hooker.

Grant did get some measure of official recognition in 2016. The state film funding body Screen New South Wales honored him with their inaugural award for trailblazers in the film industry and a $10,000 prize, presented to him in front of assembled media by his *Mad Max* director, George Miller.

In 1974, I wrote an outline for a 13 part half hour series starring Grant, to be called *Danger Freaks*. (Eventually made as 4 one hour specials.) It would incorporate sequences of Grant performing stunts against well-known backgrounds all over the world. For example, The Empire State Building. Local commercial rationale: "Aussie Daredevil in Foreign Parts." It would also help sales in those countries where the sequences were filmed. *The Stuntmen*, in which Grant had featured strongly, had rated well. Funding of a series built around him would be easier once I got Grant more visibility on television.

My first such vehicle quickly presented itself. The rating success of *World of Kung Fu* enabled me to propose a sequel to Greater Union, to be a continuing promotional aid to their slate of Kung Fu releases. It would be called *Kung Fu Killers*: the concept being—Who would succeed Bruce Lee in martial arts Cinema? Australian stuntman Grant Page would fly to Hong Kong and review the contenders. Basically another clip show, but with an engaging Australian personality escorting the audience on a tour of Hong Kong Cinema, which was turning out some 200 movies per year. It cost $13K. I presold it to Channel Nine for $19K.

I shot for a week using local Hong Kong cameramen. Grant interviewed producers and stars, including Stuart Whitman, hero of many westerns. We complimented him on *The Comancheros*, in which he costarred with John Wayne. Whitman's personal favorite was *The Mark*, in which he played an accused child molester. It was a very controversial film for 1961, and little seen. It earned him an Oscar nomination, but didn't help his career. Whitman was in town to star in the spy flick *Shatter*, a co-production between UK's Hammer Films and Hong Kong's Shaw Brothers.

The producer Michael Carreras did not want to be interviewed on camera. He had just fired the director, Monte Hellman, who "was difficult" and—cardinal sin—"had fallen behind schedule," so he was obliged to take over the reins himself. Hellman had felt that Carreras coveted the director's chair. Carreras for his part had felt the action scenes lacked excitement, the dialogue was dull, and, as he later wrote to his father, Hammer Chairman Sir James Carreras: "Hong Kong looks like a slum. I just don't know how to salvage it." Stuart Whitman was philosophical. "They keep paying me, I keep showing up." This was my first glimpse into a movie's backstage politics. In time I would replace several directors, and once be replaced myself.

At the Golden Harvest Studios we met Australian actor and onetime James Bond, George Lazenby, who had a 3-picture deal with Raymond Chow. I filmed him discussing action films with Grant, and dodging spear-wielding opponents for a film with the curious title of *Stoner*. I could see George playing the villain in my proposed action picture but bided my time. Producer Andre Morgan asked me if parts of Sydney could double for San Francisco in a car chase. Sure, I said, maybe around Watson's Bay. We discussed the traditional method in right hand drive Australia: Print street signs and license plates backwards, then flop the film in the lab. Thus right hand drive becomes left hand drive and the street signs read as intended. Morgan said he would be in touch.

Grant did rope slides off Lion Rock and performed two fights with Carter Wong, who was being promoted as Bruce Lee's successor.

Carter Wong was a nice guy, handsome, with fast fists and feet, but his career never took off outside Hong Kong. His only significant American role was in 1986 as an excellent villain in John Carpenter's *Big Trouble in Little China*. We asked a couple of local producers for their pick as the next international Chinese superstar.

They said there had been some buzz around a new actor who brought a comic touch to Kung Fu, but his first film had not been a success, so it was unlikely that Jackie Chan would become a star (ha!).

A more likely successor to Bruce Lee, they said, was Wang Yu, previously a major star at Shaw Brothers for such hits as *One-Armed Swordsman* and *One-Armed Boxer*. He had broken his contract and joined Raymond Chow's new company Golden Harvest, producing, directing and starring in eight films for GH which he shot in Taiwan out of Shaw's legal reach. Wang Yu was the biggest star in Asia before Bruce Lee, and was poised to resume that role.

I took advantage of a spare month to shoot the further sequences of *Danger Freaks*. I had self-funded little shoots piecemeal

up till then. Now I could afford to take Grant overseas to perform a variety of stunts in Tahiti, the USA, the UK, and South Africa, where Grant arranged an encounter with a leopard.

I hired local cameramen, backed up by my clockwork 3-lens Bell and Howell. We broke local ordinances wherever we shot, I say with a mixture of pride

and shame. Grant pulled off some nifty climbing feats, like doing chin ups from the top bar of the old, now replaced, Hollywood Sign, and from a street lamp outside Tower Records hanging over Sunset Boulevard traffic. He scaled the corner wall of the London County Council building barefooted.

At the Empire State Building, we timed the security guards' circuit 'round the observation deck a couple of times to see how long we would have for me to shoot Grant climbing over the concave railings to stand on the edge, looking down 1,200 feet.

Apparently, anyone caught even attempting to climb over the barrier would get a mandatory stay in a psychiatric institution. I got the shot just before the security guards returned. I know, grossly irresponsible. But I had total confidence in Grant's ability.

I would shoot the remainder of *Danger Freaks* a year later. Australia's other leading stuntmen and women had their skills and techniques recorded. Ten years later I compressed the best moments from all four episodes into a 90-minute version. My commentary is on the heavy-handed side, but you might find it an interesting time capsule.

# CHAPTER 18
## *The Man from Hong Kong*

When I had returned to Australia to edit *Kung Fu Killers*, Golden Harvest sent a small unit to Sydney for the Lazenby vehicle *Stoner*. I supervised the shoot on Old South Head Road which doubled for some San Francisco oceanside cliff highway. It went well. So I felt ready to propose to Raymond a coproduction between Golden Harvest and Greater Union, with Wang Yu as the hero and George Lazenby as the villain. I submitted a print of *The Stuntmen* as a sample of my work, along with the script I had written entitled *Yellow Peril*. "Talk about the bloody Yellow Peril," growls the drug cop as they gaze at collateral damage caused by the hero. From that line sprang the proposed title. Making prejudices explicit the better to expose them is a theme that runs throughout my body of work. To me it was ironic humor, mocking the racial pejorative when applied to a Chinese hero, who is smarter, tougher, more noble than the white guys. Raymond Chow explained to me why his audience would not see it that way. One country's irony is another country's insult. Raymond gave me a lesson in cultural sensitivity. I still had a lot of evolving to do. It's a credit to Raymond's tolerance that he persisted with me nonetheless.

Raymond suggested changing the title to *The Man from Hong Kong*. "Man From..." titles have a long successful tradition. Then Raymond made his offer: Golden Harvest would put in half the AUD$450,000 budget, if GUO came in for the other 50%. The timing was propitious. GUO was under pressure in 1974 to invest in Australian films, which had been largely absent from local screens for the better part of a generation.

Some background: 49% of GUO was at that time owned by The Rank Organization, which also owned Pinewood Studios in the UK. Rank's recommended policy toward homegrown Australian films was that they were low profit potential at best: it was better that Australia remain a distribution and exhibition market, not a production center. A similar policy was active at the second largest cinema circuit in Australia, Hoyts Theaters, which was wholly owned by 20th Century Fox, also with a studio infrastructure to support.

A relatively healthy self-supporting Australian film industry prior to WWII died because these two theater chains denied Australian-made films summer and school holiday playing time, instead reserving the prime playdates for British and Hollywood movies. Most films shot in Australia in the fifties and sixties were foreign backed. There were US productions: *On the Beach*, *The Sundowners*, *Long John Silver* being the best known. UK's Ealing Studios made *The Overlanders*, *Eureka Stockade*, *The Siege of Pinchgut*. But local producers like Lee Robinson, Chips Rafferty, Cecil Holmes, Charles and Elsa Chauvel had a hard time raising finance for movies under Australian creative control. Investment dried up.

Both GUO and Hoyts were shipping the bulk of Australian-earned film rental out of the country to the foreign companies they serviced. Consequently, film industry proponents were floating the idea of a 10% withholding tax on this exported revenue to fund Australian feature films. That worried all distributors of imported films. Greater Union, to its credit, counter proposed direct investment in production in concert with the new government film funding entity the Australian Film Development Corporation.

Once again, I found myself in the right place at the right time with the right group of people. So lucky. I wrote a proposal for a joint venture production company in partnership with Greater Union Theaters. They would provide the funding; I would provide the creative and production expertise. I gave it to John Fraser, then heading GUO's distribution arm BEF. He passed it up to Greater Union's CEO Keith Moremon, who duly arranged to meet me. I laid out my vision, in which *The Man from Hong Kong*, if successful, could lead to a slate of Australia/Asia co-productions. The fledgling Australian film industry would need to penetrate the international market to survive. Moremon was a charming knowledgeable man. We got along from the start. He genuinely wanted to help create an Australian film industry. So, despite Rank's advice against an in-house production company, a joint venture was agreed on. It would be called The Movie Company Pty. Ltd., with my parents and myself holding 50% of the shares, and BEF, GUO's subsidiary, holding the other 50%. John Fraser and I were appointed joint managing directors.

Financially, GUO drove a hard bargain, if I wanted partnership and profit participation rather than a good salary. I would receive no salary, only a low fee for each project that went into production. I would be paid AUD$5000 each to write and direct the first two projects, plus 50% of the profits after recoupment. I can hear you laughing…I could have, indeed should have, made a better deal. But it was such a monumental opportunity that I did not want to risk blowing it. There was a clock ticking. I needed to connect Raymond Chow with a committed Australian partner before some other film took his attention.

Two projects had been approved for funding in tandem by GUO: *Danger Freaks* had budgeted at $25,000 per episode. This had been a pretty safe bet because I had obtained a $100,000 pre-sale to Channel Nine. *The Man from Hong Kong* was more of a risk—$225,000, recoupable in first position from Australian distribution, matching Raymond Chow's commitment, recoupable from Asian distribution, pegging the budget at $450,000. Revenue, after sales commission, from all other territories was to be split 50/50. Raymond Chow was anxious to get the production underway. *The Man from Hong Kong* was now on the fast track.

Then Keith Moreman had a heart attack.

The night before, at a function organized by GUO, I had sat with Keith Moreman and former Minister for Customs and Excise, Don Chipp. As Customs Minister, Chipp virtually abolished Australia's outdated censorship of printed materials. He unbanned Henry Miller's *Tropic of Capricorn* and permitted *Playboy Magazine* to be imported. In 1970 he had introduced the 'R' rating, allowing previously banned films to be rerated and shown to audiences over the age of eighteen. He was a big supporter of the renascent Australian film industry.

So, being the reticent fellow that I am, I told Don Chipp that co-production with foreign countries, both English-speaking and non-Anglophone, was the key to an economically sustainable film industry. State investment would inevitably dry up one day. Local producers needed to build alliances with foreign distributors and become a regular, reliable source of product for the international as well as the domestic market. Keith Moremon could only agree, as he was about to be a partner in Australia's first co-production with an Asian film company. Then he went home and had the heart attack. I prefer to think it was unrelated to my pitch but to the accumulated stress of ten years as CEO, during which he had dramatically improved GUO's fortunes. Happily, he survived, but stepped down as CEO within the year.

Understandably, the progress of *The Man from Hong Kong* stopped dead in in its tracks. I tried to persuade Raymond Chow that this was a temporary hiccup, but I knew his interest would soon cool. Luckily, a benefactor stepped into the arena—Graham Burke of Village Roadshow Theaters, which was allied with GUO in a number of exhibition arrangements. Village Roadshow was a less conservative company than GUO, prepared to take greater risks. So Graham Burke told the GUO Board that he would assume some of their risk, and guaranteed to play the hell out of the movie through Village theaters and drive-ins. GUO reduced its risk further by requiring that I persuade the Australian Film Development Corporation to invest half the Australian commitment of $225,000. Fortunately, the AFDC liked me, so they committed to match GUO's $112,500 investment.

After a 3-month hiatus, the amber light turned green. *The Man from Hong Kong* was back on track, but before I get into the weeds of my first real feature film, a brief bizarre digression:

The first actor I told that the money for the movie had come through was Roger Ward. He had joined my crew on *The Stuntmen* and we had become good friends. Tall and brawny, he had been a wrestler and a journalist, among many colorful occupations but it was a stint in Tahiti as a non-speaking mutineer on the Brando version of *Mutiny on the Bounty* that lured him into acting. I had cast him as Sgt. Taylor and decided to drop in to his place to tell him in person that the movie was finally on. His girlfriend at the time was charming, elegant, and French, France Villachon. She cooked us dinner. I showed off my schoolboy French *avec un accent affreux*. Her English was good. She was always fun, full of husky-voiced warmth and *joie de vivre*, whenever we socialized in Roger's company. Imagine my surprise, years after she and Roger split, to learn of her conviction for kidnapping and imprisoning two teenage girls, subjecting them to physical and sexual abuse and causing the death of one of them. She served seven years and was deported. At what point does the descent into darkness become visible to others? I had no inkling. I've known two murder victims and one convicted killer. No more, I hope.

As the undercover narc partnered with Roger Ward's far-from-straight cop, I cast Royal Shakespeare Company actor Hugh Keays-Byrne. Their wry chemistry together still gets laughs at recent US revival screenings. Hugh would go on to a prolific career, known best as the iconic "Toecutter" in the original *Mad Max* and even more iconic "Immortan Joe" in *Mad Max: Fury Road*.

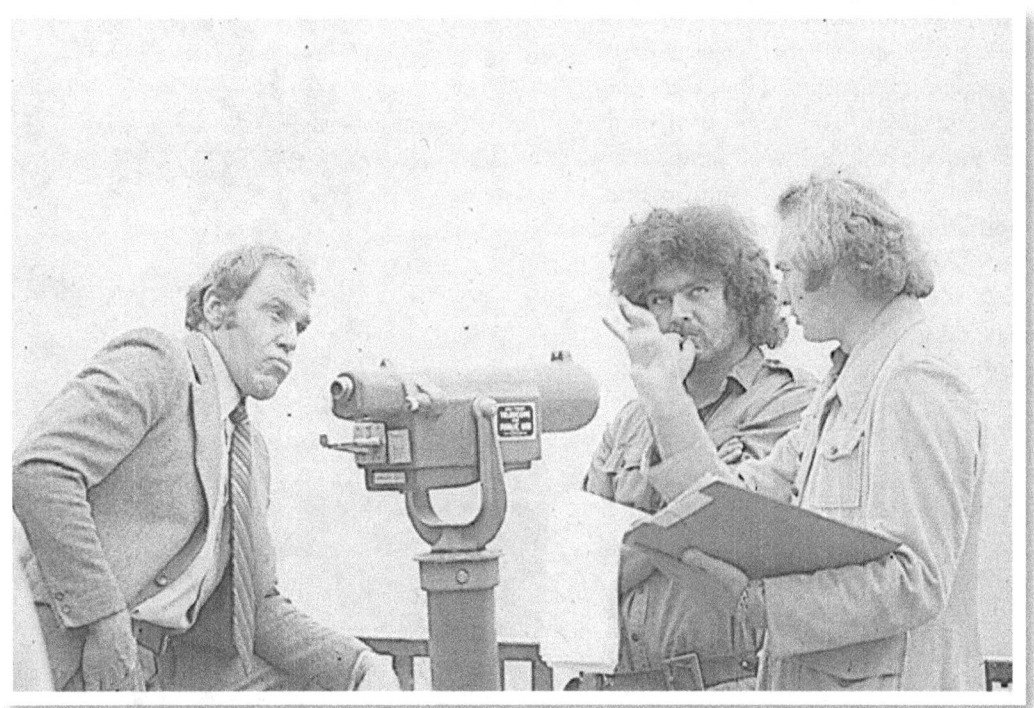

Hugh and I became close friends; his home with Christina at 16 Lang Road Centennial Park was a haven for artists, and I spent many Sunday mornings enjoying tea and toast in their excellent company.

As soon as the green light flashed, I was anxious to meet Wang Yu, or at least talk to him on the phone. Raymond Chow had assured me he spoke good English. But Jimmy was always out of reach, busy with another film, or hunting in the mountains of Taiwan. As I waited for the call that never came, I watched as many of his movies as were available and learned more about him from conversations with Andre Morgan, the Golden Harvest executive on the film.

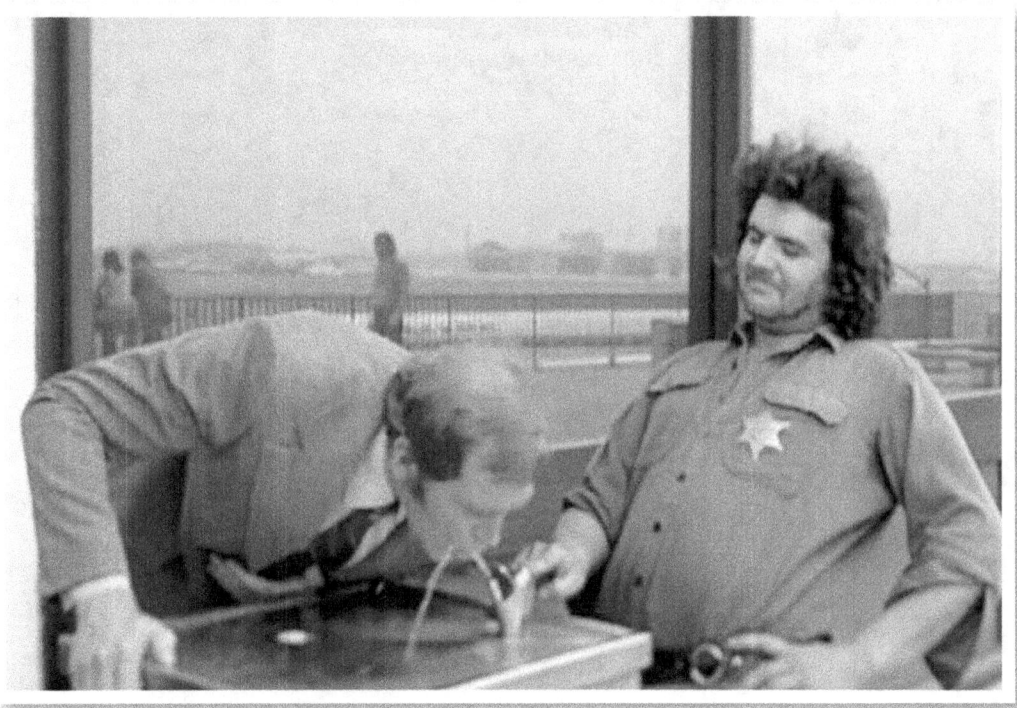

Jimmy was born Wang Zheng-Quan on March 28, 1943 in Shanghai, at that time under Japanese occupation. How different his childhood must have been compared to mine. Gifted athletically, he studied at the Shanghai Sports Academy, and became an accomplished swimmer, rider and race-car driver. Wang Yu settled in Hong Kong in the early 60s to study civil engineering in Chu Hai College. After he won a swimming championship, his athletic ability came to the attention of reigning Hong Kong movie mogul Run Run Shaw, who signed him to a long-term contract. His initial movies all did well and he rose quickly through the studio ranks.

His physical prowess and confident persona came to the attention of Shaw Brothers star Jeanette Lin Tsui, eight years his senior, and married to director Chun Kim. She and Wang Yu began an affair, which became a scandal when Chun Kim subsequently hanged himself.

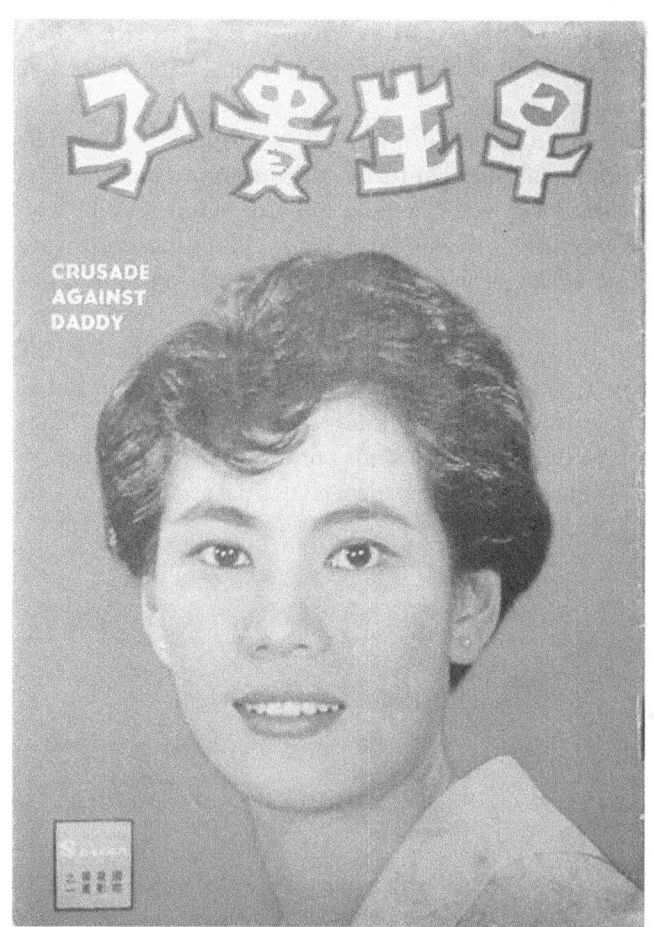

CRUSADE
AGAINST
DADDY

In 1967 Lin's influence at the studio helped get him a role in which he could shine. It was *The One-Armed Swordsman*, the first of a new kind of *wuxia* film. *Wuxia* ("martial heroes") is a genre in Chinese literature concerning the adventures of wandering swordsmen in ancient China, who fight for the oppressed and punish malefactors. Top Shaw Brothers director Chang Cheh brought a vigorous new style to a genre that had become staid and pageant like. Chang Cheh delivered rugged antiheroes and limb-hacking swordplay. *The One-Armed Swordsman* became the first Hong Kong film to make HK$1 million at the local box office, propelling Wang Yu to superstardom. In 1969, he and Jeanette Lin were married. She stopped acting almost immediately. In 1970, Wang Yu wrote, directed and starred in the first *wuxia* film to replace swords with fists and flying feet, *The One-Armed Boxer*, grossing HK $2M, and confirming Wang Yu as the number one star in Asia. His brooding intensity was likened at the time to Hollywood's Steve McQueen.

But Wang Yu chafed at the low pay, zero profit participation and creative restrictions at Shaw Brothers. He decided to break his contract with the studio and partner with Raymond Chow to write, produce, direct and star in his own films, over which he had creative control. He had become friends with Raymond Chow when Chow was the head of production at Shaw Brothers. Raymond Chow had also chafed at a salary disproportionate to the success of the films he produced. So he left the studio to found the Golden Harvest studio in direct competition with his long time mentor Run Run Shaw. There was bad blood between the mogul and his former protégé, which intensified when Chow appeared to poach Wang Yu, Shaw's top star. In the lawsuit that quickly fol-

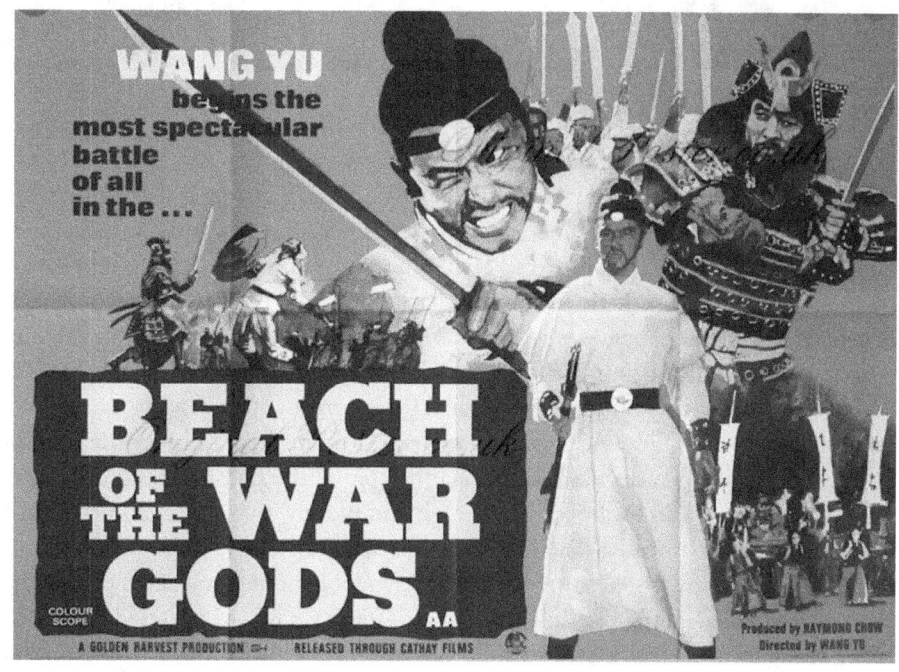

WANG YU begins the most spectacular battle of all in the...

BEACH OF THE WAR GODS
COLOUR SCOPE                    AA

A GOLDEN HARVEST PRODUCTION        RELEASED THROUGH CATHAY FILMS

Produced by RAYMOND CHOW
Directed by WANG YU

lowed, the court ruled in favor of Shaw Brothers, and Wang Yu was barred from working in Hong Kong pending a settlement. Consequently Wang Yu's films for Golden Harvest were shot out of Shaw's reach in Taiwan.

By the time of *The Man from Hong Kong*'s shoot in August 1974, Jimmy Wang Yu had directed eight movies in Taiwan or other Asian countries, all successful. One film that particularly impressed me was *Beach of the War Gods*, a kind of *wuxia Magnificent Seven* (nearly fifty years later, it's still a lot of fun.) Andre Morgan also told me Wang Yu had recently led Hong Kong Police on a high speed chase in his sports car when they tried to book him for speeding. He then got into a fistfight with two cops trying to arrest him. Tough guy on the screen. Tough guy for real.

Because of his stature in Asia, it was agreed that Wang Yu would receive codirector credit on the Chinese language version. I would be the credited writer director in all other territories, and I would in all respects be the director of my script. Raymond Chow assured me that Jimmy had no interest in directing the film, which would be his English language debut. But he wanted some control over the fight scenes. That could only be a plus as far as I was concerned. Wang Yu was an experienced martial arts director. I was making my first feature film. What could go wrong?

Jimmy Wang Yu and I finally met when he arrived in the week before the shoot. John Fraser made sure that a Cine Sound News crew covered "Asian star Wang Yu's arrival" for the weekly newsreel that was still in 1974 a regular part of the cinemagoing experience. To kick start the director/star relationship, I had arranged a trip for us to a top Surfers Paradise hotel to bond. Sun, surf, nightlife. There is probably no more serious problem for a first time director than to lose the confidence of his star. I managed to achieve this in ten days. *Not Quite Hollywood*, Mark Hartley's excellent documentary about 'Ozploitation', paints an unflattering portrait of Jimmy during the shoot. Certainly we had issues. He behaved badly at times. But looking at it from his point of view, if I had been a major star working with a first-time writer/director in a foreign country that did not speak my language, I might have been a little controlling too.

The Surfers trip was awkward. He had no particular comments to offer on the script. When we discussed the fights, I said I wanted them tough and bloody, to push the limits a bit. He agreed. His films were tough and bloody. Great. I talked with enthusiasm about the intended wry tone of the film. But I don't think he grasped my ironic approach to the invincible hero who causes prodigious loss of life, not to mention property damage, in the cause of justice. Genre satire—as opposed to comedy—was rarely a factor in Hong Kong movies at the time. It would take till the 1980s for HK's action and horror genres to develop an over the top sense of humor. I probably did not score any points with my nerdy elaboration on the subject. Perhaps my accent reminded him of the haughty British policemen he must have encountered in Hong Kong, still under colonial control from the UK in 1974.

I earnestly raved about one of his films *A Man Called Tiger*, in which there was an underwater kung fu fight. He offered to show me underwater kung fu in the hotel pool. I found myself held underwater for longer than I wanted to be. I coughed and spluttered a lot on surfacing. Later I took him to a party Clyde Packer was having in Surfers. At a bar later, Jimmy drank a series of spirits and liqueurs in quick succession without noticeable effect as if to demonstrate macho credentials. Yet I was the one that left the bar with a girl. Mistake.

Cameras rolled the next Monday with the car chase. I wanted to start with something big, so that when Raymond Chow in Hong Kong got dailies/rushes, he would see what he was getting in terms of production value. Another mistake. If possible, always start with something simple, to ground cast and crew, then tackle a big sequence. The Wiseman's Ferry location for the car chase did not photograph the way it had looked to my wide-angle eyes on survey, where I visualized the Hawkesbury River constantly in the background. But it's not what your eyes see, it's what the camera sees, lessons I found myself learning on the run, along with the difference between 16mm Academy and 35mm Anamorphic framing. The camera team of Russell Boyd, David Gribble, and John Seale taught me a lot.

The transition from directing clip shows and dramatized documentaries to a complex action picture with thirty or more people wanting their questions answered was an abrupt gear change. I was slow in blocking and selecting camera positions for the car chase. Wang Yu was unimpressed by indecision. In Hong Kong production, money is tight. Enhancements would happen at the end of the shoot if the budget could accommodate the cost. On Day One I found an unexpected, albeit trivial, detail interesting—like the spider climbing the back tire of the waiting killer's motorbike. The spider added a quirk to a standard linking shot: low wide angle behind the tire, with a view of the target, Wang Yu's van, on the road beyond. For me it was a grace note worth stopping for five minutes to shoot. To Wang Yu, not so much.

Another factor impacting this first week was that I was not in synch with the stunt coordinator Peter Armstrong. My line producer David Hannay wanted him, because Peter had handled the excellent stunt work on Sandy Harbutt's *Stone* which David Hannay produced. Obviously I wanted Grant Page, who would also play the part of the Assassin, as coordinator. At the outset, David saw Grant as more of a skilled daredevil than a professional stuntman. He would revise his opinion after the shoot and became a big fan. We compromised on Peter doing the car chase and providing the stunt driving team, while Grant handled the hang gliding, the building climb, the abseiling, and the Assassin's extended chase/kitchen/restaurant fight. I don't know what it was, but I did not have the same stunt chemistry with Peter Armstrong as I did with Grant Page. Peter gave me a list of car stunts his team could deliver for the budgeted amount with little sketches of key moments. His driving team of Max Aspin, Bob Hicks, Jerry Gausla were excellent. Some stunts that had pizzazz on paper turned out to be damp squibs on camera. After an out of control bike pinned Herbie Nelson against a parked car and broke both his ankles (he recovered and was compensated), the staging slowed down to ensure the safety of future stunts.

The net result in those first days of shooting was that the chase lacked impact. Wang Yu, whose prowess behind the wheel, both on the race track and by regularly exceeding the Kowloon speed limit, was well known in Hong Kong. Jimmy had high hopes for a *Bullitt* level car chase and was clearly disappointed with what he was seeing. He began to fear that lots of action would have to be dropped if I continued at this pace and his

English language debut would fail. So he asked that I be replaced by another Australian director who would handle the dialogue while he directed the action. I was told later that Sandy Harbutt was approached but declined. I knew nothing of this, of course. I was well aware of Wang Yu's unhappiness, and at times he treated me with open contempt in front of cast and crew. I just tried to stay cool, be accommodating, and keep hanging on to the rollercoaster. Whatever my mistakes might be, I knew I was making something special.

John Fraser sensibly kept most of the backstage politics from me. We both knew we needed to appease Wang Yu's concerns that the picture would not have enough action. John negotiated with his coproduction counterpart GH's Andre Morgan for Jimmy to be given three added sequences to direct by himself on days when we were shooting other actors. The scenes were: a new attempted ambush and short fight in a hotel corridor, an additional piece to be added to the foot chase, and another day's shooting of the car chase. This featured a sideswiping duel between two cars. I had added the gag where the car drives through a house as the climax to the chase.

The footage shot by John Seale from inside and outside the vehicles as they repeatedly slammed into each other provided a terrific buildup. I've never had a problem with someone making my idea better. Directing these three scenes appeared to satisfy Jimmy.

As shooting progressed, the tension eased somewhat. Grant Page was a helpful influence here. Jimmy respected Grant as a fellow superior athlete, and as Grant clearly respected me, Jimmy took note, and was OK most days. Grant even fixed him up with a girlfriend. Worked wonders.

I shall be forever grateful to John Fraser for standing by me at considerable risk to his career at Greater Union. If I had been fired, or the film had turned out to be un-releasable, the embarrassment to the Australian investors, GUO and The Australian Film Development Corporation (later, the Australian Film Commission) would not have been survivable either for him or for me. Perhaps I would never have had the opportunity to direct a feature film again. But I'm also grateful to Jimmy Wang Yu, difficult though he was. His stunt driving skills and the ferocious energy he brought to the fight scenes greatly contributed to the film's lasting entertainment value. And he gave a young director an educational baptism of fire.

*The Man from Hong Kong* was a complex Australian film for its day, but I had surrounded myself with gifted production staff. In addition to David Hannay, first assistant director Hal McElroy and second assistant Errol Sullivan both went on to become successful producers. I am grateful to all of them for rallying 'round and helping me find my sea legs during those unsteady first weeks. Hal McElroy particularly helped me plan each day more efficiently. We all faced a number of logistical challenges. Ninety percent of the story was set in Australia, but fifty percent of the coproduction budget had to be spent in Hong Kong. So several Australian interiors—the Martial Arts Academy, Win Chan's cell, Wilton's penthouse—were created at the Golden Harvest Studios on Hammer Hill Road. The Sydney Chinese restaurant and kitchen where Grant Page and Wang Yu have their epic fight was shot over four nights at a real Hong Kong restaurant between 11 p.m. and 11 a.m.

In one of several location hybrids, you will see me, as the luckless fellow who get punched through a glass window in the Martial Arts Academy (a studio set in Hong Kong) then run bleeding from the head into a corridor full of elevators (the sixth floor of the Greater Union HQ in Sydney) where I get further punishment after sliding down the lift shaft cable and fighting Wang Yu on top of the descending elevator. Riding those old elevators many times at GUO had given me the idea. And as my production partner and exhibitor, GUO was most likely the only company that would allow me to stage a fight on top of a moving elevator. Why did the director choose to play this role, you might ask? Partly vanity—never a good reason. Partly proof of courage. Courage should play no part in a stunt sequence. And partly because—why film an actor in Sydney, then fly him to Hong Kong for one line of dialogue, albeit an important piece of exposition, when the director himself yearns to be beaten up by a Hong Kong movie star? Save the airfare and hotel. It seemed a good idea when I wrote it.

Because we shot the Australian locations first, then moved to Hong Kong, there were continuity decisions to make out of order. In the Martial Arts Manager's fight scenes, I had to guess how much blood to put on my face as I ran into the Sydney corridor, then find a way to match it in the Hong Kong set, weeks later where my initial beating and defenestration was to take place. Raymond Chow told me later there was "too much blood." He was concerned because the Singapore censor was clamping down on violent Hong Kong movies.

But my intention was to test boundaries. Hence the 'squirrel grip' moment in the kitchen fight. Grant is strangling Jimmy with a telephone cord (remember them?) when Jimmy grabs his nuts and gives them a vigorous squeeze.

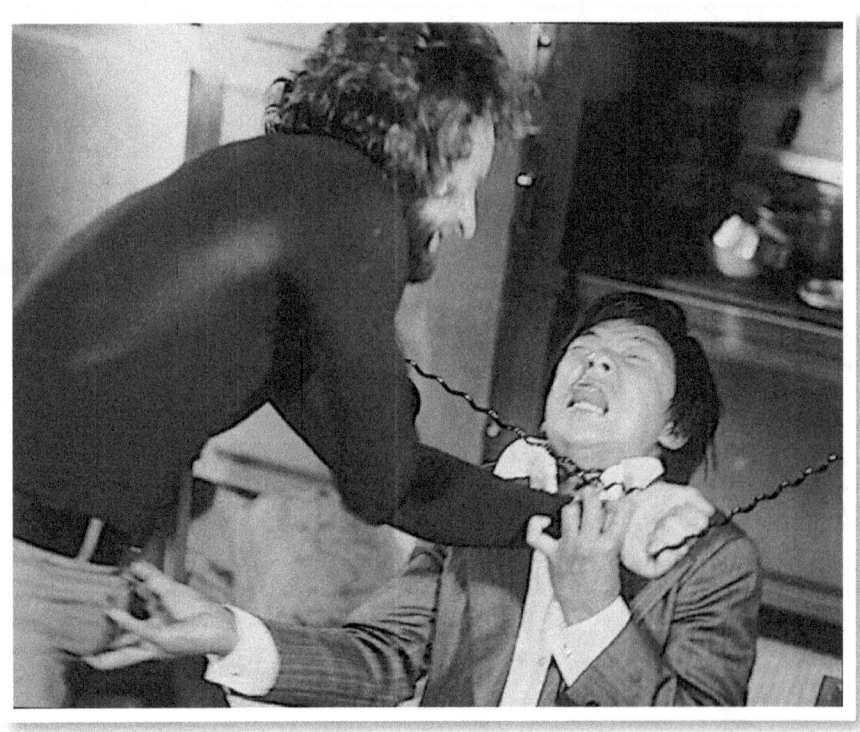

Grant's reaction always gets a huge laugh. Groin kicks were previously cut by the Australian censor, but the new 'R' rating permitted such shots. I staged the violence in the picture to be over the top, like a Kung Fu Roadrunner cartoon. But, as it turned out, the Australian Censor would not see it that way.

The Greater Union building in Sydney's Market Street also provided the location for the midnight climb Wang Yu made eight floors up the drainpipe, before entering through a window. Inspired by my climb down North Head I wrote the sequence specifically for the narrow lane between GUO and the adjacent building. It provided the opportunity for a money shot: the actual star in foreground hanging onto a vertical drainpipe up the wall of a building, with cars passing eight floors below. Look folks, no back projection, no safety net! Now here's an example of Wang Yu's determination and athletic ability. In a single shot he climbed to the third floor of the building, moving between horizontal and vertical pipes, all the while ignoring a cracked rib he had acquired the day before. Then Grant doubled him for the freehand climb up the next three floors, which was shot from a rising cherry picker (the poor man's crane). Then we secured Wang Yu with a concealed safety wire to his body harness and photographed him from the floor above, presenting his face to camera. We organized cars with their headlights on to drive through the lane below at several stages, till he reached the top floor and opened the window into the off screen Martial Arts Academy. When watched with a large audience, this sequence generates a palpable tension. Seeing is believing; though I have to confess the eagle-eyed will spot the safety wire in the last second of the shot.

Throughout the shoot I was blessed to have a fantastic camera crew. DP Russell Boyd and 2nd Unit DP John Seale have both won Academy Awards. Camera Operator David Gribble would develop a career as DP on big movies and commercials. I learned a lot about lighting and composition from them. Just about every member of that Australian crew went on to substantial careers in film and television.

The sequence on Uluru (Ayers Rock) will never be repeated. The chase, fight and car explosion would not be allowed there today. I was unaware then that Uluru was a sacred site to the indigenous people. Cultural insensitivity again. At that time, the Northern Territory was retrograde in its treatment of aboriginal Australians, who had not been included in the national census till 1967. The NT government gave per-

mission to shoot at Ayer's Rock, hoping the film would draw tourists to the region. I do not know if the NT government consulted the indigenous tribes.

22-year-old fight arranger and stuntman Sammo Hung (Hung Kam Po) played drug courier Win Chan, who gets chased up the Rock.

Sammo Hung was a great asset to *MFHK*. Since Sammo spoke no English and our interpreter had flown back to Hong Kong with Wang Yu, I communicated the desired action with sign language and by drawing in the sand. Despite Sammo's bulk, he was extraordinarily dexterous and athletic. Check out the backward somersaults he delivers in the opening of *Enter the Dragon*. Sammo went on to become a leading Kung Fu action/comedy star. His *Mr. Vampire* series is hilarious. By 1998 he had attracted Hollywood's attention. CBS created a series for him *Martial Law* which ran for forty-four episodes. For nearly four decades he has

been a successful producer/director and star of major Asian box office hits. He was particularly helpful to me in the Hong Kong fight scenes.

I arrived in Hong Kong to discover that Shaw Brothers were suing Wang Yu—again. In their ongoing breach of contract suit, the court had previously ruled in Shaw Brothers favor, barring Wang Yu from working on any movie in Hong Kong. Now he was defying that ruling. So Shaw applied for an injunction to stop any shooting of *The Man from Hong Kong* till the matter was resolved. Along with Grant Page, Russell Boyd

(DP), Lynn McEnroe (continuity), the sole members of the Australian crew to join the Hong Kong part of the shoot, I awaited the outcome in an apartment owned by Golden Harvest. In fact, the apartment immediately below ours was the one in which Bruce Lee had tragically died.

A week later the dispute with Shaw Brothers was resolved and it was all systems go on a succession of fight scenes. Choreography was by a triumvirate of Wang Yu,

Sammo Hung, and myself. Grant collaborated on the ones that involved him. For Grant's big fight, I had planned for a variety of kitchen utensils to be used. Knife, meat hook, chopper, pans, etc. At the kitchen/restaurant location additional ideas evolved. We saw a wok on the stove. By adding dry ice to water, the wok appeared to steam, and it looked like boiling water was being hurled. In this fight we used a technique pioneered by a famous Shaw Brothers director Chang Cheh. Jimmy entered the kitchen cautiously, looking for the assassin he was chasing and moved into foreground. Grant sprang from his hiding place behind him, and slashed his back with a carving knife. Jimmy spun round, revealing a bloody gash on the back of his jacket, hitherto concealed by the camera's angle. The fabric had been precut, with blood added just before I called action. The fight continued for a beat till I needed to change angle for the next piece of business.

As part of his 3-picture deal with Golden Harvest, former James Bond George Lazenby was set to play Wilton, Sydney's King of Crime. Notorious Sydney crime bosses in the 1970s were Lenny McPherson and Abe Saffron, George Freeman, Stan "The Man" Smith. Luckily I made the brief acquaintance of only one of them, but I doubt any of them had a penthouse like the one we designed with Bond-ish flavor as the villain's lair. There was a skilled Art Department at GH.

I had first seen George Lazenby on screen when *On Her Majesty's Secret Service* came into National Screen Services to have its trailer devised by Esther Harris, and its opening titles created by Maurice Binder, who pioneered the elaborate Bond title sequences using NSS's Oxberry Aerial Image Optical printer. Like Connery, George projected a wry charm, and looked ferocious in fight scenes. Sitting beside Esther Harris as she shaped the trailer on the Moviola, I had watched his key scenes. So here he was five years later co-starring in my first film. Funny how things turn out. He was easy to work with. His post-Bond experience had been humbling. George recognized he had made a terrible mistake in not signing the contract for three

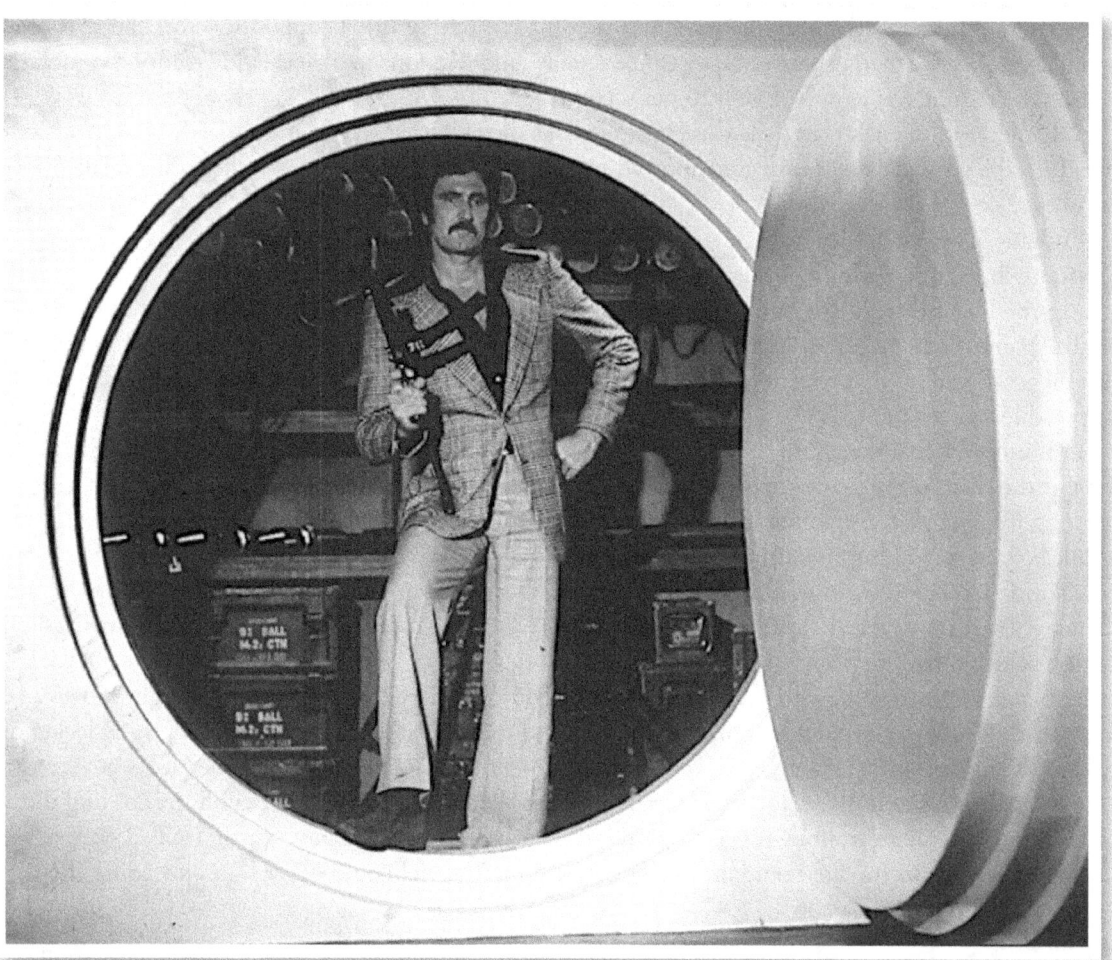

more Bonds. He had been covertly blacklisted; all the lucrative deals that were on offer had evaporated. But Raymond Chow, recognizing his potential, saw him as an ideal costar for Bruce Lee and offered him a 3-picture contract.

Mark Hartley's 2008 feature documentary *Not Quite Hollywood* is a meticulously researched, frequently hilarious account of those wild days of Ozploitation movie making. There's a section on *MFHK* with some amusing anecdotes from my colleagues, including the day I persuaded George Lazenby to have the back of his jacket set on fire in the final fight scene with Jimmy Wang Yu. In Hollywood at that time big human torch gags were performed by a stuntman, with a head-to-toe fire suit. Camera angles were framed to avoid revealing the protective facial covering. Using the fire retardant Waterjel rather than shooting wide angles of a blazing stunt double in a fire suit meant that the camera did not have to avoid the character's face. To see a former James Bond actually do such a stunt himself would be a great takeaway moment for the audience.

In *The Stuntmen*, I had very briefly set my naked arm on fire to demonstrate the effectiveness of the new fire retardant gel. I asked George to watch as I gelled up, then donned a discarded costume from the wardrobe department. My back was sprayed with fuel then set on fire, supervised by Grant Page, to show George it was safe. Of course I should not have put George in that position. How could a macho guy like George have refused after that? Murphy's Law should act as a strong antidote to a director's hubris.

The fight had been choreographed to bring George Lazenby and Wang Yu to the fireplace in the center of the room. Now the moment had arrived when Wang Yu was to kick George in the chest, making him fall backwards into the flames. George then was to lunge forward, as his jacket caught fire and continue the fight through several moves before shedding his blazing jacket. We rehearsed all the moves multiple times, then fueled George's jacket. Now the clock was ticking before the WaterJel would seep through the layers of

**165**

cotton overalls underneath George's jacket and prevent it catching fire. I told both actors there would be a slightly longer pause than usual between "Roll cameras" and "Action" to give the slow-motion cameras time to reach the require frame rate of 90-120 per second.

When everything was ready, the cameras rolled. As they whirred to get up to speed, Wang Yu suddenly picked up the adjacent fuel bottle and sprayed more on the back of George's jacket. This freaked George out a little.

"What's happening?!"

Jimmy barked something to the effect: "Not enough. Better with more."

I learned later that Jimmy had done a fire gag on a recent movie without either a fire suit or protective gel. The flames were mainly from his shoulder blades down to his elbow, but he thought they could have been bigger. Based on that experience, he decided suddenly to freshen up the fuel on George's jacket at the last possible moment.

I shouted "Back in position!" or something like that. Frankly I did not know what to say. Should I call cut? Put the stunt off till tomorrow? What were the ramifications of countermanding Wang Yu in front of his Hong Kong crew, causing him loss of face? Jimmy returned to his mark and resumed his fighting stance. I think he said something reassuring to George, but I could not make it out over the whir of the cameras. This all took just a few seconds. George said nothing and squared up. The camera reached ninety frames per second. Russell Boyd yelled "Speed." I called "Action!" Jimmy kicked George so he fell momentarily into the fire, before springing back.

His jacket ignited well, with the flames staying behind him. He carried out all the fight moves as choreographed. It looked good. Everything was working as intended till he had to tear the burning jacket off to hurl it at Wang Yu. Unfortunately, the protective layer of gel soaking the clothing beneath his outer costume made it a tighter fit round the elbows. He could not get the jacket off. I don't recall him shouting for help, but he was obviously in trouble. It was trapping his arms behind him. Grant swiftly tackled him, bringing him to the ground so the fire-retardant blanket soaked in WaterJel could cover him and douse the flames,

the planned conclusion to such a stunt. I had promised George that he would not get burned. But he was burned on the wrist where his struggles with the jacket had wiped off a section of gel. George was understandably furious. In *Not Quite Hollywood* you see Roger Ward (who was not there and relied on hearsay) state that George "punched the director" and "damned near broke his jaw."

Here's my recollection: George stepped forward balling the fist of his uninjured hand. I felt appalled by what my desire for an unprecedented screen moment had brought about. In retrospect, I realized that I should have done a dry run with a small amount of flame and tested the theory. We would have seen the flaw in the plan, how hard it was to slip the burning jacket over his gel-thickened undergarments, and made the necessary adjustment. It would have meant destroying the irreplaceable double of his jacket, meaning there could be no Take Two, but we should have done it.

As George approached fist upraised, I do remember saying something like: "I'm very sorry, George. You can hit me if you want." I don't remember him swinging at me. I recall he stopped and turned away. We immediately reapplied the gel to the burn which extended for about four inches along the inside of his wrist and got him to a doctor. The tea tree oil in the gel has restorative properties. After treatment, he was back on set to finish the scene three days later. In the meantime we shot other scenes. Grant doubled him throwing the blazing jacket at Wang Yu, so he did not have to deal with fire again. I don't recall seeing a scar on his wrist three years later when George invited me onto his yacht for a day's sailing off Long Beach. Despite the trauma I had inflicted on him, he did not throw me to the sharks.

This episode was one of several lessons I had to learn about directing stunts. Control. The ideal is to create images that look dangerous but are not. Today the director, stunt coordinator, safety officer, and all cast and crew directly involved convene to triple-guess the plan, and consider what combination of factors could cause a bad outcome. Now there are many options available to stage screen mayhem safely. Computer

animation can convincingly fake a hair's breadth escape or a lethal impact, or an actor whose face you can see being engulfed by flames. No one should be maimed or killed because they went to work.

The proposed hang gliding sequence was considered risky by the Hong Kong authorities. But it was not Grant's safety they were concerned about. They required us to take out a US $5 million insurance policy for property damage, including to any ships in the harbor during the various 10-minute flights. Grant was doubling kite flying journalist Caroline Thorne played by Rosalind Speirs, as she flies from Kowloon over Hong Kong Island and lands in the middle of the parade ground of the Police Training Academy in Aberdeen, where she would meet Wang Yu's character. The Golden Harvest contingent did not initially share my confidence in Grant. Victoria Peak, 1800 feet high, provided the best camera position for Grant to fly with a harbor vista in the background then cruise past a row of high rise apartments.

"But where will you land?" his local support team asked. Grant pointed to a tiny patch of green, way below, a small park.

"Wait for me there."

They set off for the rendezvous point, a little dubious of the outcome. But sure enough, after giving Russell Boyd's camera some great banking turns, Grant glided down and landed exactly in the middle of the designated park to the astonishment of the crew. The next day we scheduled the landing at the Hong Kong Police Training Academy in Aberdeen. It was a much more challenging maneuver. Grant took off from a nearby hill, then swooped low like a bird of prey over squads of police trainees marching in formation with rifles at the slope. With a sudden pivot lifting the nose, he glided to a gentle halt, facing away from camera, thus making an easy cut to Ros Speirs under the wing taking off her helmet. Perfection. It could not be bettered. This was the first shot that made me actually gasp with joy as I watched it happen. To the crew, Grant Page was a god. These were unique images. Confidence in the picture rose.

Back in Sydney, we waited for a fine sunny day, hired a helicopter and shot Grant, wearing Wang Yu's track suit, flying the kite across Sydney Harbor. Close ups of Wang Yu steering the hang glider had been shot with the kite tethered ten feet above the ground with a wind machine inflating the sail. The kite was not allowed to fly over the Harbor Bridge, but POV shots from our helicopter cruising over it achieved the same purpose. The footage, as in the Hong Kong fights, was spectacular. Now I knew I had a worthy climax. The icing on the cake was to blow up the top floor of the Esso Building in Sydney. Well, appear to blow it up. Bringing with me the pyrotechnic expert who later created napalm strikes for Coppola's *Apocalypse Now*,

I persuaded Esso executives to let us place small fireball mortars beside the top floor windows, and a larger mortar on the roof. Across the street from Esso was a fire brigade station. What could go wrong?

Assumption is the mother of all fuckups. We told Esso and the Sydney Fire Department that both explosions would be concluded before 4 p.m. that Sunday afternoon. Most probably at 3:30. The fireball from the windows went off on schedule, but problems setting up the big explosion on the roof caused a delay till about 4:15. The budget dictated this was an unrepeatable shot, so we had to be sure that everything was set up correctly, and with pyrotechnics you cannot rush these things. We assumed: Being fifteen minutes late is no problem. We advised the fire brigade across the street. They happily gathered on the pavement to watch. Remember the eleventh commandment: Thou shalt not assume. What we did not know was that the fire brigade headquarters changed shift at 4 p.m. The incoming shift knew nothing of the planned explosion. It was not on their log. It was assumed to have already happened. Reinforcing the misunderstanding, the outgoing shift stayed across the street to watch the explosion. Firemen on the spot. No reason not to go ahead.

Roll cameras! Speed! Action! Kaboom! A 30-foot fireball appeared to erupt from the roof of the 18-story building. In fact it came from a reinforced container directing the flames upward. It was very impressive. Both explosions worked perfectly, no damage, other than a scorch mark on a window shelf. But the roof explosion could be seen for miles. Traffic briefly stopped on the Harbor Bridge. Sydney's emergency services were deluged with calls. Within two minutes multiple fire engines raced up to the building, surprised to see a group of firemen outside their station watching the still-billowing smoke unconcerned. Oops…

Apologies all 'round, but I got the shots I wanted. Real explosions on a city high rise. Such a shot back then was generally achieved with an exploding miniature and/or a superimposed photographic effect which always looked fake. Whenever I saw miniatures, be they a blazing high rise, volcanic earthquakes, or galleons battling at sea, it jarred. Miniature waves or flames never look in proper scale to the dominant object. Such shots would take me out of the story for a moment. But I wanted a shot to end the film which would give the departing audience something to talk about in the foyer with friends, or round the water cooler next day:

"Wow! It looked like they really blew up that building!"

# CHAPTER 19
## Cannes '75

It was a race to finish editing and sound mixing *The Man from Hong Kong*, scheduled to be presented at the Cannes film market in four months. Early in the shoot it was clear that Wang Yu would have to be revoiced for the English language market. Giving a good-looking actor the best sounding voice was common at that time in the Hong Kong film industry, which did not record direct sound during shooting. The entire dialogue and sound effects were created on the soundstage.

I flew to Hong Kong and chose Roy Chiao, an Asian star of the 1950s and '60s who had a deep resonating voice to match Wang Yu's physical toughness. Roy was a well-practiced dubbing artist. He improved delivery and inflection throughout. Roy would work for Steven Spielberg ten years later in *Indiana Jones and the Temple of Doom* as the gangster who poisoned Indy in the opening Hong Kong sequence.

Next task was to work with Golden Harvest's choice of composer, Noel Quinlan, an Australian resident of Hong Kong where he was an in-demand producer of advertising jingles. Noel had become a professional guitarist at age fifteen, studied in Los Angeles under Henry Mancini and Nelson Riddle, and has enjoyed a remarkable musical career. Since *The Man from Hong Kong*, Noel has scored over forty feature films and documentaries, together with orchestral works for the Hong Kong Philharmonic Orchestra, and the Cologne Radio Orchestra. His "Middle Kingdom" series, which sold over a million CDs, features ancient Chinese melodies performed on computers and traditional instruments. So I lucked out. My assigned composer had real talent, and delivered a propulsive score with a big sound in keeping with the over the top action.

One morning during this process, I was walking down a corridor at the Golden Harvest Studio. There was Wang Yu approaching. I think he was shooting another movie in Taiwan. I greeted him cheerfully. I felt good about our movie, and asked him how he was. He told me he was sad because his wife had just left him. I felt genuinely sorry for his misfortune and told him so, but each of us was running late for respective duties. We parted, agreeing to meet later, but have never seen one another again.

I returned to Australia with the music score and the new voice for Wang Yu.

Within a month the sound was mixed, the negative matched, and a print dispatched to the London office of Cathay Films, which handled international sales. They thought the film had great prospects, which could be enhanced if the song running under the main title sequence were replaced with one by a rising British band, Jigsaw. The promotional push behind Jigsaw would guarantee the song made it into the top ten on the UK charts. I was sorry to see Noel Quinlan's dynamic song "Power" go, but there was no denying the commercial logic.

I flew to London, and met the band. Great guys. Clive Scott and Des Dyer had written a song, "Sky High," with the lyrics: "You've blown it all Sky High/By telling me a lie," which they thought would work equally well over the kite flying main title sequence and add a note of irony to the end titles after the exploding penthouse finale. Their arranger, Richard Hewson, had worked for the Beatles, Art Garfunkel, Diana Ross, and Fleetwood Mac. He helped orchestrate the 4-minute title sequence version of "Sky High". With its dynamic intro springing out of the explosive Uluru sequence, "Sky High" gave the titles a Bondish flavor that Lazenby's name would amplify. A 2-minute single version of "Sky High" was also recorded to be released in the weeks leading up to the movie's premiere. Once again I really lucked out. "Sky High" was a worldwide hit in the latter half of 1975, reaching Number 3 on the Billboard Hot 100 and Number 2 on the Adult Contemporary chart in the US. There was a well-established band in Australia also called "Jigsaw", so "Sky High" was released there under the name of "British Jigsaw," where it rose to Number 2 in the charts. It reached Number 1 in Japan two years later, where it sold 570,000 copies. Amazing. *MFHK*'s eventual share of the music royalties, underreported I suspect, was AUD$20,000.

Next came Cannes, where alongside the 10-day arthouse-driven Film Festival, there was the Marche, where scores of new commercial movies were screened in the town's regular theaters from 8 a.m. till midnight for international buyers. So many movies, so little time. *The Man from Hong Kong* would get four screenings at different times and different venues. How do you get buyers from significant territories to put your film on their calendar, with so much bigger budget, star heavy product to inspect? The major players had the money for big billboards along the Croisette and multiple ads in the trade papers. We could afford one such Trade Ad per screening. One way to get market place attention was to post flyers with the time and venue in the cafes and bars where the buyers paused for brief overpriced refreshment. I spent my first full day at Cannes visiting every *tabac* I could find persuading proprietors to permit a *MFHK* flyer on their wall or front window.

In the course of this exercise, I moved into streets further away from the Croisette, and came across a movie theater that was not catering to buyers, but was continuing its regular programming. I moved closer to see what was playing. The poster beside the box office showed a close up of a beautiful girl offering an apple. The title read *La Nuit de la Grand Chaleur*. Hmm, *Night of the Big Heat*. Wasn't that a 1967 British science fiction film directed by Terrence Fisher? Curious. I bought a ticket and entered the half-full auditorium. On the screen was Peter Cushing and Christopher Lee speaking dubbed French dialogue. It was a worn print of *Night of the Big Heat*, as I had suspected, a minor alien invasion piece not up to the standard of Fisher's Hammer films. Why would it be reissued in the South of France eight years later? Strange.

I found a seat. The scene changed to one in which Patrick Allen, a ruggedly handsome British actor was engaged in an animated conversation with Sarah Lawson, his actual wife playing his screen wife in a story of an alien induced heat wave. Husband and wife stopped talking and looked at each other. Suddenly, with an evident splice, the image changes to one in which a man and a woman are copulating vigorously, and at some length, on the floor. Their faces are hard to see but everything else is not. The rationale apparently was that the alien's heat ray induced not only unbearable heat but uncontrollable lust.

Later that day John Fraser explained it to me. The French government had, up till that year, strictly banned all hardcore porn from cinemas. Finally they gave in to pressure and permitted the import of *Deep Throat* and other porn classics, provided the importer paid a $60,000 excise fee. That was too steep for some smaller distributors, so they shot their own porn sequences and spliced them into films that they dug out of their library, thus avoiding import duty. I wonder if Patrick Allen and Sarah Lawson, happily married for forty-five years till his death in 2006, ever knew of this unique performance moment.

There was a substantial line of buyers waiting for the first screening of *MFHK*. Karate hero vs. former James Bond sounded like a promising concept. Also present were other Australian filmmakers who had movies premiering at the market. The AFDC, now retitled the Australian Film Commission, an investor in all the Australian films on offer, had set up a suite at Cannes to assist producers with sales. The projector rolled. By the time Grant Page piloted his hang glider over the marching ranks of police academy cadets, the buyers were hooked. This was a bigger film than they were expecting.

Reaction from my peers was mixed. Some praised its energy, visual flair and sense of humor. But not all of them grasped the genre homage aspect. One response that took me by surprise came from Sandy Harbutt, the cowriter, producer and director of *Stone*, for which I had made the trailer and a behind-the-scenes TV documentary. My key players Roger Ward, Rebecca Gilling, Ros Spiers, Hugh Keays-Byrne, Dereck Barnes, Bill Hunter had all performed in Sandy's outlaw biker movie. He accused me of stealing his cast in *MFHK*. I did not steal his cast. I had merely borrowed them and returned them in good order, with an international cinema release on their resumes. Sandy and I had employed the same production executive, David Hannay. I had certainly listened to David's praise for the actors in *Stone*. In mid-1974 when I was casting, the pool of actors with feature film experience was not deep. I picked from what I saw. I had also featured a crossbow in *MFHK* as Sandy had *in Stone*, which infuriated him. Another complaint was that my movie made violence look attractive whereas in his movie violence was realistic and ugly, as it should be depicted. He added that I would learn about real violence if I ever got mugged "in some back alley." Interesting critique. Sandy Harbutt was a genuinely talented filmmaker, who despite the success of *Stone*, which has a cult following in the pantheon of biker pictures, never made another film.

Cannes was a success. We sold all of Europe, Latin America, some Middle East territories, recouping about half the budget in minimum guarantees. This put us in a good negotiating position for the US & Canada. Raymond Chow made a deal with 20th Century Fox for a $200,000 minimum guarantee and a summer release. The film was to be renamed *The Dragon Flies* for its US release. Sam Arkoff of AIP (American International Pictures) had bid $150,000. As things turned out, we might have done better with the lower offer. But at that time confidence in the picture was high. Raymond Chow offered to buy out the Australian half of the copyright for double the Australian investment, plus allowing us to keep, and not share, all Australian revenue. He thought investors would find recoupment plus a minimum of 100% profit an attractive proposition. But I was not ready to sell off my firstborn film. I was going to own my piece of it forever. Raymond did not know I had the power of veto. Conversations about a sequel stalled.

# CHAPTER 20
## *MFHK:* Censors and Critics

On my 29th birthday, I flew back to Sydney to find the Australian Classification Board had screened a finished print of *The Man from Hong Kong* and given it an 'R' rating, restricting admission to those over eighteen. I had privately screened it to one of the members of the board on the dubbing stage at the end of the final mix. She warned me that an 'M' rating was unlikely without a lot of cuts. Groin kicks, testicle squeezing, blood, repeated blows, hero dunking enemy in the toilet, letting enemy burn to death, etc., plus the sustained volume and intensity of violence throughout. My argument that the violence was live action Tom & Jerry coupled with Kung Fu satire fell on deaf ears.

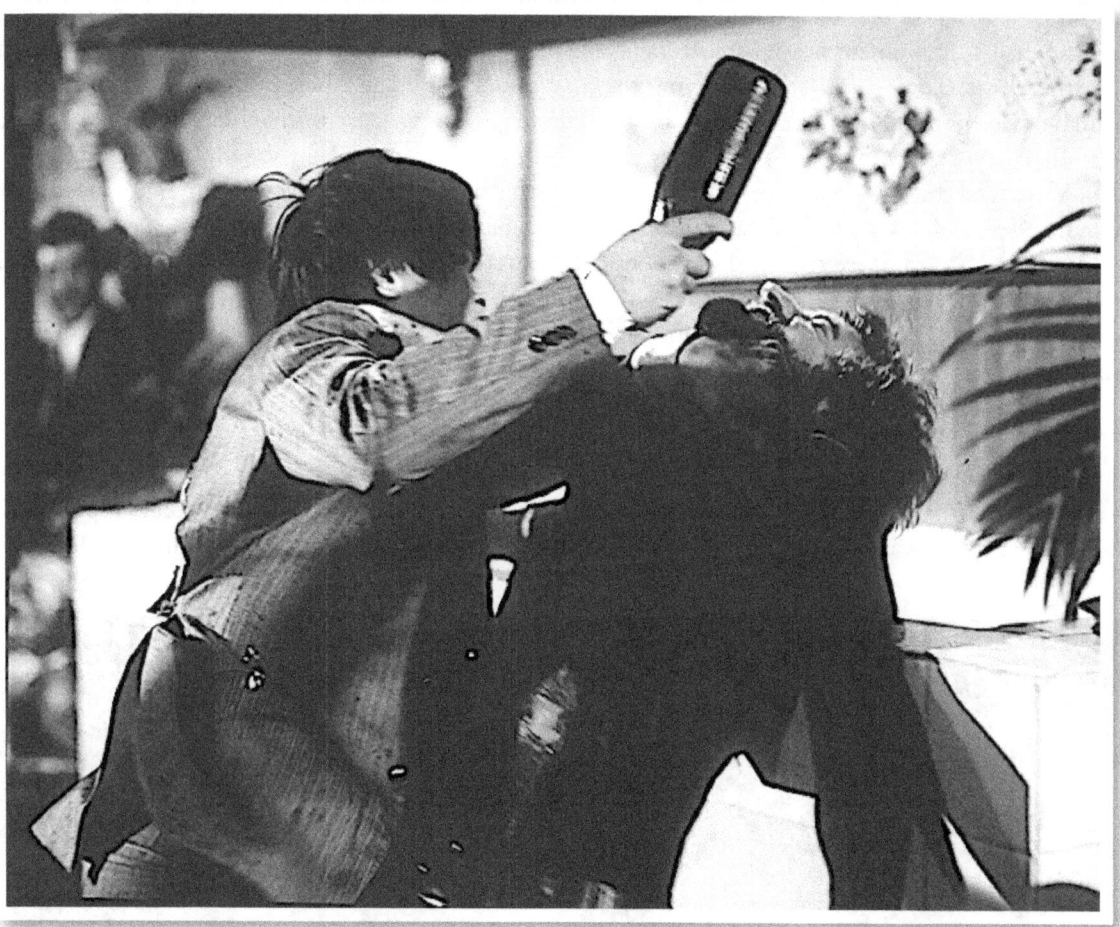

I did not want my genre cocktail watered down. We submitted the film for classification unchanged and appealed the subsequent 'R' rating, citing the cartoonish nature of the fight scenes and the wry macho fantasy tone of the piece. In essence we were told: It's acceptable for this sort of thing to happen in Hong Kong, where there is a culture of violence, but in the heart of Sydney, this many violent acts in 106 minutes? No. This film appears to normalize violence within our culture (this was an argument The British Board of Film Censors made in the 1930s against Hollywood gangster pictures). In retrospect I can understand their sense of social responsibility. There had been an uptick in screen violence internationally since 1970. The Australian Classification Board felt they had to hold the line against what they perceived as glorification of violence.

We were told that the volume of violence had to be substantially reduced to gain an 'M' rating. They supplied a list of proposed cuts. Admittedly, I had deliberately pushed the envelope to give the film more bite in international markets. Awaiting release in the US were a flood of cheap Hong Kong made 'Chop Socky' pictures—the new trade paper label for Kung Fu flicks at the time (a little racist, perhaps?). 20th Century Fox were going to release *MFHK* in August, the earliest date they could get. The violence was uncut for an American 'R' rating, allowing the under 17s to see it if accompanied by an adult.

John Fraser and I conferred. 'R' rated action pictures (Bronson flix for instance) were still doing good business in Australia, particularly in the drive-ins. I knew the film would be cut in some countries. I just wanted the Australian version to have everything in it. We accepted the 'R' rating. My artistic right, although a bad business decision. Today *MFHK's* rating is 'MA-15', following a successful appeal ten years ago. I doubt that recent fans would enjoy it so much if my excesses had been cut.

The British censor cut Wang Yu watching the assassin burning to death, and all but one groin kick, thankfully leaving the best one: Jimmy kicks Sammo in the groin, cut to pool table balls scattering. Grant Page's squirrel grip moment in the kitchen fight was trimmed but the impact was not lost. Also eliminated from the UK version—every shot involving the 3-sectional staff. The BBFC were very concerned about "imitable behavior." Clubs linked by a chain were deadly weapons, easy to manufacture by soccer hooligans. There were a few other nips and tucks along the way that niggled, but the film played well enough when I attended the UK press screening. Was I right to have resisted cuts, I wondered? Too late for second thoughts. 'R' rated posters were already printed in Australia.

Another taboo I wanted to upend was to show an Eastern hero making love to Western women, not the reverse as was the custom in these kinds of movies hitherto. Consequently in South Africa both interracial love scenes (Miscegenation! Horror of horrors!) were cut, along with groin kicks, blood squirts, the words "Shit!" and "Piss off!" and the obscene British 2-finger gesture from an outraged motorist run off the road.

A scene cut from the US version had nothing to do with censorship. 20th Century Fox just wanted the 106-minute picture to be shorter. At the gas station, Hugh Keays-Byrne's aggrieved drug cop complains about the body count Wang Yu is racking up. "This is Australia, mate, not *55 Days at Peking*," a reference to the movie of that name that depicted the Boxer Rebellion of 1900 totally from a colonial perspective. Wang Yu's response was written to be a contemptuous shrug. Jimmy told me how insulting that line would

be to Chinese audiences. That 1963 epic—full of "yellow peril"—had grossly distorted the facts of a painful period in Chinese history. His character would have to respond angrily or lose heroic stature with his home audience.

"Go ahead" I said.

Jimmy did. He gave his best glower, pointed a threatening finger and loudly growled: "Hey, don't give me any shit!"

It was a strong scene for the hero. Stupid of Fox to drop it. Another dialogue scene with some amusing lines between Royal Shakespeare Company actor Hugh Keays-Byrne and well-spoken Ros Speirs was removed on the grounds that Americans don't understand Australian accents.

I flew to London and did a round of radio and print interviews to publicize the UK release. . Outside the Cathay Films office in Soho Square, I demonstrated how a stuntman can be safely hit by a car. The driver must momentarily touch the brake, dipping the nose, just as the stuntman jumps up and rolls onto the hood. A brave Cathay publicist, watched by a shocked associate, drove the car at only 15 MPH. Wearing a leather suit, I got my legs up in time, but the impact of my shoulder broke the windscreen.

The photographer missed the moment it cracked. So the frontal shot was re- staged with the glass already shattered. Hammy performance, but good enough for Page 3. Cathay obligingly paid for the damage.

The UK Press screening, held at the London Pavilion in Piccadilly Circus, was my first ever meet the press experience, at which I mounted the stage in my then-stylish tan leather suit, and addressed the assembled media. I told them that the film was the first co-production between Australian and Asian film companies and was shot in nine weeks for half a million dollars. I hoped there would be many more such co-productions. I told them it was a James Bond/'Chop Sockey' cocktail and hoped they have fun watching it. I was brief and bubbling with enthusiasm. It never occurred to me that it was a major *lèse majesté* for a filmmaker to address critics before a press screening, as pointed out in the British Film Institute Monthly Bulletin's review, but perhaps my exuberant naïveté gave me a pass and set the UK critics up for the film's sense of humor, because the picture got uniformly affectionate reviews.

*"All action and great fun"*—News of the World
*"A really dashing adventure, lavishly filmed and smartly paced"*—Daily Mail
*"An all action job with as many laughs as gasps"*—Daily Mirror
*"Brian Trenchard Smith has hit on a winning formula: a sort of James Bond action thriller. There isn't a dull moment in his enjoyable, energetic—not to say exhausting—film."*—Madeleine Harmsworth, Sunday Mirror.

The *Observer*, one of the few naysayers, called it: "*a witless display of non-stop mayhem.*"

A reception followed the screening, where I was invited to mingle with the critics. "Make sure you pay attention to that man over there," advised my handler, "He's the cinema critic for Reuters and quite influential." I was duly introduced then left alone with a slightly unkempt, rumpled-looking, fiftyish Scotsman.

He looked at me quizzically and said: "You know I've had a lot of young directors try to show me their cock."

Gulp. What an interesting way to start a conversation, I thought.

A momentary pause.

"But you did not."

He then launched into his thesis that young directors insist upon putting scenes of explicit sex into their movies to demonstrate their masculinity. He seemed to have missed the two love scenes, one of which emphasized the hero's capacity for repeat business, the other indicating he was headed south of the border. In fact, my metaphorical cock was out there, front and center, in concept and execution of pure macho fantasy: Super tough hero clobbers twenty-eight bad guys, beds beautiful women. QED. And the UK audience responded.

*The Man from Hong Kong* opened at the London Pavilion in mid-September and grossed nine thousand six hundred and two pounds sterling, the best first week figure since *Midnight Cowboy* opened there six years earlier. The movie did good business all over Europe but was not the summer breakout hit everyone wanted. We would not see much money beyond the minimum guarantees negotiated.

In America, 20th Century Fox's August release did not go well. US critics, oblivious to the film's humor, were contemptuous of the new Kung Fu genre: "a slick, shallow, well-photographed Australian-Chinese movie which has substituted do-it-yourself decapitation with mass demolition." Fox's choice to use the word 'Dragon' in the title to suggest a Bruce Lee quality had been undermined by a glut of concurrent Kung Fu releases doing the same. The poster and TV ads underemphasized the unique hang gliding visuals, perhaps because Fox had its own hang gliding movie, *Sky Riders*, awaiting release. The opening was soft and the film soon vanished from US screens. This was particularly troubling when we learned that our partner Raymond Chow

THE DRAGON! HE'S THE ULTIMATE WEAPON IN THE ULTIMATE ADVENTURE!
The Dragon flies...The Dragon stings...The Dragon kills like no man alive!

THE DRAGON FLIES

Get ready for Jimmy Wang Yu-The new King of Kung Fu!

JIMMY WANG YU · GEORGE LAZENBY "THE DRAGON FLIES"

had decided to waive Fox's $200,000 minimum guarantee, in exchange for a lowering of commission on subsequent US TV sales. (WTF!) The risk/reward equation made no sense. But we had no say in the matter even though we owned 50% of the film's equity. World sales were controlled by Cathay Film Distributors, the London branch of Golden Harvest's exhibition partner in Asia, a company Raymond Chow would soon buy.

On July 31st, the film opened in Hong Kong under the title 直搗黃龍 *Zhi Dao Huong Long.* *Zhi Dao* translates as: "direct attack on," *huang long* is "the yellow dragon" meaning "to directly attack the root of the problem." The local gross was HKD1,087,235, not what they were hoping for.

The film premiered in five cities across Australia on September 5, 1975. Critics were largely positive, though some damned it with faint praise, and others felt that government money should be saved for more culturally enriching projects. But the popular press was uniformly positive.

There was an amusing postscript to our epic car chase sequence that I heard about a week or two into the release. During our prep period, line producer David Hannay, a persuasive fellow, had induced a Chrysler dealer to provide seven free vehicles for the chase including their latest model Valiant Charger, the only car that had to be returned in mint condition; the rest could be junked. By the end of the chase, we had done $4,700 worth of repairs to a $5,000 Valiant Charger. It once again looked brand new. The vehicle was returned to the dealership, who thanked us, then sold it as a new car. A year later the proud owner of a new Valiant Charger bought a ticket to *The Man from Hong Kong* at Sydney's Rapallo Theater. Imagine his surprise when he recognized the number plate on the vivid blue Charger that Jimmy Wang Yu carjacked. Imagine his succession of WTF moments throughout Jimmy's automotive *smashathon,* concluding with his once beautiful Charger demolishing a house and limping onto the expressway, belching white smoke. Must have been a surreal experience. He left the auditorium to complain to a bewildered theater manager. A few weeks of phone calls later, I'm pleased to say, the man became the proud owner of a truly brand new latest-model Charger.

I began to hear that cinema managers across the country were calling GUO's theater division to complain that they were having to turn away so many young customers because of the 'R' rating.

It was becoming clear by the end of September that the US distributor's gross would come nowhere close to the minimum guarantee we previously had been told was part of the deal, but had mysteriously been waived before the release. We faced the possibility of receiving nothing from the US market. I gave my views—the 'Dragon' title change was a mistake. The film should be rereleased under the original title *The Man from Hong Kong*, using the British poster (a brilliant collage that went on to win a 1975 Best Cinema Poster award in Europe). I offered to go to the US and redo the promotional material. Golden Harvest supported my view and Fox agreed.

Four days after getting back from doing publicity the UK, I flew to LA where I met with Ashley Boone, then in charge of marketing at Fox and one of the few African American executives in Hollywood in 1975.

Mr. Boone projected a lot of energy, listened to our concerns and genuinely wanted to help. He told me there were many US markets where *The Dragon Flies* had not played. I suggested that I bring Grant Page to America and do a stunt show in a few cities where the film, now retitled as *The Man from Hong Kong*, would premiere. This could boost publicity for the opening weekend with a local "happening" in cities of significant size but do not normally get "Hollywood" visitors. He liked the idea and picked three markets that did well with action pictures—Wichita Kansas, Jacksonville Florida, El Paso Texas. A strong weekend's figures might encourage a ripple of other bookings in similar markets across the country. It was a kind of *Billy Jack* approach. It was agreed, and publicity company ICPR was engaged to organize the tour. Initially they offered me to Johnny Carson's Tonight Show as The Hottest Director in Town. The curtains would part, there I'd be on fire, walking up to Johnny and shaking his hand. I was told that there was initial interest, but then NBC legal affairs said absolutely no way!

To remodel the promos, Ashley Boone sent me to the trailer company run by legendary publicist Jack Atlas, a former VP of Promotion at Columbia. He was aware of my work on Columbia trailers like *Land Raiders* in the UK when I was at National Screen six years before. I recut the trailer and TV spots with more of a Bond-ish flavor, then recorded new voice over with Ted Cassidy. Yes, Lurch, the Butler from *The Addams Family*! What an honor. And his voice was the deepest basso profundo. It gave the promos a sharper edge. Jack Atlas was sufficiently impressed with the result to offer me a job if I ever came back to America. I said thanks, but I was committed to my Australian company.

Grant Page arrived, bringing several buckets of WaterJel for the fire stunts. We needed cotton or wool costumes for the best results. Again Ashley Boone was helpful. He gave us access to the Fox costume department where dozens of green woolen jumpsuits left over from the *Planet of The Apes* series hung on racks. He also provided us with a number of breakaway bottles to smash over each other's heads during interviews.

We flew to Jacksonville Florida, did a stunt demonstration for media in the airport car park. Radio interviews were followed by a TV appearance on an afternoon show, where I set Grant on fire. The show's host was becoming anxious during our preparations while we talked about *MFHK* and stunt work in general. Upon ignition, flames rippled up Grant's back, from his ankles to his shoulder blades, and he paraded across the studio floor with a fiery trail behind him. "Put him out! Put him out!" the host screeched. While still ablaze Grant lectured him on how safe it was. A surreal moment. I wonder whether any recording has survived?

At dawn we crossed the continent to the next engagement. A crowd of 100 or more students gathered at the campus of the University of Texas, El Paso for the advertised stunt show. Grant and I warmed up the crowd by smashing toffee glass bottles over each other's heads, then I set Grant ablaze. It went perfectly as before, and the crowd cheered. Grant went off to shed his burned costume and get into his padded leathers. I was to swipe him off a motorcycle with a plastic baseball bat.

I used the time to work the crowd about the *The Man from Hong Kong*—this weekend's movie, right? A voice hailed me from behind a knot of bystanders.

"Hey, you wanna meet an actress?"

Not a hard question.

"Sure," I said heading towards the front row of the crowd, which parted to reveal a male student standing beside a slender girl with long blonde hair staring down at the pavement, her cheeks reddening with embarrassment.

Something happened as I looked at her. The air quickened. I know, it sounds like something out of a Mills and Boone romance, but it happened. I suddenly felt inexplicably drawn to this person in a way that was separate from her physical beauty.

We were married sixteen days later.

# CHAPTER 21
## Margaret

OK. I just wanted you to be as surprised as everyone else in my life was. Rewind to that moment when I first met Margaret. It only happened because her French class finished early. The unfathomable randomness of life.

The man who had hailed me from the crowd introduced his blushing companion as Theater Arts major Margaret Enger. "Do you have any advice for a young actress starting out in the business?" he asked.

I found myself saying: "Whatever you do, don't lose your soul."

In fact, at that stage of my life, I hadn't spent much time on spiritual introspection or even self-exam-ination, as you may have noticed, but don't lose your soul is what I said and I meant it. Many aspire but few succeed in the acting profession, and the quest can be corrosive. My concern for her soul resonated with Margaret and it alleviated her embarrassment. Her friend had blindsided her with this introduction. We chatted for a moment. I found her both enchanting and smart. Grant Page then rode up on a rented motorbike ready to do the final stunt, a back fall timed to the swing of my baseball bat.

"Don't go away," I said to Margaret, wondering what was happening to me.

Grant and I lined up and I duly did my duty as a slugger. Margaret was there as the crowd dispersed. I invited her to the press lunch, where I gave her much more attention than the assembled local critics. But Grant kept them busy.

"You're good at this?" she asked as we settled into our seats.

"What?"

"Seduction."

A keen mind. I assured her my intentions were honorable. I learned Margaret had just turned twenty, was preparing to play Anne Neville sparring with the eponymous villain in *Richard III*, had won the Best Actress Award two years straight at the University of Texas at El Paso and worked part time as a nurse's aide. She was an Anglophile, a poetry lover able to recite at length from memory. She read a lot, theater was her passion, she had only seen two movies in the last two years. Be still my beating heart.

She had been struck by the thunderbolt, too. Who can explain love at first sight? The Brit/Aussie accent helped. Similarly, I have always liked the sound of Southern speech. I had a teen crush on Ellie May Clam-pett from the Beverly Hillbillies. A Southern lilt was attractive to my ear. Though Margaret's Texas accent was less pronounced than that of her six older siblings, whom I would meet later. A fascination for English literature had inflected the Texas twang. But our mutual attraction went beyond such contingencies, and neither of us can fully explain it, decades later.

After lunch Margaret accompanied us to our next engagement at a local TV station recording segments for the following morning's breakfast show. It was my turn to be set on fire. Margaret showed no sign of being particularly impressed, which impressed me. She figured these guys knew what they were doing. And we did. I was alight only from the backs of my knees to the shoulder blades, hardly any on the arms. Grant did the big ones. We knew it looks good for the camera if you rotate and the flames twirl around you, so I pirouetted. It went off without a hitch.

We went back to the El Paso Holiday Inn, and had tea on my balcony. I felt compelled to tell her that during our short acquaintance I had developed strong feelings for her and planned to postpone my flight out to spend more time with her. I had serious intentions. It's a wonder she did not run screaming out of the room. She stayed and we talked for hours. I liked her sense of humor. I sensed in her a questing spirit, like mine. At some point I invited her to join Grant and me for our evening assignment at the Juarez Dog Track just across the border in Mexico. A man you've only just met wants to take you across an international border. Hmm…Margaret certainly should have run out of the room screaming after that. Instead she calmly boarded our limousine for the half hour ride to Juarez, where *The Man from Hong Kong* was opening simultaneously in Spanish. She trusted me. And it would be an adventure.

One of the greyhounds racing that night had been named *The Man from Hong Kong*. Grant, Margaret and I were photographed with the dog, which we were told was the guaranteed winner, because all the other dogs would be carrying weights. Local PR guy suggested I bet on *The Man from Hong Kong*. I declined, which Margaret noted. We walked around the track discussing matters pertaining to a future together. Religion—raised Catholic, she was now Bahá'í. Children—definitely. Politics—at sixteen she had been a campaign volunteer for McGovern before her new faith precluded partisan politics. For my part, religious piety did not come naturally. I had voted for Gough Whitlam at the last election. Children were a new and not unwelcome possibility. At the end of the night, when I dropped her off at the family home, I was left with that feeling so well-articulated by Jack Nicholson in *As Good as It Gets*—"She makes me want to be a better man."

I wrestled with what to do. Until this weekend, I had wanted no ties. Career was my focus. I was a lousy boyfriend. I had never been struck like this before. Of course I could be prudent, go back to Australia and maintain a long distance relationship with Margaret until I could come back to America again. But I didn't want to risk the thread being broken. It was total happenstance that our timelines intersected yet we clicked immediately. I had the inescapable feeling this was meant to happen.

The next day Margaret joined me at the Holiday Inn where I introduced Grant Page's 12th floor rope slide off the roof to a group of bemused local media. They published pictures of Grant in mid-air, arms and legs spread wide, in the flying fox position. It made a good fluff piece to close the TV news that night.

We had done all we could to promote the picture in El Paso. Grant took his scheduled flight back to LA. Margaret and I took a picnic lunch to the summit of Trans Mountain Road through the Franklins looking down over the city. At sundown I proposed. After initial hesitation, she agreed to seek her parents' consent.

Meeting Margaret's parents, Richard and Mary Jane, her siblings and her extended family would make an hilarious chapter in itself. An only child, I was suddenly to become the brother-in-law of Robbie, Rick, Franny, Paul, Kristin and Thomas. Witty, intelligent, lively characters all. When I first met Paul, stripped to the waist and wielding a stage hammer, he demanded, "You take care of my sister, you hear?" Tom took one look at me and observed (ironically), "He ain't Catholic." I was cross-examined by her parents and her godparents, Ruth and Bill Reynolds, at the Reynolds' home while Margaret awaited the verdict upstairs. Somehow, I was judged suitable. Margaret and I were married at her great aunt Netta's pecan farm sixteen days after we met, nine of which I was away in Los Angeles and Kansas. Forty-five years later I am still married to an angel from a remarkable family, and she is my partner and muse to this day. Ours is a true meeting of minds, but we are a study in contrasts, too. I am irreverent and antinomian; she is pious and resolutely law-abiding. But we share a love of adventure, and while careful about small matters, we're ready to take risks about large ones. QED.

Our publicity blitz on El Paso lifted the weekend's gross a little. But the truth was we had missed our moment. In the slow churn of moviegoers' tastes, the film should have hit the screens six months earlier. Ripeness is all.

But I did not care. I was a man in love. Our honeymoon was four days in Los Angeles, three days in Honolulu, during which Margaret taught me to play chess (she still wins). Then it was back to Australia to finish editing *Danger Freaks*, do publicity for *The Man from Hong Kong*'s opening in New Zealand, and write another 60-page issue of *Movie*. The next issue's deadline was approaching fast. By that stage I had got the process of writing short blurbs, choosing pictures, and supervising layout for up to twenty-eight titles, down to a week.

In Auckland, Grant set me alight on top of the Kerridge Odeon building for New Zealand television. Margaret watched coolly but I could tell it was time to hang up my WaterJel-soaked long johns. I had learned what I needed to know about the photography and choreography of fire gags.

Back in Sydney, Margaret and I privately repeated our vows at the Bahá'í House of Worship in Mona Vale and then threw a fancy dress wedding reception for all my friends to meet her at Smoky Dawson's Ranch, a location

where I had shot the horse sequences for *The Stuntmen* and *Danger Freaks*. A team of stunt riders did saddle falls and trick riding to much applause. I reflected I had been incredibly lucky with my career to date. Three years previously, I had quit a safe job at Channel Nine, and borrowed $16,000 to shoot a 16mm stunt documentary, much of it right where I stood. Now I had a movie playing in cinemas across the world. I was co-owner of Greater Union's in-house production company. The future looked promising. What could go wrong?

# CHAPTER 22
### *Death Cheaters*
### *Hospitals Don't Burn Down*

By the beginning of 1976, long-percolating undercurrents in play at Greater Union would surface. Years before, three key executives had started their careers in the publicity department—Keith Moremon, David Williams, and John Fraser. They all got along well and occasionally threw paper clips at each other from adjacent desks, according to John. They were good at their jobs and rose through the ranks. When the post of CEO fell open, the choice before chairman Sir Norman Ridge was between David Williams and Keith Moremon. He chose Moremon.

David Williams was given charge of GUO theaters. Sir Norman promoted John Fraser to run the distribution/acquisition wing British Empire Films. When Keith Moremon resigned as CEO six months after his heart attack, David Williams finally had the job he had sought ten years before. He did not want to be saddled with Moremon's choice of an in-house production company. He wanted to choose projects from across the spectrum of up-and-coming filmmakers. I can understand his attitude. It's common in regime change. He decided no longer to fund The Movie Company. I was to deliver *Danger Freaks* and close down the company forthwith.

GUO were within their rights, but I was disappointed. I thought I had delivered a winner for them—the first coproduction between Australia and an Asian film company that would recover its investment and be profitable, which in due course it was. GUO did not do badly from the arrangement. They owned Colorfilm, the laboratory that processed all the film I shot, and charged full price for all the Australian 35mm prints and international deliverables. The movie played in GUO theaters, which retained 50% of the gross. The balance was passed on to GUO's distribution arm which took print and ad costs off the top, then 33% commission, before any money was dispersed to investors. It took a decade before I saw any remuneration beyond my original writing and directing fee of $5000. But that was the deal I had signed up for, and I had to live with it.

Probably my decision not to edit *MFHK* to an 'M' rating had a bearing on my being cut loose. My loyalty was evidently to my creative process. I was not corporate-minded enough in my strategic thinking

to be a permanent addition to GUO's culture. An 'M' rating might have added $200,000 to the Australian box office. CEOs don't get their contracts renewed for such mistakes.

With the mothballing of The Movie Company Proprietary Limited, I was, as Robert Duvall describes himself in the 1980 movie *Network* "a man without a corporation." I had to get another picture going, quick. Luckily, I had developed a relationship with the local office of an American TV distribution company, DL Taffner. I had chosen them to distribute *Danger Freaks*. They were looking to develop a movie length pilot for a series in Australia, which if successful would lead to syndicated distribution in the United States. Did I have any ideas? Who, me? It fitted perfectly into my plans for Grant Page.

I suggested this concept: infuse a dramatic narrative from a popular genre into a *Danger Freaks* episode. Stuntmen are recruited by the Secret Service to carry out missions using their unique skills, starring a laconic Errol Flynn-esque Grant Page. I also proposed to cast my American wife as the female lead, to give the American audience someone to relate to in an Australian show.

The Taffner execs, led by Australian CEO John Fitzgerald, had met Margaret a number of times. Beautiful, charming, articulate. What's not to like? They required no persuasion. I felt confident Margaret would do well. I had seen her perform Lady Anne's first encounter with Richard III at UTEP the day after we got engaged. My recollection of that scene, over four decades later, was that she had a commanding presence on the stage and she handled the text persuasively. The girl can act, I could tell. When a director casts his unknown actress wife in her first movie role, it's impossible to avoid accusations of nepotism.

I look at it this way. By marrying me at short notice, Margaret had abandoned two years as a Theater Arts major, dropped out of college, no chance now of trying her luck in New York theater. Instead she had left family and friends and travelled to a new life in Australia. The least I could do was to give her a helping hand into her profession of choice. As it turned out, acting would not be Margaret's career. Her inquiring mind led her to become a Ph.D., teaching at Loyola Marymount University in Los Angeles for a number of years.

Dr. Margaret Trenchard-Smith is a published scholar who has presented papers on Byzantine History at UCLA, Harvard, Princeton and other universities. Her theater arts skills are evident in the way she lectures. You can find one of her lectures on Utube (https://youtu.be/Iam3we_c9Ko ) She deserves a book of her own.

I wrote the original story as *Cunning Stunts*. Defending the title against the distributor's fear of accidental spoonerism, I had at one point insisted, "Nobody's going to call it *Stunning…*" Oops. It was retitled *Death Cheaters*. But I got the joke on the screen anyway, emblazoned on the T-shirts the heroes wear. It gets a smile.

I hired a writer with comedy background. Michael Cove had written episodes of *The Aunty Jack Show*, a Python-esque sketch show for the Australian Broadcasting Commission. We shared a British background and immediately clicked. Michael understood the brief. *Death Cheaters* had to serve two masters: to be a fun, action-packed but 'G' rated summer holiday movie appealing to Australian cinema audiences, but also to be the pilot for an action comedy series appealing to an American TV audience. Simple, right? On this untried business model, all I could raise for a 90-minute movie, inclusive of blow-up from 16mm to 35mm, was AUD$150,000. That was roughly a quarter of the eventual *MFHK* budget.

The Australian Film Commission invested 50K, Channel Nine bought broadcast TV rights for 50K. Roadshow took Australian theatrical distribution for a 25K advance. DL Taffner invested 25K and became international sales agent. In those days financing could come together quickly. I hurried into production because Roadshow had a slot open for a 'G' rated picture at Christmas that year if I could deliver. Shooting started on July 29, 1976.

I should have paid more attention to the script. No disrespect to the writer Michael Cove, who did a great job turning my thin storyline into a screenplay. I made a fundamental mistake in in my concept of the characters. Stuntmen Steve and Rod are press-ganged by the Secret Service into a dangerous mission. Julia, Rod's wife is the voice of reason throughout. Don't go. This conflict was intended to provide the loving couple with wry debate on machismo and risk taking. I completely missed what a Boy's Own movie audience would want. Enough with her naysaying! The girl should go on the mission, dummy! Make the guys the naysayers, refusing to take her, so she stows away, turns out to be just as good in the field as they are and saves their arses! That's much more interesting. But I didn't see it. In creating a showcase role for the woman I loved I made her a spectator with no real impact on the story.

*Death Cheaters* is a noble effort but flawed, which I examine in the DVD commentary. A gratuitous demolition derby sequence added variety of action to the trailer but nothing to the progression of the story. The flashback to the heroes' exploits in Vietnam, to fill in backstory via a production value action scene, was an insensitive use of the tragedy of Vietnam. Seems obvious in hindsight. But at the time, I was focused on giving the picture as big a look as my slender resources would allow.

In the quest for production value beyond our means, I was greatly aided by Executive Producer Richard Brennan who helped a lot of Australian filmmakers make the most out of their budget. He put together an excellent crew for a 22-day shoot, eighteen days main unit, four days reduced unit. Many of the crew were getting an opportunity to step up a grade.

*Death Cheaters* gave John Seale his first Director of Photography credit, after fifteen years as a camera operator. He had done fantastic work on *MFHK*'s second unit, and this was the best way to say thank you. I learned a lot about composition from John Seale, who would go on to become a top Hollywood DP, winning multiple awards including an Oscar for *The English Patient*.

I would have the benefit of his expertise on two subsequent pictures. As wages for all the crew were by necessity low (between $200 and $400 per week) I offered to split 5% of profits between all twenty-three members. As things turned out, they ended up with only $100 each. But I think they appreciated the gesture.

I needed favors and turned to people who had helped in the past. The Ancient and Medieval Martial Arts Society which I had featured in *Danger Freaks* arrived in chain mail with swords and shields for the opening Saxon battle sequence, revealed to be a commercial on which our heroes are performing stunts. I used my Army connections to supply, as a training exercise, soldiers and explosive engineers for the aforementioned Vietnam battle scene. Production manager Betty Barnard went one better. She had Navy connections. She got me an Orion class submarine, also as a training exercise, to sail through Sydney Harbor with our heroes on the conning tower beside the real captain. We shot scenes in the torpedo room and in the Conn around the periscope. Outside the Sydney Heads, we submerged to sixty feet. It is very quiet underwater. Another camera crew was on a boat nearby to film the sub surfacing and our heroes speeding away in a zodiac. All these favors added greatly to the look of the film.

*Death Cheaters* was a calculated paradox: an action picture without violence or blood, where no-one gets shot or even seriously hurt, but at the same time it's full of gunfire, explosions, and car crashes, the regular hardware of violent movies. Not normal ingredients of a 'G' rated Christmas release. But what 10-year-old boys would enjoy if they could get in. We had to avoid the next rating up from 'G' which was 'NRC': Not Recommended for Children. The very opposite of our demographic. To lighten the atmosphere, I gave the film a whimsical tone. I had loved the tongue-in-cheek quality of *The Avengers* TV series (1961-69) and drew on that. Here's something Patrick Macnee (John Steed of *The Avengers*) said about the approach that he and Diana Rigg (Emma Peel) took to that show's scripts:

*"But what we really did was to see what would happen if we took these perfectly straight stories and then made them ever so slightly ludicrous—because we thought that life was ludicrous anyway, which it is! To stay alive and all, you have to be slightly mad—but you also had to be basically cool. We used that, we tilted it a bit, we made it funny and the show worked."*

Despite best efforts, I never succeeded in grafting the pitch-perfect tone of *The Avengers* onto a macho action genre. But Michael Cove wrote a lot of witty lines for Noel Ferrier as Secret Service Chief Culpepper, who had fun with the role. I added an anarchic sight gag for adults accompanying their children. The camera pans across portraits proudly displayed on Culpepper's wall—a row of dictators: Hitler, Stalin, Idi Amin, and ends on a picture of the current Prime Minister Malcolm Fraser. One critic noticed.

This was Grant Page's first dramatic role, tailored for his personality. I partnered him with John Hargreaves, a gifted stage actor who went on to a fine career in Australian film. Husky-voiced Judith Woodroffe was funny and sexy. I gave Grant a basset hound named Bismarck with whom he has one-sided conversations. I could not resist evoking the famous recording industry trademark His Master's Voice. In one shot, a matching pose to the 1899 painting, Bismarck stands beside a windup disc gramophone. Being a cool 1976 hound dog, Bismarck listens to music through headphones. Yes, I was in a whimsical frame of mind.

We submitted the film to the censor. It was touch and go whether we would get a 'G'. But they heard our plea. Perhaps the silliness of the picture was its saving grace. The last DVD release was reclassified 'M'

as a caution to parents that the dangerous stunts depicted could be imitated by younger children without supervision. *Death Cheaters* opened in five carefully-chosen capital city theaters in time for Christmas and ran four weeks. Reviews were condescending at best, with the exception of Helen Frizell's in the Sydney Morning Herald:

*"Death Cheaters, a minor film, was a major surprise. This Australian spy thriller is a two-musketeers, cobbers-campaigning story of two ex-Army mates, now stuntmen, who are sent by this country's Intelligence to steal secret papers from a firm in the Philippines...This film is for 'kids' but 'kidults' (not my invention) will enjoy it. The pace is fast—car chases, hang gliding, cliff climbing and submarines—and the plot is wildly improbable. All the same Death Cheaters has originality, unusual glimpses of Sydney—from the Vaucluse Bowling Club to the Hilton and satiric glances at Intelligence establishments. I liked most the scene at Intelligence headquarters, where photographs of dictators hung on the wall—Hitler, Stalin, Idi Amin and an Australian Prime Minister...The director, Brian Trenchard Smith, is a very clever man. I wait for his next film."*

It's nice when a critic gets your wry asides. *Death Cheaters* was up against such heavyweight product as *The Spy Who Loved Me*, Tim Burstall's *Eliza Fraser*, the biggest budget Australian film to date, plus the latest Pink Panther movie. An AUD$150,000 film is limited ammunition against that kind of lineup. But I knew that going in. Where we did do tremendous business was at matinees, particularly at the Athenaeum in Melbourne. Each week's gross increased. Somehow the comic strip derring-do resonated with Melbourne kids. In its final week, despite half-price tickets for kids, the Atheneum took $12,000, an amazing figure under the circumstances.

As it turned out, *Death Cheaters* would be rejected as a series pilot in the US, the initial objective of the distributor. It languished for a couple of years before being sold to a minor video label. But international TV sales put the picture into a small profit. I was to learn that a director's first film is not necessarily the most important. It's the second film that determines whether or not he or she is just a flash in the pan.

In January, Margaret and I flew to London to screen *Death Cheaters* for possible UK theatrical distributors, citing its Australian cinema release. I used the screening in a small Wardour Street theater to shop for an agent, recognizing this would be essential if I were ever to work outside Australia. A well-thought-of UK writer's agent, Andrew Mann, attended. I became a client. Eighteen months later he would call me with a directing offer. Another invitee was producer Michael Klinger. He had produced Roman Polanski's first English language films, *Repulsion* and *Cul-de-sac*. I had met him in 1968 while working on the trailer of *Baby Love*, which he exec produced. In naïve pride I told the audience at the screening that the film cost only AUD150K. "Don't ever do that," Klinger said sagely to me afterwards, "Now they know how lowball to go."

He saw a use for *Death Cheaters*. His son Tony Klinger had made a film called *The Butterfly Ball*, shot on 16mm blown up to 35mm like *Death Cheaters*. It was an in-concert rock opera movie composed and conducted by Deep Purple bassist /composer/singer Roger Glover. The concert footage was intercut with surreal imagery. Nobody liked the film. Roger Glover hated it. And still does. Read how much on his website. It was screened for me. It was pretty bad. Michael Klinger, despite all his connections with UK exhibitors could not get the film booked at Rank or ABC cinemas. But if he could get a promotable 'U' certificate co-feature, bookings were available in independent theaters. He proposed coupling *Death Cheaters* with *The Butterfly Ball* as a 'U' certificate double bill.

I was privately dubious that the BBFC would allow two human torch sequences, even as stunt demonstrations, in a film for universal exhibition. The Australian censor had been lenient to an Australian film. The BBFC were more likely to be concerned about the imitability of the stunts by impressionable kids. Klinger wanted UK theatrical rights to *Death Cheaters* with *Butterfly Ball* taking 40% of the rental for the double bill. No advance. No minimum guarantee, just a 60/40 split of net returns. A UK theatrical run, however limited, would have elevated the picture's profile. I wanted to give it a shot, but my partners at Taffner demanded a minimum guarantee. Klinger refused. I had to turn down Michael Green's offer of distribution for the same reason. A pity. But London was not a total bust. I took Margaret to Brian De Palma's *Carrie*, and enjoyed watching her jump out of her skin at the final scene.

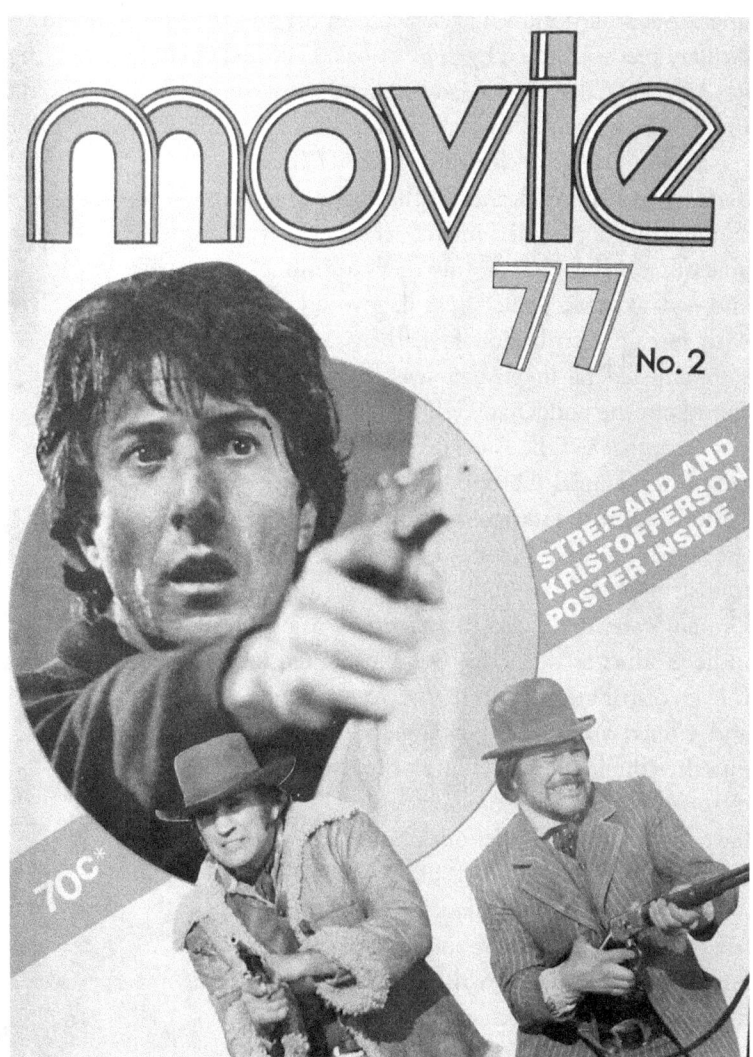

Back in Sydney, I wrote the April issue of *Movie*. The process required me to deliver copy and photo layout at least six weeks ahead of delivery to cinemas and drive-ins. We were now printing 40,000 copies per issue in Hong Kong and shipping them back to Sydney. It was enjoyable work. It paid the rent, with the added benefit of a free pass for myself and a guest to any cinema in Australia.

While I busied myself with the magazine and a couple of trailers, I thought about what my next feature project should be. When I first sailed into Sydney's spectacular harbor on the Achille Lauro in 1966, the vessel cruised past the small sandstone islet of Fort Dennison where a naval gun, originally mounted to defend the harbor in WWII, was still in place. The Fort, in early settlement times, was known as Pinchgut Island by troublesome convicts isolated there as punishment on bread and water diets. It had been the prime location for the last Ealing Studios film shot in Australia, a 1959 crime/suspense thriller *The Siege of Pinchgut* starring US tough guy Aldo Ray (*The Naked and the Dead*). He played an escaped convict who seizes the island and aims the 6-inch naval gun at a munitions ship moored across the harbor, threatening to fire if his demands are not met. Released as *Four Desperate Men* in the US, the film was not successful. But it impressed Quentin Tarantino when he discovered it on television years later, and gave it a nod by naming Brad Pitt's character Aldo Rayne in *Inglorious Basterds*. *The Siege of Pinchgut*, directed by Harry Watt, is not bad for its day, and uses its scenic location to great advantage, albeit in black and white. It seemed to me that the suspense would have been greater if Aldo Ray had fired a few warning shots causing explosions among the water frontage mansions. How about an action-packed disaster thriller update in CinemaScope and color?

This idea was to coalesce as my next proposed feature project: what if a rogue unit of disillusioned CIA operatives stole a mini nuclear weapon for an extortion plot and seized control of Pinchgut along with its artillery piece? Inspired by *Thunderball*, I wanted an underwater frogman fight among other action scenes. I got Michael Cove to write an excellent script, in which the city is defended by the heroic New South Wales Premier, to be played by Jack Thompson as a younger, sexier Neville Wran, the actual Premier at the time.

I approached Cleavon Little (*Blazing Saddles*) to play the leader of the rogue spies, through his agent Ed Limato, who was very gracious on the phone: "Just get the money and we'll work with you," he said. I would start with foreign distribution first, then see what state and federal investment would follow to round out the budget at AUD$450,000.

I approached the Australian office of Cinema International Corporation, a film distribution company started by Paramount Pictures and Universal Pictures in the early 1970s to distribute the two studios' films outside the United States. CIC also picked up occasional indie product as well. They were interested in foreign distribution rights to *The Siege of Sydney* and offered a $200,00 guarantee, but pulled out after the box office failure of the similarly terrorist-themed *Black Sunday*. A pity. I would have made a good thriller out of it.

I had read a number of books on the Maori Wars of New Zealand, which spurred me to develop a script about a biracial settler family living in peace with Maori neighbors but forced to take sides when war with British troops invades their region. I loved the true

HOSPITALS DON'T BURN DOWN!

story of rebel chief Hone Heke chopping down the British flagpole three times. I envisioned a great sequence with Hone Heke looming out the mist at dawn bearing an axe, causing the British soldiers on guard to flee before him. Again Michael Cove wrote an excellent script. I sent it to George C. Scott, who had taken me to lunch at the Friars Club in New York when I interviewed him for *Movie*. We had kept in touch and I had provided quotes for him for a proposed deep-sea fishing holiday on the Barrier Reef. George C. Scott would have played the patriarch of the settler family. The budget was $750,000. But it was too high. Nobody bit. Then unexpectedly a small project came my way—*Hospitals Don't Burn Down*, an ironic title as you will see. It was a creative joy to make.

The Veteran Affairs Department had experienced an alarming rise in fires at the hospitals they managed. Discarded cigarettes were a leading cause, compounded by poor housekeeping of flammable items. There were also concerns about the level of staff training in the event of fire. So Vet Affairs approached another government department Film Australia to make a film as an awareness raising exercise. Producer Peter Johnson hired Chris McGill and Anne Brooksbank to write a script for a 20-minute short film that would be shown to all Veteran Affairs Hospital staff, followed by a lecture pointing out the fire safety issues raised by the film. They wrote a well-researched script depicting what happens to a group of patients and staff in a multistory hospital when fire breaks out. A smoker throws his cigarette down an unmarked laundry chute when a nurse approaches. Over time the smoldering butt ignites piles of laundry in the basement. Fire spreads up the chute to the 6th floor, cutting the hospital in half.

When I came on board to direct, I said it needed to be grim. More horrific deaths. Sucker punch the target audience so they pay attention to the lecture that follows. It's a mini disaster movie like *Earthquake* and *The Towering Inferno*, where any character could die next. I set out to make *The Towering Infirmary*.

Using a crew experienced in commercials, we shot in three hospitals over eighteen nights on a budget of $90,000. I was blessed by casting Jeanie Drynan as the leading nurse, who catches a patient smoking under his bedding in the opening scene. Over a long career Jeanie would be nominated for three AFI Awards, most notably for *Muriel's Wedding*. In *Hospitals* she provided a strong empathetic presence throughout. I have seen her sobs that conclude the film bring audience members to tears.

Because we were a government-sponsored film for a worthy cause, we got tremendous co-operation. Newcastle Hospital let us put flame bars on balconies and stairwells. The fire brigade provided multiple trucks and personnel. The Bethesda Nursing home scheduled for complete remodeling let us set fire to wards, corridors, kitchens. They did not care what we scorched, as long as we did not burn the whole building down. Grant Page masterminded the human torch stunts. Monty Feiguth and Chris Murray, legendary pyro guys at the start of a great career, provided the flame effects. There were interesting production challenges. I wanted *The Cleaner* (Ralph Cotterill) incinerated inside the elevator to underscore the lesson: do not to use elevators when fire breaks out. Robina Chaffey as *A Patient* contributes a moment of visceral terror. We built a roofless replica of the interior with working doors and set it in the middle of a deserted car park. We had complete control over the spread of the flames. Grant Page delivered an impressive full burn. I provided the screams in the mixing studio. Moviemaking is such fun.

The Veterans Affairs Department was very pleased with the finished 24-minute film. Other hospitals quickly picked it up. Ultimately, every hospital in Australia would require new staff from trainee nurses to surgeons to view the film once they started employment. This practice would continue for more than twenty-five years. *Hospitals Don't Burn Down* would win Best Short Film at the Cork Film Festival and be a prizewinning entry at the 1978 US Industrial Film Festival in Chicago. Eighty prints were sold to global institutions within the first three months of its release. It became Film Australia's highest selling industrial film for the next quarter century. It prompted hospitals, hotel chains, and other institutions to initiate reviews of fire safety and emergency procedures. A few years later I heard a specific example. After screening *Hospitals Don't Burn Down*, a 4-storey hospital changed the location of its Intensive Care Unit. Keep non-ambulatory patients as close to the exit from the hospital as possible was one of the lessons of the film. Several months later, the fourth floor, the original location of the ICU, caught fire and was gutted. There were no casualties, because the ICU had been relocated at street level. That made me feel good. While the bulk of my oeuvre is pulp fiction, one of my films at least had a positive social impact.

# PART IV
## AN AMERICAN INTERLUDE

# CHAPTER 23
## *Stunt Rock*

Sometimes a filmmaker gets a wild ass crazy idea. Normally there is a robust system in place to prevent such an idea from ever reaching the screen. In this instance, the system failed.

Late the previous year, I was in the shower one morning when an idea came to me: famous stuntman—Grant Page—meets famous rock band—TBA. Much stunt and much rock take place. Let's call it *Stunt Rock*. Holiday movie. Kids will go wild. I toweled off, sat down at the dining table and immediately started scribbling on a pad. Six pages later my next vehicle for Grant Page emerged: a feature-length dramatized documentary to be shot in 35mm anamorphic. The premise: Grant is hired to do stunts on a big Hollywood TV show being filmed in Australia. He hooks up with an old buddy, a member of a major rock band, and attends their concert performances, which pepper the film. Grant meets a young reporter who wants to do a story on men who live with danger. At the same time Grant works with the band to bring stunts into their act. This would trigger multi-panel montages of stunts taken from *Danger Freaks*, underscored by the band's music. Silent era stock footage would be added to the mix. A triumphant final song, in which all the band do stunts as well as musicianship, would end the picture. It would be my professional love letter to stuntmen in general, and a vehicle for Grant Page. *Stunt Rock*, I hoped, would launch his stunt actor career internationally.

I sent my outline to a Dutch producer/distributor, Herman Ilmer, who had bought *Death Cheaters* for Holland. He had told me to be in touch if I had any bright ideas. So, how about this? He responded immediately, but he did not want the picture shot in Australia. He was keen to do a deal that would enable him to spend the freezing Amsterdam winter in Beverly Hills, California. Works for me!

American producer Marty Fink was assigned to the project. His expertise and charm were a great asset to me throughout the production. He has had a long and illustrious career including serving as Associate Producer on One Flew Over The Cookoo's Nest. By January 15, 1978 I was in an office in Beverly Hills adapting my thin dramatized documentary outline to the new requirement: that it have scripted dialogue and costar a rising Dutch actress, Monique van de Ven, who had come to international notice in Paul Verhoeven's early films *Keetjie Tippel* and *Turkish Delight*. The film had to be delivered in 4-track magnetic stereo for release in Dutch theaters by June 30th. The Dutch producer was to supply the rock band through his connec-

tions with Intersong. With the aid of young writer Paul-Michel Mielche Jr. we knocked out a draft of the re-modeled *Stunt Rock* in a couple of weeks. Then I flew to New York to meet with Foreigner who had expressed interest. They were very gracious, intrigued by the concept, but were unavailable till their current tour concluded in July. There was no moving the delivery date. Pretty soon the edict came down: "Find a band by the weekend or we shut down the picture."

An agent offered three bands—Virgin, Van Halen or Sorcery. I chose Sorcery because their combination of magic, music, and pyro offered more visual potential. They turned out to be great guys who gave 100% throughout the show. We brought in Grammy Award winner Jimmy Haskell to work with the band and produce the soundtrack, at a budget of $150,000. The movie itself was budgeted separately at $450,000,

and would have to be nonunion. We could not afford International Alliance rates. However, the IA permitted its members to work on non-union pictures provided they took positions other than their union designation. A waiver permitted us to hire cinematographer Robert Primes as DP for the concert sequences. Bob would go on to win multiple awards, including two prime time Emmys. I greatly benefited from his cinematographic expertise.

"STUNT ROCK"...

Stuntman Grant Page is a study in concentration as he executes one of his many aerial feats in the musical-action film "Stunt Rock".

"STUNT ROCK"

starring

Ann Strasburg, an experienced continuity/script supervisor, had watched enough assistant directors in action to know how to handle that job. And she handled it well. Margaretrose, costumer of Elvis, Rita Moreno and other celebrities, clothed an entire band and other cast stylishly on a shoestring budget. *Stunt Rock's* IMDB crew list is full of names that went on to fine careers.

My designated leading lady Monique van de Ven was living with her first husband cinematographer and future director Jan de Bont (*Speed*) in Los Angeles, auditioning, meeting producers and directors, trying to parlay her Verhoeven's Dutch art movies into a Hollywood career. Monique was not a member of the Screen Actors Guild. The whole cast had to be non-SAG to fit the budget. I recruited several actors from the LA Improv group The Groundlings. The late great TV comic Phil Hartman (*Saturday Night Live*, *The Simpsons*, senselessly shot to death by his wife in 1998), has a 1-line part as an assistant director. Dick Blackburn, the director of the cult classic *Lamora*, chose to play the slimy Hollywood agent. UCLA screen writing professor Ron Raley played the irascible TV director. Margaret plays the reporter.

**Tony Cecere**
Stuntman: Scream · Armageddon · Terminator · House
A Nightmare on Elm Street · The Thing · Ghostbusters

APPEARING ALL WEEKEND!
PRO-PHOTO-OPS COMING SOON!

HORRORHOUND WEEKEND
INDIANAPOLIS · SEPTEMBER 6-8, 2019
WWW.HORRORHOUNDWEEKEND.COM

Our stunt coordinator was Tony Cecere, who was Robert Blake's double on the *Baretta* TV series for five years. A good double, too. I did a shot of him in the party scene disappointed that the escapologist thrown into a swimming pool did escape alive from his chains. He flicks away his cigarette Baretta-style, repeating a trademark moment in the series. The *Baretta* bit got a laugh at the 1978 premiere. Pop culture references date quickly and rarely get a second life. But at a 2002 screening, Tony Cecere was such a good double for Blake that a disapproving gasp and hiss from the audience followed his repetition of the *Baretta* flick. Robert Blake had just been arrested for shooting his wife twice in the head. Ironically, Blake had first come to fame playing executed murderer Perry Smith, to whom he bore a chilling resemblance, in Truman Capote's *In Cold Blood*. A signature line Blake repeated throughout the *Baretta* series was "Don't do the crime, if you can't do the time." After a lengthy trial, Robert Blake was acquitted of his wife's murder, but like O.J. Simpson, was later made liable for her wrongful death in a civil suit.

Monique van de Ven was charming and embraced her character's arc: a TV star angry at the studio always doubling her with men dressed in her costume and wig for the simplest stunt. In the script, her character persuades Grant Page to teach her how to do a rappelling free fall known as the Flying Fox. (Her Dutch-accented pronunciation of that term gets a smile.) And here, Life imitated Art. Like the character she was playing, Monique really wanted to do that stunt herself. Her husband Jan de Bont said no way. He had his own reason for concern about stunt safety. He had until recently been the lead cameraman on a wild animal movie called *Roar* when a cute lion cub playfully raked his scalp with its claws, requiring 220 stitches. He no longer believed those oft-repeated words: "Don't worry. It's perfectly safe." Imagine Jan de Bont's surprise as he drove up in his open sports car, looking up to see his wife, her arms and legs spread wide, sliding at speed down a rope dangling from the roof of the Roosevelt Hotel. A high-pitched whirring sound accompanied her fall, generated by the rope coursing through the carabina secured to her belt. Grant and Tony Cecere yanked on the rope, and the increased friction through the carabina brought Monique to an easy landing at their feet. Seeing her in action, her husband's fear and annoyance gave way to admiration.

While filming the aforementioned party scene where the escapologist is thrown into the swimming pool in chains, I received an unexpected phone call. My London agent, Andrew Mann, had access to the print of *Death Cheaters* that I had left at the Australian Film Commission's office the year before. He had shown it to a Disney (UK) executive, who liked it. They had an immediate need for a director for a Disney spy/comedy telemovie shooting in England called *The London Connection*. The job was mine if I could be available immediately. I was almost through my 15-day shoot, but I had to deliver a locked cut to the mixing studio three weeks from the last day of principal photography. Yes, fully tracked and ready to mix in magnetic stereo. I would not/could not ditch my partners and colleagues and had to decline. I sometimes speculate what my career path might have been if I had done that Disney telemovie and done it well. Forks in the road, you never know where they might have led. But it was my duty to stick with *Stunt Rock*.

I edited 'round the clock with five editors to meet that 3-week deadline. It helped to have created all the split screen stunt sequences derived from *Danger Freaks* in the prep period. Editor Robert Leighton (now renowned), cut the concert sequences. A few years later, he would edit Rob Reiner's *Spinal Tap*, and then a number of his subsequent movies. I divided the rest of the scenes between Earl Watson, Beth Bergeron, Curtis Burch and Chris Lebenzon, who worked heroically to get it all done in the time. The sound was mixed on the Todd AO stage at the Goldwyn Studio on Santa Monica Boulevard. They had just finished the mix of Sam Peckinpah's *Convoy*. Fueled by alcohol and cocaine, Sam had spent thirty days mixing reel one, just ten minutes of screen time, and he still wasn't happy with it. The producers, exasperated by the latest Peckinpah profligacy, took over and finished the remaining six reels in two weeks.

"STUNT ROCK"...
Monique van de Ven sails through a rope stunt down a tall building in "Stunt Rock"
silencing the skeptics who challenge her throughout the film.

"STUNT ROCK"
*starring*
GRANT PAGE | MONIQUE VAN DE VEN | MARGARET GERARD and introducing SORCERY
Executive Producer HERMEN ILMER · Produced by MARTIN FINK · Directed by BRIAN TRENCHARD-SMITH · Screenplay by PAUL-MICHEL MIELCHE, Jr. and BRIAN TRENCHARD-SMITH
Director of Photography BOB CARRAS · Music Soundtrack Produced by JIMMIE HASKELL

We mixed *Stunt Rock* in five days, a reel per day. Admittedly, twenty-five minutes of concert sequences were virtually mixed already. Compared to mono, the 4-track magnetic stereo soundtrack made a big difference to the impact of the movie in front of a large audience. This was apparent when we rented the Academy of Motion Picture Arts and Sciences theater to preview the film before an audience from local high schools and one special guest—Emanuel L. Wolf, CEO of Allied Artists, who had expressed interest. The target audience gasped at the stunts and cheered the music. We had filled the theater with Sorcery fans. Wolf bought US rights to *Stunt Rock* the next day.

Within a few months however, the deposit wasn't paid and Allied Artists declared bankruptcy. Wolf had acquired the film to fatten his inventory in anticipation of bankruptcy. We sued to get the film back, and eventually placed it with another indie distributor, Film Ventures International. Then their chief executive Ed Montoro disappeared as did a lot of the company's cash. Some say the Mafia buried him under a construction site for unpaid debts. Others say he assumed a new identity and lived the high life on his ill-gotten gains in a non-extradition country. Then our British distributor Lancair went belly up, too. These calamities were yet to unfold. Full of hope for the film's prospects, Margaret and I boarded a flight from LAX to Amsterdam to join Grant Page in a stunt show for Dutch media and potential buyers on the day of the Dutch premiere.

The next thirty-six hours fell into the *Series of Unfortunate Events* category. To save a few hundred bucks on airfares, the Dutch distributor booked us from LAX to Amsterdam on a cheap charter flight which kept us on the tarmac of Calgary airport for five hours for a 1-hour refueling stop. We were told the packed 747 was too heavy to take off in the 90°+ summer heat. Further, the plane was denied access to the terminal to maintain internal power because the airline had contracted only for refueling not docking rights. Therefore, no air conditioning. The exit doors were opened for ventilation but no egress. The passengers became restive. The crew served free alcohol until it ran out. One drunken passenger took over the PA system and told dirty jokes in Dutch, translated in part by the embarrassed Dutch-speaking woman seated next to us. Margaret read a good book. I watched and wondered how the situation could become a key sequence in a comedy, or a thriller, or a disaster movie. Eventually we took off.

The plane had to make an unscheduled landing at Prestwick, Scotland for refueling. There was insufficient juice in the tank to sustain the remaining 30-minute flight to Amsterdam! This must have been an anxious flight for the pilot. We arrived just in time for Grant Page to perform his human torch stunt followed by a rope slide off the roof of the hotel. This was for the edification of European buyers who had gathered for a party ahead of the premiere. Sufficiently lubricated, the buyers were shown a 20-minute promo reel of highlights from *Stunt Rock*, plus one whole 5-minute song—"Wizards Council"—on a big screen TV. Well, big for 1978. This featured the impalement of the Wizard at the hands of the Prince of Darkness, followed by the Wizard's resurrection. As the Wizard extracted the sword that transfixed him, the buyers were excited. They all made offers. So far, mission accomplished…

For reasons I could not fathom the distributor chose not to premiere a 4-track magnetic stereo print. The only theaters in Amsterdam that had mag stereo sound systems were booked with other pictures, so *Stunt Rock* played to its most important audience in mono with Dutch subtitles. Compounding the error, the premiere was scheduled for 10 p.m. at a downtown theater, after the main feature had ended. Not important enough to pre-empt normal business. The screening started fifteen minutes late. The theater's night manager, unaware of the purpose of the screening, had a standing order to be closed by midnight or incur staff overtime so he ran *Stunt Rock* at a frame rate higher than the regular twenty-four per second, thus it would end a few minutes sooner, giving him more time to empty the building. A slight chipmunk quality colored the dialogue, and the music sounded tinny. I was powerless to get it fixed.

Murphy's Law continued the next day. We met up with Margaret's father in Brussels at a theater where a 4-track magnetic stereo print was playing at Friday's opening 2 p.m. session. Since the demise of 70mm roadshow epics almost a decade earlier, a 4-track mag release was a rarity. Unfortunately, the projectionist that day had no real understanding of that brown magnetic strip that ran beside the sprocket holes throughout the film. He was trained to clean any new print before its first screening, winding each reel through a cloth dampened with Freon, which would remove accumulated dust that might damage the emulsion. A mono soundtrack is not porous, a mag stripe is. The Freon penetrated the magnetic, embedding the soundtrack with continuous crackling. Then the projectionist cranked the volume up to designated concert movie levels. It was unbearable. Due to sparse publicity, only a couple of other people attended and soon left, as did we. My father-in-law, Richard Enger, who was like my father a WWII veteran, said he had not experienced such noise since he was under bombardment in the Pacific.

After the botched premiere in Amsterdam several of the buyers revised their offers downward. Nonetheless, deals were done for Europe, Latin America, Asia, that totaled, according to a telex I received, over 600K, the cost of the picture and Sorcery's soundtrack album. The promo had led buyers to expect more of a regular story rather than an improvised documentary with concert sequences. True. They still wanted the picture, but *Stunt Rock* was now a specialty release rather than a multi-print holiday movie. Some markets, like Indonesia, got with the spirit of the movie. A friend saw it with an enthusiastic audience in Jakarta, presented in deafening stereo, with fog machines and a laser show to enhance the concert experience. While it left critics at the time bewildered, *Stunt Rock's* sly sense of humor, Grant's charm, and Sorcery's musical expertise has caught on over the years, particularly in America. In the 1980s *Stunt Rock* was rediscovered on video, albeit in pan and scan VHS in the bargain bins of supermarkets. As a movie trailer/ rockumentary hybrid, it has built a loyal following in America, where it plays midnight shows. There will be a Blu Ray. Meantime I recommend you screen the DVD with a group of rock fans/70s fans & action movie geeks, fueled by the intoxicant of your choice.

# CHAPTER 24
## At the Corner of Mickey Avenue and Dopey Drive

Back in LA it was time to follow up that thwarted Disney connection. I have always enjoyed time travel movies. And alien invasion movies. Why not a combination of them? What if alien time travelers plan to conquer Earth at a time when our technology is too primitive to resist? What if the invaders come from a planet where insects and reptiles have evolved into the dominant sentient species, and despite their differences collaborated smoothly? Really? I want to see that! Expensive, but why not go for broke? I quickly wrote a 3-page outline for a spectacular Sci-fi story entitled *Time Warp*, a running battle through space and time between a party of NASA scientists and the invading Alien force. A beautiful heroine and a 12-year-old boy are caught up in the adventure. There were dinosaurs, pterodactyls. Opportunities for animatronic lizard-and-ant-derived creatures. And a big 17th century set piece involving The Great Fire of London. I wrote a ripping yarn. Andrew Mann, my London agent, sent it to Disney's head of development Frank Paris, who agreed that it was indeed a ripping yarn. He brought me in to pitch myself as writer/director of *Time Warp* to Studio Chief Ron Miller.

A former football player for the Los Angeles Rams, Miller was a burly, muscular man with a firm authoritative manner. He had married Walt Disney's daughter Diane, and after Walt died was appointed head of production. Disney had done well picking British directors. John Hough (*Escape from Witch Mountain*) Don Chaffey (*Pete's Dragon*) and their top hitmaker Robert Stevenson (a string of hits such as *Mary Poppins*). I played up my Anglo Australian roots, and made a good pitch, highlighting the visual effects set pieces which Disney would do so well. I had the effrontery to conclude by saying I wanted to be Disney's next Robert Stevenson. To my surprise, I walked away with a development deal and an office in the animation building at the corner of Mickey Avenue and Dopey Drive. It had its own bathroom, because the animation building had been a private hospital, before Walt bought it in 1940. Disney was a signatory to the Writers Guild of America, so my first American job got me into the Guild with its generous health plan, a godsend in 1981 when our son Eric was born by caesarian section.

It was not obligatory, but Disney liked having writers do their work at the studio, particularly if they handed in pages at the end of each day. The studio's early warning system for writer's block, perhaps, and for me a way to build relationships within the studio. *The Black Hole* was in production at the time. As part of my preparatory education for big budget Sci-fi filmmaking, I was invited to watch the shooting of sequences involving visual effects and attend dailies. I saw how airborne robots had to be carefully lit to avoid seeing the wires suspending them from rails above the frame line, as they weaved through large sets and hovered beside the actors.

I wanted a really big set for NASA's time travel facility. To save money on set construction, I suggested a practical location—the vast interior of the Hoover Dam in Nevada, enhanced by Sci-fi consoles and machinery. The dam was not far from Edwards Air Force Base, another planned location in my story, where Earth's fighter jets take on the Alien craft in a climactic battle. *Independence Day* would later capture what I had in mind. So I was sent to Nevada for a day to survey and take pictures. Accompanying me was location manager Dan Horton, who had been the location manager on MGM's 1959 *Ben Hur*. He regaled me with stories of Old Hollywood, and what a decent man Charlton Heston had been throughout the long arduous shoot (like others, Heston has left a mixed legacy). There was a relaxed almost small-town atmosphere about the Disney studio in the late 70s. It had its own folksy post office and memorabilia store. Occasionally I would buy humorously sentimental cards by popular graphic artist Suzy Spafford and mail them to surprise my wife. Margaret had opened up my sentimental side.

Eventually I handed in my script. After a few weeks Disney bought it for the amount specified in my development deal—$65,000. No production date was set. The studio wanted to see how *The Black Hole*, costing twenty million dollars, plus six million in marketing, their biggest budget ever, would perform at the box office. It was the first Disney film to be given a 'PG' rather than the usual 'G' rating. Two other high budget co-productions with Paramount—*Popeye*, starring Robin Williams, and *Dragonslayer*, a surprisingly gory mythical adventure, were also in production. None of these films performed to expectations. Over the years other writers would come up with similar ideas to mine, though not combined in the same script: a chase through time in *Time Bandits*; reptilian alien invaders in the *V* series and *Independence Day*. *Time Warp* was mothballed, permanently.

# CHAPTER 25
## *Dangerous Summer*

We lived in Hollywood, or South Beverly Hills, to be precise, a block from the end of the zip code, not as cool as North Beverly Hills, the beginning of mansion land. To the status-conscious of the period a class line ran down the center of Santa Monica Boulevard. From our point of view, our modest apartment at 215 South Tower Drive, adjacent to Wilshire Boulevard, was close to the epicenter of the business and we lived there for two happy years. After leaving Disney, I wrote and pitched projects with little success. You can die from encouragement in Hollywood. I paid the rent with promotional work.

I made two 35mm product reels for the Australian Film Commission to present at NATO (no, not that NATO—rather, America's National Association of Theater Owners national convention), to showcase the latest Australian feature films. So they arranged for me to present *MFHK* at the Mill Valley Film Festival, which has since become known as the filmmaker's festival. They sent key executive Danny Collins to join me there and together we were guests on various panel discussions. Unlike other Q&As I've attended, these took place under a shady grove of trees across a warm late summer weekend. Chairing the panels was acclaimed San Francisco documentary director John Korty. He and the audience were really interested in the emerging Australian cinema, which was in 1979 the *bright new thing* on the festival circuit. Danny and I were an effective double act, and we've been friends ever since.

Then a challenging assignment came in from producer Tony Ginnane in Sydney. I had already made trailers for his thrillers *Patrick*, and *Snapshot*. Prep had started on his next picture, *Harlequin*. Tony wanted to presell it at the upcoming Milan film market MIFED. But the *Harlequin* shoot did not finish until the first day of the market. Tony wanted a twenty-minute promo to present that day, completed on film rather than a ¾-inch U-matic as was the custom at these markets for unfinished movies. Tony hoped the impact on major territory buyers of a polished coherent selection of scenes projected in 35mm anamorphic on the biggest screen available would produce higher offers.

Forgive me but I'm going to get into the technical weeds here to give a window on the technology and *lab speak* of the time, now long superseded.

To deliver a composite print of picture and sound, or a *married print* by the deadline for dispatch, I calculated two weeks of intense production time was needed from the day all the material was in the cutting room. I read the script, in conjunction with the shooting schedule, marked the scenes that would be available in time, fashioned a first draft script of the promo, then flew to Australia. As each of the requested scenes was shot in Perth, the laboratory would send two additional sets of "one light workprints" to Film Production Services, my cutting room in Sydney. We used one for cutting, then, when the final edit was locked, matched the pristine duplicate positive work print to it, same process as "neg matching," thus creating a master positive, from which the lab would make an internegative. Some "grading" or color timing was done at that time. I benefited from having Christopher Nolan's future editor Lee Smith on the editorial team. Library music, sound effects, and some linking narration to plug gaps in the story from gravel voiced Alfred Sandor were laid against the cutting copy and mixed onto magnetic tape, from which a 35mm sound negative was made. Sound neg and picture neg were "married" at the lab, their offspring being the 35mm "answer print" that would be projected on a big screen in Milan. Off it went in the nick of time.

The *Harlequin* promo worked, racking up $1.2 million worth of sales for an $850,000 movie. Mission Accomplished! Over the next few years I did film market promos for *The Survivor*, *Dead Kids* (aka *Strange Behavior*), *Blood Tide*, *A Rumor of War*, *The Right Hand Man*.

In the fall of 1979, I was offered a development deal by Hal and Jim McElroy, producers of Peter Weir's movies *Picnic at Hanging Rock* and *The Last Wave*, for which I had made trailers. They wanted me to direct a thriller about an arsonist who causes a major forest fire in the Blue Mountains, north of Sydney. Bush fires are an annual problem in Australia as in America, and frequently occur in the hot months of December and January. (Tragically, their intensity has worsened with climate change.) In 1957, 600 people were left homeless by the fires over the Christmas break. Three people were killed and forty-nine buildings were destroyed. The local bushfire fighting brigade, a volunteer force, bravely tackle every outbreak each year. The producers got funding from the New South Wales Film Corporation to make a 35mm Panavision cinema documentary as a tribute to the courage and expertise of the Blue Mountains brigades.

The documentary also had another purpose. It would provide the forest fire footage needed for the proposed arsonist thriller to be called *Dangerous Summer*.

Whenever a fire broke out, I was to take a cameraman by helicopter and shoot it from the air, then

touch down in a safe area and continue to cover the Bushfire brigade on the ground as they battled the flames. Sometimes these fires burned for weeks before being extinguished. I asked my *Death Cheaters* cameraman and future Academy Award winner John Seale to shoot both the documentary and the feature film, if it was financed. We didn't have long to wait. The 1979 fire season commenced on December 17th. John and I got the call: Go to the Sydney City Helipad where a Hughes 300 helicopter awaits you. We changed into white overalls as part of the survival protocol to make it easier to find us in case the chopper had to make an emergency landing in thick bush. I gulped down a Cup-a-Soup from the vending machine while John helped the pilot take the door off the side of the chopper, then rig his Panaflex Gold from bungee cords. A Tyler mount, the usual method of shooting from a helicopter, was beyond our budget. We took off and headed for the coordinates we had been given for the location of the fire. As you have seen, I am an occasional magnet for Murphy's Law.

As we approached the ribbons of fire and smoke, we were struck by a weather phenomenon unique to Sydney known as a Southerly Buster, a hot wind from the south that can reach full intensity inside a minute

and is strong enough to capsize a yacht. This Southerly Buster caused the fire to back burn and fizzle out, ending our mission. However local airports including the City Helipad from which we had taken off were closed to all aviation till the wind had abated. Our pilot, cool and laconic as Australian aviators tend to be, simply turned the chopper into the wind and hovered pending instruction as to which airport to make for.

Despite being the son of a fighter pilot, I have not inherited my father's love of flying. As a child I would get carsick on long journeys. After ten minutes of buffeting, pitching and yawing, motion sickness set in. Soon the Cup-a-Soup was unhappy with its lodgings and anxious to leave. The pilot, while sympathetic, was under orders to maintain his position while other aircraft were diverted to different airports. He urged me to hold it. Well, there comes a time when you know that a Technicolor Yawn is inevitable. You have seconds to decide in which direction to point your mouth. I considered the options from left to right. Vomiting on a pilot while in flight is considered bad manners in Australia. Vomiting on the controls of an aircraft is also frowned upon. Vomiting on one of Australia's top cameramen…see rules relating to pilots. Additionally, John had taken the $200,000 Panaflex Gold with zoom lens off the bungy cords and was holding it securely across his lap. On my lap rested the spare magazines. No cups or paper towels. Not many choices left. So, when the time came, I leaned back as far as I could go and regurgitated in careful bursts onto my chest, while my perverse subconscious played the Barry McKenzie's song "Chunder in the Old Pacific Sea" in my head.

My companions were stoic, grateful no doubt that the flying vomitorium had one door removed. We were directed to land not at the city helipad, but at the light plane section of Sydney Airport. When we touched down, I asked the pilot where the nearest bathroom was so I could clean myself up a bit, before getting a cab to the city helipad were my regular clothes were. He pointed me towards a large hangar, advising that the bathrooms were at the back. I entered to find it full of office party revelers. At least a hundred of them. It was December 17th, midsummer in Australia. The extended Christmas party season was underway. Uniformed waiters offering wine, and trays of smoked salmon at an upscale bash for some aviation company, was now gatecrashed by a man in white overalls sporting a large stain from chin to groin, with some artistically placed food particles. The Ghost of Christmas Party Future had materialized as a warning to all those might over-indulge. I stammered some explanation, but guests looked away from a partygoer who clearly could not hold his liquor.

Finally reaching the bathroom, I succeeded in making the stain even bigger, but at least lighter in color. And particle free. Then came the task of calling a cab. In the height of the Christmas party season. An hour later a cab did arrive where I was waiting at the curb. The cabbie's eyes narrowed.

"I don't take drunks."

"I'm not drunk," I protested. "Just a little motion sickness."

He took me under sufferance. But anxious to be rid of Mr. Smelly in the back, he went like a bat out of hell for the City Heliport. The twists and turns reactivated the motion sickness, and I had to ask him to pull over.

"I bloody knew it," growled the cabbie.

The cab slewed to a halt, the back door flew open, and I slid along the plastic-lined seat, I wondered what I looked like to the passing traffic, several of whom honked their horns at the head and shoulders dry retching into the gutter. Today, it would be on Instagram in minutes.

Perhaps the best place for the telling of this tale is to fellow passengers on a helicopter in flight, which I did when sharing a ride with TV star Lindsay Wagner and her kids. We had finished a night of shooting on my killer virus melodrama *Voyage of Terror*, and were being flown from location back to the Vancouver helipad. Watching her kids howl with laughter at each icky detail was a joy.

A lightning strike had started a blaze which spread quickly. We chased it for two weeks. Fire behavior is unpredictable, as we found one late afternoon when the wind suddenly changed and the flames were on three sides of us. Ross Matthews, who was my UPM/1st AD, spun the station wagon around and we hightailed out of there at 90 mph. Ross had Grand Prix skills, which is no mean feat on Australian country roads.

We headed for the nearest fire engine which was located a few miles away defending a lone house on a ridge. The owner had sensibly cleared the brush in a wide radius around the property—another safety precaution the film promotes—so the situation did not look dire from a distance. As we arrived, we saw 70-foot flames sweeping along the opposite ridge. Gum trees well ahead of the fire front would suddenly explode in a process known as crowning, where sparks blown ahead would ignite the accumulated gum tree gases. A major blaze can accelerate at considerable speed when this happens. But from the faces of the volunteer fire fighters, we could tell they were not concerned. These were battle-hardened guys. They had hosed down the building, and were watching carefully for wind shifts. Nature obliged. The fire turned from

the ridge, down into the gully below, then up the slope towards us. What struck me more than the heat was the noise, like the roar of an approaching blast furnace.

I remember helping to steer John Seale, who was crouching low under a blanket, hand holding the Panaflex Gold, keeping pace with a burning carpet of hissing and crackling leaves that rolled towards us from the blazing tree line. The fire moved on, leaving the house unscathed. Over a 3-week period, it consumed 287,000 acres till it reached the Warragamba Dam, and burnt out at the water's edge.

I remember little of the editing. On Christmas Eve our first child, a boy, was stillborn in the fifth month of pregnancy. We sublimated our grief by throwing ourselves into work. Margaret had joined the cutting room team, and edge-numbered all the footage that came in each day. Those who have been through a stillbirth will understand what a painful period this was.

The eventual 20-minute theatrical documentary *Dangerous Summer*, was quite good, distinguished by spectacular scope photography from John Seale, Tom Cowan ( aerials) and Australia's leading female shooter at that time, Jan Kenny, who carried camera, lenses, and tripod across her back through burning landscapes as if they were a lunchbox in her knapsack. The documentary was shown in a few cinemas in the Blue Mountains and Sydney, and has never been transferred to DVD. The negative was cannibalized for use in the arson thriller *Dangerous Summer*. The NFSA has a 16mm print, but the original wide screen version is probably lost.

# CHAPTER 26
## *Día de los Assassinos*

A mistake I had made in this period was not to combine my British agent with a Hollywood agent who would have introduced me to all his contacts among LA producers. When you are a fresh face in town, you should get yourself about a bit. Relationships are key to an ongoing career. But I had focused entirely on Disney. It had seemed a perfect home for me. So when *Time Warp* stalled, I had nothing waiting in the wings. The first Hollywood agent to be interested in me was Ronnie Lief, who was well-connected, having been once married to the daughter of Universal Studio chief Lew Wasserman. Timing was perfect. He hooked me up with a US/Mexican coproduction that needed a director in a hurry. It would be my second international coproduction, a business arrangement designed, it seems, to foster mistrust between nations.

The producer on the American side, Ika Panajotovic, was in fact a Serbian attorney, who had enjoyed a distinguished tennis career. He was a Yugoslav Davis Cup player for eleven years, reaching the Wimbledon semi-finals in 1958. Then a serious car accident almost killed him. His leg was so badly injured, doctors wanted to amputate. Ika refused:

"I'd rather die than lose my leg."

Ika was a man of indomitable will. His leg healed sufficiently well for him to take a position as a coach at the Beverly Hills Tennis club. Many Hollywood actors played there. Ika had found his calling. He would become a low budget movie producer.

There were older stars on the downside of their careers who would accept starring or guest starring roles in foreign co-productions. Action-driven foreign markets would pay good money for unsophisticated genre fare, if they had even a faded US star on board. Quentin Tarantino referenced that

situation in *Once Upon a Time in Hollywood*. Often poorly dubbed, these movies, if released in America at all, would play a week in the grindhouses and drive-ins, mainly unreviewed by critics. The stars would pick up a nice chunk of change with negligible embarrassment. All Ika needed was a cheap script, and a star happy to get cash at the end of an overseas working holiday. Armed with that, Ika would find Yugoslav coproduction partners who would gladly fund the entire shoot in their native land, in return for local distribution, and a share in the international sales. Over eleven years Ika had put together five such pictures: *Bomb At 10:10*, starring George Montgomery, *Last Train to Berlin*, (Ty Hardin), *Partizan/Hell River* (Rod Taylor) *Operation Cross Eagles* (Rory Calhoun and Richard Conte, who also directed). All were shot in Yugoslavia, mostly by Yugoslav directors. The scripts were dumb and the productions looked cheap. Sales were OK but not great.

Ika knew he had to step up. He hired top TV director Leslie Martinson (who piloted the original *Mission Impossible* series) for an ambitious Germany/Italy/Spain/ USA/Iran co-production—variously titled as *Cruise Missile*, *The Tehran Incident* or *Missile X*, a Ludlum-esque spy thriller starring Peter Graves and Curt Jurgens. It was shot in Tehran eighteen months before Shah Reza Pahlavi—whom my father had once escorted around the RAF base at Odiham—was deposed. The strong cast had produced better sales, so Ika collected a gallery of names for his next production. Chuck Connors (*The Rifleman*) Glenn Ford (*Superman*) Richard Roundtree (*Shaft*) Henry Silva (*The Manchurian Candidate*) and Jill St. John (*Diamonds Are Forever*) would star in *Day of the Assassin* alongside top Mexican stars Jorge Rivero (the Latin Robert Redford), and Andres Garcia (the Latin Steve McQueen, very handy with firearms) again to be directed by Leslie Martinson.

The Mexican stars were also his coproduction partners, funding the entire cost of shooting in Mexico in return for Spanish and South American rights. Ika would get US/Canada distribution. Both partners would share other international sales 50/50. Ika's responsibility was to pay for the script, the imported stars' fees, post production in Los Angeles, and the director. Contracts were signed. Dates were set. Then Martinson bailed for a better offer when his deposit did not arrive. Ronnie Lief, who was Martinson's agent as well as mine, seized the opportunity and slotted me in. Big stars, thirty-five days of shooting! Gonna be a great movie…

A better movie might be a Coen Brothers rendition of what went on behind the scenes of *Day of the Assassins*…

All directors, at some point in their career trajectory, find themselves hanging on to a runaway train; despite best efforts, derailment threatens daily. More often than not, The Movie from Hell is a coproduction. Foreign locale, fast money, giant egos, high pressure schedule, all make a volatile witches' brew, even before you factor in deep-rooted national resentments.

Mexico, Spain, and the US were the funding partners, which meant that the Spaniards felt superior to their Mexican brothers, and the Americans felt superior to everybody. Each country gave undertakings to deliver certain elements of cast or crew. Disputes arose immediately. Because Leslie Martinson had bailed, Ika and his American co-producers, unbeknownst to me, described me, their replacement director, as "the man who made the last Bruce Lee movie," referring to the documentary I had made about the late Bruce Lee, *The World of Kung Fu*. The Mexicans thought they were getting *Enter the Dragon* director Robert Clouse. Their disappointment was palpable when this misrepresentation became clear on the first day of prep in Mexico City. Must say, my sphincter tightened a little, too. I had arrived in a war zone.

The next disappointment followed quickly. Designated leading lady Jill St. John, who had been charming to me on the phone, got tired of waiting for her deposit and took off for the ski slopes of Aspen. The Americans were in default. So Spanish coproducer Carlos Vassallo had the right to choose the replacement. He chose his wife, Susanah Dosamantes, a lovely and talented soap opera queen, still popular in Latin television today, but whose name would not generate the same foreign sales interest as the former Bond girl. Nonetheless he demanded she be paid Jill St. John's intended fee. The Americans ground their teeth.

Susanah's first shot required her to run to her getaway car across a parking lot paved with cobblestones. I set up a nice dynamic convergence dolly. Susanah insisted, because of the way she would look in a subsequent scene, on wearing impossibly high-heeled boots, against my advice. She sprained her ankle in the first rehearsal. Her husband blamed me. Naturally.

During pre-production, as the bullets continued to fly around me, I had something to look forward to. On Day One of shooting, I would be working with one of my screen heroes, Glenn Ford, already in the 40th year of his career, with so many memorable roles: *Gilda* (1946), *The Blackboard Jungle* (1955) the original *3:10 to Yuma* (1957), to name but three. His recent role as Superman's father in the Richard Donner movie had raised his profile. His fee was 100K for two days' work. Pricey, but his name would elevate the picture. He had also been promised that an actor friend of his, Taylor Lacher, would play a key supporting role. Unfortunately, the producers had also promised that role to the writer, Robert Avard Miller. He learned about it the day Mr. Ford arrived, and was summarily demoted to non-speaking villain number three.

Robert Miller was a decent man who had sustained a grievous loss, for which I felt deep sympathy. One night, while sitting beside me at a beachside bar in Ixtapa, he railed at the sky and challenged God to prove His Existence by striking him dead with a thunderbolt. Confronted by this outburst, I must confess that I shifted a little in my seat but counted on God's forbearance, or at least accuracy. But no Thunderbolt came. God had a more lingering fate in store for us: Death by Co-Production.

Glenn Ford arrived at the hotel. He was to play Christakis, a criminal mastermind who hires Chuck Connors for a dangerous mission. I was duly summoned to his suite and after cordial greeting was told that cue cards would be required for the big 6-page scene the next day. These cards would have lettering of a particular height and color; each of his lines must be preceded by the last three words of the other actor's last line in a different color. Margaret and I made the cue cards ourselves.

Arriving on location for Day One, Glenn Ford was not a happy camper. Probably because a tall campervan had been provided to him, instead of the promised trailer. Furthermore, it was parked at the side of a 6-lane highway beside the gate to the mansion location. The low arch over the gate prevented any vehicle above a certain height from entering. As I stepped inside, trucks thundered past, and the campervan shuddered. For some reason the American producers had vanished for the morning.

In addition to his unhappiness, Mr. Ford was also wearing dark glasses, which he announced he would be wearing throughout the scene.

"But, Sir, it's nearly seven pages long; you are only in one other scene when you are killed at the end of the film. The audience needs to see your eyes."

"I can't let my public sees these," he replied, taking off the dark glasses momentarily, revealing blood-shot eyes.

"What happened?"

"I was up all night in the bathroom. I'm a little better now. But I can't let them see these eyes."

I said we would get eyedrops immediately. How did he get Montezuma's revenge? Apparently, he had drunk the hotel tap water instead of the bottled water provided. In 1980 foreigners drank the local tap water at their peril, or to achieve rapid weight loss. Everybody knew this. Glenn Ford had done five pictures in Mexico during his career.

"But I like hot water…" was his explanation.

Make the star happy was the priority. I tried to get him a room in the mansion instead of the camper, but the company had hired only the large glass atrium to the building. The rest of the place was off limits and the owners were away. It took till lunchtime to get him a room in the house. In the meantime, we had to shuttle him back and forth along the driveway from the marooned campervan. The Atrium was floor to ceiling glass providing a 360-degree view of the mansion grounds. But at 4 p.m. the sun would go behind an adjacent building and the light in that direction would not match anything shot before. Nonetheless, I started shooting everything I could for as long as possible without actually showing whether he was wearing dark glasses or not, in the hope I could persuade him that his eyes were back to normal. I cited several points in the dialogue where he could shed them for dramatic reasons. The eyedrops made the redness recede but not sufficiently for Mr. Ford. The American producers, whose problem-solving technique was "Stay away, it'll blow over," returned. They did not care about the audience seeing Glenn Ford's eyes. They only cared about his name on the poster. I was falling behind for no good reason, just another director jerking off. Now both sets of producers hated me.

I was determined to get those glasses off. I went to see Mr. Ford in the room we had procured for him. He had eaten his lunch, and was lying on a sofa looking very depressed. Sitting down in a chair beside him, I started by apologizing for the campervan. This induced a sad litany of woe about his conditions, rate of pay, etc.

"I have never been treated like this," he said, expressing concern he was still feeling ill—and more seriously, experiencing a lack of confidence in his ability to play the scene, whereupon tears trickled down his cheeks.

Something made me think of my own father. I would hate to see him so unhappy. Or any man of that age. So I sat down on the sofa, and put my arms around him. I remember I said soothing words that I cannot recall while a Hollywood legend wept on my chest. About fifteen seconds later, he was feeling better. I got up, assured him with confidence that the scene would be great. Knowing, of course, that it would be at best a boring scene, full of convoluted exposition, functionally shot due to time constraints. You mean directors lie to their cast? Shocking. Finally Glenn Ford agreed he would take his glasses off at the very end of the scene. As I hurried off, Chuck Connors (TV's stalwart hero *The Rifleman*: 1958-63) who was playing opposite Glenn Ford in the scene, came in to see how he was. I left them to talk.

This was the first of several times that Chuck was my guardian angel. At the end of the lunch break, both men emerged from the room, Chuck his usual breezy self, but Glenn Ford noticeably brighter. No mention of sickness. Keen to work. Even jocular. We raced through the coverage facing the windows just in time to beat the sun. The eagle-eyed can see Mr. Ford reading his lines from the cue cards at times, despite the dark glasses. The glasses finally did come off at the end of the scene. The eyes had lost their redness. Glenn Ford's fanbase was saved from trauma. My difficulties were compounded by a fractious relationship with the Spanish DP. Neither of us knew more than a few words of each other's language. *Day of The Assassins* was my personal *Lost In Translation*.

"Well done, you beat the set," said Chuck, as we wrapped, triggering a blank look from me, reeling from the horrible Day One of 35.

"Every day the set tries to beat you," the veteran of countless TV episodes continued, "weather, lighting delays, sound problems, actor problems…sometimes it does, sometimes it don't. I saw the shit you were dealing with. You beat the set. Well done, kid."

Later Chuck told me he'd offered Mr. Ford one of his amazing stomach settling pills he always brought to Mexico.

"Is it natural?" Glenn Ford had asked.

"Totally," Chuck Connors had said, handing him some speed. It always fixed a sick or insecure actor.

Glenn Ford was in good spirits on arrival for Day Two of the *Assassins* shoot, his last scene in the picture. It also involved Taylor Lacher, the actor Ford had brought with him. They had become buddies on the set of *Cade's County*, a high profile but short-lived series in 1971.

I had actually visited the *Cade's County* set when I was promo director for Sydney's Channel Nine and had watched Mr. Ford do a brief scene with Taylor Lacher. Little did I know then, as I observed Mr. Lacher discreetly from the sidelines, this actor would, nine years later, spit on the ground in front of me as a gesture

of his contempt for a creative decision I had made. My directing style does not normally produce this kind of response, by the way. Later in the shoot I would repay the compliment with a set of full load blood squibs for Lacher's demise.

Day Two was to shoot the remainder of Glenn Ford's scenes and to finish early so trucks could take off for the next location in Ixtapa. Low page count, get it done by lunch…

So, fast forward to…Taylor Lacher has to pull a gun, harangue Glenn Ford, then shoot him. As I set up the first shot, an argument broke out between Mr. Ford and one of the producers, the one who had persuaded Glenn Ford to accept a paltry 100K for what was now going to be one and a half day's work. It degenerated into name calling, hissed loudly at each other while the Spanish-speaking crew worked around them as if nothing was going on. The first few set ups went smoothly enough, then came the actual gun firing moment. When he saw the armorer load the pistol, Mr. Ford's mood changed. He came to me agitated, stating that he had a mortal fear of firearms. Puzzling, I thought, given the number of westerns he had made, including *The Fastest Gun Alive* (1956). By reputation he had the fastest draw of any Hollywood actor, firing at 0.4 of a second faster than John Wayne or *Gunsmoke's* James Arness. Glenn Ford had been a Rear Admiral in the Naval Reserve. In 1967, he volunteered to serve three months in Vietnam, spending some of his time under bombardment, and accompanying five special forces missions. So what's the problem with the quarter load blanks? He took up hang gliding at the age of sixty-four, for God's sake!

As he was costumed in his own clothes (another brilliant money-saving decision by the American producers), he was not prepared to be squibbed. He begged me to allow him not to be in any shot in which the gun was fired. I had hoped to have him pumped full of lead Peckinpah-style. So much for that wild idea. I looked to a producer. He shrugged and walked off. Brave, brave, Sir Robin.

Of course, actors have a right to be nervous around firearms. The tragic loss of Brandon Lee has since become a safety lesson to the whole industry. You pick your battles. This was not one of them. So, I set it up with the simplest coverage:

Wide profile shot: Lacher points unloaded gun at Ford.

Big closeup of the gun firing.

Cut to Glenn Ford clutching his chest dropping out of frame.

Cut to a low wide 2-shot. He completes the fall, etc. Boring, but gotta shoot.

When I called "Cut" on that shot, Mr. Ford got up and approached me, beaming from ear to ear. He put one arm round my shoulder to hug me.

"Oh, thank you, thank you so much for doing that, I really appreciate it," I recall him saying.

Then I felt his other hand cup my balls and give them a quick but gentle squeeze. It was over in a flash.

I flinched, disguising my gasp as a big laugh, Whoa! Ho Ho! Just jocular locker room humor, nothing to see here, folks. Of course, I did not think Glenn Ford was gay. He had brought with him wife number three (out of a total of four), actress Cynthia Hayward, also a cast member from *Cade's County*. She treated my wife, another beautiful but younger woman, with lofty disdain. There was in fact nothing sexual in Mr. Ford's act of testicular solidarity, rather it was a demonstration of power, a direct metaphor for our relationship during his brief days of work. He had me by the short and curlies the entire time. Perhaps it was a parting handshake for satisfactory service. So the only way to take it was as a compliment. How many directors have the privilege of getting their balls squeezed by a star from Hollywood's Golden Age in front of the entire crew? I am deeply blessed.

This was a movie made without a completion guarantor, but with a plethora of executive producers, some of whom felt entitled to give the director conflicting notes. Their ranks expanded weekly, as the Americans sought to repair their cash flow crisis by offering potential investors executive producer credits, and a holiday trip to our Ixtapa hotel. All were given to me to look after, like lost dogs.

"Hang out with the director. Ask him anything you like." Which they would sometimes do in the middle of a take.

As relations between the coproduction partners worsened, Margaret and I wondered what might happen if the production collapsed. Because we had arrived at short notice without a work visa, our passports were taken from us for visa processing "…just for a few days." Two weeks into the shoot, they showed no sign of returning. Margaret and I developed a contingency plan should our passports be frozen because of some legal dispute. We would take a bus to Juarez and phone Margaret's brother Rick, a former El Paso police detective, who would drive across the border and collect us.

Chuck Connors had a huge crush on my wife. In my presence, he would occasionally pretend to be a vampire and try to bite her on the neck. Indeed, she had a lovely neck. It was as close as he would ever come, he said, to playing a vampire on the screen, which was in truth his heart's desire. But a hit western series had typed him solely for gun-carrying roles. Even though his politics was to the right of Attila The Hun, we got on famously. He was a true Hollywood Character. A former Brooklyn Dodger, Chuck was often guest sports commentator on NBC till he accidentally dropped the 'F Bomb' during a primetime live telecast, startling the nation, and endearing him further to his male fanbase. Chuck told us not to worry about our passports. He was an honorary Treasury Department Agent, a rank awarded to him because of the Department's affection for *The Rifleman* series. The Treasury Department windbreaker he wore in the movie was a gift from them. He would make a phone call if necessary, and we would be home.

Matters finally came to a head in the sixth and last week. Still no passports, and the Spanish producer Carlos Vassallo wanted the hero (Chuck) to participate in an armed robbery of a security truck and shoot the unresisting guards. I pointed out the damage to audience identification with the hero. So I was fired. Vassallo took over the last few days of the shoot, and gave himself codirector credit in the territories he had sales rights to. Chuck just gave me that *It's Chinatown* look.

Later he commiserated with me that night over wine and cocaine. I did not develop a taste for the latter, unlike many of my contemporaries in that period. In vino, veritas. In white powder, hubris. I prefer vino.

Passports were returned, and back in LA, I was cut out of the editing (it shows). Before long, we got a call from Chuck to see how we were. He did not drop us, as many might have. We would meet occasionally for lunch before I returned to Australia two years later. Once he picked me up in his Mercedes, with a photo medallion of the Pope hanging from the rearview mirror, and a 357 Magnum in a cowboy holster mounted on the passenger side of the drive shaft, ready for a quick draw. Once a Rifleman, always a Rifleman.

# CHAPTER 27
## *Blood Tide*

My next gig took me to London. A British film investment company had a problem. Their film *Red Tide*, shot on a photogenic Greek island, had left unpaid bills. While much of the picture negative had been transferred to the custody of the producers in London, the last weeks of shooting was frozen in an Athens laboratory until payment was made. But there were no funds left. Somehow the production company had run out of money and the Athens lab would not budge. Deadlock.

I met with the investment company and proposed a 10-minute promo reel to be made from the footage they had. The promo would screen at the Cannes Film Market a couple of months away. Buyers generally pay a 10% deposit on signature. So by the end of the market they would have enough cash to pay the Greek debts, recover the missing negative, then with a bit more investment they could fund post production and finish the movie. They told me to go ahead and watch the pennies.

I worked with Gerry Hambling, Oscar-nominated director Alan Parker's longtime editor (*Midnight Express*), to make the footage as commercially appealing as possible. The 35mm promo (using the same technique adopted for the *Harlequin* promo) was delivered to Cannes, and it did the trick. Buyers signed up, put money down. The Athens lab were paid and released the missing negative. Mission accomplished!

Then the investors asked me to take over postproduction. For whatever reason they had lost faith in both the producer and the director and wanted me to finish the picture without their involvement. I had no idea who was at fault. But I did sight the writer/director's contract with the producer, which imposed on him the most exploitative terms for a mere 15K, and locked the producer into the director's next two scripts. Outrageous. I had only met the director briefly at the LA screening of the promo. This must have been a terrible blow to him. After being denied the editing of *Day of the Assassins* I could relate to his pain.

I suggested changing *Red Tide* to *Blood Tide*. Does subtlety sell tickets? Though clearly subtlety was what the director was aiming for. It was well-acted. The shooting style was classical, well composed but static. The pacing was measured. On first assembly, it was not a bad movie. It just did not seem to be very suspenseful or horrific.

The movie's premise: An ancient Greek monster, hungry for virgin sacrifice is roused from its island grotto by a Shakespeare-quoting treasure hunter (James Earl Jones). People die. The monster goes back to the sea. Really?

The film had pedigree names in the supporting cast—Jose Ferrer (*Lawrence of Arabia*), Lila Kedrova (*Zorba the Greek*) plus up-and-comers Deborah Shelton, (De Palma's *Body Double*) and Martin Cove (The *Karate Kid* nemesis). The problem was it was a monster picture without a monster. The monster is talked about, but remains totally unseen. I wondered what their plan for this key element had been.

I proposed mounting a 4-man crew, and creating some additional horror visuals. How about the forearm of a dead victim being picked at by a crab at the water's edge? (A shot that would return to haunt me nearly twenty years later.) How about getting Deborah Shelton waking up from a dream full of bizarre images that are either freshly created or lifted from angles not used in the cut? Fairly standard enhancements, or detractions, depending on your point of view, but it might give the movie more bite. So we built a clawed arm of the creature plus a separate head and shoulders intended only to be seen in silhouette. We did some underwater photography with doubles off Catalina Island, then blew up the monster's head and shoulders in slow motion in a pond at the pyro guy's premises, where explosions were licensed. I probably did not make the film appreciably better, but I did make it more commercial. Menahem Golan's new company 21st Century Films, acquired the rights some years later.

Margaret was now pregnant again. Following a threatened miscarriage in the first trimester, her obstetrician had prescribed total bedrest for the last six months of pregnancy. So I had become the shopper and the cook, roles I enjoyed and still do. I felt like a contributor to our child's development, more than a mere onlooker. At lunchtime, I would leave the cutting room where I was reshaping *Blood Tide* to bring sushi and sandwiches to my recumbent wife. Lying on her left side for half a year, Margaret became understandably stir crazy. Her brother Paul and his wife Susan, then living in LA, helped her to maintain sanity by diverting her with games, novels and good company.

# PART V
## RETURN TO OZ

# CHAPTER 28
## Ozploitation

Anthony I. Ginnane is Australia's most prolific film producer, with over seventy credits. . He wrote, produced, and directed his first feature "Sympathy in Summer" in 1970. when he was 19. A genuine movie lover, he studied law at Melbourne University, and used those skills to raise money for movies he would produce. At twenty-four he had his first film on release—*Fantasm*, a softcore documentary about Hollywood's hardcore porn industry, made for 50K. It was hugely successful. Tony was able to leverage government funding to finance a slate of movies to be directed by up-and-coming TV directors Simon Wincer, Richard Franklin, and Rod Hardy. Tony was a fan of *The Man from Hong Kong* and had me in mind for something down the line. In the meantime, I made all his trailers. We bonded over our mutual love of Cinema, from Trash to Art. When I got back from the London gig, he gave me an American screenplay called *Turkey Shoot*.

Set in the Deep South of the United States, the script of *Turkey Shoot* was a genre hybrid. A blend of *I Was A Fugitive from A Chain Gang* (1931) and *Cool Hand Luke* (1968) played for seventy pages, followed by forty pages of *The Most Dangerous Game* (1932), a classic that spawned a quite a few hunt-the-humans derivatives, *The Naked Prey* (1966) being my favorite. Tony wanted to set it up as an Australian film enjoying the benefits available under Division 10 BA of the tax code. Obviously, the American 1930s setting would not fly, besides being costly and potentially unconvincing. My recommendation was: set it in a dystopian corporate fascist Australia, where celebrities and bureaucrats can hunt political prisoners for sport with impunity. A genre cocktail in which *Nineteen Eighty-Four* (1956) meets Hammer's *The Camp on Blood Island* (1958) and they play *The Most Dangerous Game* (1932). Make it fast-paced, big, bold and bloody. Tony bought it. Two new writers were hired to work with me (Jon George & Neill Hicks), resulting in an action-packed script that started doing the rounds of distributors.

The phone rang one evening. It was Tony Ginnane. I hoped it was news on *Turkey Shoot*. It was not.

Some background: Tony Ginnane and his partner William Fayman had started a new company, bringing in British actor David Hemmings as a third partner. Hemmings had been a star name in the mid-1960s, having played Mordred in *Camelot*, and starred in Antonioni's multi award winning mystery *Blow Up*, and MGM's big budget *Alfred The Great*. Although mainly a star character actor by 1980, Hemmings' name and Hollywood connections gave the new company an international image.

*Race for the Yankee Zephyr*, an action comedy written by the prolific Everett De Roche, was their first production. As you know, nothing is easy in this business. Australian Actors Equity had begun to oppose the importation of foreign actors for leading roles in an Australian film because it denied Australian actors the opportunity to be seen on international screens. Tony's *Harlequin* had brought in two actors from the UK, Robert Powell and the aforementioned David Hemmings along with Academy Award winner Broderick Crawford from the US. This time around Actors Equity blocked visas for *Zephyr*'s proposed imported stars Ken Wahl, Leslie Anne Warren, George Peppard, and Donald Pleasance. So Tony moved the picture to New Zealand, where there were no such restrictions.

However, the designated director Richard Franklin did not like the change of location and resigned. Everett De Roche then adapted the script for Queenstown, an adventure tourism resort in the South Island of NZ and David Hemmings took over as director. A few weeks into the shoot, Hemmings was falling behind schedule, and showed no sign of making the necessary compromises to catch up.

This put Tony in a difficult position between his partner and a nervous completion guarantor. In the next week the issue would be coming to the boil, which motivated Tony's call. Would I come down to Queenstown and help out, or take over directing the picture if Hemmings left? This posed a dilemma. When I explained that Margaret was pregnant and confined to bed and completely dependent on my help, Tony decently offered to fly in Margaret's sister Robbie as a support while I was away. It was a hard decision, but Margaret insisted I take the gig.

Ostensibly I was in Queenstown to discuss the *Turkey Shoot* project, but I was also there to take over as director, if the impasse with David Hemmings could not be resolved. In Mark Hartley's documentary *Not Quite Hollywood*, Vincent Monton, Zephyr's director of photography, makes an enigmatic allusion to this possibility. I was asked to hang around my hotel for the first couple of days to avoid bumping into David Hemmings. We had met once before when I showed the *Harlequin* promo to Tony Ginnane accompanied by Hemmings and Carmen Duncan, fresh off the redeye from Perth at 9 a.m. Hemmings thought the promo should just be a selection of scenes. No narration. I felt that having a narrator plugging information gaps would help buyers from non-English speaking territories engage with the story. Subtlety is not your friend in market promos, if you want them to pre-buy. Hemmings wanted to play with the footage himself. I pointed out that any delay could jeopardize the delivery date, knowing that was a sacred cow. Two alpha dogs politely butting heads. I don't think Hemmings and I clicked that day. Nor were we ever likely to if I were to take over *Race for the Yankee Zephyr*.

There are no secrets on location. Hemmings heard about my arrival and shot the next day's call sheet on time and continued to do so throughout the week. Soon it was clear I was not needed. Before I was sent back, I was brought to where *Zephyr* was shooting for the official reason for my visit—discussions about *Turkey Shoot*, on which Hemmings would be the supervising producer and 2nd Unit Director. He knew the real reason for my visit. We ignored the elephant in the room, but the relationship would be a bumpy ride. A pity, because David Hemmings was a multitalented man, a charming raconteur, with a wealth of Hollywood stories, like "I remember on *Eye of The Devil* when Kim Novak got so angry with Marty Ransohoff (producer) she tried to stub her cigarette out in his good eye…" We should have hit it off. But it was not to be. I returned to LA, privately relieved. Now I could be present for the last months of Margaret's pregnancy.

On April 25th our son Eric was born at Cedar Sinai Hospital Los Angeles (thanks, Writers Guild!). Due to complications, he was born by caesarian section, which I was allowed to witness after signing an indemnity form. On a previous occasion an anxious father, standing at the head of the operating table, holding his wife's hand, had fainted at the sight of her stomach being cut open, fracturing his skull on the tiled floor. But I was confident that everything would turn out well. And it did. Eric was born weighing 7 pounds, 11 ounces. I cannot adequately express our feelings of joy as he was laid freshly swaddled beside Margaret. Eight days later I had to leave to start prep for *Turkey Shoot* in Australia. It was a wrench but Margaret and Eric would follow eight weeks later when it was safe for a newborn to fly.

David Hemmings had told me the film would be shot in the state whose film commission offered the best incentives. South Australia would mean a desert setting. Queensland would provide jungle, which was my visual preference. And Queensland it was, scheduled to start prep early in May 1981. Cairns, a coastal tourist town in the tropical north, was selected as our production base. When I arrived to start prep, I found that Hemmings had already chosen the site for the prison camp an hour's drive away at Babinda, officially the wettest town in Australia with an average annual rainfall of 4279.4 millimeters. That's wet. Construction quickly bogged down in the mud which put paid to my desire to shoot in story order; all the prison camp scenes first, ground the cast in their characters, then continue with the hunt. Now I had to do the second half of the movie first to give enough time for the camp to be completed. Then our real problems began.

The 10 BA tax incentives of 150% for investors in Australian films had unleashed a flood of taxpayers eager to turn their liability into internationally liquid copyright. But the government quickly flinched at the significant drain on the Treasury this incentive would generate, so they cut it back to 133% early in our prep. Some investors who had not yet paid in their promised funds balked at the reduction so the budget kept shrinking as the shoot date approached. There were fixed costs that could not be reduced: contracted fees for creatives and stars. Savings had to be made from below-the-line items. I kept modifying the scale and number of set-piece action scenes to trim the original 44-day schedule to thirty 10-hour days. 300 camera hours.

Cut were the first ten pages set in an Orwellian city where the heroes are captured in a series of chases. Instead I had to start the film as they arrive at the prison camp. To remedy the loss of the 1984 scenes, I designed an opening title sequence welding news footage into a multi panel montage of violent clashes with police across the globe. Ironically, it's a better start to the picture, tying a dystopian fantasy to contemporary issues. Sometimes a silver lining...

Next, a 4-page helicopter chase weaving through forests and canyons had to go, along with its pilot character, the aerial hunter, to be played by TV personality Graham Kennedy. Terms could not be agreed. (He wanted 50K. Sorry.) That hurt. He had some great lines. It meant that I had to distribute his plot function to other characters in the chase. This reduced a 94 page script to 70. I made stuff up every shooting day to fill out the contracted running time. But all the action I came up with had to be achieved without incurring loadings for any stuntmen beyond their daily flat fee.

The prison camp was big. Its dimensions had been determined by the original bigger budget. For the parade ground to look full, it needed 250 extras, but now we could only afford seventy-five on our biggest day. This is where Camp Commandant Thatcher (Michael Craig, perfect in the part) addresses the assembled inmates with Orwellian doublespeak: "Freedom is obedience. Obedience is work. Work is Life." This is followed by Roger Ward as the Guard from Hell monstering innocent prisoner Oriana Panozzo, which, I learned, was Quentin Tarantino's favorite scene, when I met him at a Hollywood party fifteen years later.

Low budget taught me how to maximize extras in crowd scenes. Anchor the camera at the center of things, where Thatcher meets the newbies (Steve Railsback, Olivia Hussey, Lynda Stoner), and shoot outwards. All the wide shots in this scene on both sides of the axis featured every extra we had, filling out the background in a wedge formation. Triangles gave more depth to the crowd than a square or wall of bodies. The illusion of another wedge of seventy-five inmates just out of frame behind camera was created by placing a triangle of six extras in foreground at the edge of the shot. When I changed angle to the reverse perspective, I moved the front people to the back of the wedge and vice versa. It worked.

The budget shortfall meant we could not afford the finale in which futuristic aircraft strafe and bomb the camp. We could afford to blow up the camp, but not show who is doing it. Matte shots with miniatures of the aircraft was also beyond our means. The only solution was stock footage. The Film Australia library had 35mm footage of Australian Air Force Mirages practicing low level bombing runs. It bumped up to anamorphic just fine. I ignored the issue of why a future authoritarian regime would be using obsolete fighter jets to put down prison rebellions. These were impressive shots of aircraft thundering past camera close to the ground in terrain that matched the prison camp. Luckily, there was a stock shot of a plane releasing a bomb which provided the connective tissue to the explosions we shot demolishing all the camp buildings. The pyrotechnics were supervised by John Stears, who had performed similar duties on the early Bond movies, and shared an Academy Award for special effects on the original *Star Wars*.

I'm often asked about Alf (Steve Rackman), the mutant beast that Tito found in a circus and brings to the hunt. Alf was intended to be a kind of *Island of Dr. Moreau* human/animal hybrid, requiring elaborate prosthetic make up. Time in the makeup chair, time on the set. Time is money. Our budget shortfall meant that we could only afford hair pieces, gnarly false teeth, and weird contact lenses. His top hat added the final touch. As I pushed the envelope of the exploitation elements in the piece, I recognized the inherent absurdity of some of those genre tropes I was celebrating. Without the spectacular action set pieces, how could I make this linear story stand out from other low budget fare? I increased the level of blood and black-hearted laughs into a sort of Lucio Fulci-inspired high-camp splatter movie. Blood is cheap.

One of my more hilarious memories was the day we cut Steve Rackman in half at the trouser-belt level with a bulldozer. I wanted a shot of his bottom half, kneeling trapped against a tree, wriggling beneath the dozer blade (OK, I am a sick puppy). We had the pants suspended by monofilament, but we were running short on prosthetics. We had eaten sausages and steak for lunch and there were uncooked leftovers and lots of ketchup, so everyone pitched in to fill the Traveling Pants with a convincing set of innards, and squirt individually designed trails of tomato sauce. The things we do for Art.

The film is far from perfect. But, I argue, in a fun way. All filmmakers find themselves in situations where the playing field develops potholes, and the goalposts shift. You have to adjust. Ultimately, from a business standpoint, a good movie is a salable movie. And it was. Turkey Shoot was released theatrically across the world and became a strong seller on international home video. It was in due course profitable and became a cult movie after a new generation clicked with its dark sense of humor. The latest release is a 2-disc beautifully remastered Blu Ray. I've heard that the German language version (entitled *Island of the Damned*) captures the satirical flavor well.

Sadly, my relationship with David Hemmings deteriorated during the shoot. On wrap, after a hard shooting day, I nursed a beer in the production office. Margaret, freshly arrived from Los Angeles, joined me with our 9-week-old son Eric in her arms. Hemmings approached. After being introduced to Margaret, he bent forward and cooed over our baby.

"Nine weeks old?" he said, "He's much more mature than his father."

I poured beer over his bent head. Don't use my newborn son as a means of mocking me in front of my wife.

Taken aback, beer dripping from his chin, he spluttered: "Was that really necessary?!"

"Just demonstrating my maturity."

Not my finest hour.

# CHAPTER 29
## *BMX Bandits*

Despite the continuing changes to the tax incentives, film production in Australia was ramping up. Offers of promotional work increased at the beginning of the year, so we let our Beverly Hills apartment go and moved back to Sydney. I anticipated that soon I would be directing the arson thriller version of *Dangerous Summer*, that would use the footage I had shot for the documentary. But the producers and the financing company Filmco, which had financed *Turkey Shoot*, chose Quentin Masters, whose UK movie *The Stud* with Joan Collins, had been a big success all over Europe. (*Dangerous Summer*, released in the US as *Flashfire* did not prosper at the box office.) But Filmco, in addition to keeping me busy with their trailers, said they wanted to find a feature vehicle for me. Several other productions sought me as director pending finance. It was just a matter of time.

Then, prior to its theatrical release, producer Tony Ginnane entered *Turkey Shoot* into the Australian Film Institute Awards of 1982. When the film was screened before the voting membership normally accustomed to more high-minded fare, there was much clutching of pearls and moral outrage.

"How could you?" hissed an actress I knew well as the audience filed out.

Quite a few had scuttled for the exit early, fleeing what one pundit described as "a litany of horrors." Some thought that after *Turkey Shoot* my career in Australian features was over, that I should just stick to making trailers. But in fact *Turkey Shoot*'s action scenes influenced producers Tom Broadbridge and Paul

Davies to approach me to direct *BMX Bandits*. They had hooked up with Melbourne's Nilsen Group of companies, who had a bigger than expected tax liability that year. I can imagine the pitch: Put the $1.1M tax you will be obligated to pay into a kids' action comedy film and earn a generous tax credit, you'll get your investment back and more besides. They did. Eventually.

I persuaded producers Broadbridge and Davies to move the picture from Williamstown, Melbourne to the North Shore of Sydney, which offered greater visual opportunities through the anamorphic lens; beachside streets, harbor views, ocean views, and the slides at the Manly Waterworks, an ideal location for my approach: put BMX bikes where BMX bikes are not meant to be! So I rewrote the action scenes for specific locations. The owners of Warringah Shopping Mall, who had allowed me to run amok with a dune buggy on their property for *Death Cheaters*, were only too happy to let me do it again, this time with bicycles. A marina, a golf course, a football field with a game in progress, all lent scale to the chase sequences. If you don't have much money, find exterior locations that are cheap or free, but have high production value backgrounds.

The script originally had 10-year-old heroes, but the producers sensibly commissioned a rewrite making them between fifteen and sixteen. The writing team of Russell Hagg and Patrick Edgeworth gave the teenagers a lot of wry wit: "Two's company. Three gets us talked about." I needed a trio of newcomers who had chemistry. Angelo D'Angelo as the ever-positive PJ and James Lugton as the cynical Goose were the obvious choices at the auditions, as was then 15-year-old Nicole Kidman. There were concerns that she was taller than the two boys and skinny. Who cares? I said. She has a striking look, a shock of frizzy red hair, good instincts with dialogue, and the camera will love her. It did, in the capable hands of future Academy Award winner John Seale. His skill with available light and his innate sense of composition were once again a great help to me.

Not only did the camera love her, so did the whole cast and crew. At the dawn of her career, she knew she had talent but was as yet unaware of her personal charisma. Standup comics David Argue and John Ley, who played the bumbling criminals pursuing her, would jokingly, but with affection, refer to her as "the

mop" because of her hair, or "the bean pole" in relation to her physique. In fact, we could not find a skilled BMX stunt girl as slender as Nicole so we used an 18-year-old boy with a wig under the helmet.

Despite a budget of only $1.1M, *BMX Bandits* gave me more shooting time than I had on any other picture. Forty-one days. School hours for Nicole and Angelo and other cast members who were still fifteen at the start of production had to be accommodated within the schedule. I was blessed by a resourceful line producer, Brian Burgess, who had been Alfred Hitchcock's production manager on *Frenzy*. Everyone was excited by the project. There was a palpable energy on the set, which fed my own energy. You remember such shoots, because it isn't always that way.

Bob Hicks, one of the car chase team on *MFHK*, was now a stunt coordinator, so we hired him to oversee safety and handle the stunt driving in the extended chase sequence. Helmets were worn whenever a bike was in motion. Our young heroes were doubled by top BMX performers for anything other than simple riding. All the stunt riders did great work. No one was hurt riding, but on the last shot of the second night of the shoot, Nicole sprained her ankle jumping into an open grave in the cemetery sequence. She felt her first take was "wimpy" and asked to do it again. I should have said no. But she did make the shot better. Her foot was quickly strapped up by the unit nurse and I drove her home. As this was only the second day of shooting, Nicole was concerned I would have to replace her, now she was unable to ride for her first bike sequence the next day.

I assured her we would move scenes around till she was healed enough to peddle again. I explained how stunt doubling works, how action is broken into different angles, some to be performed by the actor, others by the professional trained in the particular maneuver required. I took her home and apologized to her parents for "breaking" their daughter. They were understanding. It was not a bad sprain, and she was limp free and peddling well within a few days. The shoot continued with no further mishaps.

*The Man from Hong Kong* car chase shows an affection for rig shots. This is where the camera is secured to the side of a vehicle, close to a wheel, with a limpet mount, as low to the road as possible, thus strapping the audience onto potential impact zones of the chase, and generating an adrenalin-charging effect. A combination of forward and backward facing mounts show the proximity of the vehicles in a dynamic way. I

wanted to apply the same car chase technique to BMX scenes. Today clamping on a 4K Go-Pro easily provides such a shot. Back then, mounting a 35mm camera, even one as light as an Arri 2C, behind a pounding pedal as the bike weaves past obstacles, was a challenge, because of its effect on the balance of the bike. So we came up with a way to rig a matching counter weight on the other side that corrected the bias. It took strenuous peddle power from our stunt riders to compensate for the added twenty pounds and get the bike up to speed, but it worked well, adding a lot to the BMX action.

My favorite traveling shots of the movie are the ones sliding with the kids and their bikes down the twisting tunnel of the Manly Waterworks Slide. At one point, a chase rampages throughout the Warringah Mall, through cafes, shops, over a fountain and finally down an escalator. As our heroes on bikes emerge from the escalator, they pass our tow-headed 2-year-old son Eric, who delivers the line: "BMX! Wow!" This experience seems to have had a profound effect. Later life Eric would become a formidable cyclist, completing the 205-mile Seattle to Portland ride in ten hours flat.

Australia's major distributors Greater Union and Roadshow did not grasp the popularity of the BMX craze, and turned the picture down as too niche. Filmways picked it up. Local audiences delivered an excellent box office result in six weeks at only daytime sessions with mainly half-price tickets. It did good business in the UK and Japan but the US distributor went belly up during the fumbled theatrical release. In the end, American kids only saw a cropped center cut image on VHS or cable TV. US fans recall as kids they would skip school early to catch the movie over and over again on HBO or Showtime or the Disney Channel, all of which programmed it repeatedly in the mid-1980s. Australian kids would play the VHS till it literally wore out. The current widescreen Blu Ray is a beautiful color-popping transfer and the best way to rediscover the movie in its intended aspect ratio.

Some reviewers criticized my cartoonish approach to *BMX Bandits*. Why wasn't it more of a realistic kid thriller? Shouldn't the crooks be realistically threatening, so the audience genuinely worries about the fate of the young heroes? But I wanted to capture the good-humored spirit of the Ealing comedies I enjoyed growing up, and apply it to Australia's new BMX culture, to make a fun family holiday movie. If you look at the basic premise of the plot, the crooks clearly want to kill the children at some point, so how do you make that palatable to an audience of kids and parents? Particularly if you must get a 'G' rating. You make the crooks buffoonish, the gang that couldn't shoot straight. Though in retrospect, the closeups of the bank robbers loading their guns was a tonal lapse. I am surprised in retrospect that the moment where John Ley menaces Nicole with a flick knife was allowed for unrestricted exhibition. I would have cut it if necessary. The current video release is rated PG .

My approach was to deliver laughs and gasps for the core audience of 8 to 14-year-olds, a neglected yet ever-renewing generation with a partiality to pratfall comedy. Show the heroes riding wherever they wished, getting the better of adults, every Australian kid's dream for the summer holidays. There were deliberately no parents in the film. Yet parents still enjoy watching it with their kids. Its longevity is due to an enduring charm, a throwback to a romanticized childhood, before texting and Instagram took over from unstructured, unsupervised outdoor exercise.

In their Blu Ray interview, the producers thought Nicole Kidman did well, but admitted they hadn't seen stardom in her future. Somehow, I had. She had a striking look, strong dramatic instincts, evident drive, but so do many actors. What would make Nicole stand out in such a competitive field? I had a gut feeling. When filming was over, her parents asked me privately whether I thought she had a future in the acting profession, about which she was passionate, to the apparent detriment of her schoolwork. I told them that normally I discourage young people from choosing such a career. I still do. The combined membership of AFTRA/ Screen Actors Guild in the US has about 116,000 "active" members. Statistically very, very, few people make a living from acting, let alone a good living. It is a profession of constant and arbitrary rejection; not for the faint of heart. But Nicole had something special, I said, and she should go for it. They were encouraged by my opinion.

*BMX Bandits* was screened to Australian Film Institute members for awards consideration. I called June Cann, the leading actors' agent in Sydney, telling her that there were some newcomers she should look at. She took on Nicole and Angelo D'Angelo the next day. I had hoped to score a trifecta because I thought James Lugton's deadpan comedy timing had potential. I am pleased that he went on to a good career in journalism.

*BMX Bandits* won the *Prix Chouette des samedis du Cinéma* in Brussels in 1985. A hardworking Australian diplomat carried the 8-kg (nearly 18 lbs.) bronze owl statue to Australia in his personal luggage. (Thanks once again!)

I showed the movie privately to Doug Netter, the Disney Channel executive on the *Five Mile Creek* series—think *Little House on The Prairie* meets *Stagecoach*, retooled for colonial Australia. I had directed a couple of episodes of the first season. Mr. Netter was looking for a teenager who could play an Irish waif in the next season. He was impressed by Nicole and cast her as a regular, and brought me in to direct her first episode.

Before *BMX Bandits* opened in Australia in mid-December 1983, I took Nicole to a dinner with the veteran showbiz reporter Matt White, who wrote about it in the *Daily Mirror*. I am sure I embarrassed Nicole by predicting she would one day become Australia's Katharine Hepburn, giving standout performances in every decade of her life.

# Twinkle, twinkle

JUST before the schools broke up for their Christmas holidays last week, a pretty young pupil at North Sydney Girls' High School named Nicole Kidman was the target for a lot of light-hearted taunting from her classmates.

"Nicole is in movies — so she says!" they jeered.

And indeed Nicole is in movies — in a big way.

She has the starring roles in two films but neither had reached the cinema screens when her schoolmates scoffed at reports that she was now Australia's youngest movie star.

Today, all that will change, as her two films have their premieres in major city cinemas, within 200 metres of each other, as well as simultaneous release in several suburban theatres.

DUO: Nicole Kidman and producer Brian Trenchard-Smith

Nicole's first film, *Bush Christmas*, is opening at the Hoyts Centre and selected Hoyts suburban cinemas while her second film *BMX Bandits* is making its debut at Village Cinema City and three suburban theatres.

And one month after finishing filming on *BMX Bandits*, Nicole was given another leading role in a television series called *Chase Through The Night* which has been bought by the ABC and the BBC.

Not bad for a 16-year-old who has just passed her school certificate and has two more years of schooling in front of her.

Brian Trenchard-Smith who directed her in *BMX Bandits* said: "I see Nicole Kidman as a young Australian Katharine Hepburn. She has the potential to become a world class actress."

He, Nicole and I were having dinner together in a North Sydney restaurant, not far from her school and Trenchard-Smith's remarks drew only an embarrassed giggle from the girl in question.

By Daily Mirror Showbusiness Editor Matt White

"I like acting, but I'm not sure I want to be an actress when I'm a grown-up," she explained.

"I wouldn't mind being a public relations officer or a barrister — or even a politician."

What then made her audition for the movies and television series.

"I've always been a show-off," she said simply. "As a little girl I used to perform ballet for the next door neighbors.

## Direction

"When I was eight I went to local drama schools at Centre House, Lane Cove near where we live and I kept going there after school until I was twelve."

Those classes gave Nicole the acting bug and she later attended The Young People's Drama Studio at the Phillip Street Theatre under the direction of Peter Williams.

Because of her qualities Nicole was signed up by model agent Ursula Hufnagl and she has appeared in several commercials as well as receiving an offer to model in Paris.

Nicole is also on the books of one of Australia's leading theatrical agents, June Cann whose clients include Jack Thompson and Bryan Brown.

The fact that she is the youngest Australian actress ever to achieve starring roles in two movies in city cinemas at the same time, doesn't impress her.

When I was with her she was far more excited about passing her school certificate, the results of which she had received earlier that day.

"Because I missed a lot of weeks at school to do film work, I'd been told I would not be allowed any more time off, and most people didn't think I would do well at my exams."

Asked how her friends at school reacted to her being a film star, Nicole shrugged her shoulders and said: "They were not all that impressed.

"After all, none of them had ever seen me in a film so they used to poke fun at me by saying 'Nicole's in movies — so she says.' I don't mind."

Brian Trenchard-Smith shook his head and laughed uneasily.

"Well, I do," he said. "And it won't be long before all Australia is talking about Nicole Kidman, our top movie actress.

"I've been asked to direct two more movies and I would like to use you again in one of them," he said to Nicole.

Trenchard-Smith paused and critically eyed the ballooning long skirt and loose jacket Nicole was wearing.

"I would like to see you as a modern miss fulfilling some stronger roles in the new year. And I'd also like to see you wearing something tighter."

Nicole bestowed a benign smile on him and gently replied: "Well, my mum doesn't think so. . . ."

All she needed was an adult role that would get Hollywood's attention. Soon enough, that role came along in Philip Noyce's stylish thriller *Dead Calm*, when Nicole's screen chemistry was fully demonstrated. I was in LA at the time of *Dead Calm*'s premiere and saw it at the Mann's Chinese a few blocks from my hotel. Her star quality was evident. There was buzz about her all over town. I phoned her parents in Sydney, recalling our previous conversation about the perils of acting, and told them she was well and truly on her way. And the rest, as they say, is history.

1983 ended with a joyous event for Margaret and me. After another difficult pregnancy, our second son Alexander was born, like his brother Eric, by caesarean section. Alex showed signs of distress in the womb, so a natural birth was not an option. Margaret opted for epidural anesthesia during the surgery. She was awake and magnificent throughout. I sat beside her head, offering words of love and encouragement. Alex was six weeks premature (4 lbs., 10 oz.) but healthy, and is now a strapping six foot three inches.

Alex was just a few months old when we purchased a home in then semi-rural Hornsby, to the north of Sydney. The seven years we spent on Maranta Street while our boys were small were idyllic. Our neighbors on either side, the Huggetts and the Becchios, were wonderful people who also had young children, and there were constant comings and goings between the three properties.

# CHAPTER 30
## *Frog Dreaming*

By coincidence Nicole Kidman was present when I was offered my next feature film. The *Five Mile Creek* series had moved its second season to Melbourne. I had just finished directing the episode which introduced Nicole's character, and had brought her to dinner at a Japanese restaurant so she could meet Kevin James Dobson, who would be directing episodes of Season Two. Nicole appreciated being introduced to Kevin ahead of meeting him for the first time on the set. Late that afternoon I had received a call from an executive at UAA Films for whom I had made trailers. She asked if I were available to take over directing a film on an immediate basis. Like tomorrow. If I were willing to jump right in, then the producers would like to meet me as soon as possible. I was unaware of the movie in question other than its title listing in the trade papers—*Frog Dreaming*. The director was Russell Haag. At that time, I did not know him personally. He had been an art director for Kubrick on *A Clockwork Orange*. He had cocreated and directed much of the hit bushranger series *Cash & Company* plus its follow up *Tandarra*—a solid professional. What had gone wrong, I wondered. But if the company was determined to change directors, I would take over, and nominated the restaurant where the producers could find me.

When they arrived, I left Kevin and Nicole to chat, and took my sushi to a nearby table where I met with Barbi Taylor, producer, and Everett De Roche, writer and coproducer of *Frog Dreaming*, a $5M film starring Henry Thomas, known throughout the world as E.T.'s best friend. Everett, tall, fit, with a beachcomber's tan, was Australia's top genre screenwriter, having emigrated from America in the late 1960s. I had made trailers for all the films of Everett's scripts to date: *Patrick*, *Snapshot*, *Thirst*, *The Long Weekend*, *Harlequin*, *Race to The Yankee Zephyr*. I had met Barbi, a smart bubbly blonde, ten years before when she was a

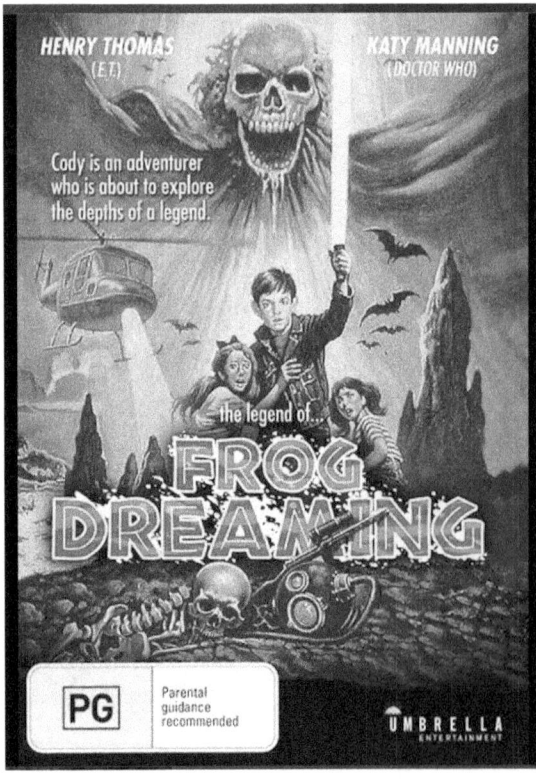

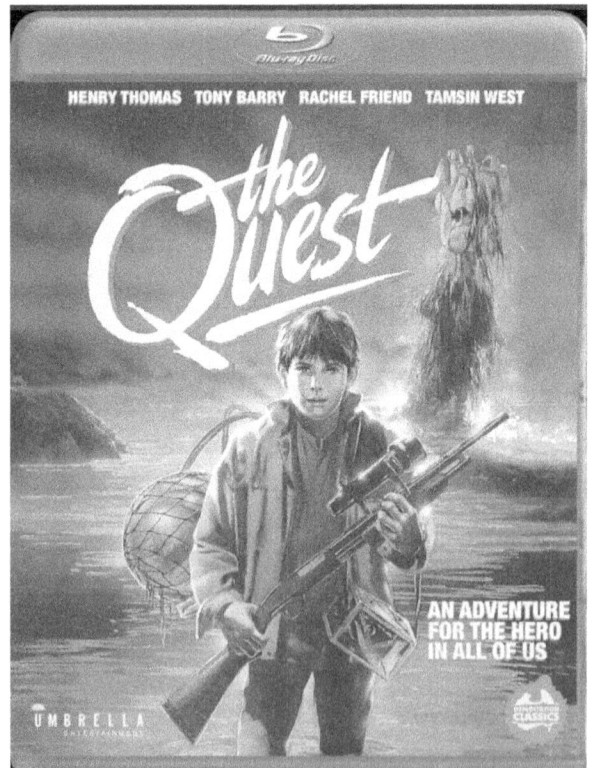

production secretary. She had been personal assistant to director Richard Franklin when he made *Cloak and Dagger* in Hollywood, in which Henry Thomas had played the lead.

Barbi had bonded with Henry and his mother during that shoot, so she developed a coming of age story specifically for him, written by Everett De Roche. Henry would play an American orphan living in an Australian country town, a precocious child inventor, who discovers signs that a monster lives in a nearby pond. Is there a scientific explanation, or could the Aboriginal myth of Donkegin be true? Great concept. Perfect role, but not a well-paid major studio movie offer that was assured of theatrical distribution in America. Henry Thomas was the most famous child actor in the world in 1984. Against the advice of his agent, young Henry, an adventurer at heart, accepted the gig, and along with his mother flew to Melbourne for an 8-week shoot. Halfway through the second week, the financiers were unhappy with the dailies. In their view, the child actors were giving flat performances, and scenes were paced too slowly. They wanted the director replaced, and as much of the existing material of the kids as possible reshot without extending Henry Thomas' schedule. I started the next morning.

*Frog Dreaming* was the first of four movies I took over as director. Others I took over in postproduction. Leadership is crucial; listen to everybody, make decisions, project enthusiasm for each challenge to restore the enthusiasm of your new collaborators. Luckily, I had already worked with two key Heads of Department on *Turkey Shoot*—1ˢᵗ AD Terry Needham and DP Johnny Maclean. They both knew my affection for low wide angles, camera movement, and thorough coverage of a scene, so we already had shorthand on the set. I had spent most of 1984 between trailers, directing two episodes each of *Five Mile Creek* and the Crawford's police show *Special Squad*. It had sharpened my efficiency. I felt confident that we could reshoot Henry's scenes within his contracted period.

Winning the trust of the demoralized cast was the first important step. As a calling card, I arranged a screening of *BMX Bandits* for Henry Thomas and interested cast and crew. Response was good. Relations between Henry and my predecessor had deteriorated which was a contributing factor to his departure.

"If I make a suggestion about a scene, will you listen to me and discuss it, or will you treat me like a kid who knows nothing?" Henry asked me, to my best recollection.

I assured him I treated all actors as adults irrespective of age and would never talk down to him. We were soon in good rapport. He did not make suggestions often, but when he did, they made the scene better. Once he asked if, instead of a closeup for an important line, he could walk forward from a full shot into foreground and make his own closeup, perhaps taking a leaf out of Spielberg's playbook. It did give the line more weight. Where his guardian Gazza (Tony Barry in an excellent performance) is demanding he stop going to the pond, Henry improvised an emotion-laced speech that made both the scene and the subsequent events at the pond all the more poignant. I cast Henry Thomas again in *Happy Face Murders* fourteen years later. He was still the intelligent actor and decent fellow I had met on *Frog Dreaming*.

Henry's partners in many scenes were 14-year-old Rachel Friend and 10-year-old Tamsin West. He confessed to me recently that he had had a crush on Rachel, who being a year older was not interested in him. He would occasionally say something intended to be cool, but it would come out all wrong. She would roll her eyes, and he would kick himself. "Why did I say that?" I think the awkwardness between them contributed to their relationship onscreen. He related better to Tamsin, whom he described as "a pistol." She reminded him of Drew Barrymore, who had played his younger sister on *E.T.: The Extraterrestrial*. Tamsin certainly had a similar sweet but feisty presence. I would cast her in the title role of my next movie, *Jenny Kissed Me*.

I reviewed all seventy-three minutes of the printed footage, and decided that only the Rockabilly dance was worth keeping, plus parts of the opening sequence, where the fisherman has a heart attack at the sight of something frightening offscreen. The scene just needed lots more images to build tension. I outlined a list of atmosphere-building shots without actors: frogs watching, bubbles spreading, windmill vanes turning and the like, to be done by a 2nd Unit under the editor Brian Kavanagh. What he added to the opening pond sequence really helped build suspense in what was previously an undernourished sequence.

The next day we started night shoots at Moorooduc Quarry, a flooded pond where the mythical Donkegin is supposed to reside. Scheduled were key emotional scenes for the climax. Not ideal for a director's first day. But the clock was ticking. We had to cram almost eight weeks of work into six. I don't enjoy total night shoots, where for a week or more, your body clock is completely reversed. (How about 120 nights of shooting for the New Zealand crew during the battle of Helms Deep in *LOTR—The Two Towers*?) I joined the crew on location at a country hotel whose east wing was literally ten feet from a construction site. Drills and jackhammers would start at 7 a.m. just when the crew were settling into bed after a hard night at the pond.

Making the monster credible was the key to the movie.

There would be no optical effects, no miniatures. The glimpses of the monster as seen by the characters had to serve two agendas: to be believable to them as a biological entity, yet later in the big reveal, be equally believable as (spoiler alert) a piece of early twentieth century mining equipment.

Donkegin (Donkey Engine) turns out to be a steam shovel left behind in the flooded quarry. Furthermore, the mechanical Donkegin had to work reliably, submerged in water, raising its weed-draped shovelhead above the surface then lowering it again on cue. Production Designer Jon Dowding and his team did a great job on a modest budget. Brian May's multifaceted score for *Frog Dreaming* is one of his best. His music unites the different elements of the picture. Suspenseful underscoring of the mysterious pond segues to a breezy old-fashioned country town flavor then transitions to the pounding rhythms of Cody's adventure theme.

When the film was delivered, executives at UAA, the financing company, were certain they had a hit on their hands. Not so fast. While distributors recognized the quality of the film, they saw it as not adult

enough for nighttime business, and perhaps a little too adult for the under-10s. The movie would only play two-thirds of the day, with most admissions at half price. Offers of Minimum Guarantees were calibrated

accordingly. Disney reportedly offered one million dollars as guarantee against world distribution, but UAA hung out for three million, and the deal went away. Pity. Eventually it played on the Disney Channel. I can hear the Standards and Practices executive now…

You cannot have a 10-year-old smoking.

You cannot have a 10-year-old ask her mother: "Can you get herpes from French kissing?" (A priceless delivery from Tamsin West.)

You cannot have a 10-year-old use words like "lost tribe of blackfellas" or call a local rock formation "the Devil's Cock"

You cannot have a 10-year-old's bedtime reading to be *The Perfumed Garden*!!!

Everett De Roche had six kids, and therefore a good fix on kidspeak. His quirky perspective distinguishes the film from formulaic examples of the genre. Greater Union did not think it was strong enough for a Christmas holiday release. They went for August School holidays with a muddled campaign. Flying Henry Thomas in for publicity was apparently too expensive. The result was an Australian gross of only $171,000.

Foreign distributors struggled with what genre their choice of title should point to. The title *Frog Dreaming* only resonated in Australia, where there was some knowledge of Aboriginal Dreamtime mythology. In the UK it was *The Go-Kids*, with a poster intended to evoke *The Goonies*. In Germany it was *The Spirit Chaser*, in Finland *Fighting Spirits*, and in France *Le Secret Du Lac*. The pre-Disney Miramax had bought the US rights, renamed the picture *The Quest*, and based their sell on the star of *E.T.*, placing Henry front and center on the poster.

Many years later at the premiere of *Kill Bill Vol.1*, Harvey Weinstein (the once and future pariah) told me that he would love to get the home video rights again. But due to UAA's bankruptcy, the film disappeared from circulation, and its copyright became clouded. I assisted Christine De Roche, Everett's widow, in sorting out the chain of title issues, and in 2017 she reclaimed her late husband's film. Umbrella Entertainment have made a beautifully remastered Blu Ray, available worldwide.

For fellow nerds of censorship trivia: The movie was rated 'PG' throughout Canada, except in Quebec, where it was rated 'G'. Apparently French Canadians raise tougher kids. In Germany it was given the age advisory of twelve on the grounds of disturbing sequences of peril, and the potential for unaccompanied moppets to imitate the hero's reckless behavior.

At the 1986 Montreal Children's Film Festival, *Frog Dreaming*, submitted under the title of *The Spirit Chaser*, won 2nd prize, which was gratifying. It's a pity it was not entered into more festivals. But over the decades, like *BMX Bandits*, *Frog Dreaming/ The Quest* has built an ever-replenishing source of fans. I think it's one of my best films.

# CHAPTER 31
## *Jenny Kissed Me*

The next picture came quickly from my *BMX Bandits* producer Tom Broadbridge. *Jenny Kissed Me* was an early script by Judith Colquhoun, who went on to a solid career writing for family-oriented TV series, and has recently published two novels. Ms. Colquoun had drawn inspiration from the 1838 poem by Leigh Hunt, which she used for the film's title and the name of the child at the heart of the story.

> *Jenny kiss'd me when we met,*
> *Jumping from the chair she sat in,*
> *Time, you thief, who love to get*
> *Sweets into your list, put that in!*
> *Say I'm weary, say I'm sad,*
> *Say that health and wealth have miss'd me,*
> *Say I'm growing old, but add,*
> *Jenny kiss'd me.*

The kiss in question was bestowed on the aging poet by a young admirer after one of his many illnesses. In the context of Ms. Colquoun's screenplay, these sentiments reflect a character's belief that the best part of his life were the six years he spent being a father to Jenny.

To my recollection Judith Colquoun and I have never spoken since I proposed script changes. She rejected them as was her right, and probably believes I went on to make a complete mess of her work. Maybe that's valid. I have sometimes wondered how it might have turned out if I had stuck to her original script, a well-written, social issue drama, with a slow, spare, arthouse tone. Too little seemed to happen. Too many valleys, not enough peaks—my first reaction. Directing the script as written would have displayed versatility, an ability to do a Ken Loach social realism piece as well as my usual popular genre fare. It might have been a good career move. But rightly or wrongly I felt the project needed to be less arthouse and more commercial, in the vein of a Douglas Sirk tearjerker. Yes, growing up, I did

Det sägs att kärleken vet inga gränser — en film Du aldrig glömmer

see Douglas Sirk movies too, between epics, horrors, westerns, thrillers. A sprinkling of melodrama might help the social issues of the piece reach a wider audience, particularly when it came time to sell to television. I engaged Warwick Hind, a former Greater Union executive and a talented writer, to give it more 'oomph'.

The original script was centered on 10-year-old Jenny. For the past six years she has been living in a rural district an hour from the bright lights of Melbourne with her mother Carol and Carol's boyfriend Lindsay, a market gardener. Jenny is devoted to her surrogate father, who pays her more attention than her mother does. Carol, feeling isolated and bored, has a quick fling with a neighbor. When Lindsay suspects the liaison, Carol vanishes while Lindsay is at work, dragging Jenny with her. They stay with her friend Gaynor, who earns good money at a massage parlor. Soon Carol is working there, too. Lindsay is the only father Jenny has ever known, but as a live-in boyfriend has no parental rights. Jenny runs away and is made a ward of the state. Lindsay, who has just been diagnosed with cancer, removes a delighted Jenny from the institution at gunpoint, and goes on the run with her. But Lindsay's cancer worsens and he has to give Jenny up. Carol redeems herself marrying him on his deathbed, making him officially Jenny's father. Jenny assuages her grief with the belief that Lindsay has been reincarnated as a tree possum on their property. Carol goes with it, and so rediscovers her maternal instinct. The bones of a melodramatic weepie were inherent to the story.

I was also influenced by producer Tom Broadbridge's casting preference. Tom had good instincts. He wanted TV soap star Paula Duncan to play Carol. Made sense. She was a good actress with six years of visi-

bility on *Cop Shop*, a prime-time soap. Nonetheless, we held auditions for the three lead roles. Paula was great as expected. Ivar Kants nailed it as Lindsay. Then relative newcomer Deborra-Lee Furness read for the supporting role of Gaynor. We were seriously impressed. I wondered whether she might not be even better for the Carol role than Paula and gave her some of Carol's scenes to study for a few minutes. She gave a stunning reading. Both she and Paula were excellent. But there was something about Deborra's persona in the role that had the edge. I suggested that Deborra play Carol, and Paula play the wayward best friend, Gaynor. Deborra had just done sixteen episodes of *Kings* and six episodes of the top rating soap *Neighbors*. I deemed she was on her way up (right about that). We had a promotable cast. Two TV-visible actresses plus

JENNY KISSED ME

torpedoed the film's prospects. The Australian Film Institute Awards had become a big deal in

Ivar Kants, of the recently released and well-reviewed, though low grossing, migrant drama *Silver City*. Producer Tom Broadbridge went along with it. Was I right? Or should Paula have played the lead? Who knows? The "what if…" of movie casting—now there's a rabbit hole. All a director can do is follow his instincts and hope for the best.

I had a hunch about an unknown actor/musician named Wilbur Wilde who auditioned for a 1-scene bit part as "delivery man." He had an engagingly wacky personality. I cast him in my next movie, too. He went on to a big career as a television and radio presenter best known for a 15-year stint on *Hey, Hey, It's Saturday*.

It was a fun shoot in many respects. *Frog Dreaming* had shown me Tamsin West would be ideal to play the precocious 10-year-old Jenny. In prep, I showed some footage to Tom. He could see what I saw in her. But the decision had not been made. We went to dinner that night at a top Indian restaurant in Toorak. As we sat down, I noticed—cue *Twilight Zone* theme—Tamsin West and her parents were there too. I had met them a couple of times during the shoot. They did not see us come in. Complete coincidence. Tom and I conferred. He gave me the nod and I walked over to their table. I remember the look on Tamsin's face—shock slowly transitioning to delight—when I offered her the title role.

Filming commenced on location in and around Melbourne in March, 1985 on a budget of AUD$1.4M. Our key grip came with a mini-gib, mounted on the back of his flatbed truck. In exterior locations, it enabled me to push in, boom down, arc around etc., and energize the visual flow without the time-consuming process of laying rail on uneven ground. 180 degrees of mini-move options. To shoot reverse angles—just swing the truck round. It helped me capture the beauty of the Dandenong Ranges.

We had arranged to shoot the massage parlor scenes at a real operating massage parlor. Such premises had been made legal only in the state of Victoria in the mid-1970s. I negotiated with the owner, a Mr. Trimbole, reputedly a relative of notorious drug kingpin Robert Trimbole, who was alleged to have ordered the contract killing of anti-drug campaigner Donald Mackay. This Mr. Trimbole had a long-healed 4-inch scar on one side of his throat. His wife, a hard-faced blonde, was very proud of the expensive remodel they had done to the establishment. Signature rooms, a small swimming pool and a jacuzzi. This is a high-class wine bar with rooms for men who need to relax, she stated. She wanted that image maintained in the film. Of course, I said, as directors do, to get a location they want. In fact, it *was* perfect. Glossy production value that did not need additional art department dressing. She also stipulated that the actual name of the brothel (renamed in the film as "The Golden Palm") and its address be listed in the closing credits.

Business was strong, said Mrs. Trimbole, a former employee of her husband, I surmised. Apparently, celebrating football teams often booked the place out. The only day she could close up for the eight hours our shoot needed would be on ANZAC Day between 5 a.m. and 2 p.m. Business was traditionally slow on that public holiday because the annual march of veterans affected traffic patterns. A one-chance location with a finite window of time is always a risk, but I took it anyway.

None of the crew (including the grip and electric department, they assured me) had ever been inside a brothel before. There was a subconscious embarrassment that rippled throughout the crew as the shoot day approached. Unbeknownst to me, a subversive idea took root. I drove up just before crew call at 4:30 a.m., and my jaw dropped. Bearded grips and electrics were unloading equipment wearing classic bustier and fishnet stockings. Inner discomfort alleviated through humor. The continuity girl came in a figure-hugging Suzy Wong cheongsam, others came in cliché streetwalker garb. That particularly irked Mrs. Trimbole, who felt her establishment was being mocked. It took some pretty fast talking to persuade her not to throw us out.

Several of the extras we brought in to play background sex workers were reluctant to enter the pool and jacuzzi used by real sex workers. It was 1985. The AIDS epidemic had entered the zeitgeist. Fear and misinformation about the disease was rife. Safe sex was a social issue the film ignored. Too soon. Too raw. A pity in retrospect.

What I intended as a refined soap opera did not prosper. A combination of phenomena torpedoed the film's prospects. The Australian Film Institute Awards had become a big deal in these boom years for the industry. Members had to see all the submitted films to be allowed to cast a vote. *Jenny Kissed Me* joined twenty-two films that year competing for nominations. The timeframe for the members to see every film was compressed into a few short weeks. Films ran two per night, and back-to-back throughout weekends. Screening fatigue amplified by alcohol set in. Some films were heckled. The privilege of viewing a film before its release had become a chore to the nouveau arts elite. A journalist attended the screening of *Jenny Kissed Me*, the second film of the night. Some of the audience were well lubricated and mocked the film's tear-jerking moments. Despite the media embargo on reviews of these films prior to their release, he wrote a piece in the *Sydney Morning Herald* about the screenings in general, and mentioned the audience's ridicule of *Jenny Kissed Me*. This had the effect of killing any enthusiasm Hoyts Theaters may have had for the movie. No awards for this one likely. It seemed there were too many Australian films being made. The market was glutted. Oz flicks were dying like flies. Hoyts fulfilled its theatrical release obligation by putting *Jenny Kissed Me* into one theater for a week, grossing $1824, then sent it direct to video, and subsequent TV broadcast on Channel Seven. Following on the earlier newspaper article, the stage was set for reviews that ranged from "misfire" to "turgid", that were barely read before the picture closed. Nonetheless the film sold well to video and television in Europe.

I acknowledge the role that critics must play as a consumer watchdog, to be a countervailing force to the distributors' hype. But some reviewers write from a position of cultural superiority, in the vein of epigrammatic scorn. Neil Jillette, of *The Melbourne Age*, for many years wielded the most poisonous pen of Australian movie critics. On February 8, 1986, he had this to say about *Jenny Kissed Me*:

" '*Jenny Kissed Me*' (Hoyts) seems to be an attempt to lure geriatric audiences away from daytime TV serials. Brian Trenchard-Smith apparently wanted a change from his usual action subjects, and so, unwisely, took on this soppy effort (which ends with Lindsay expiring from a terminal disease) He seizes every chance to inject a bit of action (even a car chase) and sex into the desultory material, but to no avail. The actors seem to be having difficulty delivering their lines with straight faces. Without giving away too much, it can be said that the plot ingredients include cancer, appendicitis, pot-smoking, coke-snorting, abduction, a car chase, a massage parlor and discussions about the nature of God and the possibility of being reincarnated as a possum. 'Jenny Kissed Me' is good for plenty of laughs, though tears might have been what the makers had in mind. With its relentless concentration on bathos and banality, it achieves a certain purity of style.*

Ouch! And I probably got off lightly. The film is reviewed with greater sympathy in John Murray's 1995 book—*Australian Film*.

*Beyond its crisp and efficient direction (with much spectacular cutting on movement), what makes the film interesting is its B-movie melodrama touch.*

I believe *Jenny Kissed Me* is a better film than its reviews indicate, but it does have a flaw that critics failed to note. I had set out to make a late 1950s glossy weepie in modern dress, a tearjerker for men as well as women, without realizing that I had made the mother too unsympathetic, and too late in her redemption, for the audience to engage with her. A lesson for the future, which I would apply twelve years later to the development of *Happy Face Murders*.

# CHAPTER 32
## *Dead End Drive-In*

The second half of 1985 was taken up with *Dead End Drive-In*, which Quentin Tarantino has kindly nominated as my best film. Due to its allegorical nature, an increased awareness of institutional racism, and its striking visual design, it has stood the test of time.

The script, adapted from a short story by Booker Prize winner Peter Carey, had been developed by the New South Wales Film Corporation. An accomplished novelist Peter Smalley, a friend of Peter Carey, had written three drafts of this quasi-Sci-fi dystopian tale for another director, who lost confidence in the proj-

ect and left. The NSWFC approached me, acknowledging the script needed work and a clarifying vision. I read the short story, absorbed its flavor, then interwove the best elements of all three drafts into a new version that everyone was happy with.

I added titles at the start of the film listing a series of potential global catastrophes that precipitated society's decline into dystopia. A nuclear accident, a race war in Africa, the biggest of Wall Street crashes, combine to destabilize the interlocking economies of the world, propelling poverty-driven urban crime into overdrive. It is eventually revealed that in an attempt to control the crimewave, the government has turned a chain of drive-in theatres into covert concentration camps for unemployed youth as a preemptive measure. If the occupants of a car claim the discount ticket offered to the unemployed (suggesting they are a crime

GETTING IN WAS EASY...
GETTING OUT IS HELL ON WHEELS.

SPRINGVALE PRODUCTIONS PTY LTD IN ASSOCIATION WITH THE NEW SOUTH WALES FILM CORPORATION PRESENT
A FILM BY BRIAN TRENCHARD-SMITH

**DEAD END**
*Drive-in*

NED MANNING   NATALIE McCURRY   PETER WHITFORD
Director of photography — PAUL MURPHY   Production designer — LARRY EASTWOOD
Original music by — FRANK STRANGIO   Edited by — ALAN LAKE & LEE SMITH   Screenplay by — PETER SMALLEY
Co-produced by — DAMIEN PARER   Produced by — ANDREW WILLIAMS   Directed by — BRIAN TRENCHARD-SMITH

risk), their car will be sabotaged while they watch the movie. They're not leaving. The inmates are allowed easy access to drugs, alcohol, junk food, exploitation films, and the latest music, everything their consumer-programmed value system has conditioned them to desire. Consequently, they are happy to stay.

Into this hedonistic dead end comes an unsuspecting young man, nicknamed Crabs ("I thought I had them once, but I didn't so it sort of stuck"). He has a job, but claims the unemployed rate to impress his girlfriend Carmen. As they watch the movie, a rear wheel is removed from their car. Once Crabs discovers he is a prisoner, he quickly decides not to play ball. He wants out. But Carmen thinks the drive-in is better than a teen runaway's life. After several unsuccessful attempts to escape, our hero's crisis of conscience comes when the government starts shipping in Australia's unwanted Asian migrant community. Racial tensions simmer between Caucasians and Asian inmates.

"They could rape me or anything," says Carmen. "They should limit the number who come here."

Prescient dialogue nearly four decades later. Against some pushback at the time, I beefed up the racial issues in the script. In the climax our hero steals a police van and busts out to an uncertain future. No surprise that I jumped at the chance of visualizing these ideas.

We had to move fast. Australian drive-ins were withering in 1985. Home video was stealing their audience. The Matraville Drive-In in Sydney's south had closed, soon to be replaced by blocks of flats. We secured the drive-in, with still-working projectors, for six weeks of prep and six weeks of shooting before handing it back to the developers. I was greatly aided by production designer Larry Eastwood and art director Nick McCallum, who made our $2.3M budget look a lot richer. Larry was nominated for an AFI Award for his remarkable production design, but did not win.

The drive-in's capacity was 400 cars. We managed to make it look well-filled with a couple of hundred wrecks. We could always fatten up the background of a shot by moving cars around. We paid the contractors who normally collected the abandoned cars from suburban streets, giving them an extra fee to dump the cars at the drive-in and collect them three months later. Loads of rubbish were also dumped there for the art department to play with. The cars were variously decorated to give a sense of the diverse culture that had sprung up within the drive-in. Neon proliferated. Tents and sunshades were added. Car parts became tables, chairs, clothing accessories. A van was gutted, turned upside down and filled with water as a swimming pool. An adjacent sign read "Club Med."

I wanted graffiti everywhere. There had been an outpouring of illegal murals on public buildings and train carriages in the early 1980s. Part thrill-seeking, part agitprop driven, a new generation of teenage artists were thumbing their noses at authority. "Don't vote. It only encourages them," was one I recall, spray painted in vivid colors under a bridge.

The BUGA UP group (Ban Unhealthful Government Advertising) targeted cigarette billboards rented in prime positions on state property by tobacco companies. Pressure was mounting on the police to clamp down on graffiti guerillas. A number of arrests had been made, and the offenders were serving their sentence at nearby Long Bay Jail. In an ironic counterpoint to the movie's concept, we were able to get a number of young inmates on day release to spray paint their art onto our long drive-in wall. They were accompanied by a prison guard and returned to their cells each night. They did a great job and were paid the same as the regular artists we hired.

One of our "at liberty" recruits was young Vladimir Cherepanoff. He tells his story on the Blu Ray extras. Vladimir was part of a vibrant graffiti community that met at Westfield Shopping center regularly on Thursday nights. They would share pictures of the art they had done, and sketches of what they were planning for new targets. One Thursday night Vladimir and other artists were discussing a plan for decorating a carriage in the Blacktown railyard. They were unaware that the meeting had been organized through an informer as a sting operation by the state rail police to arrest all the graffiti writers meeting at the Westfield Mall at once. Four paddy wagons and eight patrol cars swooped in. A total of eighty graffiti artists were taken to Paramatta police station to be interrogated and charged.

# DEAD END DRIVE-IN

Vladimir was caught red-handed with a bagful of aerosol cans and permanent markers. He was able to dispose of his incriminating sketchbook via a crack through the paddy wagon door. But, when questioned at the police station, Vladimir had a "get out of jail" card in his pocket—his first paycheck from the *Dead End Drive-In* Art Department. The spray cans in his bag were justified by his employment. The Police realized they could not make the case stick and Vlad was released. Unlike some of his companions, he avoided a criminal conviction on his permanent record.

Over the years Vladimir Cherepanoff became a seminal figure in the history of Australian Street Art. He was the founding member of Sound Unlimited, the first Australian Hip Hop band to be signed on a major record label, Sony Music. He remains a sought-after guru in the world of advertising and product design. Vladimir said in an interview: "*Dead End Drive-In* was one of the few legal jobs I did as a teen, which set me on the path to become a legit digital artist and art director. It showed me I can make a real living out of my art and I'm forever grateful for it."

I'm glad *Dead End Drive-In* made a difference to his life. As it did to mine.

All the graffiti and neon made the drive-in a great set to shoot. Paul Murphy delivered outstanding widescreen camerawork and lighting. The fact that he was not even nominated for an Australian Film Institute Award for Best Cinematography reflects the professional myopia of the AFI at that time.

I grew up on CinemaScope, VistaVision, Cinerama movies, where the wide screen encompassed my entire peripheral vision. I wanted this picture to play in the 2.35 ratio with lots of deep-focus wide angles, but in those days night photography through anamorphic lenses delivered less depth of field than spherical lenses. Anamorphic required a lot of candlepower, and therefore a more expensive lighting package. Paul Murphy came up with the solution. Again let me geek out about "old skool tek" for a moment. We rented the fastest spherical lenses, just on the market, which gave us much more background detail with less light. We achieved the scope format via a process then called Super-35. We adjusted the camera's gate to shoot on the soundtrack area, normally blocked off, thereby converting the Academy box into a rectangle with additional picture area. After the negative had been matched, and an interpositive created, this was re-photographed through an anamorphic lens on the optical printer, cropping a little top and bottom, thereby adding to the rectangle, and squeezing it back into the Academy box. Thus the master internegative, from which prints were made, was created in the desired 2.35 anamorphic format. In theaters, the squeezed image would be un-squeezed by the projector's anamorphic lens. I know, your eyes are glazing…

Wet-downs always make a night exterior more attractive. The first approach of the '56 Chevy convertible to the gates of the Star Drive-In was enhanced by seeing the giant neon sign above the box office reflected in a puddle close to camera. I like compositions that cause the viewer's focus to roam between background and foreground. My favorite piece of complicated camera operation is the shot where Crabs and Carmen wake up to see their environment in daylight for the first time.

The shot starts inside the car as Crabs opens his eyes and reacts to something. As he reaches for the switch that triggers the convertible's top to fold back, the camera slides out through the open passenger window, tracks back, then rises to a wider view of the car, as Crabs and Carmen stand up to gaze at the drive-in, still populated in the early morning by garishly dressed youths emerging sleepily from their cars.

There were extensive auditions to find the two leads. 20-year-old Natalie McCurry, a model and aspiring actress, who would be crowned Miss Australia four years later, had a great look and read well, projecting a teen runaway's vulnerability beneath a confident veneer. This was her first role. I would cast her twice more in later years.

The movie has one sex scene. Screen nudity makes most actresses uncomfortable. But the sex scene supported the notion that both Carmen and Crabs were too distracted to notice the cops taking the wheels off the Chevy till the moment the car tipped backwards. We negotiated the parameters and limited the nudity to two shots. Natalie was a sensitive, decent, unpretentious person and I was very sorry to hear of her death from cancer at the age of forty-eight.

The casting of Ned Manning was more contentious. Casting is a minefield. Everyone's an expert. It's a risk to stray from consensus. The NSWFC exec was strongly pushing Rod Zuanic, who had played the juvenile delinquent in his first movie, *Fast Talking*. He was good actor for sure, but his audition was flat. This happens to the best of actors. Ned Manning's audition projected a persona that fitted my image of Crabs better. Ned gave his age as twenty-five, the upper limit for Crabs. After the film was finished, he admitted he was really a youthful-looking thirty-four. If I had known that at the time, it would have made my insistence on his casting less defensible, and I probably would have bowed to NSWFC pressure and cast Rod Zuanic.

Ned embodied the character well, but local critics other than David Stratton did not agree. Critics did not care for Wilbur Wilde's take on the drug-crazed showoff Hazza, either. I did. Wilbur was mimicking a particular group of Melbourne loudmouths he knew, who reveled proudly in their loutishness.

All the cast made the most of their characters, but the only one who received any critical approval was Peter Whitford as the Star Drive-In's seedy manager and apologist. Well-deserved. He anchored the fanciful premise in reality.

We shot over thirty-five split day/nights, starting around 4 p.m. to give late afternoon backlight to the daylight scenes, then we would continue with night photography sometimes till dawn. In the final week we started the climactic car chases and mayhem that preceded the extraordinary truck jump through the Star sign.

Guy Norris and his stunt team handled the heavy vehicles smashing through obstacles with precision. The closer you can get the lens to the collision point, the more impact the shot will have on the audience. The camera was secured inside a thick metal fireproof housing known as a "Ned Kelly" because of its resemblance to the stove pipe helmet the Australian outlaw created from stolen plough shears, as armor for his final gunfight. Several times our cameras were clipped by a vehicle and the image tumbled end over end. Great shot till the last frame before point of impact, and no camera damage.

The time came for the big stunt. The cost of construction, rigging, special equipment, camera crews, and stunt fees for this 20-second show-stopping moment would be $75,000. Guy Norris, doubling for Crabs, would race the stolen police van up the ramp of an empty car transporter, sail over the box office, through the Star neon sign, to reach freedom on the other side. Hopefully this would turn out to be more *The Great Escape* than *Thelma and Louise*.

Guy calculated the physics of the exercise: the weight of the vehicle, the angle of the ramp, and the speed that would be necessary to travel up the ramp, get airborne, smash through the neon Star, and land however many feet beyond. For heavy duty automotive stunts, there was a steel cage built into the interior of the car so that whatever happened to the exterior, the immediate area around the driver is heavily protected. The danger from a speeding vehicle dropping to the ground from thirty feet was the impact upon the driver's spine. Heavy duty shock absorbers were installed under Guy's seat which was suspended on bungee cords within the cage.

The stunt had to be shot at the moment sunset resembled dawn. This enabled us to do the preparations in daylight. I stayed by the police van with Guy as he was strapped into his harness and all the final preparations for his safety took place. A hundred and fifty yards away, beside the ramp pointing to the Star sign, was DP Paul Murphy, monitoring the sunset for when it would look like the first rays of dawn. Once he gave the signal, we would have a 2-minute window before we would lose the matching light. Five cameras were in place, including one in the van, each set to shoot at different speeds ready to be rolled. If we missed the window, the diminishing light would require the exposure on all cameras to be adjusted. Synchronizing these converging disciplines was a little nerve wracking. There's always a tiny but vital detail that has to be fixed at the last minute. But it all came together in that 2-minute window.

Guy was ready. Roll cameras. Make sure all the high speeds are working. Pray none of them jam.

Five calls of "Speed!"

Then I shouted "Action!"

Guy took off, gathering momentum fast. He reached 70 mph at the foot of the ramp, rocketing to the top. Then, enhanced by pyrotechnics, the van shattered the neon Star sign into a thousand pieces. "The main thing," said 25-year old Norris to reporters at the time, "was getting through the sign in the right place. Left wheel will go through the S of 'Star' and my right wheel will be above the 'N' of 'Drive-In.'" Still

photographs show that's exactly where he hit. He landed 162 feet away, a world record for a truck jump of that weight. The impact folded the truck in two like a toy someone had bashed with a spade. Wow, that was a sight to behold! Guy Norris emerged unscathed. The next day he woke up with a slightly stiff neck for a few hours. He would go on to a major international career as a stunt coordinator and second unit director. His work on *Mad Max: Fury Road* was dazzling.

Most movie shoots have their surreal moments. At 3 a.m. a car full of drunken hoons, whooping and hollering, their testosterone stimulated by nightly sounds of motorized mayhem, skidded round the entry barriers and roared into the drive-in at high speed, perhaps hoping to join in the fray. We were about to do some gunfight scenes, so there were a couple of M16s on set, loaded with blanks for the next shot. I asked the armorer to hand me one. The drunks turned and sped towards us at the camera position. I shouldered the weapon. When the car was 100 yards away, I opened up full auto, prompting a screeching U-turn. As the invaders headed for the exit, a member of the stunt team drove his truck towards them at high speed, slowing just in time to let them pass. I think the invaders got their desired adrenalin rush. And for my part it amused me to step inside an action scene for a moment. Irresponsible behavior. I know. But at the time, we had a laugh. It never even made the progress report.

Every production has its crisis moment. Coproducer Damien Parer handled our potential disaster with expertise. I'll let him tell the story:

*I am in the production office at 8AM when producer Andy Williams rings me. He is in a panic. A neighbor near the drive-in site has phoned him at home threatening to shoot him because of the nocturnal noises. Gunfire, explosions, car chases had to stop. Later that morning a summons was issued demanding that the production company appear in the Supreme Court later that day. The plaintiff was seeking an emergency injunction to stop all filming after dark. And night shooting was all we had left to do.*

I quickly contacted our lawyers who secured an immediately available barrister. We dashed to his chambers in Macquarie Street for a briefing as the matter was scheduled for after lunch. The briefing was so close that the barrister was donning his wig and gown as we conferred. Off we trooped to court.

Then we appeared before the judge about 2.30PM. The complainant turned out to be a retired European immigrant who said that the noise of machinegun fire etc. had triggered World War Two flashbacks. He wanted the filming to stop at night. This man, said his barrister, was a decorated war hero. I heard my barrister groan 'Oh,

God' under his breath. We expected a total ban on filming or a big fine. But I wondered what the decoration was for. So my barrister asked about the war service. The man turned out to have fought against the Allies in WW2 and was awarded an Iron Cross. I saw the judge's expression change to a look of disdain. The judge intervened and quickly asked my barrister if we could minimize gunfire at night. I said yes knowing that we only had a bit more to do. The judge fined us $1,000 and gave us two weeks to finish filming. Perfect!

Damien was a very supportive producer. Directors want to spend; producers want to save. It could have been an adversarial relationship. But no. He did everything he could to give me the big look I was after, even squirreling away enough cash for an extra action scene – Crabs in his pizza delivery van attacked by marauding Karboys—which I dreamed up to energize the early part of the film with a burst of mayhem. Finally, we were done. The wrap party, commencing when shooting finished at dawn, offered an unique activity: Crew and director playing dodgem cars with the few remaining working vehicles in the drive-in. T-Bone that Fairmont! Rear end that Mazda! Without damaging insurance consequences. Now that's a wrap party! Those were the days.

The Australian censor initially gave *Dead End Drive-In* an 'R 18' classification, despite minimal sex and violence. Their concern was "antisocial behavior." We appealed and got the advisory 'M' rating. But it was a sign that what the film had to say was not appreciated. At its Christmas 1986 release, critical opinion was dismal. "Lame…" "Mad Max—lite…" Greater Union Film Distributors had no faith in it. In fact, in Sydney they opened the picture at the start of the Christmas holidays in a multiplex undergoing extensive remodeling. It grossed $67,000 nationwide and went straight to video. In the United States, the reviews were quite different. Michael Wilmington of the LA Times wrote:

*'Dead-End Drive-In" (citywide) is that increasingly rare surprise: a seeming piece of schlock that turns out to be exciting and offbeat. It's one of those strange grind-house classics worth looking for…Director Brian Trenchard-Smith, an Aussie adventure specialist, has given it violently kinetic action and sometimes amazing visual style, density and energy. The Star Drive-In, shown in extravagant deep-focus moving camera shots, is a triumph of design: It has a boiling, turbulent unity (you might ask, though, why it seems so ordinary when hero Crabs and heroine Carmen—Ned Manning and Natalie McCurry—first pull in). Populated by delinquents, punks, 'cowboys' [sic; he meant 'Karboys'] and desperate unemployed youth and run by an affably seedy, unctuous, sinister manager (Peter Whitford, perfect in the part), the Star really looks like a no-exit drive-in. Waste, laundry and fires are spread through the grounds in raffish riot, bizarre graffiti adorn the walls, the cars are partially wheeled wrecks. The audience-prisoners subsist on diets of malts and cheeseburgers, and every evening a succession of violent exploitationers pour down, sometimes mirroring the off screen action: war, kung fu and revenge movies (Trenchard-Smith's?), films as reflectors of the population's pathological fantasies, teasing reminders of the world that has rejected them.*

*It's a brilliant premise, and it comes close to working completely…a comic nightmare made hellishly real. It also may be one of the ultimate movies to see at a drive-in.*

That made me feel a little better. Over three decades, *Dead End Drive-In* built a following on home video, finally reaching collector status with Arrow's Blu Ray, remastered from the interpositive. The colors pop, the wet-down gleams. It's never looked so good. Reviews were appreciative. I'll conclude with one that gets into the heart and mind of the movie.

"The Ozploitation movement of the 70s and 80s largely comprised fast, trashy and loud movies – unambiguous affairs relegated to the realms of low-brow entertainment. Few attempted (or are remembered for) ambitious intellectual ideas. Director Brian Trenchard-Smith's 1986 science fiction oddity Dead End Drive-In, one of Ozploitation's most interesting productions, is a rare exception. The film has the grungy midnight look of a retro music video; the kind of garish aesthetic that could only emerge from the heart of a decade fashion forgot. But at its core is a bizarre and compelling representation of society as a microcosm. The setting – a drive-in cinema – is both unconventional and perfectly fitting given Trenchard-Smith's cult movie oeuvre. Singled out by Quentin Tarantino as his favourite film from the Aussie auteur (who made a range of daffy classics including BMX Bandits, Turkey Shoot and The Man from Hong Kong), Dead End Drive-In belongs to the camp of so-weird-it-works. Trenchard-Smith baited young audiences with the promise of brainless spectacle (the film is far from it, but its marketing material suggested otherwise) and when they sat down, they watched a film critical of their own demographic for being numbed and neutered by popular culture.

Set in a dystopian future where crime is rampant, the economy ravaged and cars are considered precious commodities, the film is based in a drive-in theatre where reprobates and layabouts are locked in forever – a kind of cinema concentration camp – and forced to acclimatize to a world built around the screen...

Dead End Drive-In is a political film dressed up (or down) as frothy entertainment. On both fronts it's a fist-pumping success.

I like the new artwork on the Arrow Blu Ray.

# CHAPTER 33
## Doldrums

While I was editing *Dead End Drive-In*, I got an offer from Tony Ginnane to direct a marauding crocodile adventure called *Dark Age*, to be shot in North Queensland as soon as I was available. I had reservations about the script. I was concerned (rightly as it turned out) whether the planned mechanical crocodile would look convincing. I had just done three pictures back to back. I did not want another three months away from Margaret and our boys. I turned it down. Mistake. Or was it? So it seemed, as 1986 progressed as a fairly dry year, sustained only by script assessments and promotional work.

At Christmastime in 1986, I was offered the Barry Humphries vehicle *Les Paterson Saves the World*. Perhaps my image within the industry after *Turkey Shoot*, *BMX Bandits*, and *Dead End Drive-In* was as an "over the top director," ideal for Barry's brand of gross-out humor. I had problems with the script, cowritten by Humphries' third wife Diane Millstead, the driving force behind the film. It wasn't the scatological humor and relentless innuendo that bothered me. It was the major plot point: Middle East dictator General Godownie (really?) plotting world domination with biologically infected toilet seats, contact with which causes a graphic pus-oozing death. This was an unwise attempt to coopt the recent panic about AIDS into the comedy. I pointed this out to Ms. Millstead when we met.

"But the AIDS joke in Barry's current show gets a huge laugh," she responded.

"What's the joke?"

"There's a newspaper billboard that reads: 'AIDS Cured. Media Fury!' "

"But that's a media joke, not an AIDS joke."

You might ask, given the political incorrectness of some of my work, why was this cheap laugh plot point a *no no* for me? Comedy is often meant to be offensive as a way to wake people up to an issue, but this was just exploitation of a global tragedy. I saw no laugh in that. Quite the opposite. Gay friends were dying. Margaret had strong feelings about the crisis and in the next year would become a volunteer at Project Ankali in Sydney, a group that to this day offers emotional support to people with AIDS. How could I contribute to the perpetuation of myths about the disease? It was a cordial discussion, but I got a strange vibe, a blinking amber light in the back of my mind. This may not end well. Despite an offer of $150K, I passed.

There were two other worthy projects to which I was attached that were seeking investors: *Blowing Hot and Cold*, with Italian star Giancarlo Giannini in the lead, and a well scripted Cold War spy thriller *The Taipan Negative*, from respected producer Anthony Buckley. One of those would be next, I felt sure. But neither was funded, leaving the next year potentially barren. At which point turning down two greenlit movies did not seem such a wise decision. Due to some distribution debacles, *Dark Age* was never theatrically released. Eventually it appeared on VHS in some counties. Quentin Tarantino is a fan and once hosted a screening of his personal print in Sydney. In retrospect I should have taken the offer. As for *Les Paterson Saves the World*, which cost AUD $7.4M, it was a colossal box office disaster, grossing only $626K in Australia, fizzling in the UK, and getting minimal release in the US after disastrous test screenings. Non-English language countries found it incomprehensible. It garnered many vituperative reviews. Some said it was "Australia's worst ever movie." As *The Guardian* drily put it, "It was a career high for nobody." Dodged a bullet there, I guess. Then again, the family coffers would have been 250K richer if I had done both projects, and perhaps I would have fixed *Les Paterson* (I doubt it). On New Years' Eve, staring at an empty calendar for 1987, I decided never again to turn down a *go* project. Just take it and run with it and hope for the best. Having family responsibilities changes one's perspective.

# CHAPTER 34
## The *Panther* Pictures

Damien Parer, the coproducer of *Dead End Drive-In*, called me late one afternoon in March of 1987. Would I be able to travel to Perth in West Australia immediately and take over two low budget martial arts movies being shot back-to-back in twenty days each? The films were privately financed, no government money involved. Four days into the schedule, the investors were unhappy with the footage and wanted the first-time writer/director replaced. I flew to Perth the next day. From this troubled start began one of my most enjoyable shoots—the *Panther* pictures.

*Day of The Panther* and sequel *Strike of The Panther* were created for the international video market. They were shot on 16mm and blown up to 35mm for theatrical release in a few foreign territories. Budgeted at only AUD$500,000 each, the movies were intended to make a star of Perth martial artist Ed Staszak, and kick off a fight movie franchise.

The stories of both movies followed a familiar formula. Part 1: Martial arts expert and undercover cop Jason Blade goes after a criminal gang, responsible for the death of his partner. He puts the crime boss and his chief enforcer behind bars. Part 2: When the enforcer escapes from jail, kidnaps the hero's girlfriend and threatens to blow up the city, our hero goes back into action.

Both Eddie and his fight choreographer Jim Richards, who also played his chief opponent, were really talented action actors, but they were not served well by the script, which was full of awkward clichéd dialogue without being fun. Producer Damien Parer was aware of these issues, but he could do nothing until there was a change of leadership. I had read the scripts overnight and again on the flight, arriving in midmorning due to the time difference. Damien screened some of the previous four days' footage. Eddie's performance was flat, and it was clear that key supporting roles were badly cast so we recast them. Well regarded stage actor Michael Carman blessed us with an amusing *Snidely Whiplash* villain. We decided to discard what had been shot and start over, adding significant new characters and a backstory explaining the otherwise unexplained secret society of 'Panthers'. But at the same time, shooting had to continue. We could not afford to lose another day. Damien had a new writer Michael Brindley on board within hours. Next morning, I started a 2-day chase/fight sequence that would not be impacted by the proposed changes to the scripts.

When an out-of-towner takes over from a home town boy, there are issues of loyalty and resentment that have to be handled with sensitivity. I told the crew I had considerable sympathy for my predecessor, but the show must go on, and I needed all their help. My philosophy is for everyone to share my enthusiasm for the work, and to have fun in the process. No crew functions at their best in an atmosphere of blame. So I try to find humor in routine mishaps and delays. We had a very productive first day, got some good action, and finished on time. They were my crew thereafter.

Damien Parer created a similar atmosphere in the production office, which had to deal with a daily-changing schedule. We were stepping into the abyss. Rewriting, recasting eight roles, and choosing new

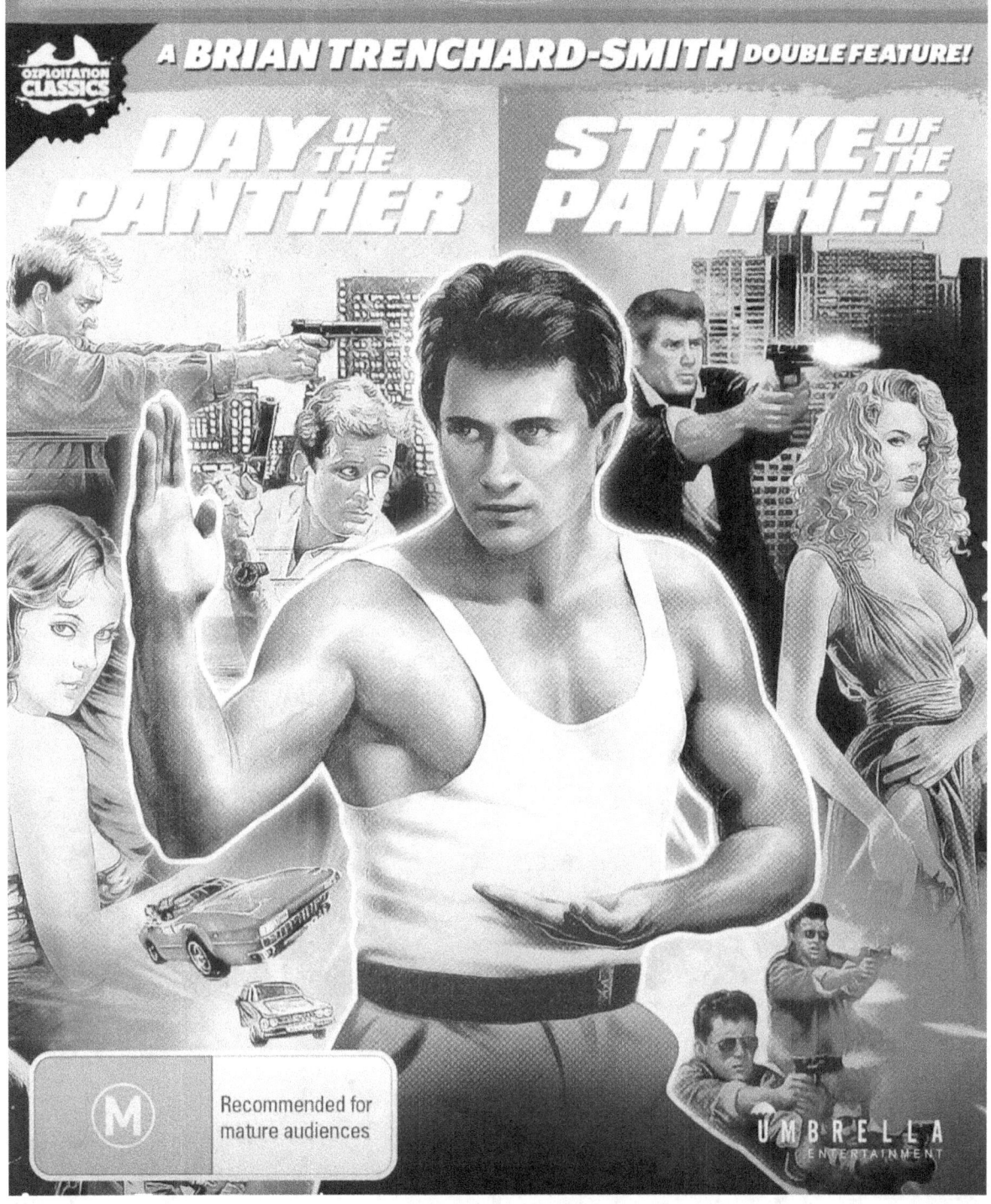

locations while continuing to shoot two movies with interwoven schedules is not the normal recipe for success, but Damien radiated a firm confidence and bonhomie at all times that was contagious. Every call sheet had panther jokes on it. Appreciation for services above and beyond the call were acknowledged. There was almost a cheerful wartime camaraderie in the office. Damien was able to persuade the investors to come up with more money to replace the lost shooting days, and add two guest stars, John Stanton and Rowena Wallace, to the marquee. Their local popularity would ensure a sale to Australian television, and indeed the Nine Network bought it a few years later. The shoot galloped along, cherry-picking scenes from both

movies, while staying at least a day behind the ongoing rewrite. One day I arrived at a location I had not seen, to work with supporting actors I hadn't met, to do a scene that still lacked credibility. But it worked out well. Directorial theater sports. I enjoyed it. The schedule soon settled down.

One complication was a shortage of trained martial arts stuntmen in Perth. Fighting for the camera requires selling the blows rather than inflicting them. There's an art to making unarmed combat convincing yet safe. There were eight fight scenes in the first film and nine in the second. That's a lot of fist-fodder for Eddie Staszak, but we could afford only three experienced stunt fighters who could handle complex choreography. They would be backed up by recruits from local martial arts clubs. But the key opponents across seventeen fights had to be played by three guys. Solution: disguises! In the first fight they wore Halloween-style Pig Mask, Geezer Mask, and Skull Mask. This concealed the beards they had grown during prep for their next appearance as New Thugs. Then they shaved their beards and dyed their hair to become fresh victims of the flying fists and feet of Jason Blade. By the time we arrived at *Strike of The Panther*'s climactic battle in the power station, the only option left was—Hockey Masked Ninjas! In one multiple combat, I had to add a similarly disguised Jim Richards to increase the numbers of assailants. He then changed costume and resumed his role as the evil Baxter for his final duel with Jason Blade.

Eddie had a catlike grace in the fight scenes. Jim's choreography was inventive and the equal of any Chuck Norris movie of the 80s. Together they delivered the goods for the core martial arts audience. On the first day of the sound mix I discovered that the soundtrack of the fights contained only sound effects, impacts, not a grunt and groan track, vocal reactions that bring the combat to life, part of the Kung Fu genre's DNA. So all the male yells and groans in the finished pictures are provided by yours truly. As each fight came up in the mix, I would lay down a track for each fighter. AGH! EURR! EEK! Great fun. The studio receptionist volunteered to do the female tracks. She performed with gusto.

I wanted the fights tough but not unpleasantly so. Characters bleed but they bleed politely. I was sensitive to the recent "video nasties" controversy in the UK and finetuned the violence accordingly. The British

Board of Film Censors gave it an '18' rating nonetheless. Guild Home Video brought Eddie and Jim over for publicity and did extremely well with both movies in the boom days of VHS. It's interesting to compare the way different countries styled their artwork.

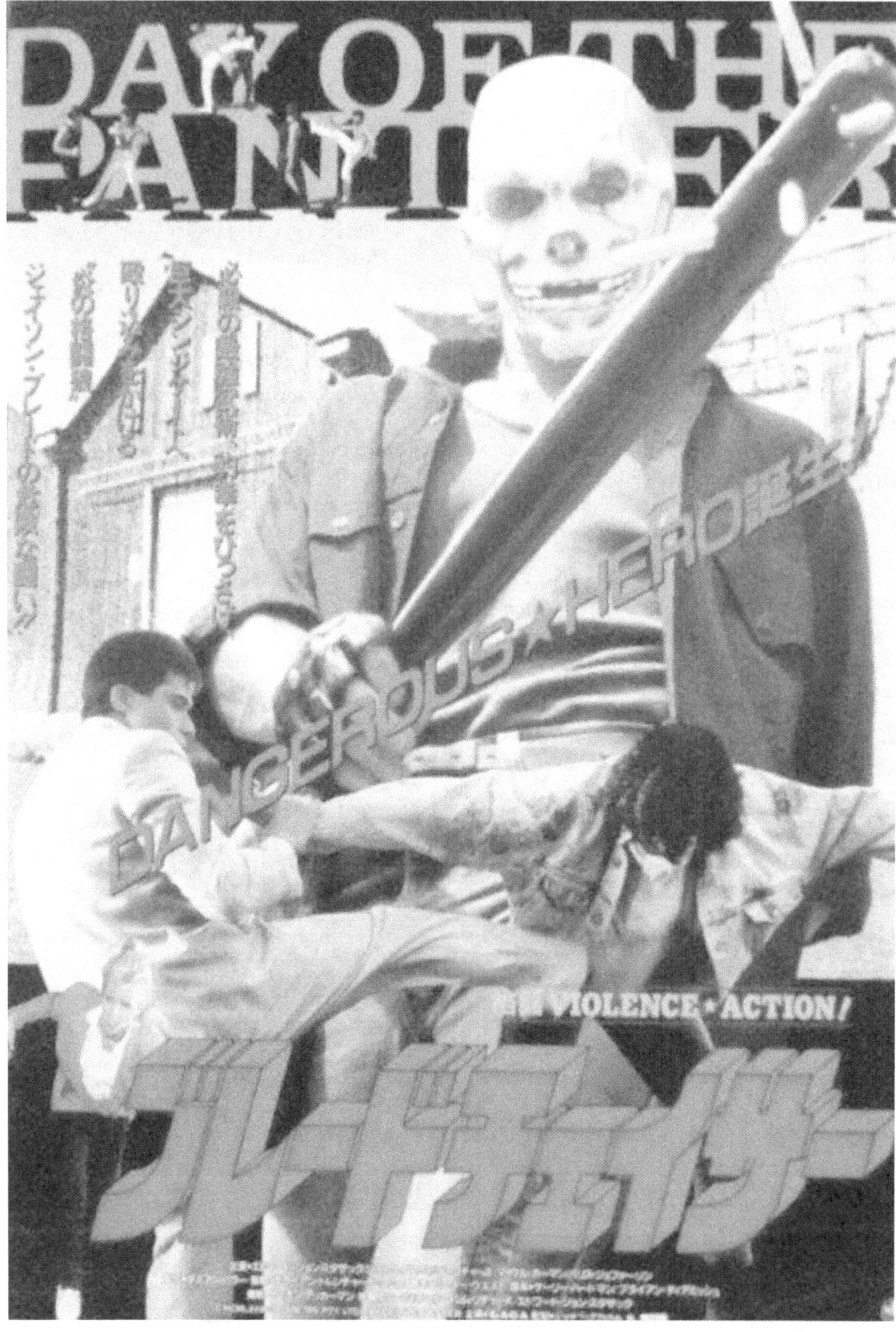

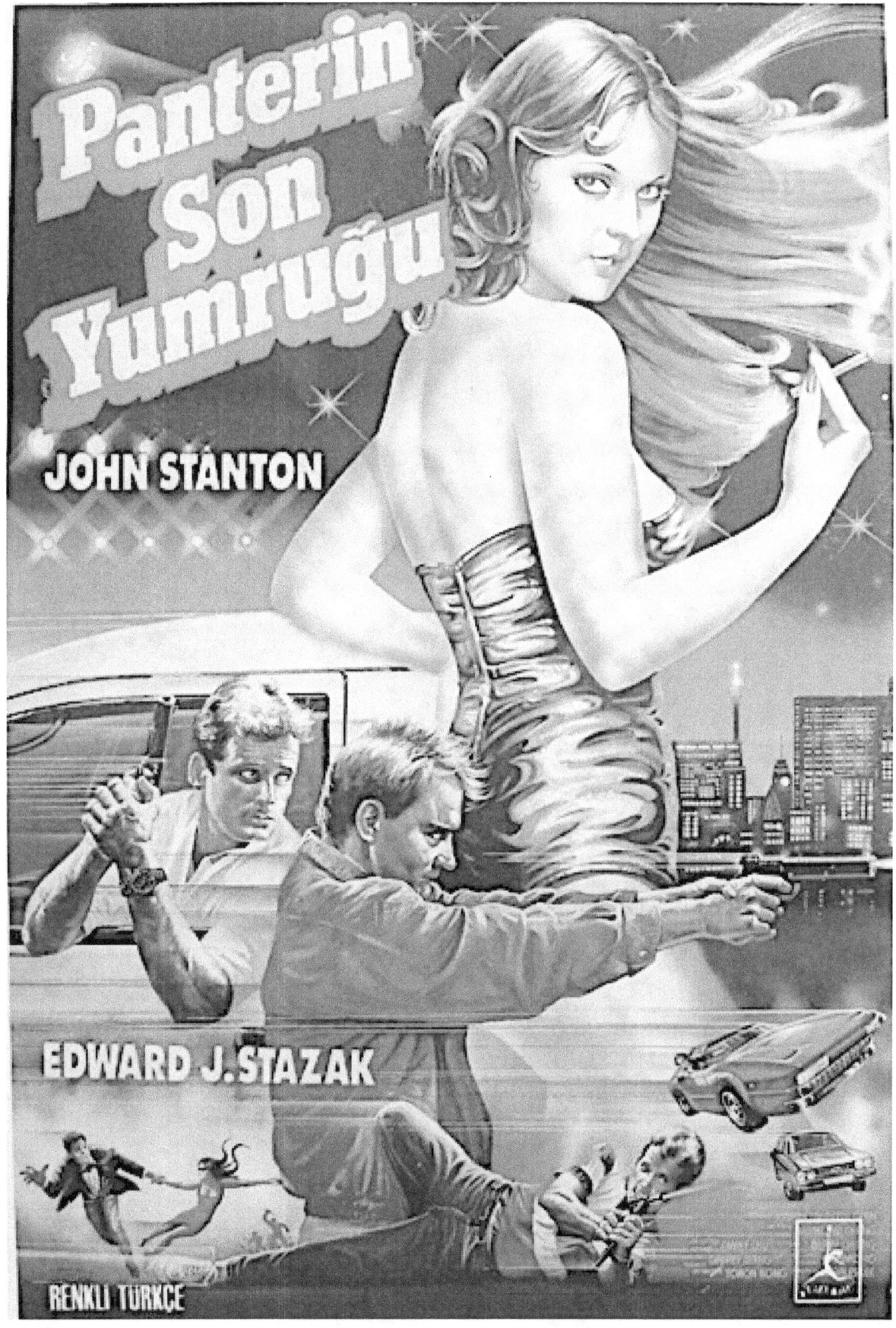

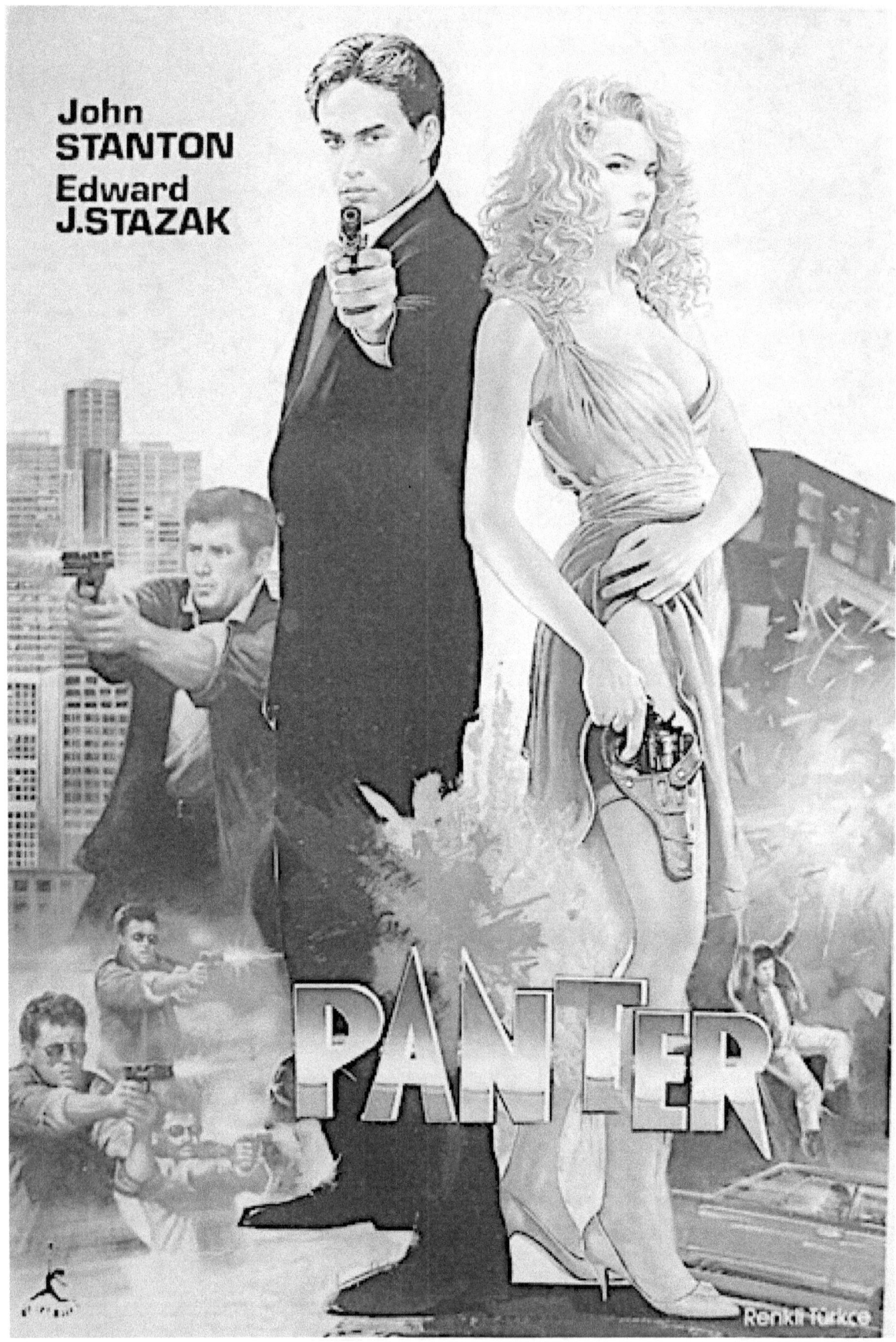

John
STANTON
Edward
J.STAZAK

PANTER

Renkli türkçe

I'm proud of the *Panther* Pictures, an 80s time capsule brimming with clichés, stereotypes, and dated genre tropes to celebrate and satirize. There's something about campy fun that seems to travel well between generations. At Portland's Hollywood Theater I was gratified to watch an audience of nearly 300 cinema geeks chortle and occasionally howl with laughter. They kept the Q&A going for forty minutes.

While editing the *Panther* pics, I got a call from my *BMX Bandits* producer Tom Broadbridge, who had put together a package of four movies budgeted at 500K each. Would I like to do one? The suggested script was a supernatural horror thriller entitled *Out of the Body*.

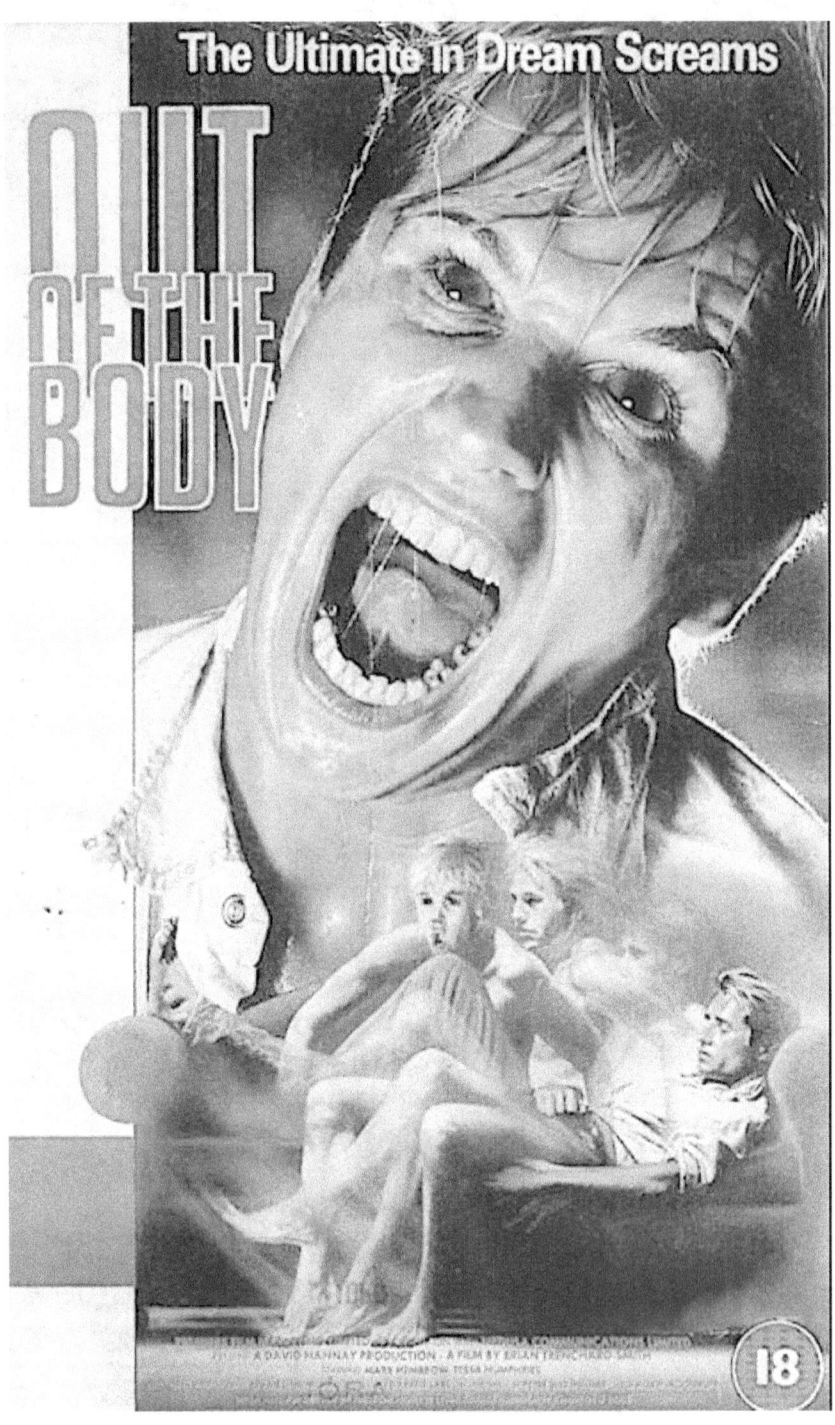

A man is haunted by out-of-body experiences in which he sees murders from the murderer's point of view. Was he dreaming or did he commit these crimes? Or has his astral travelling self been hijacked by a demon that is taking him over? To be honest, I never fully understood the whys and wherefores underpinning the story, but the script had a level of preposterousness that appealed to me. I amplified this by adding more horror moments and spookery. *The Entity*, *Poltergeist*, Hammer, William Castle, Argento were my influences, but the resulting genre cocktail does not gel. There were lessons for me to learn.

An up-and-coming actor, Mark Hembrow, delivered the best audition, and put his heart and soul into the role of a man going mad. He made some bold choices. I went along with them, believing they suited the overripe nature of the piece, so I must take responsibility. What I didn't realize till it was too late was that I had allowed Mark to play the role largely on one note. The character spent too much time complaining, wailing his agony and despair. Admittedly, he *is* being possessed by a demon, but for an audience to maintain identification with their lead character, he must show courage in adversity, not weakness. He must restrain emotion, not constantly display it. It's not Mark's fault. The director calls the shots.

I cast Tessa Humphries as the hero's luckless girlfriend, who—spoiler alert—ends up being possessed by the demon herself. She was a charming young actor with an elfin beauty. She was also Barry Humphries' daughter. I did not tell her I had turned down her father's movie *Les Patterson Saves the World*. It was not easy for her to face a local cast and crew after the horrible Australian reviews of *Sir Les…* then try to make preposterous dialogue about astral travel convincing. But she did her best.

Within the 4 week schedule, I tried to give the film multiple locations, pace, and a fluid camera incorporating a lot of colored gels in the lighting. Dario Argento, but without his budget. Like Argento's films, *Out of the Body* needed a great soundtrack to boost the unease. This was another area where I felt the film fell down. I had to leave after locking the cut to prep *The Siege of Firebase Gloria* in the Philippines. The producers supervised the sound mix. Months later I saw the finished version, I found the mix flat, and the music dirge-like. Not spinetingling. Not what The Goblins added to *Suspiria*. To be fair, that was not the brief I had given the composer. In retrospect, it should have been.

The movie does have some effective moments, such as when the astral demon forces Carrie Zivitz as the psychiatrist, to stab herself in the forehead. DP Kevan Lind shot *Siege of Firebase Gloria* for me as a result of his good work here. Fellow victims Helen O'Connor as the ex-wife, and Mary Regan as the TV presenter handle their scenes well. Shane Briant, a Hammer veteran (*The Vampire Lovers*, for which I made the trailer) was now living in Sydney and wanted to work with me, however small the part. He was effective in a brief scene as a possible suspect. The production value on a $500K budget is high. It sold well to video across the world, particularly in the UK, where it debuted at No. 9 in the video charts. But the film doesn't really deliver. I think this more recent review sits between fair and generous.

*Out of the Body is not a well-liked film. It currently sits on a soul-shattering 3.7 on IMDB from only fifty-five votes and the title of the first review I can see reads "One of the worst films I have ever seen!" Well, I can safely say that I have seen far worse than Out of the Body. In fact, I had a very good time with this one. Out of the Body is nowhere near the heights of Trenchard-Smith's best, but it is still an extremely entertaining and snappy little horror-thriller. Sure, the plot is silly, Mark Hembrow's performance is completely bananas and I could picture the film's ending after the opening ten minutes, but all of its cheesiness only adds to its charm. Trenchard-Smith knows how to stage quality action sequences and he delivers them with his usual flair. The film's ending is enormous fun* and some of the death sequences are quite impressive. The killer's victims are murdered by an unseen Evil Dead-esque force that tears them off their feet, hoisting them in the air. The epic dispatchings are captured with a keen eye and creativity that doesn't seem to exist in films today. If you are a Trenchard-Smith fan, find a copy of this straight away. It delivers if your Trenchard-Smith-expectations are kept in check.

# CHAPTER 35
## The Siege of Firebase Gloria

My next film, *The Siege of Firebase Gloria*, would meet the expectations of the war movie audience. Producer Tony Ginnane had financed what was then called *Forward Firebase Gloria* as a coproduction with a Philippine company, to shoot in and around Manila. It was a solid script. I saw it as *The Alamo* in Vietnam battledress with credit given to both sides of the conflict. My influences were Cy Raker Endfield's *Zulu*, Sam Fuller's *Merrill's Marauders*, Cornel Wilde's *Beach Red*. The script, depicting an isolated American outpost under siege during the 1968 Tet Offensive, was written by two Australians, Bill Nagle and Tony Johnson. Bill Nagle served a year's tour of duty in Vietnam while in the Australian army. Many of the incidents are inspired by stories he heard from American soldiers. What I liked was that it told the story of a battle from both sides, albeit with the American side taking the balance of the screen time. The Vietcong were not demonized. They were depicted as brave soldiers following orders, just like the Americans they were fighting.

The story begins fifteen years after the US left Vietnam. We see a boatload of Vietnamese refugees sight landfall in the Philippines. A retired Marine Gunnery Sergeant ((R. Lee Ermey), now working for the ref-

ugee processing center in Manila, is the film's narrator. He scans the latest group of boat people he is about to process. Amongst them is a face he remembers, a former North Vietnamese officer (Robert Arevalo) with whom he had engaged in hand-to-hand combat in the final battle for the firebase. This opening and closing scenes of the movie are bookends to the story of the battle that unfolds in flashback. Many of the sergeant major's men are killed. He has to euthanize his best friend (Wings Hauser). The flashback ends and we return to the refugee processing center. How does the ex-Marine feel about his former enemy? He approaches the man and says "Welcome" in Vietnamese. The men shake hands. The film is about war and reconciliation. Sentimental perhaps, but I thought it worked.

However, the distributor cut the bookends from the film shortly before the sound mix, rendering the story to be purely about a battle. Sales executives felt that from a US audience point of view there was, and I quote "too much emphasis on the gooks." They wanted the film to evoke those gung-ho Marine movies of the 1950s. "Against all odds they went to hell and back!" declaimed the subsequent video sleeve. How could I restore some of the message of the movie at the eleventh hour? I got Lee Ermey into the mixing studio. We brainstormed some additional narration to what was already there, and through his character's thoughts showed where the movie's heart lay. I dropped it into the final mix without executives noticing. Enough evenhandedness remains in the picture, which has become a favorite of a lot of Vietnam vets. I'm proud of it as it stands, but it would have been a deeper-themed film with the intended bookends. Local Philippine star Robert Arevalo' moving performance as the North Vietnamese commander is all the more remarkable for being learned phonetically.

I took Margaret and our boys with me to the Philippines. Eric and Alex were then aged seven and four. We settled into the Intercontinental Hotel in Manila, close to a Montessori school which our sons attended. Our ten weeks in Metro Manila, Los Baños, and Pagsanjan was an eye-opening adventure for us all. Margaret was to play Captain Flanagan, the medical officer on the firebase. The production could only afford local supporting actors at Manila prices. The role needed to be played by an American, not by a Filipina, because all the Vietcong were being played by Filipinos. Margaret held her own in scenes with Wings Hauser and Lee Ermey.

We filmmakers are obsessive folk, often oblivious to the perils of shooting in foreign parts. Within a few days, I was taken to survey a location two hour's drive out of Manila, accompanied by First AD Carding Guzman, Production Designer Toto Castillo, and Production Executive Mike Fuller. Miles into the countryside we passed a guard tower at a crossroads, its elevated platform cocooned in netting, conjuring the image of a robot beekeeper.

"What's the net for?" I asked.

"Grenades, sir," was the deadpan reply from our driver.

In 1988, the Philippine Islands were still in the grip of two insurgencies, an Islamist guerilla war on the southern island of Mindanao, and the communist New People's Army (NPA) on the main island of Luzon where we were. Hmm. An hour's drive out of Manila we were already crossing the perceived border beyond which lay NPA-contested territory, and we had an hour's driving to go.

"Don't worry about the NPA, sir, they are The Good People."

I mistook this for character evaluation. In fact, the Good People was a line item in all Filipino movie budgets at the time. Ostensibly, it referred to security staff for locations outside Manila. Indeed, who better to protect you from the NPA than the NPA themselves? I was told that they were better than the Philippine military. Or the police. They did not get drunk, or bring their cousins demanding they get paid as well. They were therefore The Good People.

Our car eventually arrived at the top of a hill with a good view of surrounding countryside, the recommended choice for the firebase. Worked for me. We awaited the arrival of the NPA representatives. Toto Castillo outlined his plan for the layout of the defensive perimeter and bunkers.

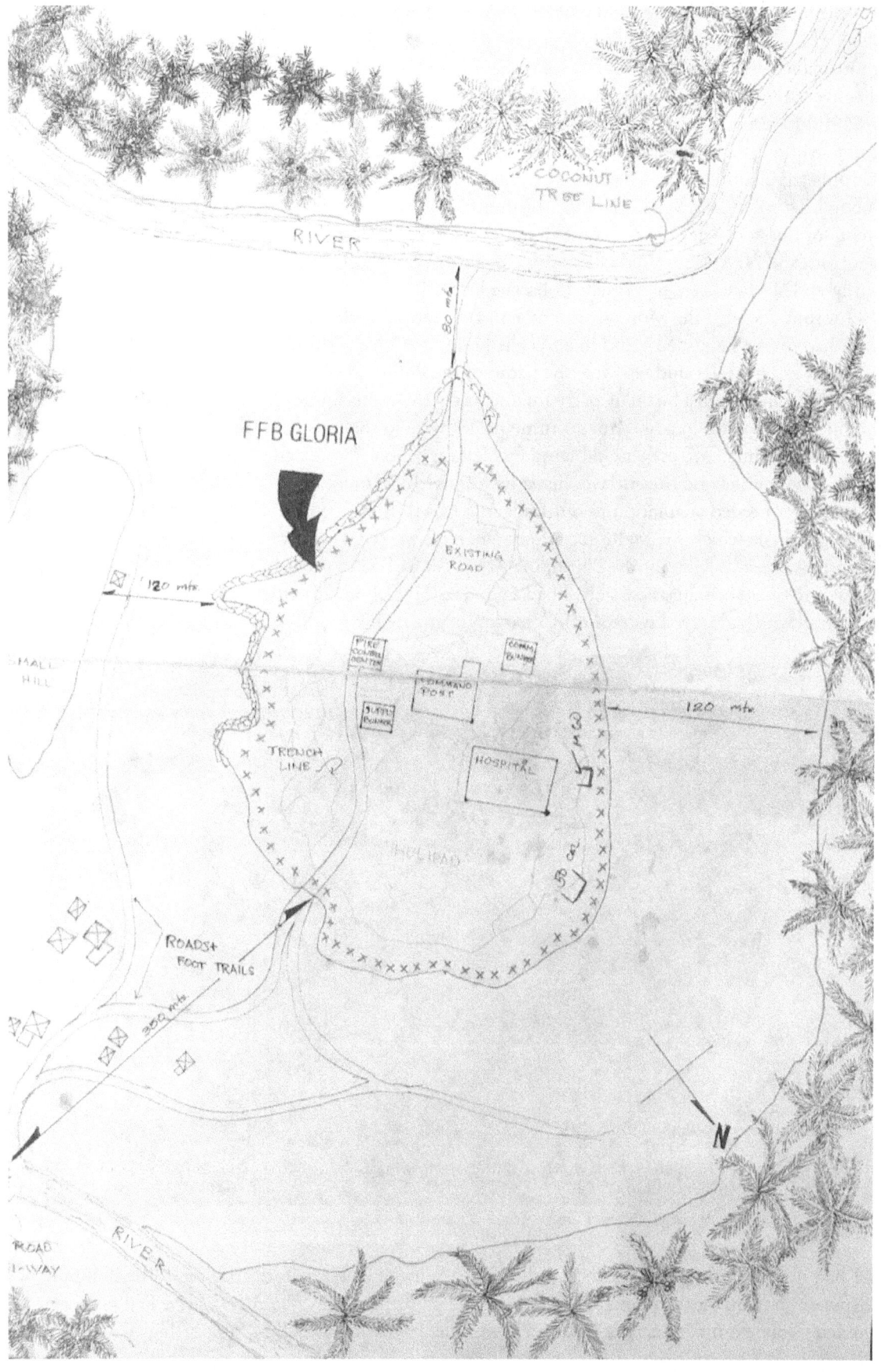

A pickup truck approached and parked. Two armed men with bandanas round their faces got out. Mike Fuller and I realized our Philippine colleagues were also armed. Apart from a moment of frisson at the sight of more loaded weapons, I did not feel we had anything to fear. It had a routine vibe to it. And indeed, cordial conversation in Tagalog took place, a deal was made, and the NPA were on their way again. We would pay $5000 for each month of our stay in their territory. They would protect us, ensure that local bandits did not strip our firebase set each night, etc. They even volunteered to be Viet Cong in our battle scenes. Their only stipulation was this—when we brought in the Filipino Army helicopter gunships for the strafing and bombing scenes, we would give the NPA notice so they could make themselves scarce. The Army were grateful for this, too. They did not want an unnecessary fight, either. This was indicative of a level of popular support for the NPA, purported champions of the poor in the Philippines, where social inequality in the recently-ended Marcos era had reached obscene levels.

Our sons attended the Montessori school in Dasmariñas within Metro Manila. As at other public places, you had to pass an armed guard to enter the building. Once within, the school was light and bright and its teachers excellent. Its students were the scions of the Philippine élite of Luzon in 1988. On one occasion, the boys were invited to a birthday party for a schoolfriend at his home. Or rather, mansion, of mind-blowing opulence. An actor in a Skeletor costume played ogre to the kids while security with submachine guns patrolled the perimeter to prevent kidnapping. Helium balloons were tied to small baskets containing coins, alms for the poor beyond the enclave. Just a typical day in Manila…

The script needed adaptation to our budget ($1.6M) There were attacks by tanks and armored hovercraft in the finale which we could not afford. We replaced them with the Air Cavalry. Vietnam era Huey helicopters were still flying for the Philippine Army. All we had to do was put US decals on them. I wanted the movie to be as accurate as possible. I had a good barometer of authenticity in costar R. Lee Ermey, a Marine veteran who had served two tours in Vietnam before being invalided out with shrapnel in his shoulder.

I had not met either of our stars, Lee Ermey or Wings Hauser, before arriving in the Philippines, but had spoken to them on the phone. Lee's astonishing performance in *Full Metal Jacket* had just earned him a Golden Globe nomination. The Boston Film Critics gave him their Best Supporting Actor award. I encouraged Lee to come to Manila a week early, which he did. Luckily, he approved where we had placed the firebase, because construction was well underway. The role of Sgt. Major Haffner was written to be Army. Lee said he would be much happier playing what he knew best—a Marine Gunnery Sergeant. Fine by me.

When I phoned Wings Hauser in the US, he felt his role was undernourished, and he had ideas on how it could be improved. I got the sense that he expected to be the focus of the movie, being the bigger name, with a growing fanbase.

After starring in the hugely successful *Vice Squad* six years earlier, he had done a string of well-paid 'B' movies, and recently received excellent reviews for his role as the crazed cop in Norman Mailer's *Tough Guys Don't Dance*. He would bring some of that to the crazed Corporal DiNardo. I assured him we would work together to give his character more texture and opportunity.

Lee did not think of himself as a star. He had been a technical advisor to Vietnam war movies shot in the PI, while acting small roles. He had been elevated to the showcase role of Sgt. Major Hartman in *Full Metal Jacket* when Kubrick watched him train the actors playing recruits in full-throated foul-mouthed Marine lingo. Kubrick immediately replaced Tim Colceri, whom he had hired to play the drill sergeant, with Lee, who

SEASON HUBLEY. GARY SWANSON. WINGS HAUSER

VICE SQUAD

DIRECTED BY GARY A. SHERMAN

On the street, the real trick is *staying alive*

"Sensationally Brutal" –*New York Times*

had actually been one. Lee delivered an award-winning performance. He was a proud yet humble man, surprised by his sudden good fortune but not expecting it to last. As I listened to Lee telling stories about the Marine Corps, just like Kubrick, I fell under his spell. I had to find opportunities to put Lee's brand of Marine patois into the movie.

When Wings Hauser arrived, fresh off the plane, he had ideas to put into the movie too. He suggested that in the final conflict he would strip off all his clothes—"I don't bare my ass for just any movie, but I'll do it for this one…"—and run naked into the middle of the battlefield, screaming "Stop!" And both sides do stop shooting.

"Then a single shot rings out, and as I die, I say 'At least I stopped the war'. What d'ya think?"

"Very interesting, Wings. Thank you. Let me discuss it with the team…"

I attributed this curious concept to a 19-hour sleepless flight, and hoped it would be forgotten in the morning. It was. Ultimately, I gave him a much better death scene. Wings needed his character to have an emotional focus, which the script did not provide, in order to show the inner humanity of the hard bitten Corporal DiNardo. So I made him the guardian of an orphaned Vietnamese boy, a character that was almost cut on the first morning of the shoot.

In the opening scene, the Marine patrol discovers a massacred village. The only survivor is a 5-year-old boy. They take him to the firebase, and leave him with the nurses in the field hospital. In the course of the final battle, the Viet Cong commander scoops the boy up and carries him back to his retreating troops. The child, wearing traditional black pyjamas, is a metaphor for Vietnam, taken by Americans, taken back by Vietnamese. It was a non-speaking, largely passive role, that would still require reactions to specific situations, primarily surprise, curiosity, and tears.

I met a number of Filipino kids from acting families. One 5-year-old seemed the most confident and malleable. His parents duly brought him to our Day One location. He was needed for the first shot. We presented him with the black pyjamas that would be his costume. He absolutely refused to put them on. Threw a tantrum. His parents remonstrated with him, which only made matters worse. We were at a standstill before film had even rolled through the camera. This did not bode well. I needed the child to represent Vietnam as a country and a people. It was put to me strongly that maybe "the child thing" was impractical on our budget and schedule. It would be better to drop the character now before the first shot, rather than do it later, and have to reshoot any kid scenes without the kid. Then I heard a voice.

"My boy will do it."

A small crowd of fishermen from the nearby village had gathered to watch the filming. One of them, a Mr. Cruz, stepped forward, holding his 4-year-old son Michael by the hand. Why not? I thought. I asked for the black pyjamas to be brought over. Young Michael Cruz got into them immediately. I think the other boy was freaked out less by the black pyjamas than by the sight of the men in uniform, standing around carrying weapons. So we paid his parents for the day, and proceeded with Michael, who turned out to be a natural. His moments with Wings were effective, and he delivered a chilling moment I improvised, playing with a (dummy) fifty caliber bullet,  muttering "Boom, boom , boom…" as if it was a plane on a bombing run, as if war was a natural part of life. On the last day of the shoot, I presented him with the biggest Voltron action figure available. In his teenage years, Michael became an actor and is credited on a couple of Manila TV shows. I hope he is having a good life.

Friction with Wings arose early when I set up a tracking shot along soldiers in the trench line tensely waiting for the attack. Nicely backlit, it was to be the last shot of the day. Then it occurred to me I could use this setup also for an additional pre-battle moment: the sergeant giving his men an appropriate pep-talk as he walked along the trench line. In fact, it would be a great place for his "There's no such thing as an atheist in a foxhole" routine. I called Lee over, and within fifteen minutes we had a great take in the can.

*"A little religious communications might not be bad idea at this stage of the game. Now myself, I don't take any chances. I talk to Mohammed, Buddha, Mr. Jesus H Christ, and any other religious honchos I can come up with... You can rest assured that you will not go into that bag until I have said a few appropriate words over you."*

Lee's flair for dark humor would be a major asset to the tone of the film. Wings felt I was favoring Lee over him, that I had broken faith. Of course, he was right. I was favoring Lee. But Lee's natural persona would give the movie something unique and I was going to run with it. My favorite of all Lee's improvisations is the "severed heads" scene which we brainstormed while the crew were setting up the lights. In the script, the scene ended with the gruesome discovery of the beheaded soldiers. I wanted to throw the focus back on Lee's character and his leadership qualities. Why don't you show severed heads to the troops as the consequence of inattention?

*"Does anyone know who these belong to? This is Corporal Miller. He's dead. Hell, the whole goddam gun crew is dead, and to add insult to injury, Charlie took the fifty fucking caliber machine gun with him... Pay attention, stay alert, stay alive. It's as simple as that."*

Wings felt he should be offered similar opportunities, so I invited him to write a performance scene for himself which we would shoot on our last day. Wings had received story credit on another Vietnam film, *Uncommon Valor*. I was sure he would write something useful. And he did. He wrote a good, if slightly overwrought, scene, that, late in the film, fleshed out his character revealing how the death of his own young son had tipped him into craziness.

This helped support the death scene I had in mind for Wings. As the final battle rages, he sees the orphan boy being carried from the battlefield by a North Vietnamese soldier, in fact the commander Cao Van. He rushes to intervene and Cao Van shoots him down. Wings volunteered to be squibbed in the groin to motivate his character's subsequent request to be euthanized. I was happy to oblige.

The promise of this personal scene ahead did not stop us clashing a number of times. Wing's behavior did not endear him to cast or crew. His resentment of Lee Ermey manifested itself in little ways. Lee was patient but finally he spat the dummy (that's Australian for "he threw a fit").

"Goddammit!" he yelled, throwing his cup of coffee to the warehouse floor. He then gave Wings a good Gunnery Sergeant chewing out.

"You got to call people on their shit," Lee said to me later. It cleared the air and it was plain sailing for his final scene. The day after Wings flew back to the US, the Filipino crew printed a Firebase T-shirt on which was emblazoned "We can fly without Wings."

Despite our friction, Wings did deliver a compelling performance as a PTSD time bomb, for which he deserves and has received considerable praise. As a method actor he put himself through the wringer

to create the tortured character and his effort shows. The producers considered the scene Wings wrote as a performance moment for himself too sentimental and suggested I cut it, but in that matter, I kept faith with Wings and the scene stayed. I think it's effective. The whole experience gave me some tuition in the challenges of cast management.

*The Siege of Firebase Gloria* contains five major battle scenes, and the fulfillment of a childhood ambition. I shot my first battle scene on 8mm in which two squads of the Wellington College Cadet Corps overran a trench line. Now at last I had 200 extras (on my biggest day) to assault the firebase.

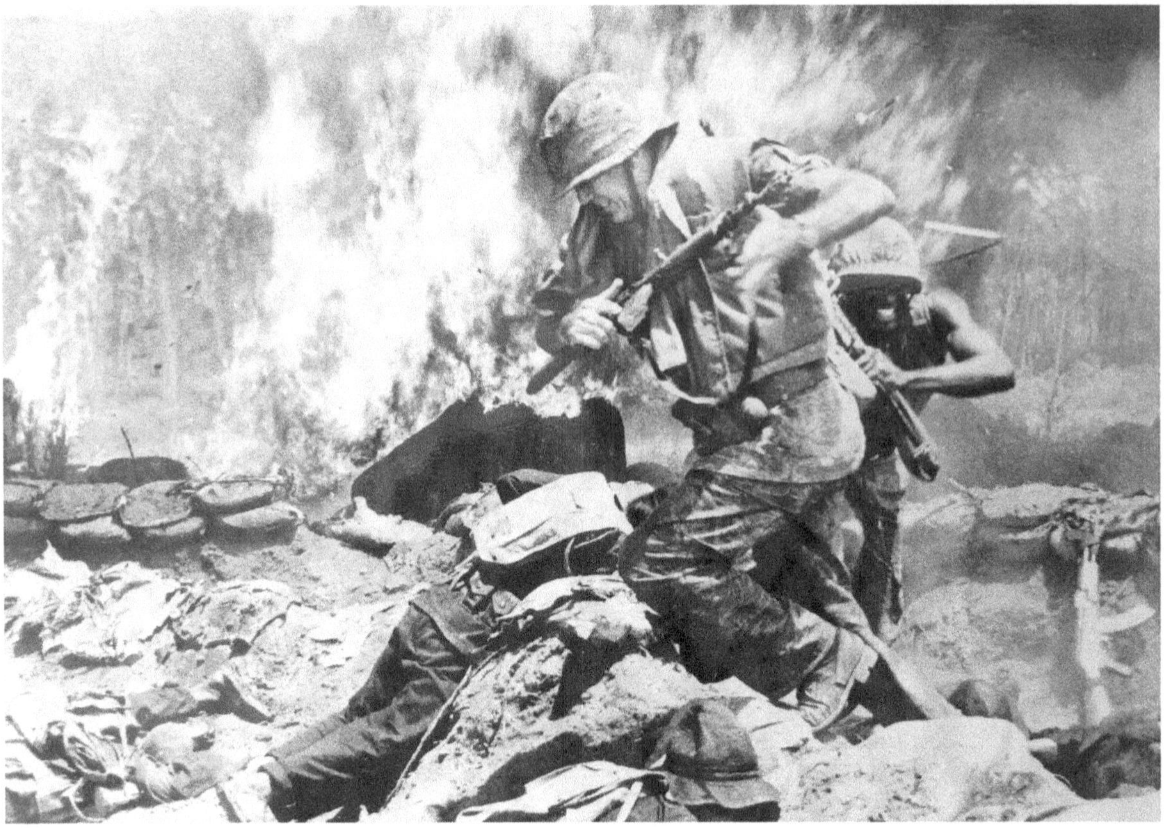

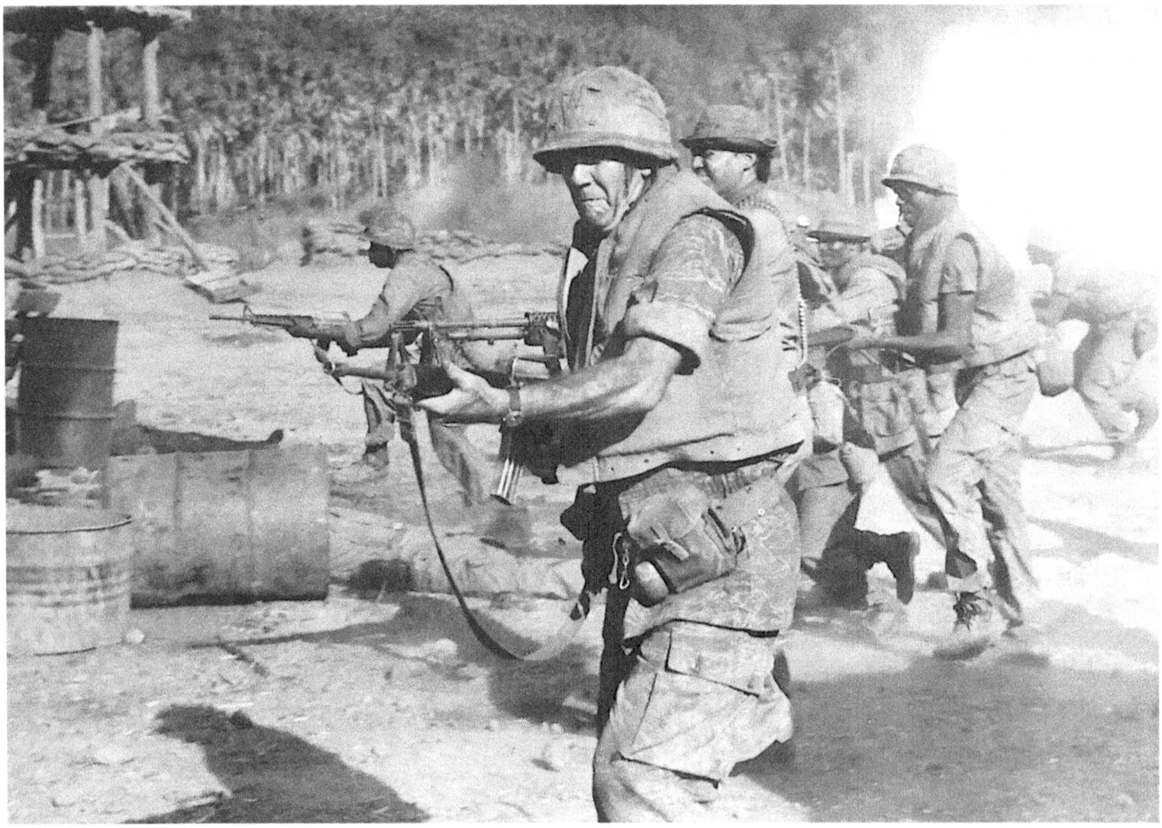

Battle scenes need coverage and momentum. Lewis Milestone's trademark tracking shots—*All Quiet on the Western Front*, *A Walk in the Sun*, *Pork Chop Hill* amongst others—inspired me to do similar. I tracked behind a trench line, as the defenders took fire from approaching attackers. Some defenders were squibbed with exit wounds and recoiled as the camera passed. Cut to a tracking shot facing the defenders returning fire, as squibs punctured sandbags beside them. Cut to a tracking shot along squibbed attackers as several fall. Cut to tracking shot behind the attackers showing how close they have got to the defenders' trench line, more fall. Intercutting these angles, when combined with vigorous staging, can give a battle a lot of drive. I was greatly aided by editor and 2$^{nd}$ Unit Director Andrew Prowse, who stayed on with the extras after I had cleared the actors from the firebase location, and delivered excellent scenes of helicopters strafing the Vietcong camp that I did not have time to do. Danny 'Boom Boom' Dominguez, as he was known locally, did a great job with the pyrotechnics. He told me that we ultimately let off more explosions than *Hamburger Hill*!

I have a motto: if in doubt, blow it up, or at least set fire to it. Fire is always good production value and relatively cheap. We had built An Lap village in a field and would have to dismantle it, and clear the debris.

Why not burn it down first as a funeral pyre for the massacred inhabitants? This provided a nice tracking shot with the patrol somberly walking away with the village blazing in the background.

Cashflow was erratic throughout the shoot. The Lab processed our negative but would not make work print for our inspection without payment. I shot the last three weeks of the film without being able to see the result till I was back in Australia. I found out that the stunt team were owed two weeks of backpay. Apologizing to me that they had no choice, they went on strike in the middle of a battle scene. The Philippine coproducer drove to a racecourse and borrowed cash from his friends to pay the stunt team. A couple of hours later, filming resumed. They were a great bunch and fun to be around.

One day I was down to 700 feet of Kodak stock at the start of another battle scene. No sign of replenishment. Veteran Director Andrew V. McLaglan (fifty-seven movies, countless TV episodes) was shooting *Return to the River Kwai*— his last film—in a nearby paddy field. I sent a messenger asking to borrow some stock, to be replaced. He sent me 3000 feet of Fuji film as a gift.

Vale: Andrew V. McLaglen (1920 - 2014). A class act.

When the Main Unit moved on to Metro Manila, leaving the 2nd Unit to continue, the company was late in paying the NPA for the next month's security. 2nd Unit Director Andrew Prowse was warned by his Filipino crew to stay in his Pagsanjan hotel, or he would be taken as a surety.

Here Andrew (far right) is taking a break with one of his camera team and associate producer Mike Fuller. Within a couple of days, the 5K was delivered and the 2nd Unit continued to get great stuff.

During a tough night shoot, I wandered away from the lights of the set so I could gaze at the brilliant stars and recover some inspiration. One of the NPA security people at our perimeter told me it was not safe to go any further.

"But you're The Good People," I said.

"There are good Good People, and there are bad Good People, especially at night," he replied. "Best stay back."

OK. Got It.

But I don't think that I really *Got It* till the night we were relaxing having dinner in the only Western-style restaurant/bar in the tiny town of Pagsanjan (where much of *Apocalypse Now* was shot). At the only street lit section, this bar was adjacent to the police station. Twenty yards walk from door to door. Margaret and the boys were there that night. She was seated opposite our friend Mark Neely (Private Murphy in the film), who faced the front door. Mark's eyes widened and he muttered *sotto voce*, "Get the kids out of here." The local Police Chief had entered the bar. He wore a bandolier and a sidearm, and a submachine gun hung from a strap around his neck. Ammunition pouches and grenades dangled from his belt. All this firepower to go twenty yards?! Grenades?!! Was everywhere outside of the walls of the police station a free fire zone? Wordlessly, Margaret walked to where the boys were fooling around with the drum set at the back of the restaurant and led them, protesting, away.

Some days later, outside the bar, two of the Police Chief's men monstered one of our cast, Clyde Jones, who plays the radio operator Shortwave.

"What are you doing in the Philippines?" they demanded.

"I'm making a movie!" said Clyde, with as confident a smile as he could muster.

"What do you do?"

Clyde replied, "I'm an actor."

"An actor?" one cop asked. Turning to his fellow officer, he commanded: "Shoot him!"

Clyde Jones is African American. For a few heart-pounding seconds Clyde really thought they meant it. Two liquored-up cops, thousands of miles from the US, in a town with three street lamps…who would ever know what had happened to him? Then they roared with laughter and let him go. No joke to Clyde.

When the army helicopters were scheduled for the strafing and bombing sequences, we duly informed the NPA, who melted back into the jungle. But the helicopters were five hours late. The Captain in charge apologized. They had been on a mission against the NPA 100 miles to the north.

"We will now change to blank ammunition," he said.

"Excellent idea!"

The army guys laughed. But my quip masked a twinge of guilt. We were doing simulated war, while further north people were dying in real war, compatriots perhaps of the local NPA who had treated us well.

Back in Manila, I staged the 1968 attack on the US Saigon Embassy, at a rundown Foreign Business-men's Club, a passable match to photographs of the original building. After Take One of the initial assault, with Viet Cong shooting up the sentry box and driving in hurling grenades, we suddenly found ourselves surrounded by police and army units. It turned out that President Cory Aquino and potential rival General Ramos were meeting in a hotel a couple of blocks away. Upon hearing the explosions and gunfire, they thought that another revolution had broken out. We were shut down for two hours while I persuaded the authorities that we had no plans to overthrow the government of the Philippines…

Despite all the stress, we had a great time in the PI. Even the reptiles were friendly.

The Siege of Firebase Gloria sold well across international markets mostly to home video, as was its fate in Australia. Although the film was written, produced, directed, photographed, sound recorded, edited, scored, and dubbed by Australians, the Australian Film Institute refused to allow it to compete in its annual awards, because it had an American cast. Animus towards producer Tony Ginnane within the Arts/Culture circles was a factor. They deplored Ginnane's international casting approach to movie making. And Tony had a tendency to flaunt his success, which did not endear him to some contemporaries. But his prolific output gave many directors, actors and crew opportunities to build a life long career. In America, Fries Entertainment gave the film a token theatrical release, mainly in drive-ins as the supporting feature to Dolph Lungren's *Rambo* clone *Red Scorpion*. LA Times critic Michael Wilmington's review was full of praise for the "feisty little B movie," adding that *Red Scorpion* should be supporting *Firebase*, not the other way 'round. Over the years, the film has developed a loyal following among veterans, many of whom regard *Firebase* as the movie that evoked their Vietnam experience most truthfully. In an *Entertainment Weekly* interview, Quentin Tarantino was kind enough to call *Firebase* one of my best.

# CHAPTER 36
## Taking Stock

1988 continued to be a busy year, although that wouldn't last. After finishing postproduction on *Firebase* in Sydney, I got a call to direct an episode of the *Mission Impossible* TV series. The writers' strike in the US had prompted Paramount Pictures' TV division to generate product offshore using Australian writers. They set up two series—*Dolphin Cove* and *Mission Impossible*—at the new Village Roadshow Studios on the Gold Coast. Paramount sent top executive Jeffrey Hayes to be the showrunner on the reboot of the *Mission Impossible* series. Jeff and his wife Lisa are pictured on the next page with Jonathan Chase, the star of their 2012 series *Chemistry*.

While playing golf with respected actor Nick Tate, then on the *Dolphin Cove* series, Mr. Hayes asked for recommendations of good Australian television directors. Because Nick had enjoyed our time on a *Special Squad* episode four years earlier, he recommended me.

"Is he fast?" asked Mr. Hayes.

"He's the fastest," was Nick's reply, he told me.

The episode I got, "The Pawn," a reworking of the 1968 episode "A Game of Chess" in the original *MI* series, was fortunately a good script. As an episodic director, you are only as good as your script. Jeff

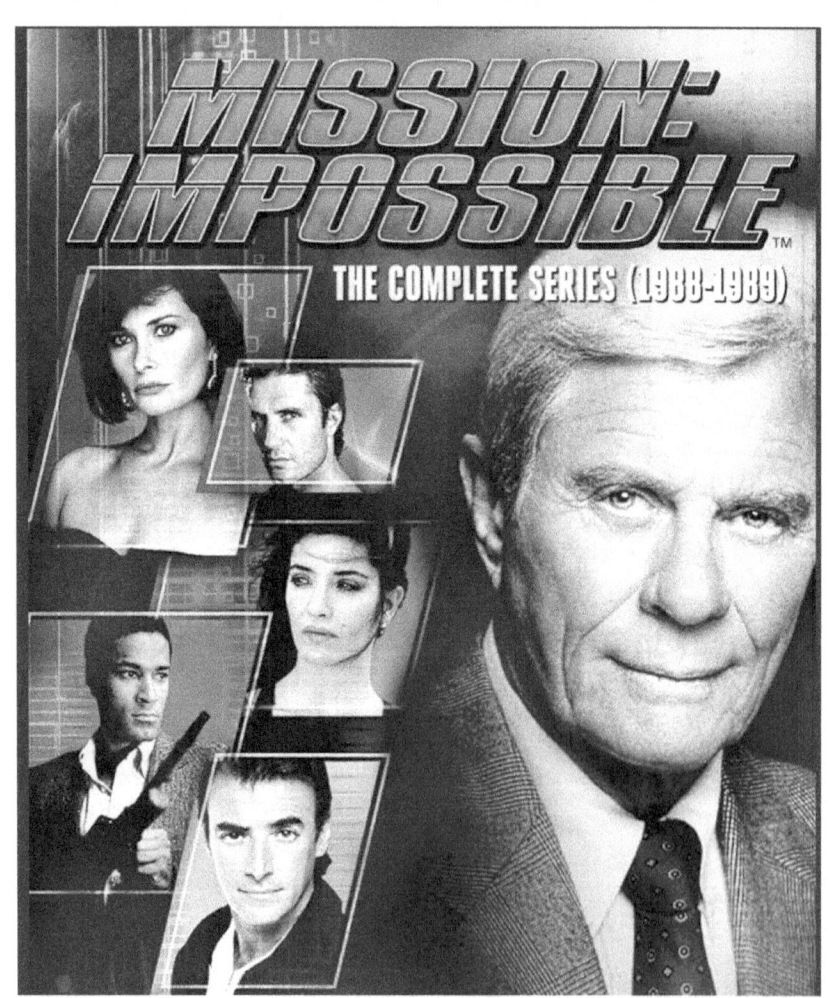

Hayes thought I did well, and booked me for another episode in the next season. So began a professional relationship from which I learned a lot about the running of a TV series. Over the next twenty-five years he would hire me six more times.

I returned to the Philippines to direct an action horror thriller called *Demonstone*, again with Lee Ermey, partnered this time by Jan-Michael Vincent, who was struggling with alcohol. I became ill and handed the reins over to Andrew Prowse. Throughout the year, I sensed the winds of change. None of my personally developed feature projects, all reaching for higher budgets, had found favor with Australian distributors, or federal and state funding bodies. Seasons change. The zeitgeist

had shifted from what I was known for. Perhaps I was just the lowbrow action guy in their eyes, not qualified for more elevated material. At the Sydney premiere of *Crimes of The Heart*, I complimented director Bruce Beresford, for whom I had made three trailers, on what was a superb Southern Gothic black comedy. "Probably not enough car chases for you," was his response. It was just a friendly joke, but it reflected a perception.

Ozploitation, the term Quentin Tarantino would subsequently coin, was out; more high-minded or nationalistic projects were in. Nothing wrong with Art or Patriotism. I would have loved to have done one of the great historical miniseries that Australia produced in the 1980s, but I was not perceived to be artistically qualified.

I had an eye-opening conversation with a visiting British producer Stanley O'Toole ( over 20 credits including *The Boys From Brazil, Enemy Mine*), He wanted to shoot a number of films in Australia with Australian directors. He visited the Australian Film Finance Corporation and asked who were "the good directors". He told me he was shown the A list, the B list, and the C list. My name was on the C List.

I spent the last months of the year turning the 4x50-minute *Danger Freaks* episodes into a 90-minute compilation of its best moments, writing a new narration track, which Nick Tate delivered with his usual skill. I got the composers of the *Panther* pictures to create a new score, in return for ceding them all music publishing revenue. For less than a 5K upgrade I had given this historically valuable material a new lease of life in the marketplace, first on VHS, then DVD, now on download thirty years later and still being rented. I would in due course buy out GUO's equity in *The Man from Hong Kong, Dangerfreaks* and *Kung Fu Killers* and ensure their preservation.

# DANGER FREAKS

IN A QUEST FOR THE ULTIMATE STUNT!

# PART VI
## BACK IN THE USA

# CHAPTER 37
## Starting Over

Since childhood I had dreamed of making largescale movies across the genre spectrum. I was now forty-four years old. In ten years, I would be dealing with ageism. Perhaps a successful Hollywood film or two would make me a valuable filmmaker in Australia again. So in early 1990, I moved the family to Los Angeles to start over. We intended to be in the US for only a few years. But it was a wrench for all of us. And a financial risk. Still, it was now or never.

As I flew out of Sydney, I was possibly a medium-sized fish in a small pond. Landing at LAX, without a recent US theatrical release to herald my arrival, I immediately became plankton. It would take many years of navigating Hollywood's shark-infested reef before I evolved into a clownfish, playfully cruising through a variety of genres.

Don't panic. The aquatic metaphors are now concluded.

So how do you start from scratch in Hollywood without a coinciding theatrical release of your latest Australian film to prompt meetings…?

You have to get a good agent.

Here's a scene I'd like to shoot.

EXTERIOR. BLAZING HOUSE. NIGHT

A modest suburban home is fully engulfed. A struggling filmmaker parks his beat-up hybrid, as his distraught spouse runs up.

WIFE

Your agent came over and set fire to the house!!

FILM MAKER

(awestruck)

My agent came to my house…?

Agent jokes—we've all heard 'em. Love 'em or hate 'em. You've got to have someone out there spruiking for you: "My guy's better than his guy!"

I had secured an agent the previous year when I was sent to Los Angeles by the New South Wales Film Corporation to make a 25-minute promo reel incorporating twenty-two of its films. I asked around. Two agents were recommended to me, one specializing in episodic directors. I chose the other older agent, Jerry Adler, hoping that his longevity in the business would produce the widest range of connections. After returning from service in the Korean war, Jerry Adler started as assistant to the legendary Lew Wasserman at Universal, before becoming a producer, then an agent. He was quite a guy. Within three months Jerry got me a gig: *Delta Force 3: The Killing Game* [a.k.a. *Young Commandos*].

"We got a big-name cast: Cassavetes, Douglas, Peck, Norris, Penn…"

I can imagine such a producer's pitch to buyers at the American Film Market that year. *Delta Force 3* would in fact star Nick Cassavetes (son of John), Eric Douglas (son of Kirk), Tony Peck (son of Gregory), Mike Norris (son of Chuck), Matthew Penn (brother of Sean Penn?) This last was the producers' assumption. Wrong. Matthew was a relatively unknown New York stage actor, the son of Arthur Penn, acclaimed director of *Bonny and Clyde* amongst other classics. When they found out his true lineage, they shrugged, figuring the audience would make the same mistake. It was to be a Sons of Stars movie, which came about because Chuck Norris had not wanted to reprise his role in *Delta Force 1 & 2* a third time. He suggested his son Mike could provide the link to its successful predecessors. Matched with other Big Name Sons looking to build their careers, the third in the series could generate publicity in its own right.

It was a fairly derivative script; in fact the plot seemed remarkably similar to *Iron Eagle 2*, released four years earlier, in which a hastily assembled joint US/Soviet fighter squadron enjoy stereotypic cultural conflicts, while stopping a major terrorist plot in the Middle East. *Iron Eagle* had morphed into *Iron Tank*.

I had met the *Delta Force* producer Christopher Pearce in 1978 when he helped provide crew for my nonunion shoot of *Stunt Rock*. His then-girlfriend Ann Strasburg was my 1st AD. He had grown up in England a few miles from me, though we had never met. He made a name for himself as a unit production manager on low budget films, and when we met, had just started working for two Israeli producers new in Hollywood—Menahem Golan and Yoram Globus. He rose to be the head of production at their Cannon Films throughout the company's Hollywood A-Go-Go years. (Check out *Electric Boogaloo*, Mark Hartley's documentary on the craziness of Cannon.) When Golan and Globus split, Chris Pearce partnered with Globus, and formed Global Pictures. *Delta Force 3: The Killing Game* was to be their first movie, shot in Israel on a budget of US $3.5M. Eight weeks of photography. All under a producer who knew and liked me twelve years ago. What could go wrong?

*"I have a reputation for fighting with directors. I am the Ax Man."*

A memorable moment from one of my many phone conversations with Chris Pearce, during which, I soon learned, it was wise to take handwritten notes, which I eventually collated as The Quotes of Chairman Pearce. A sample:

*"I am not as bothered by the script as you are. Just a bit of tweaking, and it will be fine."*

A few days later…

*"This script is terrible. He just phoned it in."*

I wrote an opinion on the script for Christopher Pearce and his coproducer Boaz Davidson. Boaz had directed several successful films, both Israeli and American, for Cannon, and was functioning as Chris's development executive, though I heard little from him initially. Naïvely perhaps, I expressed myself with the same candor I employed in script assessments written for the Australian Film Commission.

*"Transpose bomb attacks on Secretary General of United Nations and The Pope. Kill the Secretary, not The Pope. A big proportion of the foreign market audience is Catholic. US Catholics a factor also. Assassination of The Pope to whom so many are deeply emotionally attached tends to throw a shadow over the rest of the story; whereas greater dramatic value lies in keeping The Pope as the end target."*

Chris's written response was firm:

*"I want to shock the audience in the first scene. We are going to blow up The Pope. Religious people aren't gonna come to this film anyway. That's not our audience. No way am I going to lose that scene."*

I eased into the next point with greater success.

*"Kadallah is an unwise choice of name and deeply offensive to Muslims, as it contains the word Allah or God. Let's avoid a Salman Rushdie style response from Islam to the film, and change the name."*

The name became Kadall. And Chris had to reverse himself over the Papal immolation.

*"Yoram says if we blow up the Pope we cannot sell the film in Catholic countries…"*

Then there was the issue of the female Russian commando. I wrote:

*"Why have a girl, if you don't do something with her?… Right now, our hero is prejudiced against her, thinks she will screw up, because she's a woman! and then, in effect, she does screw up! and needs to be rescued!"*

"Oh, we have a director with ideas…" exclaimed executive producer Harry Alan Towers, with some misgivings, I am told. Harry Alan Towers was a legend. A prolific writer and producer (114 credits), Harry was an eccentric, lovable rogue who successfully worked the low budget market for half a century, still wheeling and dealing till his death at eighty-eight. He had one movie left of his multipicture deal with Cannon. *The Killing Game* was the script he delivered.

During this early period, I was becoming aware of some internal tensions within the production. Chris Pearce had made a favored-nations deal with the Sons of Stars cast: you each get equal pay— $60K. Except for that secret side deal with Eric Douglas, for an extra $20K. Why? It was the only way Chris could get Eric Douglas to sign. An arrangement on which Eric promised confidentiality. Not for long. He mentioned the $80K fee in conversation in front of fellow cast members, who immediately hit Chris Pearce for an extra $20K apiece. Chris had considerable animus against Eric:

*"Douglas is trouble. I'm going to fire his ass off this picture. He came to my office in Cannes, with his lawyer, and demanded money from the 15th of May. And I told him you gave up script approval on this project when you*

*accepted it. How about we change your part to a whiney little faggot who gets fucked in the ass on page 3? You will do the part or we will sue you…"*

As Chris told it, Douglas and his lawyer were gob smacked, backtracking immediately. He told me to beware of Eric, that he would try to manipulate me into swapping his role, the explosives expert, with the Delta Force team leader's role, a bigger part, currently assigned to Nick Cassavetes.

Soon after that, Eric called me before I left for prep in Tel Aviv and invited me to join him in the Douglas family box at the next Dodgers game. His father Kirk and stepbrother Michael would be there, and he would like to introduce me. I wondered whether this unique opportunity would put me under some obligation in the future. Feeling I should take the producer of my first US gig seriously, I made an excuse and declined with regrets. Eric was clearly nonplussed by my refusal. With the advantage of hindsight, I made a stupid decision, one that weakened my defenses in the shoot, rather than demonstrated my integrity. What was I thinking?

Chris finally decided that he had always been unhappy with the script. Driving with him to a location survey, I suggested Neill Hicks, one of the writers of *Turkey Shoot*, could fix the script.

"See if he is available," said Chris handing me a satellite phone. I called Neill, and by the time the car arrived at the location we were surveying, Neill was hired for a "two-week polish" and booked on a flight to Tel Aviv the next day.

Upon arrival, we set to work at the Dan Hotel. Chris had radical new ideas for the start of the story, which he offered much as dictation. Here's my recollection.

*"I want a scene where we start in a hotel with our hero in bed with a beautiful woman. Cut to an axe smashing into the door. It's her husband.. Hero leaps out of bed, grabbing his clothes. Didn't tell me you were married. You didn't ask, she says. The axe smashes open the door. Jealous husband bursts in. Hero just makes it out the window in time to escape. That's a strong opening."*

Happily, this *"adulterous hero runs away"* introduction was abandoned. But there were a few such "producer's scenes" that Neill had to accommodate. One such had the Delta Force team and the Russian commandos sharing a communal shower while simultaneously singing competing national songs. "Taking care of business" was the song allocated to the Delta Force, while the Russians sang "The Song of the Volga Boatmen." Hmmm...

Two breathless weeks ensued with regular scene-by-scene notes from Chris and latterly Boaz Davidson. Finally, Neill, who had been hired for a polish, handed in his third draft of a page one rewrite. Chris didn't like it. Boaz Davidson didn't like it. A new writer was needed. Neill was sent back to LA, feeling ill-used.

As I was the one who had suggested Neill, it was put to me that I should be the one to fix the lousy script my suggestion had produced. It wasn't lousy; in my view, it was better than the draft Neill had been given, while incorporating the insisted-upon "producer scenes." I duly set about a rewrite while casting the local supporting roles and choosing locations.

Given the state of Israeli/Palestinian relations in 1990, locations in Palestinian areas were challenging to finalize. An ancient monastery or abandoned Arab fortress was essential for the terrorist HQ. I would hand in a draft written for a particular location with geographic aspects specific to the plot, then find that permission to shoot there had been withdrawn. Not surprising, given the unflattering portrayal of Arab characters in the storyline.

The budget kept fluctuating. For one draft I was told to write big desert action with tanks and mechanized hardware. Bargain production value per the Israeli Defense Forces. Whoopee! But the next week, the script had to become urban and smaller because of an availability (or cost) problem with the Israeli Defense Forces. It was an exhausting process.

Compounding the problems of prep was the May 31st Palestinian Liberation Front speedboat attack targeting beachfront hotels in Tel Aviv. I was at a beachside café as IDF attack helicopters streaked across the shoreline. Only one of the six terrorist boats reached the shore, where the attackers were quickly killed or captured. Libya had financed the failed attack. US media gave it front page coverage. Tony Peck dropped out of the cast as a result, citing security concerns. There was talk of replacing him with Chad McQueen, son of Steve McQueen. An agent offered Griffin O'Neal, son of Ryan O'Neal. In 1986, Griffin was driving a speedboat that killed Francis Ford Coppola's son Gian-Carlo. Griffin was acquitted of manslaughter but convicted of negligent operation of a boat and was required to submit to drug testing. Chris's view was clear.

*"I would prefer we didn't use O'Neal, because he could be as much trouble as Douglas. I know Cassavetes would prefer him because, I think, they're friends. It's up to you but that's what I prefer."*

I did what the producer preferred, ignored Nick's wishes, and passed on Griffin O'Neal. I was in enough conflict over the ever-changing script as it was. It was decided not to spend the money to purchase another Son. I was instructed to eliminate that character.

Then a good piece of casting came our way: British soap opera actor John Saint Ryan as the Russian commander. He was a Muay Thai kickboxer, and had the screen presence to match Nick Cassavetes in their clashes over command. I enjoyed the way he channeled Sean Connery's Scots/Russian performance in *The Hunt for Red October.* John did pitch-perfect Bond imitations and even resembled Connery enough to be his photo double in *Medicine Man.* He left acting a few years later, in favor of a safer career breeding and training competition horses.

After the shoot had been pushed back twice, the lead cast started arriving, each with a different viewpoint on the latest draft, and on their place in the cast pecking order. Mike Norris made everyone aware of his famous father. The Norris name had financed the picture, apparently. He and I did not click. He was often moody and short-tempered. He felt I should be giving him more action opportunities. The more I tried to get through to him, the less it seemed he liked me. I believe he thought that his uncle Aaron Norris, who had directed *Delta Force 2,* should have been the director. Mike Norris has since become a successful writer, producer, director of Christian-themed movies.

Nick Cassavetes was at a transitional stage of his career. His parents John Cassavetes and Gena Rowlands had been the indie movie power couple, acting together in semi-improvised relationship dramas,

hailed by critics, while still getting well-paid mainstream roles from the studios. Nick told me he felt the weight of his father's reputation as an actor/director titan, but that he planned to follow in his footsteps, anyway. He hoped to put aside formulaic roles, such as the one he was about to play, and write and direct quality movies. Nonetheless, he was going to give 100% to the character of the Delta Force team leader. He wanted to wear green contact lenses for the part, which he brought with him. It was certainly a different look that could be good, but I pointed out the producer would have to approve.

"Just do it anyway. After the first day, they won't want to reshoot."

But as it turned out, Chris Pearce liked it, or didn't care, and the contact lenses stayed. Nick did go on to realize his ambition. So far, he has directed eight films, including the hugely successful weepie *The Notebook*, which scored a world theatrical gross of 115 million dollars. Nick refers to it as his worst film.

Eric Douglas finally checked into the hotel, even though, as he told me, the company had not yet put the deposit in his bank account. Having been unable to see me in LA, he had regularly faxed me script, music, and casting suggestions, and was frustrated by my lack of response. I had been instructed not to send him any draft or even pages of the script. Eric was shorter than I had anticipated; father Kirk and stepbrother Michael each seemed to have such stature on the screen. Eric had a restless, mercurial presence, with self-assurance thinly papered over insecurity. In him I could see the painful downside of being the Son of a Star. He revealed his self-loathing through "I am Spartacus" jokes and disparaging remarks about his stepbrother.

Eric was always a little hyper, yet showed no sign of the drug problems about which I had been warned. He needed approval, which I tried to give him. On his first scene, he had problems with a speech. I spoke soothingly to him at each fluff, till he nailed it. He sent a signed photo as appreciation for my patience.

I got along well with Matthew Penn. He had a New York actor's seriousness about his craft, grateful for the gig with which his surname had erroneously gifted him. He would go on to a substantial career producing and directing for TV series like *Law and Order*. As I passed through NY on my way to start prep in Israel, he suggested I look at his girlfriend, fellow stage actress Candace Brecker, for a small but important supporting role. No obligation. She

Thank You! Eric Douglas

was a good actor and right for the part, so I cast her. She and Matthew subsequently married. So, one good thing came out of *Delta Force*.

Then coproducer Boaz Davidson arrived from LA. He felt the script needed a major overhaul and took over the writing. I felt humiliated and demoralized. I sensed a change in attitude towards me from the Israeli crew. Was I a Dead Man Walking? Four days later we started eight weeks of shooting, Sunday through Friday.

At the end of the first week, Chris Pearce flew in, knocked on my hotel door, and congratulated me on my handling of an Eric Douglas scene. Eric could be really good. When the camera turned, he often had his father's charisma. I was reassured by the response.

At the end of the second week Chris Pearce flew in, knocked on my hotel door, and summarily fired me, on the grounds the cast and crew had lost confidence in me. I asked for examples. He spoke mainly in generalities, with specifics such as this.

*"Nick Cassavetes said you made him run away in a battle scene."*

A location had been switched on me in the last day of prep. I had difficulty choreographing the action to the new geography. The day ended with the scene incomplete. Nick's retreat to fight again from a better position would enable us to pick it up at a new location later in the schedule. I tried to justify my decision, to no avail.

*"If you fight me on this, I will produce affidavits from key crew saying you are incompetent. I could have them by tomorrow."*

No doubt his regular Israeli crew would do what was expected of them. Why wouldn't they? Not a fight I could win, and fatal to my attempt to break into the US market. I was to be replaced by Sam Firstenberg, who had made a number of ninja movies for Cannon in the 1980s. Ironically, he was originally intended by Chris to be my 1st AD, till the shoot was pushed back and he took another 1st AD job in Jerusalem. He had just become available and started shooting as the director of *Delta Force 3* the next day.

This was devastating to me on many levels. I had replaced the director of three films, and now I was being replaced. The firing lasted less than a minute. Chris left my hotel room. I had dedicated every waking hour of the last three months to the best interests of this film, so I was profoundly shocked.

My dismissal had precipitated another problem—my ability to return to my wife and children in Los Angeles. I no longer had a valid visa to do so. Australia and the UK were the only countries I could immediately reenter. Why? Before I got the *Delta Force* gig, I had been granted provisional US residency by spousal application. I would receive the official green card within six months. During that period, residency applicants may not leave the United States or their application is canceled and they have to reapply from outside the US. When I had signed on to the movie, Chris had promised that the company would handle the reapplication. Would he honor that promise now? Not without horse trading. So I waived any further payment for the movie if he funded the mechanism necessary for me to reenter the United States as a resident alien and maintained my accommodation and my $100 per diem till the process was completed. To his credit, he honored the bargain. He flew Margaret and the boys to Tel Aviv where she applied afresh for my green card at the US Consulate. Although expedited, the process would take three weeks. We were flown to London and given Harry Alan Towers' apartment to stay in, to be flown back to Tel Aviv when the final paperwork was ready. A Cannon employee told me I was lucky. Chris had once fired someone in the middle of the Namibian desert, and told him to find his own way home.

I licked my wounds in England. My confidence had taken a major blow. The love of Margaret and the kids sustained me. I realized Hollywood was not the Australian Film Industry I grew up in. I would have to toughen up.

The scenes I directed that remain in the picture are mostly the mission training sequences and the beach landing/minefield incident. Judge for yourself if they are any better or worse than the rest of the picture.

Nick Cassavetes denied that he had pushed for my removal. He suggested it was more likely that Mike Norris had been the initiator. Maybe he had told his father things were not going well. Maybe Chuck Norris called Yoram Globus to ask what's going on? Maybe Yoram told Chris, his partner in the new venture, we need Chuck for future projects, make Chuck's son happy. Maybe. I will never know.

"I stayed out of it," said Matthew Penn. He and John Ryan were the only cast members who contacted me with sympathy. While a child, Matthew had accompanied his father Arthur Penn to Paris when he directed *The Train*. Burt Lancaster had fired Penn a couple of weeks into the shoot. Matthew understood my pain and was sympathetic. Eric Douglas sent me handwritten letters full of self-help homilies. But he did not fight to keep me. We would meet ten years later at a Showtime premiere. We exchanged pleasantries. Eric stated proudly that after ten years of arrests and rehab, he had conquered his drug addiction. He was now doing a standup routine 'round the comedy clubs of New York, making fun of the Douglas family and the vicissitudes of being a Son of a Star. He seemed genuinely cheerful. I wished him well. Sadly, he died of an accidental drug overdose four years later.

My agent Jerry Adler took my firing in stride: "They're a *facockta* company. Pearce is a bastard. We move on." *Delta Force 3* spluttered at the US box office and went straight to video in most territories under the title of *Young Commandos*. The reviews on IMDB speak for themselves. Global Pictures never produced another movie, though Chris Pearce would exec produce more direct to video pictures till his retirement in 2000. I ran into him at a restaurant in 1994. He introduced me to his companions as an old friend and a great director…

I would have been protected from summary firing if I had been a member of the Directors Guild of America, one reason for the producers wanting a non-DGA director. Hiring a Guild director meant extra cost. Production manager and assistant directors had to be Guild also. Directors' fees were tied to budget level. Health and pension contributions had to be made. The Guild would arbitrate disputes. There were producers who could not afford the extra expense or were philosophically opposed to trade unions. For such producers, I was an experienced non-DGA director with thirteen English language features and seven episodic credits to my name. Through my British passport, I qualified for EU coproductions. Jerry Adler set about selling me on that basis. Soon enough he found a show where my resume ticked the necessary boxes. It was the first of a series of animal adventures.

# CHAPTER 38
## Animalflix

So far, I've told my story in sequence. The best way to deal with the projects I've made since moving to the US in 1990 is to group them by genre. I'll deal with the animal flicks first.

Producers Max and Micheline Keller had bought the TV series rights to the Edgar Rice Burroughs' character Tarzan. They put together a France/Canada/Mexico co-production, with shooting in Mexico, post production in Toronto, directors and lead cast from Canada and EU countries.

Canadian Wolf Larsen (Tarzan), was born Wolfgang von Wyszecki in West Berlin. That made him a moveable component in a coproduction cocktail that could fatten the required quota of either Canada or the EU. Casting by passport is a factor in the way these things come together. For trivia fans, prior to Tarzan, Wolf Larsen's physique got him gigs with Chippendales, the all-male dance revue that performed polite striptease routines for female audiences. Wolf Larsen is also the only actor to play Tarzan who had an MBA and taught business and economics at college level. Wolf worked hard on the show and we got on well.

Lydie Dernier, from Saint Nazaire, France played Jane. She came to the US as a successful model, got small parts in movies and TV, but Jane Porter was her first big break, costarring in 64 episodes. In 1995 she was engaged for a while to J. Christopher Stevens, the US ambassador who was killed in the 2011 Benghazi attack.

Malick Bowens (Simon Govier), born in Liberia, also had a French passport. He was best known for playing Meryl Streep's loyal steward in *Out of Africa*. Here he played the only African in the series. The producers wanted to avoid the inherent racism of the Edgar J Burroughs original creation, which persisted, albeit under the surface, in the movie and TV series versions. In prior Tarzans, from Johnny Weissmuller though Gordon Scott to Ron Ely, the stories consistently depicted the white "noble savage" solving the problems of his African neighbors. But the first season's scripts unwittingly undermined the

producers' good intentions by having Malick regularly deliver packages to Jane's house as a reason for them meeting in an African jungle that was mysteriously unpopulated by Africans, the price of shooting on the Yucatan Peninsula. Malick felt his character was little more than a servant, a messenger of plot points, and he left the show after the first season.

When a script ("Tarzan in the Sacred Cave") called for flashbacks to young Tarzan at two different ages, my blond sons Alex (8) and Eric (11) were an excellent match for Wolf Larsen. They joined the ranks of twenty-three actors who had previously portrayed Tarzan. They received no credit, because, under coproduction rules, only Canadian, Mexican and EU actors could be credited. Happily, neither son caught the acting bug.

The Mexican coproducers had selected Palenque, in the state of Chiapas, for the show's location because the local Mayan ruins offered a spectacular backdrop. Archeological authenticity, who cares? That pyramid sure looks good, was the rationale. As soon as we had trekked thousands of miles to the bottom end of Mexico, the state of Chiapas denied us permission to shoot at the pyramid because it would be culturally offensive. Why was I not surprised? But there were the highly photogenic falls at Agua Azul.

There were many difficulties shooting so far from Mexico City. The convoy of trucks from Churubusco Studios bringing camera, lights, the generator, honey wagons, the whole circus, was regularly harassed en route by various police departments, demanding money for a permit to let the convoy continue. Consequently, the journey took twice as long as planned, arriving the day before shooting was to start.

I cannot speak highly enough of the Mexican crew. They knew their business, and worked hard in 100° heat. I had tried to learn some basic Spanish from cassettes in the month before I flew in. Despite my alarming grammar, syntax, and vocabulary, it meant a lot to them that I had made an effort. They helped me learn other useful phrases like "Dónde está el gringo pendejo?" and "Hijo de la chingada!" (My Spanish improved to such degree that when Margaret joined me ten weeks later, I was able to impress her by ordering dinner in Spanish: "Quisiera la carne bien cochina." Mistake. I meant "bien cocida", not "bien cochina". Margaret explained that I hadn't asked for my meat to be "well-cooked" but to be "really filthy.")

We worked 6-day weeks shooting on 35mm. The producers had scored a million feet of cheap Agfa stock. Each director shot a block of three episodes over a 12-day period, then prepped his next three episodes over the following twelve days, and so on. After a while I would know the regular sets and locations so well, I did not need the prep time. The producers would send me to Toronto on a twofold mission: to do some editing, and to bring back future episode's props as personal luggage. Airfreighting the props in—the normal procedure—involved permits and permits could be unaccountably delayed, unless money changed hands. Ultimately, I directed twelve of the twenty-five episodes in Season One, and a couple of days of wildlife footage at the Cuernavaca Wildlife Park to be sprinkled throughout the show. For four months I had enormous fun. Sometimes there was more human comedy going on behind the camera than in front of it. If the Coen brothers were to make a *Day for Night*-style movie about shooting an animal picture, this might make a good scene:

EXTERIOR. CHIAPAS JUNGLE, MEXICO—DAY

An episodic film crew makes the final preparations for a complicated shot. Dolly track has been laid to converge on a tree with sprawling roots.

The Director looks at his watch.

The Guest Star Who Has Seen It All stands nearby with bemused interest.

The Director looks at his watch again, as if willing the minute hand to stop, and if possible, go backwards.

Fluff and Buff, the hair and make-up artists, dab sweat from the brow of The Actor, standing at the base of the tree. Given that the temperature is over 100 degrees, this is a noble but futile effort.

DIRECTOR<br>
Don't worry about the sweat, he's meant to look scared.

ACTOR<br>
I *am* scared.

DIRECTOR
Don't worry. This is totally safe.
Nothing is going to go wrong.

The source of the Actor's anxiety arrives on the set, his partner in the scene, a male with dangling testicles each the size of grapefruit. Sudan, a large African movie lion, is led out of the bushes on a chain by two Trainers. Two other Trainers follow, carrying short poles. As the Trainers tether the lion to a spike embedded beside the far end of the dolly track, Sudan yawns, and licks his lips to cool them.

ACTOR
Has he been fed today?

TRAINER
If we feed him, he won't work.

The Actor's jaw tightens further.

GUEST STAR
I've brought an apple for him.

Humor is no comfort.
TIME CUT to:
Everything is in place for the take. The Trainers have been positioned out of shot to protect both the Actor and camera crew, should the lion stray from his designated path. The collar round Sudan's neck is concealed beneath his shaggy mane, and the trailing leash masked from camera by his body. The Actor has practiced limping backwards while swinging a burning firebrand to deter the advancing beast. The dolly grip and operator have rehearsed the camera move that will keep the lion on screen right with his retreating victim on screen left. It's a traveling geography shot that will add tension when intercut with compatible dolly shots on the faces of the lion and the Actor.

The Director wants the audience to see the lion and the Actor in the same shot; but not a static shot, which could be achieved by the elements being photographed separately with a locked-off camera, then fused in the lab, with the vertical join disguised by a tree in the close background. This would spare the Actor any proximity to the King of Beasts. No. The Director wants a Movie Shot, not a *get-it-done-move-on* episodic approach, but a sense that the camera is almost mounted on the flank of the lion as it slowly closes in on its prey. The time for this glorious cinematic moment has arrived.

DIRECTOR
So, on action: slowly hobble back, wave the firebrand,
shout at it to back off…feel free to improv…

ACTOR
Back off, you fucker?

DIRECTOR
Something like that, but without the fucker…

Here we go, roll camera.
The Prop master lights the firebrand again. The 1st AD calls for camera turnover in Spanish.

The crew, a well-oiled machine, commence their respective duties. The Chief Trainer calls commands to the lion.

TRAINER
Sudan! Go! Slow Sudan! Slow! Good Sudan! Good!

The Director hovers beside the camera, which keeps pace with the ambling lion. Sudan is fascinated by the firebrand, and reacts to its movements. The Actor is In The Moment! Everything is working perfectly.

At this point the Transportation Captain arrives on set to watch the shot. The 1st AD sees him, and a long simmering feud chooses this moment to erupt.

1ST AD
(curtly)
No ha puesto los camiones en donde le dije!

Apparently, he hadn't put the trucks where the AD told him.

TRANSPORTATION CAPTAIN
Cree que es el jefe? Yo soy el capitan de transporte!
Los camiones parquean endonde digo yo!

It's a territorial dispute. You believe you're the boss? I'm the Captain of Transportation! The trucks are parked where I say they are!

DIRECTOR
Guys! Sshh!

They neither see or hear him. They are in a world of rising steam.

1st AD
Stupido!

Whoa! Bad word in Mexico. Serious escalation. The tension-meter on the set spikes. Hungry lion, anxious actor handling fire, two departments inching towards civil war, complex dolly shot, etc. It's understandable. But the net effect of the expanding angst is to push the Actor into the truth zone. It's a great performance, swinging from fear to rage and back again. Meanwhile, the other drama continues.

TRANSPORTATION CAPTAIN
Chinga su madre!

The AD is instructed to fuck his mother.

1ST AD
Chinga tu madre!

The AD returns the instruction less politely.

Oh, boy! Now they're at DEFCON 4, soiling each other's mothers. The conflict moves to the next stage…The Slap.

The Transportation Captain slaps the 1st AD's face, not to inflict physical pain, more of a formal gesture, a challenge.

Some men go red with anger. The 1st AD's complexion goes pasty white. His eyes blaze. Detonation is imminent. Luckily members of both departments seize the potential combatants and hustle them to separate corners of the jungle.

The Lion sits down at the end of his leash, awaiting reward. The Actor has started to enjoy himself. Lions? Hah, they're pussies. The Director calls for Take Two. There's no producer on the set to stop him.

Whimsical screenplay scenes periodically crawl out of my Id, but this one actually happened. The Actor was Canada's Chuck Shamata, whom I have cast in two movies since. The Guest Star was former Tarzan Ron Ely, cast as a nod to the fans of his 1966-68 series. The Lion Trainers were the incomparable Boone Narr and Hubert Wells, and the Director obsessed with getting a tie-in shot was yours truly.

In every movie, good intentions are fused under pressure with powerful egos. There Will Be Blood, if you do not head these situations off at the pass. I had ample warning that the clash of personalities was gathering momentum, but regarded it as a producer problem. Naturally Murphy's Law applied, at the most precarious moment. So I lost an excellent AD, Rene Villareal, fired regardless of the rights and wrongs of the issue, lest the transportation department immediately get in their trucks and drive back to Mexico City

without us. I have learned over the years to develop an ear for seismic pre-shocks, and use diplomacy, humor, bribery, alcohol, whatever it takes to help the parties see each other's virtues. Part of a director's job is to set the tone in the workplace, encourage communication, and make everybody's hard work FUN.

Dogs snout me. Cats leap onto my shoulders. Animals like me, and the feeling is mutual. So I have always been attracted to animal projects. CGI animals get more photo real every year. But there was a time when the actual animal and the lens were all you had to work with. In the pre-CGI era, I was lucky enough to stage sequences involving an African lion, an American puma, cats, dogs, elephants, snakes, chimps, spiders, scorpions, cockroaches, a dolphin, a mud crab, a pigeon, and a frog.

Working with All Creatures Great and Small requires planning, flexibility, and infinite patience. I hold in the highest regard the trainers who helped me deliver the shots. Safety of the animal and the crew is the governing issue when working with exotics. They are wild animals after all, and things can go wrong. Has anyone seen *Roar* (1981)? Arguably, the most dangerous animal film ever made.

I learned a lot from Hubert Wells and Boone Narr, two of the premier animal trainers of their day. Hubert started training animals in Hungary during the 1950s and soon moved to Hollywood, where he amassed thirty-one movie credits before his retirement in 2006. Perhaps his most skilled work with lions can be seen in *The Ghost and the Darkness* (1996), and with tigers in Jean-Jacques Annaud's *Two Brothers* (2004). Boone Narr started as the orangutan wrangler in Clint Eastwood's *Any Which Way You Can* (1980) and did animal training on seventy-five productions. They helped me break each sequence down into individual shots they could train the animals to do.

I was often a paw swipe away from Hubert's principal lion Sudan. Never had a problem. Or was I lucky? Hubert told me about his close call with Sudan's brother. The lions had been captured together as cubs when Hubert acquired them. Training went well as they grew into adulthood. Then one day Sudan's brother nuzzled Hubert's leg in a gesture of feline submission, then suddenly bit him in the thigh, a playful nip to the lion, but a painful puncture wound to Hubert, who nonetheless made a full recovery. He gave the lion to a wildlife park.

Despite this unfortunate incident, Hubert and Sudan had a very trusting relationship. In one scene I directed, he doubled an actor who was meant to be killed by the lion. As the cameras rolled, Hubert, in the actor's costume and hat, showed Sudan a chunk of raw meat concealed in his hand, held it beside his throat. He ordered Sudan to charge by loudly calling his name. On cue, Sudan loped forward, gathering speed. He knocked Hubert over, then nibbled at the meat which Hubert held beside his throat. Through the lens, with Hubert's legs kicking violently, it really looked like he was getting his throat ripped out, a little unusual for a family TV show. If they write it, I will shoot it.

Food plus positive reinforcement is what movie animals work for—a reward after each take. We could only work Sudan every other day. We needed him to be hungry and motivated after a day on short rations. Not too many takes, either. Once he was sated, he just wanted to lie in the shade. So we had to get the difficult shots first. Boone Narr said the most important part of his job is casting. Just like a director.

*"Finding the right animal, with the right look and aptitude can take time. Then it's largely a matter of training the animal to react to visual or aural cues, and to move from A to B, which is where you make your edit to the next action in a change of angle. It is prudent to choose locations and set decoration that take into account the behavior range of the animal in question. You always need a back-up for your lead animal. Animals may look alike but they have different skill levels and different personalities. Sometimes every performer has a bad hair day, and is uncooperative. Bring on the double.'*

We brought two chimps to Palenque. Archie was a very smart simian who would peel his bananas slowly and savor every morsel, whereas Kiko, his backup, would just stuff it, skin and all, into his mouth. Kiko was capable of much less than Archie. The trainers on *Tarzan* indulged my need to be close to the animals. Normally they prefer the animal's relationships to be solely with themselves

as the alphas, and with the cast with whom they interact. Too many humans in their lives can confuse the animals and make the trainers' task harder.

I helped wrangle the 10-foot female boa constrictor. They have thicker girth than the male. The problem was that the snake did not want to squeeze the life out of Tarzan. No interest in celebrity. The boa just wanted to get out of the 100° heat into its nice cool box. Wolf held the snake gently behind its head, positioning it so they were face to face, while pretending to struggle free from its coils. The snake handler, being short and slight of build, needed help. We squatted below camera winding the reluctant reptile back round Tarzan's body as it kept uncoiling. It took a lot of quick closeups of slithering to make Tarzan look threatened. Eventually we faked Tarzan freeing himself and the snake returned to air conditioning.

Getting inimical species to perform in the same shot is about the hardest task a trainer has. Chimps are mortally afraid of elephants who are inclined to stamp on them. Archie was no exception. Some scenes required Tarzan to ride the elephant with Archie in his lap. But Archie could not bear contact with the elephant's skin. Wolf Larsen had to carry Archie on his shoulders, his legs crossed tightly under Wolf's chin. Wolf earned his pay that day, and every day.

I particularly enjoyed working with the elephant. You steer with the ears. Want to go left, tug on the left ear. I sensed that I was riding a sentient being that enjoyed interacting with humans. But a decade later, I met Jane Goodall at a fundraiser for a wildlife charity. I admired her courage and her lifelong dedication to her work and still do. Foolishly I told her how much I enjoyed working with chimps in movies. She looked at me askance, and gave me something of a lecture on how the use of animals for entertainment is physical and emotional cruelty under any circumstance. She said that when I require an animal to be trained to perform tricks for the camera I am just as guilty of cruelty as someone running a circus or a zoo. I am not often tongue lashed by iconic figures. So I thought about the range of animal rights issues Ms. Goodall raised. It's

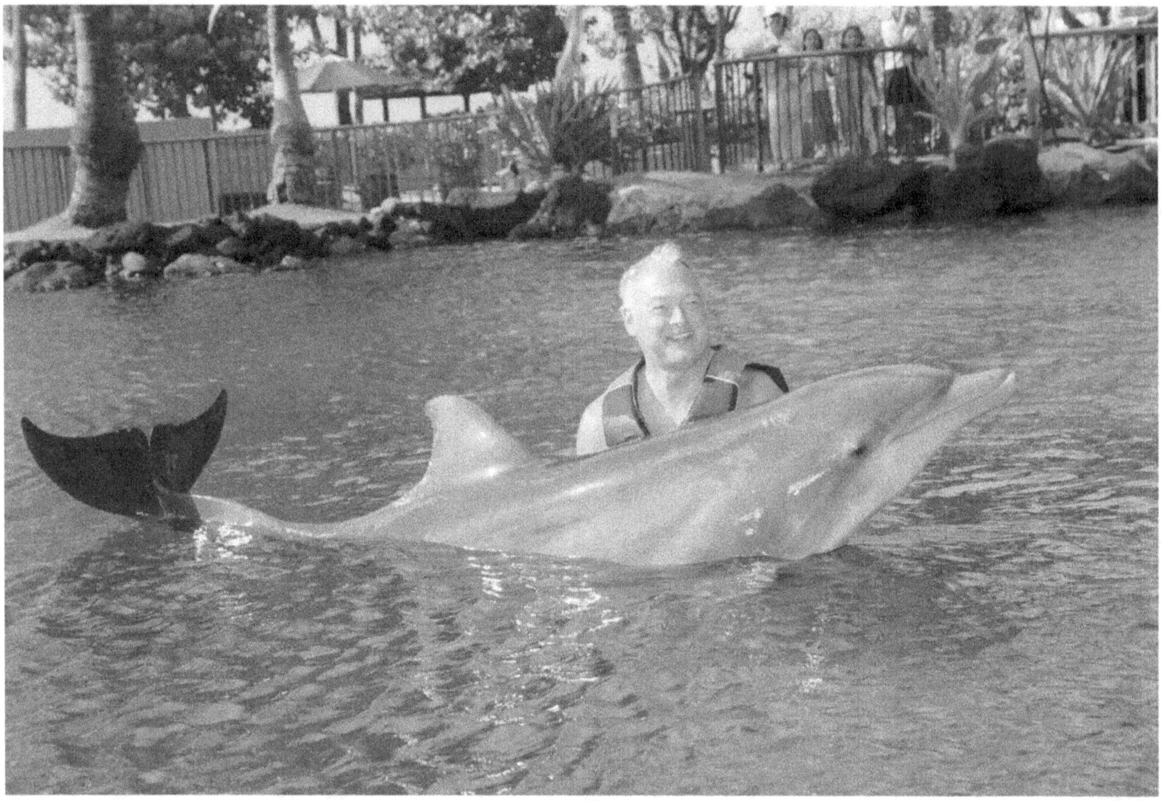

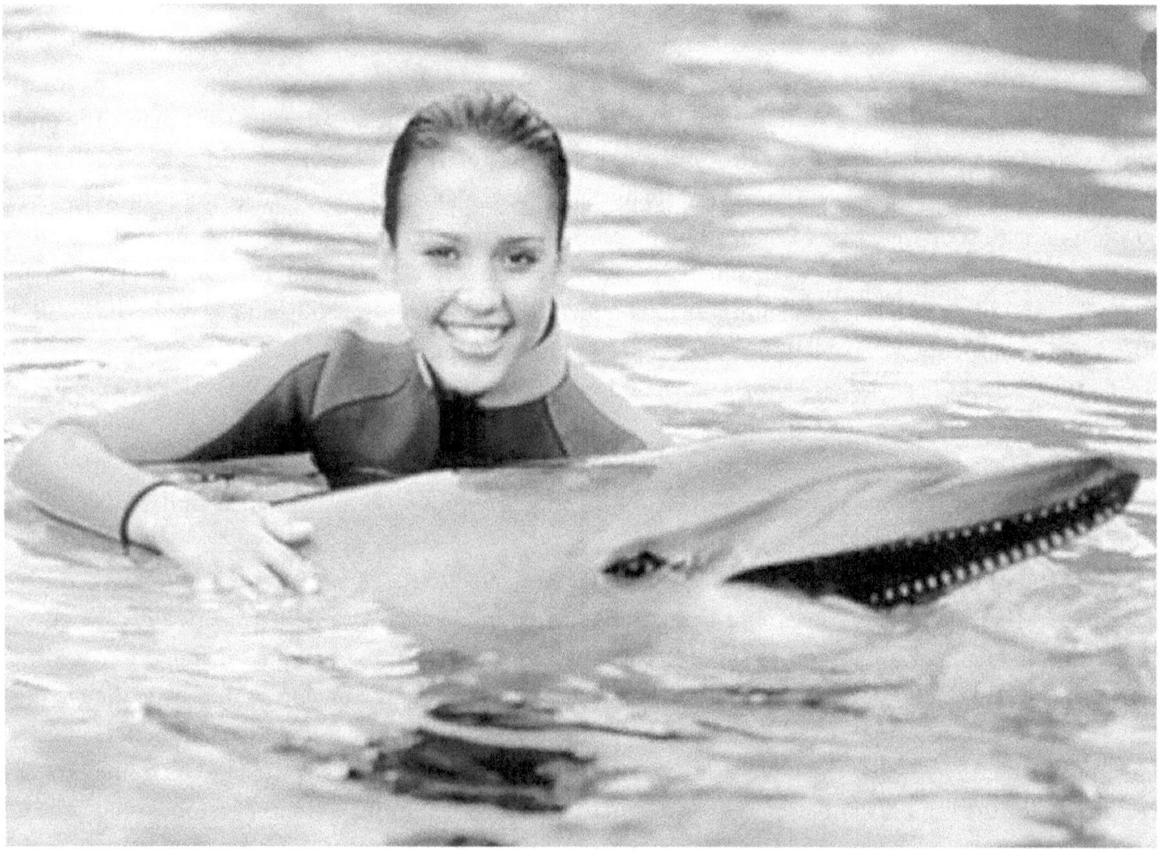

a complex question. I don't know the answer. But it would be a sad day for Cinema if animal performers were banned from movie sets altogether, and only digital creatures remained on our screens.

My next animal adventure would be the TV series, *The New Adventures of Flipper*, for which I made the 2-part pilot and three episodes between 1995 and 1996.

*Flipper* had started shooting in Florida, which quickly proved to be too expensive, so the series was moved to the Village Roadshow Studios with Jeff Hayes in charge. I was brought over to direct the 2-part season opener in which a corrupt Cuban resort owner kidnaps Flipper to use as an attraction. The heroes have to infiltrate the less-than-friendly country and rescue Flipper. It was a fun script and I had fifteen days in which to shoot it.

Jessica Alba's casting has ensured the longevity of the series. She was a director's dream, always prepared, always enthusiastic. She had great eyes and swam like a dolphin. There was a spark to her. Everyone knew her career would one day blossom.

Australia's Gold Coast is an ideal location to shoot marine-based stories like *Flipper*. The producers were experienced at maximizing the look of a TV series. They made a deal with Sea World for access to their dolphin pens as a regular set. They chose locations for their vista potential; ocean views, harbor views, river views, skyscraper views. They had characters who flew a helicopter…

The producers also created some challenging action scenes involving Flipper, that noble aquatic mammal, constantly coming to the rescue of hapless humans. The approach in the 1960s *Flipper* series was to integrate actors with dolphins, both above and below the water, but only in a controlled marine park setting. The updated series had scripts that put Flipper in open water, in the estuary and the ocean. This was going to require the building of an artificial dolphin. Ultimately, we used four different replicas for shots integrating the dolphin with humans. There was a full-size Styrofoam rubber skinned Flipper, which offscreen handlers would drag through frame either in front or behind the actor. The fin and the top inches of the dolphin's back was convincing enough if you did not hold it too long. He was known as Stiffy-on-a-Wire, or Stiffy for short. Then there was Head-on-a-Stick. Literally. Operated by two divers, Flipper's head would break the surface of the water in foreground, its snout facing away from camera towards the actors on the deck of a boat. They would call out to Head-on-a-Stick. Then the editor would select an above surface closeup of Flipper from the library of stock shots that had been acquired along with the rights to the 1964-67 show. Shot on 35mm, the underwater material was an invaluable resource. The editor would insert the appropriate dolphin reaction shot, and lay the sound of a chimpanzee cackling over it. (Yes, that's the original derivation of Flipper-speak.) The audience for this show preferred anthropomorphism over science. The next upgrade was Three Quarter Dolphin, full scale but missing its tail. Torso Dolphin, as I called it, was secured to an outrigger on the camera boat, and photographed from the deck in profile cutting through the water. These were dynamic images particularly if Flipper was keeping pace with an adjacent swimmer or water craft. The next development was an animatronic Robo-Flipper, full scale, rigged to move its tail up and down, for angles of Flipper in motion along the surface without being attached to the camera boat. It had cost 40K. Its maiden voyage, on one of my episodes in Season Two, was nearly its last.

Consider this scenario: We were shooting from our camera boat a couple of hundred yards off the beach in a secluded bay. Flipper had once again rescued a member of the human cast, in this instance Gus Mercurio, a former US Marine and professional boxer who had a long career as an actor in Australia. As often happens, I'm doing the money shot of the sequence last, as the light is failing. We had got the shots of Gus clinging to Robo-Flipper, waving to a descending helicopter. We've got the POV of the chopper descending. Then we replaced Gus with his stunt double, pulled the camera boat back to get a wider perspective of the chopper hovering and Whip Hubley's double jumping twenty feet into the water to land beside Gus and Robo-Flipper. This meant that the divers handling the animatronic had to pull back out of frame. Gus's stunt double was left to manage Robo-Flipper to which he was secured by a length of rope wound round his wrist. I was assured that the hatchway to Flipper's internal machinery was leakproof and sealed shut. Unfortunately, when the downdraft from the chopper churned up the water, the waterproof animatronic stopped

Someone's been a very bad dog.

atomic dog

being waterproof very quickly and started to sink pulling the stuntman with it. In the ensuing struggle he lost hold of the rope holding them both together. It was Flipper's turn to be rescued, but he had vanished from view. In fact, our $40K prop was slowly rolling along the sea floor twenty feet down on its way with the outgoing tide to New Zealand. Mass panic ensued. Zodiacs crisscrossed the area. Our divers combed the sea floor as the sun hit the horizon. Visibility was near zero. Luckily one of the divers felt something brush along his leg. It was the rope. He grabbed it just in time. Phew! Even when blameless, directors are tarnished by mishaps on their watch.

My 2-episode season opener went well. Former Miss USA Laura Harring contributed some deft comedy with a hint of Charo as a feisty Cuban who befriends the Americans trying to recover their stolen dolphin. Six years later she would score her most famous role in David Lynch's *Mulholland Drive*. I attended the presentation of my director's cut to the distributor Sam Goldwyn Jnr. Like his legendary studio boss father, he had great instincts. His fundamental note was: cut to the fish (I know, a dolphin is a mammal). The show's called *Flipper*, he emphasized. Wherever you can, cut to the fish. He was right. We had been afraid of doing it too much. An easy fix. He asked me if there were extra shots I would have done to enhance the dolphin action if there had been time. I said I would write a specific shot list to enhance a half-dozen sequences for the 2nd unit, operating alongside the main unit, to fit into their work schedule over the next few weeks. The added angles really helped. The pilot delivered. The show ran for four seasons.

Here's US artwork for my third animal adventure, which was shot in Canada (Calgary, Alberta) for Network USA, a cable station affiliated with the Sci Fi Channel for whom I also directed *Official Denial*, discussed later. *Atomic Dog* was intended as a family friendly *Cujo*. Seemed like a contradiction in terms to me, but hell, I'd give it a shot.

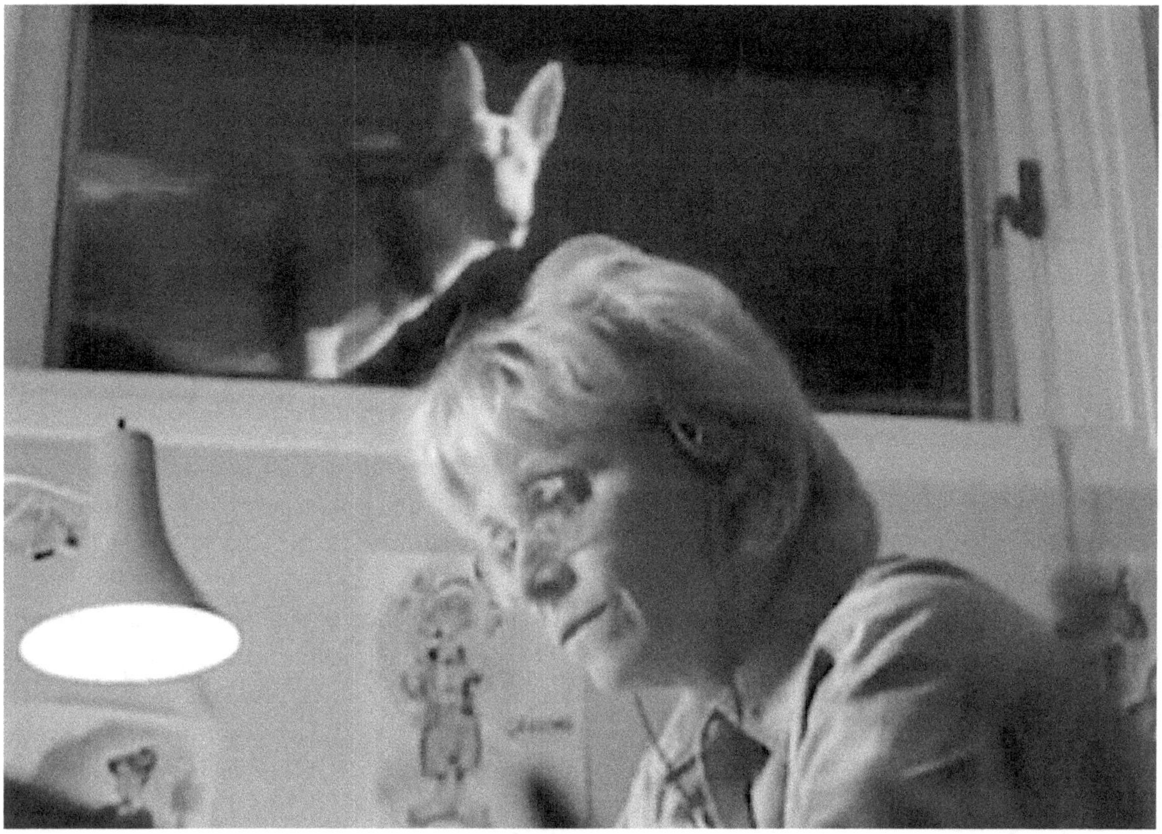

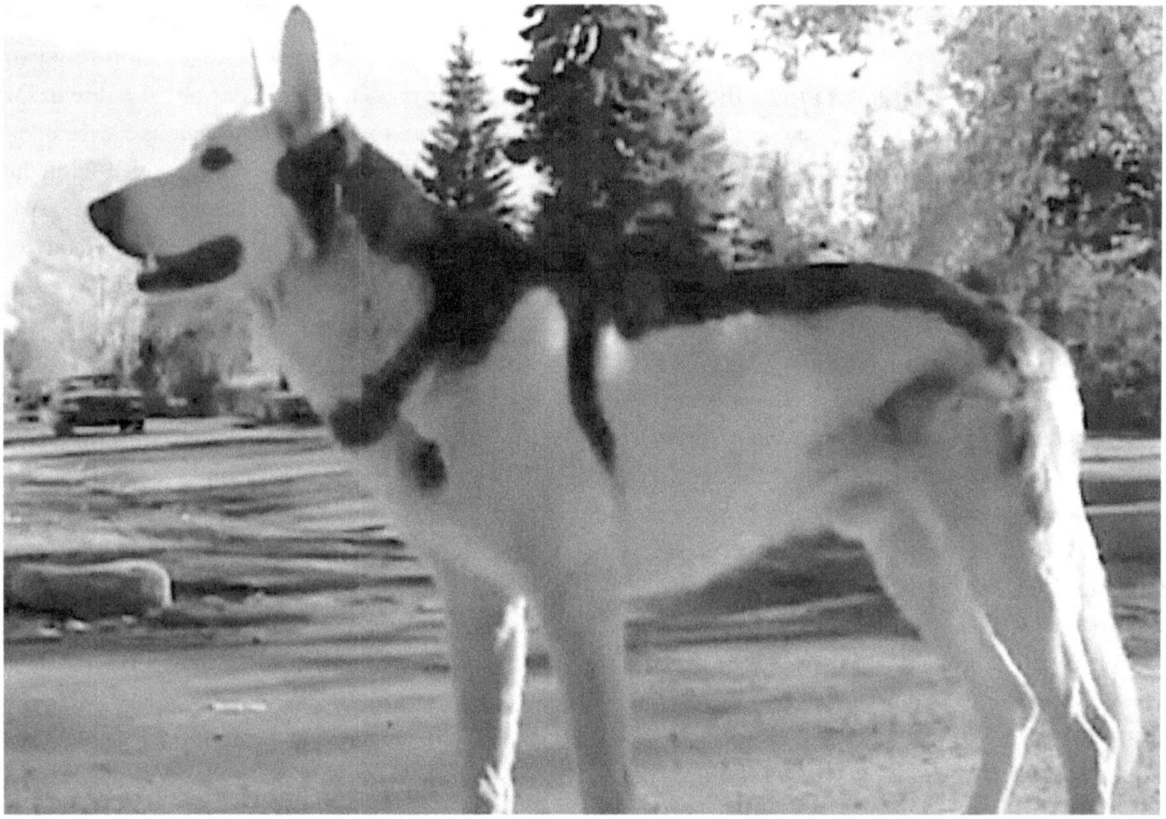

The premise was this: a puppy grows up in a nuclear power plant, abandoned after a radiation leak. Instead of causing death by radiation poisoning, the leak somehow enhances the dog's strength and intelligence. Fully grown, the dog leaves the plant and mates with the dog of a local family. She dies giving birth to a litter of cute puppies which the family adopts. Atomic Dog wants his babies back and starts to terrorize the family. Sound like a family movie to you?

Perhaps executives fell in love with the title first, then got the writer to fashion a story for it. *Atomic Dog… sounds cool, everyone'll watch that, right? Atomic Dog* is also a funky song by George Clinton; unaffordable and inappropriate for the intended *Cujo* thriller approach. Yet the initial ad line: *"I know he's radioactive, but can we keep him?"* had the wry tone the project should have adopted. But it's also indicative of how issues of nuclear credibility were unimportant in the development process. Although irradiated over a period of years, Atomic Dog apparently spreads no contamination wherever he goes. This speedbump is never satisfactorily addressed.

The more serious problem for the audience with this story, in contrast to *Cujo*, is that we are emotionally on the dog's side. He's a father who wants to take care of his kids and will do anything to get them back. It's actually a tragedy, with potential to examine animal rights issues, but the network was having none of that. They wanted a simple monster picture…for dog lovers.

There was much network agonizing over what the dog should look like. Should he glow? Are you crazy? Well, what if his eyes just glow? Like Dracula. The cost of rotoscoping individual frames (30 per second) soon shot that one down. The network finally settled for painting dark uneven markings on the white fur of the dog. One viewer posted this opinion. *"Frankly, I don't think the dog's aggression came from nuclear mutation—He just hates the paint job the makeup artists did on him. He looks like his mother mated with the Ace of Spades."*

I was allowed to tinker only with dialogue. Chief beneficiary was Isabella Hoffman the "specialist in carnivore behavior" conveniently living next door to provide exposition to the beleaguered family. I gave the character a sense of humor (it invariably helps). Daniel Baldwin visited the set one day. He seemed unhappy, so we barely spoke. Baldwin and Hoffman had become partners while working together during two seasons of *Homicide: Life on the Streets*. They had a child the previous year. The network wanted Baldwin for the lead, and knowing they were a couple, had offered the second lead to Isabella Hoffman as a sweetener. But they did not make her casting contingent on his acceptance. So she said yes to the firm offer, while he declined, so they were stuck with her. As it turned out she brought some charm and eccentricity to the part, so I had no complaints. The network scrambled to find a lead actor with as much wattage as the Baldwin name had at that time. After getting several passes, they booked Daniel Hugh Kelly, who had costarred in the 'R'-rated *Cujo*, hoping the association would draw that movie's fans. This was unlikely at the 'PG-13' level, which I was instructed to hit.

Luckily, I had a supportive producer Mark Ovitz, experienced in network politics. He is the brother of Mike Ovitz, the former super-agent and cofounder of CAA. The brothers were not estranged, but: "Mike has never done anything to help my career and he never will," Mark told me over sushi one evening. Despite being far from either coast, sushi was both fresh and cheap in Calgary, where the multi-Asian community comprised 20% of the population. We ate well. Mark's negotiating skills got us an ideal venue to house and train our dogs. Stampede Park, home of the famous Calgary Stampede, closed till next season, was spacious and quiet, just what we needed.

When I first broke down the script of *Atomic Dog*, it had close to 300 individual animal actions. Yikes! Many sequences were complicated, requiring special ramps and platforms. When the dog looked at the closed driveway gate, then ran and leapt over it, clearing its iron spikes—that worked out to be six different animal actions, six changes of camera positions, to be rehearsed and executed at night.

Viewed through the bars of the gate, the dog approaches at the run.

Low angle—the dog jumps over the camera onto a platform behind it.

Profile angle on the spikes of the gate—the dog leaps over the spikes from one offscreen platform to another.

Reverse angle through the bars of the gate—the dog jumps down to the ground from the repositioned offscreen platform.

Wide angle of gate—the dog runs from gate past camera.

By maintaining left-to-right screen direction in every shot, the sequence knits together as one fluid action.

We had an excellent animal trainer in Ray Beal, who had just performed similar duties on the live action version of *101 Dalmations*. His best dog, a part wolf/part German Shepherd named Rambo was a remarkable performer. Take a look at the scene where he climbed up a children's slide in the garden, leapt onto the adjacent shed, and from there onto the roof of the house. Rambo then pushed open a bedroom window, jumped on the bed and ripped the bedroom pillows to shreds. A lot of separate shots but Rambo was a quick study.

But there was a flaw in the casting of the Atomic Dog. Rambo, with his long snout and pretty eyes, had an appealing face. Not the squashed face of Cujo. It would be hard to hate the good-looking Rambo, however much snarling he does.

Incidentally "snarling" shots were achieved not by making the animal angry, but by installing a rubber band around Rambo's upper jaw, raising the lips to expose his incisors. Rambo is not in fact snarling. The sound of snarling is added in postproduction. Dogs tolerate this well if done quickly and rewarded with a treat.   Rambo's double (I forget his name) was not on Rambo's level but he was good enough for the simple stuff. As with the over-the-gate sequence I was able to run a separate dog unit simultaneously within walking distance of main unit and direct both and exchange dogs when necessary. It made the 20-day shoot more productive.

Ray Beal, Stacey Basil, and Cheryl Harris did an exemplary job of training and care for the dogs. Rambo's biggest stunt was to escape the house by smashing through a window. How was this achieved with no injury to the dog? First, we replaced the window in the room with one divided into four panes of glass. From the point of view of the cameras positioned outside the window, Rambo would be jumping through the top right pane. A platform was built inside the room flush with the targeted pane to give Rambo a straight run at it. Initially the pane was empty of glass. Rambo was encouraged to run down the platform and leap through the open section onto a padded landing spot just out of camera shot where he was rewarded with a treat. Once Rambo was comfortable with the jump, the empty pane was fitted with tightly stretched kitchen wrap. Rambo was shown how easily he could push his head through the transparent barrier, then encouraged to run at it, slowly at first, but he soon got the hang of it and began to leap through the wrap at speed to get his reward. Then a pane made of the thinnest toffee glass, was slotted into the frame. On a signal from Ray Beal, Rambo repeated his run along the platform, lowering his head as before and smashing through, scattering shards of apparent glass towards the lens. Rambo landed in the usual spot. He knew that something had changed, but he was not hurt or traumatized in any perceivable way, and continued to respond to his trainer's commands on subsequent shots. Later in the schedule, Rambo was retrained from

scratch in the procedure and repeated the stunt. This added two more slow motion angles, enhancing the sequence. Rambo and Ray had an unique relationship. The level of communication and bond of affection between them was heart-warming to watch.

I did everything I could to goose things along visually. *Doggie-cam* helped give personality and intelligence to our leading character. I think the trombone shot (*dolly in/zoom out* or vice versa) on the little girl reacting to her first sight of the dog is effective, though I acknowledge it has become a visual cliché. I did it in *Escape Clause* on Andrew McCarthy hearing that his wife has hired a hitman to kill him. It needs the right music accompaniment. But in the case of *Atomic Dog*, whatever I did was insufficient to disguise a neutered Cujo in a clichéd family drama. Here's a dog movie in which three out of four dogs die. Not to mention a well-meaning veterinarian. The network did not like the movie—"Not scary enough." True. I did my best and had a great time. A special bonus was the arrival of the Northern Lights near our location during our last night. I suspended shooting for fifteen minutes, so cast and crew could watch the dancing emerald lights live as they spread across the night sky.

# CHAPTER 39
## Fight for Survival

Sadly, my agent Jerry Adler developed leukemia and died in 1992. Other agents would follow, but they were not like him. Jerry was a Mensch, and I mourned his passing.

I had invaded Hollywood in 1990 with a small war chest. Despite the debacle of *Delta Force*, I remained confident that next time would be different and that somehow I would make it all work. At the time, a mortgage in California was little more than monthly rent. It was a good time to buy a house, and mortgage brokers, hungry for customers, wanted to make it easy. To qualify for finance, one of us had to have paid employment. Margaret quickly got a waitressing job on the nightshift at the local Denny's. This got us approved to buy a nice 3-bedroom tract home in Westlake Village, a suburb considered good for kids, with lots of parks and good schools for our sons, and less than an hour's drive from Hollywood. To pull this off, I had taken out a second mortgage on our Australian home.

I set up a loan-out corporation for my creative services and named it Barrenjoey Films Inc. as a nod to my Australian heritage. I was determined to hold property on both continents (blame it on my ancestors—it was the fatal Anglo-Norman mistake). Given my unexpected reversal of fortune earlier in the year, was I crazy? Apparently. Australian interest rates swiftly rose to 18%. We were ultimately forced to sell our beloved home Down Under.

I created cash flow by shuffling increasing numbers of cash advance/deferred interest credit cards, paying off each one with the next just before the interest spiked. (Unlike most who played this game, I won.) Survival was maintained by a few episodic gigs: *Time Trax*, *High Tide*, and a delightful detective show called *Silk Stalkings*, where a pair of good-looking cops solve crimes of passion among the mega-rich of Palm Beach, Florida.

For cost reasons it was shot in San Diego, an adequate facsimile. The show was being shared between CBS and USA Channel, in a rare collaboration between a free-to-air network and a pay cable channel. USA played a 48-minute version at 9 p.m. CBS played a 45-minute version as part of their 11:30 p.m. Monday to Friday "Crime Time after Prime Time" slot. The episodes were tightened for CBS not for reasons of censorship, but to cram three more minutes of commercials into the hour. Mitzi Kapture and Rob Estes were a dream team to work with, always had their lines down on 10-page days of wall-to-wall chat. I did five episodes of which

"The Sexiest Cop Team On TV!"
-*TV Guide*

*Silk Stalkings*
THE BEST OF SEASON ONE

Specially Chosen By Series Creator
STEPHEN J. CANNELL

*Lady Luck* and *Blo Dry* were considered the best of Season One by creator Stephen J. Cannell, and David Peckinpah, the head writer, and coincidentally the nephew of Sam Peckinpah. He had some stories to tell.

Low budget episodic television—generally shot in six days an episode—is the most high-pressure, cost-focused assignment a director can take on, often shooting ten pages of script per day. I've notched up forty-three episodes in five countries over the years. I've had repeat business from most producers, but you cannot please everybody.

INTERIOR. EPISODIC DIRECTOR'S OFFICE—EVENING

The Director stands in the open doorway, staring at the neatly printed paper sign on the door that has replaced the previous designation: DIRECTOR'S OFFICE.

It now reads: "DIALOGUE & BLOCKING CO-ORDINATOR."

He considers tearing it down, but restrains himself. Turning towards his desk, he sees another neatly printed sign mounted on the wall behind it:

"COVER EVERYTHING BUT DON'T SHOOT ANY FILM."

Hmm. Is his producer trying to tell him something?

FREEZE FRAME—Some context: Digital photography has substantially reduced the cost of television production by eliminating raw stock, processing, and telecine transfer. But in the early 1990s the technology required for capturing the image was a significant manufacturing cost. In today's prices, a 1000-foot roll of 35mm would deliver eleven minutes of images at a cost of $860 per roll. Assuming the director shot a 4 to 1 ratio (that's tight), the 45-minute episode would burn through about $12,600 worth of raw stock. Then processing all the exposed negative cost about $3500. The telecine transfer of the entire processed negative to digital files at a cost of $250 per hour added another say $4500. So quantity of film exposed was a reasonable concern.

CUT TO:

INTERIOR. LINE PRODUCER'S OFFICE—EVENING

The Line Producer and the Associate Producer are chewing out the Director.

PRODUCER

Every day you shoot more than the budgeted allowance of raw stock. Sometimes a little, sometimes a lot. Like 1000 feet more. Don't you realize what that means in stock, processing, and extra telecine time? So why are you doing this?

DIRECTOR

Well, these are 10-page days, a lot of dialogue, multiple characters, each with a different agenda whether they talk or not; if you want to make it interesting, all their reactions have to be covered.

PRODUCER

It's your job to make it interesting with the stock allowance you're given and that's all. Just feed the last sentence of each speech to the unimportant actors if they have a line in reply. Just cover that moment.

DIRECTOR

Which are the unimportant actors?

PRODUCER

All actors are important. Just some actors are more important than others.

DIRECTOR

Animal Farm.

PRODUCER
What? There are animals in this episode? Shit!

DIRECTOR
Sorry, George Orwell… just an Orwellian reference...

PRODUCER
You trying to be clever?

The Director knows he is doomed.

DIRECTOR
No, I would not dream of doing that. So please tell me—on which actors should I have limited the coverage?

PRODUCER
Tossle, for instance. He had one line in the party scene. You covered him through the whole thing

DIRECTOR
But shy, quiet Tossle is the real killer. The audience knows this, the other characters don't. His reactions to everything builds tension. The audience needs to see how he is scooping up information.

PRODUCER
The audience doesn't NEED shit. I don't give a flying fuck what they need. This is episodic television. Video wallpaper. It's just product. When Joe & Mrs. Sixpack get tired of fantasizing about humping the lead girl or lead . guy, the show gets cancelled. And we move on to another show. What I NEED is the stock ratio to come down so I don't get some accountant at the network with a bug up his ass calling me about the cost report. What I DON'T NEED is a lot of artsy fartsy bullshit. For the next 3 days, shoot less. Do a bunch of "one-ers".

The Director is concerned. Whole scenes in one shot can be wonderful, but limit editorial flexibility.

DIRECTOR
The actors will notice.

PRODUCER
Actors are children. Short attention span. They'll get over it.

DIRECTOR
They'll lose faith in me.

PRODUCER
Am I supposed to cry now? It's your job to manage them. And remember the "one-ers" are your idea, not mine. Tell 'em it's a brilliant concept that was always your plan for these remaining scenes, they'll love it when they see it, etc. I don't want

them whining in my office. I have to live with these people every day for the rest of the goddam season. You're just a visitor. And if you want to visit again, get the stock ratio back on budget by the end of the episode

The Director leaves. The Line Producer turns to the Associate Producer.

> PRODUCER
> Take a Polaroid of this guy.

> ASSOCIATE PRODUCER
> Why?

> PRODUCER
> Because you're never gonna see him again.

Somehow, I lasted one more episode because the show runner liked my stuff. But the day I left, my Polaroid was in the unofficial rogues gallery of The Departed.

# CHAPTER 40
## Sci-Fi

I had hit a dry patch that lasted for six months in '92. Early in '93, with only speculative prospects in sight, our financial position was becoming untenable. As mentioned, I had found myself obliged to do the unthinkable: sell the home in Australia my wife and two sons loved. Credit card debt was accumulating. And if I did not get a major assignment soon, I might lose our American home too, which was worth a little less than we had paid for it due to a real estate slump. Speaking of real estate, Margaret had developed serious academic ambitions and was enrolled fulltime at UCLA, but had to drop out for a quarter at this point

to work as a receptionist for a local realtor in Westlake Village. Everything I had built up since I had gone freelance twenty years before might be wiped out, as the price of ambitious overreach. I could not let that happen. *Never give up. Never surrender.* To quote the wisdom of *Galaxy Quest.*

I beat the bushes and managed to get four weeks in New Zealand, shooting one episode of *High Tide*, a private eye syndicated series, and shooting pick-up scenes for several unfinished episodes. It was a pleasure to work with lead actor and Grammy Award winning recording artist Rick Springfield. David Soul (*Starsky & Hutch*) was the episode's guest star. Luckily, my next gig came soon afterwards, and stabilized the family finances.

*Official Denial* was the first movie especially written for the new Sci Fi Channel (now SyFy). Noted Sci-fi writer Bryce Zabel had delivered a great *alien abduction/cosmic mystery revealed!* script. The network could not get the budget to hit the right number in the US, but Australia with its favorable exchange rate (USD$0.66 bought AUD$1.00) allowed the US dollar to go a lot farther. Jeff Hayes, who had hired me on the new *Mission Impossible* and *Time Trax*, had become the go-to guy for US-targeted production in Australia. The Village Roadshow studios on the Gold Coast became his headquarters for many years. He started a lot of careers there, and he certainly helped mine.

*Official Denial* had a great premise: When the US Airforce shoot down a UFO, a man, haunted by memories of alien abduction, is

forced by a secret government agency to try to communicate with the surviving alien, which he succeeds in doing telepathically. The alien reveals he is from the future of an ecologically devasted planet Earth, warning that human life will soon die out unless the world reforms its ways. A strong environmental message, a little in your face, but who cares—it's *E.T.: The Extraterrestrial* meets *Back to the Future*! A Sci-fi movie for parents and kids to watch together. It has a kind of goofy charm. Its warning is increasingly relevant.

One of the disappointments, inevitable in network-controlled television, is when your favorite shot gets cut out. Here's an example. You'll never see this shot, but forgive me if I get excited about it again.

Parker Stevenson (*The Hardy Boys*) played the haunted hero. Erin Grey (*Buck Rogers in the 21st Century*) played his disenchanted wife. The opening scene of the script has them standing on a river bank fishing. Parker muses whether fish feel anything when we catch them. He is brooding about his abduction, which no one believes happened. Erin reacts—here we go again—their conversation reveals a troubled marriage.

I decided the opening shot of the movie would start underwater prowling past weeds till it fixes on a fish. This was achieved by shooting through the glass of a small aquarium tank in the production office. The camera then rose up and, before the top of the aquarium came into view, was blended invisibly in postproduction with a shot taken at the river location. There an underwater camera mounted on a hot head similarly rose to break the surface of the water, revealing the couple fishing from the river bank beyond. Parker then casts his line to splash down near the lens and commences his dialogue about the feelings of fish. I thought it was a good way to start the picture. However, the marital discord revealed in the opening scene is similarly conveyed in the couple's next scene together. So the network cut the fishing scene. My cool opening was gone. Like it or not, moving the story forward often takes precedence over grace notes.

I admired Parker Stevenson's commitment to character. In the story he gains the trust of the alien by shaving his head to appear similarly bald. Instead of concealing his hair under a skull cap—as many actors do, and which the audience can generally pick—Parker elected to shave it all off. He was married to Kirstie Alley at the time. He told me when he returned home the day after the shoot, Kirstie freaked out at the sight of his chrome dome: "OMG! You're a Conehead! You're a Conehead!" He told me it required some hair growth before conjugal relations resumed.

*Official Denial* gave me my first opportunity to work with computer-generated imagery. Obviously, by today's standards some shots are a little crude. A new Australian company Photon Stockman (clever name) could see the future of this technology and invested in the necessary infrastructure. The driving force behind Photon Stockman was Dale Duguid. His pioneering work was recognized in 2001 when Queen Elizabeth II awarded him the Australian Centenary Medal for his services to the film industry. I learned a lot from Dale, who gave me a good grounding in both the creative and economic possibilities of CGI.

In those early days, shots with a locked-off camera were cheaper than shots in which the camera panned. It was less time consuming for the CGI artist to create the matte line within a static shot; for example, along the peaked roof of the hero's house as the alien spaceship hovers above it. But a moving camera can enhance the credibility of a CGI shot. I panned with a column of vehicles as they reached the high wall of a pumping station, dressed to be a secret military HQ. CGI then placed large satellite dishes on top of the building. The camera's movement distracts the eye of the viewer from focusing on the meld between the photographed element and the artificial element. I learned how interactive light can help unite these elements. If the CGI hovering spaceship emits a pulsing light, then, during the shooting of the background plate, an offscreen lamp should be set up to direct pulsing light onto whatever is below. Then the CGI artist will synchronize the computer-generated pulses with the live action pulses. *Official Denial* was my introduction to storyboarding, a vital tool in VFX, so that all departments can look at a proposed image and give input. For optimal results, it's important to work out all the details in advance. You can't *fix it in post* if you've shot the plate wrong. Now, nearly three decades later, there are software programs that can track anything, fix anything, but at a cost.

One of my creative contributions was the alien's floating POV. We mounted a wide pencil-cam lens onto a pole, and ran it between pipes and past objects in the military HQ that a 35mm camera could never navigate. We recorded these shots onto ¾-inch U-matic. American-made television movies were not mixing video and film formats in those days. The resulting distorted image, treated further in post, looked cool. I would use the same technique as *doggie-cam* in *Atomic Dog* and *ghost-cam* in *Sightings: Heartland Ghost*.

*Official Denial* got a good review from *Variety* and rated well on its November 20, 1993 premiere for the new Sci Fi Channel. In October the following year, *Official Denial* was a finalist in the Environmental Media Association Awards. The certificate was made out to Brian Trenchard-Smith "for raising environmental awareness in Television Movie of the Week."

My next Sci-fi film (in 1997) was *Doomsday Rock*, (aka *Cosmic Shock*) the first that I directed for Regent Entertainment. Showtime executive Sharon Byrens had recommended me to them.

CONNIE SELLECCA  ED MARINARO  WILLIAM DEVANE

HISTORY FORETOLD IT.
SCIENCE IGNORED IT.
NOW NOTHING CAN STOP IT.

COSMIC SHOCK

Regent need an experienced director immediately, one who could handle low budget science fiction but was not a member of the Directors Guild. Regent, at that time operating on a tight budget, did not want to become a signatory to the DGA, with its obligation for health and pension contributions. That made new directors with foreign experience attractive. The driving force behind Regent was Paul Colichman.

After graduating from UCLA, Colichman had taken an entry level job at Fox. By age twenty-four he had become head of late-night programming and created the *Joan Rivers Show*. He left Fox to partner with Miles Copeland III, who managed Sting's career, in the film company I.R.S. Media.

Then, in partnership with tax and real estate lawyer Stephen Jarchow, he founded Regent Entertainment. The initial business plan was to finance low budget movies with a popular hook. At the high end, their *Gods and Monsters* ($3M) won an Academy Award. At the bread and butter end, it was genre movies for US basic cable and foreign TV/ Home video, produced in Vancouver to benefit from Canadian subsidies. The publicity surrounding forthcoming releases of big budget disaster movies *Deep Impact* and *Armageddon* would ensure strong TV sales of similar-themed material like *Doomsday Rock*.

The storyline went like this: An astronomer (William Devane) believes an asteroid the size of Mount Everest is on a collision course with Earth. All other scientists point to orbital calculations showing the rock easily passing by. But Devane believes the asteroid will collide with a comet and be knocked off course straight towards our planet. Why is he certain of this? Because of Australian aboriginal cave paintings, of course, showing the Earth will end via impact from a "Demon Rock" near the end of the 20th century (WTF!). Devane is sufficiently convinced (again WTF!) to lead a bunch of militant environmentalists to take over a nuclear silo (bloodlessly) with

the intention of firing an ICBM at the incoming asteroid. The Secretary of Defense (Jessica Walter) regards the environmental activists as a terrorist group and wants to preemptively nuke the silo. The scientist's estranged daughter (Connie Sellecca) is brought in to negotiate. Ultimately Russia collaborates and both countries fire missiles destroying the asteroid. The buyer, the Family Channel, thought it was great.

Sometimes these pictures are rushed into production as close to the predetermined air date as possible, often due to topicality of the subject, but also to minimize financing charges. We had to start shooting in Vancouver in three weeks. There had been a huge uptick in shows coming to Vancouver. That month 20 movie and TV crews were working across the city. *Doomsday Rock* had to put together the 21st crew. Many were stepping up a rank in their department or it was their first job right out of film school. They did well under the circumstances.

An accelerated schedule has its challenges, particularly when compounded by network micromanagement which was prevalent in the telemovie business at that time. What follows is *inside the writers' room* stuff, but it highlights a problem that many directors have faced particularly in episodic television—the late arrival of scripts. For non-filmmaker folk, your eyes may glaze, but perhaps you could compare TV's management of the architect's blueprint, the script, with other manufacturing industries.

Let's flash forward to the final production meeting. Shooting would start the next day. There was only one problem. We did not have a script. What we had was an outline of every intended scene, but no dialogue. Sets were being built for the all nuclear silo scenes, and locations chosen for the rest. Costuming and props were rented. Supporting roles had been cast based upon earlier drafts but all actors had, as yet, no network approved words to speak.

How did this happen? The network "loved the concept," but after "rereading the script," decided the plot had holes, the science was bogus, characterization and dialogue clichéd. All true, but were they expecting Arthur Miller from an *Armageddon* derivative? The original writer kept trying to carry out the notes. The network would respond with more. They did not really know what they wanted. So the network had hired a new writer, Mike Norell, and had sent him to Vancouver a few days before shooting had to start. He had penned the scene outline that we were studying at this production meeting. Mike Norell had significant episodic credits. He was noted for the quality of his comedic 'banter' dialogue in the *Love Boat* series. He had never previously written science-fiction, but I welcomed the arrival of a seasoned professional.

Throughout the increasingly uncertain prep period, my mantra became: "Put it before me and I will shoot it." Project confidence, and others will feel it too. While we juggled how the proposed 100 pages of the work-in-progress script could be scheduled in eighteen days of photography, Mike Norell was holed up in a nearby hotel writing scenes for the next day. He was good with character, and came up with what drove the heroine's relationship with her celebrity scientist father: she wanted recognition from her high-standards Dad. She wanted her " 'Attagirl!" moment from him, and at last she gets it. Now there is an arc to the relationship. We scheduled a car chase for the first day to give Mike more breathing space to stay ahead of the shoot. Luckily, he lived up to his fast reputation.

After five days of shooting, we had a draft of the full script and Mike went back to LA. I thought he did a great job with the material. After reading the draft the committee at the network decided they did not like some of the witty repartee dialogue for which Mike Norell was known, and presumably a factor in his hiring. They started rewriting the dialogue themselves. Revisions were faxed to Vancouver each day, were vetted by the on-site producer before being sent to me (an added level of filtration with which my impatience was growing), then distributed. As per custom, each new set of revisions were identified by a new color: starting with blue, then green, pink, brown, and goldenrod then repeated as needed. On the last day of shooting, revised pages reached quadruple goldenrod!

Once the network rewrote a scene we had already shot. Sometimes their new material had little regard for the ripple effect of changes. For example, I noticed the network had pulled dialogue forward from a later scene and placed it in the scene to be shot the next day. This meant that Connie Sellecca's character would now know something she was not meant to find out for another ten pages. Such knowledge at this stage would have changed her performance in the intervening pages, some of which had already been shot.

I pointed out the discrepancy and shot the original perfectly adequate version. All the network revisions had to go through a supervising producer before they came to me. A former agent, he would sit beside me at the monitor and after a performance moment he liked, he would mutter "Oh that's good" loudly enough for it to be heard on the soundtrack. His more serious distraction to the performers was his refusal to turn his cellphone to silent before the camera rolled. Several times it rang in mid-take and he would start answering before he had completely left the set. On the second Friday, he decided that he disliked the network's new dialogue for a particular scene so much that he withheld the expected pages from me and said that nothing had been received. He suggested the actors improvise the scene, and oversaw a few attempts during the lunchbreak. He then flew back to LA, intending to return on Monday morning, leaving some papers behind which included the missing script page. In fact, a few tweaks were all the dialogue needed. I finished the day on time (just) but this situation could not go on.

I called the company's head of production in LA, Jeff Schenck, with whom I related well. I recounted the day's events and requested that the company not send this producer back again on Monday. If he came back and repeated Friday's behavior, I would regard it as a threat to the budget and would be obliged to inform the completion guarantor. On my first gig with a new company, I was challenging a senior executive. Was I committing career suicide? We had eight days of shooting left, and more than eight days of work to shoot. The picture would have some serious holes in it if I did not take control of the creative process. I felt it was my duty to say so.

The executive in question did not return the following Monday. Instead, CEO Paul Colichman and Head of Production Jeff Schenck arrived. Would they subject me to summary execution? No; rather, in breaks between shots that morning, they listened to my plan and gave me the authority I needed. But I knew that I had better deliver the goods. Paul Colichman persuaded the Family Channel to leave further revisions to the team in Vancouver, which they did, probably because their focus had shifted to their next production. Things settled down, to everyone's relief.

Our leading lady was Golden Globe nominated Connie Sellecca, a born-again Christian married to composer, musician and sports announcer John Tesh. She had segued from fashion modeling to a successful acting career. After eighteen telemovies, and five seasons of *Hotel* opposite James Brolin, Connie was highly sought after on the TV drama circuit. She was a sweetheart and a team player. Her only stipulation to me was to photograph her only from one side of her face in any angle closer than medium shot. So when working out the blocking of her scenes I made sure we had swung the axis to her designated side when we moved in for closer coverage. To me she was beautiful from all angles. But I recognized that Connie's modeling career had given her an understanding of how her face worked best for camera. Besides, you do not argue with a television diva on such a personal issue, so I was happy to adjust my staging.

Costar William Devane (*Marathon Man*) played a grouchy astronomer but was an amusing fellow between setups. While the lighting was being adjusted, we were sitting side by side in the row of chairs reserved for cast, discussing script changes. Devane talked of his time on Alfred Hitchcock's final film *Family Plot* when he too was sitting beside the director waiting for the set to be ready. Costar Karen Black approached, a little excited.

"Mr. Hitchcock," she had said, "I want to add another line here, and then I want to go over to the window…" she continued, showing him the script pages, suggesting further shadings to her character. Devane saw Hitchcock's hand drop out of Karen Black's view, below the arm of his chair, his fingers scissoring—snip-snip-snip—as he mentally deleted her additions. Hitchcock's editorial control was legendary. While shooting *Rebecca* (1939), he would put his

Steven Leon
Vice President Programming
The Family Channel

A Division of International
Family Entertainment, Inc.

June 9, 1997

Brian Trenchard-Smith
c/o Shavick Entertainment
116 East Second Avenue
Vancouver, BC  V5T 3B5

Dear Brian,

For everyone at The Family Channel, I wanted to thank you for the phenomenal job you did during the production of *Doomsday Rock*. I know this film was made under extremely tough circumstances, but the work you did was extraordinary. Both Tom Halleen and I thought the film looked terrific.

Thanks again for all the hard work that you did on this.

Best regards,

Steve Leon

hand over the lens to exclude parts of a shot he did not want David O. Selznick to use, when the notorious control-freak producer would inevitably reedit his cut.

In television, however, the network has the final cut. Two editors had been assembling scenes throughout the 18-day shoot. I would come in on weekends and give notes. Once shooting was over, I had seven days to deliver my director's cut. A Family Channel executive Steve Leon came up to Vancouver and sat down with me, Paul Colichman and Jeff Schenck to watch it on the editor's Avid. Steve was pleased that I had played so much of Connie Sellecca's performance in close up. The network were counting on her considerable fanbase to swell the ratings. My cut passed with flying colors, and Family Channel greenlit further Regent Entertainment productions. The supervising producer I sidelined ultimately forgave me and we worked together harmoniously on another film in 1999. Variety forgave the inherent absurdity of *Doomsday Rock* and called my direction "taut". Well, I do like to move things along.

*Doomsday Rock* premiered on August 31, 1997. Early in the broadcast, a banner crawled across the bottom of the screen *Princess Diana seriously injured in Paris car crash*. Millions, including Connie Sellecca's entire fanbase, switched to news. The hoped for ratings evaporated. Such are the ironies of life; just a blip for the network, a bonanza for tabloid media that contributed to Diana's death, and a terrible day for British people.

***

Ten years later, another Sci-fi film came my way. Jeff Hayes, who had been my producer on *Official Denial, Sahara,* and *Flipper*, asked whether I would like to make a dinosaur movie. Would I ever?

Back in 1968 I had made the trailer for Ray Harryhausen's *cowboys versus dinosaurs* flick *Valley of Gwangi*, getting an inside peek at the stop motion master's work as it progressed through the final stages. Now I would have my chance at a prehistoric monster picture. The movie was for the SyFy Channel, as part of their Saturday night series of high concept/low budget creature features. I had just reedited and supervised visu-

DELL
15¢
01-880-912
MOVIE

THE VALLEY OF GWANGI

MONSTERS!!
Prehistoric Monsters!

The Most Terrifying of All—
GWANGI!

al effects (as "creative consultant") for SyFy's recent production *Ice Spiders*. They felt I had made a big difference, so Jeff Hayes had no trouble getting me approved. The script of *Tyrannosaurus Azteca*, subsequently retitled *Aztec Rex*, was written by veteran *Farscape* writer Richard Manning. His screenplay was substantially more literate than the average SyFy original feature, though no less preposterous. The storyline was as follows:

The year is 1518. Ruthless Spanish Conquistador Hernán Cortés is on a scouting expedition in Mexico to see if the country is worth plundering. Cortés (like us) is on a low budget. He can only afford a troop of six soldiers. And a cannon. Within a remote valley he makes a startling discovery. The fierce local Aztec warriors live in tenuous harmony with a line of Tyrannosaurus Rexes, whom they placate with virgin sacrifices (seems a shocking waste of virgins, if you ask me). When the Conquistadors' brutal quest for riches upsets the balance, the T-Rexes begin a killing rampage. The invaders must slay the giants or become human sacrifices themselves…

I saw *Aztec Rex* in genre terms as a fun blend of two old favorites of mine: the aforementioned Ray Harryhausen's *Valley of Gwangi* and Hammer's 1962 summer holiday hit *Pirates of Blood River*. This low budget Hammer swashbuckler was a favorite movie of my 16th year, double billed with RHH's *Mysterious Island*. Somehow that matinee session at the London Pavilion struck such a Boy's Own Adventure chord within me that Hammer and Harryhausen became tied together on my future movie wish list. Richard Manning's script ticked all the boxes. Greedy rogues get their comeuppance from giant teeth and claws. It's a *Jurassic Park Eats Apocalypto* cocktail served with a dash of *Aguirre, Wrath of God*. I saw it as an absurdist tale that should be played with all the ripeness its genre tropes provide. However, the key to persuading a creature feature audience to accept such a nonsense premise is a convincing creature. The producers planned to shoot two of these monster pictures back to back, and wanted a bulk VFX deal from one supplier. I strongly pitched BFX Imageworks, who were approved by the SyFy Channel for past productions like *Chupacabra* and *Ice Spiders*, but they were underbid.

SyFy's deal was that their license fee covered half the budget of each film; the producers had to find the rest. At that time Hawaii was offering substantial tax breaks to owners of multistory apartment blocks with high property tax bills, if they invested their tax liability in local film production. The producers cleverly got their two SyFy Channel creature features funded this way. But funding came at an increased production cost. Hawaiian crews are full union: DGA, WGA, IA, Teamsters. It would have been more authentic and cheaper to shoot in Mexico, but Hawaii was where the money was.

This was my second shoot in Hawaii, and it was just as much fun as the first. There's something about being surrounded by so much beauty, a kind of *joie de vivre* in the Hawaiian air. Paul Atkins, who had done a great job on *Tides of War/Phantom Below*, was again my DP and brought a strong crew with him. The producers rented two houses side by side near our principal location, the Kualoa Ranch on Oahu's windward side. One was a production office, the other a group home for producers Dennis Duckwall and David Dwiggins, writer Richard Manning, Designer Cameron Bernie, Andrew Prowse (directing the other SyFy movie *Heatstroke*) and myself, plus visiting wives and girlfriends. One big happy family. We could walk across the 2-lane Kamehameha Highway, and within twenty feet, step into the ocean. Nightly BBQs. The camaraderie of men on a mission, working hard on a tight budget, but having a good time doing it.

There's always a creative ripple effect to a budgetary squeeze. An animatronic Tyrannosaur head, as per the original *Jurassic Park*, was way beyond our price. No even a foot or a claw to frame in foreground was affordable. The T-Rex would be 100% digital. The movie had to be shot in 15x11-hour days on a below-the-line budget of around 900K. We could only afford six Conquistadors and six Aztecs. The large Aztec village in the script had to become "an outpost." The SyFy Channel executives, accustomed to crowds of extras costing $10 per day on their Bulgarian shoots, responded to the first dailies with unhappy emails. My attempt to explain to the network executive the cost difference between production in eastern Europe and the fully union state of Hawaii was not appreciated. Also, more extras mean more costuming. While Aztec Rex was primarily a visual effects action picture, it was also a hair and makeup show, elements that can really slow a director down if they aren't well coordinated.

Here's a conversation to avoid:

"The cameras are ready, we should be shooting, where's the cast?"

"They're still in the makeup trailer."

"Why?"

"Six Conquistadors need their unwashed, sunburnt, bad dental hygiene look. Six muscular Aztecs need their body paint markings. It takes forty-five minutes per character. We don't have enough makeup staff to get them all ready in time."

The result: lost camera time that you never get back. The remedy: smart scheduling. Hats off to the producing team of Duckwall and Dwiggins, together with 1ˢᵗ AD Matt Locey, for their grasp of this issue. Fortunately, we had Bryan Furer, Hawaii's top makeup artist and his team on board. Bryan's other particular talent was gore, which I wanted as graphic as time and money would allow. Two human hearts are ripped out, a leg is bitten off, intestines are spilled, ribs are shredded, a half-eaten corpse falls onto wet sand, etc. Load up the burger. That's what the SyFy Channel audience wanted to see in this kind of picture, and Bryan delivered the goods.

SyFy Channel selected Ian Ziering as Cortés. He had a following from the Beverly Hills 90210 series, and was a semifinalist on *Dancing with the Stars*, where once hot TV names go to kickstart their careers. I covered his blonde hair with a Steve Tyler wig and he played Cortés as an egotistical rock star of his day. Ian had a tremendous physique so I made sure we got his shirt off for one big scene. The internet trolls scorned his casting as much as they ridiculed the CGI T-Rex. But I think Ian Ziering did well with the material he had. I was pleased to see his subsequent casting in six *Sharknado* movies that ensured his iconic status.

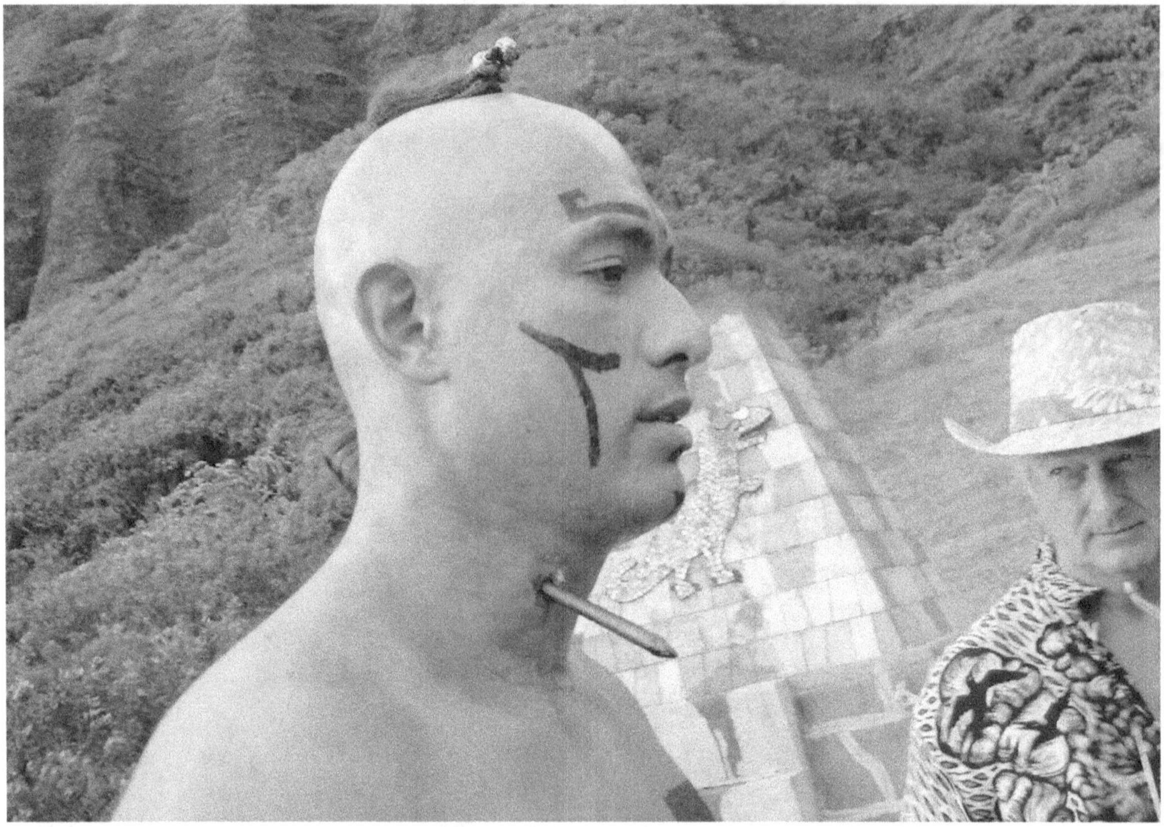

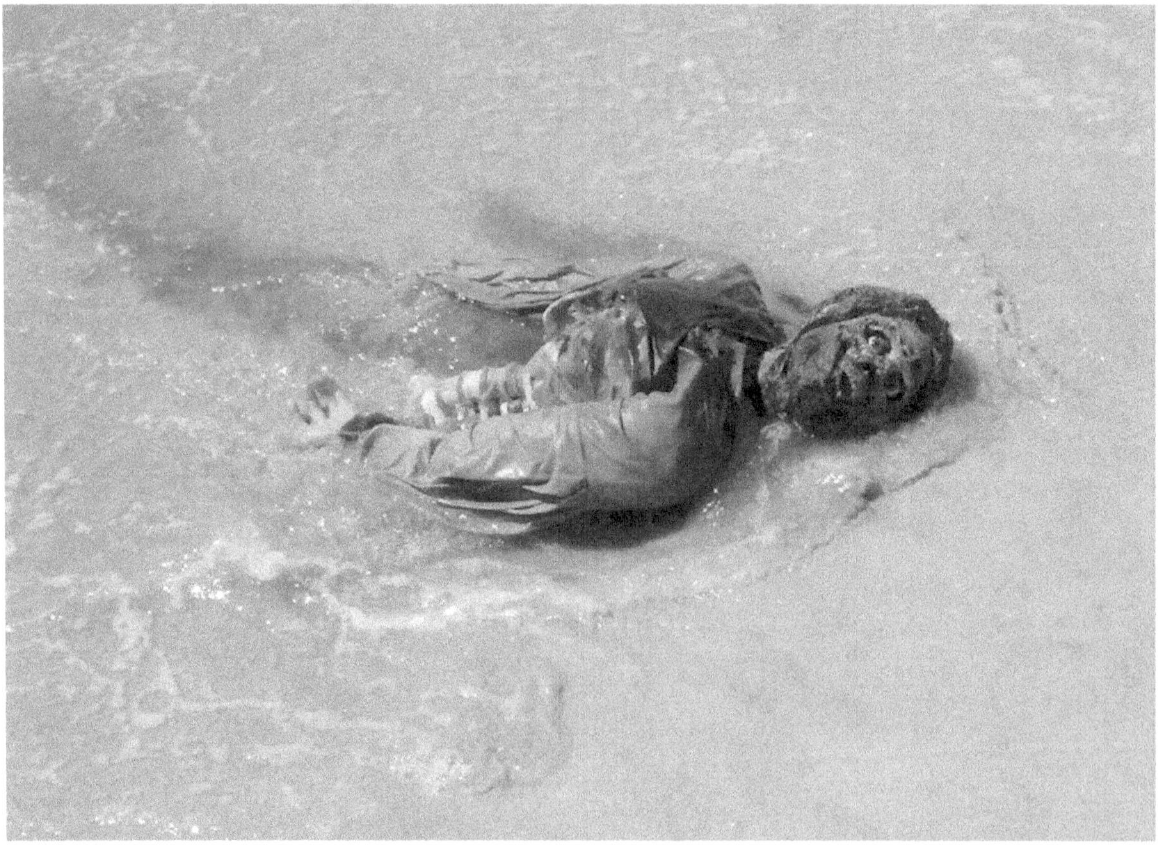

Another target for undeserved online snark was Australian/Tibetan actress Dichen Lachman, as the Aztec princess. Her previous experience was two seasons of the Australian soap *Neighbors*. For a sweet-natured girl, she sure can cut a heart out with relish! Again, I think she did well with a tissue-thin character. It didn't stop Joss Whedon casting her in two seasons of his *Dollhouse* series. She has since played a regular or recurring role in seven other series, most recently Season One of *Altered Carbon* on Netflix. In fact, Dichen had not been my first choice. I was unaware of her at the time. I chose two Hispanic actors to play the young Hispanic conquistador and the Aztec princess with whom he falls in love. Their audition showed real chemistry, but the SyFy executive in charge rejected them. I wrote an impassioned email in their support. Not appreciated. Keep looking, the executive said. So we did, and Dichen was clearly the best of the new auditionees.

Having grown up on Errol Flynn swashbucklers, and having been a fencer since the age of thirteen, I had always wanted to shoot a sword fight. *Aztec Rex* provided a perfect opportunity, so I built one into the script. If characters are carrying swords, they should use them. We could not afford the weeks of training and photography that made *Rob Roy*'s climactic claymore versus rapier clash between Liam Neeson and Tim Roth so exciting, so I threw something together that could be captured in two hours of shooting. My duelists, Marco Sanchez and James Locke, had no real fencing experience. Their swords were not sharp, but they were pointed and heavy, their boots were uncomfortable, and the ground was uneven, so care was necessary. I staged it in short blocks, lots of circular parries, and sweeping movements which look good for camera. The actors rehearsed the choreography of each section slowly till they had internalized the rhythm. As confidence grew, they gradually increased to full speed, then cameras rolled. I covered each block with a wide profile, plus over-the-shoulder shots. It's a passable sword fight, it adds diversity to the action menu, but most importantly—not a scratch.

Postproduction took place in LA. John Blizek did a great job as editor. With Dennis Duckwall, we spent long hours wrestling with the limitations of our CGI budget. We could not afford the rotoscoping necessary to show the T-Rex's feet interacting with the ground, kicking up dust or crushing the grass. Those shots had to be framed above the creatures' ankles. Similarly, we could not show the T-Rex brushing aside foliage as it moved forward.

It could appear from behind big tree trunks, which provided an easy matte line, but otherwise the T-Rex had to move in foreground through open spaces. It is to the animator's credit that he delivered the sheer number of shots the story needed. The compositing of those shots was the problem. In many of them, the T-Rex looked pasted on. The creature effects—the *raison d'être* of a Jurassic Park derivative—were roundly scorned in online reviews.

The SyFy Channel executives hated the picture. It was too talky, the T-Rex was unconvincing, etc. They decided I was to blame and dropped me from their list of approved directors. I had to step aside as director of Regent's next production for SyFy—*Malibu Shark Attack*—for which I had already shot background plates on Malibu's private beaches. (Sorry, not a great respecter of boundaries)) .

Early in *Aztec Rex*'s post-production, I turned down another telemovie that had an immediate start date so I could stay with the picture through the tricky VFX process. No good deed will go unpunished. That's Showbiz.

On November 5, 2007, the Writers Guild of America, of which I am a member, began a strike which lasted three months. Till the issues were resolved, no WGA member could carry out script writing work for hire. On the picket lines, writer Peter Hyoguchi had a novel idea: invite writers to create their *own* shows directly for the internet, premiere them on a new online network Strike TV, and donate a portion of that network's proceeds to help out industry workers (other than writers) idled by the strike. *Aztec Rex*'s writer Richard Manning wanted to ease the withdrawal pains of genre TV fans temporarily deprived of their favorite shows by the strike. To scratch as many different "genre itches" as possible—a broad-spectrum "quick fix" as he put it. Richard cheerfully borrowed familiar elements from dozens of shows and concocted a fusion of science-fiction, mystery, romance, action, police procedural, and horror, and called it, what else: *Fusion*. He asked me to direct the *Fusion* pilot, in which a homicide cop and a forensic psychologist, each cursed with an unearthly ability, combine to solve a murder.

Together with fellow *Aztec Rex* producer Dennis Duckwall, we put together an all-volunteer cast and crew, happy to work a weekend for food. Location hire, props, and postproduction brought the total cash outlay for the 11-minute pilot to $6,500. On Saturday we shot in a rented morgue set, and adjacent streets. On Sunday, the Writers Guild provided their empty underground car park for the remainder of the scenes. This was my first taste of guerrilla filmmaking since the early 1970s and I enjoyed returning to it. My thanks to the cast: Julianna Robinson, Chris Cleveland, Kevin Fry and Dennis Pratt. It's amazing what a committed crew of six can achieve.

*Fusion* screened at the American Cinematheque's Egyptian Theater on Hollywood Boulevard as part of a festival of indie shorts, before premiering on the Strike TV website where it played for a number of years. The site is dark now, so *Fusion* only exists on Richard Manning's website. We had hoped it would attract a network's attention, but no. It's still a great idea for a series.

2009 was consumed by directing a Canadian/Australian co-production, *Arctic Blast*. It had been set up by prolific Australian producer Tony Ginnane, in conjunction with equally prolific Canadian producer Pierre David who had executive producing credits on more than 200 films, including three directed by David Cronenberg—*Scanners*, *Videodrome* and *The Brood*. Pierre David had mainly concentrated on the made-for-TV market, and most of his recent films had been low budget thrillers. He wanted to try his own kind of genre hybrid, a marriage-in-conflict drama fused with a disaster movie, intended to be attractive to both SyFy and family viewing platforms, and thus broadening the movie's value in the marketplace.

He cast Michael Shanks, one of stars of the SyFy series *Stargate SG1*, in the lead role. Here's the storyline:

(Jack Tate Shanks), a brilliant but unorthodox physicist based in Tasmania, provides the land-based support for an American research vessel in the Antarctic Ocean. Complicating his life is a messy divorce from local medical examiner Emma (Alexandra Davies) and his strained relationship with bratty teenage daughter Naomi (Indiana Evans).

When Jack learns about the terrible deaths of his colleagues on the research vessel in a sudden blast of sub-zero air, he discovers that a rip in the ozone layer has allowed the freezing mesosphere to rush in, potentially triggering a new ice age. But his boss Winslaw (Bruce Davison) at the Climate Research Center in Philadelphia HQ, refuses, considering Jack's maverick past, to contemplate his radical solution. With parts of the South Pacific in deep freeze, the frigid air mass heads toward the west coast of the United States, flash freezing every living thing in its path. Meanwhile, his daughter Naomi has gone missing. As the mesosphere punches more holes over London, Tokyo, Moscow and the US, can Jack Tate save the planet, his marriage, and become an awesome dad?

The movie was shot in sixteen days in Hobart Tasmania, then two subsequent days in Ottawa, Canada for the US scenes with Bruce Davison. Publicity releases state the budget was $5M, puffing it up for sales purposes. Try $1.6M and all the creative compromises that budget implies. However, I'm quite proud of the film. It's a strong example of its microgenre, and I had a good time making it. I enjoyed working with young cameraman Marc Windon, whose father and brother had distinguished cinematography careers. Brother Steve Windon has shot five movies for *Fast & Furious* director Justin Lin. Marc and I shared an affection for the mini-jib with its variety of angles and moves the rig provided from a fixed position or on a dolly track. The mini-jib got us through nine pages of dialogue in a big set on Day One.

Assurances were given that the climate science in the script was basically defensible. A barrage of internet scorn said otherwise. Earth's warm atmosphere would have soon melted the ice fog before it travelled too far, among other complaints. Jack and his daughter outrun the fog on foot, yet when driving away at top speed, it is sitting right behind them. Hey, it's a movie! Think the ad line for *Jaws 4: The Revenge*: "This time it's personal…" Certainly it's straining credulity if the temperature is -70° and the hero's car still starts. This was a producer driven requirement. Pierre David felt it was essential to give Michael Shanks another hero building moment in the final fifteen minutes. After getting his daughter to the comparative safety of his lab, the hero must risk his life to save his assistant (Saskia Hempele) from a diabetic coma by braving the freezing fog, and breaking into a pharmacy to get insulin. Several diabetics have posted that giving an insulin injection to a diabetic suffering from excessively low blood sugar would kill her. Again, I was told the medical science involved was accurate.

Adjusting actor's expectations to reality in low budget is always a diplomatic tightrope. Pierre David, bless him, had told Michael Shanks before he arrived in Hobart that his science lab scenes would be shot inside a big refrigerated truck, so that when the lab freezes, cold breath would come out of the actors mouths naturally, not requiring *Titanic*-style CGI. Cool, thought Michael. Then when he saw that we were shooting those scenes in the Tasmanian Emergency Services HQ, full of expensive computer equipment and hence no refrigeration, he threw a polite fit, understandably. Actors hate "cold acting" almost as much as they hate being cold on the set. His faith in the movie was shaken, but he soldiered on, a true professional, and gave it all he had. I was particularly impressed by how he handled the meteorological gobbledygook required to explain the continually escalating disaster phenomenon. Michael could make recitation of algebraic equations interesting.

As a kid I always liked those *panic in the streets* scenes in Ray Harryhausen movies, and (an early favorite) *Gorgo*; here the pursuing monster is the freezing fog. We had limited funds for extras, but we got some nice shots of the panicking crowd rushing past camera in the bottom half of the frame with the roofs of buildings in the background.

Our intrepid special effects crew then built miniature cardboard outlines of those roofs, painted black and positioned them in a black limbo. We rolled camera in slow motion as an offscreen fogger pumped a white cloud rising over the line of roofs, and curling downwards. The two elements would then be composited by a company in Montreal. Certainly, it was a challenge to make what looks like a bank of thick morning fog feel scary. We could see *cause*; we needed more *effect*. More graphic freezings perhaps, where victims toppled and broke into pieces. But that would have disturbed the family side of the audience, at whom the climate change message was aimed. The *Attack of the Deep Freeze* sequences were bolstered by good use of stock images..

*Arctic Blast* got some acknowledgement in the review by Urban Cinefile:..

*Trenchard-Smith does orchestrated chaos well, and the sense of panic—crucial to conveying fear to the audience—is dynamic, and well served by Mario Sevigny's score.*

To make it a bigger sequence, I wanted multiple locations, so on days when I had ten or more extras for other scenes, I piggybacked these shots onto the call sheet for the splinter unit to do in a nearby street. My coup, if I may boast, was in persuading the administration of St Mary's College, a Catholic Girls' school in Hobart, to let us stage a brisk but orderly evacuation of a hundred or more pupils and staff. All the school asked for in return was that I deliver a 90-minute lecture to the school's drama students, ranging in age from 10 to 17. They asked lots of good questions about showbiz. I gave cautionary advice, without dampening their enthusiasm, about the uncertainty of an acting career, and urged them to get the necessary educational qualifications to develop a parallel career in case acting did not work out. But mainly I tried to introduce them to black and white classic movies, with which their generation was unfamiliar, in particular the work of Alfred Hitchcock, which I illustrated via extracts from DVDs. I know some girls rented *Strangers on a Train* as a result. Did any of the class get lucky and make a career in the performing arts? I'd love to hear.

The cooperation of the school was mirrored all over town. The Tasmanian Emergency Services provided multiple vehicles and rescue personnel for the *beached ship* scenes. I met many members of the Tasmanian Fire Services who had seen *Hospitals Don't Burn Down*, my 1977 fire safety film, still going strong on YouTube. It's a favorite film for firemen all over the world.

Strangely, *Arctic Blast* did not sell to the SyFy Channel except in Australia; too much family drama, not enough Sci-fi, not enough kills. Nor did Lifetime or Hallmark pick it up; too grim, too foreign. But in foreign markets it did surprisingly well. When it premiered on cable in Spain for instance, it scored a 15.6 market share meaning it was seen by over 2.5 million viewers. The producers emailed me ratings from France's TF1 and Germany's RTL 2 which they described as "stellar".

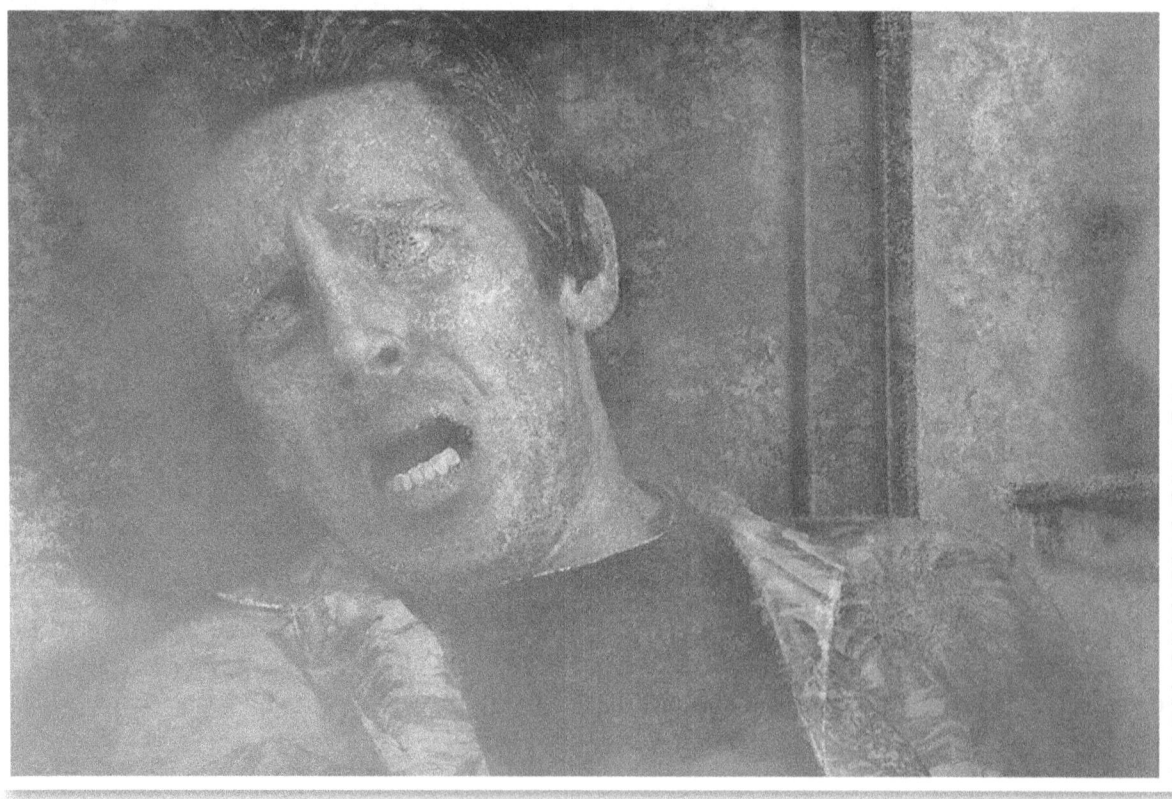

# CHAPTER 41
## Horror Comedy

After *Silk Stalkings* in 1992, it had seemed I might roll straight into another production; the showrunner David Peckinpah had liked the way I handled two of the episodes he wrote, and so he gave me a spec thriller he had written called *The Paperboy*. Think *Bad Seed* on a bike. He attached me as director and told me to find a way to get it made. I took it to a trio of producers I had met the year before, Walter Josten, Jeff Geoffray, and Henry Seggerman, partners in Blue Rider Pictures, who had made three pictures with director Kevin Tenney.

But the only way they could get it financed was as a Canadian production. Many US productions were going to Canada, which offered a favorable exchange rate and tax incentives. To qualify, if the script was American, a Canadian director was required. The producers gave me $5000 to bow out. However, their next production was a sequel to their successful 1988 horror film *Night of the Demons* for Republic Pictures. I was invited to audition.

As mentioned, I'm *good in the room*, an item agents list when categorizing clients' abilities. It's a necessary skill in Hollywood. Just get me *in the room* and I'll do the rest. I came to the head of production's office at Republic brimming with ideas for cool shots, creepy moments. According to the executive, other auditionees with better-known horror credits than I had coasted through the interview without having studied the script in detail, so she gave me the gig. Always go the extra mile.

The producers had made *Night of the Demons* in 1988 as their second film. Snappily directed by Kevin Tenney, it had earned four times its budget. For some reason, probably trivial, Republic had fallen out with Tenney over his previous film *Witchboard 2*, and he was not asked back. He nonetheless went on to write and direct several successful Sci-fi and horror films over the next decade.

*NOTD 2*, nicely scripted by Joe Augustyn, the writer of the original, followed the pattern of several horror sequels. A relative or friend of one of those sliced and diced in the prior movie is somehow brought to the same venue. So, another bunch of dumb teenagers decide to visit Hull House, the abandoned funeral parlor, where the original slaughter took place. They drag along, as a cruel prank, Melissa (or Mouse as the Mean Girls call her), the virginal sister of Angela, the only victim of the Hull House Massacre whose body had never been found. Why no corpse? Because Angela did it, of course! Now she's a homicidal demon, following in the footsteps of Michael Myers, Jason and Freddy, lying in wait for fresh victims. Abandon hope all ye who enter here.

The victims in *NOTD2* are all students at St. Rita's Academy for troubled teens, under the thumb, or

Cristi Harris — Christine Taylor — Zoe Trilling

rather the yardstick, of stern Sister Gloria. Initially Ellen Travolta, sister of John Travolta, did a killer audition. Surely, I thought, the Travolta name on the marquee would raise the movie's profile. But the Republic executive in charge said John Travolta's career was over, and the Travolta name would mean nothing by the time the film was released. A year later *Pulp Fiction* came out, reigniting John Travolta's career. So we auditioned until we got an actress who grabbed us as much as Ellen Travolta did, and that was Jennifer Rhodes.

She struck the perfect tone as the authoritarian Sister Gloria who transforms into a Ninja Nun in the climax, wielding rosary beads as 'nun'-chuks, and spraying demons with holy water from an Uzi Super Soaker (borrowed from my sons). Jennifer had to conduct a clever mating dance with the audience. The very qualities you loathe about Sister Gloria at the beginning give her the ability to be the courageous hero at the end. We lucked out with her and all the cast.

Amelia Kinkade returned as Angela, playing the female Freddy with lip-smacking relish. Zoe Trilling delivered a great Mean Girl. Merle Kennedy was endearing as the Mouse that ultimately roared. Rick Peters added some prescient improv in his first scene with Christine Taylor: "What's your problem, Marcia?" he said as he squeezed into the car beside her. Christine had a strong resemblance to Marcia Brady in the original *Brady Bunch* TV series. Three months later, auditions were announced for the movie version of *The Brady Bunch*. Christine was cast as Marcia.

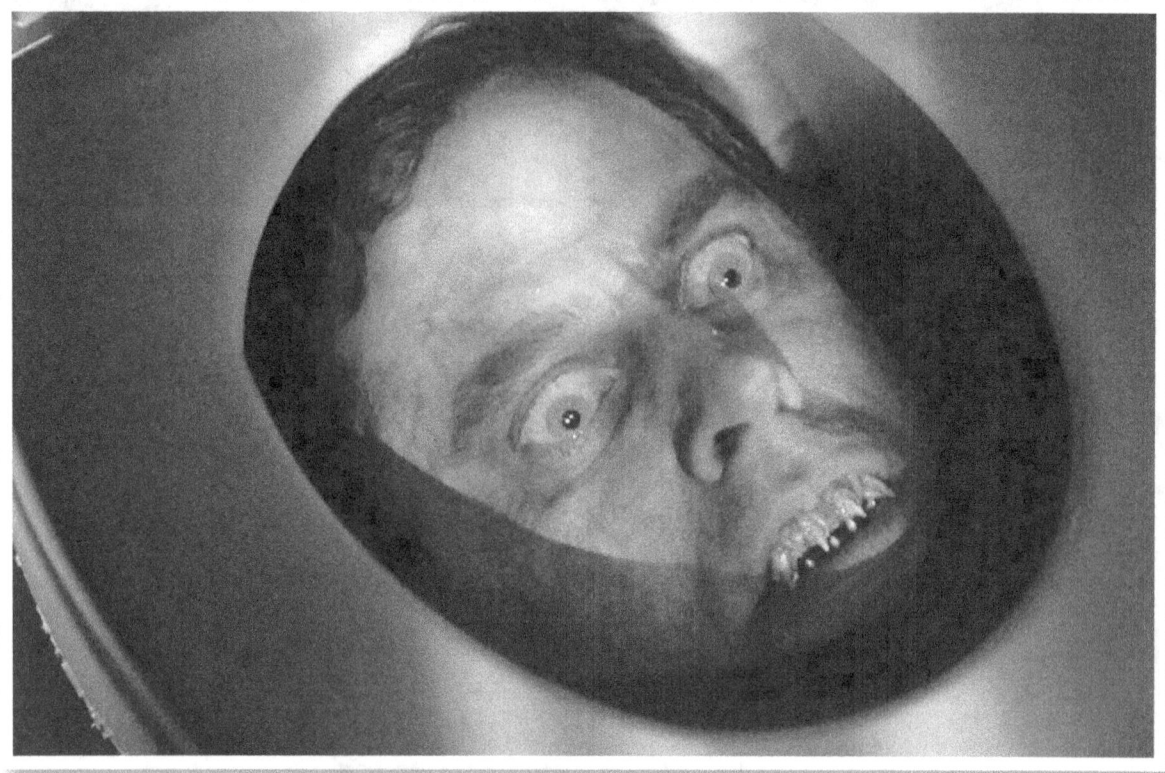

This was the last screen role for our friend Mark Neely (*Firebase*), who segued into a career as a motivational consultant, where he was able to quip that his acting career ended in the toilet. The wackiness of the script was terrific, like the demon practicing basketball with his own head, and I added some more, such as the Rambo-style montage of Sister Gloria strapping on her Holy Weapons, and the Demon repeatedly stabbing Father Bob while reciting the Act of Contrition. One of my additions was more subtle. As Demon Angela enters the sleeping girls' dormitory during a thunderstorm, lightning flashes, illuminating a foreground clock at the 6th second of the 6th minute of the 6th hour.

As was the custom then in low budget horror, there had to be nudity. In fact, an executive attended the relevant scene to ensure that the director did not succumb to an attack of good taste, and the required boobs were displayed. Cristi Harris handled it with stoic professionalism. I didn't want more sex, but I did add more sexual outrageousness, like the mistaken identity/hand job scene, where Ladd York's character thinks his masseuse is Christine Taylor, but the audience can see it is Angela's demonic hand that has pushed through the car seat between his legs, and unzipped his fly. When he realizes that both of Christine's hands are round his neck, he recoils, looking down. Angela's hand gives him the finger then disappears back into the car seat. I think the LA Weekly review got what I was after:

*"Have we really gone as far as hand jobs?... Night of The Demons—Shrimping The Undead? Freud reigns supreme as hot young kids are eviscerated for releasing chaos through their percolating sexuality. Nuns, haunted houses, bad Catholic schoolgirls. You get the idea. What's different here is the degree to which the film makers really and truly don't care about social conditioning—there's a real glee for evil, a sweet sense of fun as the taboos shatter."*

I know. I am a sick and wicked puppy.

In a horror sequel, you can't just deliver a retread, you have to top the moments the audience loved in the first one. A great assist in this regard came from Steve Johnson. Since creating the inventive prosthetic effects that distinguished the first *NOTD*, he had continued to devise new tricks. For *Innocent Blood* (1992) Johnson innovated contact lenses that could glow and change color on command without digital effects. These were scleral lenses coated with silicone glass and Scotchlite. When light was projected on them through a color wheel, the colors would bounce back toward the camera. Clever and cost effective. Steve also created the alien creatures for the climax of James Cameron's *The Abyss*.

Ten days into the 18-day shoot, Republic executives began to realize they might have a movie originally intended for home video that could get a limited theatrical release, so they said to us: what if we gave you two more days of shooting and more money for prosthetic effects, adding 150K to the budget, could you come up with an additional climax that would top the one already shot? In other words, the heroes would leave the room where Angela had just melted down, walk into the next room and there she would reappear, in some new form, even more powerful than ever. Steve Johnson came up with a 15-foot long snake woman.

Drawing on his experience working with Vegas magicians, Steve used a teeter totter or seesaw to make Angela rear up from a hole in the wall and stand apparently eight feet tall with more tail implied, coiled unseen behind her. Equally clever was the use of a false floor constructed two feet above the location's actual floor, with a sliding section to accommodate Snake Lady Angela's advance on the heroes while lashing her 10-foot tail. This allowed Amelia Kinkade to crawl forward on padded knees beneath the floor, with the sliding section of the floor fitted around her waist. Her seven-breasted prosthetic torso was invisibly connected to the above-floor tail writhing behind her, which was manipulated by wires from offscreen crew. Many in the biz thought these had to be CG sequences and wondered how we could have afforded them.

This climactic scene took up much of the last day of the shoot, which went for twenty hours; though, for Amelia Kinkade, with her early makeup call, it was a 27-hour day. What an amazing trooper she was throughout the movie. The same applied to the crew, particularly DP David Lewis, who was indefatigable.

The last shot was the multicamera slow motion fragmentation of Angela, for which a dummy of the Ang-ie-Snake infused with primacord was prepared. Doing a major interior pyrotechnic effect in the 20th hour of work was probably not wise, but without the shot, the movie had no ending. I had faith in the team. We blew Angela to bits at 120 frames per second. It went off perfectly.

There was no doubt that the film would get an 'R' rating. In fact, it was a market necessity for horror at the time. 'PG 13' horror films relying on jump scares rather than gore were not yet in vogue. However, the MPAA were traditionally tougher on independently made horror pictures than big budget studio fare. The major studios who fund the MPAA had greater powers of persuasion, shall we say. My strategy in editing was to double the number of gore shots in key scenes, so the MPAA had something to cut out and justify their existence. In fact, from a creative standpoint, these extra shots unbalanced the flow of the scene, making it feel like an assembly cut rather than a fine cut. The list of deletions came back along expected lines: *"Considerably reduce the shots of blood spurting and the severed head rolling…"* was the response to Angela's ("How about a little head, Tiger?") beheading of Ladd York. In each instance I took out the gratuitous shots I had put in, and good editing was restored.

*Night of The Demons 2* opened in a few theaters on Friday, May 13, 1994 to excellent reviews.

*"A smart, amusing horror picture, boasting a capable cast and first-rate special effects… under the swift, stylish direction of Brian Trenchard-Smith"* proclaimed Kevin Thomas of the Los Angeles Times. Hey, I won't argue. The movie, once destined to go straight to VHS, got a 'platform' release in about twenty cities, doing particularly well in Detroit, before earning a decent amount of money on home video and internationally.

The challenges of the *NOTD 2* production bonded me with the producers Jeff Geoffray and Walter Josten, who immediately invited me to direct their next production, *Leprechaun 3*, commissioned by Trimark to conclude their *Leprechaun* franchise as a trilogy.

People have asked me why did you make those *Leprechaun* movies? Agents and managers suggested I take those titles off my resume. A *so bad it's good* franchise does your image as a serious filmmaker no good. Perhaps. But I needed to work, from both an economic and a psychological standpoint. Besides these movies were an opportunity to have some laughs. I grew up enjoying the absurdist humor of *Monty Python's Flying Circus* on BBC. So why not Absurdist Cinema? The concept of the mid '90s *Leprechaun* franchise was proudly ludicrous—a little person Jason/Freddy/Chucky amalgam with an Irish twist terrorizes and kills most of the supporting cast. But he was never really scary. I decided to embrace the absurd and make it as much fun as the formula allowed.

Angela's Throwing Another Party.

Trick or Treat, Sucker.

NIGHT OF THE DEMONS 2

Jeff Geoffray and Walter Josten suggested to Trimark *"How about sending the little guy to Vegas, the capital of greed and broken dreams..."* Jeff had a perfect place to shoot it—the once grand, then abandoned, Ambassador Hotel, a location that could be redressed as a rundown old Vegas casino. Trimark only wanted to spend $1.2M on *LEP3*, 300K less than *LEP 2*. A script was commissioned that created the basic plot and characters, but I wanted it to be funnier, more satirical of Vegas culture. Trimark executive Dave Tripett was supportive of my humorous approach. To help me rework the script, I brought in a writer I had met through our mutual agent.

Dennis Pratt bears a passing resemblance to Boris Karloff. This is because he is the great-nephew of Boris Karloff, whose family name was Pratt. Dennis had served in the US Air Force, became an actor, then a produced playwright, before writing the screenplays for *American Justice* and *Kickboxer 3*. Dennis is a movie buff, whose John Wayne, Jimmy Stewart, Kirk Douglas impersonations are pitch perfect. We clicked at our first meeting and have collaborated on countless projects over the past twenty-five years. We also shared an ironic sense of humor and a mistrust of authority. Our first collaboration, a crime drama spec script, showed me how good he was at writing characters from the shady

side of the street: grifters, gunmen, gold diggers. Ideal skills to help me with the Vegas ambiance.

Together with Jeff and Walter, we did some clever production planning to turn sections of LA's Ambassador Hotel into a seedy Vegas casino. We based ourselves there and prepared for the 14-day shoot. The plan was for a skeleton crew to go to Vegas on the 15th day. The Ambassador Hotel's famous Cocoanut Grove nightclub, where Frank Sinatra, Barbra Streisand, and countless great singers performed for decades, became the venue where Fazio, the most incompetent magician in Vegas, gets sawn in half. We filled the lobby with rented roulette and blackjack tables. It was harder to get that row of slot machines into Los Angeles as their movement out of Vegas were highly restricted. I plead the fifth.

I beefed up the humor overall with limericks, and put much of *LEP's* dialogue into rhyme. "For playing me this trick," says Warwick, swinging an axe, "I'll chop off your…" Whack!  Blotting out the last word, the axe lands between John Gatins legs, an inch from inhibiting his social life. Crotch gags abound in my movies—see *The Man from Hong Kong* as an early example. There was a satirical vein of sexist humor, too. Caroline Williams, an awesome comedienne, embraced it with joy. She made the most of every scene as the blowzy croupier seeking magical transformation into traditional male expectations of female beauty. Careful what you wish for…

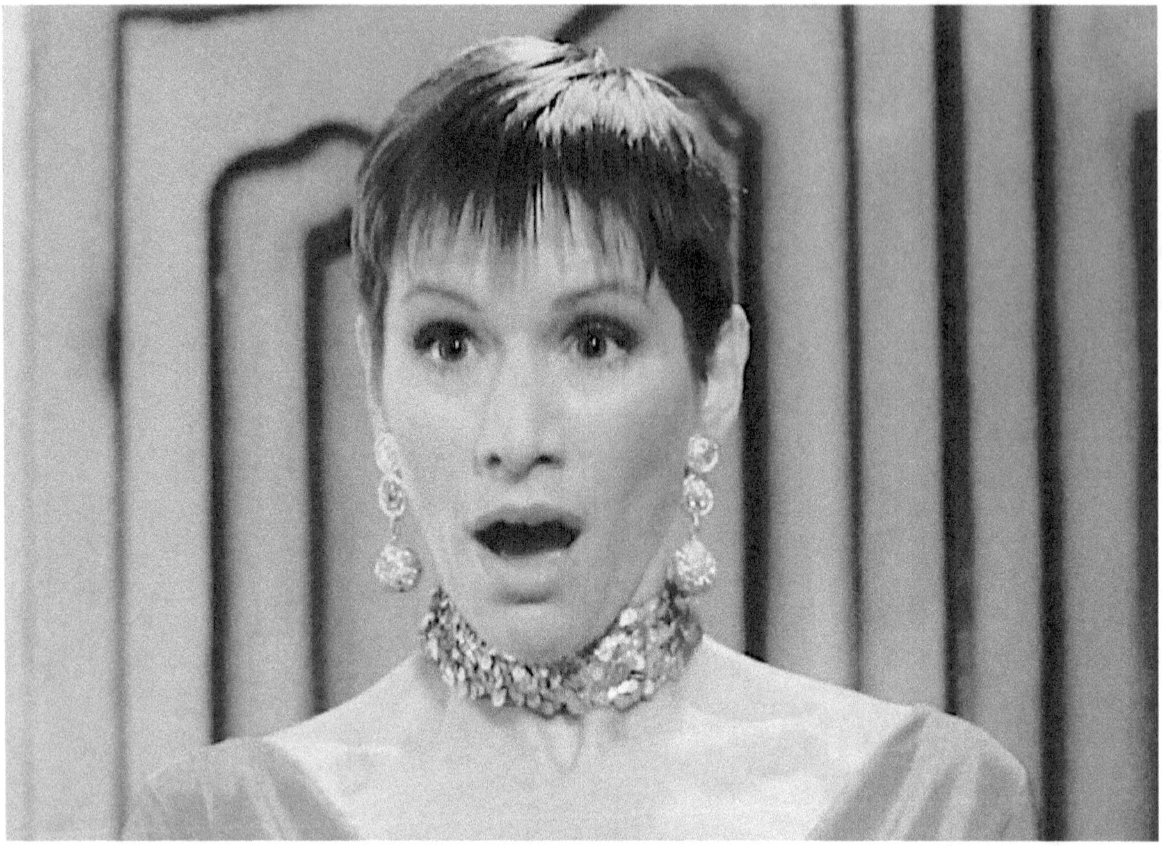

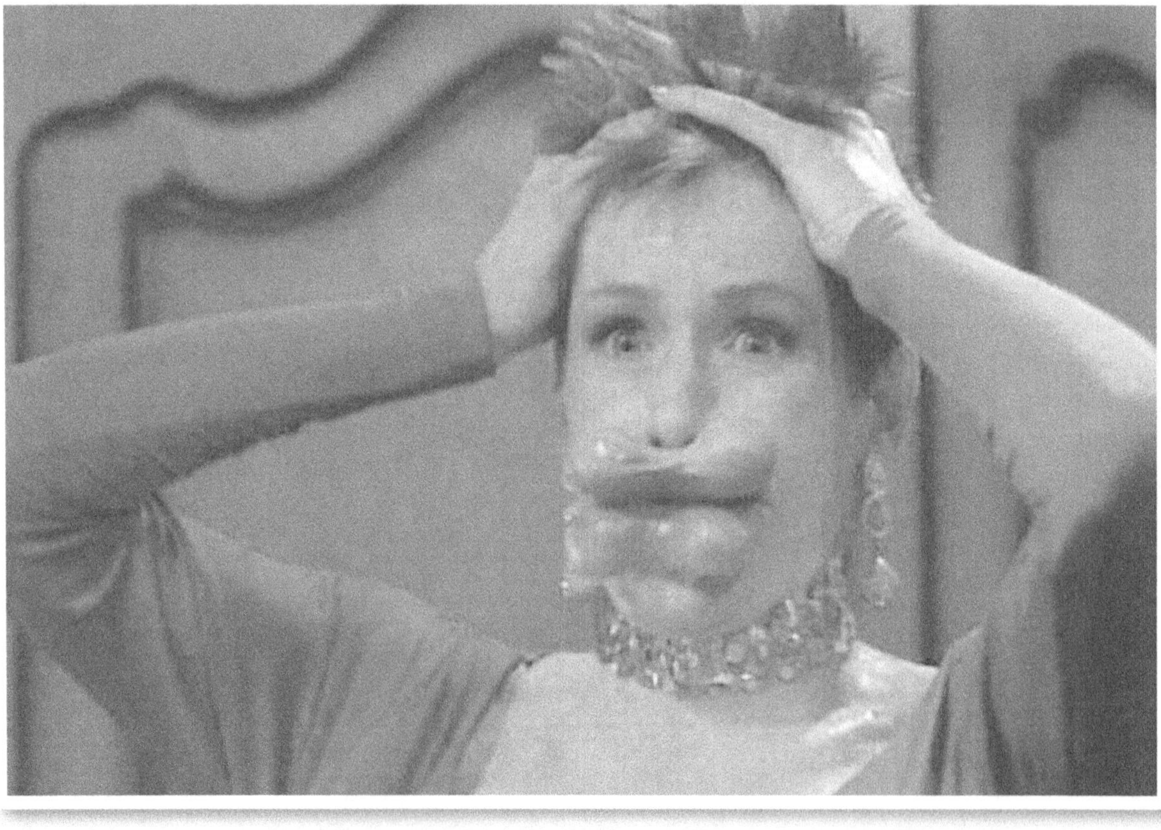

Warwick Davis (*Star Wars*, *Willow*, *Harry Potter* films, etc.) a consummate actor, was wonderful to work with.

I have such respect for his ability to create nuances of facial expression through the prosthetic appliances that covered his face.

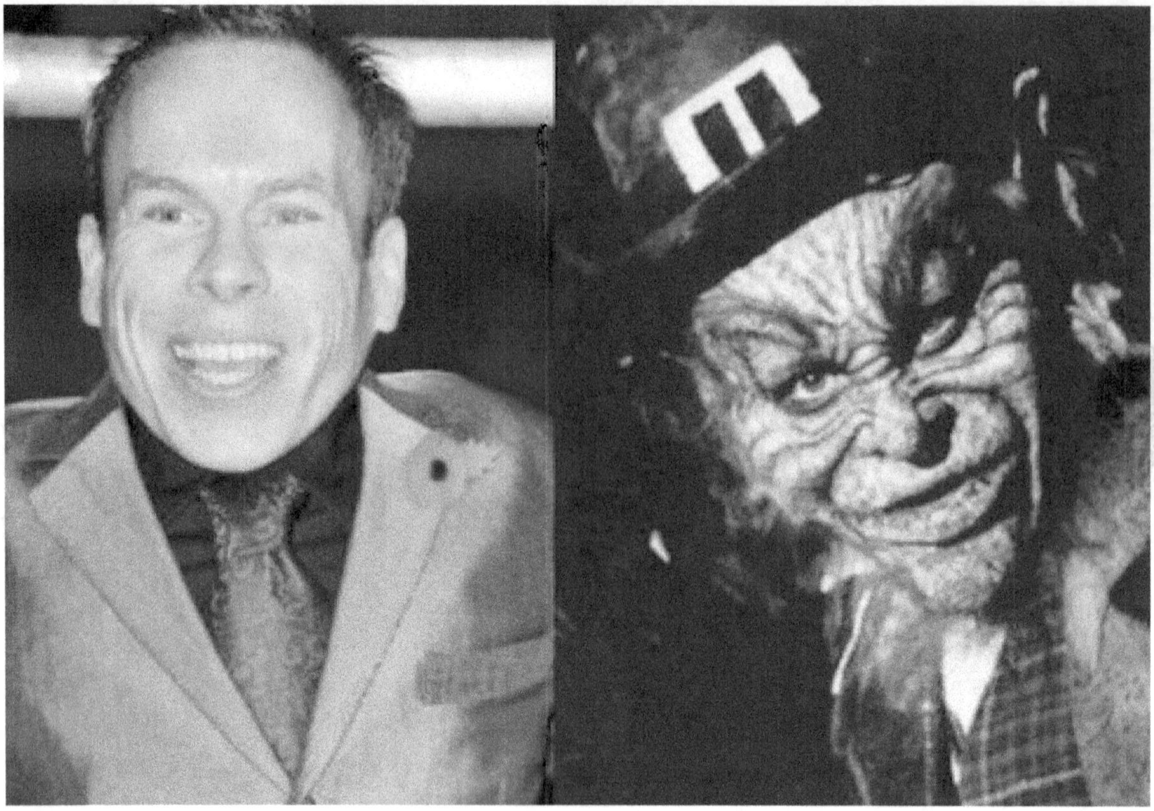

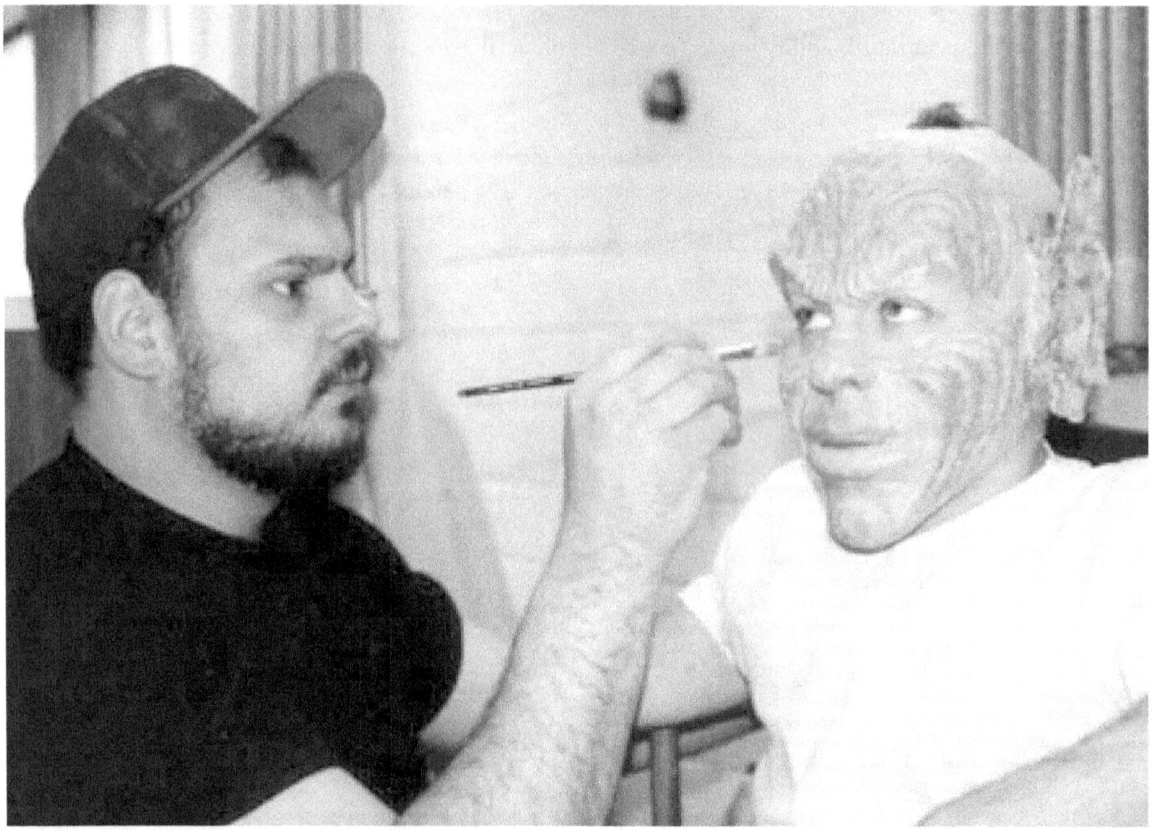

He felt he had been underutilized in *Leprechaun 2*. He appreciated the opportunity to embellish his character with spoof TV commercials in which he portrayed an ambulance chasing lawyer, a psychic, and a fire-and-brimstone televangelist. His patience and dedication every day during nearly three hours of makeup

application (and up to forty minutes removing it) was heroic. Gabe Bartalos, who created the Leprechaun makeup, also devised great new prosthetic gags, like the lethal Femmbot that crawls out of a phone sex ad on the TV screen to straddle, then electrocute lecherous casino owner Mickey Callan (*Cat Ballou, Mysterious Island*), who added the line: *"Oh, you want my heat seeking moisture missile…"*

Casting director Tedra Gabriel, who cast all Blue Rider Films at that time, brought me a great selection of talent. Lee Armstrong showed a real flair for comedy. She deserved a bigger career.

I thought our lead actor John Gatins, who gets bitten by the Leprechaun and starts turning into one, would also go on to a career in comedy. Instead he became a screenplay writer with ten credits so far including *Flight*, for which he was nominated for an Oscar.

Despite the fact that the roles were small, Tedra persuaded two well-regarded comedic actors, Tom Dugan and Roger Hewlett, to play the loan shark guys who want their money from sleazy casino owner Mickey Callan.

We improvised most of their scenes. For instance, I had fifteen more minutes of the shooting day left, and one shot to do: the mob guys waiting impatiently for Mickey Callan to show up. No written dialogue. I said: make some small talk for about twenty seconds. The off-the-wall *"jocks vs. briefs"* dialogue is what followed. Years later they joined me on stage for a *Leprechaun* Q&A after a St. Paddy's night "Leprathon". A recording is on YouTube. It certainly shows how much fun we had on the movie.

There was one gag I decided to drop on the grounds of taste (rare for me). As the Leprechaun disposes of the mob guys, Tom Dugan improvised a Wizard of Oz reference as his dying words: "What was Judy Garland really like?" Warwick, a dab hand at improv himself, shot back with feigned malevolence: "She was a bitch!" then delivered the *coup de grâce* with his shillelagh as the button on the line. We all laughed, but in the cutting room I felt it might hurt Liza Minnelli's feelings (I know, she was unlikely ever to see a *Leprechaun* movie). If anyone was bitchy to the munchkins on *The Wizard of Oz*, I thought, it was the studio brass, not her mother. I cut the line, but with some regret. Warwick was hilarious.

Thanks to speedy cinematographer David Lewis—DP on four of my films—the shoot went well in the Ambassador, despite the fact that the empty decaying hotel was simultaneously rented to three movie companies. I would bump into Martin Sheen occasionally between scenes of his period gangster movie. Tia Carrere and Eric Roberts were doing a thriller set in a nightclub. We worked around each other efficiently enough, due primarily to my 1st AD Lynn D'Angona, who had done an awesome job on *NOTD 2*. Lynn wanted to direct one day, so I made her my 2nd Unit Director on two subsequent films.

I felt a little guilty about shooting a morgue scene in the kitchen area. I had first arrived in the United States on June 6th 1968, the morning after Robert Kennedy was assassinated. Twenty-eight years later, I found myself staring at an X carved into the floor tile beside the elevator, marking the spot where Kennedy's head lay, bleeding from a wound behind his right ear. But the kitchen was the only area with white tiles and fridges that we could dress as a morgue.

On the fourteenth day we finished the Ambassador shoot at 2 a.m., then flew to Vegas at noon with Warwick, Gabe Bartolis, and a guerrilla crew of five for a dusk-till-dawn shoot, setting the Leprechaun against real Vegas backgrounds for brief scenes that would pepper the movie. We had been refused permission to shoot outside major casinos like the Golden Nugget, believing that a horror film tainted their noble image, but we did it anyway. *"Golden Nugget? I'd like one of those!"* exclaimed Warwick, as the low angle 14mm lens made him appear to tower over the building. Such was the penetration of *Leprechaun* into popular culture that people came up to us: *"Are you making a Leprechaun movie? Can we be in it, please?"* Free extras! Several followed us from shot to shot. Thanks!

One disappointing scene is the Leprechaun's demise, flying round the room on fire, coming, as it does, after the gutsy scene of the magician Fazio being sawn in half. Although stuntman Arturu Gill did a great job, the flying fire gag is

weak by comparison. A movie's climax should deliver a bigger finish, but we had simply run out of time and money to do anything more elaborate. But apparently the audience forgave us. *LEP 3* shipped 55,000 units, making it the highest-selling independent made-for-home video of 1995. So Trimark decided to extend the franchise.

As the next chapter, Trimark had originally wanted to put the Leprechaun aboard Apollo 13. "*Trimark, we have a problem*"—an idea that started as a joke poster for their Christmas party. I thought the *Aliens* formula—space marines hunting down a deadly creature—would offer more scope. Also, a variant on the iconic 'chestburster' moment had formed in my mind.

An appointment was set for myself and Jeff Geoffray to pitch it in front of Trimark's boss Mark Amin. This was not a slam dunk. There were other executives around the table who favored other concepts. Mark Amin entered, dressed dapper casual and exuding a quiet authority. I noted the general change in body language around the table as Mr. Amin sat down.

Here's my somewhat hyperbolic recollection of that meeting.

I suggested that Apollo 13 was a very small environment for the Leprechaun to wreak his havoc. Why not use "Aliens" as the matrix? Space marines hunting down a creature, which happens to be the Leprechaun.

Mark Amin said: *Tell me the best scene.*

Jeff and I had not discussed my vision for the movie beyond an overall framework that could be achieved for the budget. The pitch was now veering into unknown territory. But Jeff seemed unconcerned, thinking no doubt that I never seem to be at a loss for words on the subject of film. In fact, sometimes it was hard to get me to shut up. He knew I would think of something.

BTS: *There are so many great scenes to choose from…but how about this? If you are going to do an ALIENS homage, well, you've got to have a scene where the creature bursts out of a character's body, right?*

MARK AMIN: *That scene has been copied many times.*

BTS: *But not like this. You see…*

EXECUTIVE 1 (interrupting): *The Leprechaun is 3 feet tall. How does he get into the man's body without him realizing it?*

Another Executive grabs the coattails:

EXECUTIVE 2: *Are you going to do the whole face hugger thing? We're looking for originality here.*

Oh, you guys are a tag team? You want originality? OK.

BTS: *The Space marines ambush the creature on a desolate planet, blowing him to pieces. Then, in a gesture of marine pride, the most macho marine decides he will piss on one of the body parts. So we do this shot from behind his spread legs…*

The voltage in the room goes up a notch. The golden shower of Farrelly Brothers bodily function comedies had not yet rained down on Hollywood. But I charge on, oblivious.

BTS: *The actor squirts an unseen tube of amber fluid down onto, say, a dismembered leg…*

In the morality of Cinema, severed limbs are not offensive. Urine streams are. The Execs steal glances at their CEO, who remains attentive, but impassive.

BTS: *But what the marine does not see, and we do, courtesy of our CGI guys, is a tiny glowing green ball traveling upstream, so to speak.*

Oh Boy. Executive jaws tighten around the table.

BTS: *So, the pay-off comes back on the ship when this guy and a sexy lady marine find a quiet corner to get it on. She's got her hand in his pants, and suddenly he's saying not so rough, you want to take it home with you? And she can't understand, because she has a diploma in hand jobs…*

I suspect by now there were some "Glad you brought him in, not us, pal" looks being exchanged. Jeff and I did have one Trimark executive supporter at the table, Jonathan Komack Martin, who had never been a fan of playing *Leprechaun* straight, and had supported our comedy approach to *Leprechaun in Vegas*. He could tell where I was going with this.

BTS: *Suddenly the marine recoils backwards, his pants start to bulge and pulsate—via tubes and bladders, of course… Then he sinks to the floor, so special effects can get access from below. He screams as the Leprechaun erupts out of his pants on an invisible wire, flies through the air and lands in front of them both saying: "Next time, m' lad, you should use a prophylactic!"*

The last line came in thick Irish brogue. Stunned silence. Who let this lunatic into the building? They look to the boss. His expression is studious.

MARK AMIN: *So the Leprechaun comes out of… the man's penis…*

BTS: *Yes!*

Perhaps too much enthusiasm.

Pause.

MARK AMIN: *Ah, huh…*

Another pause…

MARK AMIN*: I like it!*

A massive reversal of body language ripples through the Executive ranks, followed by Rapture at the Brilliant Scene! Our supporter, Jonathan Komack Martin, went on to a great career with twenty-five producing credits to date, including *Deadpool 1 & 2*, both a comic and a movie franchise, that like *Leprechaun* treats an archetype with fond irreverence.

And that was how *Leprechaun (4) In Space* was green lit. Green being the operative word. I have always felt a debt of gratitude to Mark Amin and Jonathan Komack Martin for following their gut instincts and allowing me to make, unfettered, my wackiest genre cocktail. In addition to *Alien*, multiple influences include *Full Metal Jacket*, *Dr. Cyclops*, *The Fly*, *Land of the Giants*, *Terminator*, *The Magic Christian*, etc. See how many you can find. Buoyed by the response to the comedy in *LEP 3*, I pushed *LEP 4* a step further into farce incorporating Sci-fi homage and parody moments.

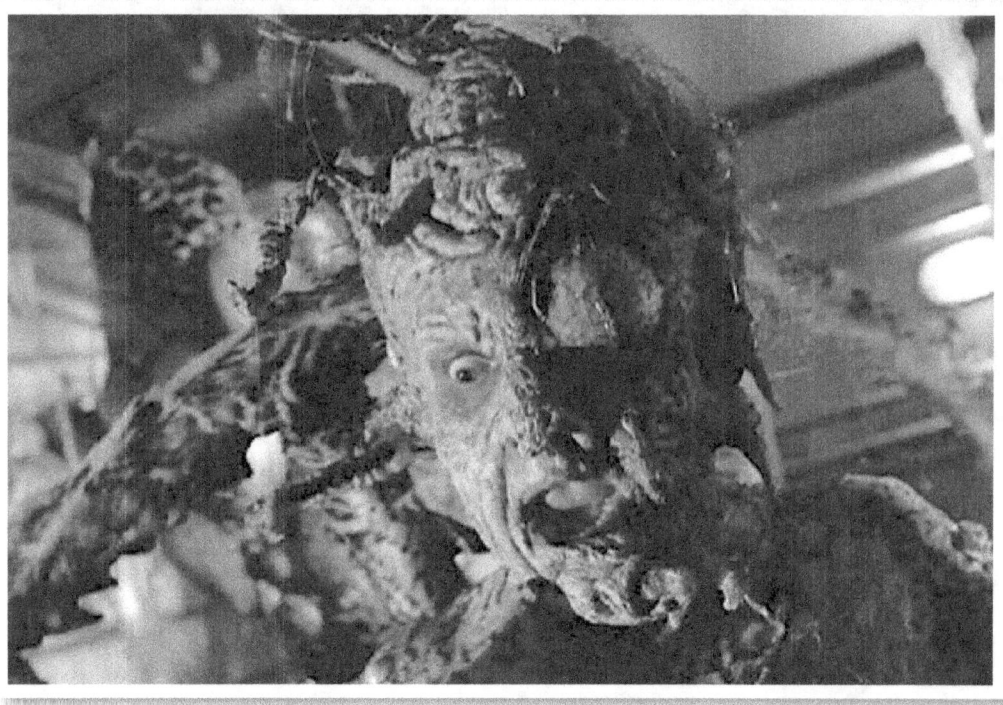

When Dr. Mittenhand (yes, really) becomes a giant spider/scorpion (brilliantly realized by Gabe Bartalos on low dollars), he squeaks the final line from *The Fly*: *"Help me!"* before being blown to pieces. The evil Dr. Mittenhand, was played as a kind of Nazi Dalek by Guy Siner, an old schoolfriend of mine and a star of BBC's classic WWII long-running comedy series *'Allo 'Allo'*. Guy channeled Colonel Klink and every possible Gestapo movie cliché.

Cinephiles smiled at the movie references, but the core audience wanted more horror, and I should have paid greater attention to their expectations. Also, by relocating a mythological creature into a space travel future, as *Jason X* did, the film destabilized the foundations of a good horror movie: ordinary people in the real world menaced by the supernatural. The characters were a pastiche of Sci-fi tropes, limiting audience identification. It was a risky experiment, which occasionally mocked the requirements of the Made for Home Video market, such as the obligatory topless moment that had to be worked into the story—a firm demand of US video distributors at the time. So writer Dennis Pratt came up with the most absurd reason for nudity. On Princess Zarina's planet, when a member of the royal family exposes her breasts, she is pronouncing a death sentence to those standing in front of her.

*"You may find this cruel but you leave me no choice,"* she says opening her bra wide. *"Look upon them and know you are forever doomed…"*

Brave Rebekah Carlton brought her mother to the set that day, then handled the chore with dignity and aplomb.

Among the many disparate ingredients stirred into this B Sci-fi cocktail was the *Full Metal Jacket*- style Marine drill sergeant, played with gusto by Tim Colceri. As previously mentioned, Stanley Kubrick had cast Tim Colceri as Sgt. Major Hartman in *Full Metal Jacket*, then replaced him early in the shoot with ex-Marine technical advisor R. Lee Ermey. Lee got a Golden Globe nomination, went on to a great career, and graced three of my movies. Though Kubrick gave Tim Colceri the role of the mad machine gunner as a consolation prize, Tim had felt the loss of this career-making opportunity keenly. So I gave him the chanc

to play the role of the kickass drill sergeant he had been denied, albeit in a low budget movie. Tim did a terrific job. The scene where he flips back and forth between maniacal marine and cross-dressing crooner is a balls-out *tour de force*.

Warwick Davis is the heart and soul of the series. Stars set the tone of the shoot. He never complained about long hours in the makeup chair. He's a lovable personality with great comedic flair. In *LEP 3*, Dennis and I had given him limericks and rhyme. In *LEP 4* we upped the ante to faux Shakespearean speeches from *Richard III* and *Henry VI* Part 1.

"It was madness," Warwick said in an interview, "Brian Trenchard-Smith, he's a brilliant but eccentric director. I got on really well with him. I actually loved the humor he brought to *3* and then with *4* he kind of—yeah, he went a step further. But I enjoyed all the little nods to popular Sci-fi and those sorts of things."

A good space movie parody needs good visual effects to anchor the satire in an accepted reality. Sadly, the CGI in *LEP 4* was disappointing. I did not feel we got our 80K worth. It was a new company and it didn't last long. Because of our budget, the first render was sometimes the final render. My 14-year-old son Eric created a fine original drawing for the spaceship, but the way it was composited against space backgrounds was pretty awful (video noise at the matte line).

Where the film's visual effects excelled was in the vanishing art of miniatures. Today, set extension is all CGI, but to create the venue for the Leprechaun to be thirty feet tall in the ship's cargo bay, we went back to old Hollywood techniques executed by veteran model makers. By building an enclosed miniature set, with a roof measured to fit Warwick's height, the cargo bay looked vast as the now gigantic Leprechaun searched for the hidden heroes. By mounting the camera on a skateboard, we could track with Warwick as he prowled past the miniature cargo containers.

These were perfect miniature replicas of the full-sized rows of containers in the studio, where we had previously shot all the material with the actors. To integrate the full size with the miniature set, we did a few locked-off plate shots in both sets that placed the heroes and 'Lepzilla' in the same frame. It's a fun sequence.

Feeling certain that the upcoming release of *Leprechaun in Space* would be a success, I proposed *Leprechaun in the White House* to Trimark. It starts, I pitched, with a giant *Independence Day* spaceship suddenly appearing over the White House roof. Evidently some space garbage they picked up—disembodied parts of

a creature—had given the Aliens a lot of grief. They had to get rid of it. The spaceship spits down a block of ice. The reassembled Leprechaun thaws and gets into the White House crawlspace. He observes the dysfunctional but sympathetic First Family; the President with a zipper problem, the ambitious First Lady, and the First Daughter—a rambunctious college girl (heroine) with the hots for a Secret Service agent hero.

The Leprechaun learns of Fort Knox and plans to steal all the gold. Trimark's response to the idea was: 'No, you're getting too wacky.' They preferred *Leprechaun in the Hood* for the next chapter. In January 1998, the Monica Lewinsky scandal broke. I left a voicemail on the relevant executive's direct line and said, "Hi, remember my *Leprechaun in the White House* idea? Wouldn't you like to have 1200 prints ready *right now*?" I never got a reply.

*LEPRECHAUN 4 IN SPACE* cost 1.6 M. It shipped about 40,000 units, a drop from *LEP 3*, the result of my favoring parody over horror. But it did not kill the franchise, which continued for three more movies. However, Trimark never hired me again. With creative risk comes the potential for failure, but we gotta try…

Twenty-five years later, with screenings every St. Paddy's Day on TV and revival theaters, *Lep 3 in Vegas* and *Lep 4 in Space* are still making people laugh at moments unlikely to be repeated in the history of Cinema. It gives me satisfaction to know that Lionsgate, who acquired the franchise, have a nice little St. Paddy's Day earner for the rest of time. My percentage is forever stalled in the *rolling break even.*

It has been said that the movie's final shot— the Leprechaun's severed hand floating in space, flipping the bird to the heroes, accompanied by 2001's *Thus Spake Zarathustra*-like chords and drumroll, reflects my view of the cynical *reductio ad absurdum* nature of low budget horror sequels. Then again, I like absurdity.

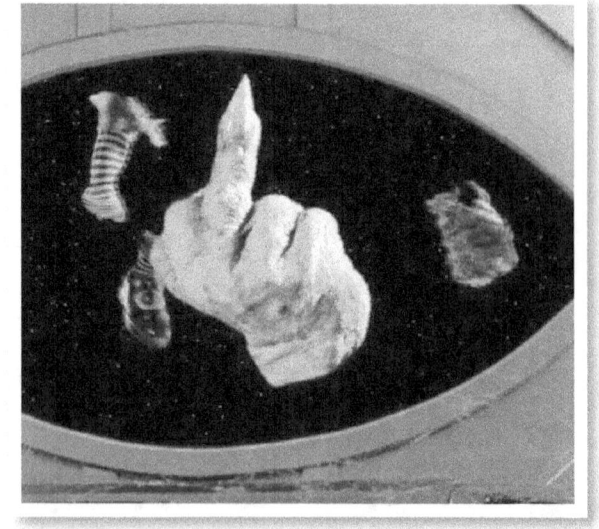

# CHAPTER 42
## War Films

For my career to prosper in Hollywood, I knew that I had to originate material to which I was attached as director. Between gigs in 1991-1992, I devised an 8-part documentary series, *Battles That Changed the World*, later retitled *Men of War*. My inspiration was Peter Watkins' BBC docudrama *Culloden*, about the battle in April of 1746 that crushed Scottish independence, told in the style of TV war reporting. I saw it in 1964 and have wanted to make something like that ever since, so finally, I thought, here goes. Each episode examined a decisive battle involving a major historical figure. Alexander, Hannibal, Julius Caesar were obvious choices, followed by lesser known soldier/statesmen, all with great stories rarely explored at that time on TV: Saladin, Shogun Ieyasu Tokugawa, Clive of India, Duke of Marlborough, and Shaka Zulu. The production technique would combine actor portrayals, and comments by historians, with battle reenactments, amplified by stock footage and manga-style animation. The look and feel of the show would be visually slick. More MTV than History Channel, but it would have a tragic tone.

*"The series will use the exploits of these remarkable men as a means to examine the root causes of war itself. Mass combat as a method of resolving disputes, is as inefficient as it is tragic, yet war has been a central institution in human civilization since history began.*

*Each episode will contrast the propaganda of the time with the agenda of the combative parties, and explore the psychological impact of war on soldier and civilian alike. Other recurring topics will be the impact of technology, the cost of military campaigns, and the evolution of battlefield trauma medicine. It is not the intention of this series to glorify war, rather to put it into the context of the development of humankind."*

I peddled my illustrated pitch document to A&E, PBS, and every new basic cable network that sprang up in the 90s. Come on, guys, bloodshed and spectacle guarantee you ratings, but how about a moral perspective as well? Quixotic wish, no doubt. Every network said no, then did their own simpler *famous battles* series. My high-minded approach was the kiss of death on the heels of the 1991 Gulf War, and again ten years later after 9/11. Pity; this was a show I could have done well.

I had evolved politically since making my documentary about Australian Victoria Cross winners in Vietnam, which was unquestioning of the war itself. I have come to see war between nations in simple terms. The ruling elite of one region covet the resources and sphere of influence controlled by the ruling elite of another region. A pretext is found. An inciting incident created. Bloodlust aroused. God is generally invoked by both sides. The rich send the poor to do the fighting. Countless are maimed or die. Many are psychologically traumatized. Then the cycle is repeated. Of course, my antiwar rhetoric must seem out of step with my enthusiasm for staging battle scenes. It's complicated.

In 1994, a project I had helped develop for two years reached a crisis point. *The Last Bullet* had been set up as an Australian/Japanese co-production. The story depicted a duel in the jungle between two expert snipers, one Japanese, one Australian, in the final days of WWII. They meet again as old men and greet each other as friends. It echoed themes I had explored in *The Siege of Firebase Gloria*. Australian producer Georgina Pope was fluent in Japanese and had built a production liaison career in Tokyo. The Japanese producer was Hiroaki Yoshida who had written and directed *Twilight of the Cockroaches*, a fusion of anime and live action, aimed at the arthouse market. With another Japanese writer, Yoshida wrote a screenplay with flashbacks to the snipers' prewar lives. When American companies turned down offers of coproduction, Georgina Pope suggested "How about Australia?" and set about putting the pieces in place. The project was 50% backed by Japanese national broadcaster NHK. Australia's Nine Network picked up the other half of the budget. Australia's Beyond Films acquired international sales. I was signed to rewrite and direct the original Japanese script, making the American soldier an Australian serving in the Solomon Islands. A condition of NHK's involvement was that the production would not be shot on film, as was the custom for telemovies, but be recorded on NHK's new system of Hi-Def video, where the cameras had to be cabled to an outside broadcast truck. The maximum length of the cables determined the position of the truck on location. Un-cabling, moving the truck, re-cabling was time consuming. There were challenges ahead.

Co-productions (see earlier) are a recipe for international mistrust, and this was no exception. The relationship between two strong-willed writers from different cultures obliged to collaborate on a movie about a war between their countries was bound to be fraught, particularly if one writer had been signed to direct, and the other, the coproducer, had always wanted to direct. After more than two years of development, matters came to a head. I felt that the Japanese producer's proposed changes to my fifth draft, which like every draft I wrote had incorporated his latest input, was a significant regression from what we had agreed. The changes, in my view, softened the core message of the reconciliation of enemies. I expected Japanese control over the Japanese characters' side of the story, but now creative control was seeping into the Australian scenes as well. I was told I could make minor tweaks, but that was it.

So I wrote an impassioned comparison of the two drafts (a copy is held by the National Film and Sound Archive of Australia) and included an analysis from the sales agency Beyond Films which substantially preferred my draft. By doing that I was not only challenging coproducer Hiroaki Yoshida, I was challenging NHK, the national broadcaster of Japan. What was I thinking? Why choose this hill to die on? My father, a WWII veteran, influenced my thinking. His opinion of a WWII film I directed was important to me. And he was living a few miles from where the movie would be shot on Australia's Gold Coast.

Predictably, the stakeholders had a deal in place, and that was more important than the creative concerns of the cowriter/director. I was paid for a rewrite and asked to step aside, which I did. In effect, I had committed professional *seppuku* over a point of honor. I shared script credit with Hiroaki Yoshida, but the incoming Australian director Michael Pattinson brought his own writer in for a new draft, which I am happy to say corrected many of the script's problems. Michael did a great job directing *The Last Bullet* under difficult circumstances. The film won the Golden Rembrandt at an Amsterdam festival for movies shot on the new Hi-Def format. It rated well for NHK but its Australian ratings were not as high as expected.

There is some irony in what followed my departure. Showtime had commissioned an end-of-WWII anniversary film to be broadcast on August 7, 1995. Jeff Hayes was brought in to produce a remake of the WWII classic *Sahara*, which had starred Humphrey Bogart. Happily, he chose me to direct. The film would be based at the Village Roadshow Studios on the Gold Coast, and shoot at the same time as *The Last Bullet* and on a substantially higher budget. I was flown in and lodged, by complete coincidence, at the same hotel as Hiroaki Yoshida. You should have seen his face when we passed in the lobby.

\*\*\*

Remaking a much-loved Bogart classic? Columbia's highest grossing movie of 1943, taking $2.3M at the US box office. No pressure, right?

We set out to be as respectful as possible to the original. To that end, we compared the 1943 film to its shooting script, which ran 150 pages. There were scenes in the script that were not in the movie, and scenes in the movie not in the script. We worked with a top Australian writer, David Phillips, to distil the best elements from both, while replacing propagandistic dialogue with realistic responses that were still faithful to the period.

The story—a group of soldiers, lost in the desert, fight to survive against overwhelming odds—has an interesting movie lineage. It was first written as a bestselling novel by a WW1 veteran Phillip Macdonald, based on his experiences serving in Mesopotamia. It was immediately filmed as a British

silent movie *The Lost Patrol* in 1929, then filmed again with sound as an American story by John Ford in 1934.

Then Soviet director Mikhail Romm borrowed the basic idea, set it in the Central Asian desert during the Basmachi Revolt, and added the element of the heroes defending an empty well from an enemy desperate for water to delay their advance. It was released as *The Thirteen* in 1937.

In 1943, Philip Macdonald added *The Thirteen*'s plot device of the fought-over well to a reworking of his original story, setting it in the Libyan desert just after the Allied rout at the battle of Gazala. It was filmed as *Sahara*, starring Humphrey Bogart. In 1953, Andre De Toth remade *Sahara* as a western, *Last of the Comanches*, starring Broderick Crawford channeling Bogart. The story has proved to be a great formula for a ripping yarn.

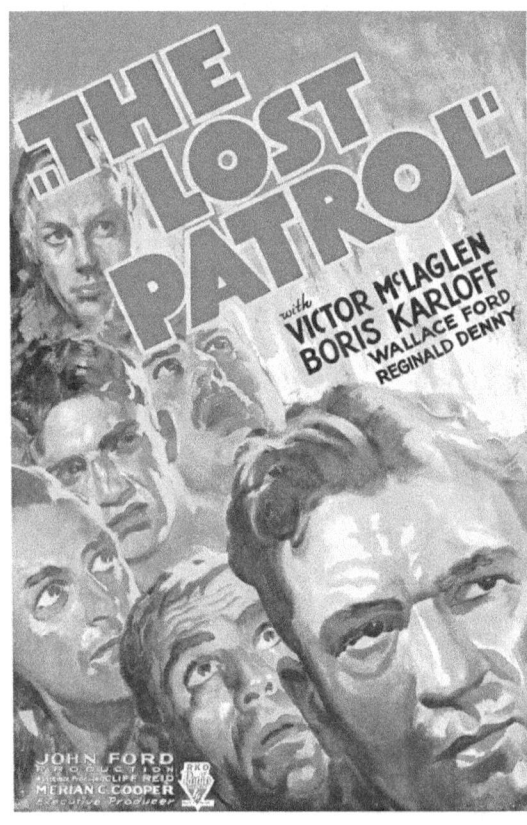

The reader may recall that as a small child I had spent several years in Libya, where my father commanded the RAF base outside Tripoli. One day, my parents had taken me to the top of the Garian (Gharyān) Plateau, which had a commanding view of the desert around Benghazi, where battles had raged just five years before. It was an awesome sight for a small boy experiencing his first mountain view. Another awesome sight followed at an abandoned Eighth Army barracks, the Gharyan Lady, painted in engine oil across a 30 foot white wall by American volunteer ambulance driver Cliff Saber. Initially he painted a nude to amuse his mates. He worked without scaffolding, rotating platforms of army crates, painting six inches from the wall. But standing back to inspect his handiwork, he found that the top outline of her body coincided with the coastal line of North Africa. He decided to turn it into a humorous morale boosting mural celebrating the endurance of the Allied forces. In his 1959 memoir Cliff Saber explained:

*"I marked her off as the Middle East from Tripoli (Lebanon) to Tripoli (Libya) and named parts of her body for nonexistent wadis: Wadi you hiding? Wadi you doing? Wadi you say? Wadi you know? It makes no claim to being a complete history of the whole desert campaign in North Africa, although it can be used as a reference. Its purpose is to depict the everyday life of the British 8th Army soldier (or Desert Rat)"*

I was too young to understand the immense importance of what had happened below the Gharyan plateau. If the Afrika Korps under Rommel had been able to push through and seize the Suez Canal, Hitler could have stalled the Allies long enough to perfect the atomic bomb. WWII has fascinated me all my life, chiefly because it was my father's war, and also because its issues of right and wrong were so clear cut, in contrast to the wars that followed. What a stouthearted, dutiful generation my father belonged to. I was making this film for them.

Australia has a variety of desert locations to choose from. *Road Warrior/Mad Max 2* was shot in the rocky desert of Broken Hill. But because "thirst" was a major story point, we did not want an overnight shower to cause little sprigs of green to appear dotting the parched landscape, as can happened to *Mad Max - Fury Road*, resulting in a move to Namibia. We needed pure unfertile sand. We chose Port Stephens on the New South Wales coast. There was a strip of sand twenty kilometers long and one kilometer wide separating the ocean from the bushland. Plenty of space to get angles of limitless desert. A local hotel offered us generous rates—it was off-season. Port Stephens was less than a 3-hour drive from Sydney where WWII museums and collector societies were keen to contribute authentic military vehicles. But the only authentic M3 Lee tank was in Perth, the other side of the Australian continent.

After WWII, the Australian government sold a variety of war surplus tanks to farmers, who cut the turret off the tank, leaving it where it fell. They used the body of the machine as a haulage vehicle, or installed a bulldozer blade. Paddock bashers, they called them. Over the next fifty years, these old tanks joined their abandoned turrets to be overgrown by brambles and weeds. But one enterprising man dug out tank tracks, a chassis and a turret. He set about restoring a fully working M3 Lee. It had cost him 25K. Get it to us a week before shooting, we offered, and we'll rent and return for 25K. The precious tank, the only working M3 Lee in Australia arrived on a transporter the day before shooting started, and completed a successful test drive. The next morning, I set up the first shot of the film. The ignition turned, the tank spluttered into life and promptly died. Nothing could coax Lulubelle, her nickname in the movie, back to life. I had only four members of the cast available, the rest were arriving during this first day. I pored through the script to find scenes I could do either around or inside a stationary tank with the four actors I had.

A director must be sufficiently prepared to stage any scene in the script at a moment's notice. I managed to fill out the day with minimal loss of page count allotted to Day One of the schedule. Mechanics worked throughout the night to make the tank operational by call time the next morning. Breakdowns thereafter were few and short lived.

When the German battalion crests the horizon to attack the well, and the defenders get their first glimpse of the numbers they face, I am channeling *Zulu*, as many war movie filmmakers have. It's still an amazing battle movie with acerbic comments on colonialism.

As extras we used 130 members of the Royal Australian Air Force in Afrika Korps uniforms. They knew how to handle weapons like professionals. They were a great bunch and performed with discipline and enthusiasm.

One afternoon, while they were taking a water break between shots, I asked which of my Australian films they had seen. *MFHK* and *BMX Bandits* scored high, but almost every hand was raised for *Turkey Shoot*.

These days, when staging a fighter flying low over the desert to strafe a tank, computer generated effects can take care of the hard part. The plane would be digital and fly at the precise height and speed the shot required. Digital muzzle flashes would be added to the wing guns, followed by digital bullet trails kicking up two parallel lines of sand, then stitching the turret of the tank. Current CGI software can make it photo real. Well, almost. On *Sahara*, we did these shots the old-fashioned way.

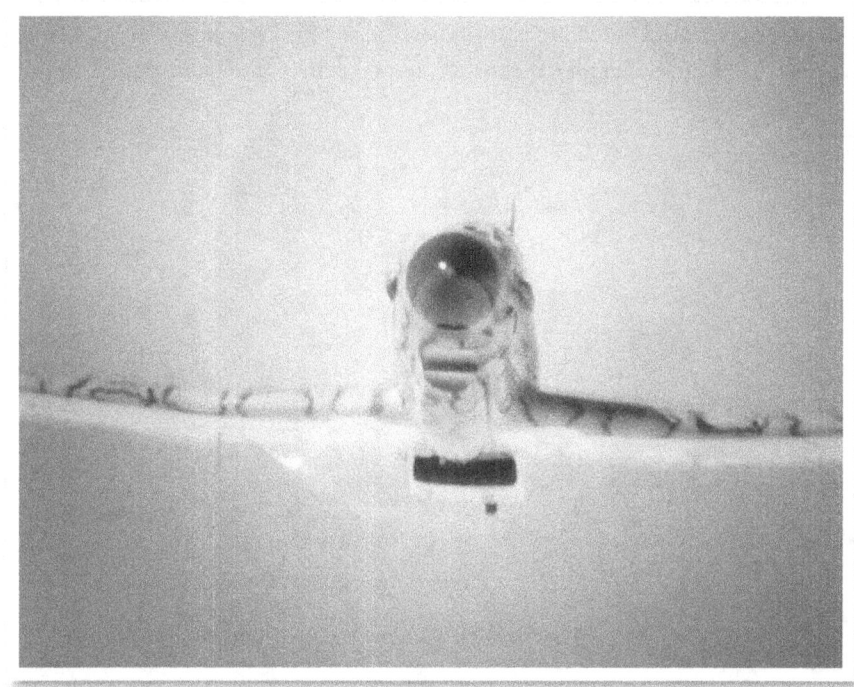

We used a Fiat G.59 painted in Luftwaffe desert camouflage. It was in fact smaller than the Messerschmidt Bf.109 G it was representing. No difference would be noticed in the air. We buried lines of squibs in the sand leading up to the tank, connecting them to spark hits on the turret. These would look good in a low wide angle that would also capture the fly past.

Coordinating the approach of the plane with the start of the bullet trail was the tricky bit. There was a narrow margin between too early and too late, as calculated through the camera lens. Cued too late, the squibs might chew up the sand too close to the plane passing overhead for the trajectory of the bullets to be believable. It is the director's responsibility when to cue the pyrotechnics. We could afford the Fiat for a limited amount of time. As we rehearsed the strafing runs, we got all the close ups of the plane we needed. Then we set cameras for the angles that connected the plane with the tank. The pilot had to fly towards the tank on a path perfectly aligned with the buried bullet trails of squibs. I stood beside the wide-angle camera position, the one that would integrate the soldiers taking cover behind the tank with the approaching plane beyond, and on rehearsal calculated at what point in the plane's approach I should

trigger the bullet trail.

Getting the timing between the elements right on Take One was the objective. Resetting such lengthy bullet trails could take a minimum of fifteen minutes while the plane has to keep circling, burning fuel. The movie gods smiled on us. Then we repeated the process on the other side of the tank, as the plane swung round for a second attack from the opposite direction. Moving the cameras closer, we captured Jim Belushi returning fire at the departing plane, which belched smoke on cue. The final challenge was to create the optical illusion of the plane crashing. Through the perspective of a long lens compressing the image, we rehearsed the angle of the dive and calculated the point of impact behind a designated sandhill, where we set a mortar loaded with a fireball. The Messerschmidt duly dived low, disappeared behind the ridge of sandhills, followed by Kaboom! As fire and smoke erupted from behind the sandhill, the plane flew on unseen. The union between flight path trajectory and explosion bent the laws of physics slightly but with editing it passes. That was an exciting couple of hours.

The original *Sahara* was shot in twenty-five days. On our budget we could only afford eighteen days spread over three 6-day weeks. Ten pages of dialogue scenes were scheduled on some days, to compensate

for battle scene days, where the page count was barely three. Also, in the Australian winter, we had only ten hours of viable light for a film that was 90% exterior. Every minute of shooting had to count. How could we speed the process? Rehearsal was key, a vital component so often denied in television movies. From the point of view of the studio number crunchers—why pay the actors for extra days when they are not yet before the camera? We too were in that cost-saving straitjacket, but were blessed with a committed cast, led by Jim Belushi. After each shooting day was done, we would have dinner at the hotel, then the cast, Jeff Hayes, and I would convene in Jim Belushi's room to discuss, then rehearse the next day's scenes till everyone felt comfortable with their approach. This meant that after the predawn breakfast we hit the ground running each day.

To take on an iconic role created by Humphrey Bogart is a risky proposition for an established star. Jim Belushi played Sgt. Gunn as a gruff, tough career soldier, no-nonsense yet sentimental, hard-bitten yet compassionate. He imbued the part with his own persona but avoided his familiar mannerisms. His performance was well-received by the majority of critics. The New York Times said: *"James Belushi...less Bogey than Hackman, delivers a terrific*

*performance with stunning authority."* Another critic called it *"…a powerhouse performance, one of the best of his career."* One reviewer had kind words for me too. *"The battle scenes are spectacular and exciting. Brian Trenchard-Smith's particular genius is getting you to care about each member of this motley band as an individual, so that his fate and possibly his sacrifice are charged with meaning and emotion. 'Sahara' is a remake, but it is second to none."*

During the 1943 shoot in the Mojave Desert, Humphrey Bogart posed, kneeling at left, with officers of Fourth Armored Division who supplied troops, and members of the Hollywood crew in front of the tank. Jim Belushi joined us atop the tank for our crew photo.

The movie rated well on Showtime. A couple of weeks later, Jim wanted me to have his opinion of my work. He sent me a fax from his company Whitehorse Productions Inc.

JAMES BELUSHI in
Sahara

The Colonel (that's what I call him) is one of the best directors of ensemble acting that I have worked with. He is not afraid of letting his actors go and guiding their vision to the overall vision of the project. He was inspiring to all the actors and rekindled the passion for acting in me. He is also an encyclopedia. Ask anything and he knows the answer in length. He should have his own PBS talk show.

That was kind. I am proud of *Sahara*.

But the person whose approval I sought most was my father, whom I was able to visit during production. *Sahara* was a tribute to him, and to his generation. A week after the shoot ended, Wing Commander (Rt.) Eric Trenchard Smith died of a heart attack on the golf course, while playing, according to his friends, his best round of golf in months. Dad had collapsed and died instantly at the 13th hole.

I had just started editing *Sahara*. It was a wrenching time for me and my mother with whom, although they were separated, my father had always remained friends. At his funeral I told his many golfing friends about his escape attempts as a POW, and his eventual service, attached to MI6, helping to plan and co-ordinate spy flights and leaflet drops behind the Iron Curtain. This was all news to them. My father, a genuine hero, was a modest man who had never liked to talk about his RAF career. His time at MI6 was a secret even to my mother. She had thought that when he caught the early train to London that he was just going to the Air Ministry. My father took the Official Secrets Act seriously, and only felt released from it, he had said, because the Cold War seemed to be over. He had told me about his time at MI6 just before I went off to shoot *Sahara*, perhaps because he could sense the end was not far away. I played the Air Force March at his funeral. For some years, the 13th hole at the Tweed Heads Golf Club where he died was named for him.

I returned to work. Although Jeff Hayes would have permitted me to step aside to have more time to mourn, I needed to see this project through to completion. both to honor my father and because he would have expected me to resume my duty. The production had a tight deadline, with financial implications if it was not met. We had to deliver an NTSC master copy to Viacom/Showtime in LA by midnight June 30th, the last day of the Australian tax year. Crucial investor tax benefits were at stake, requiring a signed receipt from the buyer prior to midnight on the last day of June for the film to qualify. It was a rush. The editor, my friend Alan Lake, fell sick during the process. I completed it with his assistant, to whom coediting credit is given. Due to a snafu at the lab, a delay did occur and an associate had to fly to LA with the film as luggage. The document was signed with only hours to spare. *Sahara* garnered excellent reviews as Showtime's 50th anniversary film to mark the end of WWII

During *Sahara*, I had gotten to know key Showtime executive, Sharon Byrens, who would champion me to direct a number of productions. In 1997, she put me "in the room" with the principals of Regent Entertainment, for whom I would make seven films over eleven years. Of these, two had military themes: *Tides of War* and *In Her Line of Fire: Airforce 2*.

Nearly ten years elapsed between the making of *Sahara* and *Tides of War*. Sexual mores had become more tolerant; subscriber-based TV channels could deliver to niche markets. Regent Entertainment partners Paul Colichman and Steve Jarchow invited me in for a meeting. They were starting a parallel venture to their production company. This was *Here! TV*—a premium television network available nationwide targeting LGBTQ audiences. We're queer and we're here! Paul is openly gay in a long-term relationship, Steve Jarchow is a heterosexual, proud supporter of gay rights. Me, too. The network's program slate included past gay and lesbian feature films, along with talk shows, cooking shows, documentaries. To be comparable to other premium cable channels like Showtime or HBO, *Here! TV* would offer gay-themed original movies specially made for the network. There would be suspense thrillers, action thrillers, disaster movies, standard genre fare, the difference being that the heroes or heroines would be gay. Their sexuality would be expressed clearly but discreetly by dialogue, a kiss or caress, no explicit sex scenes. Paul Colichman's political objective in the culture wars raging at the beginning of the new century was the normalization of gay relationships in entertainment; an end to the coy network promo warning of *"a very special episode of…"*.

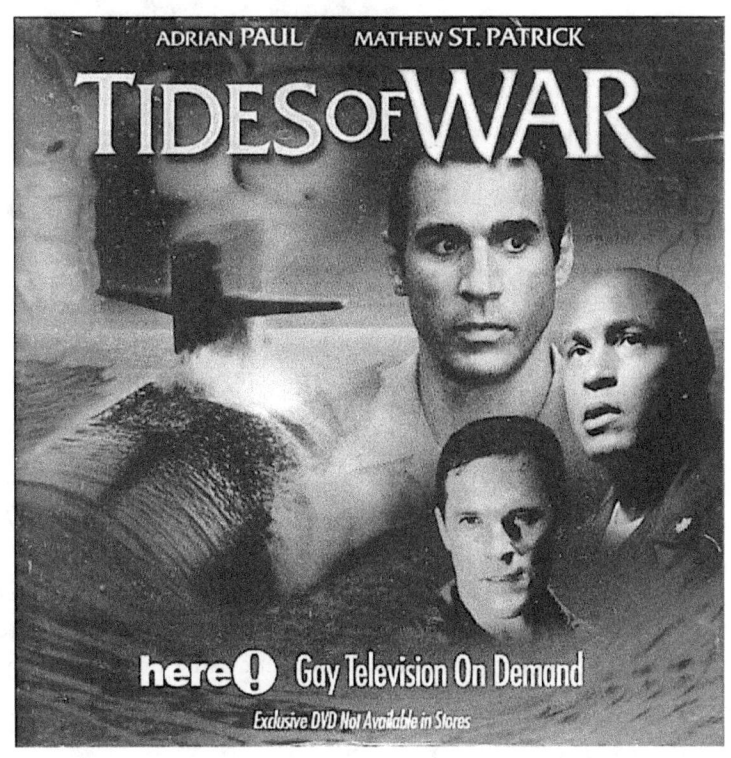

These movies, as proposed by Paul and Steve, would not be high end coming out/gay pride/gay injustice message pictures like *Brokeback Mountain* or the Academy Award winning *Gods and Monsters* which Regent had produced. They would be low budget B movies unashamed of their derivative genre tropes in which the heroes of each adventure just happened to be gay. Would I like to produce and direct *Here! TV's* first original movie?

*Tides of War* was an exciting screenplay by Mark Sanderson (*I'll Remember April*) from a story by Regent partner Steve Jarchow. It goes like this:

Nuclear submarine Commander Habley lives in Honolulu with his Executive Officer (XO) Lt. Commander Palantonio. On shore, privately, they are lovers. On board the sub, in the *don't ask, don't tell* era, their relationship is strictly professional. Patrolling the waters off North Korea, they are surprise-attacked by a new kind of North Korean stealth submarine. Executive Officer Palantonio is killed, a terrible blow for Habley, who has to hide the extent of his grief, his pain compounded by the Navel Court of Inquiry seeking to blame him for the damage to his boat.

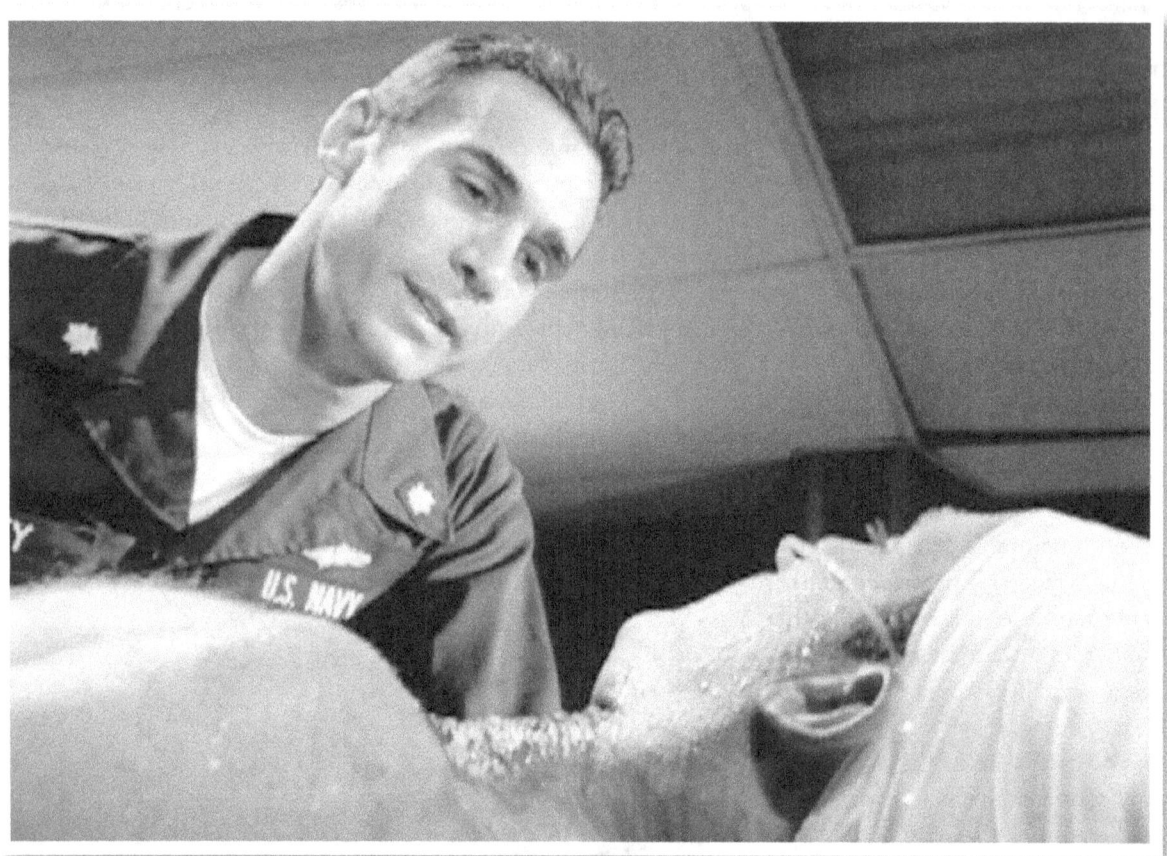

Lt. Palantonio's sister, Lt. Trifoli, serving with Naval Intelligence, blames him too, and has discovered love letters from Habley to her brother. Habley is sent back to the South China Sea to destroy the stealth sub. But Naval Intelligence assigns Palantonio's sister to the mission, along with a new by-the-book XO to take over if they deem Habley unfit to command…

With Paul Colichman's connections, we were able to attract a good TV cast. Adrian Paul (TV's *Highlander* for seven seasons) as Habley. Mike Doyle (*Law and Order*) as Palantonio, Catherine Dent (*The Shield*) as his sister, along with Matthew Saint Patrick (*Six Feet Under*) Matt Battaglia (*Queer as Folk*) and Kent McCord (*Adam 12*; this was his third military role for me).

I saw the movie as a *Run Silent, Run Deep/Crimson Tide* cocktail. My favorite sub movie was Wolfgang Petersen's *Das Boot*, which cost $14M in its day. I was allotted $1.6 million to make two versions of the movie, one gay and one straight. Regent had a presale to a Japanese DVD & TV distributor who was looking for a submarine movie to cash in on the release publicity for a forthcoming big budget Japanese submarine drama and was offering double the normal direct-to-DVD price, in a notoriously hard to sell market. But the Japanese company did not want the gay version at all. Back then, European TV paid little for gay-themed programming, particularly gay male content, if they bought it at all, because they couldn't play it till after 10 p.m. European TV would pay a much higher price for a straight version of the same movie they could play at any hour. So *dual purposing* would be the means of recouping the cost of production. The policy was not a cynical sell-out, just good economics that made the project viable.

I devised six places where the versions would diverge. All the other scenes would be common to both films. The opening sequence provides a good example of the approach:

A newspaper lands on the lawn. Headlines about the North Korean crisis.

Habley (Adrian Paul) wakes and gets out of bed.

<u>Gay version:</u> Adrian dives naked into his backyard swimming pool, where his lover Palantonio (Mike Doyle) challenges him to a race. It's a dead heat, after which they kiss passionately.

Cut to the kitchen: Palantonio, bare chested wearing a sarong, cooks breakfast. Habley enters in his Commanders uniform. They watch an update on the North Korean crisis on the TV.

Cut to the driveway where two SUVs are parked. Palantonio, now wearing his Lt. Commander's uniform follows Habley out. They each get into their respective vehicles and drive off. Cut to the submarine underway, where the last revelation is that his lover is also his Executive Officer (XO).

Straight version: Habley swims alone, has breakfast alone watching TV, drives away alone. On the submarine he greets his XO as a subordinate but a good friend. Alternate content shot from the same camera positions.

In other scenes, alternate dialogue replaced references to Habley's sexuality. The shot where Habley sits alone by his pool and is overwhelmed by grief at the loss of the love of his life was replaced by one of more stoic sadness.

The production was challenging. We were denied Defense Department co-operation, not because the sub commander was gay, but because his lover was his XO. The Department of Defense (DOD) had moved with the times by 2004. Having gay Servicemen in a script no longer disqualified the project for co-operation. It was the *fraternization* with a serviceman of different rank that was the problem. That was an absolute no-no, yet it was integral to our plot. Otherwise I could have shot on an actual nuclear submarine undergoing maintenance. I was given a tour through a Virginia Class nuclear sub. Spectacular, yet incredibly cramped. What a difference such an authentic location would have made to the movie. The visual potential of wide-angle lenses, Steadicam, floor lighting with colored gels was evident. I salivated at the prospect on the tour. But it was not to be.

I could have staged many submarine interior scenes on the USS Missouri, the decommissioned battleship operating as a museum in Pearl Harbor. The ship no longer belonged to the DOD, but it was berthed on naval property, and the film was not granted access. So I divided the submarine interiors between sets

constructed in a warehouse, and a floating dry dock location which gave us corridors, cabins, crew bunks, galley, ladders, and naval-looking machinery.

We built the best Con (nerve center where the periscope is stationed) from the best materials that Home Depot could provide, supplemented by props shipped in from LA. It was a magnificent achievement by a resourceful art department.

Once again, I turned the last day of prep into an expanded 2nd Unit day. First, we got dawn shots of Pearl Harbor, then we went to a courtyard between two office blocks. There we mingled extras in naval uniforms with the Saturday morning visitors, getting production value establishing shots for a Naval Administration building.

Then we moved on to an area where we could get shots of ships entering the naval base. Such photography was prohibited after Pearl Harbor in 1941 and the law has remained in place ever since. To get to that excellent vantage point we had to cross through an area of military housing before reaching the water's edge. We were setting up for a shot of a naval cargo ship sailing into harbor, when we heard sirens. We knew we were on DOD territory. *Mea culpa*, but sometimes the best angle is over the fence. Before NCIS arrived, the hi-def tape of that morning's irreplaceable shooting was hidden in a backpack, and replaced by a blank tape for the expected confiscation. My Hawaiian crew under DP Paul Atkins were familiar with this problem and ahead of the game. When asked what we were shooting, I decided a tourism documentary for Australian TV invited fewer problems than a story of a gay nuclear submarine commander and his battle with a North Korean submarine. Claiming that we were just setting up to shoot the beauties of the harbor, I showed the officer in charge through the camera's viewfinder that there was nothing on the tape in the camera. Totally blank. As producer I took responsibility, was duly cited for "Federal Trespass," let off with a warning. The officer was kind enough not to confiscate the blank tape.

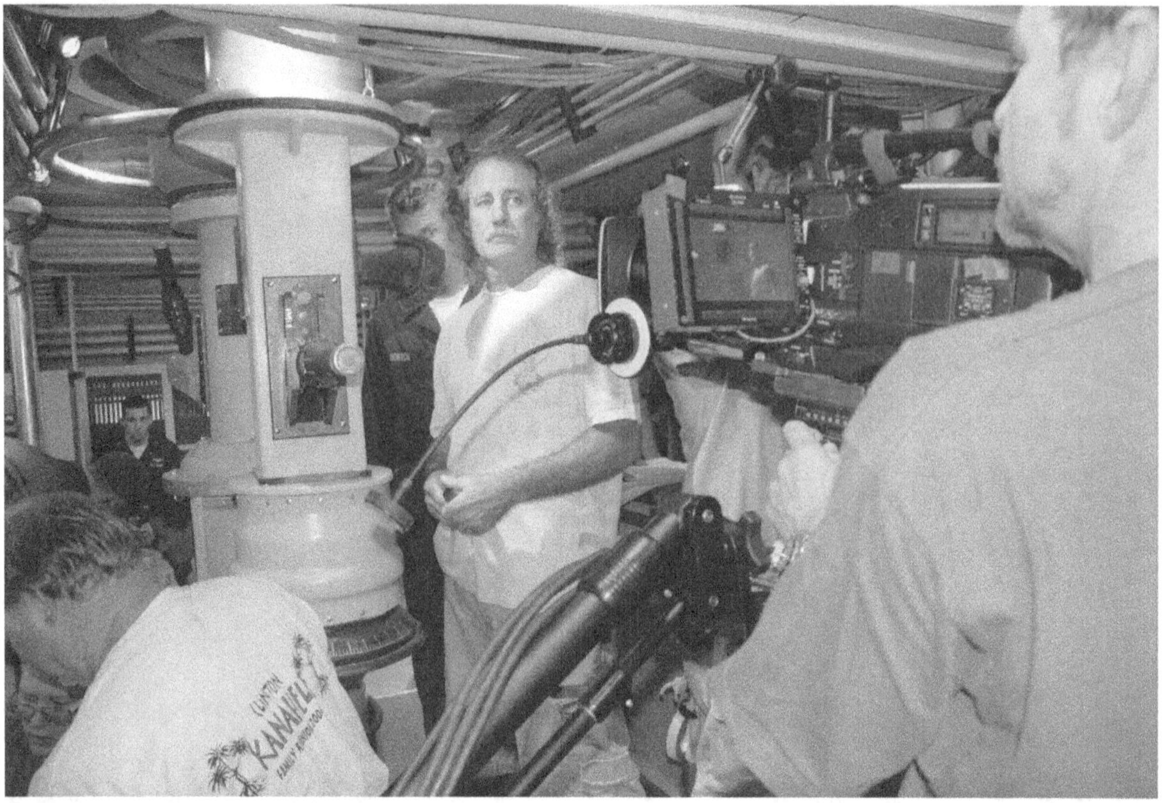

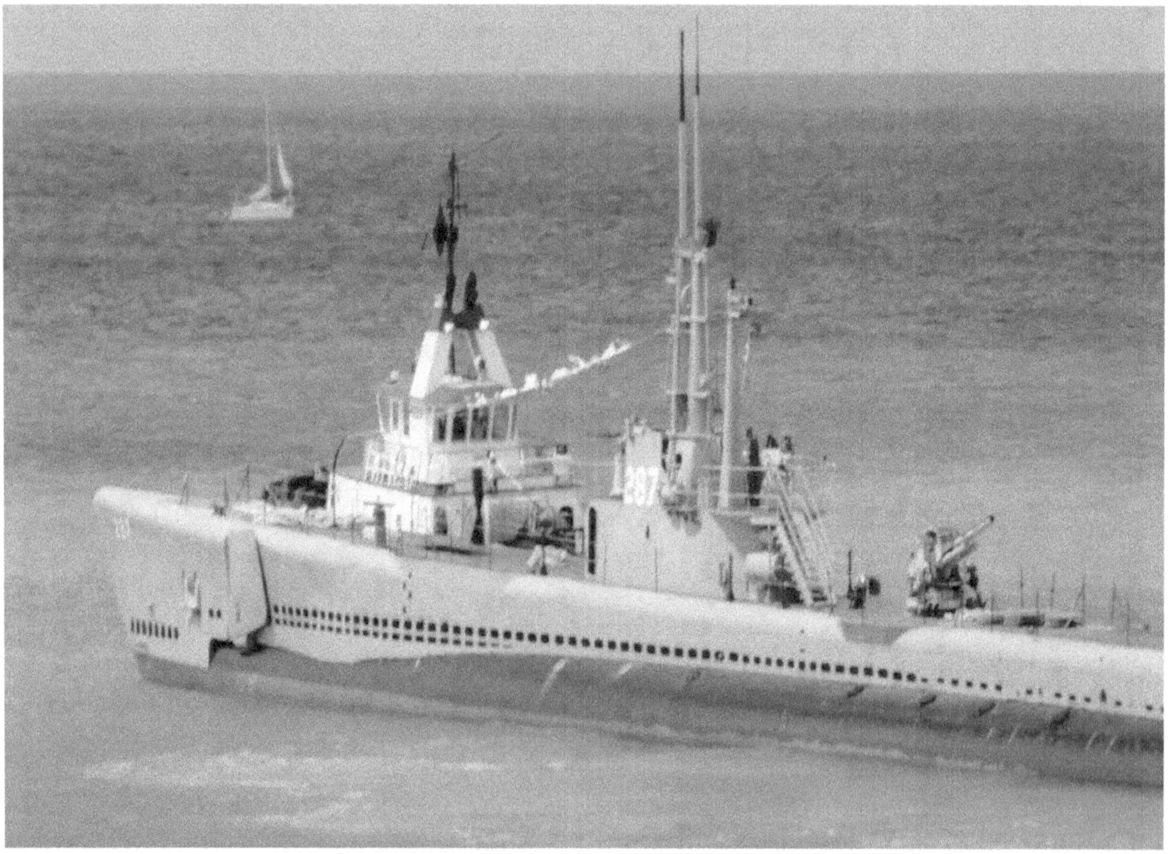
287

*Tides of War* contains a shot never likely to be repeated. The USS Bowfin, a WWII submarine, nick-named the "Pearl Harbor Avenger" for the amount of Japanese shipping it sank, was by happenstance leaving the floating dry dock we hired as a location. The boat had been undergoing maintenance before sailing to its final resting place in Pearl Harbor at the USS Bowfin Submarine Museum & Park. Now it was making its last voyage, a memorable shot for fans of the Silent Service if we could incorporate it. Just in time we got a camera in place to integrate Adrian Paul in uniform watching the historic boat pass by.

Another unexpected visual blessing occurred when we were shooting on the windward side of Oahu in the National Guard Cemetery, access to which an influential gay veteran finagled for us on the first day of main unit shooting.

I had set up a low angle tracking shot of Adrian Paul walking somberly past foreground gravestones and floral arrangements to his lover's grave, with the morning sun lighting up the mountain range beyond. Suddenly it started to rain, a windward side phenomenon the Hawaiian crew call 'liquid sunshine.' Umbrellas appeared in a flash to protect the actor and camera equipment. Just as suddenly the rain stopped. Then a rainbow appeared over the mountains beyond. Umbrellas away and roll camera! The rainbow stayed just for the few seconds we needed to add a touch of LGBTQ subtext to the shot.

I was blessed by a crew who were fast on their feet throughout the 15-day shoot. The only weak link was the costume department. The Navy would not give us a technical advisor so I depended on the costume supervisor to ensure the ranks and uniforms were correct.

*"Why can't the people in Hollywood get the US Navy rating structure correct"* growled one critic. *"The CO of the boat, Adrian Paul, is wearing Silver Oak Leaves, the rank insignia of a commander on his collar, while wearing shoulder boards of a lieutenant commander. Ms. Dent is wearing a Chief's cover with an officer's crest."*

These details may be missed by the general public or seem unimportant, but such mistakes offend Navy personnel. I should have double-checked before the first shot locked us into continuity of insignia, but in the rush, it got by me. A Navy film should get the Navy stuff right. Grrr! Never trust a civilian on military matters.

A submarine movie is by its nature claustrophobic. Appropriately chosen stock footage would let air into the picture and add production value. I accessed my bulk deal with the Paramount library and chose fifty-three shots from *The Hunt for Red October* and *Top Gun*. For example, I wanted a burst of action early in the film to emphasize the North Korean threat, so the duel between two US F-14 Hornets and four Libyan MIGs in *Top Gun* became—with a little digital enhancement—a dogfight with North Korean fighters. I wrote radio communications between the F-14s and an aircraft carrier to knit the sequence together.

This movie introduced me to Steve and BenniQue Blasini, a husband and wife team of visual effects animators, who did an amazing job with the software available at the time on nearly 200 shots of submarines, torpedoes, and explosions amid craggy underwater landscapes.

We could not afford to build a torpedo bay for a short shot, so I recorded sailors against a green screen and they digitally created the rest.

I used their company BFX Imageworks whenever I could thereafter. They're wonderful people; a lasting friendship developed between Steve and Benni and my family.

Speaking of family, it was great to have my son Eric with me in Hawaii during preproduction.

The cast gave their all, particularly on election night 2004, our last day of the shoot. Imagine Adrian Paul, Catherine Dent, Matthew Saint Patrick, Matt Battaglia, Mark Deklin and six supporting actors, a cast uniformly of lefties like myself trying to beat the clock.

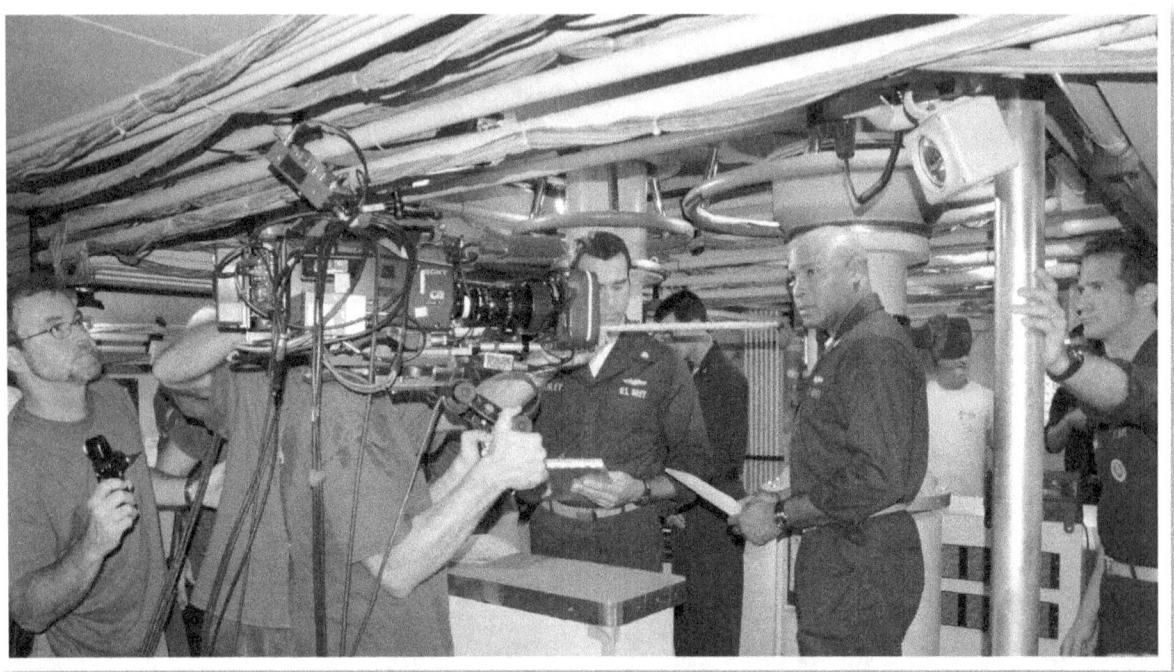

We were crammed with two cameras, sound and lighting crew into a small set in a hot warehouse with nine pages to complete, while early election results came in from the mainland on the green room TV, showing the Democratic demise. Much rending of garments, wailing and gnashing of teeth between set-ups. But like the pros they were, the actors delivered. Perhaps the angst helped the tension of the climactic torpedo battle. Certainly, it was the most interesting election night I've ever had. Until Trump, of course. Ugh. Don't get me started.

The gay version of *Tides of War* premiered at the 2005 Hawaiian International Film Festival to modest acclaim, praised more for worthiness than originality. The straight version was sold to Sony Home Video for 200K, and shipped a lot of units. Japan was happy with its version. For me, the gay version delivers better drama and underlying tension, because the hero has a secret he dare not reveal. The movie has a message. Tolerance. To cash in on the publicity emanating from the remake of the iconic *Poseidon Adventure*, Sony retitled the straight version as *USS Poseidon – Phantom Below*.

*Phantom Below* would have been a much better gay title…

My next assignment for Here TV was to produce and direct a Lesbian *Rambo* derivative to be called *In Her Line of Fire*. The straight version, a clever piece of dual purposing devised by production VP Jeff Schenck, was titled *Air Force Two*, to piggyback on the popularity of the Harrison Ford hit *Air Force One* (obviously). The premise was simple.

Air Force Two, the Vice President's plane, goes down in the sea just off a remote Pacific island. I wrote a shot list requiring eighteen digitally created images of the crash, which were nicely executed by Blasini Imageworks.

By extraordinary coincidence, local insurgent forces are being trained on the island by a rogue American mercenary. The Vice President, a former marine, is captured and held for ransom. It is up to his lesbian Secret Service Chief and the cute Press Secretary she has a crush on to rescue him. I'd buy that for a dollar.

The movie was originally set in Latin America but was to be shot on Grand Turk Island. Due to a change in financing, it became a New Zealand/Canada co-production, relocating the setting to the Pacific, requiring a rapid re-write. The reduced budget,

down to $1.2M, bought me two six-day weeks of shooting in Auckland, then two days in Vancouver, where the interior set for Air Force Two was stored.

My vision for the movie was this: What if Cannon Films of the 1980s had made another *Missing in Action* derivative, and instead of casting Chuck Norris or Michael Dudikoff in the lead, they had cast Mariel Hemingway as a kick ass ex-Marine Sister of Sappho, to liven up the classic tropes of that subgenre?

A news commentator's voice over the opening titles sets the scene of an Utopian Washington where Congress has just passed universal health care by unanimous vote, and at the same time the Vice President

is flying off to some world environmental conference. We wish. The opposite of politics in the Bush era in the middle of its second term. This sets up the Vice President before we even meet him as likeable, forward thinking, unlike the VP of the day.

I wonder if Dick Cheney, who has a lesbian daughter, saw this movie? I am certain he saw his depiction in my *DC 911: Time of Crisis* docudrama. In a nod to the Cheney family it amused me to have David Keith's dry humored Vice President actively encourage the seduction of one lesbian by another.

"You're a Marine. Go for it."

Mariel Hemingway, a joy to work with, played the secret service chief with fierce determination. Mariel, who is straight, had lesbian cred because of her role as the bisexual athlete in *Personal Best*, and for kissing Rosanne Barr on an episode of her sitcom. Jill Bennett, the in-the-closet Press Secretary, was in fact publicly "out" and a regular on Here! TV's supernatural soap *Dante's Cove*. David Millbern, who went to the gym assiduously for the role, was effective as the unhinged rogue mercenary, one of the best roles of his career.

New Zealand producers Grant and Dale Bradley were able to put together a crack crew at short notice. Many were veterans of *Lord of the Rings*. Twelve days is too short a schedule for a film with this much practical gunfire to be carried out safely, so I opted for digital pyrotechnics, commonplace today but pricey and rarely photoreal in 2005. From front and side angles I shot muzzle flashes for each weapon, poked through a hole in a black curtain, and sent them to BFX Imageworks for compositing. The Blasinis made guns blaze, cartridges eject, bullets chip trees and kick up sand. The digital approach to pyrotechnics provided two spinoff benefits: no safety issues from live firing, and because there was no noise and no damage, the best locations were easier to get.

After a breathless 12-day schedule in Auckland, we moved to Vancouver, Canada, and shot the Air Force Two interior scenes on a studio set, up until the moment of the crash. There was a small empty

swimming pool near the studio. We paid to have it filled, after installing a piece of the Air Force Two set in it that could be lowered to simulate rising water. An underwater camera crew captured key moments of various characters escape from the sinking plane. Editing commenced in Vancouver. I gave a new editor Asim Nuraney his first action picture. He did a great job, and has edited about twenty movies since. BFX Imageworks delivered an impressive CGI plane crash. There's a restrained campiness about the movie, blithely enjoying its own absurdity.

A couple of reviews called it a throwback to 80's gun porn. Yes, it was a nod to those movies where the hero mows down swaths of fellow human beings who were just following the orders of the villain, only this time it's a girl blazing away at the cannon fodder. What captures my ironic tone best is the MPAA's "Rated R for two lesbian kisses and the deaths of several dozen men."

The *New York Times* said the gay version entitled: *"In Her Line of Fire"*— *produced to be shown on the gay cable network Here!—flaunts its Sapphic*

*subplot (all five minutes of it) like a pesky contractual obligation."* In fact I would have liked to have explored the lesbian angle more, but in fourteen days there simply wasn't time to shoot many alternative scenes. As with *Tides of War*, the gay-themed *In Her Line of Fire* is a more entertaining movie than *Air Force Two*, its straight counterpart.

*Variety* said: *"Paced briskly by telepic vet Brian Trenchard-Smith…with Mariel Hemingway a credible Sapphic Stallone, this passable action trash should satisfy as fun original programming for gay-targeted Here! cable net. What it's simultaneously doing on scattered U.S. hardtop screens is puzzling."*

The 2-screen theatrical release in New York and Palm Springs was a marketing plan to publicize Here! TV becoming available to subscribers in those areas. Here! rented the smallest screens in two multiplexes for a week. Ticket sales were irrelevant. But not to me. A theatrical release, however small, still has its box office reported. *In Her Line of Fire*, produced and directed by myself, grossed, according to *Variety*, "$884 in worldwide theatrical release." Not something I could offer proudly at an interview. Optics are key in Hollywood. "How much did his last picture make?" Normally a theatrical release enhances a director's career. While my Lesbi-

an *Rambo* demonstrated an ability to stretch a dollar, and give an old genre a wry twist, it did not help my representatives move me up the budgetary food chain where there are better scripts and more money for visual style. I was becoming pigeonholed in low budget TV. The only way to break out was to write a screenplay that a studio, like Dimension, would want to make. So I wrote a script for a movie in the $20M range which would eventually become my first novel, *Alice through the Multiverse*. More about that later.

# CHAPTER 43
## Supernatural Thrillers

Who doesn't like a good ghost story? In 1999, while working on another production, I received an offer from Jerry Offsay, Showtime's president of programming, to direct a screenplay based on true events entitled *Sightings: Heartland Ghost*. Jerry agreed to wait till I was available. As soon as I was, Showtime sent me to Calgary, Alberta, Canada which would double for Kansas where the actual events took place.

The origin of the story was the long-running reality TV series *Sightings*, which investigated a wide variety of paranormal events, to either debunk or explain the reported phenomena. The most famous case concerned a 128-year old house in Atchison, Kansas, which a young couple had bought as a fixer upper, only to discover it was haunted by a hostile entity. The *Sightings* crew duly arrived, examined the property from top to bottom and conducted interviews. Several members of the crew were freaked out by the atmosphere in the house. This wasn't their first rodeo, either. The field producer refused to set foot in the house again. The ghost in America's heartland became *Sightings'* most popular investigation, returning in six more episodes.

Paramount, who owned the series, and Showtime, a sister company in the Viacom constellation, decided to make a semi-factual movie from the point of view of the investigators

and their crew. They offered the screenplay to John Carpenter, Tobe Hooper, and several other feature directors with scary movies on their resumes, but nobody bit. Well, lucky me.

I viewed the relevant *Sightings* episodes and studied the interview tapes. Here are some of the phenomena the young couple described. Both husband and wife reported seeing shadows moving in their peripheral vision. In what soon became the baby's room, their dog growled as if threatened. Photos taken in the baby's room would come out black, while shots of other rooms on the same roll would be perfectly exposed. Their baby would giggle and smile towards an empty corner of the room. Lights in different rooms turned on and off in front of hitherto skeptical visitors. The husband's brother was present when the musical carousel above the baby's crib started playing music without being wound up. For a week the oven timer would ring intermittently. Stuffed animals and bean bags would change their position from the day before. A small vase flew off a shelf narrowly missing a visitor. The husband claimed he actually saw it change direction in midair before smashing against a wall.

There were several instances of spontaneous combustion: candles, a coat, the ears of a toy rocking horse. A small flame sprouted from a teddy bear sitting on top of the TV. While the husband was carrying it to the kitchen sink, the flame went out. One night he saw for a brief moment a little girl dressed in "...*not 1993 clothing. She looked just as real as you and I; innocent looking and sweet. She had a surprised look on her face.*" He dropped the glass he was holding. As it smashed on the floor, she vanished. He immediately drew a picture of the girl he saw, short, with big eyes and brown hair .

These were just a few of the dozens of phenomena the couple reported to the *Sightings* staff when inviting them to investigate. What most attracted the show's researchers to this tale of poltergeist activity, was the claim that the entity would unexpectedly attack the husband, leaving scratches on his body, and on a couple of occasions, sexually molest him in his sleep.

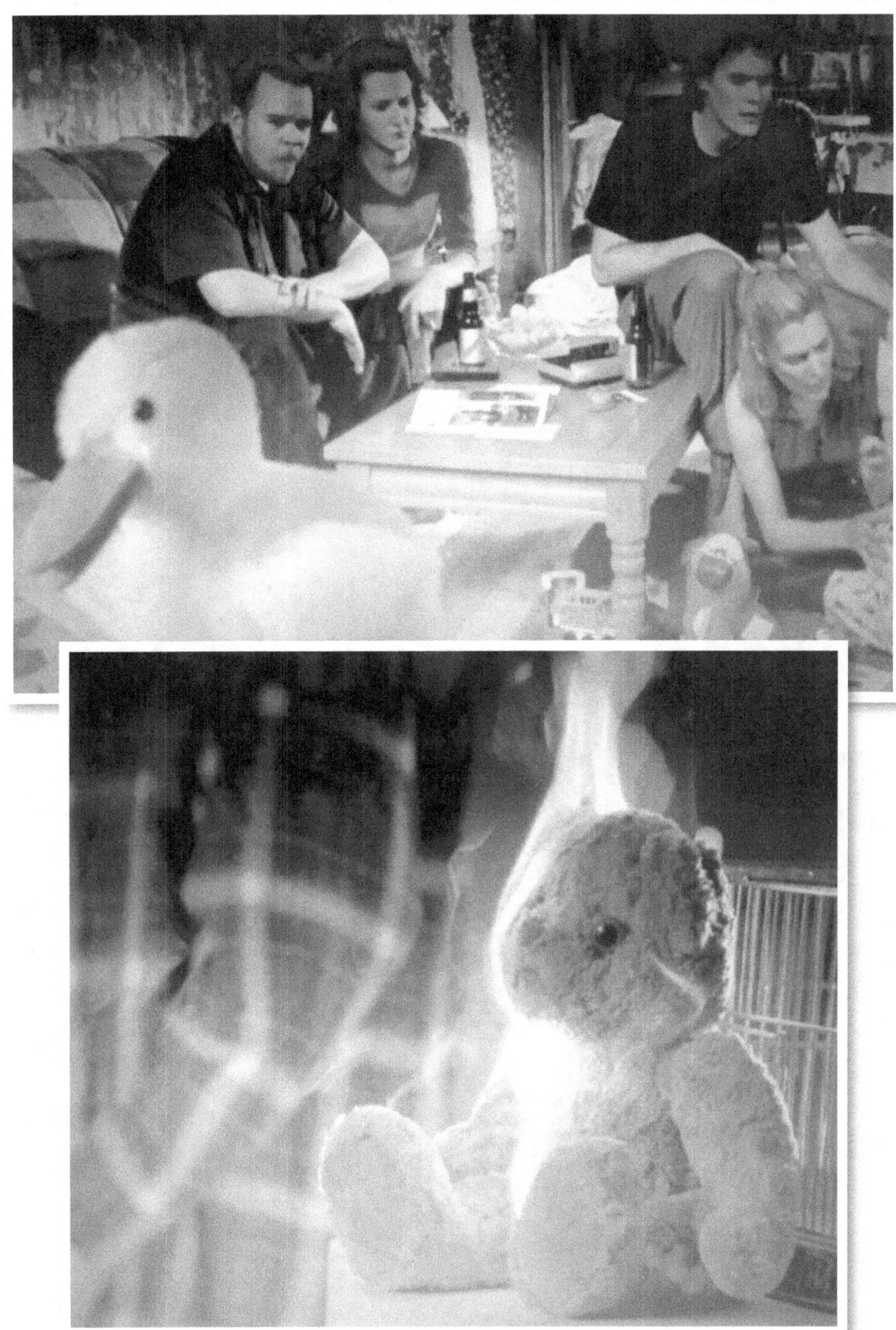

In the original interview tapes, something occurred right in front of the lens that I could not explain. *Sightings* might shape a story, but never faked evidence or allowed a participant to fake evidence without exposing it. Prior to recording an interview with the husband, the *Sightings* team would check every inch of his skin for signs of a pre-arranged scratch. On this occasion, as before, there was no sign of anything suspicious. He quickly dressed and the interview began. Before long he winced with pain.

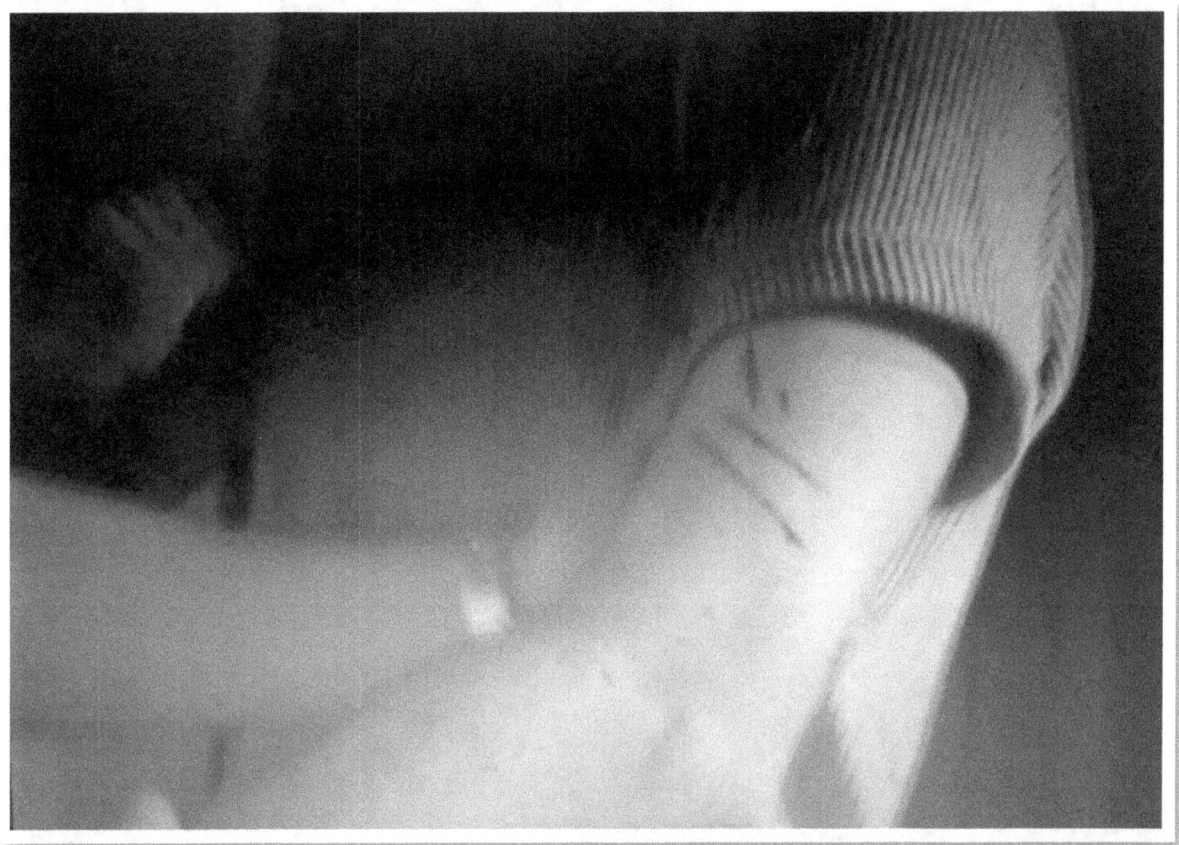

He removed his shirt and pointed to a red mark a couple of inches long that had not been there a few minutes before. He stood up. The camera zoomed in on the mark on his skin and held the shot for nine minutes during which the scratch got redder and lengthened several more inches. *"When a cold spot goes through you, you feel sad like you are going to cry,"* he commented later. Psychosomatic? Autosuggestion? Or what?

The original *Sightings* crew maintained a 24-hour vigil. Cameras were positioned in every room, relaying to a bank of monitors. When one camera showed signs of interference, a crew member was dispatched to check it out. He reported feeling a strong sense of dread while standing outside the door as if something was telling him—don't go inside. Thermal imaging cameras pick up cold as blue. When one of the crew felt a sudden chill, they turned the camera on him, and captured a wisp of blue surrounding him. Within a few seconds the husband received another scratch.

*Sightings* brought in a psychic with no knowledge of the area or the case. He established a level of psychic prowess by saying he sensed train tracks nearby. Local research confirmed that there was a disused railway line long forgotten and overgrown near the house. On one tape, the psychic is seen challenging the entity: "I am not afraid of you. Stop this now." Then he flinched from what he described as a mild electric shock. At that same moment, a definite 'pop' can be heard on the soundtrack. The psychic sensed there were three conflicting spirits in the house: a woman, a child, and someone "very medical."

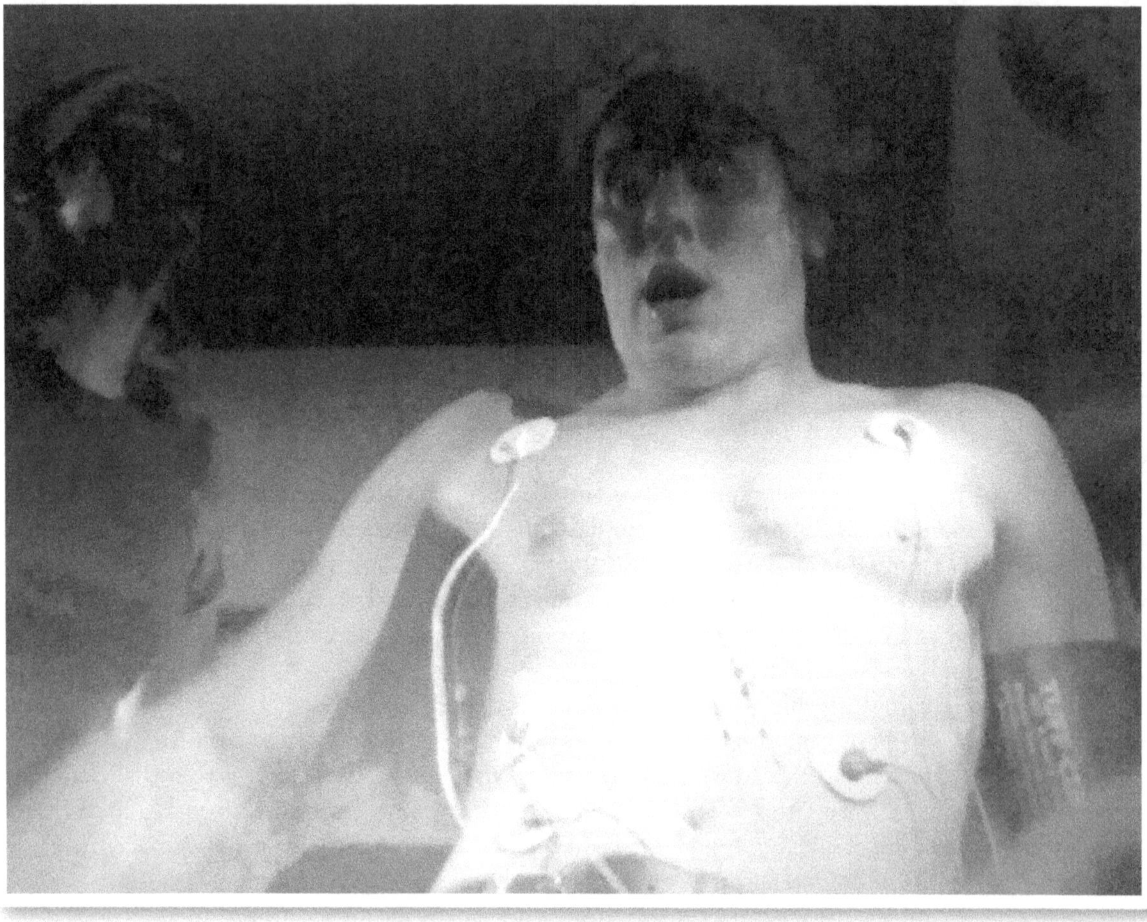

One of the original owners of the house, and some twenty adjacent properties, was a Dr. Finney. He employed a number of freed slaves and their descendants for fifty cents a day. He had a controversial reputation, and was once arrested for beating a neighbor with his cane. He became the town mayor, but was forced to resign after it was discovered he operated a secret tavern for the town's elite. Kansas was a dry state. The house next door, which the Finney family also owned, was occupied by a mentally disturbed woman, given to fits of violence, who was committed briefly to a mental institution on Dr. Finney's recommendation. She later attempted suicide by gas, but succeeded only in killing her 6-year-old son. Three people had died in the house the contemporary young couple had bought to restore. There was plenty of scandal and tragedy across all the adjacent Finney properties to justify "troubled spirits."

Translating what is, in essence, a documentary into a 3-act drama with character arcs is a challenge. I read the three previous drafts of the screenplay Showtime had developed prior to my coming on board, and made some mix-and-match recommendations, but the network seemed set on what they had. The final explanation of the origin of the phenomena is a little fanciful, but I accepted the mission: balance the factual with the speculative as believably as possible, but keep it entertaining for a ghost story audience.

Because of the slavery element in the backstory I suggested changing the female investigator to African American. Nia Long was cast, and was helpful in making dialogue about racial conditions in 1890s Kansas more accurate.

Beau Bridges played the lead investigator as rigorous skeptic, who sees every paranormal claim as a hoax. There's always a rational explanation for every "sighting". His outward charm almost masks his inner sense of superiority. So we enjoy his humbling moment when confronted by psychic phenomena he cannot explain.

Miguel Ferrer (*Robo Cop),* son of Jose Ferrer (*Cyrano, Lawrence of Arabia*), was an amusing foil as the psychic. His intense look gave credibility to the scenes of paranormal manifestation.

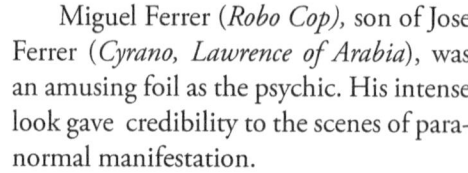

Showtime wanted to reward Thea Gill, from the cast of their long running series *Queer as Folk*, with a movie role. She was fantastic as the distraught wife.

I brought back Stephen Myers, who had cut *Atomic Dog*, as editor, and Bert Dunk once again as DP. We used pencil-cam and fly-cam to convey the spirits moving through areas of the house inaccessible to a 35mm camera. Luckily, we found a late Victorian Gothic house in Calgary that perfectly fitted the needs of the script. My producers Ann Daniel and Henry Winkler (The Fonz) were excellent. It was a smooth 20-day shoot.

A sequence I am proud of is the husband's nightmare, which suggests a possible cause of the haunting.

I mixed color with black and white, jump cuts, distorted images and eerie sound effects. We paid a lot of attention to sound and the film received a nomination from the Motion Pictures Sound Editing Guild. I often use this sequence as a discussion piece when I lecture to film students. Overall, I'm pleased with the way the tension builds throughout the movie to an ending that gives the ghost story audience satisfying closure.

The Hollywood Reporter was kind to me:

"*It's filmed with skin crawling style by director Brian Trenchard-Smith and given a disturbing visual acuity by DP Bert Dunk…a stirring, well produced ghost story that smartly undersells the effects.*"

Noted horror director Mick Garris (*Psycho 4: The Beginning*, *Sleepwalkers*, *The Stand* and *The Shining* miniseries) pictured here with his wife Cynthia, called to invite me to direct an episode of *The Others*, a paranormal series for Dreamworks and NBC. The show featured a group of psychics who use their different abilities to try to prevent tragedy. Mick had directed the pilot in Canada, which got a 13-episode pickup from NBC. Dreamworks boss Steven Spielberg suggested Mick and the creators John Brancato and Michael Ferris select directors with horror-themed theatrical releases in their resume, each to do one episode. Toby Hooper (*Texas Chainsaw Massacre*). Bill Condon (*Gods and Monsters*), Tom McLoughlin (*Friday 13th Part 6: Jason Lives*) were among other directors selected.

When NBC greenlit the series, they moved it to the Paramount Studios in LA. To enhance the *X-Files* flavor of the show, NBC brought in *X-Files* show runners Glen Morgan and James Wong as executive producers to "share" the show running with the original creators. As their pilot director, booked for two episodes, Mick Garris similarly saw his creative authority diminished, along with the directors he brought in. When I walked into the production office to prep Episode 3 (A dream come true—I'm directing on the historic Paramount lot!), *I sensed a climate of fear.* Something I am sure any episodic directors reading this can relate to. Tread carefully though the minefield of a show in the grip of a power struggle. My creative choices had to be run past two sets of showrunners. The 1st AD I had been assigned was not interested in riffing about film, only concerned that I did not cause a production problem on his watch.

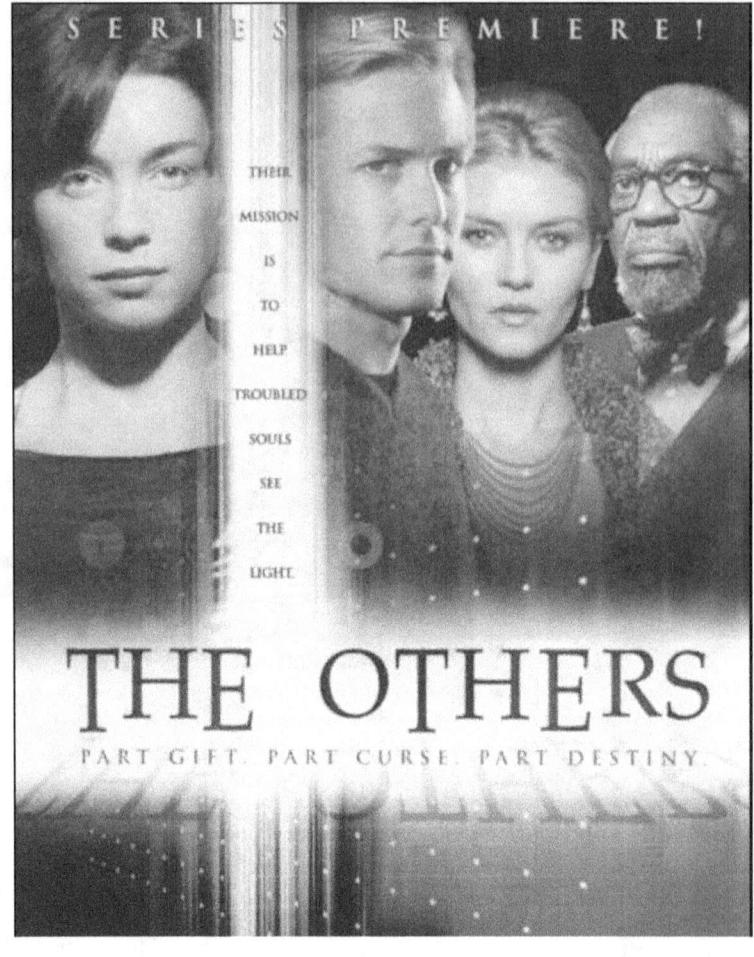

SERIES PREMIERE!

THEIR MISSION IS TO HELP TROUBLED SOULS SEE THE LIGHT.

THE OTHERS

PART GIFT. PART CURSE. PART DESTINY.

Compounding my unease was the fact that, from the first meeting, a key executive clearly did not care for me. I recognized her as a volunteer on the 2-day additional photography shoot I did when doctoring *Blood Tide* in 1980. I had needed to punch up the horror of a scene in which the body of a major character whom the unseen monster had attacked while swimming is discovered washed up on the rocks of a Greek island. Only a close up of her "dead" face resting between rocks had been shot, nothing full length of the corpse, and there was no money to bring the actress from New York. We did have a prosthetic severed foot, which we shot washing ashore. A tight shot of a girl's forearm lying on the wet sand would help, too. Having a live crab crawling towards the arm, or even on it, would give the shot more potency. I had asked the only woman on our skeleton crew to be the arm. She was not keen, afraid the crab would claw her, but I had cajoled her into doing it, and should not have. Being so focused on "getting the shot," as directors tend to be, I was oblivious to the fact I had hurt her feelings. Meeting her again twenty years later, the power differential was reversed.

I would reap what I had sown. She had opposed my hiring, I would find out later, on the grounds there were much bigger and better directors to be found. When supporting role regular Missy Crider was more than an hour late, resulting in overtime to clear the location, it was somehow my fault. Work around her! We did, till we ran out of scenes. At the end of the week, I was berated for going an hour over on the Friday night, making the crew late for their weekend. The overtime was unavoidable in my view. The key sequence involved a child actor J.T Larsen levitating at the edge of a 40-foot drop. Ensuring the safety of a minor in the presence of his mother took longer than expected. The race against the clock in episodic TV is all the harder when compounded by safety issues. We proceeded carefully, the kid had fun, his mother felt secure, and I got the shots.

The regular cast all shone in their respective ways. Julianne Nicholson, who understood the constraints of episodic, really appreciated me letting her have another take when we were on the cusp of a meal penalty. She gave a new reading charged with genuine emotion, and thanked me sincerely. Positive feedback means as much to a director as a performer. I gave a new actor his first TV role. As the insane kidnapper of a paranormal child. Zachary Quinto brought a palpable menace to an underwritten part.

His versatility quickly caught on. Seven years later he would be the new Spock in the *Star Trek* reboot.

Another series regular who would do well was Gabriel Macht.

After years in the trenches, he would at last strike it big with the hit series *Suits*, co-starring Meghan Markle, now the Duchess of Sussex (he attended her wedding). Unaware of the connection, I would subsequently cast his father Stephen Macht as Wolfowitz in Showtime's *DC 9/11: Time of Crisis.*

I had just signed with a new agent at the William Morris Agency (now WME/ Endeavor). Within six weeks I had brought in an episode of network television through my own relationships. While a little exposition heavy, I thought the episode came together quite well. My agent should be encouraged, I thought. But apparently the executive had given me a bad report, which she said she would repeat to anyone asking for a reference. So he discharged me as a client, even though I had left CAA to join him. He claimed it was orders from the new head of the agency to get rid of any clients who were not already booking 200K and upward each year. As it turned out, there was a silver lining. Being fired by my agent saved me $20,000. That's the commission I would have paid him for my next feature film (*Megiddo*) had he still been my agent two months later.

# CHAPTER 44
## Whodunits and Action Thrillers

*Sahara* in 1995 had proved my worth to Showtime, so they hired me to direct a suspense whodunnit called *Escape Clause*. which targets insurance industry hypocrisy and deceit. It was a spec script by well-regarded writer Danilo Bach (*Beverly Hills Cop*) that had nearly been made as a theatrical feature a number of times, but each deal had fallen through. Showtime offered to make it as a cable movie on a 20-day schedule in Toronto for $2.9M.

Showtime's president Jerry Offsay gave me some advice on working with a fellow strong-willed writer/producer. *You're the director but remember—all writers have is their words.* As it turned out it was a honeymoon relationship. Danilo Bach welcomed my idea for beefing up the climax: The villain had trapped the hero's child in a car and stalled it across the rail tracks. The train approaches at speed, watched by the villain, who recites the act of contrition for the crime that is about to happen. The hero races his SUV to the rescue, and pushes the car off the tracks in the nick of time. But the train clips his back wheel, flipping the SUV. Hero crawls out and takes on the villain. A bit *Perils of Pauline*, you might say, but in fact, it's organic to the insurance issues raised by the script, By adding a 5 camera team to the crew, we managed to shoot the complex train chase, crossing crash, and final confrontation between Sorvino and McCarthy in one day, made all the more visual by showers and sleet. It's a good sequence.

ANDREW McCARTHY   PAUL SORVINO

ESCAPE CLAUSE

"a shot in the arm for the suspense thriller"
—SHOWTIME

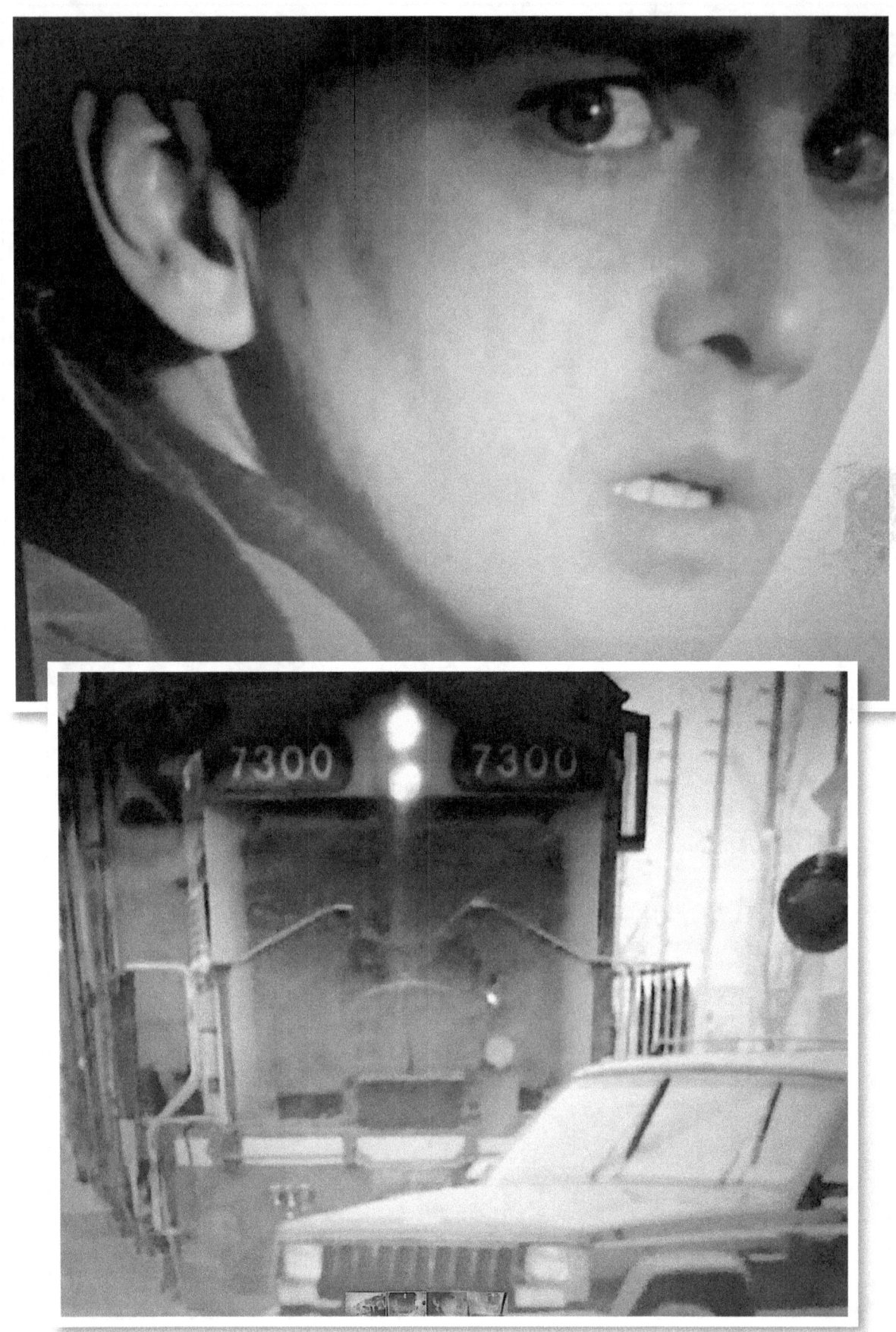

Andrew McCarthy plays a successful insurance executive, Richard Ramsay, whose philosophy that accidents are generally the victim's fault has facilitated his rise up the corporate ladder. He has a loving wife and two small children. His world collapses when he gets a call from a purported hitman who claims to have been hired by Ramsay's wife to kill him, but will refrain for double the fee.

When both his wife and the hitman are murdered, and secrets about his past are revealed, Ramsay becomes the chief suspect. And the police could be right…

Andrew McCarthy always came to the set knowing his lines and ready to go. Paul Sorvino (*Goodfellas*), playing the homicide detective assigned to the case, would arrive pretty uncertain of the text. A 108-page script with multiple locations meant a tight 20-day schedule. An hour after crew call, you should be shooting something. Some actors in television prefer to fine tune their memory of the text in rehearsal. If I had planned to start the scene with a moving camera covering the opening chunk of dialogue, it was unwise to start with that shot. I would have to pick up at a point where Paul's character was static, and place the camera over his shoulder linking him with the other participants in the scene. Next would be closeup coverage of those actors, with Paul Sorvino off camera feeding them lines. In these shots, Paul did not give the other actors much to react to in his delivery. But when the camera turned around on him, Sorvino was magic. Every nuance and flavor that the dialogue held he exploited. By then he was thoroughly warmed up, and I could shoot the opening dolly shot as planned. If there was time.

Andrew McCarthy was unhappy with this approach, but he adjusted. Every actor has his or her process, and a director must learn how to harmonize differing approaches. Andrew's off-camera resentment, as vented to me, served his performance well. He's a fine actor. Many actors have played the moment when they view a loved one's body in the morgue.

Andrew's reaction was searing, like a knife going through him, yet we are not sure whether or not he is her killer. Finely judged. Andrew and I discussed director/actor relationships. He told me of working with famed French filmmaker Claude Chabrol when he was cast in *Quiet Days in Cli-*

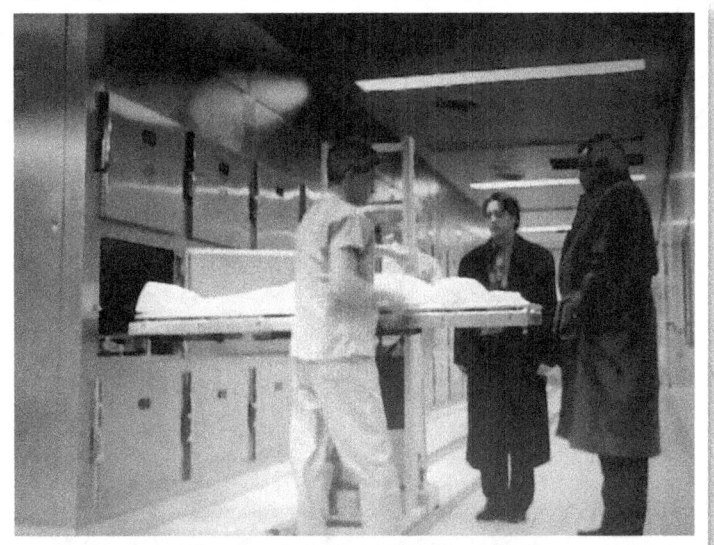

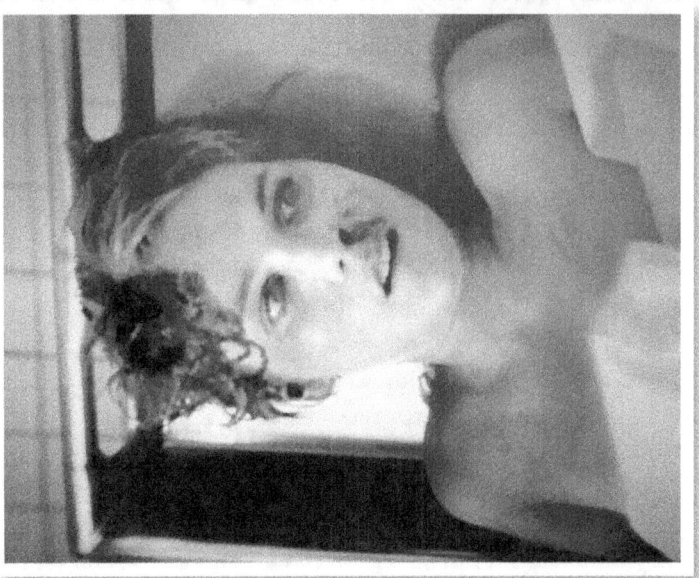

*chy*. According to Chabrol, there were, in essence, only four words of guidance a director needed to say to an actor: *Faster, slower, louder, softer*. The actor should then examine how a softer, louder, slower, or faster reading of the speech would reflect the character's response more truthfully. Andrew's grasp of drama has given him a substantial parallel career as a TV director. I admired what he brought to *Orange Is the New Black*.

Connie Britton, coming off the indie hit *The Brothers McMullen*, was cast the former flame who might be a suspect. After we started shooting, she learned she was a runner-up for the female lead in *Jerry Maguire*. The other contender was Renée Zellweger. They were each offered a table read of the script with Tom Cruise, sort of a casting bake-off, conducted on separate days. We adjusted Connie's schedule so she could

fly from Toronto to New York one night and return the next. Afterwards, I asked her how the bake-off went. She told me she thought she did well. I asked her if she spent any time with Cruise outside of the table reading. Is he any different in person than he is on the screen? Connie said he talked about his wife Nicole the whole time, what an amazing person she was. That was his only topic of conversation outside of the script. Cruise chose Zellweger, who was adorable in the role as I'm sure Connie would have been in her own way. *Jerry Maguire* lifted Renée Zellweger onto the studio feature list and her career took off. Connie Britton went on to a great career of her own, starring in long-running series like *Friday Night Lights* and *Nashville*.

*Escape Clause* starts with Andrew McCarthy's insurance executive character at a seminar outlining his *no such thing as an accident* mantra watched by a Suspicious Man. OK, intriguing. Cut to Andrew making early-morning love to his wife, nicely played by Kate O'Neil. MGM, Showtime's partners in the project viewed my cut, then summoned writer producer Danilo Bach and myself to a notes meeting. They wanted to start the movie with Andrew and Kate's sex scene, and place the other scene somewhere later on. '*Starting with sex will get the audience's attention and ensure that they don't hit the channel changer*' was their guiding philosophy.

Danilo vehemently opposed what he saw as a cheapening of the project. I supported him, which may seem uncharacteristic, given my exploitation background. I argued that someone paying a subscription of $10 per month (in 1996) for Showtime is not going to ditch the movie because there was no sex in the first three minutes.

The opening scene established the protagonist and set the movie's premise with a hint of foreboding. It has direct relevance to the climax of the picture. The script was intended to work on a more Hitchcockian level than a formula erotic thriller. Given Danilo Bach's stature and adamant objection, MGM backed off. Sometimes the creatives win.

ADVENTURES IN THE B MOVIE TRADE

# ESCAPE CLAUSE

*Escape Clause* rated several notches above the previous month's premiere movie. But TV's punditry class was becoming jaded with the deluge of telemovies that had spread from free-to-air networks to the new subscriber-based cable channels. It was too much work. So the reviews ranged from faint praise to snark:

" *Escape Clause tries to be Double Indemnity*" - No, it doesn't - " *but director Brian Trenchard-Smith is no Billy Wilder.*" True but irrelevant. It's a competent whodunnit with a strong vein of criticism for insurance industry practices.

Showtime were happy with *Escape Clause.* The executive in charge of the project, Sharon Byrens, lifted my career to a new level. She would champion me to direct two more Showtime projects, one of which was a true-crime black comedy for which I have an especial affection, *Happy Face Murders.*

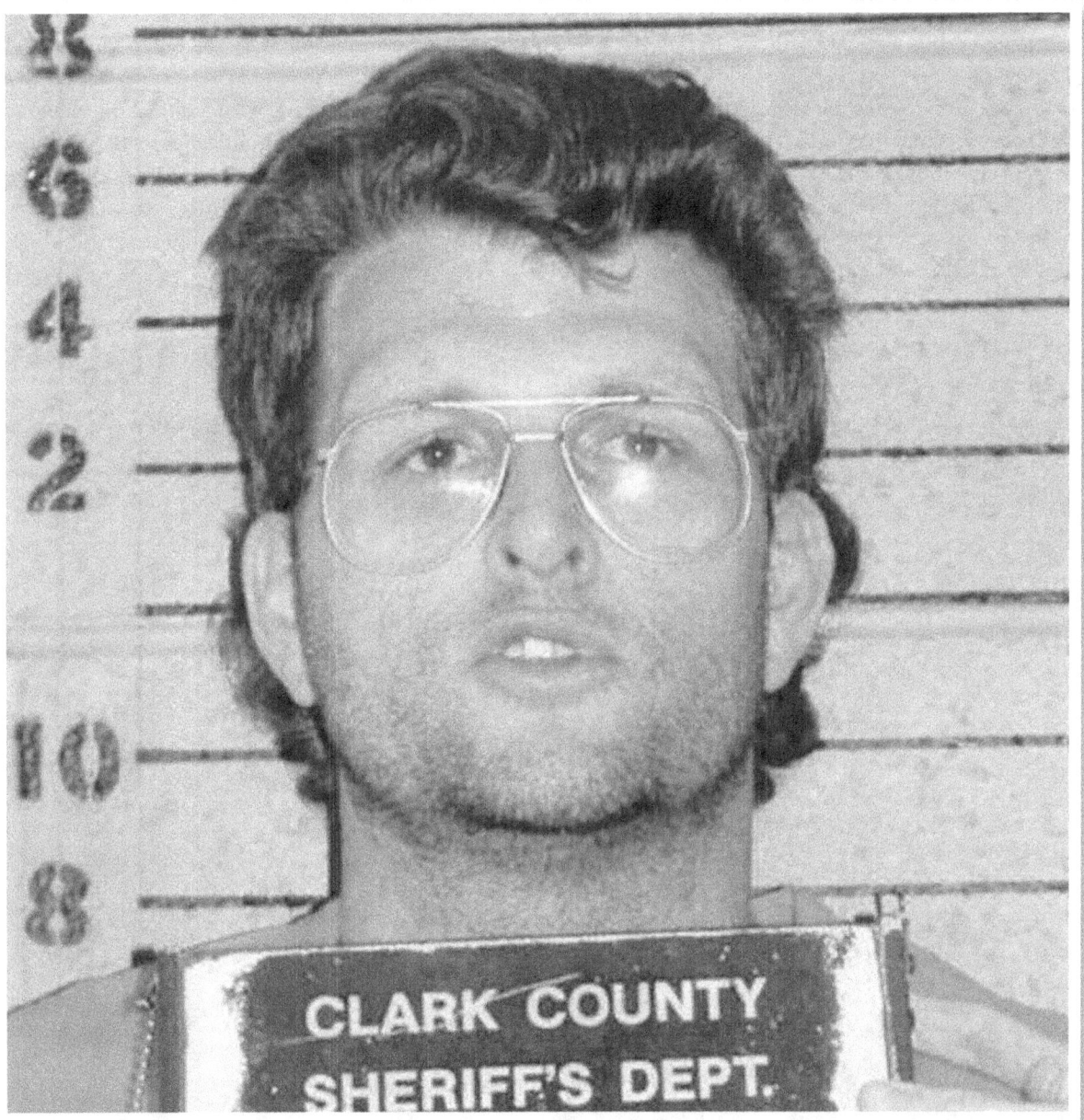

*Happy Face Murders* is based on the bizarre events surrounding the first of at least eight murders committed by serial killer Keith Hunter Jesperson. He raped and strangled his first victim, a girl he met in a Portland bar, on January 23, 1990, dumping her body on open ground. The intense TV coverage that followed was watched by Laverne Pavlinac, a 60-year old woman trapped in an abusive relationship with her alcoholic live-in boyfriend, John Sosnovske, almost twenty years her junior. She saw a means to get him out of her life by calling detectives and implicating him in the crime. She used details from media reports, supplemented by an understanding of investigative procedures gleaned from detective shows like *Perry Mason* and *Matlock*, of which she was a lifelong fan. However, this was not enough to trigger his arrest. In desperation, she changed her story to one where Sosnovske forced her to help him rape, murder, and dispose of the body. That was enough for the investigators. Pavlinac and Sosnovske were both arrested, and put on trial. Sosnoske, with his history of alcoholic blackouts, confessed to avoid the death penalty. Laverne recanted her confession, saying she made the whole thing up.

This came to the attention of Jesperson, the actual murderer, who wrote to the prosecutor claiming Sosnoske and Pavlinac were innocent and providing details of the murder that only the killer could know, signing with a Happy Face. He followed up with further confessions, one written in marker pen on the wall of a truck stop toilet stall, also signed with a Happy Face. Defense counsel had that section of the stall cut out and presented in court. The anonymous confession was ignored. There was political pressure to close a high-profile murder case. Sosnovske received life in prison, while Pavlinac was sentenced to a 10-year minimum. After Jesperson was finally arrested for his eighth murder, he repeated his confession and directed police to where he threw away his first victim's purse containing her ID. This was enough to get Pavlinac and Sosnovske released after nearly five years in prison.

Showtime had hired a top writer John Peilmeier (*Agnes of God*) and he wrote a compelling script. But Showtime did not greenlight the picture. It was a favorite project of creative exec Sharon Byrens, who had liked what I had done with *Escape Clause*. She gave me the script and asked for my ideas to get it out of limbo. It was a well-written true crime police procedural with neatly managed plot twists. The hard-bitten detective character driving the investigation contributed to a dour tone. What was needed, in my view, was to inject an underlying sense of humor, a dark, ironic, bemused look at human folly, via the impact of mass media on the criminal justice system. In my report I suggested:

*"… an increased media presence in the film. I don't mean an additional character, but rather a Robert Altman approach to the soundtrack. Scripted television and radio sound bites could constantly be in the background and occasionally watched by characters. Perhaps, during the domestic quarrel on page two, that introduces the*

*grandmother and her drunken boyfriend, the TV is playing professional wrestling as ironic counterpoint…Media coverage of an upcoming state election would certainly justify the rush by prosecutors to buy Laverne's story, and close a high-profile case."*

I pointed out the danger of introducing the real killer too early ("not before page 68"), because when Laverne makes her last painful confession, we must believe her. This time it's the truth. Till it's not.

But my strongest recommendation for a rewrite was to give Detective Jen Powell, our guide through the bizarre story, an endearing sense of humor rather than a weary cynicism. Such a part would attract the level of star we needed.

I met with the producers John Cosgrove and Terry Muerer (182 episodes of *Unsolved Mysteries*). They were initially concerned that Showtime was recommending the director of *Leprechaun* movies, but we had a good meeting. I won the execs 'round, and they were great to work with.

John Pielmeier agreed with the key points I made. The rewrite he delivered took the project from turn-around to casting. And what a great cast we got.

Academy Award winner Ann-Margret as the conniving granny. Canadian TV star Nicholas Campbell (eight seasons of *Da Vinci's Inquest*) was perfect as the abusive boyfriend. Marg Helgenberger (soon to star in *CSI*)) was cast as Detective Powell. The new script made her a dog lover, naming her rescue pooches after dubious politicians. I cast Henry Thomas as the criminology student foisted on her investigation; I had not worked with Henry since *Frog Dreaming/ The Quest* fourteen years earlier. He had navigated the rocky path from child star to adult roles, and he was still the same modest yet remarkably talented actor I remembered.

I'm picky about locations. I wanted a house for Ann-Margret and Nicholas Campbell's characters that reflected their doomed relationship. As I crisscrossed a working-class Vancouver suburb street by street, a house came into view, a single-story clapboard, with a huge water tower looming over it like a three-legged *War of The Worlds* Martian machine about to stomp. I wanted to give the story a quirky look, to distinguish it from other crime dramas shot in made-for-TV style. I hired top Toronto cameraman Bert Dunk, known as Digital Dunk because he would take a picture on his hi-end still camera, transfer it to his computer, and color time it in front of you, as a preview of the end result. Not common in 1998.

Bert introduced me to the newly-developed Frazier lens, designed by Australian photographer Jim Frazier. It delivers massive depth of field, in which both extreme foreground and background of an image are in focus. Additionally, the lens has an extended tube with a rotating prism, which enables the camera to shoot from previously inaccessible positions. Cinematographers then rotate the prism to correct the horizon. We got a couple of cool shots that way.

One night, Ann-Margret put my directorial acumen to the test. Up till that point she had invariably come to the set with a clear idea of how she was going to handle each scene. She had the essence of the character down, a seemingly sweet frumpy grandmother, a little bit daffy yet shrewd and manipulative. Ann-Margret had warned me at our first meeting that she would always be flat in rehearsal. She only turned on the juice when the cameras rolled and sure enough every time the cameras rolled the juice was flowing. So on this particular night I expected nothing different. We were shooting the scene in which the investigators, played by Marg Helgenberger and Henry Thomas, record her confession to being an accomplice in kidnapping, torture, rape, and murder. This is the third time she has changed her story to the police, but it is critical that we believe her this time, so that the next big twist—the real killer kills again—comes as a total surprise.

I blocked the scene simply, set up a 3-shot of them on the sofa, while the other camera covered Ann-Margret in closeup. When all was ready, she called me over to sit beside her and then whispered in my ear:

"I don't know how to play this scene. I don't know how I should be feeling. Please help me."

Luckily, in preparation for working with her, I had read Ann-Margret's autobiography *My Story*, which chronicled her journey as an immigrant child from Valsjobyn, Sweden, to stardom in Hollywood and Las Vegas. It is clear from her writing how much she loved her father and how important his approval was to her. But you cannot escape the impression that she never quite got enough approval from her father as she wanted before he died.

So I thought for a moment, and then whispered back something to this effect: the things you are admitting to are among the most shameful acts any human being could commit. Imagine you are confessing your shame to your father.

After a beat, Ann-Margret nodded. I got up, hand signaled "Roll 'em," and took my position beside her closeup camera. Ann-Margret built the speech to a heart wrenching, emotional climax.

Showtime liked *Happy Face Murders*, and it earned them the highest rating for an original movie in twelve months. It didn't do Marg Helgenberger any harm, either. She played a similar character on *CSI* for the next ten years. There was an unexpected spinoff benefit for me, too. The Director's Guild of America were unhappy with Guild signatory companies like Showtime's parent company Viacom sending non-DGA directors like myself to Canada, paying them at lower than DGA rates, to direct pictures that would normally be directed by members of the DGA or of the affiliated Directors Guild of Canada. The dispute came to a head as I started prep in Toronto. This resulted in Viacom agreeing to making *Happy Face Murders* under a DGA contract, requiring me to become a member. I had to be sponsored by two DGA members in good standing. My producer John Cosgrove supplied one signature. Russell Mulcahy, who was directing a Christopher Lambert thriller at the same studio, kindly supplied the other.

My pay for the movie jumped by 25K. I had residual payments for the reuse of my work. Most importantly, I had a pension plan and top health coverage for my family. Membership in the DGA was key to a long-term directing career in Hollywood. It had taken eight years.

$1.95

# DAILY VARIETY

**WEDNESDAY**
OCTOBER 6, 1999

## HIGHEST RATED SHOWTIME ORIGINAL PICTURE IN 12 MONTHS!

# ANN-MARGRET

The Hollywood Reporter
Ann-Margret's colorful (more like delec-table) performance holds the pieces together.

Associated Press
Dowdy, aged or evil, Ann-Margret isn't afraid to take roles that are counter to her attractive image. Like Bette Davis, Ann-Margret believes it's the role that counts, not how she looks.

THE WALL STREET JOURNAL
Ann-Margret carries the film with a bewitching performance.

Some things are just
too unbelievable to make up.

## happy face murders

### INSPIRED BY ACTUAL EVENTS

SHOWTIME and PARAMOUNT NETWORK TELEVISION Present
ANN-MARGRET  MARG HELGENBERGER  "HAPPY FACE MURDERS"  HENRY THOMAS
Director of Photography BERT DUNK, ASC, CSC  Executive Producers JOHN COSGROVE and TERRY DUNN MEURER
Written by JOHN PIELMEIER  Directed by BRIAN TRENCHARD-SMITH  [R]

SHOWTIME

In 2001, Carlton America, the US subsidiary of a UK broadcaster, wanted a TV action picture, which they would make in conjunction with Australia's National Nine Network. Carlton's international buyers had suggested a *Die Hard* clone; a rugged hero, played by a US star, trapped on a runaway train with a bunch of terrorists and a girl. Sounds like Steven Seagal's *Under Siege 2*. Apparently, being a derivate of a derivative did not matter. Broadcasters felt comfortable with formulas. The premise given to me was this: an American agent comes to Australia in pursuit of a criminal mercenary, who plans to unleash deadly nerve gas on a Sydney-bound train unless he's paid a $25M ransom. Somehow hero, villain and henchmen all find themselves on the potentially doomed train. Let the games begin…with plenty of action we can afford on a TV budget, and a cliffhanger before every commercial break. The working title was *Terror on the Rails*, subsequently changed to *Seconds to Spare*. I brought Dennis Pratt in to cowrite with me, while I handled the editing of *Heartland Ghost*. On the basis that formulas work, we left no cliché unturned.

After several drafts, our script found favor, and I flew to Australia to scout locations. The Queensland Government wanted our budget spent in their state, so Queensland Rail offered us the cooperation we needed for a train movie. They would supply locomotive and carriages, access to the platforms of several country stations and to the Redbank Railway Workshops outside Ipswich. The mile-long loop of rails that ran 'round the facility had both curves and straight sections for testing repaired locomotives. Shooting from inside the loop, we could get shots of the train passing by a bushland background, while shooting from outside the loop we could set the train against an urban industrial background. Queensland Rail would even let me blow up a train. No CGI. That's a real locomotive and real pyro. My cup runneth over…

Prep was going well. I had a good dinner then returned to my apartment just before 11 p.m. and switched on the late news. On the screen was a live feed from America showed smoke pouring from the North Tower of the World Trade Center in New York. I dialed my home in Los Angeles, where it was 6 a.m. Margaret, hearing the urgency in my voice, immediately turned on the TV. Like countless others, we were just lamenting what must have been a terrible accident, when another airliner appeared in the shot and smashed into the South Tower. Oh my God! We both wept for the murdered souls. The world we all knew had changed forever.

The production was put on temporary hold. US Airports were closed for three days; I took a flight back as soon as they opened. At LAX, no vehicles other than shuttles and taxis were allowed in. Long lines of frustrated passengers formed, eying the passing taxis, many of which had drivers of Middle East or South Asian origin.

"Why can they get in here and my brother can't pick me up?" said a man standing in line nearby.

"I bet some of them got relatives who did this," responded the man beside him.

A bleak angry mood had settled on the country. It was comforting to be home with Margaret and the boys at this anxious time.

After a hiatus, Steve Davis, Carlton America's CEO called me to say the production was going forward as planned. The title would be changed from *Terror on the Rails* to *Seconds to Spare*. But our potential star Dolph Lundgren, whose wife was soon to have a baby, decided he wanted to stay in America under the present circumstances. Understandable, but a loss. Dolph was physically imposing, perfect for the part of a hard-bitten federal agent on the vengeance trail. But the production clock was ticking, a start date for the shoot had been set and Carlton needed to find a star quickly who made the buyers comfortable. Antonio Sabato Jr.'s agent was pushing him hard. His father, Antonio Sabato Sr. had starred in a number of spaghetti westerns and cop dramas in Italy. The family name had visibility in Europe, where distributors had done well with some of Sabato Jr.'s direct to videos, like *Operation Wolverine*. Antonio did not have the cachet that Dolph had, but it seemed he was on the rise. So he was cast.

Antonio and I met just before I flew back to Queensland's Gold Coast to resume prep. He was, if it is possible, even more good-looking in person than on the screen. He had a devilishly charming smile. Of course, the hero he would play has little cause to smile throughout the story. He's a framed, disgraced, then jailed former FBI agent, now freed and hunting the rogue agent who set him up. Antonio asked how recently had his character got out of jail. Maybe a couple of weeks, I estimated, enough time to regroup, and locate his nemesis' whereabouts, an Australian country town.

"So he would have a prison haircut." Antonio felt just to survive inside, his character would have tried to look like the most dangerous inmate.

"Maybe," I countered, hoping the idea would go away, because I thought his present hair length complimented his bone structure well. "But not too short. We'll do it once you arrive at the studio."

Antonio duly arrived four weeks later with his hair prison-shorn to barely an inch. It helped him get into character, he explained.

It diminishes your good looks, I didn't explain…

Channel Nine's pick for the female lead was Kimberly Davies. Her 172 episodes of *Neighbors* ought to attract the non-action audience in Australia. She was a good actor, looked stunning, worked hard, but could do little with the stereotypic role of the innocent blonde in peril, hiding from the bad guys while helping the hero. Our first draft was more edgy, less predictable, but it did not fly. USA Cable was the American target audience, and they wanted their action adventures linear, easy to follow after commercial breaks.

The other female lead was Kate Beahan. She played the well-intentioned ecoterrorist intending to expose a secret repository of nerve gas, illegal on Australian soil. She hires the wrong team and pays the price. Kate was a good actor, and like Kimberly, did her best with the material.

The scene stealer in the cast was Jerome Elhers who played Sabato's nemesis. He chewed on the part with relish, in the Alan Rickman style. I wrote a letter of support for Jerome's application to US Immigration for an H1 Visa, stating he could make a career just from playing smooth talking villains. I would cast him again in *Drive Hard* in 2013. Sadly, he died a year later. He would have done well in Hollywood. In the thirty years since landing in LA, I have written a number of references on behalf of Australian actors and cinematographers seeking access to Hollywood. It's a tribute to the talent of Australian film professionals how many, from a country of around twenty-five million people, have secured international movie careers.

The most important document a television director must work on during prep is his shooting schedule. How many days of photography are to be allotted to each location or studio set? How will the hours of the day be divided between the scheduled scenes? The schedule becomes the roadmap through the minefield of high-pressure production. By the last day of the schedule, every scene in the script must be shot. Therefore, it is important that a director sign off on a schedule he believes he can accomplish. This may mean trimming or dropping certain scenes or pieces of business that require too much camera time for their worth in the overall episode or movie.

But what if, after the number of scenes are reduced, three into two still won't go? We had a standard telemovie 20-day schedule. Action scenes that are both effective and safe take time. It is a lot slower to repo-

sition a train for camera than a car. My script, after pruning, scheduled at twenty-three days. So I suggested we steal the last day of prep—Friday, before start of principal photography on Monday—and shoot some simple scenes that did not involve the train. Antonio and Kimberly were already on site for camera test and wardrobe fitting. Virtually all the crew were already on deck. Why not put together five pages of scenes that can be shot in adjacent locations in a 10-hour day? For instance: Let's call a realtor and offer to rent a swanky waterside mansion for that last day of prep, one that's been fully furnished for an open house. No dressing required. There we can stage the opening scene where Antonio beats up a suspect to extract information. At a restaurant on the adjacent marina, we can shoot Antonio and Kimberly reuniting for lunch at the end of the movie. The plan was accepted and worked perfectly.

I saved another day by moving scenes, like the fight in the car carrier, to a separate small splinter unit. I would direct this unit for four hours before the main unit clocked in. Then I started a full day of scheduled scenes, divided between day and night shooting. Three split day/nights followed in the railway repair yard. The splinter unit worked on stunt shots adjacent to main unit, and I jumped between the two. Cumulatively, this approach absorbed the work of another day. My producer Matt Carroll was most helpful in coordinating all the moving parts.

I got the picture back to twenty days at the very end of the schedule by undertaking to shoot thirty-three pages of dialogue in one set over two days instead of the originally scheduled three. Luckily, I had my regular Queensland DP John Stokes. During *Sahara* and *Flipper*, we had developed good shorthand together. These scenes, scattered throughout the movie, were set in the war room of the Australian Anti-Terrorism Task Force, an impressive studio set dominated by the operations chief Commander Haggerty who did most of the talking.

Veteran stage, film and TV actor Nick Tate was the perfect man for the part. As of 2020, he has 115 acting credits on IMDB. Nick had the interpretive skill to keep those thirty-three pages interesting. We had first worked together in 1984, on a *Special Squad* episode (*In the Cause of Justice*) I was impressed by his charisma and versatility. Later he did voiceovers for some of my Australian trailers. His vocal dexterity earned him a lucrative career in the US narrating trailers and TV campaigns, often in the *thunder throat* style of legendary trailer maestro Don LaFontaine (for further insight into this Hollywood subculture, see Lake Bell's delightful comedy that uses the LaFontaine trademark opening line as its title: "In a world…"). Stage-trained, Nick Tate had no trouble with lengthy dialogue.

The game plan was to maximize the coverage as efficiently as possible, while still getting the necessary dramatic result. Instead of shooting each scene one by one, I would rehearse a number of consecutive scenes as one continuous block, complete with pauses, entrances and exits, then shoot it from multiple roving camera angles. To make these scenes more visually interesting, the war room had a big screen, on which prerecorded material was always on display. This ranged from a permanent live feed from the helicopter tracking the train, to FBI files on the terrorists. A highlight of the night attack on the train is the commando helicopter's onboard camera output. The girlfriend of one of the commandos witnesses the chopper's destruction on the War Room screen, a poignant moment nicely played by Alyssa Jane Cook. Block by block, with a bit of overtime, we got through the thirty-three pages in two days.

But each of these stratagems were a risk, so I am grateful to then-CEO of Carlton America, Steve Davis, who attended the whole shoot and allowed me to push the envelope each day. *Seconds to Spare* became Carlton's highest-selling movie of 2002. Steve is now Executive Vice President and Chief Content Officer of Hasbro Studios. They are lucky to have him.

I would produce and direct another thriller/whodunit in 2012, *Absolute Deception*. Here are some observations on the funding process at that time: It was set up by the executive producers as an official Canadian/Australian co-production, thus garnering subsidies for investors in both countries. But in order to qualify in Australia for the highest benefit—40% of local spend—the film had to be theatrically released in a number of cinemas across at least three states, otherwise, if it went Direct to Video (DTV) or broadcast TV, it would qualify for only 20% of local spend. Exhibitors were hardly begging for low budget movies shot in fifteen days. So a local distributor would be engaged to book the film onto the necessary number of screens, where it would run for a week with minimal promotion in mainly empty halls, but the regulatory criteria would be met at least on paper. The cost of such a release was considered worth spending to ensure the full 40% rebate. But it seemed an unnecessary expenditure, money that might be better spent on international marketing. The DTV movie was a grey area in the regulations. I wrote a letter to Screen Australia in which I argued that

DTVs should be regarded as feature films, because they are the equivalent of drive-in movies, exhibited instead, due to market changes, in the customer's home.

*If the qualifying definition of theatrical release for the higher rate of Offset is: <u>projected for a season in the local multiplex or art house,</u> (my paraphrase) then that term needs to be redefined in the light of the seismic changes that have been re-calibrating market response to product in the last 5 years and continue to do so. Such a rigid definition—one based on previous market custom—will greatly inhibit the financing of lower budget product that has a shot at profitability. It is not a definition that is in tune with the times.*

*In 10 years you may see the principal method of exhibiting films to the public will be internet download onto your 80 inch home cinema screen, or your wristwatch computer. Either way, you are watching a feature length film delivered to the public for exhibition.*

Screen Australia remained adamant in its definition of theatrical release:

*A feature film is the only format which receives a 40 per cent offset. The term feature film is intended to mean a film of at least one hour in length that is screened as the main attraction in commercial cinemas.*

Ultimately *Absolute Deception* was screened in the requisite number of Australian commercial cinemas, where audiences were no doubt disappointed to have paid to see a TV movie. Reviews were predictable:

*"Trenchard-Smith handles it with anonymous efficiency, but he—and we—deserve better … it's really sad to see him slumming with forgettable junk like this."*

Appreciate the sympathy, but a gig is a gig. Do the best you can with what you're given.

Distribution of *Absolute Deception* outside of Australia and Canada was split between two companies. Sony took US rights, Voltage handled foreign sales. Voltage had been sold a Cuba Gooding action picture, with shootings, punch-ups and "at least one explosion." Sony wanted a feature-quality female-driven thriller that, after the DVD release, they could sell to the Lifetime Channel with the added benefit of Academy Award winner Cuba Gooding Jr. as the star. My job was to make something that would satisfy all parties.

Cuba was cast because his name on the marquee guaranteed a certain level of sales in the United States, European and Latin American DVD/TV market. However, Cuba's daily quote meant that the budget could only afford him for eight days of shooting. So the script had to be adjusted to reduce his scenes. Cuba of course knew nothing of this. He told me he would have given us more days if he had known. It was all handled by his agents, managers, and lawyers. Cuba read the script for the first time on the plane down to Queensland's Gold Coast.

The script was Canadian and had, shall we say, adaptation issues. But under coproduction rules, the Australian director could rewrite it without credit, thus preserving the appearance of creative parity between the international partners. In the development process my first rewrite, with a healthy assist from my writing partner, Dennis Pratt, had attempted to create twists and turns to a standard murder mystery: revealing that the FBI agent that Cuba plays was in fact the mastermind behind the whole conspiracy. Now there's some meat for the star to chew on! Not what Sony wanted—I was told. So back to formula, the FBI agent had to remain the hero.

So here's the eventual story we shot: When FBI Agent John Nelson's (Cuba Gooding Jr.) key informant, Miles, is abducted and shot, all that's left is a severed finger. In order to find a new lead, Nelson travels to New York City to inform widowed magazine reporter Rebecca Scott (Emmanuelle Vaugier) that her long dead husband, Miles, had, in fact, only recently been murdered. He had faked his first death. Perplexed, Ms. Scott joins Agent Nelson in the wealthy enclave of Australia's Gold Coast to investigate her late husband's secrets, but the two become the target of unknown attackers.

Sounds like a 90s Lifetime movie, doesn't it? As for the final twist—the dead guy is not really dead, he had faked his demise for a second time—you can see it coming, because, well, it's been done a few times before. What I hoped would spark up the material was chemistry between the two leading actors. I liked Canadian actress Emmanuelle Vaugier's self-assured performance as the no-nonsense reporter/widow. As for Cuba, he brought a wry charm to his world-weary cop. I thought some of their banter worked quite well.

I had been told that Cuba Gooding Jr. could be "difficult", but he never was. Cuba enjoyed visiting his favorite haunts in Surfers Paradise, where he had spent time with Paul Hogan on *Lightning Jack*. He appreciated my shooting all his scenes each day in a block. I organized the schedule so that he could arrive, work continuously till done, then have free time to enjoy. He had no problem working a full day, either. He just wanted to work the whole time he spent on the set. We quickly had a good rapport. We talked about the ups and downs of our respective careers, how we both found ourselves stuck in DTV. He talked about the movie roles he wished he had not turned down: *Amistad*, *Collateral*, *Hotel Rwanda*, particularly Taylor Hackford's Ray Charles biopic, for which Jamie Foxx earned the best actor Oscar. Later I was glad to see that Cuba's role as O.J. in *The People v. O.J. Simpson—American Crime Story* miniseries gave his career a well-deserved boost.

Back in LA I took him to the Beverly Hills Fencers Club, outfitted him with jacket, mask and glove, then introduced him to epée. Cuba had studied Japanese martial arts as a teenager, so he had a natural aptitude. I showed him the basics, how to take the blade, to parry and riposte. Then, *en garde*! It was an interesting moment. From the first clash of blades, we changed from collaborators to competitors. It was a fun duel. Fencing, (*L'escrime*) allows you to indulge your warrior instincts without inflicting injury on your opponent, to feel the adrenaline rush of what was once hand-to-hand combat with a deadly outcome, while conforming to the rules of a sport. Nothing like the satisfying sound of the buzzer when the tip of your blade fixes on your opponent's wrist. Cuba enjoyed it. We've spoken a couple of times since. Cuba gave me a good report when John Cusack called him to ask: "How was that Australian director you worked with?"

When my name was first submitted to John Cusack as the proposed director of a movie to be shot in Australia, he looked at my recent credits—direct to video and cable movies—and rejected me. Then apparently someone who knew my work said to him: "Why don't you look at *Dead End Drive-In*?" Which he did. That turned *no* into *maybe*.

Rewind for the backstory: An American script entitled *Hard Drive* had been acquired by the Canadian coproducer of *Absolute Deception*, who planned to set it in Australia. I was told it had been written as a vehicle for action star Jason Statham as a master thief who robs the corporate criminals who framed him for a robbery he carried out on their behalf. He books a driving lesson with a former racecar driver now working as an instructor, longing to race again, then tricks him into becoming his getaway driver, after he robs the corporate crooks, a fractious Odd Couple bromance develops as they evade both cops and crooks.

There was some car action but the script mostly featured Jason Statham style punch ups and gunfights. There were echoes of Martin Brest's *Midnight Run*, where Robert De Niro's bail bondsman and Charles Grodin's escaped embezzler squabble and bond while on the run from corrupt cops,

The producers sent it to Jason Statham, but he passed. They moved on to Jean-Claude Van Damme. The script was retooled accordingly, eliminating Statham-esque British idiom and lengthy speeches. But JCVD passed. Then in March we got a hot tip. There was a gap in John Cusack's schedule. A deal could be made, it transpired, with three stipulations: Cusack had director and costar approval, the last script intended for Jean-Claude Van Damme had to be rewritten to his satisfaction, and Cusack's scenes had to be shot by Saturday June 22nd, so he could meet his scheduled date on a David Cronenberg movie. After initially rejecting me, then being persuaded to see *Dead End Drive-In* and apparently some other titles, Cusack was ready to discuss the script with me. We were still at the *maybe* stage. I've enjoyed every decade of Cusack's work and recognized that it would be an honor to work with a seasoned star whose screen persona is always interesting. We met at his elegant Malibu beachside home on April 4th. His annotated copy of the script indicated he had issues with almost every page.

```
 you wanted!

Roberts shakes his head.

                    ROBERTS
          I never wanted this.

                    KELLER
          It's not a game, Roberts!

                    ROBERTS
          I'm not the one playing with other
          people's lives!

                    KELLER
          Yeah, well, you didn't seem to mind
          until you blew that guy's chest out
          two miles back!  Shit, or get off
          the god damn pot, man!
```

*Do better*

*sloppy writing*

He wanted changes to suit his screen persona and make the bank robber less physical and more cerebral. He was not particularly interested in either Van Damme or Statham style fights. I saw some books on the table by anti-globalization activist Arundhati Roy. Her latest was *Capitalism: A Ghost Story*. Hmm. So I suggested to John Cusack that the bank robber character would be more interesting if he espoused Cusack's own political world view, as expressed in his published op-eds: "The game's rigged." He could point the finger at the perpetrators.

The conversation took off from there. The original script had a Bond/Blofeld-style international criminal mastermind who ordered the garroting of a subordinate in his presence at a board meeting, while he took a phone call. The Bond franchise and its derivatives have done this scene many times. Cusack wanted to make the villains corrupt bank executives—*banksters*—upon whom he was exacting revenge. After five hours of brainstorming, Cusack told me he was happy for me to proceed with a draft. Cusack's stop date of June 22nd meant that I had to get the rewrite approved by him and in time for prep to start on May 15th with the shoot three weeks later. My writing partner was once again a great help. We had a first draft by May 1st. Cusack gave us notes. The process continued during prep and throughout the shoot. During the rewrite, we looked for an actor to play the reluctant getaway driver. Cusack liked the idea of Don Cheadle (*Hotel Rwanda, The Guard*), but Cheadle passed. We then chose Thomas Jane (*Boogie Nights, Deep Blue Sea*), whose three seasons of HBO's *Hung* showed a flair for comedy.

Cameras rolled on June 6th. D Day was certainly on my mind that morning! I had good reason to feel I was battling considerable odds. The Australian producer and the Canadian producer were in conflict from the moment the picture was greenlit. There had only been time for two weeks of fully staffed preproduction. Yet I did not get a 1st AD till the second week. Funds were slow in arriving. But regardless of whatever goes awry in every film—and plenty does—it's essential for a director to maintain outward calm. You are visualizer, brigade commander, occasional therapist. Everyone wants to feel the movie will be great. Regardless of your private misgivings, it's your job to convince them it *will* be great, and indeed to make it so. The budget provided for 18x10-hour days of shooting. 180 camera hours. So when it rains all day on the traveling car dialogue scenes intended for sunny backgrounds…go with it, shoot through the wipers. In fact, it added texture to the scene.

I have always enjoyed working on Australia's Gold Coast. I was told my plan for a beachfront chase would be prohibitively expensive in location and parking fees. But if you approach local government officials in the right way, they can be your project's best friend. The Surfers Paradise City Council let me run a car chase along the esplanade and onto the beach, because those officials as kids had enjoyed the chases in *BMX Bandits*. Sometimes your past comes back to haunt you in a good way. Total location and parking fee for the day: a generous reduction to $750. Nice.

After evading the police in a driving instructor's car, the heroes swap to "a special car" for the rest of the journey. It had to be something appealing to the benched race car driver for him to be tempted to continue as getaway driver, yet not a vehicle that would attract attention like a Ferrari. I made the mistake of choosing a reconditioned 80s muscle car, that turned out not to have been reconditioned enough. It was constantly breaking down, and worse, incapable of reaching the expected speeds of a car chase. Imagine you're shooting a Roy Rogers western and Trigger goes lame. Compounding the problem was the fact that we could not afford to damage any of the vehicles. Stunt choreography had to be in tune with that imperative: the stunt of the near miss was the order of the day. The exploding SUV was a stock shot. Camera and editing tricks helped a little, but our heroes' getaway from the biker gang lacks credibility.

When Thomas Jane came on board, the comedic chemistry between him and John Cusack was immediately apparent. I incorporated input from both of them, and encouraged improvisation. The scene where Cusack calls the bank executive who is his target of revenge and spews a list of hilarious scatological insults aimed at the man's wife is pure Cusack. Thomas Jane's ability to adapt to the moment was evident in the scene when he leaves the getaway car and tries to surrender but runs back to the car when met with a hail of police bullets. Somehow, on take one, the car door wouldn't open, so without skipping a beat he leapt feet first through the open window into the driver's seat and roared away. We didn't bother fixing the door for Take Two. Magic. It was a joy to work with such gifted actors. At the end of the 18-day shoot, we all thought we had a quirky character-based action comedy that would provide amusement on DVD and Netflix.

But Voltage did not like the picture. The original Statham/JCVD script they expected to see on the screen had been full of stunts we could not afford, and was skewed more to hard action than comedy. What Voltage got was an Odd Couple action comedy with a wry tone throughout. They hated the Mad Grannie scene, where a septuagenarian tries to arrest them wielding a .357 Magnum, probably the funniest sequence in the film, but it supplied the .357 Magnum, vital for the next scene, so it survived, thankfully. There was tinkering nonetheless. They cut out the shot of sheep watching as Cusack and Jane have their absurd standoff in the field next to them, which got a big laugh at the preview Voltage attended. This and other nips and tucks were supposed to reduce the comedy level. How would that help sales? To emphasize action, they lengthened the marina chase with repeated angles, which diminished the impact rather than added adrenalin. They got the composer Bryce Jacobs to throw out the quirky music score he had composed and start again with classic Zimmer-esque driving rhythms. He followed the brief well, but the film lost some originality as a result. Greater quirkiness would have mitigated the implausibility of the plot. As an author I felt thwarted in the finer details of the creative process.

Let me put "author" in context. A director is as much an author as a screenwriter, although of a different kind. A screenwriter generates stories; a director interprets those stories with images and sound to form a coherent narrative, calibrates tone, chooses visual style, guides collaborators both behind and in front of the

camera, to realize the authorial vision. The greater the control a director has over these elements, supported by an adequate budget, the closer that he or she gets to its realization. Each director has a unique take. Give ten directors the same script, and adequate resources, and ten quite different movies will be made. Clearly, some versions would please audiences more than others. Management want to protect their investment by conforming the product to what they perceive will lead to a successful outcome, which is not unreasonable. However, the best product comes out of an honest and mutually nurturing relationship between management and creatives.

In France, respect for the director's contribution to the process has always been high. Even so, French directors are still subject to the traditional law of the marketplace: it's your vision, but if the public reject it at the box office, you will have trouble getting backing for your next project. A French director is the author of his film, a mandate that has not caused the sky to fall in on the French movie industry.

*Drive Hard* was made as a Direct to Blu Ray/DVD, with subsequent sales to streaming platforms across the world, though action fans taken in by the artwork were sorely disappointed. In the US, the movie was given a 1-week theatrical release in a dozen or so theaters across the US, where critics pounced on it as a cynical deal-driven exercise. They had been sharpening their knives for John Cusack anyway because of his recent lower budget DTV movies, so they did not find the film funny at all. Further fueling their scorn was trade paper publicity listed the budget as a handsome $12M. In fact, the audited budget was under $5.6M. Cast fees took up 2M of that. I was told I only had a $2M below-the-line budget to actually shoot the movie. Not sure where the rest went. The credits contain seventeen executive producers. At Cannes that year a Voltage executive advised another sales company against approving me for a bigger budget movie I had written with Dennis Pratt. No good deed will go unpunished.

"Never give up. Never surrender," to quote my favorite Sci-fi comedy *Galaxy Quest*. Again.

# CHAPTER 45
## TV Melodramas

I was lucky enough to direct two films in 1998. *Happy Face Murders* was one. A second was made for Saban's Family Channel, set up as a Canadian/German co-production and pre-sold to Germany's ARD network. I qualified on the EU side. Conceptually it was a *fear of pandemic* movie, written under the title *The Fourth Horseman*, referencing the fourth horseman of the Apocalypse, namely pestilence. In this case, the disease strikes a cruise ship. The proposed title was way too obscure for a mainstream audience. There's a memo from an executive proposing the title: *Sea-sick: Epidemic Afloat*. Sanity prevailed, and the new title became the generic but promotable *Voyage of Terror*. In view of the 2020 coronavirus spread within the cruise ship Diamond Princess, the premise has proven to be unfortunately prescient. (The most gripping realistic fictional film made about the spread of a pandemic is Steven Soderbergh's *Contagion*.)

The premise: An infectious disease researcher is on a holiday cruise with her truculent 15-year-old daughter when an Ebola-type virus attacks the ship's passengers and crew (you know the kid's gonna catch it). While politicians wrangle about the risk to the mainland population, the ship gets quarantined offshore, if necessary, till everybody dies. Can she find a cure?

There was a good development executive on the project, Amy Goldberg. She wanted to explore the moral and political issues inherent in the story by expanding a subplot about the White House's management of the crisis. For some reason the writer had sole credit but was unavailable to make the changes the network wanted, which were considerable. I offered a new outline in which the President's chief advisor plots to discredit the President to boost his own career by manipulating the crisis. Politically nonspecific, but critical of government. Opportunities for guest stars with some meat to feed on. Ms. Goldberg went with it.

Shooting had to start in five weeks. I was given eleven days to complete a new draft, which must also incorporate input from the German network. Once again, I

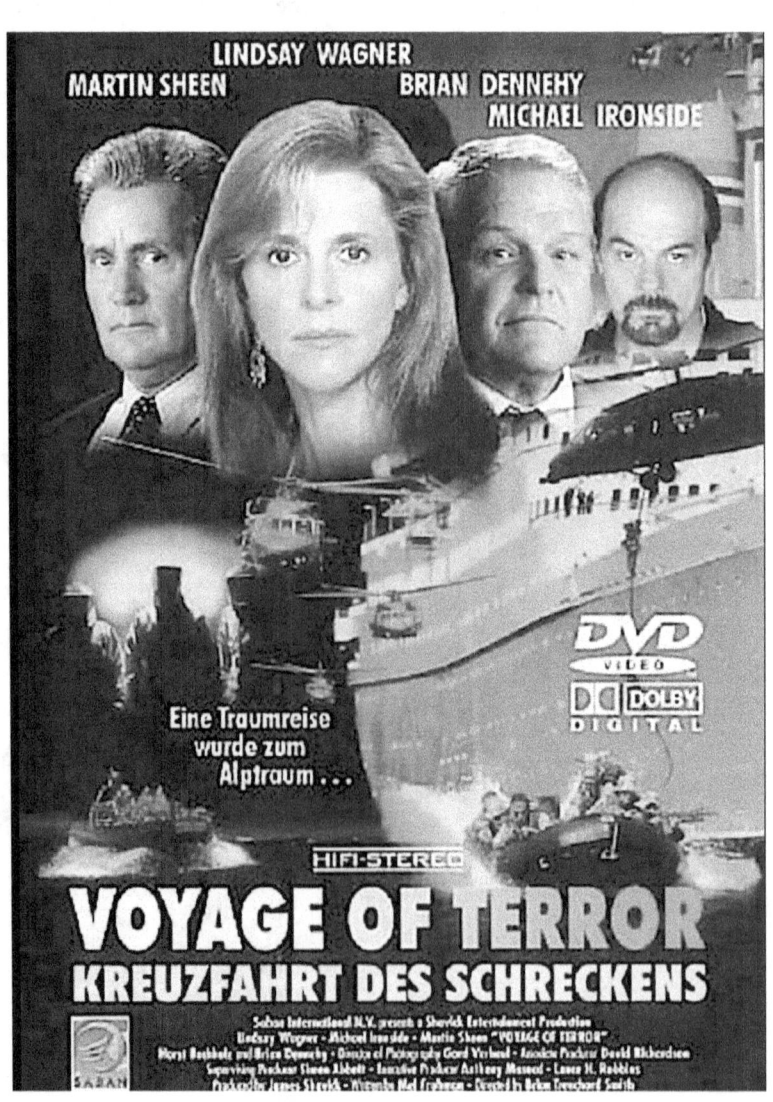

LINDSAY WAGNER
MARTIN SHEEN
BRIAN DENNEHY
MICHAEL IRONSIDE

Eine Traumreise wurde zum Alptraum ...

HIFI-STEREO

# VOYAGE OF TERROR
## KREUZFAHRT DES SCHRECKENS

brought in Dennis Pratt as a consultant. Luckily the new screenplay was good enough to snag Lindsay Wagner (*The Bionic Woman*) as the scientist, Brian Dennehy (*First Blood*) as the President, and Martin Sheen (*Apocalypse Now*) as his evil Iago, Michael Ironside (*Starship Troopers*) as the mutinous first mate.

As a bonus for shooting in Vancouver, we picked up William B. Davis (*X Files'* Cancer Man) for a key supporting role. As Lindsay Wagner's daughter we cast 17-year-old Katharine Isabelle, soon to star in the

hit horror franchise *Ginger Snaps*. That's a good marquee for basic cable in 1998, but quite a complex production in eighteen shooting days.

No cruise line was going to let a *virus movie* shoot on one of their ships. Really? No, the shots of the liner on the ocean would have to be CGI. For the exterior deck, we were able to secure a ferry tied up to the dock, that nonetheless provided some open water backgrounds. As for the interiors, a cruise ship is just a floating hotel. Using common design elements like Orion Star Shipping Line signage, I was able to unify a combination of locations—hotel suites, corridors, dining room, swimming pool, even shopping mall escalators—into a believable cruise ship. To that end, I did a sequence that roamed throughout the ship, showing the spread of the infection, from the initial mosquito bite (an extreme closeup stock shot) through handshakes, food sharing, sneezes and kisses. Studio sets were built for the ship's bridge, ballroom/hospital and the Oval Office. Choosing locations, finding the look of the film is a part of the process I particularly enjoy. It grounds me in the story and how to shoot it.

Brian Dennehy was perfect as the US President. He had a natural gravitas. Whenever he came onto the Oval Office set for his next shot, our ever-chatty Canadian crew fell silent.

It was great to work with Martin Sheen, a truly admirable man: excellent actor, idealist, and political activist. He's been arrested many times for protesting social injustice. In May that year, he had gone through the trauma of his son Charlie's arrest and near death from repeated drug overdoses. He initiated an intervention to force his son into rehab and separate him from his enablers. I offered to introduce Charlie Sheen to the sport of fencing, with its naturally-induced high and good fellowship. Martin thought it was a good idea, but nothing came of it.

Lindsay Wagner was a dream to work with, a consummate actress able to make the most expository dialogue natural and interesting. She would occasionally spoof her Bionic Woman character by running onto the set in slow motion. Like all stunning TV divas of a certain age, she was very particular about her lighting in medium and close up coverage.

"I can take any amount of frontal light," she told me and cameraman Gord Verhuel.

She produced a mirror to check the light level on her face then signaled for two lamps to be brought closer. You don't argue with your leading lady on how she should be lit. We came up with a fast solution for future occasions: hang a white sheet in front of her and blast it with lamps on a dimmer. Dial up, dial down as she dictated. She loved that.

It's interesting when two actors playing characters that are in conflict clash at first sight. All cast were seated ready for the table reading of the script. German star Horst Bucholz, whose remarkable body of work was unfamiliar to many people in the room, arrived late with a brief apology.

"Does anyone mind if I smoke?" said Horst, pulling a cigarette out of a pack.

"Yes, I do," Lindsay said firmly. Tobacco smoke would make her ill and she would have to leave. Round One to Lindsay. Horst played the proud captain of the cruise ship, with whom Lindsay as the epidemiologist repeatedly clashed. In fact, their personal friction worked well for their scenes together, and they parted the best of friends.

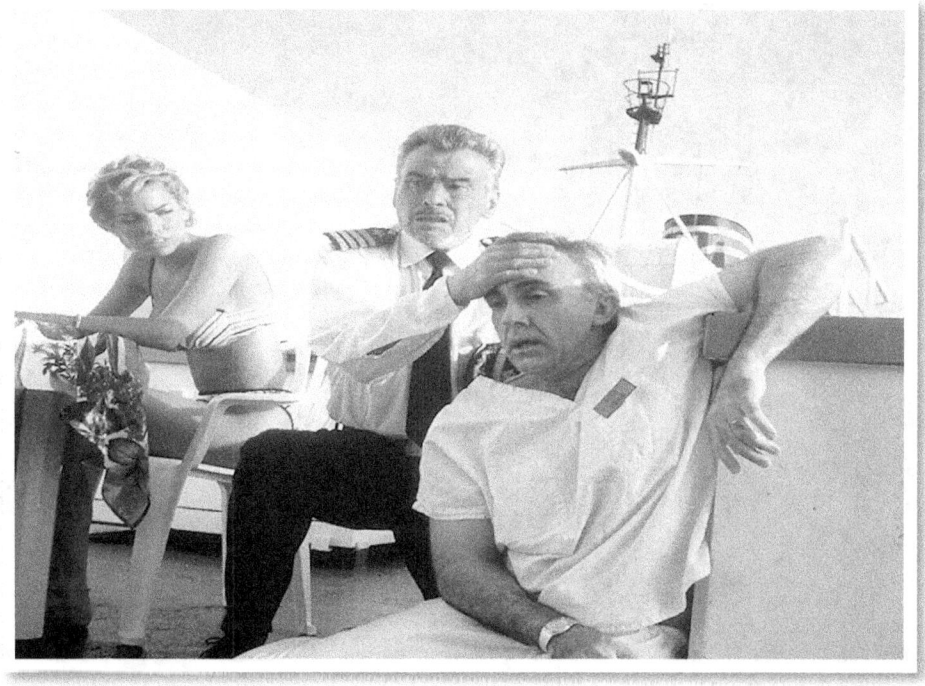

I wanted to make Horst feel appreciated upon arrival, so I booked a special table at a top Vancouver eatery appropriate for a visiting German movie star. He greeted me warmly, sat down and lit a cigarette. A waiter stepped up and told him smoking was not allowed in this restaurant nor any in Vancouver, but out of deference to an apparent celebrity he offered to move us to a small screened-off anteroom. "We will look at this room and see if it is suitable," Horst stated in an imperious tone. In fact, anywhere he could satisfy his nicotine craving was suitable, even a table screened off by the kitchen door. We sat down to an excellent three-course meal with tobacco breaks. Horst was a good actor, a decent fellow and a great conversationalist. He had had a remarkable life. Born in 1933, evacuated to Silesia during WWII, and later Czechoslovakia, he developed an interest in languages. At seventeen he returned to the rubble of postwar Berlin and started working in theater. His ability to speak other European languages including English got him into film work by doing foreign-language voice dubbing. Supporting roles in German movies followed. After a juvenile delinquent movie, *Teenage Wolfpack*, Horst Buchholz was being promoted as the German James Dean.

His first English-language movie, opposite burgeoning child star Hayley Mills, was *Tiger Bay*. His performance as a Polish seaman on the run brought him to Hollywood's attention. Horst moved to LA. With his enormously appealing smile, he was hot for a while. But regardless of talent, happenstance can affect a career. He was offered the role of Tony in *West Side Story* (1961) and Sherif Ali in *Laurence of Arabia* (1962) but schedules of both movies clashed with films on which he was already booked. He particularly regretted that on his agent's advice, he turned down the Clint Eastwood role in *A Fistful of Dollars*. Just one of those movies would have confirmed Horst's A List standing. Horst told me that his particular look, high cheekbones with olive skin, enabled him to play different ethnicities: the wannabe Mexican gunfighter in *The Magnificent Seven*, the Hindu assassin of Gandhi in *Nine Hours to Rama*, Marco Polo in *Marco the Magnificent*. Horst recounted how Orson Welles played Marco's tutor in what was intended as a 2-day role. Welles kept fluffing his lines on the second day, holding up shooting, requiring him to be hired for a third day. Orson confided to Horst that of course he knew his lines; he just needed the additional $25K, his daily rate, to finance shooting on his next personal project.

Hollywood heat wanes, and by the seventies most of Horst's work was in European movies and television, where he was in constant demand. The year before *Voyage of Terror* he had played a key supporting role in the Oscar-winning Italian film *Life Is Beautiful*. Horst was one of the few German actors to become, albeit briefly, a Hollywood star. I'm surprised more has not been written about his remarkable 50-year career.

*Voyage of Terror* ended up a serviceable TV melodrama, undermined by poor CGI. After spending more than was customary on cast, it would have been prudent to give the Canadian VFX vendor an extra 30—50K on better visual effects of the ship, helicopters, submarines etc. Budgetary restrictions to these sequences undermined the credibility of the story.

I would make a second *fear of pandemic* melodrama in 2002. Both films now seem even more superficial and exploitative in the wake of Covid-19.

*"THE PARADISE VIRUS is a dull epidemic-on-an-island TV movie from a director who really should know better."*

So wrote one reviewer from his lofty perch, ignoring the realities that face a filmmaker competing for work in Hollywood. While developing worthy projects, you still have to pay the bills, and that means accepting firm offers with imminent start dates, even when you know the project is creatively flawed

*Deadly virus sweeps tropical island* would seem a strange Valentine's Day programming choice for the faith-and-family based PAX network whom Regent Entertainment were courting. Vomiting and bloody sores were out. Plague-lite would have to be the approach. The emphasis would be faith in God, rather than dependence on medical science. I had made one virus telemovie for $2.8M at a Vancouver studio. I would have to make this one for around $800K. The odds of creating a silk purse out of a sow's ear, were probably not good; but why not give it my best shot?

The storyline was familiar. Or as one critic called it, a bucket of clichés. Just like *Voyage of Terror*: "…*a brilliant and beautiful virologist must interrupt her holiday to stem the spread of a deadly virus that could claim her child among its victims.*" I brought Dennis Pratt in to help me enliven the formula, but we were working in a creative and budgetary straitjacket.

The casting strategy was to give the role of "*beautiful, brilliant virologist*" to a soap opera star, in the hope that she would bring her daytime audience to nighttime. Susan Lucci (Emmy Award winner for *All My Children*) said no, Melody Thomas Scott (*The Young and*

*the Restless*) said yes. A good choice; like Lucci, she had a big following worldwide. We matched her with Lorenzo Lamas, whose nine years in the nighttime soap *Falcon Crest* and five years in the action series *Renegade* would draw both male and female viewers.

Sadly there was no dramatic reason to give him shirtless scenes.

The key supporting role was the local religious leader Joseph, who refuses medical attention on the grounds that only God can save him. He survives, and thus becomes patient zero from whom a serum can be made. You see, just leave it to God… Best not to think about all the people who died before the serum was created. At the auditions in LA a seasoned but relatively unknown black actor knocked it out of the park. He was short, wiry, bald, with a quiet yet commanding presence. Sud-

denly Joseph's dialogue had meaning, nuance and conviction. I could see him as the local Gandhi. He was perfect. There was hope for this movie yet. But not for long.

There had recently been a sharp downturn in prices offered by European networks for run-of-the-mill American telemovies. The market was glutted. Regent was struggling to make the foreign presales hit the required number. The current lead cast did not score highly enough. The solution was to cast a German actor whose name would get a higher price from Germany, and enhance all European sales estimates. My choice for Joseph was overruled before his deal memo was issued and he was replaced by Ralf Moeller, a six-foot-six former bodybuilder friend of Arnold Schwarzenegger. He had been in *Gladiator*, then played TV's *Conan* for two seasons on syndicated TV. A gigantic white man giving spiritual guidance in a guttural accent to an island of mainly black people? Really? Sales dictate casting, too often. My heart sank.

The designated location was Grand Turk Island, part of the Turks and Caicos Islands, less than an hour's flight from Miami. The Islands are, in fact, British territory, thus, at that time, eligible for EU tax benefits. This enabled a German group to provide financing to Regent Entertainment for this and several other films. My British passport fitted into this arrangement. Regent made me producer as well as director. Due to a 6-week delay in the arrival of the promised funds, *The Paradise Virus* became the fastest movie I have ever made. Funds may be late, but the designated air date February 14th was not going to move. Finally, just before Christmas, we were off to the races.

Here's how it went. I arrived on December 26th with a few key people for six days of frantic prep. Shooting (on 35mm) started on January 2nd for two 6-day weeks. Then I flew back to LA, where two editors had been assembling the footage. We had five days to make a director's cut for the network to view over the weekend. Their minor notes arrived Monday, and were carried out by Tuesday. Composer David Reynolds whipped up an excellent heart-tugging score in two weeks. The sound was mixed and the film delivered on February 11th, three days before its Valentine's Day premiere. Seven weeks from start of prep to broadcast… Phew!

Grand Turk Island, three miles long, one mile wide, is a world-renowned scuba diving destination. I had time for one dive, exploring a shallow wreck, cruising over startled sandworms that quickly shrank from sight, following a turtle as it did lazy circles around me. Only one movie had used Grand Turk Island as a location before we did.

In June 1941, *Bahama Passage* starring Sterling Hayden and Madeleine Carroll was shot there by Paramount in beautiful Three Strip Technicolor. Hayden and Carroll were secretly engaged yet never kissed in

the movie. Hayden's most memorable performance came late in life as the paranoid Brigadier General Jack D. Ripper, in Stanley Kubrick's *Dr. Strangelove*. One of Grand Turk's inhabitants who watched *Bahama Passage* being shot in 1941 still lived on the island. She was, in 2002, in her late sixties. We were introduced. She told me how she had watched Sterling Hayden (who has his shirt off for most of the movie) playing scenes with the beautiful Madeleine Carroll. I invited her to be an extra, and featured her in the hotel garden scenes with Melody Thomas Scott. It made her day.

The 2-week shoot was a wild exhilarating ride which I had the pleasure of sharing with our younger son Alexander, then about to start college. Directors or executives who bring their progeny to location purportedly to work on the movie often inflict a burden on the production staff, when their kids just treat it as a vacation, but Alex showed he was an asset as a general production assistant, running errands, painting sets in prep, and handling craft service during the shoot, not an easy job on a shoestring budget. I was (and am) so proud of him.

We were lucky to start shooting on the designated Monday. If we hadn't, I doubt if we would have made our delivery date. The camera/lighting package had arrived by barge at the island's dock a few days before, but the crane to unload it had broken down, requiring a replacement part. Things work on island time in the Caribbean. The port authorities seemed in no hurry to repair the crane until they learned that the island's beer supply was nearly exhausted and the new consignment was in the barge along with our equipment. At 10 p.m. on New Year's Day we got our cameras and lights. No time for lens tests. Day One started the next morning.

Not an auspicious start, either. There were, and probably still are, wild dogs on the island, as well as wild horses and donkeys. Script supervisor Lisa McNeil on her way from her hotel to the pre-dawn crew call, found herself being stalked, then chased, then bitten on the leg by a wild dog. We had her flown to Caicos for medical examination to ensure she did not get rabies. She bravely returned.

Melody Thomas Scott and Lorenzo Lamas both did solid jobs making their characters appealing to the audience. Lorenzo displayed more emotional range than his regular roles offered and was pleased for the opportunity. Many ladies on the island were fans of *The Young and the Restless*. Melody, always gracious about

autographs, was sometimes mobbed by admirers, calling out her feisty soap character's name: "Nikki!… Nikki!" Hey, what if *The Young and the Restless'* wild card Nikki, the parricide, alcoholic, much married, divorced and widowed stripper, with PTSD and multiple sclerosis etc., yes, what if that Nikki had come to the island and cured the outbreak? Now there's a movie…

Ralf Moeller can be very effective in the right role (*Gladiator*). Arnold Schwarzenegger left a "break a leg" message on his voicemail before Ralf's first scene. Ralf was a nice guy, easy to work with. I helped him all I could. He knew he was miscast and did his absolute best. He just could not overcome the unlikelihood of being the leader of a religious community on a Caribbean island.

My local liaison was Arthur Smith, a charming black man around fifty, with a shiny bald head. At our first meeting, he said: "Your name is Smith, my name is Smith. We must be related."

"Brothers under the skin," I responded. Our wry sensibilities clicked.

On our third meeting, Arthur said to me: "You know, you should be bald like me. You would look good. You should try it."

He gestured his two companions, tall, muscular, and shiny bald like Arthur.

"Sure, perhaps I should, someday," I said playing along.

"How about tomorrow?"

Arthur pulled a round plastic container from his pocket.

"This is what I use," he said, "depilatory cream, better than shaving it every day. You just rub it in…"

Arthur explained the process, assuring me the cream was non-toxic.

"Go on, be bald…like us…"

"OK…" I said, hesitantly.

"Bald, at breakfast tomorrow," said Arthur, pressing the container into my hand. He and his friends turned and left. It seemed I had been set a test. Are we brothers under the skin?

I arrived back at the apartment which I shared with Alex and Dennis Pratt. I rubbed the solution from the container into my hair till it became a thick lather. After the ten minutes designated by the instructions, Dennis and Alex took a pair of spatulas from the kitchen and scraped my skull clean of hair. The few snippets that escaped fell to the razor. I entered the predawn crew breakfast next morning in my customary baseball cap. As I approached Arthur and his friends with no sign of baldness, I sensed a look of disappointment. Then I doffed my cap with a sweeping low bow, revealing my polished chrome dome. Arthur gave me a hug. The crew applauded. The island was ours thereafter.

With Arthur's seal of approval, I got on the local radio station to request volunteers for our mass evacuation scene. A dozen pleasure boat owners were only too happy to rush along the marina for our cameras, carrying hastily-packed suitcases, dragging wives and children. They piled into their expensive watercraft and powered towards the open sea. Good production value sequences for a round of drinks at the hotel. And everyone had a good time.

Except, perhaps, those in America on Valentine's Day who said to their beloved: "After our romantic dinner, let's go home and watch that virus movie!"

The French DVD offered a serious virus movie

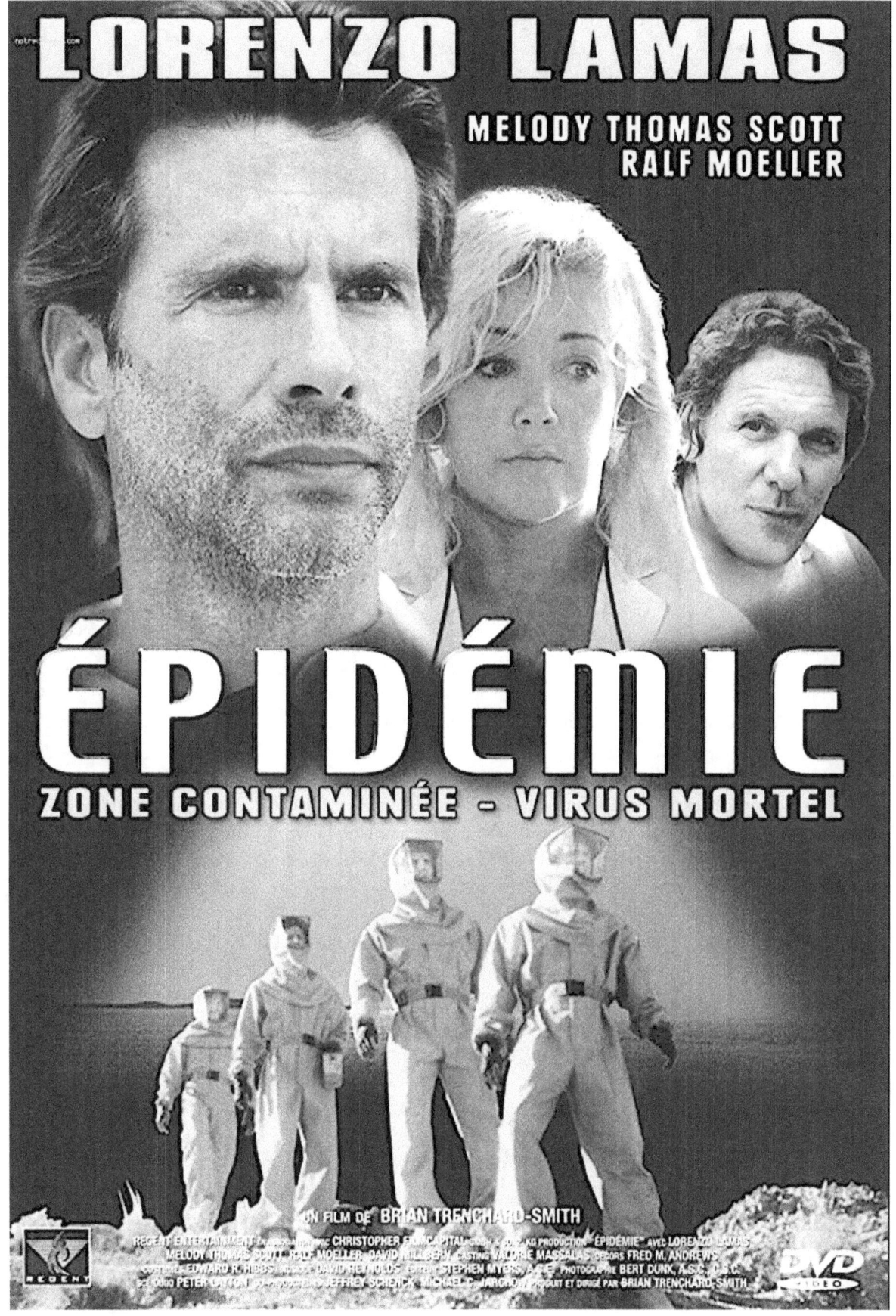

In Asia the artwork was digitally altered to add blood for a horror sell. Boy, were those customers disappointed…

A third melodrama, of which I have fond memories, is *Long Lost Son* (2006).

Regent sent me back to Grand Turk Island. I recall being in the bar of the Grand Turk Hotel after a tough shooting day. I was stating my position about a problematic location deal to 1st AD Quentin Whitwell and German executive producer Andreas Hess, whose company, in conjunction with Regent, was funding *Long Lost Son* for the Lifetime Channel.

"We can't let them dictate the terms," I said,

"No," agreed Andreas, "We dictate the terms. We Germans make the best dictators."

Jaws dropped all round. Then Andreas turned from Buster Keaton stone face to Cheshire Cat grin. Andreas' sense of humor was always taking us by surprise. I was tempted to offer my *Fawlty Towers goose stepping and don't mention the war* routine, but I exercised restraint. Andreas was also an accomplished scuba diver, and a well-connected man across European television networks. His wife and business partner Sylvia produced his films. This was the second telemovie I was making for them on Grand Turk. They trusted me. Trust is invigorating to a director.

Our first film together, *The Paradise Virus*, shot in twelve days, had been a foreign sales success. Now I was getting a leisurely fourteen days to shoot *Long Lost Son*, a script presold to the Lifetime Network in the US by a trio of talented US producers. These producers and the German producers initially did not see eye-to-eye on a lot of matters, and I sometimes found myself playing diplomat between grumbling parties during prep. But once we got going and people liked the dailies, (which because of our remoteness, we had to view via FTP site each night), things settled down. Everyone could see they were going to get a saleable film.

The premise was this: Kristen (Gabrielle Anwar) has made a painful adjustment to the loss of her 4-year-old son Mark, after her estranged husband Quinn (Craig Sheffer) had taken him for the weekend and had gone sailing in a dangerous storm fourteen years previously. Both were presumed drowned. She has remarried and moved on. But while watching a vacation video friends took while on a remote Caribbean island, Kristen sees a brief glimpse of two faces in the background of one shot—the faces, she is convinced, are of ex-husband Quinn and her son Mark (Chase Crawford), now eighteen. Kristen immediately flies to the small Caribbean island. Nothing is going to stop her finding her *Long Lost Son*.

That's a great hook for a heart-tugging weepie, dedicated to devoted mothers everywhere, and I went for the emotional jugular. The star who accepted the leading role was Gabrielle Anwar (*Scent of A Woman*, *The Tudors*, *Burn Notice*).  She loved the script, but informed us two days before flying to join us that she hated most of her dialogue and was rewriting it herself. The two producer groups were not happy. It took some fancy footwork to lower the emotional temperature and persuade them to give her some creative freedom. Good actors are good detectives. They analyze the whys and wherefores of every beat in a scene, looking for inconsistencies or opportunities. Gabrielle dumped contrived moments, eliminated bad lines, and strengthened her character while I made sure that none of the lump-in-the-throat power of the story was lost in her changes.

Craig Sheffer (*A River Runs through It, One Tree Hill*) played her estranged husband. The onscreen fractious chemistry between them derived from the fact that they had lived together in the 1990s and had a 13-year-old daughter, whom they brought to the island. Gabrielle's current husband and their two infant children also visited (he and Gabrielle divorced later that year). Quite an ensemble. Chinese movie proverb: may you live in interesting *dinner* times. Ah, well.

I liked Craig Sheffer, straightforward, talented, no-nonsense. He had been Showtime's original choice for my *Sahara* remake, in the Jim Belushi role. After a few scenes with Craig, I rewound *Sahara* in my mind. Yes, Sheffer would have been great, too. I enjoyed working with him. Likewise, Gabrielle—a sharp-witted, irreverent free spirit.

Everybody loved her. On a day off, Gabrielle and a bunch of us went via a conch fisherman's boat to nearby Gibbs Cay, where baby stingrays gather in the shallows to be fed by hand.

They are docile creatures, particularly towards food providers. The fishermen supplied chopped squid pieces which the rays vacuumed from our fingers. On the way back we spotted a pod of dolphins swimming alongside. Gabrielle pulled off her T-shirt and dove in to swim beside them. I believe one dolphin did allow her to run her hand along its flank before swimming off. Communing with friendly creatures is a great mid-shoot stress reliever.

I was adopted by one of Grand Turk's stray dogs, who would be sitting at my door every night I returned to my garden apartment. I would always bring back enough dinner for two. Abandoned by her owner, she had a tumor and was dying, so neighbors told me. She would sit beside me on the sofa with her chin on my lap watching CNN, as I did my shot list for the next day. She craved human companionship and affection. She would even go swimming with me on my days off. Directors under pressure benefit from pet therapy. Terminally ill animals need human therapy. Fair exchange. I was glad to have been of service. She was well cared for till she died not long after I left.

As is the custom in American television, the network casts the leads. I was allowed an opinion, and requested unknown Chace Crawford for the role of the long-lost son based on his knockout audition via FTP site. Back in LA, the hierarchy chose another actor, then happily dithered before making the offer. Suddenly their choice was gone to another project. So I got my first choice, and the movie got Chace Crawford, the future star of five seasons of *Gossip Girl*. From his first scene, I could tell this lad had a future.

A major production challenge was that the first twenty minutes of the story took place in LA, a certain amount of it written to be in heavy rain, but all fourteen days would have to be shot on sun swept Grand Turk. We could not afford even a day of 2$^{nd}$ Unit in LA. The Grand Turk Fire Department were happy to relieve their boredom by providing the rain for the few LA exteriors we could fake in local locations. Beyond that: Stock footage to the rescue! I went into the Paramount library and found what I needed: coastal aerials/heavy surf/Venice, California at dusk with storm clouds/aerials of Marina del Rey at night/the storm hitting a boat/ the search helicopter hovering over water at dusk. In earlier searches, I had come across excellent shots of sharks cruising for prey. Now I had a use for them. I created a sequence where choppy seas cause Gabrielle to fall out of her dinghy while travelling between islands. Shots taken on the surface and underwater of Gabrielle frantically swimming back to her boat were intercut with the sharks cruising the ocean floor then rising towards the surface, implicitly towards her. It's a nice little suspense sequence.

A creative challenge was the *time transition* moment, from fourteen years before to 'present day.' This was my approach:

We hear a 1993 news broadcast about President Clinton over the aerial stock shot establishing Kristen's California coastal house. The interior of the house (a Grand Turk location) is furnished and decorated in keeping with that era. Several scenes later, after Kristen hears by phone that there is no hope of finding her ex-husband and 4-year-old son alive, the camera tracks back to a wider angle as she staggers to the living room sofa and collapses in a meltdown of grief. Cut. Lock off the camera, wedge it so it cannot move, and leave it fenced off with tape. The shooting crew is done for the day, replaced by the art department who repaint the walls a different color, mingling new furniture, rugs, and décor with the old. A new TV is now where the phone used to be. The 14-year upgrade takes most of the night, during which the art pixies take care not to bump the locked off camera or tracking rails. If the focal plane along which the lens points is shifted by a fraction, the planned match dissolve will be misaligned.

The next morning the shooting crew returns. I position three new characters. We roll camera on the same locked off angle we left the night before. In a long dissolve, Gabrielle weeping on her old sofa fades away, is replaced by the same angle of the redecorated home. Tying the images together are strong structural elements common to both, like the open doorway in the background. There is now a man and a woman sitting on a brand-new sofa positioned in exactly the same place as the original one. Another man in his early 40s stands beside the new TV. The couple on the sofa chatter and laugh at their home movie of their recent Caribbean holiday, playing on the screen. The man standing beside the TV tries to disguise his boredom. A title is superimposed: "14 YEARS LATER." Are these people the new owners of the house, you wonder, till Gabrielle enters from the doorway beyond, in a new dress, with her hair tied back in a clip. The camera tracks in, to give her emphasis, reversing the pull back from Gabrielle on the old sofa shot the previous day. Dialogue quickly reveals the man standing by the TV is her new husband, and the couple are their rather tedious guests, whose insistence on showing more of their holiday videos triggers her search. I think it worked; succinct, smooth, and it propelled the story.

Post production went well. BFX Imageworks added a firework display, originally shot in 1964 for Audrey Hepburn's *Paris When It Sizzles*, to the sky above a traditional Caribbean parade, a nice splash of production value. Thirty-seven shots in all, under my bulk deal with Paramount, a bargain for $9250.

Regent introduced me to a new editor, John Blizek, who had excellent editorial taste and cut a number of my subsequent films.

The Lifetime Network got a 2.5 rating for *Long Lost Son* with almost no paid publicity. It was, for a while, among the network's most requested repeats. It was my second venture into Douglas Sirk emotional melodrama territory (*Jenny Kissed Me* in 1985 being the first). A throat-tugging score from David Reynolds, his fourth for me, helped a lot. The film is not perfect—some supporting actors were not great—but it delivered the goods for a particular audience's sensibility in the mid-2000s. Then Lifetime's management changed, along with their programming policy. No more would "Lifetime: Television for Women" be tagged in trade papers as "a place where former A-listers go to retire and D-listers dream of being discovered." Lifetime was now the channel for "couples" seeking smart, hip entertainment, not gender specific, with strong roles attractive to bigger stars. Budgets for cast were increased substantially, which meant, typical in Hollywood, that directors of their previous low budget fare were not approved for the new 'upscale' projects.

In 2010, I had the pleasure of making a light comedy with the multitalented Lea Thompson. The Hallmark Channel had commissioned a by-the-numbers family vacation movie entitled *The Cabin*. It was to be filmed in Ireland, doubling for Scotland. My British citizenship qualified me as an EU director in their financing plan. This was a great opportunity to visit the land of my maternal grandfather, whom I had never met.

The concept was this: Two American single parents of distant Scottish ancestry have each brought their children to a remote Scottish resort to attend the Meeting of the Macs, a traditional celebration of the Highland Games, caber tossing, hammer throwing and all. They are both divorced and strangers to each other, but because they both have the surname MacDougal, they are accidentally booked into the last cabin available, as if they are one family. Highly competitive, with different parenting styles, naturally they can't stand each other...at first.

Predictability was what the Hallmark Channel of 2010 wanted. As defined by their executives, the Hallmark core audience was fifty years and upward in age, and enjoyed an unchallenging movie where they could visit the kitchen for five minutes, and be quickly caught up in the story on return. I saw its clichés as an opportunity to homage two 1968 blended family comedies *Yours, Mine, and Ours* (Lucille Ball & Henry Fonda—a big success) and *With Six You Get Eggroll* (Doris Day & Brian Keith—a modest success). It's what used to be called "wholesome entertainment." Hey, I can be "wholesome". My job is to please the target audience.

My writing partner Dennis Pratt wrote the first draft but Hallmark found it too quirky and lacking in predictability. A new writer was brought in and delivered what they wanted, and he did a decent job, given the brief. In this draft, there was a subplot where one of the children had smuggled into Scotland his pet snake, which ultimately caused the cabin's finally united families to win the Tug of War event, by running up the leg and under the kilt of their strongest competitor.

Some slightly "unwholesome" images spring to mind, don't they? For different reasons I opposed this development in my notes:

*Now that Connor is American and flew in from the United States, not the UK, how did the snake escape scrutiny by airport security? I know the snake pays off in the final tug of war scene (103). But that should trigger an obligatory moment of moral correction—cheating is a bad example to kids—that muddies the family victory. Certainly, we need a reason in scene 104 or later for Connor to ask: "Why are you trying to make me a better person?"*

The network's response was to turn the snake into a tropical frog. Aviation security problem solved, right? A small frog in hand luggage would not be noticed. And that cheating thing, well, the frog gets loose by accident. You work it out…

Frogs are not the easiest thespians from whom to coax a performance. With some difficulty I achieved all the shots needed to get the frog onto the shoe, up the socks and under the kilt. When the network saw the cut, they finally recognized the inherent absurdity of their idea and instructed all shots and dialogue about the frog be cut. As it happened, in the hope that reason would prevail, I had shot the scenes in a way this could be easily done. Protect the network from itself. All part of the service.

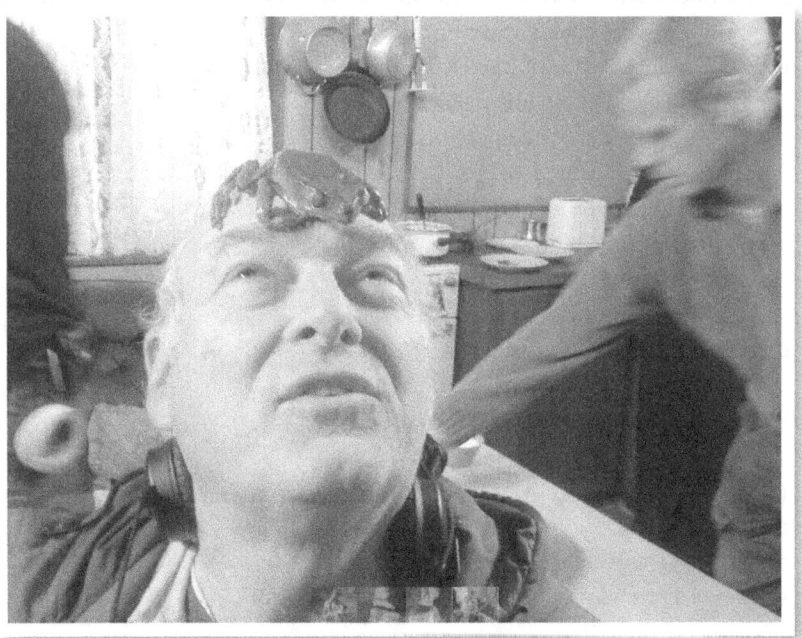

This kind of material depends on the charm of the players. Lea Thompson (*Back to the Future, Caroline in the City*) and Steven Brand (*The Scorpion King*) played the single parents. Both were highly skilled actors and worked hard to find the smiles in every scene. Lea does "adorable" very well. She's been a star for over thirty five years, yet she remains a genuinely down to earth person. Our rapport was enhanced by the fact that she was a director herself, having helmed the last two telemovies in which she had starred. There was no clash of creative wills, rather a mutual enjoyment of common skills. Lea went on to direct multiple episodes of her next series. I enjoyed her feature directing debut *The Year of Spectacular Men*.

Among the actors playing the kids, it was clear to me that 18-year-old Bel Powley, playing fourteen quite convincingly, had a future. She's been working ever since. In 2015, she starred in the indie hit *Diary of a Teenage Girl*, winning best actress at the Gotham Awards. Two Dublin actors Orla O'Rourke and Stephen D'Arcy delivered scene-stealing performances as a pair of Highland Games fanatics. It was a joy to watch them make seemingly mundane dialogue funny. Like so many I have worked with, their real talent should have earned them better careers. The acting profession is a cruel lottery.

Ireland was beautiful: 50 Shades of Green. I had such a good time. There were fans of my movies among the crew, even for my celebration of groanworthy Irish stereotypes *Leprechaun 3 & 4*, but *Turkey Shoot* was the general favorite. The production services company in Dublin was a well-oiled machine, *The Cabin* was the third in a line of five telemovies shot back to back with the same crew, each in 20x10-hour days. It all went smoothly. My one stylistic flourish by Hallmark standards was to do a training montage in multi-panel split screens. The reviews were as predictable as the film:

*"The plot is contrived, predictable, almost unworthy of a Hallmark movie."*

*"…despite being on the corny side 'The Cabin' does still entertain with Lea Thompson and Steven Brand making for appealing single parents…"*

Hey, there's nothing wrong with movie comfort food.

# CHAPTER 46
## Sex Comedies

A hard-to-find piece of my oeuvre—and perhaps it should be—is *Porky's-The College Years*, ultimately released on pay per view as *Pimpin' Pee Wee*. When I was approached, I was told the project was intended as a modernized remake of director Bob Clark's 1980s teen sex comedy franchise.

The original *Porky's* grossed $107M in the US and Canada, fifth highest box office of 1982. *Porky's* would now be regarded as retrograde for its objectification and degradation of women. Back in '82, I saw it (mea culpa) merely as an exaggerated portrait of sex-starved American teens in the repressed 1950s that both satirized and celebrated stereotypes of the genre. Sound familiar? I thought it would be fun to get in on a franchise reboot.

Margaret was less than enthusiastic…

Backstory: Mola Entertainment had optioned the rights to *Porky's* but would lose those rights if Mola did not make a *Porky's* movie by a certain date, fast approaching. So Mola decided to make a *Porky's* as cheaply as possible to fulfill that obligation, and retain the rights for a further period. The film would

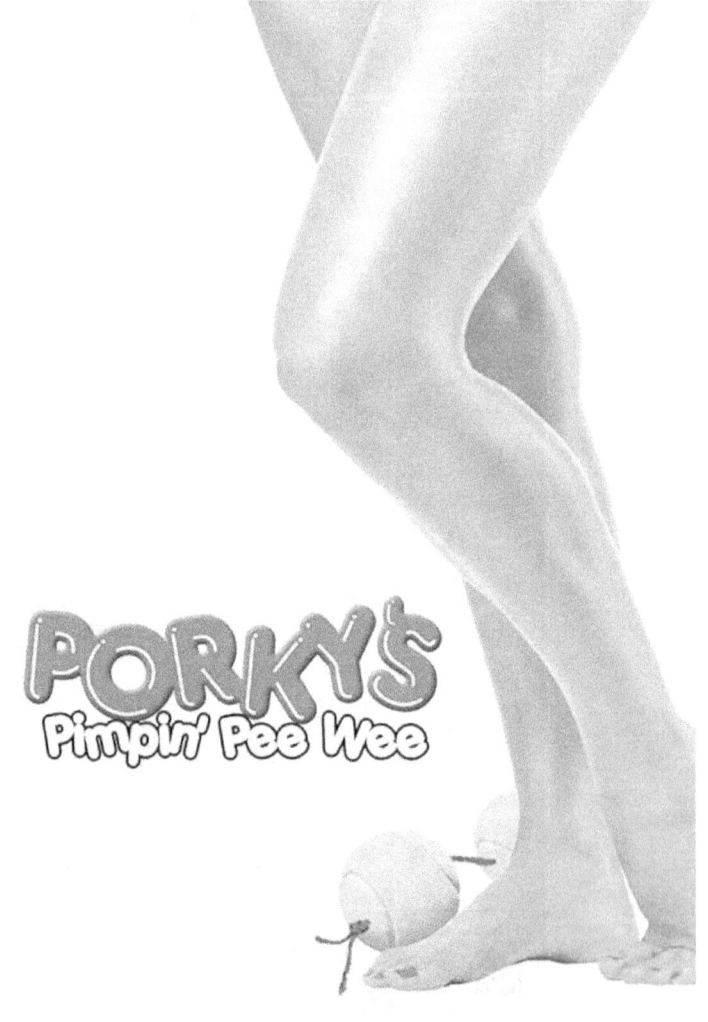

premiere on VOD in the hope such exposure would kickstart the franchise on a higher budget. The original characters of Porky, Pee-Wee, Tommy and Meat would return, as if their high school days in 1954 happened yesterday. Steven Niver wrote a script in three weeks that gene-spliced the original *Porky's* with a *Risky Business* derivative; the kids' wild party trashes a mansion, so they start a brothel there to pay for the damage before the owner gets back. The *American Pie* franchise had indicated there was still a market for raunchy youth humor. But *The Joy of Sex* had driven the original *Porky's*, in this storyline, it was *The Joy of Money* with an amusing subtext of male sexual panic.

The movie had to be shot by Christmas. Prep started as soon as the first draft came off the printer. Writing continued till we started shooting on December 2, 2008 at the Larry Levinson studio in Simi Valley on a budget that could not exceed $500K. That was the ceiling for the *ultra-low budget rate* permitted by SAG/DGA/WGA. I think we came in at $487,000. Not much meat on

**Keep an eye out for the funniest movie about growing up ever made!**

PORKY'S

You'll be glad you came!

MELVIN SIMON PRODUCTIONS / ASTRAL BELLEVUE PATHE INC. Present BOB CLARK'S "PORKY'S" KIM CATTRALL SCOTT COLOMBY KAKI HUNTER NANCY PARSONS ALEX KARRAS as the Sheriff SUSAN CLARK as Cherry Forever Executive Producers HAROLD GREENBERG and MELVIN SIMON Produced by DON CARMODY and BOB CLARK Written and Directed by BOB CLARK

those bones. However, Larry Levinson's studio had a range of standing sets to adapt. In an act of pop cultural desecration, a major set from the family detective show *Diagnosis: Murder* became the interior of Porky's whorehouse. The wild party mansion-turned-brothel was a rented location in Canyon Country where I experienced what a director dreads on a tight schedule: theft of a vital prop just before the scene is to be shot.

I had set up an *Austin Powers*-style hide-the-penis gag in a dimly lit room. Meat's enormous erection would be seen rising from his reclining body as a backlit silhouette, accompanied by Zarathustra-like chords evoking Kubrick's *2001*. Boom, Boom, Boom, Boom etc. You see, Meat was having trouble getting laid because the sheer size of his member frightened prospective candidates. A porn star comes to the rescue in his payoff scene, which would be a bit *blah* without a sight gag, and this was the best I could come up with. The aroused member was a stone phallus, acquired from a Hollywood sex toy shop, mounted on a rod secured to a C-stand. From the camera's point of view, the shadow of Biggus Dickus was positioned to align perfectly with the silhouetted outline of Meat's loins. On cue, the rod would be slowly rotated from horizontal to vertical. We had it all set up, ready to go after lunch. That's when Murphy's Law kicked in.

During the lunch break, someone, perhaps an extra, walked off with our distinguished phallus. It being mid-December, this would have made an ideal Christmas gift for that special someone, but for us, it was the centerpiece of a key scene. The nearest sex shop was an hour away in traffic. We were in cock-blocked Canyon Country. Luckily, we had a resourceful props man in the hot seat, Mike Marquez. With the clock ticking, Mike rapidly sculpted a replacement for the missing member matching the necessary dimensions with gaffer tape! He got us shooting within twenty minutes and the shadow of Meat's mighty member rose in perfect alignment. Props departments rarely get enough recognition for what they contribute to the texture of a film. Appropriately, I added the following reassurance to the end titles: No dildos were harmed in the making of this motion picture.

Why were cast and crew doing this movie? Their reasons were like mine. Work breeds work. The same company gave me a wholesome family comedy a couple of years later as a reward for services rendered. From the actors' point of view, it's a SAG credit, providing, with luck, at least one good scene for their reel; and it helps an agent talk up the client—"She's the co-lead in a franchise reboot that's shooting right now…" But the actors knew in their hearts, as I did, that they would not have been doing this movie if there had been any better career choices out there at the time the offer came through. So how do you help them to do their best work with this disappointing truth gnawing at them? You make it fun. I told the young cast I wanted their characters to represent a vapid, self-absorbed generation in a hypersexualized world, without being totally unsympathetic. And they did. These young actors, while they continued to get roles, did not have the screen careers their talents deserved. I'm going to sing their praises so that there is an acknowledgement somewhere that they excelled at their craft. I wish I had the space to do that for all the talented yet unrecognized actors I have directed.

None of the lead female characters appeared nude or did simulated sex. We could not have recruited such good actors otherwise. Whitney Anderson worked with a sketch comedy group, so her improv ability was well-honed, and she offered some nice zingers. Sandra McCoy had a reaction to every beat of another actor's dialogue. So useful when editing. Russ Hunt, as Meat, 6 foot 4 and built like a linebacker, understood how to make a doofus endearing. You have to be smart to play dumb. His improv "Talk to the gland," in the *blowjob from hell* sequence, got a good laugh. John Patrick Jordan, channeling Ray Liotta, turned the leader of the buddy trio into the type of the charming manipulative college bad boy who always got his friends into trouble.

Adam Wylie (Pee Wee) is a seasoned actor, having started as a child in sixty-seven episodes of *Picket Fences*. He is also an impressive magician who often performs at LA's Magic Castle, as well as an acro-

bat, so I added these abilities to his part. I put it to Adam at our first meeting that the whole movie rested on him making the character of sex-obsessed semi-virginal Pee Wee appealing in his fecklessness. No pressure, Adam…But he was unfazed. He had the character down from the moment the cameras rolled, channeling Woody Allen with a splash of Robin Williams.

I also want to acknowledge the talent of the late veteran character actor Vic Polizos, who played Porky. In the scene where a hooker vomits on his fancy shoes, I told him to riff on his outrage, so he did:

"They're made from the foreskin of a rhinoceros. You can't get that shit anymore!"

The *Porky's* cast embraced the un-PC wackiness the movie needed. It was a fun three weeks. Editor Lawrence Klein was in tune with my sense of humor, and the finished version is a guilty pleasure for those who like that sort of thing. This was not a film that would do my career any good, but I could not afford to turn down a greenlit project, particularly one that might earn residuals a year later from the promised DVD release. But subsequent litigation between the parties involved over the rights put paid to that.

2008 brightened when I attended the premiere of *Not Quite Hollywood: The Wild, Untold Story of Ozploitation!* as a guest of the Melbourne International Film Festival. The film, which examined the quirky variants on exploitation cinema in Australia's film industry renaissance between 1970-1989, had been a decade-long passion project of writer/director Mark Hartley.

He interviewed over eighty Australian, American and British actors, directors, screenwriters and producers, including Quentin Tarantino, who coined the generic term "Ozploitation". He had some nice things to say about my films of that period.

*Not Quite Hollywood* was tightly cut, irreverent and hilarious and won best feature documentary at the Australian Film Institute Awards. It's an excellent companion piece to this book. I did a lot of interviews for the film over the next twelve months as a guest of a variety of festivals: Fantastic Fest in Austin, Texas, Toronto International Film Festival, Paris Cinema, Karlovy Vary in the Czech Republic. This helped raise my profile.

PRAVO — PAGE 4 ENG

**FESTIVAL DAILY**
THE OFFICIAL ENGLISH DAILY OF THE 45TH KARLOVY VARY INTERNATIONAL FILM FESTIVAL

# The hottest director in town!

Jaroslav Švelch

Director Brian Trenchard-Smith's films *Dead-End Drive In* and *The Man from Hong Kong* form part of KVIFF's Midnight Screenings: Ozploitation! section. The films are featured in Mark Hartley's documentary *Not Quite Hollywood: The Wild, Untold Story of Ozploitation!* which is also screening at KVIFF.

■ Has Mark Hartley's film changed people's perception of Ozploitation movies?
Oh yes it completely opened the eyes of cinema-lovers all over the world to the forgotten treasure-trove of eccentric B-movies. B-movies have not always had much respect, but Mark Hartley showed that there was professionalism, there was real creative invention that can be achieved within the B-movie budget and formula.

■ B-movies have a reputation for being all about sex and violence. Would you say that your movies pushed that genre in another direction?
*Dead-End Drive In* has an undercurrent of political comment as well as classic exploitation values. It could have had more nudity. It could have had more violence, but to me that wasn't what it was about. It was a socio-politi-

*Brian Trenchard-Smith gives two fingers to the establishment.*

For instance, Elizabeth Stanley, Joe Dante's partner in their Cinema History website Trailers From Hell, invited me to join their contributors. I have since curated over ninety movies for their site, and continue to do so. I was also invited by noted horror director Mick Garris to join his Masters of Horror circle alongside other top horror directors of Hollywood. *Turkey Shoot*, *Dead End Drive-In* and *Night of the Demons 2* had

earned me a place. A couple of times a year we get together at a famous old Hollywood restaurant in Burbank and swap war stories.

Incongruously, throughout that year I was researching and writing draft after draft of a spec script that I hoped would attract an upscale cast and a production company with a track record in historical drama. The subject was *Richard the Third*, arguably the most maligned King in history.

As Shakespeare tells it, Richard murdered his brother, three of his in-laws, a cousin, several friends, countless rebels, and, most heinously, two nephews, the Princes in the Tower, in a blood-drenched plot to steal the throne of England. He then poisoned his wife, in order to marry his niece. Well, Shakespeare got it wrong. He fashioned Tudor propaganda into one of the greatest plays ever written. Then, like alchemy turning gold into base metal, drama transmuted Richard's reputation into accepted history. What I had in mind was a film, styled as a political thriller, which would rebut the commonly-taught version of Richard as the ultimate wicked uncle, by sticking as closely as possible to historical record. There were many

other contemporary accounts of the Wars of the Roses that painted a different picture of Richard as a devoted family man and idealistic lawmaker trying to unite a divided country in an era when politics was truly a blood sport.

If the most infamous child murders in English history were to be tried, this movie would be a case for the defense. In 1997 three Justices of the United States Supreme Court held a mock trial of Richard III for the murder of the Princes in the Tower. Chief Justice William H. Rehnquist and Associate Justices Ruth Bader Ginsberg and Stephen G. Breyer ruled that Richard was *Not Guilty*.

The script attracted the attention of a British producer based in Hollywood with strong connections with UK companies. He thought my best chance was with BBC Films or Working Title. BBC Films thought the script was too fawning on Richard, and they had plans for their own big budget series on the Wars of the Roses. Working Title passed, opining that "bad Richard" was more fun. Because there was a good response to the writing, there was brief interest in me from a development executive at Tom Cruise's company, who was seeking an action writer, but nothing came of it. I still think my script of Richard III's story would make a great movie or miniseries.

A man can dream…

I thought *Porky's* would be my only sex romp. But in 2011 producer Jeff Hayes, who had hired me five times before, offered me four episodes of a series for Cinemax called *Chemistry*. I ended up doing seven of these.

Need I report that Margaret opposed this?

The show had pedigree writers. Norman Steinberg had cowritten *Blazing Saddles* with Mel Brooks. Richard Christian Matheson, who did most of the writing, has had twelve of his scripts produced as feature films or mini series. His high school comedy *Three O'Clock High* became a cult favorite. He has published 2 novels, 3 collections of stories, one a #1 bestseller on Amazon. Richard is the son of legendary science fiction writer Richard Matheson; the apple did not fall far from the tree.

He is also a talented musician, the drummer for Pearly King and the Temple Thieves. photographed here by David Pascal, of Pascal Records while recording their latest album Fool Skool. His sense of rhythm showed in the dialogue's repartee.

" Lawyers and cops. Two sides of a bad argument" muses our hero, the sole lawyer among cops at the cabin of his paramour's psycho ex-boyfriend.

INT. JUDD'S CABIN - A STUFFED CARIBOU - CLOSE

On a wall. The final indignity. PAN down to find Michael and Liz in bed, naked under covers. He looks unnerved by the other stuffed, glassy-eyed game; a taxidermized Veldt.

> MICHAEL
> Tellin' you, I'm next.

> LIZ
> Judd *is* the jealous type.

> MICHAEL
> What does he have to be jealous of?

> LIZ
> I don't know. Decency. Sanity. Whatever isn't his.

> MICHAEL
> Including you.

> LIZ
> It was the perfect arrangement. Until I actually got to know him. He
> has no boundaries. Woulda boned Mother Theresa if he could've
> figured out how to get her scarf off.

The executive producer behind the enterprise was Bill Haber, one of the founding agents of CAA, then a successful packager of shows like *Rizzoli and Isles*, which ran six years on TNT. Veteran guest stars Chad Everett (*Medical Center*) who I cast in *Official Denial,* Morgan Fairchild (*Falcon Crest*), and Sally Kellerman (the Altman classic *Mash*) were on board. If these esteemed industry professionals were not ashamed to have their names on a 'Skinemax' series, why should I be? Money was also a factor. As it turned out, three months' work took care of most of the year's expenses.

*Chemistry* was set in a high-end Los Angeles law firm where all the attorneys, their wives, and girlfriends seem to be untreated sex addicts. Untreatable, probably. More couplings a day than British Rail.

The star attorney (Jonathon Chase), while engaged to the senior partner's daughter (Ragan Wallake), commences a torrid affair with a loose cannon LAPD detective (Ana Alexander).

His best buddy at the firm (Jeremy Kent Jackson) is engaged to the senior partner's other daughter (the hilarious Augie Duke) but they both practice polyamory.

I loved working with the regular cast. They told me I was their favorite director on the show too. There were regular bursts of nudity and simulated sex, though genitalia were avoided. I chose a female 1st AD to set the tone on the set. Women filled many crew positions. This helped create a nurturing atmosphere for the sex scenes. My experience on *Porky's* had shown me how to make such scenes comfortable for actors who had never been naked in front of twenty people before. On one erotic-heavy day, the AD team wore false moustaches. Humor helps.

The saving grace of the scripts was the wit that Richard Christian Matheson infused, as he rewrote every episode during prep. Lots of lawyer jokes. Punctuating each episode were wry monologues delivered to camera by various characters, offering cynical comments on contemporary sexual mores. The best of these came from guest star Sally Kellerman (the original Hot Lips in *Mash*) as a sex guru of indeterminate age, who claims to have blown Freud. She was fun to work with.

Mea culpa, but the whole non-PC show was fun to do. My best episode, if you are interested, is episode eight - *Night on Bald Mountain*.

# CHAPTER 47
## Epics

While I was making *Happy Face Murders* in 1998, Regent Entertainment called with a project to be shot in the UK. Trading on the popularity of James Cameron's *Titanic*, this would be a TV movie about her equally doomed sister ship Britannic, which sank four years later in the Aegean Sea during WWI. History records that one young woman was actually on all three ill-fated ships of the White Star Line…

Regent were not yet happy with their script and invited me to give my take on the material. Forgive me if I briefly explore a writer's dilemma. What is Truth? And whose Truth? Different perspectives on the same event will offer different truths. How true can a photographed reenactment of a past event be, anyway? Should History be protected from distorted representation onscreen? Holocaust denial and slavery rationalization would be obvious examples of cinematic moral transgression, but on a less significant level, is it OK to fictionalize events for dramatic effect? What standard of accuracy should a filmmaker be held to when shooting a story "based on true events"? For example: the miniseries *Feud,* which pitted Jessica Lange's Joan Crawford and Susan Sarandon's Bette Davis against each other in an 8-episode catfight during the making of *What Ever Happened to Baby Jane.* What right had the filmmakers to represent the late producer/director Robert Aldrich as a stock Hollywood manipulator, a sweaty, pathetic, pretentious hack? Those who worked with Aldrich wrote about him quite differently, as an auteur whose artistry and humanism is

reflected throughout his body of work. No evidence supports this demeaning portrayal, roundly criticized by the Directors Guild of America. Yet the makers of *Feud* had no such qualms.

In *Britannic* I played fast and loose with history too, but with fictitious characters inspired by true events.

First, some facts about the actual events on which *Britannic* was to be based. After Titanic sank, the White Star Line implemented a major safety upgrade to their third Olympic class liner Britannic to prevent the ship sinking if the hull were punctured. At the start of WW1, the British government requisitioned the nation's merchant fleet, and turned Britannic into a hospital ship, to bring soldiers wounded in the Gallipoli campaign back to England. Before Britannic's sixth voyage, the German Government claimed Britain was using hospital ships on their outward journeys to carry munitions or troops, cargo normally deemed legitimate targets, yet shipped in vessels protected by the Geneva Convention. Naturally, the British Government denied these allegations.

Eight miles from the port of Kea in Greece, the Britannic suffered an explosion on her starboard bow. This occurred during one of the short periods each day when the bulkhead doors throughout the ship were opened to facilitate a shift change. The doors near the explosion jammed and could not be closed. Water flooded in. Then a secondary explosion occurred. When the Captain increased speed hoping to beach the vessel on the nearby coast, it had the effect of pumping more water into the hold. Compounding the ship's vulnerability was the fact that portholes on the lower decks had been opened to let in fresh air prior to reaching the harbor and were now letting water flood in. As the ship began to list, the Captain gave the order to abandon ship. It all went smoothly till one lifeboat was caught in the whirlpool surrounding the now-exposed propellers and chopped to pieces. Thirty passengers died. One young woman was thrown clear and survived. Her name was Violet Jessop. By some extraordinary quirk of fate, this was the third time she had been on board a White Star Line vessel during its brush with maritime history.

Violet Jessop had been a stewardess on White Star's first superliner Olympic when it collided with HMS Hawke in Southampton Harbor in 1911. Her bow punched a nasty gash into the Hawke extending below the waterline, but the ship did not sink. No casualties, but red faces all round. She declined to discuss the incident in her memoirs.

The next year, Ms. Jessop was assigned to the Titanic on its fateful maiden voyage. When boarding a lifeboat, she was handed a motherless baby. She took care of the child until they were rescued by RMS Carpathia. According to Ms. Jessop, while on board the Carpathia, a woman, presumably the baby's mother, grabbed the baby she was holding and ran off with it without saying a word.

In 1916 Ms. Jessop was on board what had become His Majesty's Hospital Ship Britannic as a trainee nurse. Once again disaster struck. In her memoirs she described what happened when she realized her lifeboat was being sucked into the thrashing propellers.

*I leapt into the water but was sucked under the ship's keel which struck my head. I escaped, but years later when I went to my doctor because of a lot of headaches, he discovered I had once sustained a fracture of the skull!*

She went on to describe the last moments of the Britannic: "

*The white pride of the ocean's medical world...dipped her head a little, then a little lower and still lower. All the deck machinery fell into the sea like a child's toys. Then she took a fearful plunge, her stern rearing hundreds of feet into the air until with a final roar, she disappeared into the depths.*

After WWI, the unsinkable Ms. Jessop continued working for White Star and other passenger shipping companies till 1950. Years after her retirement, Ms. Jessop claimed to have received a telephone call, on a stormy night, from a woman who asked her if she saved a baby on the night that Titanic sank.

"Yes," Ms. Jessop replied.

"I was that baby," the voice said with a laugh, and hung up.

Her friend and biographer John Maxtone-Graham thought it was probably some child in the village playing a joke on her.

She replied, "No, John, I had never told that story to anyone before I told you now."

Despite being diagnosed with tuberculosis as a child and being given months to live, Violet Jessop lived to the ripe old age of eighty-four. Four years later, the undersea explorer Jacques Cousteau discovered the hitherto unknown resting place of the Britannic, eight miles from the position designated in the British Admiralty report on the sinking. For many years the cause of the initial explosion was debated. Was it a mine? Was it a torpedo? Or was it sabotage?

What an amazing true story. I could see a *portrait of an era* movie in the vein of *Upstairs Downstairs* (proto-*Downton Abbey*) using stately ships rather than stately homes. It would be a Brit-focused tale of a girl from a humble Irish/Argentine background, transcending gender and class prejudices, showing heroism in a succession of deadly situations on the open ocean, her life concluding with the heart-warming phone call from the child she saved on the Titanic. Maybe this could be a studio vehicle for a major female star, or a 2-part miniseries for PBS or the A&E Network. Those were my initial thoughts for dramatizing the true events. Then I read the script. It wasn't bad. But it wasn't Violet Jessop's story.

The writers had opted to transfer the *Titanic* formula to the Britannic, featuring a group of passengers with different aspirations, agendas, and conflicts, one of whom—a surrogate for Violet Jessop—was a Titanic survivor. In the script, Titanic's impending iceberg became Britannic's lurking saboteur, who would cause the explosion. Although historical records indicate that a German sea mine was the likeliest culprit, a human villain has more dramatic potential. This script provided a number of possible suspects, including a handsome sailor rescued from a *Lifeboat* (thanks, Hitch) containing survivors of a torpedoed vessel. Is he not what he seems…? Naturally the female lead was going to fall for him. Additionally, there was a Suspicious Doctor and an Unsinkable Molly Brown character in the mix. The writers tried hard, aware of TV's budgetary limitations, but to me, it lacked drive. Formula genre better have drive.

I understood the commercial rationale behind the script policy. Sticking with the known facts, telling Violet Jessop's life story, would have made a great movie. But there was no way Regent was going to go back to the drawing board on the project. Now at a proposed $3M budget, Britannic was going to be an expen-

sive television movie for its day. To recoup, it had to cater to the broadest possible audience across the world, and particularly in the US, where Regent's best client was The Family Channel, soon to be Fox Family Channel in a short-lived partnership between Haim Saban and Rupert Murdoch, a man who, I suspect, did not share toys well as a child. Fox Family Channel would favor familiar genre tropes in a *Titanic* derivative over a more PBS/BBC approach. Formulas work. I'm fine with formulas, if I can add fresh ingredients.

So my principal input on the script was: if you are going this route, make it more fun. Add more action, and elements from similar genres, such as classic British naval warfare movies. Let's see a torpedo attack, failing by inches to hit the Britannic.

Introduce the antihero saboteur on page one, I suggested, killing the ship's chaplain and assuming his identity, thus the least likely suspect on the ship.

The next scene should introduce the female lead (now named Vera after my mother), nervous at boarding Titanic's sister ship. Why? An early flashback to that fateful night tells us why, and provides the audience with a taste of the set piece disaster sequences that will climax the film.

Soon we learn that Vera is not just a governess to Lady Lewis's children, she is a British agent in search of a German spy suspected to be on board. Vera and the Chaplain become attracted, each unaware of the other's agenda. Think *Eye of the Needle* threading *Titanic*.

Regent accepted my pitch. I brought in my longtime story consultant and writing partner Dennis Pratt to help with several drafts of the rewrite while I went to Canada to direct *Happy Face Murders*. One challenge was to make a WWI story in which Germany sinks a hospital ship accessible to the German audience. The trick was to make the saboteur an honorable spy, following orders, hoping to carry them out with minimal loss of life. His plan, once he confirmed there were forbidden munitions on board, was to conspire with Irish stokers bitter about repressive British actions in Ireland. They would take over the ship and sail to a neutral port where the evidence of British falsehood would be exposed. When the mutineers are killed, the Chaplain's identity as a German agent remains undiscovered. Using a secret radio, he initiates his next plan. He gives a German submarine the Britannic's position, so that a torpedo can cripple the "unsinkable"

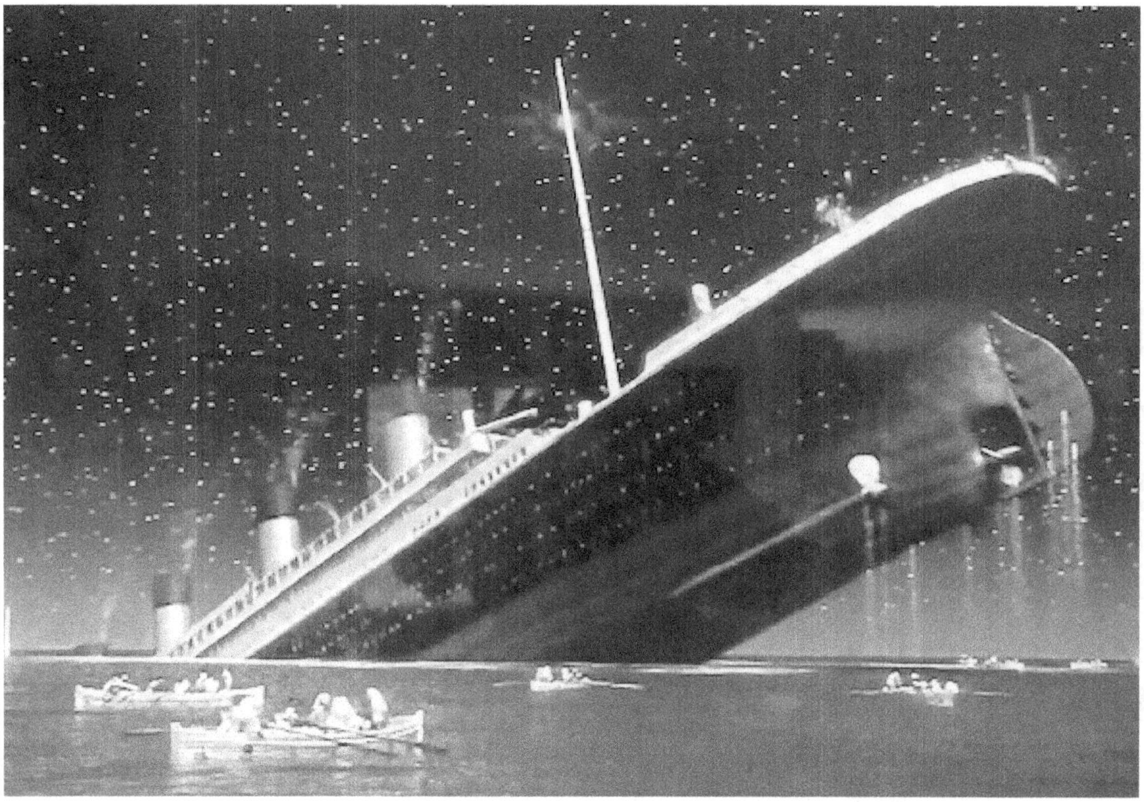

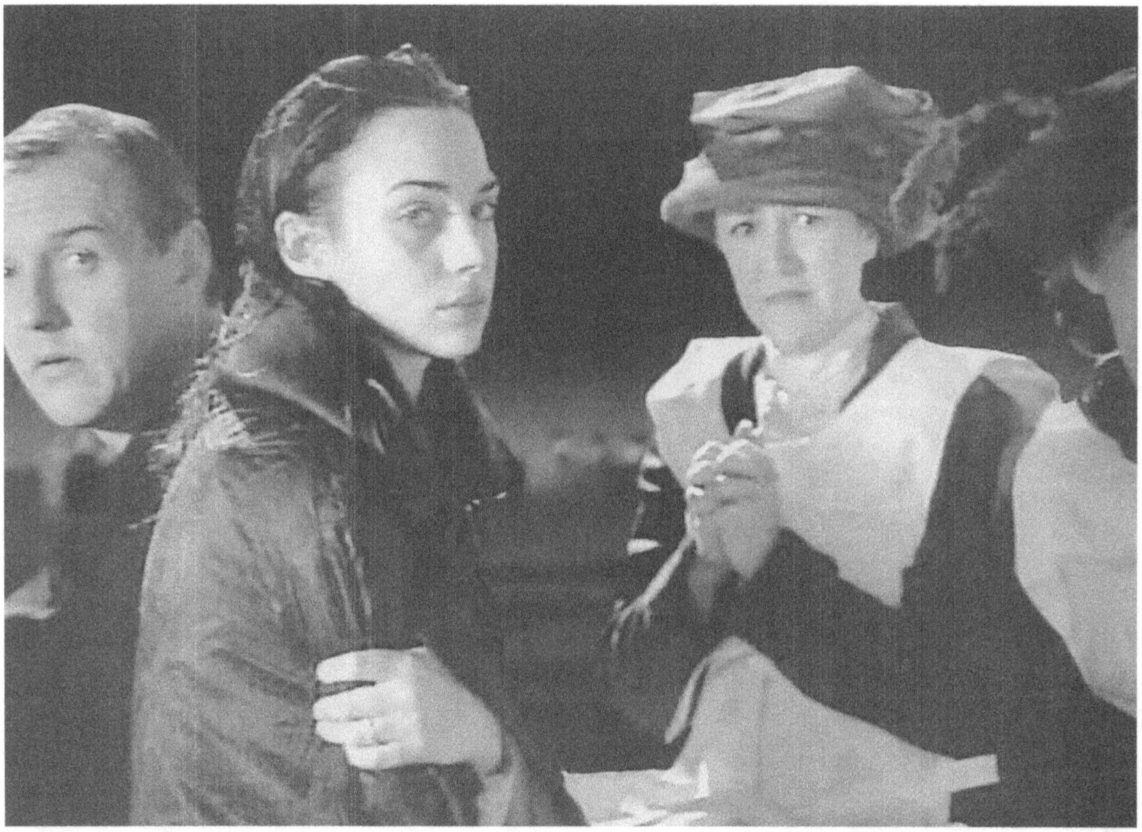

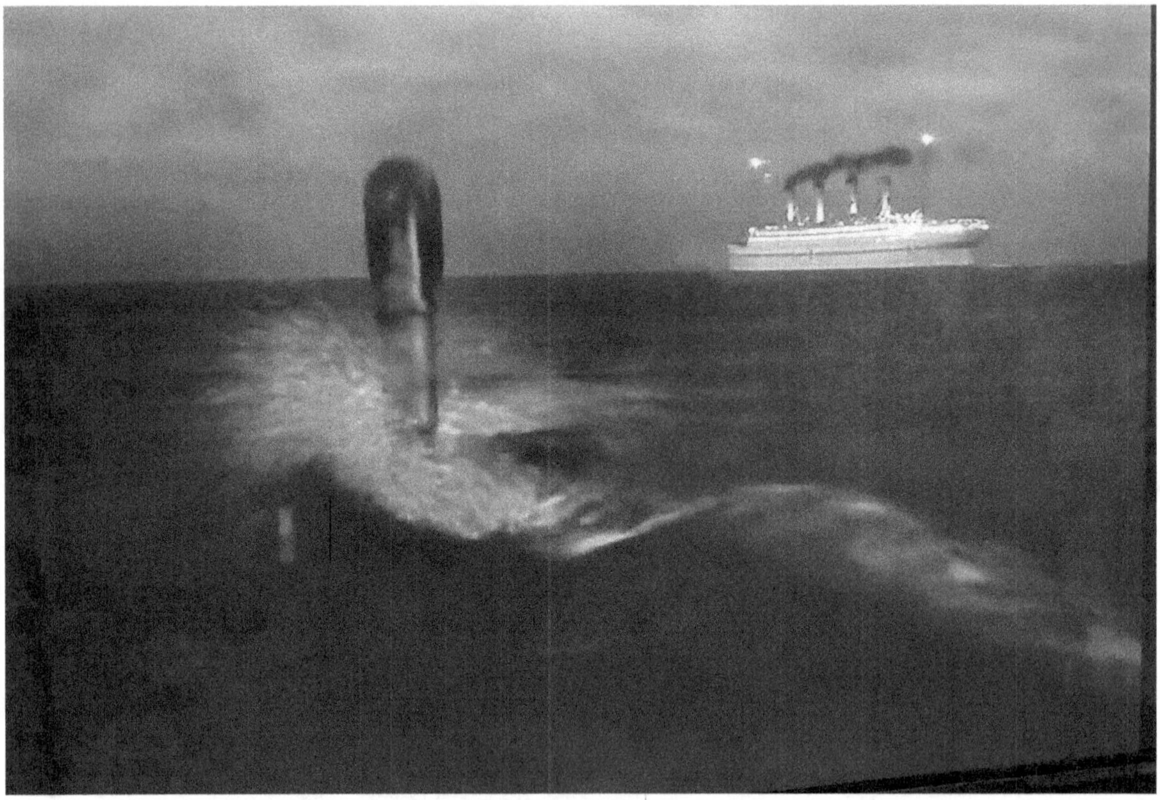

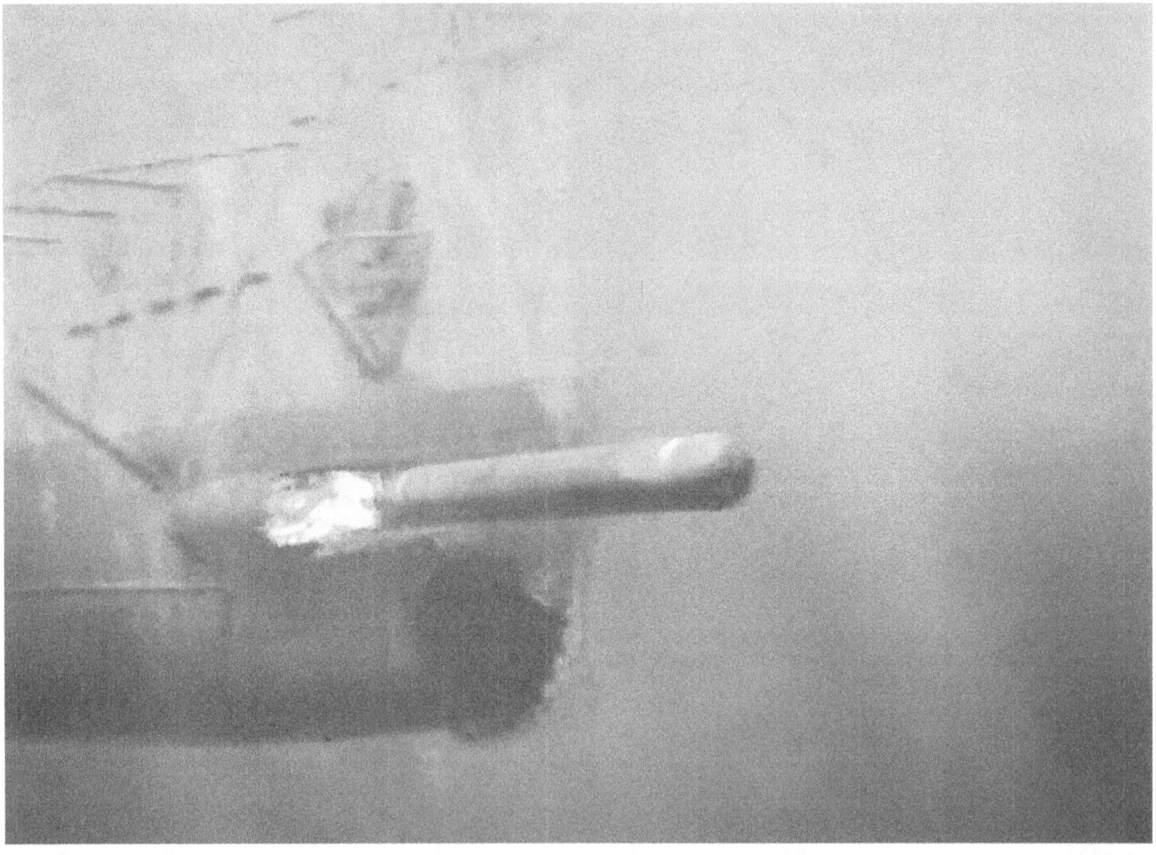

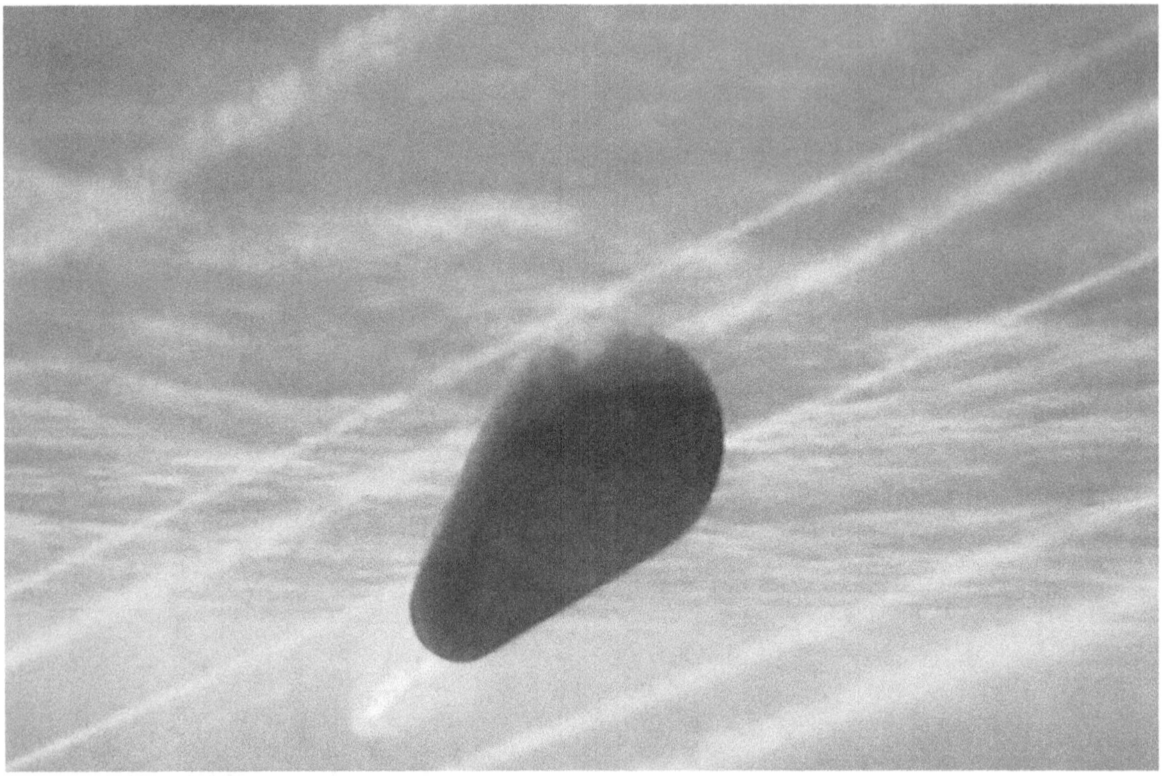

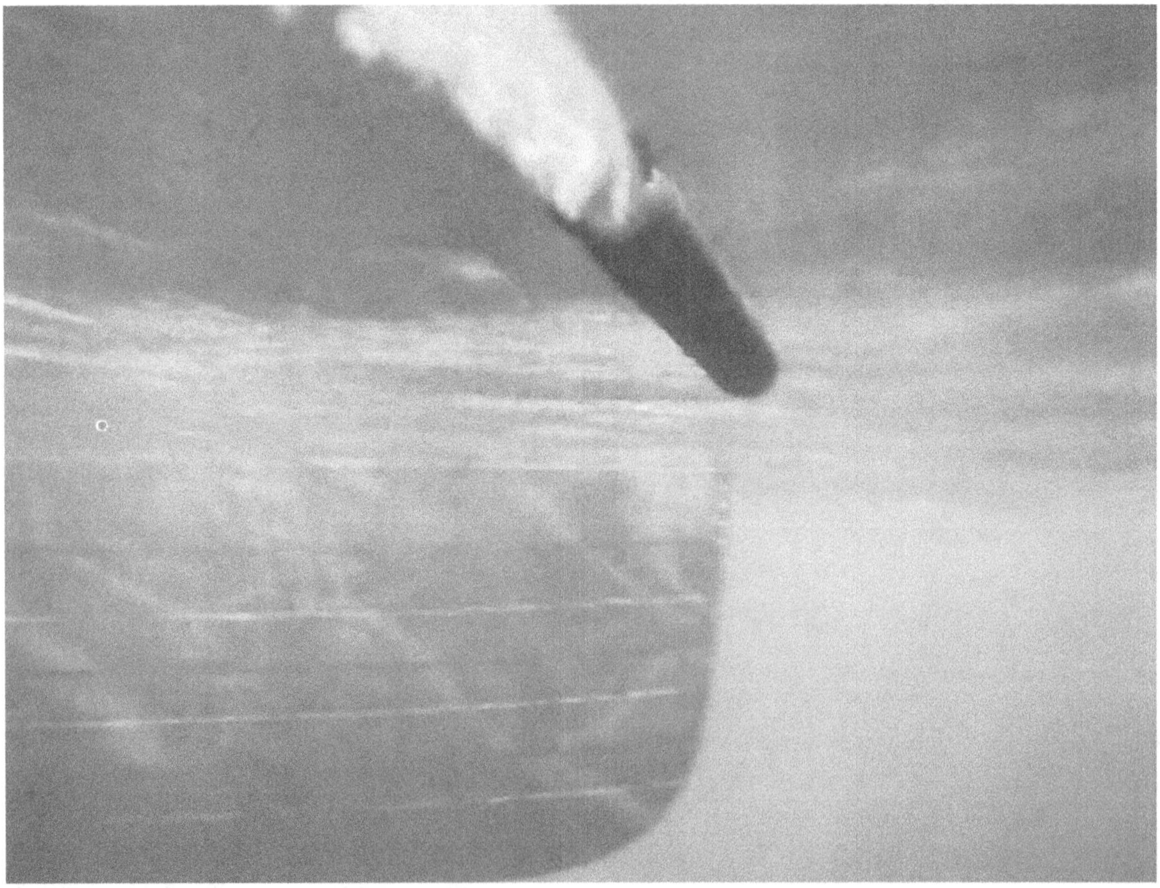

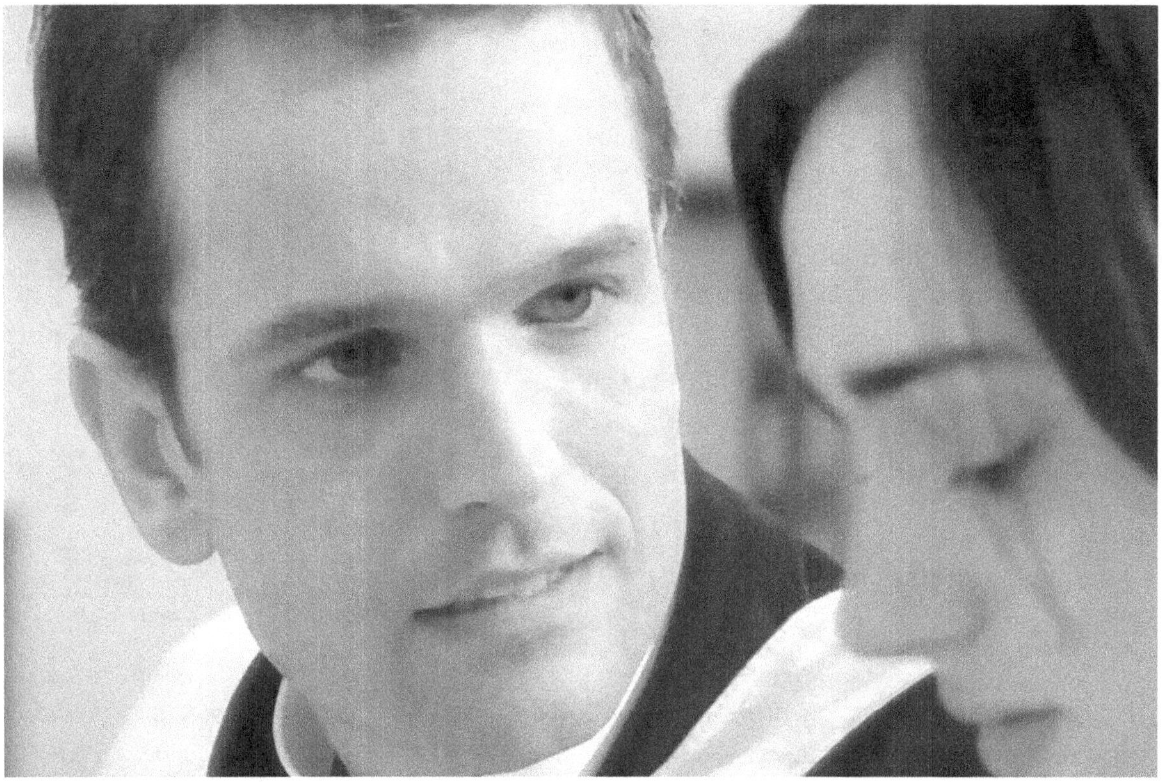

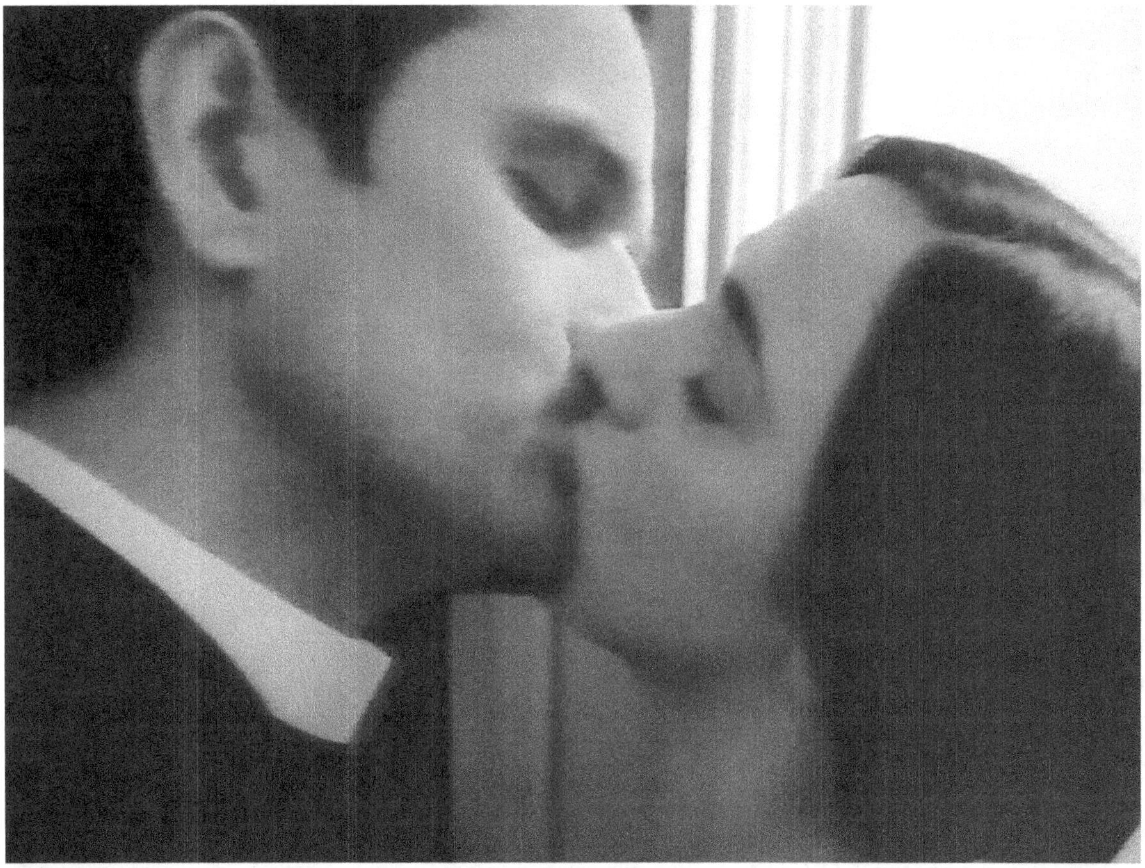

ship and prevent the munitions delivery. That plan also fails when a British warship sinks the submarine.

His duty compels him to undertake the sabotage himself. The stage is set for a cat-and-mouse game, Spy vs. Spy. In the end, out of love, the German spy sacrifices himself to save her life and reputation.

The new script gained some traction. I took the train from Waterloo Station via the Channel Tunnel to Paris to meet Jacqueline Bisset, a star of sufficient wattage to get sales projections to the right level.

She was initially uncertain about a *Titanic* derivative, but luckily, I persuaded her to play Lady Lewis, wife of the British Ambassador to Greece, who was a passenger on Britannic. When we added Bruce Payne (*Passenger 57*) Ben Daniels (*Aristocrats*) and John Rhys-Davies (*Shogun*, soon to be Gimli in *Lord of The Rings*), the production was greenlit.

You can imagine my pleasure when Bray Studios, where the Hammer's classics were filmed, became the production base. I stayed across the road at the Oakley Court Hotel, once a grand Victorian Gothic country house, which Hammer leased in 1949 and used as a location for countless movies.

As a kid, I had dreamed of working for Britain's top genre film company. Eventually I made some trailers for Hammer. Now finally I walked the same studio floors as Peter Cushing and Christopher Lee, and directors like Terrence Fisher, John Gilling, and Roy Ward Baker. Hallowed ground for Hammer fans.

The production was run well by British producer Judith Hunt (*Loch Ness*) who introduced me to the perfect production designer of period material, Rob Harris (*Hornblower, Poirot*). Another boon was lighting cameraman Ivan Strasberg (*The Killing Fields, Bloody Sunday*). I was impressed not only with Judith's producing skills but also her understanding of the stress level a director is under while shooting 6-day weeks. She arranged on the company's tab for a skilled masseur to come to my hotel room every Sunday night at 6 p.m., and tune me up for the week ahead. No happy ending, strictly professional, and effective. It helped. Smart. And kind. Actually, kind is smart.

The cast fell into place quite quickly. Our Violet Jessop surrogate, now called Vera Campbell,

was played by up-and-coming Amanda Ryan (*Elizabeth*) who brought a lot of moxie to the role.

Edward Atterton (*The Man in the Iron Mask*) played the German spy with a mixture of handsome charm and ruthless resolve.

The whole cast were excellent actors. If the performances had a flaw, it is that I allowed John Rhys-Davies to play Britannic's captain with an excess of Dickensian gusto.

As it turned out, my approach to a German antihero worked. ARD bought German and French rights for $1.3M. Fox Family paid $1.5M for US broadcast rights. Sales were strong all over the world. Regent got a good price in the UK's ITV for making *Britannic* as a qualifying British film.

The question you must be asking by now is how on earth were you going to make a *Titanic* derivative in twenty-four days for $3M and change? Particularly as the *Titanic* 4-hour miniseries with George C. Scott and Catherine Zeta Jones, shot two years earlier, cost north of $13M. I had a top British crew, particularly in set design and costuming. A small but skilled visual effects company in New Jersey—Corbitt Visual Design—did all the CGI work. They had contributed effects shots to *Doomsday Rock*, then offered to create a sweeping shot of *Titanic* on the open ocean as a sam-

ple to measure against the photo realism James Cameron achieved. It looked just like a shot lifted from *Titanic*. The 188 visual effects shots Pat Corbitt, Dan Dipierro and their team delivered covered a wide variety of challenges both above and below water. Here's a small *before and after* example: When the ship started to sink, they added digital water rising up the stairwell as sailors and nurses hurry up to the deck. Simple and effective.

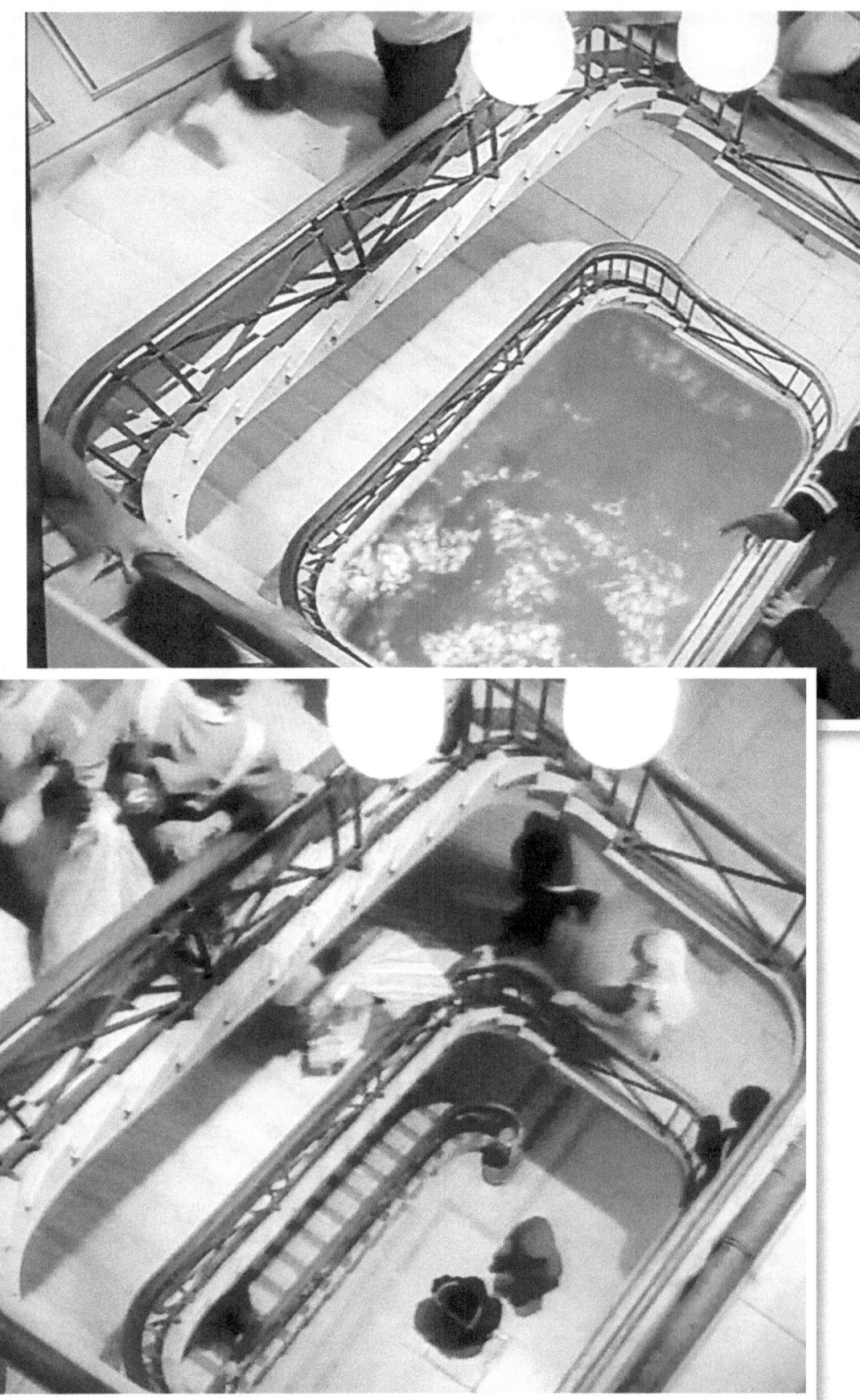

With twenty plus years of visual effects hindsight, there are shots you could certainly criticize, but they were pretty good for the TV screen in 1999. In 2011, the Directors Guild held a 3D symposium with James Cameron, Steven Spielberg, and Jeffery Katzenberg as guest speakers. After talking briefly with Steven Spielberg about a shared actor—*E. T.*'s Henry Thomas—I found myself walking into the auditorium alongside James Cameron. I was in a jocular mood. I wondered if he had seen my *Titanic* derivative. After introducing myself, I told him "I made *Britannic* on your catering budget." He gave me a wry smile. After a beat, he added: "You know, there was some quite good CG in that film." I thanked him, then he walked to his seat. Pat Corbitt's team had done a great job, so a year later I brought them in on a CGI-heavy movie.

*Britannic* was the second recent television drama to trade on James Cameron's *Titanic*. Inevitably it was a critical target. But *Variety*'s review was not too bad.

"*Director Trenchard-Smith proves adept at stirring the melodramatic pot that is 'Britannic,' stylishly whipping the action into a frothy frenzy (supported by some especially intense scenery chewing from John Rhys-Davies as the Britannic's captain). There's also some nifty underwater work from director of photography Ivan Strasburg and his team, though many of the accompanying visual effects tend to fall on the cheesy side. 'Britannic' is, no doubt, precisely what an H2O movie made for roughly 5% of the budgets accorded 'Titanic' and 'Waterworld' should feel like.*"

Britannic is more enjoyable than the reviews indicate. My handling of the visual effects sequences provided a good audition piece for a big budget opportunity that soon came my way.

*Megiddo: Omega Code 2* is an interesting film to analyze from various perspectives, so forgive me if I go through its director issues from soup to nuts.

Again, I was the beneficiary of the kindness of others. While Margaret was undergoing coursework for her doctorate at UCLA, I had joined the university fencing club. There I met a talented young writer, David Baxter, who was doing his Masters in the Producers Program. David would go on to sell several screenplays and produce two films, and is now a key executive at Legion M, a fan-owned production company. Five inches taller than I, he was a formidable épée opponent and still is.

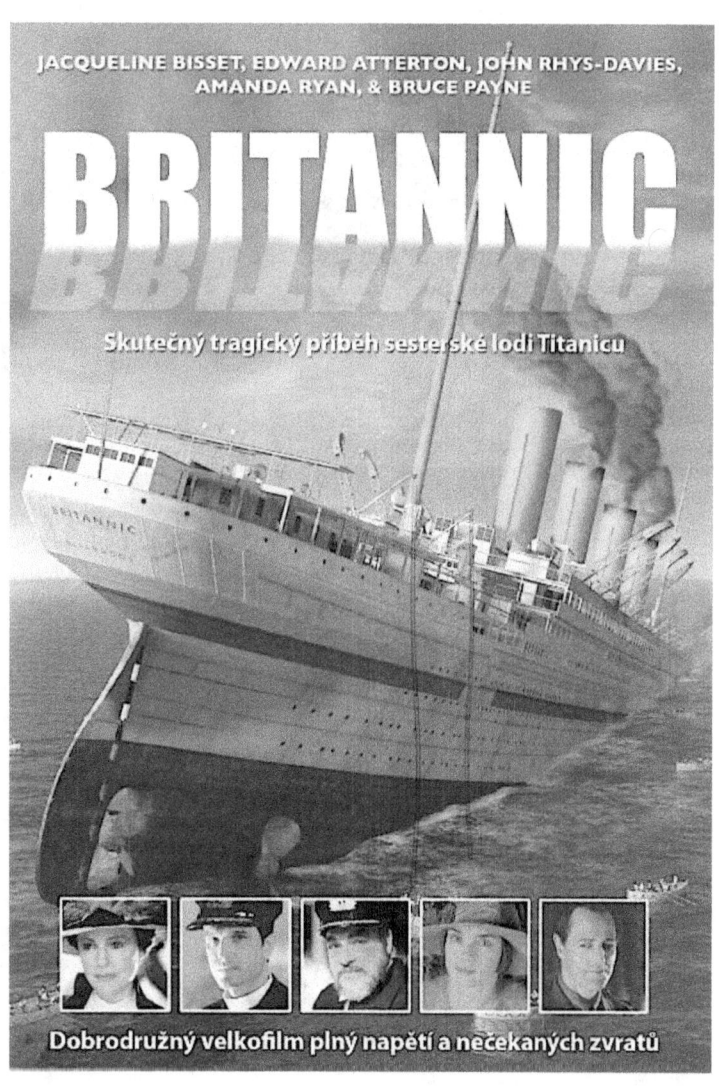

JACQUELINE BISSET, EDWARD ATTERTON, JOHN RHYS-DAVIES, AMANDA RYAN, & BRUCE PAYNE

BRITANNIC

Skutečný tragický příběh sesterské lodi Titanicu

Dobrodružný velkofilm plný napětí a nečekaných zvratů

David Baxter had become friends with celebrated British actor Michael York, whose body of work is full of iconic titles—*Romeo and Juliet*, *The Three Musketeers*, *Cabaret*, *Logan's Run*, the *Austin Powers* franchise, amongst 165 credits in film, television, voice acting and audio books. His honeyed-yet-commanding British tones made him an ideal candidate to play The Antichrist in a little independent movie *The Omega Code*, financed by the world's largest Evangelical Christian network, Trinity Broadcasting.

Founded in the 1972 by Paul and Janice Crouch, TBN preached the "prosperity gospel" with great success. Their twice-yearly praise-a-thons on TBN generated as much as $90 million a year in donations, mostly in small amounts from lower-income Americans. "When you give to God," Crouch said in a typical appeal, "you're simply loaning to the Lord, and he gives it right on back." At the urging of their younger son Matthew, the Crouches began financing Christian-themed movies. Their first production, *The Omega Code*, costing $6M and starring Michael York, was a hit, grossing twice its budget in the US theatrical release alone. Now Michael York was being asked to repeat his role as the Antichrist in a bigger budget sequel. But he was demurring; he had not enjoyed working with the previous *Omega Code*'s director. This issue was on Michael York's mind when he had lunch with David Baxter.

"Do you know any good directors?" Michael asked.

David, bless him, grabbed the opportunity to enthusiastically talk me up. Michael requested my director's reel be sent to his manager Gavin Polone for evaluation. Polone approved. Thus I passed the first gatekeeper, one I would never have reached without David's help. Michael arranged to meet me at a book signing he was attending. Aided by our common English background, we clicked immediately, as Michael points out in his book *Dispatches from Armageddon*: "...five minutes later I could see that Brian was a man I could do business with."

Margaret begged me not to make this film. But the family coffers needed to be refilled.

So I had to win the hearts and minds of the producers, principal among whom was Matthew Crouch, the 39-year-old younger son of the founder of Trinity Broadcasting, Paul Crouch.

His father, encouraged by the success of the first *Omega Code*, wanted to fund another, this time incorporating the final conflict—Armageddon. He would put up $12.5M, twice the budget of the previous film. After a screening of *Britannic*, Matthew Crouch agreed to meet with Michael York's recommendation for director. There were other contenders. Michael left the choice to him—just not the last guy. I was sent the script, which I read a couple of times, as is my custom, once straight through, then again for notes. The next day I arrived at a diner in Studio City and sat down in front of Matt Crouch, and fellow producers Gary Bettman, (Line Producer), Laurence Mortorff (Business Affairs & Legal) and Thomas J. Cook (Visual Effects Producer).

First, here's a summary of *Megiddo*'s basic story:

Daniel Alexander, owner of a multibillion-dollar media empire, has two sons. The older boy, 8-year-old Stone, unsuccessfully tries to burn alive his newborn baby brother David in his crib. Stone is sent off to European military school. Years later, kid brother David has become the Vice President of the United States, while big brother Stone has risen to be the head of the European Union. Stone is trying to compel America to join his proposed United World Federation, which has divided the planet into nine economic zones. Stone is, as you've guessed, The Antichrist. Satan, aided by a rogue Catholic priest, is now challenging God for control of the Earth. Stone murders his father, inheriting an influential media empire from which to pump propaganda. Next, he assassinates the US President and unleashes earthquakes, meteor showers, ecological disasters, to bring the United States to heel. Corrupt politicians across the world flock to join the Antichrist's elite. Russia provides troops. David Alexander, now the President, is betrayed by Congress, who order his arrest for the murder of his father on the basis of a faked video. David escapes and goes to war against his brother. His only allies are Latin America and China. The stage is set for the final conflict, the battle of Armageddon, fought in Israel as prophesied in the Bible on the hill of Megiddo, from which the word Armageddon is derived.

Spoiler alert: God wins! And we can also see where God stands on US foreign policy issues. European Union—bad. World government—bad. The Papacy—bad. Politicians—bad. Russia—bad. US, China & Latin America—good.

The meeting with Messrs. Crouch (pictured here), Bettman, Mortorff, and Cook began with cordial greetings and praise for *Britannic*. I felt my only choice was to be brutally honest, even if it cost me the job, because the script was that awful:

*"I would really like to direct this movie, but I have to be frank with you. The script is weak, hard to follow at times, and if you shoot exactly what is written here, the film will fail."*

I produced my notes and cited the script's problems. It was, frankly, a dog's breakfast—all over the place. Rambling, confused, with plot elements introduced, then dropped. A passive hero. Grandiloquent speeches substituting for relationships. It took forty pages for Michael York to appear. The story started in present day then jumped thirty-five years ahead for the next seventy pages. What financial impact will that have, I asked, on production design, and most importantly, the future weapons of war for the battle of Armageddon? Apparently, Trinity Broadcasting's patriarch, Paul Crouch Sr., who was to finance the movie, had not liked earlier scripts, so a well-regarded Hollywood screenwriter and script doctor John Fasano was brought in. He had contributed to a long list of studio movies including *Another 48 Hours, Die Hard with a Vengeance, Tombstone, Judge Dredd*. He understood screenwriting. He was just what the project needed. Unfortunately, he was not allowed to run free. What Fasano told me was that Crouch Senior basically dictated the succession of scenes he wanted, and Fasano was told to flesh them out. I could not help noticing there were some curious parallels in the screenplay with the dynamics of the family producing the film.

It was to Matthew Crouch's credit that he appreciated my candor. Matthew knew the script was a mess. But if he told his father that his version of the story was not working, Crouch Sr. might fly into a rage and pull the plug. I suggested to Matthew that he let me fix it without credit as part of my directing duties.

*"Will your father really remember every detail of his script input six or nine months from now when the movie is finished?"* I suggested.

Matthew asked me to come down to TBN headquarters in Costa Mesa to meet with his parents and use the budgetary problem of creating a world thirty-five years into the future as a means to get "some small changes" in the script, and my position as director approved. John Fasano had warned me that the patriarch of TBN was a control freak. He was grooming younger son Matthew for leadership but often overruled his decisions, which Matthew resented. Tread carefully.

I duly arrived at TBN's iconic headquarters in Costa Mesa, which looked like a mashup of Disneyland Castle, a wedding cake and the White House. It was no secret in LA that TBN manipulated charitable Christians into funding a lavish lifestyle for its founders.

I did not believe for one moment that a sequel (more of a reboot, really) to *The Omega Code* would result in a wave of new converts to Trinity Broadcasting's brand of Pentecostalism, or make one iota of difference in the political tug of war between Left and Right. Such a film would preach solely to the converted. However much I disagree with Trinity Broadcasting's worldview, surely Pentecostals are just as entitled as secular audiences to have their views propagated in an entertainment medium.

Actually, I'm an ethical hedonist, an agnostic who would in fact be happy to discover that there actually is a God. But I have a problem with contradictory belief systems that make war upon one another in His Name. All religions are different cultural expressions of the same search for the meaning of life. Different faiths should be in harmony not conflict. Empathy should make the world go 'round, not money; naïve, I know, but a philosophy common to all the great religious teachers. However, that's not the way the world currently works. The ruling elite retool their prophet's teachings into a patriarchal control system for their own economic benefit. I don't understand why a just, all powerful God lets this and other human misery happen. I don't believe Satan is real. He is a fun movie character, but, like Jason and Freddie, does not exist.

Matthew Crouch ushered me into his father's office. It was not hard to sense that Matt had that mixture of love, fear and resentment that many an adult son

has for an authoritarian father. Paul Crouch Sr. sat at the head of a giant oval table, hand-carved in Italy with ornate matching chairs and shipped in sections to be assembled at TBN headquarters. I had not got the job yet but was already visualizing scenes. The table would be a perfect piece of set dressing for the Antichrist's office, when he meets with world leaders. Sitting beside her husband was his cohost of TBN's *Praise the Lord* show Janice Crouch in a dress that matched her trademark pink-tinged cotton candy wig.

I was duly introduced by Matt and the interview commenced. British stuff seemed to impress them, so I played it up. I mentioned my schooling at Wellington College, founded in the name of the Duke of Wellington, hero of Waterloo. The special relationship between Britain and the US, and so forth. Once I sensed they were getting comfortable with me, I raised the economic issue of so much of the script being set thirty-five years hence. The same script would work just as well if the timeline were slid back, starting the Antichrist's childhood and adolescence just before the election of President Kennedy, jumping to the present, concluding with the battle of Armageddon when the available US Army tanks would still seem credible weapons of war. My logic prevailed. Crouch Sr. said I could make such changes as Matt approved. Mission accomplished.

As we left, I mentioned to Matt that I wanted to use that extraordinary boardroom table in the movie. Matt said that he had requested it for the original *Omega Code* but his father had refused, fearing damage in transportation. Disassembly and reassembly were complex and could only be done by experts. Never to be moved, said the Patriarch, and that's final. But Matt was tempted. He wanted to see his father's face when the never-to-be-moved table appeared on the big screen. As it turned out, Crouch Sr. was away for the first week of the shoot, so I was able to stage corrupt world leaders sitting around his unique table as the Antichrist gave orders. And Matt was able to one-up his father.

I explained to the producers that my rewrite would keep all the markers Paul Crouch Sr. had laid down in the previous script but I would reorganize the material in a more commercial, coherent, actor-friendly

way while adding action and visual effects sequences. It was in TBN's interests for the film to reach the widest audience possible. A multi-genre action epic, with 'PG-13' horror trimmings, was the best way to reach beyond the faith-based audience. *The Omen* meets *Air Force One* in the *End of Days*. They fight the *Battle of the Bulge*, and are rewarded by *The Second Coming*. That would make an interesting genre cocktail. I wanted to do my honest best to make their Pentecostal allegory as entertaining as possible. Maybe then, they will get their money back, because the rule used to be: *don't spend more on the sequel than the first one, because most sequels earn less than the original hit. Omega Code 2* was initially set at $12.5M, twice the budget of the original. If the production came in on that budget, I would get a 50K bonus. During prep the schedule was cut from forty-four days to thirty-nine, because of unexpected cost increases. I duly shot it in thirty-nine days, with very little overtime. Somehow the eventual cost came in at $20M and change. Hmm. How did that happen? Goodbye, bonus.

With help from Dennis Pratt, a script was delivered three weeks later that Matthew Crouch and his fellow producers were pretty happy with.

Michael Biehn (*Terminator, Aliens, Tombstone*) had been offered the Vice President's role but had passed on the old script. He didn't want to take the part until I could make his character a more active hero. I promised to do what I could, but it had to fall within TBN guidelines. His character is not permitted to do anything on his own initiative to cause the tables to be turned and the forces of good to prevail, unless it has been divinely preordained. The real hero of the movie is God, its human protagonist merely His tool. Despite these restrictions, Michael Biehn, a gifted actor, did a solid job with the material. Nonetheless he lists *Omega Code 2* among his bottom five worst movies.

Michael York's part was easier to fix. I decided that Satan should have a wicked sense of humor, quote the Bible and make wry Shakespearean asides (not unlike an approach I had taken with the Leprechaun).

*"We should kill him."* A husky whisper from Udo Keir, (*Flesh for Frankenstein*, among many cult titles) playing Satan's little helper.

*"Unnatural deeds do breed unnatural troubles,"* quoted Michael York, drawing from Macbeth.

It added to the ripe tone I was creating throughout. We gave the populist Anti-Christ some prescient lines: *"Television, wonderful invention. It does the work for me!"*

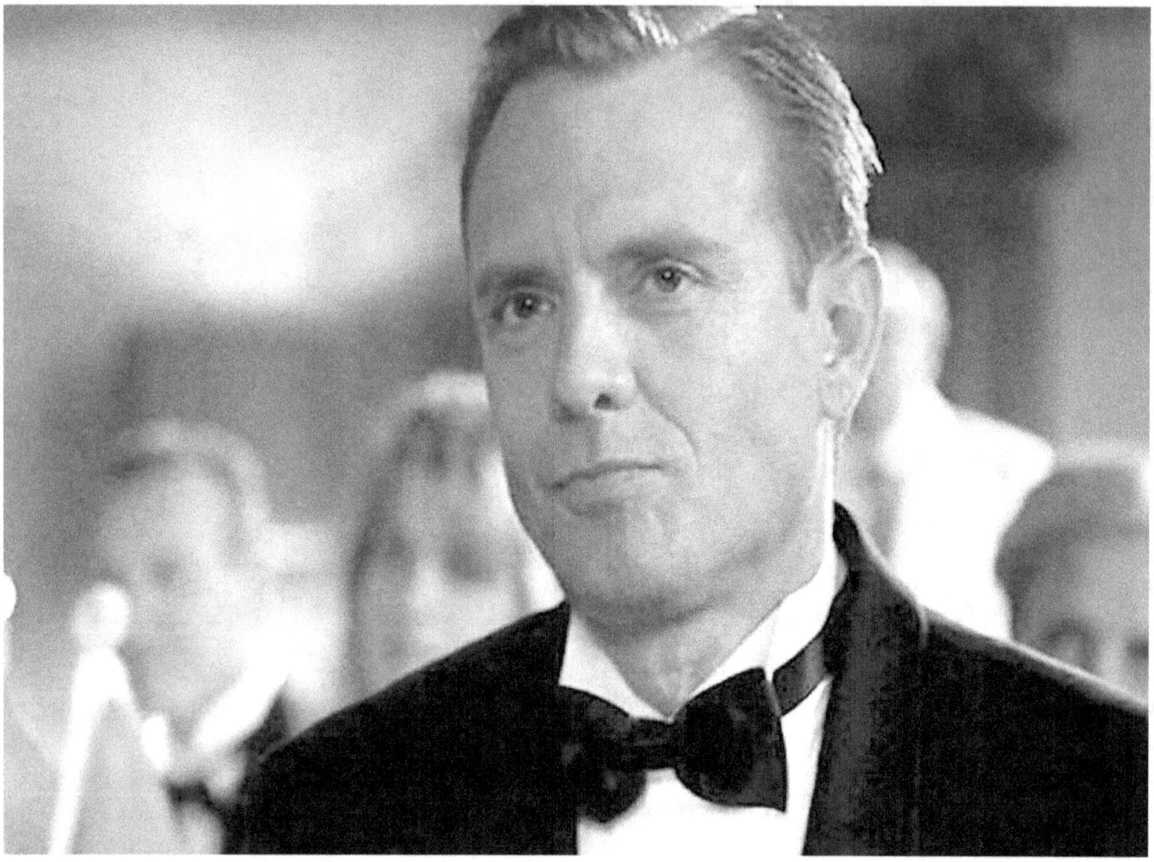

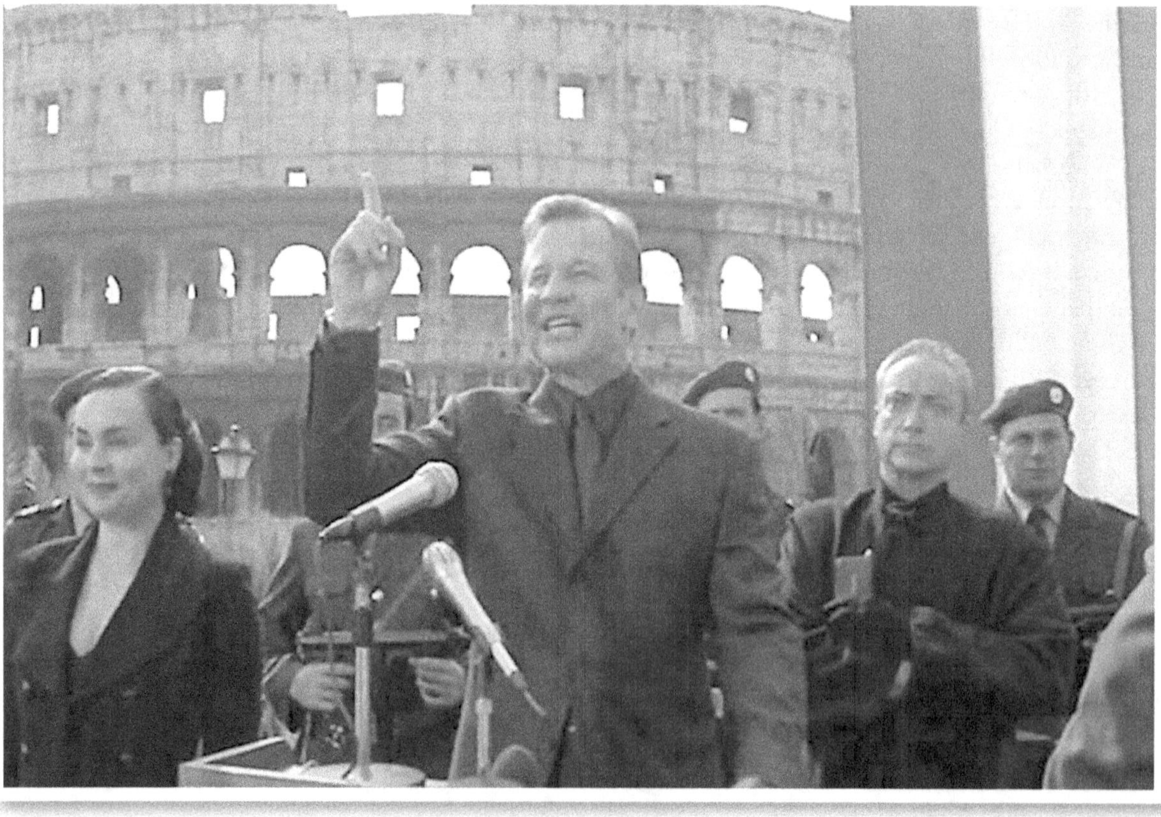

Udo Kier gets a dynamic demise in the apocalyptic finale, worthy of his cult status. Inspired by Christopher Lee's time lapse demise in Hammer's first *Dracula,* I had his face digitally disintegrate.

In his book *Dispatches from Armageddon,* Michael York described my directorial style.

*"I like his no-nonsense brand of direction, treating the actor as a colleague, not a pawn."* Common sense, really. It's a collaborative medium. I don't see the director as puppet master; rather, as the conductor of an orchestra.

TBN wanted me to hire Paul Crouch Jr., Matthew's older brother, whose experience was in video photography, as the 2nd Unit cameraman on a 35mm shoot. Hmm. OK. But in fact he did well, and never reflected his privileged position. I was allowed

to bring back key personnel who had always delivered the goods for me: Bert Dunk (*Happy Face Murders*) as Director of Photography, whose work on the film would receive a Canadian Society of Cinematographers nomination; John Lafferty as Editor, Lynn D'Angona, my former 1st AD, as my 2nd Unit Director for the second time. Corbitt Visual Design, which created all the CGI on *Britannic,* did two segments of the huge visual effects shot list—the President's heart attack and the helicopter attack on the castle. Jerram Swartz became my new 1st AD, very efficient and hardworking. They all did a fantastic job.

The shoot started in LA for two weeks, using such iconic locations as the gothic Park Plaza and Greystone, the former Doheny Mansion built in 1928. Big, bold architecture suited the movie I had in my head. The controversial "baby burning" scene was shot in that magnificent faux-Tudor building. (Spoiler alert: the little tyke is unscathed.)

Brief pause for child endangerment issue. No, we did not endanger a newborn in the burning crib scene; the wriggling foot an inch from the flames was a doll's foot in a matching jumpsuit manipulated offscreen. The baby was never on a set where there was smoke and flame. California has the strictest regulations for newborns in movies; specific hours of the day, no more than twenty minutes of work total, no more than thirty seconds at a time under hot movie lights. We obeyed child labor laws to the letter. But because the scene is so convincing, so discomfort-inducing, people have suspected otherwise.

Then we moved to Rome, where we made good use of the Colosseum as a background for several scenes, including its destruction by a comet. We assembled as large a crowd as we could afford, then at magic hour, shot them running in panic away from the majestic structure. Computer graphics added the converging comet up to the point of impact.

The scene was completed in LA under the supervision of visual effects supervisor Rob Bredow (*Solo: A Star Wars Story*) who had wisely chosen miniatures over digital. We created a 6-foot-tall replica of the front side of the Colosseum, out of separate blocks stacked one upon the other, with thin layers of sandstone grit in between. Three cameras were positioned, then the structure was hit from behind by a blast from an air cannon.

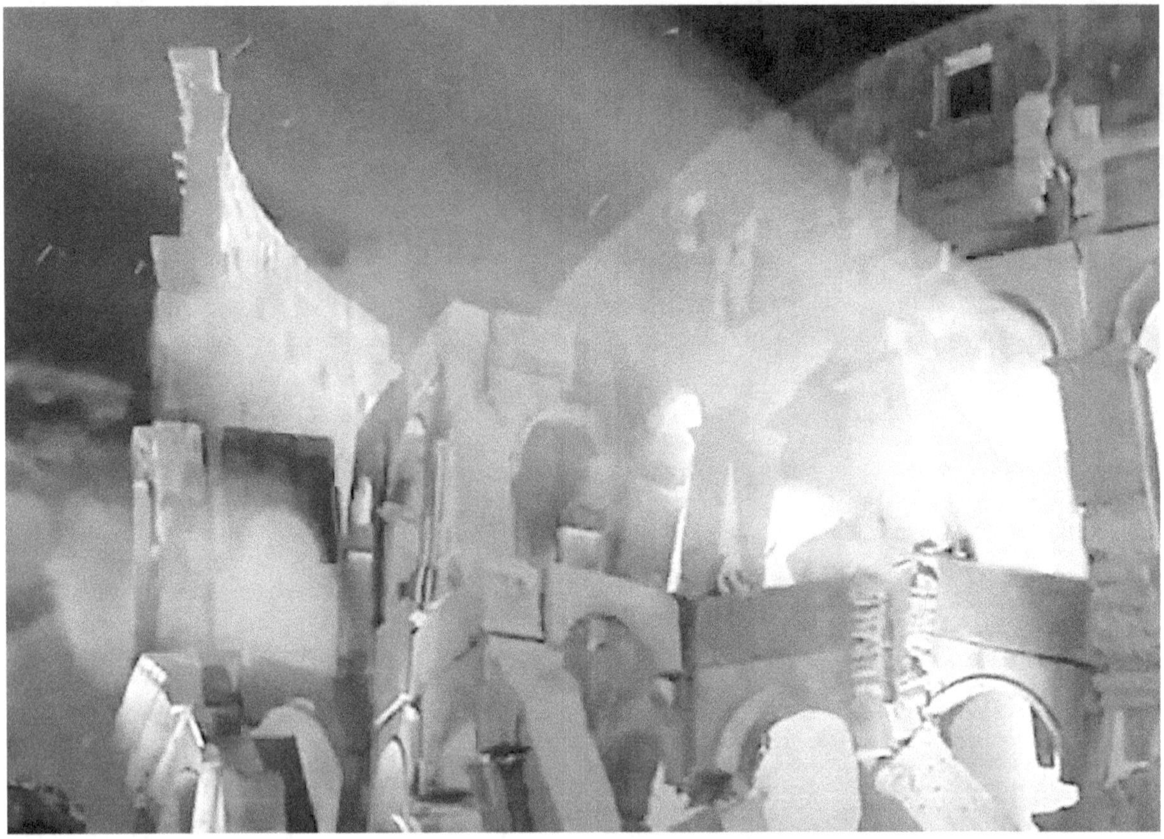

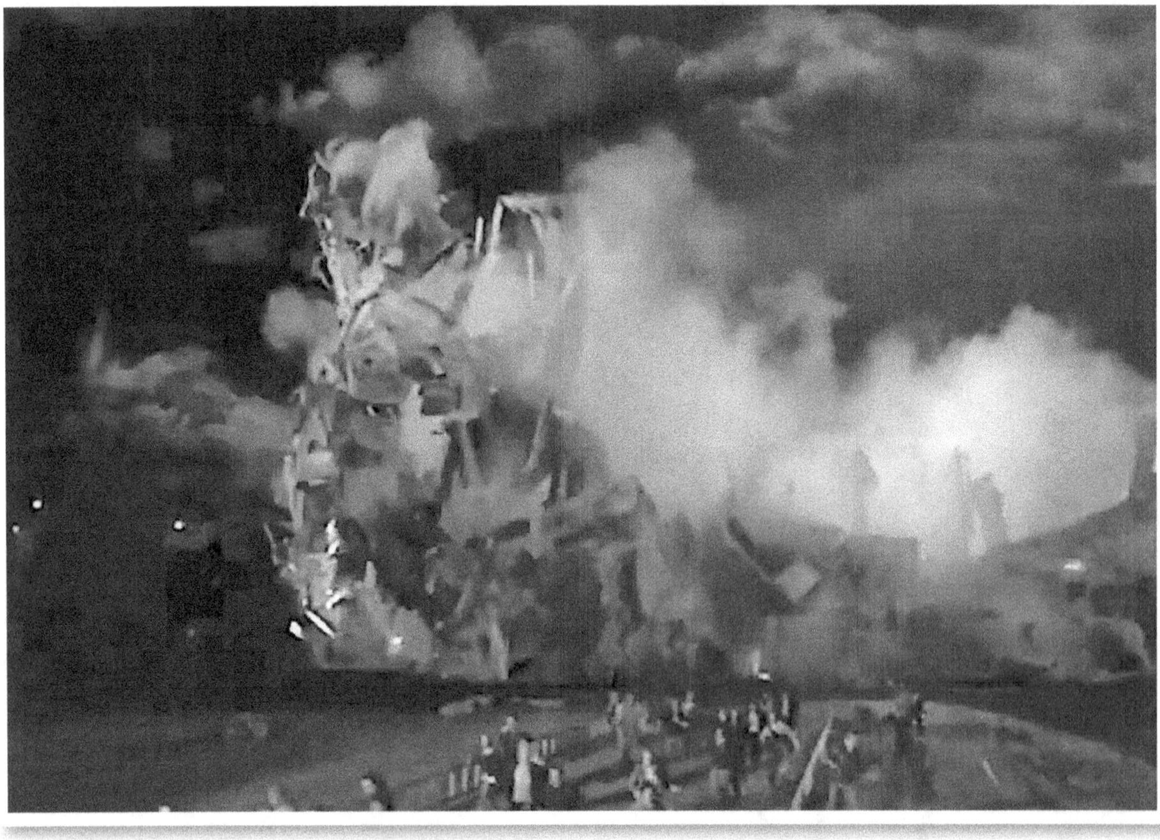

The blocks tumbled both past and onto the cameras. By using an air cannon, rather than explosives, we did not destroy our miniature. We just had to reassemble it, touch up the paintwork, choose three new angles, and go again. Similar techniques were utilized in the destruction of the Sphinx.

My friends at Corbitt Visual Design (*Britannic*) delivered a couple of great shots too. They handled the *Satan vomits hornets* moment. Then they fly over the Great Wall of China. Really.

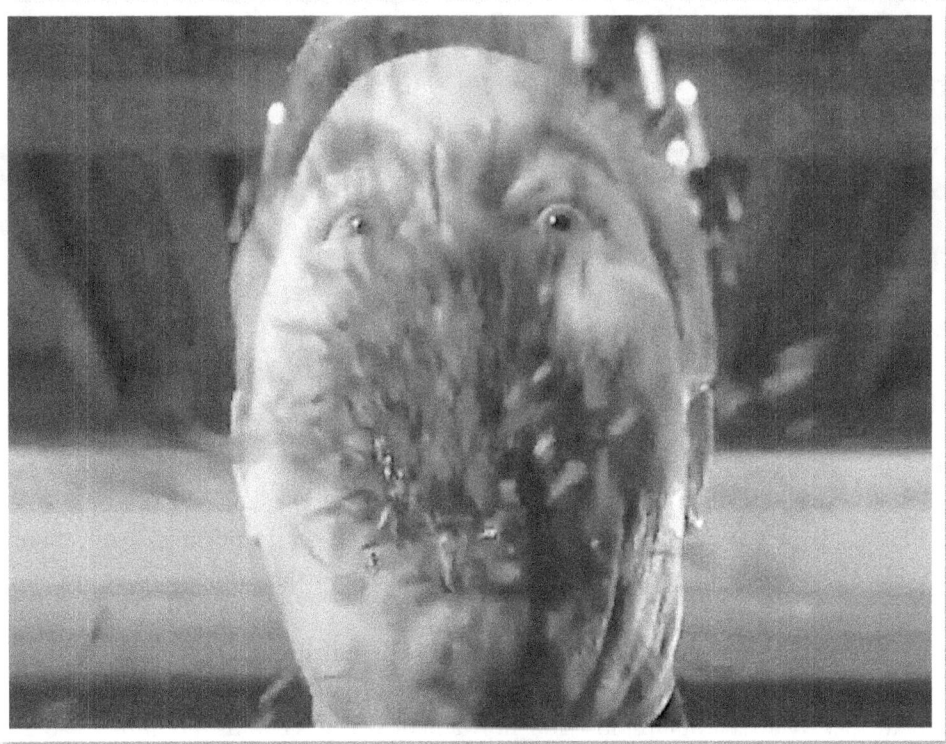

Almost two weeks of the shoot took place at the castle in Bracciano, an hour's journey from Rome. Tom Cruise would later rent the castle for his wedding to Katie Holmes. Built in the 15th century as both a fortress and a residence, it was the frequent site of conflict between the Colonna and Borgia families. Pope Alexander VI sent a papal army to capture it and failed. There are still the pockmarks of cannon ball strikes against its walls. It is now a museum, with medieval weapons on display. I hefted a sword and practiced a few moves. It was a lot heavier than I expected. Those soldiers were strong.

There is an anachronistic paintball battle sequence at the Italian military school, set in 1975, whereas paintball competitions began in 1981. Matthew Crouch, a keen competitor, led his team to victory in the California State Paintball Championships, and he wanted such a scene in the film. I had no objection.

Peripherally the scene demonstrates the Antichrist's ruthlessness (if we were still uncertain) and his grasp of military strategy (surprise the enemy from behind). It gives the film a burst of visual energy before a bunch of wordy scenes.

In *Megiddo: Omega Code 2*, three of the leading characters start as young children then become adults at not one but two different ages in life. This represents a casting challenge. For each character, there must be plausible physical and facial matches between the actors chosen as they age. The character of David Alexander starts as a baby. That part's easy. When we see him, he's 18-year-old Chad Michael Murray (later, the good son in *One Tree Hill*) Finally, it's Michael Biehn as Vice President David Alexander for the rest of the movie. Similarly, with Stone Alexander, he starts as a Bad Seed 6-year-old, played with an eerie quality by 8-year-old Gavin Fink, who was then a stand-in on the *Malcolm in the Middle* series. Stone is next seen as a 24-year-old military school graduate played by Noah Huntley. Noah's facial bone structure and British accent was a good match for Michael York, who will appear twenty-five years older in subsequent scenes.

I wanted to do a child-actor-to-adult-actor transition in one unbroken shot. Bracciano Castle's Hall of Weapons provided the ideal opportunity.

Franco Nero (*Camelot, Django*, etc.), playing the headmaster of the Italian military school to which young Stone has been sent, is giving a lecture on the evolution of weaponry to assembled first year students, including Stone Alexander. The boy loses interest and drifts away. The camera tracks with 8-year-old Gavin Fink, who disappears behind a life-sized statue of a knight on horseback. The camera continues tracking alongside the horse. At the same time the sound of Franco Nero's voice changes to a new, younger voice in mid-sentence. The camera continues, to reveal the now 24-year-old Stone (played by Noah Huntley) stepping out from behind the horse's head, in military cadet uniform, lecturing to a class of teenage students. It was a neat transition.

It was great to work with Chad Michael Murray. I could tell he was going places and he soon did.

It was gratifying to cast David Hedison as the media mogul father. Hedison had costarred with Vincent Price in 1958's iconic Sci-fi horror hit *The Fly*. I was a big fan of his hit TV series *Voyage to the Bottom of the Sea*. I saw him again at a convention, not long after his daughter Alexandra married Jodie Foster. David Hedison continued working until his death at age 91.

Franco Nero gave a solid performance, and graciously arranged a special guided tour of the Vatican for the producers and myself. I'll be forever grateful to have experienced the astounding art on display.

With the Rome shoot concluded, we returned to LA. Initially the plan was to stage the battle of Armageddon in Israel using Israeli Defense Force's military equipment. This was abandoned when the Intifada started during our location scout. Posing as a small documentary crew, we shot VFX plates in Jerusalem for a day then left. Producer Gary Bettman hired a small plane, cruised over the outer Los Angeles area and found the perfect location, Mystery Mesa in Santa Clarita County. Fortifications were built, reenactors hired to be the troops, Gulf War tanks marshalled, and battle commenced, with great pyrotechnic assistance from Paul J. Lombardi and his team.

As part of the attack, I wanted an homage to the *Rat Patrol* TV series with machine gun mounted jeeps blasting through rows of tents. I gave that one to Lynn D'Angona, who did her usual first-rate job.

A particular visual effects coup was devised by Matt Crouch and VFX producer Richard J. Cook. I wanted one shot showing a vast panorama of the battle of Armageddon, stretching to the distant horizon. They had a concept. For $8K they managed to hire a Lear jet with a camera port in its tail and installed a 35mm camera. A 25mm lens delivered a wide angle, with no distortion. Roll camera! The plane took off down a long runway at a remote deserted airfield in the Californian desert. The Lear rose from the tarmac, then switched to the steepest possible ascent, rising ultimately to 8000 feet, from which the camera captured a vast area of the desert below.

The shot was then scanned in reverse. Now the camera seemed to be plunging down from a great height to level off and scud along the desert floor. This VFX plate was given to the CGI artists, who filled the sky with dueling fighter jets. The shot follows an air-to-air missile destroying a plane, then plunges down towards the tank war raging all over the desert. Coming up behind a low-level bomber, the shot concludes as it drops a bomb. Cut to an explosion in foreground from the main unit shoot of the battle scenes. Now we have gone from God's point of view down to the thick of the fight. It is a clever shot.

During the battle scenes, a camera crew from TBN arrived. I was required to wear a wire for a few days so that my directorial instructions could be recorded at any time regardless of where their camera was. Hmm… I never saw those broadcasts but don't think I featured very often. Each night the footage their crew shot would play on TBN, coupled with raw VHS dailies, with visible timecode, from the previous day's shoot. Kind of like showing the future DVD extras before the film is finished. Prefiguring Kickstarter

funding, Paul Crouch Sr. used these visual progress reports on the movie to request further donations towards its cost.

On the final night of the battle scenes, Matt bussed in 200 Pentecostal volunteers to swell the ranks of the reenactors. It was freezing cold. Groups of them huddled round small gas heaters for warmth singing Christian songs between set ups. I went over to one group to thank them for their contribution. They decided to give me a blessing, crowding round me, laying their hands on me, even though I told them I was agnostic. They prayed that I might find God like they had. They were genuinely happy people. The Pentecostals that I met throughout the movie all sincerely believed that their brand of Christianity was the way the world would be saved from despair. I saw their charities in operation. I met crack and heroin addicts they had rescued from skid row who were now living happy productive lives. I accepted the blessing. It was very sweet. I was touched. Did it make me a better person? I'm still same ethical hedonist. Perhaps it stopped me getting any worse!

Postproduction began in November just after the election of George W. Bush, who achieved the US Presidency with a big assist from Evangelical Christians. Matthew Crouch and his associates were exultant. The Bush victory was part of God's plan to save America from liberal decadence. Evangelical Christians of a variety of denominations tipped the balance in the 2000 election. They would do it again in 2016.

I hired John Lafferty as editor. He had been the visual effects editor on *Britannic* and we had developed a good rapport. Together we now adopted a trailer-cutting approach that would speed along the opening twenty-four minutes of backstory before the star Michael York appeared. We started the movie with a title card quote from the book of Revelations:

*"The Beast shall ascend out of the bottomless pit, and they that dwell on earth shall wonder when they behold the Beast that was, and is not, yet is…" Revelations. 17.8*

Michael's unique voice delivered the text with a wry quality, perfectly setting the tone for the movie. Next we placed a scene between Michael York and Udo Keir, lifted from later in the movie. Atop the hill of Megiddo, they survey their armies camped below and enthuse over their forthcoming victory with a degree of moustache twirling. OK folks, big scenes are coming. Time for a flashback to show how this all came about. Buckle up. Cue fiery Megiddo title!

I got along with Matthew Crouch well enough, but naturally there was creative conflict over my director's cut. Two Type A personalities…what do you expect? Under DGA rules I had eight weeks after the editor's assembly to deliver my director's cut and the right to show nothing to producers till that date. But I've always found it to be wise to let producers view an early work in progress, get input, before the editor and I homed in on the director's cut. Shortly after we started, we discovered that one of the producer's staff had access to the digitized dailies and was also editing the film on his computer in an adjacent office. "Cutting behind the director" during the director's editorial period is a clear violation of DGA rules for which the producers could be sanctioned. It all got resolved quickly. I stayed involved well beyond my allotted time and was happy enough with the final cut. I adopted some of their ideas, and John Lafferty used his editorial experience to talk them out of the worst of theirs.

I was shooting *Heartland Ghost* in Calgary when *Megiddo* was mixed. The most disappointing change they made was to the soundtrack during the battle sequences. To help the audience to understand the military strategy of both sides, I had a succession of radio communications from troops on both sides laid into the soundtrack to blend with sound effects and music. But it was dropped, a decision which diffused audience involvement in the ebb and flow of the battle.

At the final cut stage, the producers decided to substantially increase the number of visual effects shots. Much of the CGI was good. But the key, most expensive, effect - "The Beast," a 10 foot tall, horned-and-hooved Satan—was disappointing in design and barely Play Station in execution. But it did add to the campiness of the piece.

In an unfortunate coincidence, *Megiddo: Omega Code 2* was booked into 400 theatres across America to open on September 21, 2001. A big Hollywood premiere had been planned; red carpet, live TV coverage, the works. After 9/11, there was talk of changing the red carpet at the premiere to a black carpet. (OMG) Michael York refused to attend such a premiere so it was sensibly cancelled. In fact, the release should have been postponed till the nation had time to recover. The Arnold Schwarzenegger antiterrorist movie *Collateral Damage* was pulled immediately from release, resurfacing four months later. Several films showing the World Trade Center underwent reediting. But TBN decided to stick with the planned release on September 21st despite all theaters in New York and Washington, DC canceling their bookings, reducing the number of playdates to 300. I heard that GoodTimes, the movie's home video distributor, would not move their VHS release date scheduled for March 2002.

Matthew Crouch issued the following statement.

*"So as to be sensitive to a grieving nation, we have examined the possibility of delaying the release of Megiddo. After much staff prayer and consultation with pastors, we are convinced that we must stay on schedule to release Megiddo around the world. The overwhelming consensus is that we are releasing a movie containing an answer to the question that we did not even know would be asked. The horrible tragedy that was September 11, 2001 has left our national leaders uttering statements like 'We are witnessing the battle of good versus evil' and 'Is this the end of the world?'—sublimely echoing Megiddo's tag line, 'In the beginning…the end had a name.' Millions around the country are turning to prayer and are calling on God as our only hope.*

*We know that the heart of God weeps over the suffering of His people. He does not crush buildings with His hand nor blow airplanes off their course with His breath. Yet in the midst of tragedy, God in his ultimate love and compassion is seeking to give an answer for hurting people everywhere. Gener8Xion Entertainment is humbled to think that twenty-four months ago the production of a project was set into motion that we now pray He can use to this purpose.*

*Who could have foreseen that on September 21 we would be releasing a motion picture dealing with events prophesied in the Bible that are shockingly similar to what this nation has just experienced? Who could have foreseen that it would be a motion picture that rallies the resiliency and determination of the American people in the midst of catastrophe? Megiddo offers the hope of an ultimate triumph over all acts of evil and presents a glorious future without sorrow, fear or pain. It's God's very nature to open His arms and embrace a world that through its weeping, anger, and despair is questioning 'Why?'*

*In the fullness of time, God may have prepared Megiddo to be an answer.*

*Out of tribulation…hope arises. Know that we are praying for all of you."*

*Sincerely,*

*Matthew Crouch*

*President - Gener8Xion Entertainment*

Hmm…

I went to a Burbank theatre on the first Friday for the 7:30 session. It was a full house split more or less evenly between devout Christians and secular customers, including some crew members. Michael York's dry asides got laughs from both sections of the audience. There was a collective wince at the shot of the undamaged Pentagon. But at the end of the film when God starts smiting the forces of evil, the Christians started cheering and it spread across the whole theater. Opposites united by gung-ho action. I got some satisfaction from that. R. Lee Ermey, who played the US President, took family members to the film a couple of times in Palmdale, a strong Christian community. He said the audience was particularly vocal in their approval. Some were there for the third time. They enjoyed seeing the Book of Revelations as a glossy, VFX heavy, faith-based action adventure romp. But hardline Christian critics objected to its genre tropes and preposterous politics, as did most secular critics, though Harry Knowles's *Ain't It Cool News* review got what I was doing,

*"…the kind of overtly high camp old fashioned B movie that they basically don't make any more."*

True, it's a 1960s-style religious epic. Compared to the *Left Behind* franchise, *Omega Code 2* is the crown jewel of the Godsploitation genre. And it's a lot of fun If you don't take it seriously.

However, ten days after the carnage of 9/11, the wound was too raw. Secular audiences were not attracted to a film with the tag line: "In the beginning the end had a name—Megiddo—That time is now…" Now? Really? If TBN had been able to hold the release till March 2002, when US forces had struck back against Al Qaeda, and American spirits had been lifted, then a film about the triumph of good over evil would have generated substantially bigger box office.

In a 4-week run, Megiddo grossed just over $6M, not bad for 300 theaters, but half of what its predecessor took. However, it did ship at least 450,000 video copies in the US and Canada alone, before playing repeatedly on TBN.

As mentioned, Paul Crouch Jr. was the 2nd Unit DP. He worked hard and did a good job. Whenever I visited the 2nd Unit, I found him to be a modest man for the elder son in a billion-dollar multi-media empire, which Paul referred to as "the family business." Over the weeks in our conversations, I got a sense of tensions within the family dynamic, the stresses and strains of working for a domineering father, and now for his younger brother. I couldn't help thinking this will not end well.

TBN would have its share of tribulations, although its end times have not yet arrived: "Molestation scandal is latest setback to once-mighty Trinity…" was one of a series of stories in the *Los Angeles Times*.

Ah, what a wicked web we weave… Behind the scenes of *Megiddo—Omega Code 2* would make a powerful movie. Shakespearean tragedy, Jacobean revenge drama, with Cain and Abel, Jacob and Esau among Biblical parallels; it's all there. Time will sharpen *Megiddo's* allegory. Inevitably, *Megiddo* was roundly damned by critics. Yet in the era of Trump, a movie about a demagogue's rise to power though media manipulation seems more relevant than ever.

Speaking of US presidents, in 2003 I directed the *DC 9/11: Time of Crisis*, only the second film at that time to be made about a United States President while he was still in office. The first, released on June 19, 1963, was *PT 109*, which depicted the actions of Navy Lt. John F. Kennedy in WWII.

Joe Kennedy had maneuvered Warner Bros into the production as a none-too-subtle way of kicking off his son's reelection campaign for 1964. JFK had approval of Cliff Robertson's casting and is said to have liked the movie—but remarked that it could have been shorter. He was assassinated five months later. What a different world we might have lived in.

Jerry Offsay, then Showtime's president of programming, called me late at night with a problem. Over ten years he had greenlit more than 300 television movies, including three of mine.

He asked me to take over a movie shooting in two weeks because its veteran director Daniel Petrie Sr. had fallen ill. The film would depict the first ten days inside the Bush administration after 9/11. Timothy Bottoms had been cast as George Bush, a reasonable lookalike and a great actor. The script was written and would be produced by conservative film maker Lionel Chetwynd. Not a word of his script could be changed without his permission, because that was the deal Showtime was obliged to make when acquiring the project. Jerry, like myself, was of a left-of-center persuasion. He knew the political purpose of the movie (like *PT 109*) was intended to polish the President's image before the 2004 election, but he was obliged to make it anyway. Would I step in as director? The opportunity to make a fact-based docudrama was irresistible.

Initially Showtime's senior management had wanted a prestige director to take over and made an offer to Roland Joffé (*The Killing Fields, The Mission*), but Joffé wanted more prep time, and to change the script. No script changes. No deal. The clock was ticking. They needed somebody now. Jerry Offsay was aware I had taken over three movies in the 1980s when they were already in production. He got me approved, and I was on a plane to Toronto within two days.

This was another film Margaret pleaded with me not to make but Jerry urgently needed my help.

Showtime knew the movie was going to be controversial. To prevent picketing by Canadians unhappy with the U.S. president's policies, preproduction had started in Toronto under the innocuous title of *The Big Dance*. Dancing silhouettes graced the company letterhead. Shooting in Toronto had to start in two weeks without fail. Nearly fifty supporting parts were still uncast or unconfirmed, some of them requiring lookalikes of Cabinet members, Cheney, Rumsfeld, Wolfowitz, Rice, Ashcroft, Mineta, and Secretary of State Colin Powell could be cast with US actors. The rest had to be found from the Canadian talent pool.

Check out my lookalike choices for FBI Director Bob Mueller, and for fireman Bob Beckwith, who stood beside Bush during his "bullhorn" moment at Ground Zero.

My biggest production challenge was the SARS epidemic which broke out soon after I arrived. People began wearing surgical masks while walking the streets. The public buildings chosen to simulate Washington were suddenly withdrawn as locations on the grounds of public health safety. Someone among the cast and crew just might be one of "the infected." Covid-19 has since shown how easily a virus can spread. When we lost our choice for FBI headquarters at the last minute, I heard of a police procedural TV series on hiatus with a big standing set. Our fearless art department had it re-dressed and ready in the nick of time. How to simulate the rubble of Ground Zero was a major conundrum. Luckily, by the end of the shoot, we found a large demolition site which worked well. Each day was a scramble, but I loved every minute of it.

The script, written by the producer Lionel Chetwynd, a rare and proud Hollywood conservative, was intended to show how a decisive, well-informed, articulate President took charge of government and rallied the people in an unprecedented crisis. Each scene was based on me-

dia reports, Cabinet records and handwritten notes taken by Karl Rove and White House House Press Secretary Ari Fleischer. I saw some of these documents and the script reflects them accurately, but they were shaped to convey the president's analytical powers and off-the-cuff eloquence. We have not seen such a whip-smart Bush on the TV screen before or since, said one critic.

Chetwynd told me that the White House had granted him a 15-minute interview with President Bush to get his personal feelings on the crisis as it unfolded. The conversation ran over. In fact, Chetwynd noticed, as he left the Oval Office, the next scheduled visitor, former UK Prime Minister Margaret Thatcher, had been kept waiting for forty-five minutes. His meeting with Bush convinced Chetwynd that the president's intellect and grasp of world affairs were underestimated by the media.

Many scenes have an issue or spin that continues to divide Left and Right; I hope that the intervening years give the film new a perspective, particularly in light of the Donald Trump's conduct of the presidency. Erik Lundegaard's *Huffington Post* article, "DC 9/11 is the new *Reefer Madness*" sees the film as a Monster's Ball of ideologues, whose pronouncements now drip with dramatic irony: "This is a movie that *actually celebrates the worst foreign policy decisions we've ever made*. It's like finding a 1964 film celebrating the Gulf of Tonkin resolution or a 1943 film celebrating the internment of Japanese Americans." In his review, J. Hoberman identified which category of Propaganda Tool *DC 9/11: Time of Crisis* represented: Stalinist "Father of Our Nation" myth movie. Another critic described *DC 9/11: Time of Crisis* as a Project for the New American Century infomercial, as approved by Karl Rove. But my view of propaganda is that it is a double-edged sword. It often reveals more about the propagandists than they realize. With hindsight, they might regret some of the hubris sprinkled throughout.

So, Rumsfeld actually said at a Pentagon breakfast on the morning of the attacks: "Something's coming, something big …" Hmm. Speculation or information? Ninety minutes later American Airlines Flight 77 struck the west wall of the Pentagon. Scanning through video coverage of the event, I found a wide angle showing Rumsfeld helping stretcher bearers evacuating the wounded. So I staged a closer angle with John Cunningham in matching clothing, which I intercut. We had access to everything Fox News shot during 9/11, enabling me to have live news always playing on TV screens. Some iconic images were digitally composited with live action. All my experience selecting stock footage for dozens of shows came in useful on this one.

Bush actually said: "This will decidedly not be another Vietnam."

Hmm, I wondered, as I read the script over and over, do they really want to be on record as saying some of these things? The Cabinet meeting on the night of the attack in the subterranean PEOC (President's Emergency Operations Center) clearly shows Bush had his sights set on Saddam Hussein from the get-go. I knew I was directing a film that would only find favor with rightwing media, yet, with the passage of time, it would have historical value as an authentic example of neocon thought, styled as advocate docudrama. So I wish my film a long and fruitful autopsy.

The invasion of Iraq started during the shoot. It was surreal to enter my Toronto hotel room after twelve hours of filming characters in the embryonic stage of planning the Iraq war, then switch on CNN and watch those plans being carried out. Don't they realize, I wondered, that this will not be as easy as they claim? They might be blowing up the entire Middle East! And they did. The cast, almost all lefties, expressed similar disbelief, but like me, had a duty to honor the contract we signed to shoot the script as written. I encouraged each actor to find tone and quirks that could operate beneath the surface of the dialogue. A moment that I was allowed to get away with was this shot of Karl Rove, Ari Fleischer and Andrew Card reacting to an awkward moment in the President's first TV address after the attacks. My direction to the actors was: See no evil, hear no evil speak on evil.

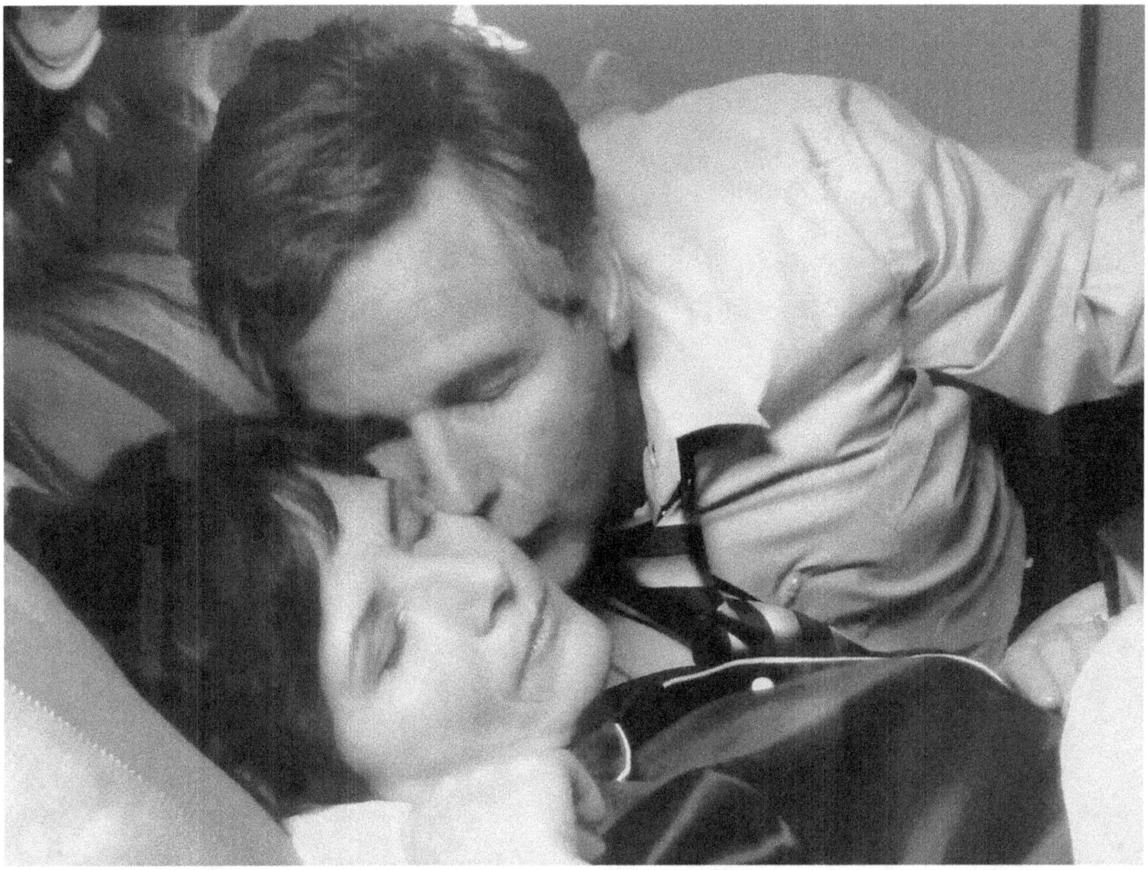

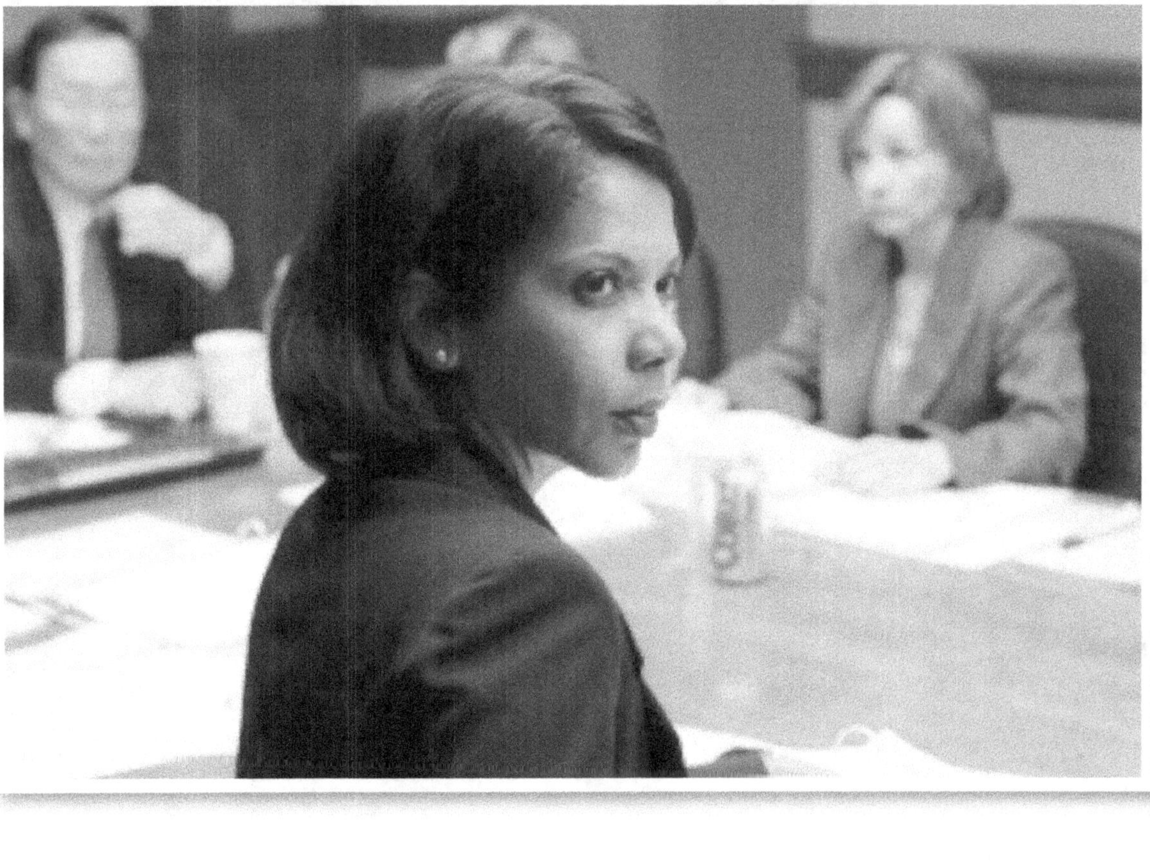

I think Timothy Bottoms convincingly captured the Bush swagger. To show his tender side there were scenes with his wife Laura, nicely played by Mary Gordon Murray.

The centerpiece of an ensemble effort. Timothy Bottoms's performance of a role built from Lego blocks of political exposition is nuanced and masterful.

I was lucky to get Penny Johnson Jerald as Condoleezza Rice. She had a big part in *24* at the time, but was willing to be shuttled back and forth between LA and Toronto. She played Condi with a mixture of personal warmth and steely grace. She would play her again in 2006 mini-series *The Path to 9/11/.*

John Cunningham nailed the patronizing Secretary of Defense Donald Rumsfeld. He had the voice, the cadence, the look. He really brought the text to life.

Lawrence Pressman captured the cold blooded Chaney. This was the "shoot it down" moment.

The " *I'm a war President* " scene was written to counter media reports that Chaney not Bush was running the Presidency. Pressman subtly conveyed Chaney's disappointment.

Stephen Macht's Paul Wolfowitz brought flavor to an underwritten part. His 'weapons of mass destruction' speech selling Bush on the Iraq war was cleverly handled.

Karl Rove's Machiavellian instincts are clearly visible in Alan Royal's cunning interpretation of the Senior Advisor to the President. I heard later that Mr. Rove did not care for the performance. He joked that he had hoped to be played by Brad Pitt. But I think he got the point.

PAUL WOLFOWITZ
DEPUTY SECRETARY OF DEFENSE

A sidebar: I am sure the change in director—to a liberal with a slew of wacky, irreverent movies in his repertoire—was a concern to Rove. Was there a cuckoo in his nest? During the shoot, and for a couple of months afterward, when I called my wife from Toronto, our home phone would sometimes make clicking sounds during calls. A couple of times during postproduction, I would switch on my computer and find my email momentarily resorted. Just a coincidence, of course…

*DC 9/11: Time of Crisis* was the first time I shot digital and not film. It was liberating not to have to worry about stock and processing costs. It was a timesaver, too. Instead of changing 35mm magazines which ran out between ten and twenty minutes depending on their load, I could keep the camera rolling through fifty minutes of tape if I wanted to. It was helpful for several scenes where twenty people were gathered around a long conference table and each one needed coverage of some kind.

After getting establishing shots of the conference, I would lay a rail along one side of the table, shoot one actor or group of actors' reactions and dialogue, then when the scene ended, I would not call "Cut", resulting in the crew talking, a new scene number being slated etc., thus breaking the mood. Instead, the camera would slide down the rail, and frame up on the next group or actor I wanted to feature, while the scene remained fresh in their minds, and I would tell them to start the scene again from the beginning. If an actor fluffed, I would quietly ask him to do it over till the line was right. In less than half an hour in one continuous take, I got all coverage needed for that side of the table. Then I would repeat the process on the other side.

It's important to let some air into a picture that's largely composed of interior dialogue scenes. Wherever possible choose locations with the biggest look.

Arrivals and departures also help in these circumstances. Via CGI, I added pilots getting into position to protect Air Force One.

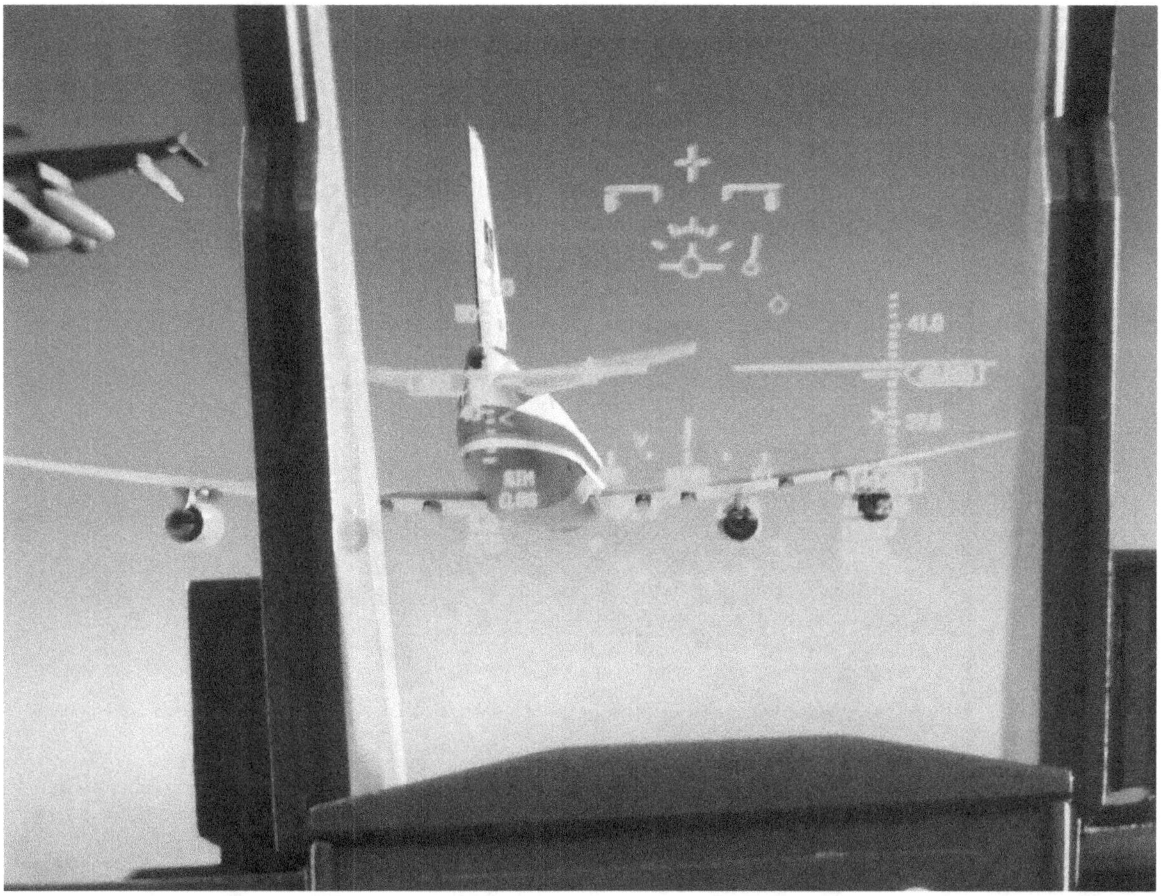

UNITED STATES OF AMERICA

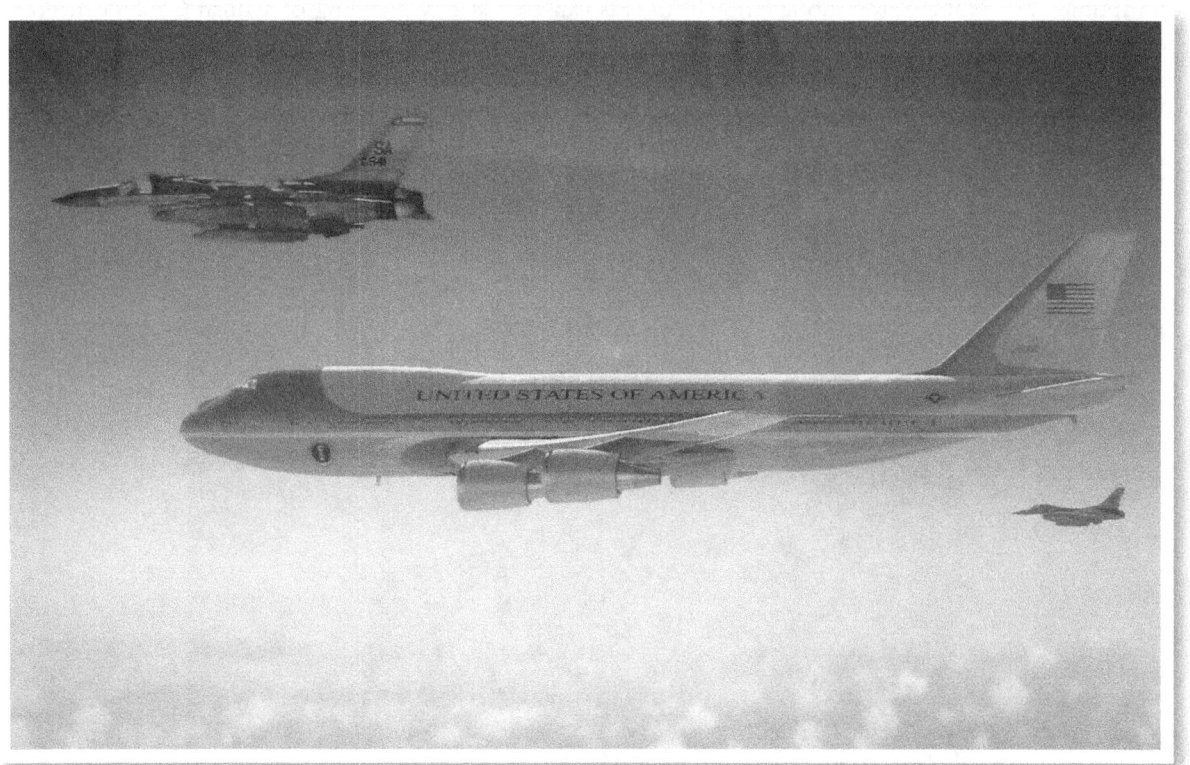

Video of Air Force One's take off from Florida that morning indicated a steep *angle of attack* as it climbed. The pilot was no doubt anxious to get the President out of range of a possible surface to air missile. Intelligence surveillance had discovered that that day's code word for Air Force One appearing in chatter on terrorist networks. In hindsight, a coincidence, but in these opening hours all threats seemed possible. This gave me an idea for a shot to reflect the central character's challenge and resolve. As the plane rises sharply, a pencil rolls back down the President's desk. He blocks it from falling off. It was the first shot on Day One and it convinced the hierarchy that the replacement director was not going to phone it in.

Due to the SARS outbreak, my producer remained in LA. He vetted dailies remotely and was generally complimentary. None of the subtle embellishments caused a stir. My staging of a Bush Cabinet meeting with the president striding back and forth beside the conference table issuing assignments to his key lieutenants like a brigade commander was ruled a good choice, not ironic hyperbole.

I emphasized the arrogance of Greg Itzin's smoothly conceited John Ashcroft by shooting a key speech in low wide angle. But adjustments were ordered from time to time.

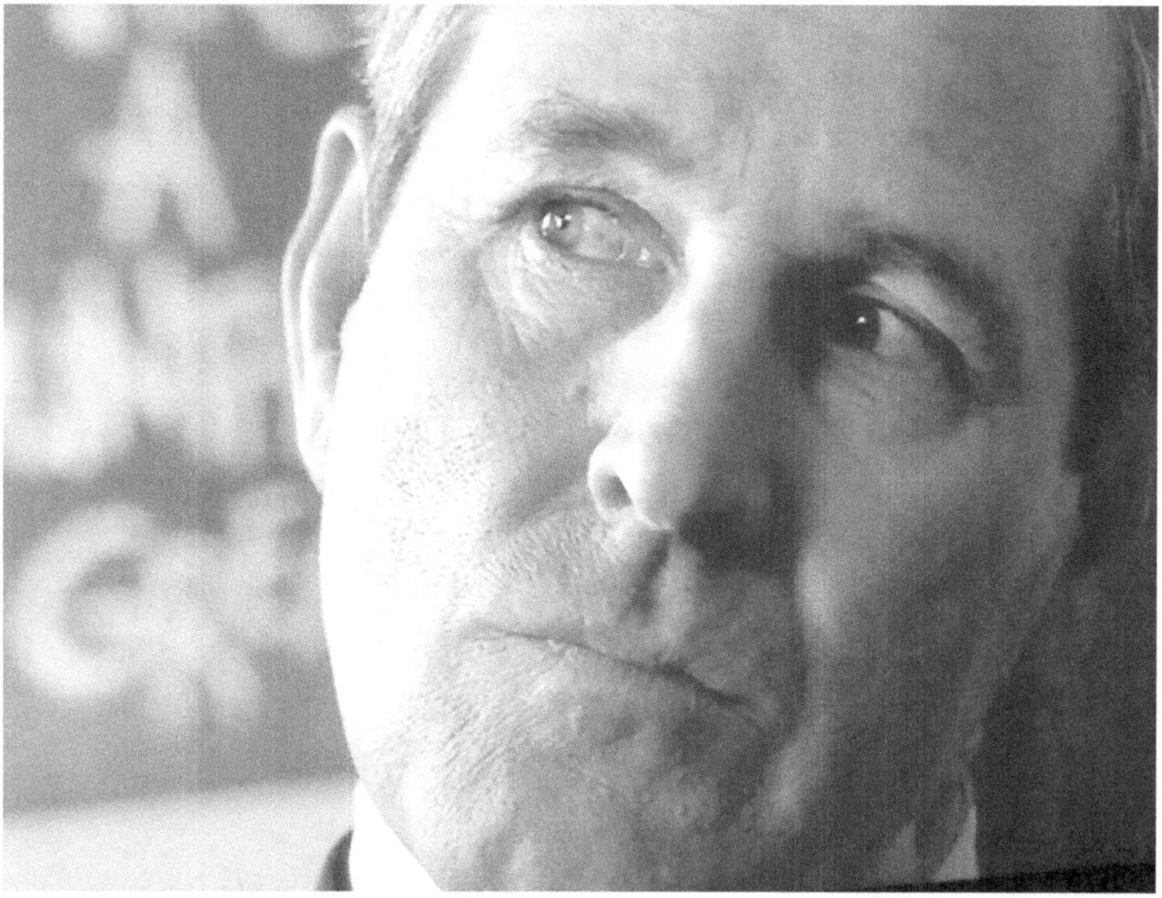

EMMA E. BOOKER
ELEMENTARY SCHOOL
SARASOTA, FLORIDA

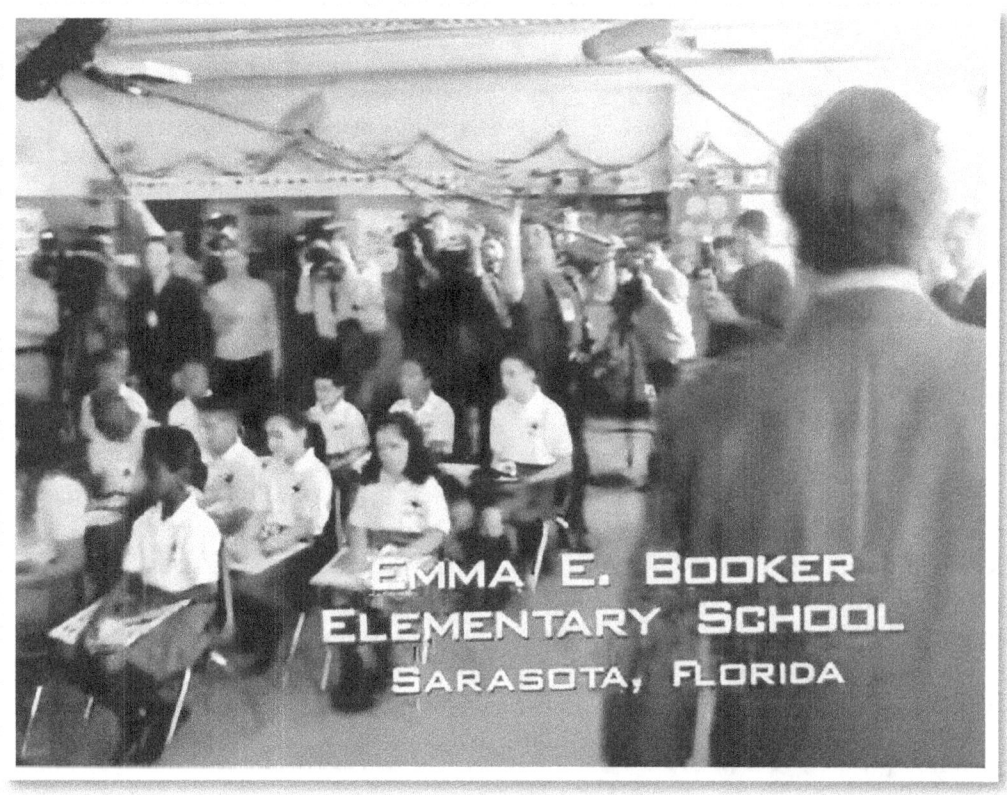

A battle I lost in the editing process was not being allowed to reflect the length of time Bush continued to read to the schoolchildren after receiving word of the crash into the second tower. I wanted to superimpose a title indicating how many minutes he waited. The word came down from on high: *absolutely not.* The issue was ultimately glossed over by a dissolve. And perhaps Bush was right to sit tight and remain outwardly calm till more information had been gathered, then make an exit.

On Day Two, I had apparently allowed Bush to be too angry in an outburst on Air Force One: "Brian, the President would not lose control like that …" Presidents have human moments too, I countered, to no avail. I had to reshoot parts of that scene on our last day. The original performance was more truthful. The eagle-eyed will notice Timothy Bottoms had gained ten pounds during the month between medium shot and closeup.

The weight of responsibility on Timothy's shoulders every day of the shoot was monumental, but he always carried out the brief with dedication and expertise. On that last day, the inner liberal Tim had to bust out. After all, he had played Bush for comedy in the short-lived series *That's My Bush!* On the final take of the scene in the Marine One set, while the camera was still rolling, he jumped onto the window seat, pulled down his pants and mooned New York (as a green screen) while uttering a derisive stream of Bush-isms relating to international consensus. I think those tapes have since been destroyed.

Showtime were happy with the movie. The change in directors had not been a disaster. They had dodged a bullet. I felt confident that after four films, and particularly this last tricky assignment, I would continue in their circle of regular directors. But I was wrong. Jerry Offsay, president of programming, had been tasked with making bricks without straw. For years he had to compete in the ratings with heavily promoted HBO movies with a third of their production costs and publicity budgets. Offsay's ten year contract had come to an end. Viacom decided they wanted a change in Showtime's programming policy, shifting the emphasis from original movies to series, which generate more hours of programming for the same publicity expenditure.

Viacom replaced Jerry Offsay with Robert Greenblatt, who has a record of developing network-defining hits such as *The X-Files*, *Ally McBeal* and *Beverly Hills, 90210* at Fox. Under Greenblatt's aegis, Showtime would launch *Dexter*, *Nurse Jackie*, *The Tudors* and *Weeds*, all very successful. I managed to get a meeting with Mr. Greenblatt shortly after his appointment, at which I pointed to the many genres I had handled both in longform and episodic and offered to be useful. He gave me a cordial hearing, and said he would get back to me. I never heard from him or any Showtime executive again. It's a common Hollywood custom to discard the retainers of the old regime. This was a serious blow. Showtime had given me quality scripts, with quality casts, on above average TV budgets. Finding a new sponsor on that quality level was going to be hard, particularly after *DC 911: Time of Crisis* had received such a critical drubbing for political reasons.

For six months after making *DC 9/11: Time of Crisis*, my agents had trouble getting me meetings with network executives. "I'm not hiring the guy that made the Bush movie" was one comment. Another said to me directly, "I can't forgive you for helping Bush get a second term." Critics praised or reviled the movie along party lines. To liberal executives, I became the Leni Riefenstahl of cable movie directors, guilty of making *Triumph of the Swill*. I am not ashamed of taking on *DC 9/11*. Diverse sides of political and social issues are entitled to have their stories told. I've served clients as dissimilar as Pentecostal Christians and a gay Video On Demand channel. I'm a professional filmmaker. It's what I do.

# CHAPTER 48
## Film Doctoring

In addition to direction, Regent Entertainment hired me to carry out a succession of film doctoring jobs (*Sanctimony*, *The Ghost*, *Dante's Cove*, *Hotel Mystique*, *Ice Spiders* and *Crash and Byrnes*). Here's some doctoring detail about the last-mentioned.

Regent had shot a film in Canada, written by and co-starring Wolf Larsen, whom I had directed in the first season of *Tarzan*. We had enjoyed working together. Regent had intended the project as a low budget theatrical and at the same time the pilot for an action comedy spy series entitled *Crash and Byrnes*. Yes, you guessed it—the names of the two leading characters. Wolf, together with British actor Greg Ellis, play mismatched agents forced to team up to hunt a terrorist (Joanna Pacula) with a bomb. The Regent team were not yet happy with the film and invited my help. It had some good scenes but the chief problems were pace, plot coherence, and the young female lead was unconvincing. To be fair to the director, he had too much to shoot in only eighteen days. The film reminded me of the earnest campiness of my 1987 *Panther* pictures. My instinct was to finetune it in that direction.

I flew to Vancouver and recut the film with the editor. We tightened flat patches, and dropped unnecessary scenes, reducing the running time to eighty minutes. To achieve the needed 90-minute running time,

I inserted title cards describing new scenes to be shot, and—a saving grace in movie resuscitation—selected stock footage. The Regent executives authorized two more days of shooting with limited cast, crew, and equipment.

During my *Mission Impossible* period in 1988, I had had brief dealings with a lady in the Paramount stock footage department. A decade later, she was now in charge of supplying Paramount stock for TV and home video productions. I proposed a bulk purchase arrangement which continued over six subsequent projects. If I bought a minimum of twenty-five shots under ten seconds in length per production, the license fee for world video and TV would be $250 per shot. Theatrical excluded. I bought thirty-five very helpful images. They ranged from picturesque establishing shots to the building blocks for new action scenes.

At one point, *Crash and Byrnes*, quarrelsome spies on the run from rogue agents, jump out of a building into a river (well, their stunt doubles do). After a dissolve, we see Wolf Larsen and Greg Ellis clambering out of the river onto the rocky riverbank. Here was an opportunity to extend their escape. How about black ops helicopters appearing and chasing them into the forest? Can we afford that on a pickup budget? Stock footage to the rescue.

In new scene specially written by Wolf we see: Crash and Byrnes bickering (they do that a lot) as they walk along the shale bank to the river, from which they had emerged in the original shoot. Then they react to an off-screen noise and look up.

Cut to a stock shot from the 1995 virus movie *Outbreak* where two choppers appear over the tree canopy ahead.

Cut to Crash and Byrnes running for cover.

Cut to another stock shot from *Outbreak*. The chopper wheels round. The location looks identical to where Crash and Byrnes were walking. River, forest, sand and shale. Add pilot's voice reporting the fugitives have been sighted.

Intercut multiple dynamic angles of Crash and Byrnes running through the forest with stock shots of the choppers flying low over the trees, reporting progress of the pursuit in VO. Although there were no pyrotechnics, this device sparked up the energy level and added production value. Good for the trailer, too. In all, I used seven shots from *Outbreak*, and it worked because the location I chose for the new shoot was an excellent match to the stock. The shale river bank was right beside a sound mixing studio I had frequented. It was a pleasant spot for lunch breaks. With future location potential, I thought. Everywhere you go is a location to a film director.

In two days, we shot new material that boosted clarity, gave Joanna Pacula more to do, and exploited the genuine comedic chemistry between Wolf Larsen and Greg Ellis. Regent were pleased with the faster, more energetic movie. *Crash and Byrnes* played on Showtime, and sold well internationally but no buyer saw its series potential.

Thirty stock footage shots from the Paramount library helped enliven *Ice Spiders*, further enhanced by creature effects by BFX Imageworks' Steve and BenniQue Blasini. In one effect, the Blasinis took a stock shot of a skier crashing on a slope, and added a digital giant spider leaping onto his back, causing him to wipe out. It's a spectacular shock moment.

Another film I reedited was writer director Uwe Boll's first English language film shot in Vancouver, entitled *Sanctimony*. Think *Seven* gene-spliced with Bret Ellis Easton's *American Psycho*, with Casper Van Dien in the Christian Bale role as the bored stock broker who becomes a serial killer. I designed a punchy new opening credit sequence using stylized animation of lurid newspaper headlines about the murders. Ruthless cutting clarified confusing narrative development and tightened lethargic pacing. Ultimately, the best version of Uwe Boll's nihilistic movie that could be achieved ran only eighty-six minutes. "Tighter than a rattler's tail…" said the *Variety* review.

I acted as a bag man on a subsequent film doctoring job. Let me explain…

Early in 2005, I got a call from Jeff Geoffray and Walter Josten of Blue Rider Pictures. Would I fly immediately to the Greek island of Rhodes and report on a movie for which they were supplying bridge financing? There were cash flow problems due to a significant chunk of the financing promised by the producer either falling through, or delayed in delivery. If it all turned to custard, Blue Rider could be on the hook for about nine million dollars. They needed eyes and ears on the ground. Given our past association on *Night of the Demons 2*, *Leprechaun 3* & *4*, Jeff and Walter felt I was the right man to be their representative (spy) and, if absolutely necessary, replace director Elie Chouraqui, a former assistant to famed French director Claude Lelouch, if he was unable or unwilling to shoot the movie in a shorter schedule than the original allotted time due to the budgetary shortfall. I hoped that it would not come to that.

It was a passion project for Elie Chouraqui, who had made a couple of European movies with American leads. Scott Glenn starred in his *Man on Fire*, which Tony Scott remade in 2004 starring Denzel Washington. When he found out that I was not just *a suit*, but also a director, he was not happy, and avoided speaking to me as much as possible. But he shot the schedule from then on.

*O Jerusalem* was also a passion project for producer Andre Djaoui. Born in French Tunisia, Andre came to France at age five. He found his métier in publicity. After ten years as a top executive of the Havas agency, he quit to put his showmanship talents to work as a film producer, successfully specializing in co-productions. He was well connected with the French Cinema elite. One day I came into his office, a bungalow in the hotel grounds, while he was on the phone to Anouk Aimée, French Cinema royalty, star of such classics as Lelouch's *A Man and a Woman*.

He passed the phone to me. She spoke perfect English elegantly phrased with a sexy rasp. I gushed like a hopeless fanboy about *Les Grands Chemins* (1963), a movie of which she had no recollection.

Andre's film was based on the acclaimed nonfiction book *O Jerusalem* written by Dominique Lapierre and Larry Collins, that depicts the 1947-49 Palestine war and the end of the British mandate. The story centers on two Americans, students at NYU, one Jewish, the other Arab, who are good friends. When the United Nations votes for the creation of the state of Israel, both are pulled into opposing sides of the conflict, where finally they come face to face on the battlefield. *O Jerusalem*, the movie, was a $15M coproduction blending France, Italy, Greece, UK, Israel, USA into a classic example of *Euro-pudding*.

The Medieval Old Town on the island of Rhodes (a key location in *The Guns of Navarone*) was an ideal place to recreate the streets of Old Jerusalem in 1948. The surrounding Greek topography passed for Israel perfectly, and it was a safer place to stage the struggle between Jewish and Arab forces. The twenty-nine producers on the credits (Really? Yes.) included veteran film executive David Korda, the son of Zoltan Korda who directed the 1943 Humphrey Bogart version of *Sahara* (six degrees of separation again). I sent him a DVD of my version.

O JERUSALEM!

'A SUPERCHARGED, SPELLBINDING TALE OF ISRAEL'S BATTLE FOR IDENTITY'

LARRY COLLINS
DOMINIQUE LAPIERRE

AUTHORS OF THE FIFTH HORSEMAN

David Korda had been brought in early to stabilize the production, which he had done, but the erratic cash flow was threatening to bring shooting to a halt. There had been two work stoppages when wire transfers of salary to the international crew did not go through as promised. This resulted in the crew forcing the movie to become *a cash picture*. No more receipts for cancelled wire transfers, thank you. Cash on the barrelhead at the end of each shooting week or we don't work. And payday is Thursday.

André Djaoui assured us that funds would arrive in time. Just. It was so large a sum of Euros that the local bank needed twenty-four hours to get actual cash flown in from the mainland. David Korda and I took a taxi to the bank, instructing the cabbie to wait. We were shown into a small flimsy office that jutted out into the customer area, a remodeling afterthought, in which was secured the bank's only safe. We watched as 400,000 neatly bundled euros were counted, recounted, and counted again, before being stacked by the manager in a paper shopping bag. Two employees bearing messages to the manager came in and out. The second one left the door ajar. Is the town of Rhodes more trusting than other cities, or is the Island of Rhodes a hard place to leave if they don't want you to? We found this out, when the hotel finally lost patience with non-payment and threatened to lock all cast and crew out of their rooms, then advise the airport and ferry terminals of the passport numbers of the bill-welching absconders. But that was to come later.

Right now, we had a bag of money to keep funding. We left the bank, elated, adrenalin-charged, almost as if we had robbed it. As we walked to where we had left the cab, we took turns carrying the bag, feeling the weight of 400,000 euros in cash, an amount few people in Rhodes earn in a lifetime. The cab was not there. We wondered whether advance word of our cash transaction had spread to the local underworld. An uneasy moment. Luckily the cab, obliged to find another parking place, appeared 'round the corner and took us back to the hotel.

Among many bizarre happenings on the movie was the arrival of the Bedouins who would participate in the Arab Council scenes, speaking in their native tongue. Elie would not settle for Arab actors. He insisted on real Bedouins. There are close to 200,000 Bedouins enjoying their traditional way of life in the Negev region of Israel. Twelve Bedouins were duly imported to the hotel in Rhodes for a week of shooting, with a fee and all expenses paid. Their experience of television was slim, I suspect, but they soon discovered the two pay-per-view adult channels on the hotel TV. This was clearly a new experience. In six days, twelve Bedouins racked up more than $3000 in adult movie charges on the company's account. But they did look good in their scenes.

The shoot continued as did the financial difficulties. There was soon another cash flow cliffhanger and I accompanied the production accountant to the bank to collect 250,000 euros. This time a member of the Israeli crew joined us at the last minute for 'security'. Patting his jacket pocket, he said he was ex-Mossad. Producer André Djaoui was not a trusting man. Perhaps that was the legacy of half a dozen co-productions.

Andre and I had a few contentious conversations as I represented my clients' interests. I presented him with the final amount of bridge funding he was going to get until he delivered the money that he promised. He expected bridge financing to continue as long as the movie needed it, and complained about the usurious rate of interest. He was in general a charming fellow, but given to grand hyperbolic statements. When the possibility of legal action against him arose, somehow aquatic metaphors entered the conversation.

"If one drop of water touches my face," he said, "I shall respond with Niagara!"

I scribbled this on my pad.

"You are writing this down?"

"Of course."

"I can do worse!"

I promised to convey his complaints to my principals. I was careful not to criticize his stewardship of the picture in our dealings. I was just the messenger, there to help. My job was to lower the temperature, not to raise it. André was convinced he was being robbed by the Greek production services company. I could not tell who was robbing whom, but this long-simmering grievance came to a head, as they so often do, on the last day of shooting.

David Korda and I were present when the Greek producer Dionyssis Samiotis came to André's office to demand the payment of arrears. He had been patient for weeks, accepting of every excuse, but as the shooting was to conclude that day, the company could skip town and leave him with a significant debt. Unless his company was wired the funds immediately, he would tell the Greek crew to unplug the power to all equipment and shut down the shoot. The critical climactic scene of the movie, the scene in which the Jewish and Arab friends meet on the battlefield, was being shot. It

was time to get this matter resolved. But André said he still needed more proof of the various expenses listed on the bill; he was not going to take Dionyssis' word for it. To say Dionyssis was a big man would be an understatement. He was built like a bear. Dionyssis felt he had been called a liar, and let out a primal scream of rage that rattled the window panes of the bungalow. He strode outside, yelling imprecations in Greek. He was soon on the phone to his unit manager, ordering him to stop the shoot.

David and I knew we had better get out there fast, preferably ahead of Dionyssis. The single vehicle at hand was about to ferry the lead actor JJ Feild out to the set. We could not strategize in front of him or give any indication something was amiss in front of an actor about to perform a crucial scene. But I had a plan.

Dionyssis drove up just after we arrived. Work had stopped. Director Elie Chouraqui was fuming that the climax of his film was being jeopardized by "the Greeks." A moment later Dionyssis appeared across the set. Elie called out to him demanding that filming resume. Dionyssis remained calm and said the producer had left him no choice. As the conversation continued, the temperature quickly ratcheted up on both sides. Elie strode up the slope, He was mid-fifties, lean and wiry, with a tough guy reputation. As the two men converged, so did David Korda and I. David came around from behind Dionyssis, and I stepped up beside Elie. I have a memory of raising the palms of my hands towards each of them, as a gesture to keep them apart, and saying something like: "Gentlemen, gentlemen, there is a solution to this. Let me discuss it with Dionyssis…"

David took a growling Elie back to his trailer. I asked Dionyssis if he would accept the negative that had been shot today as a surety against what he was owed, on condition, of course, that he let filming continue. Now leverage for his claim had been restored. He accepted. Then I went back to Elie who was on the phone with David to André at the hotel. No way, said Elie and André on speaker. David and I pointed out that the situation was dire. If the scene was not shot today, they would have to regroup in Israel, build the

same fortification in matching topography, and shoot the scene again when actors were available. Such an operation could end up costing another $200K.

I outlined my plan, explaining that we would not in fact give Dionyssis the exposed negative. Instead Elie's Italian camera crew would hand over thousand-foot rolls of unexposed raw stock in cans marked as exposed negative for the relevant scene number. No way to tell the difference till the film was processed. O wily Odysseus! The camera crew were to discreetly bring the actual footage to us back at the hotel. The British transport crew offered to smuggle it back to London and deliver it to the lab. André and Elie reluctantly agreed to the arrangement, which David and I conveyed to Dionyssis. Shooting commenced immediately, and the scene was concluded by sunset.

My conscience was clear about deceiving Dionyssis. He was going to be paid the full amount sooner or later because his company held Greek distribution rights for the movie. They could sequester all income from *O Jerusalem*'s Greek box office pending payment. This was a clash of personalities that got out of hand. I liked Dionyssis and I would use my influence to see he was paid. But my duty was to protect the bridge financiers. Having agreed to the plan, André just could not bring himself to trust the outcome. He sent his ex-Mossad associate to go to the camera truck at picture wrap to collect the shot footage from the camera crew, who complied thinking the plan had changed. After the handover was seen, he hightailed it for the Hotel, with Dionyssis, furious at his betrayal, in pursuit. The cans of negative were lodged with André in his garden bungalow, just before Dionyssis and several associates arrived and camped outside. A stand-off ensued. I counseled Dionyssis against taking the film by force, while David Korda got on the phone between the parties and negotiated a rather neat solution.

We both felt that more pressure had to be put on André to complete funding his end of the budget. We were sure that Dionyssis would get paid eventually. We were more worried that the hotel bill, once again substantially in arears, would not be paid. The manager was losing patience. His job was riding on the outcome. He was threatening to lock all of us out of our rooms and maroon us on the island unless immediate payment was made. He had previously padlocked the rooms where the costumes worn by the extras playing both European refugees and Arab soldiers were stored, before they could be washed and returned to Bermans in London. Regrettably, the extras had spent time crawling through fields and scrub, their costumes acquiring a variety of insect life along the way. The room was now infested with bugs, presenting a potential health hazard to the hotel. David Korda offered the hotel the cans of negative as surety, provided they were kept in a safe in an airconditioned room, not to be released until payments were made to both the hotel and Dionyssis' company. André, not wishing to spend the night guarding his office, reluctantly agreed. The costumes were fumigated and released. André left for Israel to hunt down more money.

Within days sufficient funds arrived to placate both Dionyssis and the hotel. I was free to fly to Paris where the bridge financiers insisted that I be granted a viewing of the assembly to date. The film was slow, with long debates about the political issues. The performances were patchy, the worst being from Elie Chouraqui himself, the co-writer, co-producer, and director. He was also the camera operator in all scenes in which he was not performing. He had a significant part, and delivered long speeches in severely broken-accented English. When I asked the editor what the plan for this was, the reply was that Elie's performance would be much better when he dubbed himself into his native French for local release. The US and UK markets seemed to be unimportant. My view, expressed to Jeff and Walter at Blue Rider Pictures, was that they should not even consider converting a portion of their bridging finance into equity. Happily, they recouped their loan with interest. The French version, running 160 minutes bombed critically and commercially. The English language version, cut to 100 minutes, did no better.

*"Characters converse in stilted, expository mouthfuls that smother emotion,"* said the NY Times.

*"This bloated historical epic flatlines early and never regains a pulse."* Chicago Reader.

Its worldwide theatrical gross was $2,724303. What a pity. A great non-fiction book, promoting the concept of peace between Israelis and Arabs, was filmed on a substantial budget, but without the grasp of drama necessary to reach the audience the subject deserved.

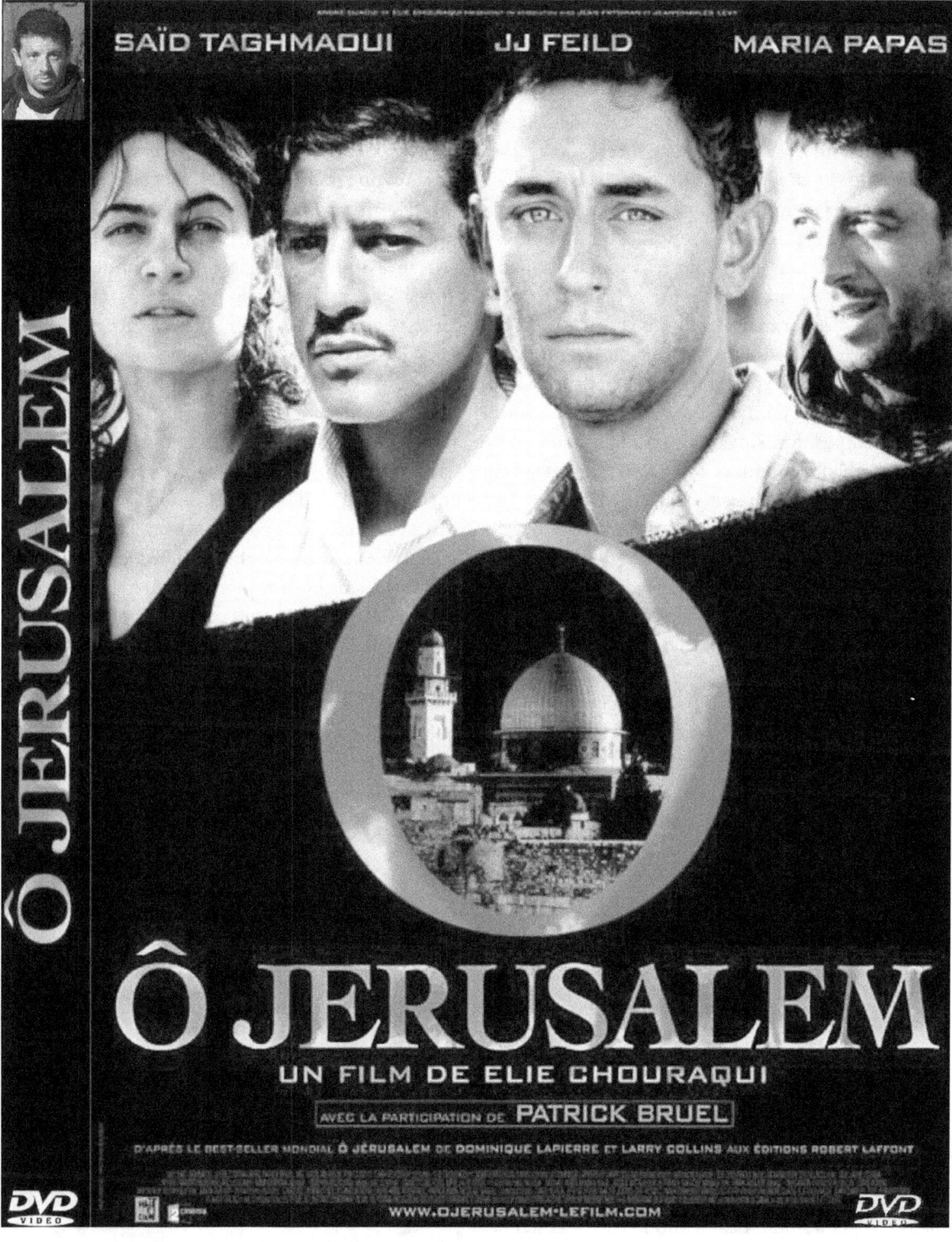

# CHAPTER 49
## *Alice Through the Multiverse*

Movie ideas come to me at unexpected times. *Stunt Rock* came to me in the shower. Watching Bruce Lee's first three Chinese movies in quick succession sparked *The Man from Hong Kong. The Executioner's Daughter* came to me in a dream. I don't often remember my dreams. Yet one morning in 2002 in the moments immediately after waking, striking images replayed in my mind: a riot overwhelms a medieval execution…A teenage girl flees through a forest in a blinding thunderstorm… She wakes up in a 21$^{st}$ century psychiatric institution… That's all I could remember. Strange. If a dream is the subconscious putting out the trash, what tortured region of my inner being did this come from? Or was it just psychic screen grabs evoking movies I've seen, or maybe a movie I would want to see? The potential for a genre cocktail intrigued me. A time paradox "fish out of water" adventure. Hmm. I groggily jotted down what I could remember, then ruminated on the concept during my then daily swims in the pool at UCLA, where Margaret was undergoing the tortures of the damned (a.k.a. doctoral studies).

As I lapped, for sometimes up to an hour, characters and plot twists would come to me. I named the girl Alice, then set about creating a world that was no Wonderland. Is Alice the daughter of the executioner, perhaps? Does the psych hospital have a deadly agenda? I would scribble bullet points on my hand as soon as I reached the locker room. The story developed its own momentum and a screenplay poured out of me, entitled *The Executioner's Daughter*. Two girls, five centuries apart, swap lives. They are zapped back and forth without warning, plunged into frightening conspiracies in both time zones. Are they skipping across parallel strands of the Multiverse? Or is Alice insane? It was a wacky genre cocktail with paranormal trimmings, part Medieval (rather, Early Modern, my historian wife insists) Palace drama, part Jason Bourne spy thriller.

The script was optioned twice for good money, but was never able to attract a star big enough to trigger the finance the project required. Reluctantly I relinquished the director's chair to a talented German filmmaker who had more sizzle at studios than I.

Christian Alvart, was fresh off a hit German thriller *Antibodies*, and would soon to direct Renee Zellweger in *Case 39*. He showed me his director's cut. It's a well-made supernatural *Bad Seed* movie, but it sat on the shelf for a year. Paramount at that time did not know how to market horror, and squandered its potential. It's a pity because Christian has a strong visual style and would have done a great job on my script. These days he makes back-to-back movies and miniseries in Europe. But even with Christian on board at the height of his Hollywood visibility, we could not get any of the rising female stars du jour (Keira, Scarlett, etc.) to sign on to an independent Euro-shoot movie without a studio deal. And we could not get a studio deal without a star's Letter of Intent. The script languished through eleven further drafts, trying to please different distributors till the option expired.

ALICE THROUGH THE MULTIVERSE

BRIAN TRENCHARD-SMITH

I went on to direct several more films, but Alice's story still gnawed at my liver. So I adapted the screenplay as a novel, something I had never done before, but I found the medium liberating. I had the space to explore the character's thoughts, make wry comments on the culture and politics in both centuries, and give the reader two hundred and fifty pages of blood and thunder amid time twisting paranormal thrills. What's not to like? No publisher was interested. Only one bothered to reply. Again I put it aside. Then a couple of years ago, I said dammit—I'll self-publish. During the novelization process, the environmental and corporate conspiracy themes in the script grew stronger. It became a chase thriller/parallel universe/ripping yarn sprinkled with nuggets of agitprop and an alternative history ending intended to provoke debate. A fun ride had developed a soul, which I entitled *Alice through the Multiverse*, to emphasize its paranormal elements. Finally, closure; after fifteen years, fragments of a dream became a published work, albeit not in the originally intended medium.

If *Alice* plays like a movie in your head, that's the idea.

# EPILOGUE

After *Drive Hard* in 2014, I redoubled my efforts with three different producers to get projects in the $3—5M range funded. A WWII bomb disposal story called *Sacrifice* looked promising for a while with money from India, but it fizzled, as did the South African co-production *Shaft 6*, a supernatural thriller set in a gold mine. *Blood Reef*, a sci fi action piece, and *Jammed*, a claustrophobic thriller, similarly fell short after initial enthusiasm. Dennis Pratt and I retooled our *Blowback* script for Tony Ginnane as a female-driven crime and espionage streaming series which we are still pitching. No luck so far. But there was still the joy of creating the blueprint, which, I came to see, could be done anywhere.

Margaret and I like adventures. We have roamed the world, based first in Australia, then for twenty-five years in the heart of Los Angeles. It was time for a change. Much though we loved our life in Australia, returning full time was not really an option, though I continue to visit frequently. Our sons have established careers and lives in the United States. We are a close family, and it's easier to be close on the same continent.

And Now for Something Completely Different in the Life of Brian…

Encouraged by our son Eric, we moved to rural Oregon, where the air is clean, the water pure, and deer come to visit twice a day.

We live on a magnificent hill shadowed by Douglas firs. In garden, field, and forest a myriad of potential images wait for my camera phone. I like to cruise past foreground flora to reveal the subject of the shot, which might range from a pollinating bee to a herd of elk. Composing for available light, maintaining smooth camera moves in awkward positions while not spooking the critter in question is a challenge I enjoy; a technological update to the three lens clockwork wind Bell & Howell of my Danger Freaks days. It's not important whether anybody sees what I shoot. My joy is in practicing the craft for its own sake.

Our neighbors are tremendous people and we have all become close friends. In this environment, Margaret has researched and written two significant articles for historical publications, and she and I are commissioning music based on poetry she has written. Here I wrote the novel that sprang from *The Execu-*

*tioner's Daughter* screenplay. There are a couple of other books forming in my head, and I will continue to contribute to Trailers From Hell. I still pitch my scripts *Blowback, Richard The Third*. and *Alice through the Multiverse* as streaming series. The show ain't over till it's over.

In 2016, the Fantaspoa International Fantastic Film Festival flew Margaret and me to Porto Allegre, Brazil, where I screened *Turkey Shoot* & *Dead End Drive-In* and received a Lifetime Achievement Award. It's nice to be king for a day.

Maybe a few of my films will continue to be seen, regarded, in terms of microgenre and social subtext, as entertaining time capsules. In reviewing my career for this book, I am constantly reminded how incredibly lucky I have been throughout my life. When so many are born into inescapable misery, I am given a life of privilege and opportunity. Why me? I still wrestle with the existence of God. In my view one's moral compass should be guided by common sense not dogma; treat others as you would want to be treated. That's not so hard. Spiritual matters should be a source of worldwide unity not conflict. I lean towards God being the creative force of Life itself, indefinable, arbitrary yes, but ever replenishing, everlasting. We spring from it. We return to it. Having spent the last five years on a forested hill surrounded by an abundance of plant and wildlife, I am awed by my tiny part in the vast natural world. Nature gives me more spiritual comfort than religion, a feeling of oceanic mysticism. I will know the answer to the conundrum of faith sooner rather than later. Not too soon, I hope, because there is more I want to do.

I am so grateful to all those who helped my career along the way, starting with my parents for the sacrifices they made to give me a good start in life, and for never discouraging me from chasing my dream. But most of all, I am grateful to Margaret and our sons Eric and Alex for their love and encouragement. If you strive to make your mark in any field of endeavor, there is no better inspiration and comfort than family.